THE NEW POLITICS OF THE
BUDGETARY PROCESS

THE NEW POLITICS OF THE BUDGETARY PROCESS

Fourth Edition

Aaron Wildavsky
University of California, Berkeley

Naomi Caiden
California State University, Los Angeles

New York San Francisco Boston
London Toronto Sydney Tokyo Singapore Madrid
Mexico City Munich Paris Cape Town Hong Kong Montreal

Publisher: Priscilla McGeehon
Senior Acquisition Editor: Eric Stano
Associate Editor: Anita Castro
Marketing Manager: Megan Galvin-Fak
Supplements Editor: Mark Toews
Production Manager: Denise Phillip
Project Coordination, Text Design, and Electronic Page Makeup: WestWords, Inc.
Cover Design Manager: Nancy Danahy
Cover Designer: Keithley & Associates
Cover Illustration/Photo: Photo Disc
Senior Manufacturing Buyer: Dennis J. Para
Printer and Binder: Maple-Vail Book Manufacturing Group
Cover Printer: Lehigh Press

For permission to use copyrighted material, grateful acknowledgment is made to the copyright holders on p. 363, which is hereby made part of this copyright page.

Library of Congress Cataloging-in-Publication Data
Wildavsky, Aaron B.
    The new politics of the budgetary process / Aaron Wildavsky, Naomi
Caiden.—4th ed.
      p.   cm.
    Includes bibliographical references and index.
    ISBN 0-321-04255-7 (pbk.)
    1. Budget—United States.   I. Caiden, Naomi.
HJ2051.W483   2000
352.4'8'0973—dc21   00-038462
                                                                      CIP

Please visit our website at http://www.awl.com

ISBN 0-321-04255-7

2 3 4 5 6 7 8 9 10—MA—03 02 01

To

Mary Wildavsky

Gerald Caiden

Contents

Chapter Four
The Collapse of Consensus   69

Chapter Five
The Politics of Dissensus   93

Biographical Note[1]

Aaron Wildavsky

Aaron Wildavsky was born in New York City in 1930, the son of Russian Jewish immigrant parents. He grew up in Brooklyn and graduated from Brooklyn College. He wrote his first book on Australian politics and, following a doctorate at Yale and assistant lectureship at Oberlin College, joined the Department of Political Science, University of California, Berkeley. He remained there for the rest of his life, except for two years as president of the Russell Sage Foundation in New York. At Berkeley, he was chair of the Department of Political Science, the founding dean of the Graduate School of Public Policy, and he was also president of the American Political Science Association. He died at his home in Oakland in August 1993.

This brief recital of a life's chronology does not communicate the vibrancy and fullness of the life itself. It was a life of accomplishment, reflected in the publication of hundreds of books and articles. It was a life of intellectual endeavor and enjoyment, a continuous reflection on the interplay of ideas and experience. It was a life of collaboration and research, a perpetual voyage of discovery into political behavior, values, and institutions.

Aaron's mind was restless, tackling fresh issues, inventing new concepts, and mapping out and achieving ambitious agendas for research. His findings and conclusions were written in provocative, lucid, and eminently readable prose. Aaron was a master craftsman whose influence stemmed not least from his expressive use of the English language to capture ideas, arguments, perspectives, and realities of political life and change.

Beyond scholarship, Aaron will be remembered for his personal qualities. Many are indebted to him for acts of kindness and consideration. He was honest and unpretentious. He honored his deeply held values and obligations as a Jew, a citizen, and to his family. He was realistic yet optimistic.

Through his writings, professional activities, and life, Aaron Wildavsky touched and influenced an extraordinary number of friends, collaborators, colleagues, students, researchers, practitioners, and others. He was generous with ideas, time, resources, attributions, and encouragement.

---

[1]Taken from Naomi Caiden, "Foreword," in Naomi Caiden and Joseph White, eds., *Budgeting, Policy, Politics: An Appreciation of Aaron Wildavsky* (New Brunswick, N.J.: Transaction Publishers), 1995, pp. 1–3.

Preface to the Fourth Edition: Curiouser and Curiouser

In the words of Alice in Wonderland, the world of federal budgeting has become "curiouser and curiouser." In the five short years since the appearance of the third edition of *The New Politics of the Budgetary Process*, there have been more than enough surprises to keep researchers, journalists, and just plain observers busy and astonished. Who would have forecast that the long–dominant theme of federal budgeting—the deficit—would have vanished abruptly, replaced by surpluses as far as the eye could see? Or that both political parties would compete to outdo each other to "protect the social security surplus" (even if they did fudge a little or a lot)? Or that conflicts over appropriations bills would be so intense that they would be almost routinely preempted by last minute highest level negotiations over huge omnibus bills, consisting of thousands of pages, whose complete contents were really known only to very few? Or that despite the deep ideological chasms and political bickering between the parties, they would agree on a bipartisan Balanced Budget Act, let alone welfare reform? And why did a favorite cause for so many years, the executive line item veto, come and go with so little to show?

Less dramatic, but no less interesting, are unfinished developments from the last edition. The fate of the Republican "revolution" to roll back social programs and cut back government, is a story in itself. Managerial reforms have now had sufficient time to permit at least preliminary evaluation. Broad trends in revenues and outlays have revealed changes in the balances among the major components of the budget: defense and domestic discretionary spending, entitlements, and interest.

How may these developments be interpreted? On one reading, not much has changed. Over two-thirds of the budget is accounted for by prior commitments such as entitlements, interest payments, and contracts. Even the so-called discretionary spending is not really open to radical change. For all their sound and fury, conflicts add up to a few billion here and there, out of a $1.7 trillion budget. In this sense, Aaron's original insight was accurate: Budgetary politics *is* incremental because it leaves untouched decisions about the great bulk of revenues and spending. The main budget story lies in the ongoing budgetary commitments, whose growth is largely determined by social and economic trends.

Moreover, the differences between the parties may not be as great as they are sometimes portrayed. Faced by an electorate that seems to prefer stability to radical changes, the parties have staked out similar positions on such issues as the need for entitlement reform, effective defense, improved education, the fight against crime, research on health, more transportation funding, welfare reform, and balancing the budget. Both parties also still enjoy pork spending, despite their protestations to the contrary. A major exception is the issue of tax cuts, but even here both parties favor some cuts in taxation, though they disagree on their level and nature.

A second interpretation would discount such agreement as superficial, masking not only deep differences between the parties but also the multiple lines of fissure within them. This interpretation carries through Aaron's theme of political dissensus, a pattern of dynamic conflicts so deep that they threaten the viability of budgetary institutions altogether and produce deadlock, shortcircuiting of established processes, and blurring of roles. Agreement on entitlement reforms has been impossible. The Balanced Budget Act included provisions that would clearly prove infeasible later down the line. The pledge to "protect social security" has been decried as fallacious and cynical by reputed economists who dismiss charges that social security has been "raided" to pay for other spending. Budgeting is rife with fictions, gimmicks, and evasions. Appropriations debates are lengthy bitter wrangles, some of which find resolution only in high-level negotiations. Budget processes are complicated not only because of formal procedures, but because they do not seem to work the way they were intended. The budget process seems more opaque than ever.

A third interpretation sees both conflicts and agreements as symptoms of deeper currents. All over the world, governments are grappling with unprecedented challenges arising from economic, social, and technological changes. In Western industrialized countries, a rapidly aging population is forcing decisions on social security, pensions, and long-term health care. In the United States, a boom economy masks the growing gap between rich and poor. Globalization has changed the structure of economies and is related to such developments as environmental pressures, large-scale immigration, worldwide business mergers, international organized crime, and volatile capital markets. The fast-moving communications changes constitute a virtual revolution whose ramifications are still to be fully comprehended, while other technological developments, such as those in biotechnology, are no less destabilizing and discomfiting. Meanwhile, the prospects of universal peace promised by the end of the Cold War have dissolved into regional ethnic conflicts, and new armaments buildups threaten.

All of these, and more, demand responses from government, but the direction of response is not clear. Both the old doctrines of classical social democracy and neoliberal or radical conservatism seem to offer inadequate answers. There is a growing consensus on a "Third Way," which emphasizes effective government, strengthening of civic society, partnership of government and the private and nonprofit sectors, decentralization, and reduction of bureaucracy. Government has a leading but not exclusive role in guiding the economy, providing a social safety net, ensuring a safe and healthy environment, participating in resolving international issues, and encouraging social investment.[1] Many recent policies seem to fit within these general guidelines. But the basic issues in budgeting—Who pays and who receives? What should be publicly financed and what should be privately financed? And how much?—continue, and are likely to do so indefinitely. The politics of budgeting, by their nature, will find no definitive resolution or end, though their intensity might diminish.

The writing of the third edition was very much overshadowed by Aaron's recent and unexpected death, which still leaves a large gap. Ours is a continuing and unfinished collaboration, but it is perforce a one-sided dialogue, in which I do not pretend to take his part as well. Aaron "taught us how to read the world differently."[2] Even as the budgetary world fills with new events, I have endeavored to preserve his insights, which stretched well beyond commentary on what was happening at the time.

Once again, there is the problem of selection. While adding new material, and revising to take account of changes, I have omitted detail that no longer seems important. Even so, some readers may find in the recounting of events more than they wish to know about the intricacies of budgetary debates, positions, and conflicts. My response is that if we wish to understand the politics of the budgetary process, it is necessary to study the stuff of politics in budgeting—the who did what to whom. Without the substance of the living world of budgeting, the subject is sterile and unrealistic. I have tried to avoid overwhelming the reader, while still providing an impression of what really happens to make federal budgets.

In making revisions, I have tried to keep in mind two main considerations. First, the book should remain a comprehensible account of the federal budget process, available and understandable not only to those who lived through the same times and events as Aaron, but also to a later generation no longer familiar with that context. Second, *The New Politics* should be a record of what has happened. It is all too easy to take for granted what we see in front of us, and to take the next step of assuming that this is always how things have been and that they will never be any different. Aaron believed that understanding institutions and processes required knowledge of their history, and the new edition of *The New Politics* honors this perspective.

To retain Aaron's insights, historical development, and currency, it has been necessary to reshape some of the chapters. As before, the book is divided into a chronological account of the development of the federal budget process, and four analytical chapters. Chapter 5 now ends before the Gramm-Rudman-Hollings Act, so as to characterize more closely the politics of dissensus of the 1980s. Chapter 6, "The Politics of Balancing Budgets," now discusses three major efforts in trying to deal with the deficit: the Gramm-Rudman-Hollings legislation, the 1990 Budget Enforcement Act, and Clinton's first landmark budget. Chapter 7 is the final chapter of the third edition, dealing with the 1995 Republican revolution and its fate. The two entitlement chapters have been combined into a single

---

[1]See Anthony Giddens, *The Third Way: The Renewal of Social Democracy* (Oxford: Blackwell Publishers, 1998), pp. 99–128.

[2]Cynthia Ozick, "The Impossibility of Being Kafka," *New Yorker*, January 11, 1999, p. 80.

Chapter 8, which brings together Aaron's theoretical material on entitlements with an updated analysis of the political dynamics of entitlement programs. Chapter 9 has updated the discussion of defense budgeting to take account of post-Cold War changes. Chapter 10, "Reform," includes material on later developments, including the Chief Financial Officers Act, the Government Performance and Results Act, and the line item veto. Chapter 11 contains a new discussion of the surplus in addition to the existing material on the deficit. Finally, a new Chapter 12, "A Budget of Opposites," takes stock of the federal budget process at the beginning of the new millennium. I think that had I been able to explain what I have done, Aaron would have approved.

There is no single story to relate. *The New Politics of the Budgetary Process* is a narrative that includes change and continuity, centralization and fragmentation, ideology and opportunism, division and agreement. It is a fertile ground for students of political science, economics, public policy, and public management, as well as those who would like to know how some of the most important decisions affecting United States government are made.

Thanks are due to a number of people who made this book possible. I should like to thank Anita Castro of Addison Wesley Longman, whose help and patience were always encouraging to me during the revision process. L.R Jones of the Naval Postgraduate School at Monterey, Calif., was extremely helpful in the revision of the chapter on defense, as well as providing valuable comments on the third edition, but responsibility for the final account is of course mine, not his. My especial thanks are due to Nancy Weckwerth, lab manager of the Faculty Instruction Technology Support Center at California State University, Los Angeles, for her patience and courtesy in helping me to produce the final manuscript, and to George Taylor, associate director of the FITSC and the student assistants. My daughter, Miriam, typed much of the manuscript and deserves my gratitude for her persistence in finding her way through the complexities of the revisions. My other daughter, Rachel, provided essential encouragement without which I could not have continued. Finally, I should like to thank my husband, Gerald, for his unswerving support and confidence, which enabled me to undertake and complete this revision.

Naomi Caiden

Los Angeles, January 2000

Preface to the Third Edition

For over 40 years, Aaron Wildavsky researched, wrote, and spoke about public budgeting. His contribution was to transcend the narrow world of budgeting and to transform its study into a central concern for political scientists. Budgeting was not just a technical realm for experts, but a critical manifestation of politics. For Aaron, budgeting *was* politics, writ large in basic questions of how a society organized itself to determine the relative domains of the public and private, who gained and who lost, who benefited and who paid. What would he have made of the great budget revolution of 1995, if indeed it is a revolution? Would he have welcomed it as a vindication of much of what he had written ever since *The Politics of the Budgetary Process* appeared in the mid-1960s—the overreaching of government, the need for limits, the restoration of balance? Or would his sharp mind, honest logic, and trenchant wit have analyzed critically a phenomenon in which all is not as it appears, decried accelerating dissensus and polarization, and laid bare hypocrisy, opportunism, and ideological politics? Or would he have taken the progression from the old politics of the budgetary process to the new yet one stage further—to confront us with a new vision, a different way of looking at reality, a fresh vocabulary, so that readers would immediately recognize his insight to exclaim "yes, that is how things are"?

We shall never know the answer to these questions, but we do know that had Aaron Wildavsky lived to respond to the events of the past five years since the last edition of *The New Politics of the Budgetary Process*, he would have taken the moral high ground, sifted the significant from the clutter of detail, related the story with accuracy and the highest standards of scholarship, and produced an understandable, readable, and stimulating account of events. I have endeavored to do the same. While I cannot know how Aaron would have felt and thought about all that has transpired, I have tried to be faithful to his general approach. But in the intervening years since the second edition, while much has remained the same, much has also changed, and what has changed requires in some measure reassessment, a fresh perspective on both past and present.

The Politics of the Budgetary Process responded to V. O. Key's famous question "On what basis shall it be decided to allocate X dollars to activity A instead of activity B?"[1] Aaron's answer was framed in political and behavioral terms. The different aspects of incrementalism combined to portray a world in balance, secured through the unwritten rules observed by its participants. This was the world of classical budgeting, whose norms were annualarity, unity, and balanced budgets.

In *The New Politics of the Budgetary Process*, the balance had gone. The rise of entitlements eclipsed the previous norms, which no longer acted to control the budget. Huge budgets overwhelmed the capacity of government. Dissensus about the kind of society we want and the role of government strained political processes and politicized the budget debate. Appropriations—once the very stuff of budgets—were dwarfed by entitlements that grew without restraint. Developments in processes—the Congressional Budget Act, Gramm–Rudman–Hollings, the Budget Enforcement Act—were all attempts to stuff the genie back into the bottle again and to restore previously unwritten norms through legislative fiat.

This interpretation of budgetary politics has been challenged. An ongoing debate about the existence of incrementalism in different contexts has been a staple of academic research for decades, with inconclusive results.[2] A recent study of federal budgeting by Roy Meyers questioned whether a "classical" period of budgeting really existed, and suggested a more complicated and dynamic set of strategies and tactics than that present in *The Politics*.[3] More trenchant was the charge by Allen Schick that the focus of analysis was narrow and limited, failing to take account of the broader political context against which budgetary politics in Congress was played out.[4] The closed "classical" world of budgeting was a world of insiders, and the notable growth of spending that was already beginning, even as *The Politics* was being written, reflected greater participation in American political life by groups previously excluded. The expansion of entitlements did not take place simply because of a desire to avoid the appropriations process, or to increase government spending, but in response to perceived demands—even if all of these were not equally fulfilled.

In the preface to the second edition of *The New Politics*, Aaron acknowledged the transformation of the budget process to deal with major policy issues, and the expansion of the budgetary arena to include more participants and more complex political divisions. He wrote about the emergence of a politics of ideology, the looking to budgetary reform to solve political questions, and the necessity for agreement on limits to make the budget process workable again. The current budgetary

---

[1]V. O. Key Jr., "The Lack of a Budgetary Theory," *American Political Science Review*, Vol. 34 (December 1940), pp. 1137–40. Reproduced in Albert C. Hyde and Jay M. Schafritz, eds., *Governmental Budgeting: Theory, Process, Politics* (Oak Park, Ill.: Moore Publishing Company, 1978), p. 20.

[2]See Joseph White, "(Almost) Nothing New Under the Sun: Why the Work of Budgeting Remains Incremental," in Naomi Caiden and Joseph White, eds., *Budgeting, Politics, Policy: An Appreciation of Aaron Wildavsky* (New Brunswick N.J.: Transaction Publishers), 1995, pp. 111–32.

[3]Roy T. Meyers, *Strategic Budgeting* (Ann Arbor, Mich.: University of Michigan Press), 1994, pp. 1–14.

[4]Allen Schick, "From the Old Politics of Budgeting to the New," in Naomi Caiden and Joseph White, eds., op. cit., 133–42.

turmoil reflects these themes, though its outcome is uncertain, but also adds a further dimension to them: an attempt to reverse the domestic role of the federal government and at the same time balance the federal budget.

Neither of these aims is new: The Reagan administration had similar objectives, and the last edition of *The New Politics* covered in detail the deficit issue and the politics surrounding the Omnibus Budget Reconciliation Act (OBRA). Now it is time to add new material to cover developments during the Clinton administration, beginning with the deficit reductions of his first budget in 1993, and continuing with the efforts of the Republican Congress to reshape the budget in 1995 through unprecedented cuts in taxes and mandatory and domestic discretionary spending. But whenever I thought I had completed the manuscript, some new and interesting development occurred. I was able to take the narrative to the end of January 1996, before the new president's budget. In this wonderland of budgeting, who knows what more awaits us? But books, like budgets, demand closure, if only to be reopened.

We live in an era of limits, and even classics have limits if they are to remain alive and relevant. It has therefore been necessary to cut as well as to add, and also to take account of changing emphasis. Details of earlier reforms, such as Gramm–Rudman–Hollings, are now primarily of historical interest. Some of the arguments and speculation in the second edition have been settled or superseded and deserve less space. What appeared new or astonishing only a few years ago is now accepted, or regarded as only one element in a broader trend.

Yet history is still important. Aaron used to ask, "How do we know where we are, if we do not know where we have come from?" Facts and examples do not lose relevance because they occurred a few, or even many, years ago. For this reason I have tried to retain enough of the experience of budgeting as Aaron observed it for the reader to understand and appreciate his insights. While we may have difficulty in interpreting the present, the past record enables perspective, comparison, and deeper appreciation of consequences.

Another issue is that of opinion. Aaron and I did not always agree, but I have not changed his conclusions. I have also left some of his first-person references as they stood. "I" means Wildavsky. "We" is used in the conventional sense of all of us.

I should like to acknowledge the support of California State University, Los Angeles in granting sabbatical leave to enable the writing of the third edition, and of Margaret Loftus and her colleagues at Addison Wesley Longman for their encouragement and expertise. I would also like to thank the following individuals, who took the time to review the draft manuscript: John A. Hamman, Southern Illinois University; L. R. Jones, Naval PostGraduate School; Andree Reeves, University of Alabama; Diane E. Schmidt, Southern Illinois University; Fred Thompson, Willamette University; and Jacqueline Vaughn Switzer, Southern Oregon State College. Their comments and suggestions were greatly appreciated. Finally, I should like to thank Mary Wildavsky for suggesting that I undertake this revision.

Naomi Caiden

Preface to the Second Edition: Expanding the Political Meaning of Budgeting

The first edition of this book was considerably more complex than its older sibling, *The Politics of the Budgetary Process*. The reason was that the process itself had grown more complicated, with much being added and nothing being taken away. The new chapters (Chapters 11 and 12) in this second edition seek to draw lessons about budgeting from the maneuvering around the problem of reducing the deficit. It also seeks to explain the new parts of the budgetary process put in place by the Omnibus Budget Reconciliation Act of 1990 (OBRA). True, this time, a little has been taken away or, like Gramm–Rudman, placed in suspended animation. But much more has been added. Now there are three sequestrations, for instance, instead of one. We could pretend that OBRA doesn't exist. The upside would be that there would be less to learn; the downside, however, would be that for the next five years budgeting would be unintelligible. Are we to study the process that exists or the much simpler one of our distraught imaginings?

Through all the maneuvers, and the maneuvers based on other maneuvers, the same political struggles that animated the first edition of *The New Politics of the Budgetary Process* shine through. There is still deep budgetary dissensus. And these ideological differences about the kind of government and society America ought to have are still being played out through the budget. Only now these conflicts are sharper. Therefore, those who wish to understand politics must acquaint themselves with budgeting if they want to know what is going on.

In *The Politics of the Budgetary Process* I sidestepped the problem of defining "the politics" part by saying that the book was "concerned with budgets as political things" and by focusing on the budget as a record of outcomes and a process of decision making:

> Taken as a whole the federal budget is a representation in monetary terms of governmental activity. If politics is regarded in part as conflict over whose preferences shall prevail in the determination of national policy, then the budget records the outcomes

of this struggle. If one asks, "Who gets what the government has to give?" then the answers for a moment in time are recorded in the budget. If one looks at politics as a process by which the government mobilizes resources to meet pressing problems, then the budget is a focus of these efforts. (p. 4)

Because what we the people decide to politicize is what constitutes "the political" at any one time, this evasion has merit.[1] Enough time has passed and sufficient experience accumulated, however, to begin to put more flesh on the bare bones of politics.

Whether the nation will gain from the political maneuvering that led to the passage of the Omnibus Budget Reconciliation Act of 1990 is an open question. But I have no doubt that the coexistence of a Budget Summit made up of the congressional leaders of both houses of Congress and top officials of the Bush administration and OBRA are good for analysts of political aspects of budgeting. Evaluating the outcomes in these two arenas will enable us to separate those aspects that the national government leadership agreed on in both arenas from those that were altered in OBRA. Thus we can distinguish between the politics that separates elected politicians from the citizenry and the politics of ideology that separates these politicians from each other.

The question of "Who will bear the cost of change?" is of enduring importance. Senior legislators, especially those on appropriations committees, have come to believe that their committees and the agencies for which they are responsible have been getting short shrift. Therefore, they have succeeded in writing into OBRA "hold harmless" provisions that make them more responsible for changes in taxing and spending they initiate but take them off the hook for changes outside of government (war, famine, flood, depression) they feel cannot control. This withdrawal of responsibility is not as foolish as it sounds. As the continuing debate over the savings and loan collapse indicates, it may be that Americans have been disposed to have government insure them against change (by guaranteeing deposits) while no one worries about who is going to uphold government. Nevertheless, the question of whether it is desirable to have government escape responsibility for what presidents choose to call external changes while citizens must cope with them should be more widely debated than it has been, for it has hardly been discussed at all.

The noticeable speeding up of budgetary reform is convincing evidence that a politics of ideological dissensus is on us. From the Budget Act of 1921 to the Budget Act of 1974 took a little over half a century. Then the act of 1974 was substantially modified as the Gramm–Rudman–Hollings Act (GRH, or Gramm–Rudman in short), with significant new elements added, in 1986, a bare twelve years later. Now OBRA has come a mere four years after Gramm–Rudman. This speed-up, I think, is due to heroic but failing efforts to replace the classical norms of balance, annualarity, and comprehensiveness with new procedures that provide by legislative stipulation what used to be done by informal understandings. The Budget Resolutions of the 1974 act, the deficit-reduction targets of the 1986 act, and the stipulated agreements of the 1990 act (containing, for two years at least, the equivalent of both resolutions

---

[1]For a discussion of this point in the context of political cultures, see Michael Thompson, Richard Ellis, and Aaron Wildavsky, *Cultural Theory* (Boulder, Colo.: Westview Press, 1990).

and reductions) give legal directions providing overall ceilings, divisions among major programmatic areas (i.e., between defense and domestic, entitlement and appropriation), and provide pathways for adjusting to new circumstances. The more precise these instructions become, the more they straitjacket the budgetary process, however, the more fragile they are. With basic differences over policy left standing, these surface to weaken and then destroy the most carefully wrought paper plans. Even now, as I write in mid-March 1991, Republicans are talking about holding off on previously agreed tax increases due to the recession and Democrats are using loosely worded portions of OBRA dealing with supplemental spending to bring in items that would not count against the totals they previously agreed to support.

The expansion of the political agenda to include social issues such as abortion, with its budgetary implications for whether government ought to help poor women afford this choice, should make us aware of the desirability of conceptualizing political values more broadly. The old divisions between left and right, liberal and conservative, were useful at a time when the major political cleavage was between supporters of somewhat larger or somewhat smaller welfare programs. Since both Democrats and Republicans are now divided as well over questions of abortion, of defense, and of prayer in schools, it is desirable to have a way of conceptualizing policy differences that accommodates a wider range of issues. That is why I have introduced cultural language carving the political scene into three unequal parts, namely, egalitarians who believe in diminishing power and resource differences among people, hierarchists who wish to maintain differences with the understanding that the individual parts ought to sacrifice for the collective whole, and individualists who wish to substitute self-regulation for authority. If individualists agree with egalitarians that government ought not to regulate people's personal lives, but disagree with egalitarians about the extent and desirability of regulation of economic activity, the pattern of political conflict we observe should now make better sense. If individualists desire limited economic regulation and hierarchists agree because they want every person to fulfill the duties of his or her station, yet they disagree about the hierarchists' willingness to intervene in individuals' personal lives, we can understand both the rationale behind their coalition in the Republican party and the precarious nature of that coalition should attention shift from economic to social issues.

From the Budget Summit we learn that Republicans wanted lower taxes, thereby enabling their constituents to hold on to more income, and Democrats wanted higher taxes on higher-income people so as to achieve the more egalitarian objectives on which their party is agreed. From OBRA, which opened up the Summit agreement to legislative preferences after House Republicans defeated the Summit, we learn that rank-and-file Democratic members of Congress are more egalitarian than their leaders. No one who listened to the congressional debates over whether the United States should use armed force to make war in the Persian Gulf, or whether having begun with an air war it should begin a ground war, can have failed to notice that the disagreements were not only about the Persian Gulf itself but also about whether such a war, however successful on its own terms, was a lesser priority than redressing inequalities in American society.

Individual leaders do not matter. President Bush's popularity plummeted when he abandoned his promise not to raise taxes, arguing, instead, the greater national need to reduce the deficit. Bush's popularity soared to historic heights when the war ended much sooner and with far fewer casualties than pessimistic forebodings suggested. As Bush stumbled by bringing down on himself maximum disapprobation on the budget, he arose tall during the war when his guidance was both sure and successful. It may be that President Bush's enormous war-gained popularity will confer retrospective validation on his budget-balancing choice, wiping out the fatuity of "read my lips" and replacing it with the vision of "our president doing his best for the country." If the political dissensus theory that animates this book is on the right track, however, the president's personal popularity, except on matters rather directly connected to that war, will not extend to agreement with his less-than-wholly egalitarian views.

If there is now less consensus and more dissensus, how is the budgetary process affected? There should be more disputes over larger amounts that take longer to resolve. And so there have been.

The Politics of the Budgetary Process was animated by a quite different vision of budgeting as an incremental process. This understanding is reflected in Chapter 3 "The Dance of the Dollars: Classical Budgeting" under the straightforward rubric that "budgeting is incremental." My major purpose in introducing this term to budgeting was to make readers aware that comprehensive consideration of the budget as a whole, each item compared to all the others, went beyond the possibilities of human calculation. Were it tried, comprehensive calculation would also make agreement on the budget much more difficult. And so, at a time of budgetary dissensus, it has done. The need established by the Budget Act of 1974 to relate total spending to total revenues from the top down has indeed exacerbated conflicts. It does matter greatly when many more major matters are disagreed. Why else would the budget process be so stultified, taking up so much more time and room, often to so little effect?

Consensus means that there is agreement on the budgetary base; when that consensus dissipates, so does incrementalism. Just as the notion of incrementalism depended on the prior existence of a fairly fixed base, which depended on historical continuity, which, in turn, depended on political consensus (see Chapter 3), so budgetary dissensus gravely weakens reliance on the past and opens up policy direction as well as amount of money to change. That is why there is now much more attention to budgeting than before, but by no means more agreement. Just as budgeting was incremental because it was consensual, and consensual because incremental, so dissensual budgeting leads to larger and more rapid changes, which increase disagreement.

Aaron Wildavsky

Dead on Arrival? A Preface to *The New Politics of the Budgetary Process*

Confronted with the vast array of figures in the Budget of the United States, one is likely to think of budgeting as an arid subject, the province of stodgy clerks and dull statisticians. Nothing could be more mistaken.

In introducing the old *Politics of the Budgetary Process* in 1964, I began in all innocence by sharing my most important discovery: Budgeting was interesting. Amazing but true; far from being the preserve of mere technicians, budgeting was the lifeblood of government, the medium through which flowed the essential life support systems of public policy. No one then seemed to object to being told the obvious.

Today, when budgeting has become the major issue of American national politics, admonitions about its importance, like being told to breathe regularly, have a superfluous air about them—essential but unnecessary. For taxing and spending, resource mobilization and resource allocation, now take up as much or more time on the floors of Congress than all other matters put together. How large government will be, the part it will play in our lives, whether more or less will be done for defense or welfare, how much and what sort of people will pay for services, what kind of society, in sum, we Americans want to have—all these are routinely discussed in budget debates. The importance of conflicts over the size and distribution of the budget—failure to pass a budget on time or at all has become a sign of inability to govern—testifies to the overriding importance of budgeting. Nowadays the State of the Union and the state of the budget have become essentially equivalent.

As the sheer volume of budgeting has risen along with increasingly higher stakes and ever-changing procedures, the need grows apace for an up-to-date account of the new process through which spending decisions are made. As I write (April 1987), there is no contemporary account of how budgets are made. Events have outdistanced all books. Yet I believe a description and analysis of the budgetary process that focused solely on what is happening now would be inadequate, even misleading. Indeed, it is possible to convey an adequate understanding of contemporary budgeting only by comparing it with what has gone before. Since my belief in the indispensability of a historical approach accounts for the organization of the "new" *Politics* and informs its analysis throughout, the reader should know why I have not simply done the best I could with the budget of the day and left it at that.

What is it that no longer exists and is still with us? The substantial changes in budgeting that have taken place in the last 20 years have not really replaced anything; rather, the new has been layered onto the old. There is more of everything—more programs, more money, more debt, more spending devices, more control mechanisms, more participants, more procedures. It is necessary to know about the past because it is still with us. The decentralized, fragmented, legislatively centered budgeting process that stems from its 200-year-old origins still distinguishes the American budgetary process from that of any other democratic nation. The classic dance of the dollars in the appropriations process (memorialized in Richard Fenno's *The Power of the Purse* and my "old" *Politics*) remains: Spending estimates still wend their way from bureaus to departments to the central budget office to the president to the House, Senate, and conference committees, even if some participants have changed roles and new actors are pushing in different directions.

Appreciation of the new depends on distinguishing it from the old. Deciding how much should be spent *in toto,* how much revenue ought to be raised, and whether a surplus or deficit would be desirable or possible, for instance, seems straightforward. And so it would be anywhere else. But not in America. Not until 1921 did departmental spending estimates go to the Bureau of the Budget (now the Office of Management and Budget) for review before being sent to Congress for consideration. Not until 1974 did Congress commit itself to pass resolutions establishing targets for total spending and revenues. Not until the late 1970s did the president's budget message, which used to set the starting point for congressional action, cease to perform that function; nowadays it is pronounced "dead on arrival."

Here, in the extreme volatility of the budgetary process, we have another reason for taking a historical approach. No one can say whether the Gramm–Rudman–Hollings Emergency Deficit Reduction and Balanced Budget Act of 1985 (GRH) will remain in force (it is now in limbo). It has survived so far not because it is considered desirable but rather because there is no agreement on more sensible alternatives. Whatever happens, GRH's provisions for counting federal credit toward the deficit or, in the Senate, for requiring offsets (new revenues or spending cuts) in order to raise spending beyond the budget resolution, may matter a good deal. It is also possible for the very newest changes to undo the merely new changes; some argue that the 1974 reforms, such as the requirement that Congress make budget resolutions and therefore set up budget committees, make it more difficult to reach agreement. Amid this flux, it seems wise to hold on to a variety of budget procedures, as history has presented them to us, on the chance that practice may well revert back to what it once was.

Whatever form of exposition is adopted, the major omissions of the old *Politics* must be remedied in the new version. Since entitlements (legal obligations on the Treasury to provide people who qualify with stipulated benefits) now amount to just under half the budget, no book on the subject should neglect it. Yet, aside from an excellent article by Kent Weaver,[1] there is no generic study of entitlements. Nor is there a chapter in a text that can be considered a guide to budgeting for national defense. I shall remedy these lacks here.

This book begins with a discussion of the multiple meanings of budgeting as well as a description of key terms and actors in the process of resource allocation. In order to compare past procedures with contemporary practices, the second chapter surveys the history of budgeting. Here I emphasize the enduring characteristics (from a devotion to budget balance to fragmentation of power) that distinguish America from other nations, and the failing efforts of reformers to provide through the budgetary process the centralized control absent from U.S. politics.

The third chapter on the classical period, roughly 1946 through 1973—now sufficiently remote to wear the patina of time—presents a summary of salient aspects of budgetary calculations and strategies drawn from the old *Politics*. The point made then was that budgeting is so complex—so many items interacting in numerous ways, involving difficult subjects—that budgeters had to simplify by adopting aids to calculation. Certainly the problem of calculation has not gotten any easier; on the contrary, the growth of government (meaning more programs) and the decline of agreement (meaning more closely contested choices) has made figuring out what to do more difficult. The convergence on past agreements that once constituted the base from which calculations proceeded has been eroded; focusing on incremental departures from the base wavers when one cannot agree on where to start: Is it last year's outlays, the president's budget request, the current services budget, the House or Senate budget resolutions, the conference committee recommendation, the continuing resolution, or what? As annual budgeting gives way to continuous revision, agencies cannot be sure of keeping what they were promised nor, given stalemate among the politicians, can they count on getting funds at the stipulated time. Anyone who doubts the increased complexity of the process itself need look only at the Gramm–Rudman–Hollings sequestration procedures (which call for sequential, across-the-board reductions in budget authority when deficit reduction targets are not met) or at the different Senate and House rules for the 302(a) and 302(b) provisions of the 1974 Budget Act, as amended, that, when implemented, shape the rules under which the budget is broken down in Congress. Without such understanding, one cannot tell which subcommittee can handle what items within certain guidelines, or how amendments from the floor can be considered so that it can be known when proposed laws conform to or depart from the agreed spending total—if one exists.

Students of budgeting are safe in studying budgetary calculations, which have merely become more complex; but surely strategies for securing funds must have changed qualitatively. Yes and no. All the old strategies—from the camel's nose to the cultivation of clientele, as the reader will see—are still with us. As is true of the

---

[1]Kent Weaver, "Automatic Government: The Politics of Indexation," typescript, 1986.

budgetary process itself, new strategies have been grafted on to the old. Strategies based on having the House Appropriations Committee assume the role of guardian of the Treasury, with the Senate acting as an appeals court, have to change when those roles reverse and a newcomer, the budget committees, takes over what is left of guardianship. Participants are bound to have more trouble figuring out the "fair share" for their agency or program when the multiplication of spending sources—loans, loan guarantees, tax preferences, provisions for indexing spending to price changes, annual versus multiyear versus permanent appropriations—makes it so hard to determine who is getting how much. Relationships have to change when the Office of Management and Budget reduces its contacts with agencies in order to conduct continuing negotiations directly with congressional committees.

Chapter 4 provides snapshots of contemporary history that reveal how and why budgetary consensus declined. Entitlements threatened to drive out other spending. Federal credit grew astronomically. Agreements on a balance between revenue and expenditure weakened under the impact of strained economic circumstances and under the theoretical guidance of Keynesian economic doctrine. As economic distress made budget conflicts more severe, other standard practices—agreement on a budgetary base, confining conflicts to incremental departure from that base—began to erode. Reaction to President Nixon's impounding and to Watergate gave Congress reformed procedures under the Budget Act of 1974 but not agreement on how to use them. And the election of Ronald Reagan brought to the fore deep differences over taxation and welfare and defense spending that sharpened budgetary conflict.

The institutional manifestations of this budgetary dissensus, described in the fifth chapter, include transformations in the role of OMB and the appropriations committees and the appearance of the new budget committees. Strategic innovation becomes imperative as agencies and their clientele contemplate new rules of the game. No one and nothing are as they were.

Dissensus, as Chapter 6 shows, brings out both the worst and the best in budgetary procedures. Gimmicks, soft appearances substituting for harsh realities, dismay even those who use them. Across-the-board cuts in GRH substitute for intelligence. Yet there is another side to GRH. When faced with the need to recommend cuts in other programs or tax increases (rather than just asking for more), due to Senate offset provisions, interest-group lobbies begin to engage in previously unheard of behavior; they become interested in cutting other parts of the budget. Thus an objective that reformers were never able to achieve by exhortation—considering and comparing programs as part of a larger budget—has, for the time being in the Senate, been achieved through the offset mechanism. Were agreement ever reached to limit total spending and to choose the most desired programs within that limit, budget reformers have had a real-life lesson in what to do.

In the seventh and eighth chapters on entitlements, changes in strategies begin to be visible. It is better for program advocates to have funds guaranteed until Congress decides to make a change, than to chance the viscissitudes of the annual appropriations process. It is better for recipients to have their benefits tied to a generous index of rising prices, so that cost of living adjustments are automatic, than to have to ask Congress every year to hold constant the purchasing power of retirees or the unemployed. Unfortunately, such stability for beneficiaries is achieved by risking the instability of government. What is strategically rational for program advocates—indexed permanent entitlements with expanding benefits and beneficiaries—is irrational for budget controllers who find themselves unable to make large cuts in the relatively small remainder of the budget. Since entitlements make up just under half the budget, freeing them from having to be considered for cuts makes budgeting quite a different game. How to be "entitled" rather than "controllable" is of the strategic essence. Yet there is no budgetary safe harbor. Entitlement status is no guarantee either of rapid growth or of protection against cuts. That is why, in addition to high flyers, I also look at entitlements that failed.

Just as being technically listed as "uncontrollable" in the sense of not being subject to the discipline of annual appropriation does not prevent entitlements from being continuously adjusted, the fact that defense spending takes up the lion's share of "controllable" (i.e., annually appropriated) spending need not signify it will bear the brunt of reductions. But it is large, tempting, and, occasionally, vulnerable.

A chapter on defense spending follows entitlements because it is the second largest type of expenditure. Indeed, with social welfare (mostly entitlements) taking up some 46 percent of total spending, defense 28 percent, and interest on the debt 14 percent, only 12 percent is left for the rest of the budget. These figures constitute the indispensable starting place for any intelligent consideration of contemporary budgeting.

I would be surprised if anyone claims to comprehend fully defense budgeting. Huge dollar figures, long lead times for weapons built out of complex technologies, feast and famine in resources, a rapidly changing world scene, all combine to create confusion. Is there too little oversight or too much micro-management? Are defense managers prevented from doing their best, dragged down by the sheer weight of regulation, or are the services preparing to fight their wars alone so they require much more constraint? All of these are true under some conditions. As with allegations of "waste, fraud, and abuse" in welfare programs, the general modicum of truth does not tell one where to draw the line between harshness and leniency, initiative and control. If all we care about is having what we need when we need it, and expense is no object, duplication is desirable. Since "how much" affects "what for," the cost influencing the amount and kind of troops and weapons, budgeting is crucial to defense. You tell me: Is it better to learn to live with the faults of defense budgeting, like "goldplating" and "stretchouts," because they are a part of real life and therefore likely to be always with us? Or should we try once again to reform the process because there has to be a better way? What I can do is explain why every administration complains about the sins of its predecessors and then proceeds to do exactly the same.

The tenth chapter is about proposals for reform of the budgetary process—the line-item veto, constitutional spending limits, statutory balanced budget requirements, and more. The difference between the treatment of reform in the old and new books lies in a much wider perspective. The old *Politics* was virtually bereft of history; although I was astonished at the degree of informal coordination achieved under the old process, I did not pursue its roots in the achievement of balance, annualarity, and comprehensiveness. The new chapter on reform begins with the grave weakening of these norms that once had facilitated coordination of spending and revenue, had lent predictability to budgeting behavior, and had enabled budgeters to minimize their disagreements. Whereas the politics of the old process operated under considerable consensus, so that the importance of agreement on substance was played down, the new politics in a time of dissensus is about grand questions: How much, what for, who pays; in sum, what side are you on? Where before reformers were concerned with improving efficiency and effectiveness in the pursuit of agreed-on objectives, these micro-questions (touched on under such designations as performance budgeting, program budgeting, and zero-base budgeting) now have given way to more solemn macro queries: Can we govern? Is there sufficient agreement among the nation's political elites about what kind of society they want in order to do the one thing every government must do—pass its budget? Reforms look quite different if one assumes that changes in political personalities or in budget procedures will produce consensus, rather than fearing that the political visions separating the contestants are too wide to be bridged by anything less than a fundamental change in political alignments. Since I adhere to the latter position, which stresses ideological dissensus, I am less sanguine than others about budgetary cures for political ailments.

Let me put it this way: When there was (mostly) agreement on the base, the old *Politics* stressed conflict over the increments. The new *Politics* stresses the base because it is often disagreed. Conflict is now about fundamentals.

In one respect, neither I nor the budgetary process can go back to where we once were. *The Politics of the Budgetary Process*, circa 1964, has been praised beyond its merits. The budgetary process then was simple; anyone who stumbled on to budgeting could quickly get a grasp of it. Alas, budgeting is no longer so transparent. I have tried to make understandable such previously unheard of subjects as the ability of the federal financing bank to tumble credit off and on the budget, but I cannot guarantee that others will think so. The importance of federal credit is now so manifest—the credit budget, so to speak, being comparable in total to federal spending—that its dimensions cannot fail to impress. After all, credit is money too. So are tax preferences and other forms of resource allocation that do not appear in the budget.

Nearly a quarter of a century ago, budgeting was different, and so was I. Closer to students in age (and far closer to them in understanding than my confident prose might suggest), I faced no serious problem of selection; everything I knew about budgeting is in that book. Everything. But no more than the budgetary process can shrug off the accretions of time, can I recapture the days when budgeting meant appropriations and everyone, myself included, took for granted the understandings that made procedures seem so simple. In the old volume, politics was mostly internal to the budgetary process itself. Outside forces figured only through the operations of interest groups and the perceptions of participants as they assessed the political moods of the day. The new volume (in which all is entirely new except for one chapter and a few pages on the nature of budgeting) is much more concerned with the impact of external political forces on the budgetary process. The interests are still there, but they are now joined by ideologies connecting individual programs to the general purposes of government. When budgeting was a sideshow, albeit an important one, political stability could be taken for granted. Indeed, that stability made budgeting less vital. The emergence of budgeting center stage signifies its increased dependence on shifting political alignments.

When budgeting operated under a hidden consensus, the subject was considered too dull to attract readers. Nine publishers, by my recollection, turned the book down; budgeting was easy to describe but hard to sell. Now that budgeting has acquired some of the interested audience it deserves, the subject unfortunately has become difficult to describe. I hope again to show that the effort to understand is worthwhile. Budget, budget, budget, as members of Congress complain, is all we can do unless and until we Americans once again agree on what kind of society and which sort of government we want.

Aaron Wildavsky

Acknowledgments to the Second Edition

Without the extraordinarily favorable reception of the old *The Politics of the Budgetary Process* (Little, Brown and Company, 1964, first edition), I would not have been encouraged to undertake the many studies that have led to this new version. Nor would I have had the material for Chapter 3 on the classical period. Without my collaboration with Carolyn Webber on our *A History of Taxation and Expenditure in the Western World* (Simon and Schuster, 1986), it would not have been possible for me to write the second chapter on the historical development of American budgeting. Without my continuing collaboration with Joseph White on "The Battles of the Budget: From the Last Year of Carter through Gramm–Rudman–Hollings, and Tax Reform," I would not have known enough about contemporary budgeting to write the fourth through the sixth chapters. Without the many papers on entitlements prepared by students in my seminars on budgeting, Chapters 7 and 8 could not have been written. Without the research assistance of Ronald D. Pasquariello, Dean Hammer, and John Gilmore, Chapter 9 on defense budgeting would have been much poorer. Blake Edgar read appropriations hearings so as to supply me with up-to-date versions of budgeting strategies. Readers will benefit by his good taste.

Truly this book, even more than most research, is a collective enterprise. As always, I have benefited from continuing conversation with participants in budgeting. Congressional hearings and GAO reports and the works of scholars have proved invaluable. Far more than in earlier times, I have learned a lot from work by reporters who specialize in budgeting and from periodicals, like the *Congressional Quarterly* and *The National Journal*, that cover the subject. Newsletters—*Inside the Administration* and Stanley Collender's *Federal Budget Report*—and periodic reports from Carol Cox's Committee on a Responsible Federal Budget have helped me understand what is happening as it happens.

After a draft of the manuscript had been completed, I asked Dean Hammer to stand in for all those who did not know about budgeting but wanted to learn. As my lay reader, he helped me simplify my presentation, add material where it was missing, and generally reorganize the manuscript. If I have achieved a level of exposition appropriate to a beginner in the study of budgeting, I owe that to Dean's unremitting efforts to set me straight.

The award for help above and beyond the call of duty goes to colleagues who read the entire manuscript—Naomi Caiden, Mark Kamlet, David Mowery, Jonathan Rauch, James Savage, and Joseph White. They have saved me from many errors and their criticisms have sharpened my perceptions. All of them will have an opportunity in their own work to set the world straight on matters budgetary.

John Ellwood provided a critique of my use of budgetary terms, and Gordon Adams helped improve the chapter on defense. I am grateful to these immensely knowledgeable students of budgeting.

Marie-Ann Seabury edited this book for me with her usual eye for my infelicities. Doris Patton, my secretary, not only typed several drafts of the manuscript impeccably but also prepared research material. No doubt she wondered whether the mountains of note cards would ever diminish. Neither the budget nor budgeting shows any sign of diminishing, so why should studies of the subject decline?

For the first time I am fortunate in having colleagues on the Berkeley campus who are themselves students of budgeting. I am grateful for conversations on the current trends with David Mowery in the Haas School of Business and for a variety of source materials and detailed comments on the last two chapters by John Ellwood in the Graduate School of Public Policy.

Stanley Collender of Price Waterhouse; Robert W. Hartman, Senior Analyst for the Budget Process of the Congressional Budget Office; and Joseph White of the Brookings Institution provided me with detailed comments on Chapters 11 and 12. I am especially grateful to Joe White, who helped me organize these chapters in a more coherent manner. Truly, he has learned more than he was taught. Other reviewers who offered helpful suggestions include: James W. Fossett, State University of New York, Albany; Mark S. Kamlet, Carnegie Mellon University; Alfreda J. McCollough, College of Charleston; Kevin V. Mulcahy, Louisiana State University; David J. Olson, University of Washington; and R. D. Sloan, Jr., University of Colorado, Boulder.

A.W.

Chapter 1

Budgeting as Conflicting Promises

The word that originally meant a leather bag or pouch used for carrying money has, through the years, taken on a larger meaning. Today we still find etymological traces of the word "budget" when we hear, for example, about the "budget package" put together by Congress and the president. We have come a long way since the days of carrying the budget by hand, though we may regret it. Not only has the pouch expanded considerably, but it has become rather amorphous. No single document represents "the United States budget." The only document that resembles a formal budget is a book representing the president's preferences—his asking price, so to speak. When we hear that this budget is "unrealistic," we learn that many of these preferences are unlikely to be realized. The same can be said of House and Senate budget resolutions specifying how much should be spent in total, and on major programs, as well as how much revenue should be raised. These, too, may be only pious hopes. In the end, we are left with a variety of pieces of legislation—spending through appropriations, entitlements, credit, tax preferences, and more—that taken together constitute the budget.

What do we mean when we speak about the budget? At one level a budget is a prediction. A budget contains words and figures that propose expenditures for certain objects and purposes. The words describe types of expenditures (salaries, equipment, travel) or purposes (preventing war, improving mental health, providing low-income housing), and the figures are attached to each item. Presumably, those who make a budget intend there to be a direct connection between what is written in it and future events. If requests for funds are granted, if they are spent in accordance with instructions, and if the actions involved lead to the desired consequences, then the purposes stated in the document will be achieved. Budgets thus become links between financial resources and human behavior in order to accomplish policy objectives. Only through observation, however, is it possible to determine the degree to which the predictions postulated in budget documents turn out to be correct.

In the most general definition, budgeting is concerned with translating financial resources into human purposes. A budget, therefore, may also be characterized as a series of goals with price tags attached. Since funds are limited and have to be divided in one way or another, the budget becomes a mechanism for making choices among alternative expenditures. When the choices are related to one another so as to achieve desired goals, a budget may be called coordinated. Should it include a detailed specification of how objectives are to be achieved, a budget also may serve as a plan of work for those who assume the task of implementation. If emphasis is placed on achieving the most policy returns for a given sum of money, or on obtaining the desired objectives at the lowest cost, a budget may become an instrument for ensuring efficiency.

There may be a wide gap, however, between the intentions of those who make up a budget and their accomplishments. Although the language of a budget calls for achieving certain goals, through planned expenditures, investigation may reveal that no funds have been spent for these purposes, that the money has been used for other purposes, that quite different goals have been achieved, or that the same goals have been reached in different ways.

Viewed in another light, a budget may be regarded as a contract. Congress and the president promise to supply funds under specified conditions, and the agencies agree to spend the money in ways that have been agreed upon. (When an agency apportions funds to its subunits, it may be said to be making an internal contract.) Whether or not the contract is enforceable, or whether or not the parties actually agree about what the contract purportedly stipulates, is a matter for inquiry. To the extent that a budget is carried out, however, it imposes a set of mutual obligations and controls upon the contracting parties. The word *mutual* should be stressed because it is so easy to assume that control is exercised in a unilateral direction by superiors (members of Congress, department heads, and so on) over those formally subordinate to them. But when an appropriations committee approves some expenditures and not others, when it sets down conditions for the expenditure of funds, the committee is also obligating itself to keep its part of the bargain. A department head (to choose another example) who hopes to control the actions of her subordinates must ordinarily follow through on a promise to support some of their requests or else find them trying to undermine her. A budget thus becomes a web of social as well as of legal relationships in which commitments are made by all parties, and where sanctions may be invoked (though not necessarily equally) by all.

The web of interactions involved in allocating resources suggests the manifold difficulties that may arise during the budgetary process. Agreement is difficult because people want different things (or different amounts of the same things). People may also judge the future differently, partly because they prefer different futures, and this will lead them to disagree about what limits (and opportunities) the group faces. In the household, different guesses about next year's food prices and income will justify buying more or less expensive furniture; in government, different guesses and desires about the next year's inflation and revenues will justify buying more or less expensive battleships. Even people who can agree on what to buy may disagree on who should pay for it. The two incomes in a household could contribute equally to the rent, or the rent could be divided proportionately to the incomes. Each person may attempt to pay less by getting others to pay more. But preferences for different ways of life—for more competition, order, or equality—also play a part. Whether one prefers equality of condition or equality of opportunity—the richer subsidizing the poorer or the poorer trying to work their way up, or some combination of the two to maintain social stability—makes a great difference to one's view of desirable public and, therefore, budget policy.

Budgeting in any group is a process in which various people express different desires and make different judgments. In order to construct agreement on a range of items, group members resort to arguments about what is right and just. Now no one makes these values up; they come out of a worldview, an array of preferences about how people ought to live with other people. When these values are not merely ethereal (e.g., brotherhood) but lead to action—more for them, less for us—we see that budgeting is really about opposing and reconciling different ways of life. Sometimes people's preferences are dictated by principles (for example, that each should pay according to his ability; or that she who makes the largest contribution should have the most influence). It is hard to tell when people are sincere in invoking principles, for sometimes a principle is just a convenient excuse for a preference that has some other ground. In either case, ideals are invoked in order to persuade others; we have all been involved in arguments where the "principles" seemed to cause more furor than the action (Who will wash the dishes tonight?) would seem to justify. It is one thing, for instance, to argue that defense or social welfare spending is too high; it is another to contend that it would be morally wrong to provide the funds. More or less is easier to compromise than right or wrong. Because it raises questions about how people should relate to each other, budgeting can encompass disputes larger than their seeming subjects.

The desire not to disappoint or anger others makes planning to ensure that promises are kept important. Agreement in advance on spending (the promises in budget legislation) has two advantages: It bypasses continuing negotiation about each purchase, and it allows each member of the group to plan activities with assurance that the others will cooperate. Budgeting is part of the process of cooperative action in which commitments to contribute resources are joined to commitments as to their use. When promises cannot be kept for a year or more, budgeting breaks down.

Always, in the background, questions of authority—Who has the right to decide for whom?—and legitimacy—Do we trust our institutions to act for us?—overlay each choice. "Papa knows best" is different from majority rule or each person making the best deal. The greater the legitimacy accorded institutions, the more disposed are participants to accept outcomes as authoritative. When consent as well as content have to be hammered out on each and every matter, decision making becomes onerous. The process slows down both because many more choices are likely to be contested and because their significance has been enlarged from "how much" and "what for" to "who has the right to decide."

The budgetary process is further complicated by the many different implications for policy in the budget. There is a fiscal policy implication in which the total amount of spending and its deficit or surplus relationship to revenue are designed to stimulate or restrain the economy—to fight unemployment or inflation. The budget is indicative of the role of government; the budget summarizes the balance between public and private sectors of the economy—that is, what proportion of gross national product (GNP) consists of federal government spending—in short, how much federal government we have. The distribution of spending in very broad categories describes the kind of government we want: one that emphasizes military might, or protects the middle class, or helps the poor, or builds for the future. The assumptions in budget resolutions, and action on appropriations or entitlements or tax expenditures, also mean that the budget is a package of thousands of specific programs: how much to invest in airport safety; which people, if any, should receive special nutrition benefits; how many F–16s the Air Force needs.

All these policies are controversial. Some—unemployment versus inflation, the size of government, emphasis on military or social spending—are those that best distinguish Democrats from Republicans, liberals from conservatives. Yet budget politics need not cleave on these lines alone. Not all Republicans are conservatives; many Democrats are not liberals. The choices in budgeting pose trade-offs that make it hard to predict all choices from party or ideology. Greater military expenditure without corresponding cuts in social spending means bigger government and larger deficits; being a conservative or Republican will not tell a member of Congress whether he or she should prefer budget balance to defense. Party lines will also be blurred by contradictions between different preferences: Liberals usually like defense contracts for their districts, budget balancers can nevertheless like mortgage subsidies, conservatives can see good in social security or food stamps. Nevertheless, knowing a politician's party is a better guide than any other single factor to predict whether he or she is likely to vote for larger welfare and less defense.[1]

Just as it is made up of many policies, the budget also has many meanings according to one's institutional position in the government. To the ordinary citizen, budgeting is both mysterious and simple. It is so hard to understand that its complexity may be ignored in resorting to a simple test of virtue: Can the government balance its books or not? Is it in control of itself? For a federal agency—and for the state, local, and semiprivate organizations largely funded by the federal government—the budget is the irrigation system that provides the water without which an agency and its products would parch and wither. Interest groups may see the many steps of budgeting as opportunities or obstacles and budgeting institutions as allies or enemies. Some parts—an appropriations or authorizing subcommittee—may be "captured," but there are too many centers of decision to capture them all. If interest groups can simply try to get more for their favored programs, their strategies may be straightforward; if the budgetary process is arranged so that desires of various groups conflict—more for one of them means less for others—it is harder for each group to figure out what to do.

For the budget and appropriations committees, budgeting is their purpose and their power; their members must work to preserve that power. Since budgeting often encroaches on the turf of authorizing committees, they may view the budgetary process as a threat and an intrusion. For members of Congress with strong issue preferences that have been stymied by the relevant authorizing committees (committees whose domain is to recommend programs and activities for congressional approval), budgetary action may provide power. The budget resolutions, appropriations, and occasional debt-ceiling increases are trains that must

---

[1]See James L. Payne, "Voters Aren't So Greedy After All," *Fortune* (August 18, 1986), pp. 91–92.

run, and there may not be time to kick off the stowaways. Appropriations especially become targets of opportunity for "riders"—opposition to abortion and military aid to Central American forces, for example. Budget resolutions provide chances for votes on issues that might not otherwise reach the floor (e.g., public works funding or increases in veterans' benefits). For partisans, particularly leaders, of the Democratic and Republican parties, the totals for big programs in the budget resolutions measure their party's influence on the course of American government; short of the actual organization of the two houses (election of the Speaker, committee assignments), no other action is potentially of as great moment to the party leadership. The battle of the budget is the test of generalship. The ability of the parties to stay together in the final encounter (apart from the vote to organize the houses along partisan lines) is now their ultimate test of cohesion.

To those members of Congress who identify with the institution—and this, depending upon the issue and challenge, ranges from a few to all of them—budgeting is a test of Congress. Can Congress choose, can it enforce its will? In short, can Congress govern? The president asks the same questions, slightly changed: "Can I govern the agencies? Can I govern Congress? Can I govern responsibly and maintain public support?" Both president and Congress must ask, "Do we make policy or do the policies control us?" And, "Can any of us control events?"

The complexity of the federal budgetary process—the large numbers of wide-ranging yet uncertain consequences—reveals that the purposes of budgets are as varied as the purposes of the people who make them. One budget may be designed to coordinate diverse activities so that they complement one another in the achievement of common goals. Another budget may be put together primarily to discipline subordinate officials within a government agency by reducing amounts for their salaries and pet projects. And a third budget may be directed essentially to mobilizing the support of clientele groups who benefit by the services the agency provides. Nothing is gained, therefore, by insisting that a budget is only one of these things when it might be any or all of them or many other kinds of things as well.[2] One may, however, adopt a particular view of the budget as most useful for the purposes one has in mind. Without claiming to have found the only right perspective, or to have exhausted the subject in any way, I would like to propose a conception that seems useful in talking about the budgetary process as a phenomenon of human behavior in a governmental setting.

Taken as a whole, the federal budget is a representation in monetary terms of governmental activity. If politics is regarded in part as conflict over whose preferences shall prevail in the determination of national policy, then the budget records the outcomes of this struggle. If one asks, "Who gets what the government has to give," then the answers for a moment in time are recorded in the budget. If one looks at politics as a process by which the government mobilizes resources to meet pressing problems, then the budget is a focus of these efforts.

---

[2]A good discussion of the nature and variety of budgets may be found throughout Jesse Burkhead's *Government Budgeting* (New York: Wiley, 1956). See also the illuminating comments in Frederick C. Mosher, *Program Budgeting: Theory and Practice, with Particular Reference to the U.S. Department of the Army* (Chicago: Public Administration Service, 1954), pp. 1–18.

The size and shape of the budget is a matter of serious contention in our political life. Presidents, political parties, administrators, members of Congress, interest groups, and interested citizens vie with one another to have their preferences recorded in the budget. The victories and defeats, the compromises and bargains, the realms of agreement and spheres of conflict in regard to the role of national government in our society all appear in the budget. In the most integral sense, budgeting—that is, attempts to allocate scarce financial resources through political processes in order to realize disparate visions of the good life—lies at the heart of the political process. That there are visions of the good life enables people to make commitments to one another through the budget; that these visions conflict means that not all such promises can be kept.

BUDGETS ARE CONFLICTING COMMITMENTS

Our government makes different commitments to people and to other units of government, and these commitments take varied forms. All the commitments ultimately are shaped by law (and therefore by Congress, the president, and the courts). Some of these laws, *appropriations acts,* constitute permission for agencies of the government (e.g., the FBI or National Institutes of Health) to either spend or contract to spend specific amounts of money during the coming year or years. Other laws, such as the 1935 Social Security Act with its numerous amendments, contain promises to individuals that the government will pay specific sums to those who meet certain criteria. These laws, frequently called *entitlements,* differ from appropriations acts in four crucial ways:

1. Entitlements do not specify spending totals. Total spending under these programs, such as unemployment compensation, is simply the sum of the legislatively mandated payments to individuals. Administering agencies may withdraw from the Treasury whatever funds the law and the situation require.
2. Since totals are not legally mandated, they can be "guesstimated" but cannot be known in advance. Actual figures will depend on the number of people who qualify for the program and the amounts to which they are entitled. Payments for unemployment compensation, for example, depend upon both the number of unemployed and their previous base earnings, neither of which can be known exactly in advance. Not only are totals not directly chosen, they can only be known in retrospect.
3. The authority to spend is not limited in time. Rather than being authorized for use in the coming fiscal year, funding is available so long as a program exists; no ending date is established.
4. Unlike the relationship of other agencies to the budget process, the process for creating and amending these programs does not, in any meaningful way, involve House and Senate appropriations committees.

"Once enacted," a General Accounting Office report summarizes the differences, "entitlement legislation may automatically authorize an administrative agency to spend the funds for making the prescribed payments without advance appropriations from the Congress, thereby effectively relinquishing congressional control through the normal appropriations process."[3] The differences between appropriated and entitlement spending mean that legal authority for spending is the product of decisions taken by different kinds of committees at different times. Entitlements proposed by legislative committees have been adopted and amended separately over the years. The appropriations acts themselves, recommended by a separate set of committees, moreover, are not all considered at the same time. Every year there are at least 13 of them, each considered by a different subcommittee of the appropriations committees in the House and Senate, often at somewhat different times.

There is also a combination of these two commitments: the *appropriated entitlement.* As in the case of Aid to Families with Dependent Children, authority to make payments was enacted in the authorizing statute, but Congress had also to make an annual grant of spending authority in an appropriations bill.

Among the most important misunderstandings about federal government appropriations is the belief that they ordinarily enumerate the specific projects on which money will be spent. They may, but they often do not. Instead, money is appropriated in lump sums for general purposes with particular projects listed in conference committee reports or the reports of House or Senate Appropriations Subcommittees.

The nomenclature of budgeting adds to the difficulty in understanding the process. Laws that commit the government to spend money create budget authority. Budget authority (BA) is just what it sounds like: authority granted to some agent of the government to spend money. When the money is spent, it is called an outlay. Outlays cannot be made without budget authority.

The federal government cannot provide money to individuals or other units of government unless Congress gives legal authority to do so. This authority is defined in most cases (although not in all cases, as with loans and loan guarantees) as budget authority. The statutes that grant budget authority are of two general types: appropriations bills and "backdoor authority," which occurs outside the normal appropriations process. The most common forms of backdoor authority are borrowing authority, contract authority, and entitlements.

Appropriated funds are not necessarily all spent in a given year; the acts provide budget authority, but each year's outlays (i.e., actual spending) result from a combination of this year's and previous years' authority. For example, an appropriation may allow the Urban Mass Transit Administration (UMTA) to commit $200 million for a rapid transit extension in Chicago. This budget authority allows UMTA to enter into an obligation (i.e., contract) to spend that money. The money will, however, actually be outlaid (spent) over a period of years as the extension is built and material, labor, and design paid for.

In retrospect, outlays or actual expenditure for a given fiscal year are known. In prospect, they can only be estimated. Jonathan Rauch says it well: "Where Congress is concerned, budget authority is law, and therefore solid; outlays are staff estimates of the probable effect of the law, and thus are slippery."[4]

---

[3]Report to the Congress by the Comptroller General of the United States, "What Can Be Done To Check the Growth of Federal Entitlement and Indexed Spending," March 3, 1981, PAD-81-21, p. 10.

[4]"Senate Budget Panel Leaders Wage War on 'Budget-Busting' Appropriations Bills," *National Journal* (November 30, 1985), p. 2706.

This difference between budget authority and outlays is a primary source of confusion for people who follow federal budgeting. Congress votes on BA, but each year's spending, and thus fiscal policy and the deficit, depends on outlays. Members of Congress have some idea about the size of outlays that will result from their votes on BA, but, as we will see, the estimates can be controversial. What they vote on—authority—therefore, is not quite what they fight about—outlays. The distinction between budget authority and outlays allows all sorts of tricks, traps, and maneuvers, some of them inadvertent. Why, then, does it exist?

This situation results from the nature of many federal programs and the problems in administering them because of the size of the federal government. In our early history, the size that mattered was geography. Before the telegraph and the locomotive, communications were much slower. The federal government did not do very much, but what it did often took place a long way from Washington. Federal agents—customs officials from Boston to New Orleans; postmasters or army units spread from the Northwest territories to Florida—could not possibly be directed closely from the center. Slow communications meant that in the War of 1812 the Battle of New Orleans was fought weeks after peace had been made. In those days the government had to let its agents incur costs as they came along; then auditors would check the records in slow and excruciating detail. Congress provided authority to spend and under the Treasury Department chiefly controlled the honesty and frugality of actual outlays through its accounting system. Smaller local governments could vote on annual outlays directly because their work was closer at hand, and errors could be corrected if necessary by getting the legislature, say, a city council, together for a special meeting. Gathering Congress was more difficult. The kind of annual focus on outlays that concerns us now was impractical, at least for much of the nineteenth century.[5]

Later, change from a focus on budget authority to one on outlays was inhibited by established congressional routine and the nature of many federal activities. The organizational structure of federalism had become important. An organization that does its own work, like an individual spending only on himself, can change spending plans more easily than can one that works through obligations to others. The federal government has always done a lot of its work through others; contractors carried mail through Panama or built dams; in later years, state and local governments received federal funds for everything from law enforcement to caring for the poor. Working through third parties meant that federal planners had less idea of how work would be scheduled, while recipients of money needed some guarantees about federal action for their own planning. The organizational complexity, the layers of federal administration, therefore, encouraged a system in which funds were committed annually but their use was not restricted to a strict annual schedule.

In short, Congress's focus on budget authority rather than outlays arises chiefly from the difficulties of managing federal activities. Those difficulties in

---

[5]See Leonard D. White's histories, *The Federalists* (New York: Macmillan, 1961), *The Jeffersonians* (New York: Macmillan, 1951), and *The Jacksonians* (New York: Macmillan, 1956). See also Frederick C. Mosher, *The GAO: The Quest for Accountability in American Government* (Boulder, Colo.: Westview Press, 1979); and James Sterling Young, *The Washington Community, 1802–1828* (New York: Columbia University Press, 1966).

turn inhibit control of the deficit. The annual balance sheet—the outlays—is not the same as commitments—the budget authority.

Among outlays based on entitlements, outlays based on previous years' appropriations, and outlays voted and spent that year, each year's spending is based on commitments made at different times. In fiscal 1980, according to the Office of Management and Budget, only 27.3 percent of outlays were determined by the appropriations process for that year. In addition to interest on the debt and prior year's authority, most of the rest was made up of entitlements, and these in turn were largely composed of payments to individuals. Government has gotten good at writing checks.

TAX PREFERENCES

What is true of spending is more true of taxing: Tax law is an accretion of years of decisions. Like entitlements, tax law is open-ended in that individuals are obligated to contribute according to various criteria, rather than the government being guaranteed some sum of revenue. Revenue may be influenced and estimated but, in these circumstances, not decreed. When economic or demographic conditions change—how many people at which incomes fit into certain categories—revenues rise or fall accordingly.

Tax legislation is handled by the House Committee on Ways and Means and the Senate Committee on Finance. These committees also have jurisdiction over many entitlement programs, such as unemployment compensation and the massive Old Age, Survivors, Disability and Health Insurance (OASDHI) system. OASDHI includes the old age pensions we normally call social security, disability pensions, and medicare, the largest programs in the budget. The tax committees have jurisdiction over these entitlements because, by their design, these programs directly relate taxes to benefits. People earn the right to benefits by contributing to the system, thereby making the program look like insurance (you pay premiums to insure against the risk of being old, sick, or unemployed). The contributions are earmarked for trust funds, and benefits are paid out of each program's fund.

Such contributions are taxes: If you meet the criteria for paying them, but fail to do so and are caught, you may go to jail. While payments to individuals in some of these programs, like medicare, have little to do with the amounts contributed (and the Treasury is obligated to make up any shortfall through its general revenues), the trust-fund financing device requires that decisions about benefits be linked to financing. That link is accomplished institutionally by giving the revenue committees jurisdiction over benefit levels as well. The insurance (real or hypothetical) mechanism of these programs also deepens their character as obligations that may not be changed: People have paid for their benefits. Of course, people also have paid for appropriated programs, but in the social insurance programs, recipients can argue that they individually contributed for the specific purpose of personal insurance.

The committees have another type of spending jurisdiction—"tax preferences." These provisions of the law reduce taxpayers' liability to the government so long as they are engaged in some activity that the government wishes to encourage. Tax preferences are used to encourage certain industries or to promote widely desired individual goods (the tax deduction for mortgage interest encourages the construction industry as well as home ownership). Also they may be justified in terms of the wider national interest (credits for energy exploration serving to reduce dependence on foreign oil). Those who do not like tax preferences call them "loopholes," "gimmicks," or "tax expenditures." The metaphor suggests money escaping or being diverted from its intended use, and is misleading. Such loopholes are passed by Congress and are as intended as any other legislation (although, as with other legislation, there may be unintended consequences so that a group that was not originally supposed to receive tax preferences is able to qualify). The mortgage interest deduction and the nontaxation of employee health benefits (which, after all, are equivalent to income) are examples of tax decisions that involve many billions of dollars and major social policies. Because tax preferences affect many groups, the tax committees are petitioned for aid by a huge array of constituencies, all trying to get something out of a given tax bill.

Tax preferences and entitlements are similar in that it is hard to imagine either of them being subject to substantial annual review. In each case, large numbers of people make commitments on the basis of government policy—to invest under certain depreciation rules; to save at a certain rate because social security exists. Entitlements in particular involve commitments that politicians view as substantially different from those made by appropriations; the consequences will come up in Chapter 8. Our discussion so far should establish that taxing may look like spending, and spending may be many different things.

For most of American history, as in the old *Politics*, appropriations were what people meant when they spoke about the budget. We can understand this if we review some of the power stakes in appropriations.

APPROPRIATIONS: THE POWER OF CONGRESS AND POWER WITHIN CONGRESS

Americans have long feared oppression by the political executive. Members of Congress have long seen themselves as the bulwark against such oppression. The public, judging from opinion polls, trusts Congress no more than the presidency, but members of Congress still see themselves in a protective role. Their major weapon is the "power of the purse"—the fact that, as the Constitution states, "No money shall be drawn from the Treasury, but in consequence of Appropriations made by law." The power of the purse is, then, a legislative power in that no money may be spent without the granting of budget authority by Congress.

The process of annually appropriating funds for federal agencies is intended to enforce dependence upon Congress of those agencies' officers. Unless an agency justifies itself each year, it risks losing funding. If the agency behaves in ways that upset Congress, it has an annual opportunity to bring the agency into line through threats or actual changes in appropriations. The agency does not have the advantage of delay, as it would if Congress needed to legislate a change because funding was permanent or multiyear unless otherwise altered. Unlike entitlement funding, annual appropriations mean that delay will cause funding to run out and the agency's activities to cease. Appropriations acts are privileged in floor consideration because members of Congress do not ordinarily want maneuvering or logjams to shut down programs.

The House Appropriations Committee, being larger in number but with fewer duties (and therefore more specialized), has always paid more attention to detail than has its Senate counterpart. Not all details are incorporated into the annual act or report, but intensive review enables members and staff of the appropriate House subcommittee to judge whether an agency is using the money as Congress intended, or as its members intend, rather than in the political interests of the current administration or the desires of administrators.

The appropriations process is in part a response to the very problem of designing expenditure controls in a system full of advocates. We may ask why budget oversight, just like the rest of oversight, is not left to the authorizing committees—those, such as Armed Services or House Energy and Commerce, which write the legislation that creates and gives power to the agencies. The answer is that they do not have budget powers because Congress does not trust them to control themselves. Other members of Congress believe that the authorizing committees have very strong incentives to ally with the agencies they authorize. By looking at their job, we can understand both this belief and why members of Congress act on it by regulating themselves.

Members of Congress, as Richard Fenno emphasizes in his *Congressmen in Committees,* have multiple goals: They want to make good policy, have personal power, keep Congress strong (their power depends on the institution's), make voters happy, and please people who can influence voters (by giving money or publicity or other campaign help). The congressional committee system helps members pursue all of these goals, but with some drawbacks for budgeting.[6]

The committee system divides the labor—of attending to the facts, and of assessing the group preferences involved in hundreds of policy issues—because most members can develop expertise only in a tiny portion of policy matters. But they can look to the committees for guidance on other legislation and they expect others to look to them for guidance in their own fields, where they have power and the attendant chance to make policy.

Committees do not always get their way. They cannot push through Congress legislation that a majority finds obnoxious; committees that persist in trying risk losing the benefits of deference from their colleagues. Other members, however, rarely are familiar with the details of legislation in a committee's jurisdiction and therefore may not even know that they do not like it. There is a large gray area in which a committee will have discretion.

Further, legislation needs committee approval to reach the floor. Therefore, the committees have a virtual veto over, and largely shape, policy initiatives in their areas. While it is possible to bypass committees through such devices as a discharge petition, the immense effort, as well as hard feelings, discourage most efforts. Hence those concerned—farmers and the USDA for agriculture, the Federal Communications Commission and broadcasters for Energy and Commerce, for example—greatly value influence on those committee members.

Often members sit on a committee because they bring to Congress a special interest in that subject. Sometimes the clientele served can provide helpful support (or damaging opposition) for reelection. Members may seek to do the most

---

[6]See Richard F. Fenno, Jr., *Congressmen in Committees* (Boston: Little, Brown and Company, 1973).

good, however conceived, and that may well mean doing good for those people and in that policy area over which, as committee members, they have the greatest influence. Interest groups encourage such attention, whatever its origin, with campaign assistance; agencies respond to policy suggestions even if not incorporated in legislation; and over time there develops a mutually supportive, three-point relationship among committee members, interest groups, and agencies. These alliances have been called iron triangles, and critical observers hold that these bonds cannot be broken by outsiders. Actually these triangles are of widely varying strength (as a study of entitlements will show).

When the House Ways and Means Committee and the Senate Finance Committee report legislation on social security and unemployment compensation, they may simultaneously be spending and supporting that spending with revenues. When legislative committees authorize spending without specific revenues, as in entitlements such as kidney dialysis, other members fear this spending may be excessive. Since members of individual legislative and appropriations committees do not know the needs of other committees as well, and since they are particularly aware of and concerned by needs in their own areas, members of Congress fear that each of their committees will ask for more funding than they, as a body, are willing to support. The total requested may be more than Congress is willing to vote in taxes.

All members of Congress care about the relation of spending to taxing, and so do voters; they fear the consequences, both for their own reelection and for the institution, if they continually spend more than they can raise. For that reason the appropriations committees were constituted with extensive powers. Members of authorizing committees have delegated to members of appropriations committees the power (subject to floor votes) to limit spending. Thus the appropriations committees are in an inherently adversarial relation with the rest of Congress. They are protected by confidence in their discretion; when they are believed to have overstepped their bounds, they might lose their power (as happened in both House and Senate in the last quarter of the nineteenth century). The late-nineteenth-century experience, however, was not deemed a success, and since 1921 the appropriations committees have been among the more powerful in Congress.

Budgetary policy is determined by both authorizing and appropriating legislation. Louis Fisher has described the standard model of the relationship:

> As a general principle, authorizing committees are responsible for recommending programs and activities to be approved by Congress. The committees establish program objectives and frequently set dollar ceilings on the amounts that can be appropriated. Once this authorization stage is complete, the Appropriations Committees recommend the actual level of "budget authority," allowing federal agencies to enter into obligations. This, of course, is an idealized model. Actual congressional operation is substantially different.[7]

And it is different because appropriations now fund substantially less than half the budget.

The old authorizing-appropriating dichotomy no longer works so neatly. The old relationship does not apply, mostly because presidents and Congresses have

---

[7]Louis Fisher, "The Authorization-Appropriation Process in Congress: Formal Rules and Informal Practices," *Catholic University Law Review*, Vol. 29, No. 5 (1979), pp. 52–105.

wanted to spend more by guaranteeing payments to individuals. Appropriations acts are so complicated, moreover, that the appropriations subcommittees develop substantial independence from the parent committee, thus limiting the potential to trade off spending among the activities funded by the acts. The authorizing committees, unsurprisingly, sometimes resist and try to reverse appropriations committee action on the floor. Almost always this is done to increase spending.

The boundaries between authorizing and appropriating decisions are hard to maintain in practice. A decision not to fund an activity, or to fund it under certain conditions (e.g., abortions allowed only in case of rape or serious threat to the life of the mother), looks much like a policy decision. Unfortunately, the many possibilities for undermining appropriations and authorizations exacerbate power struggles among committees. They also create incentives to complicate appropriations legislation with floor amendments ("riders" that the authorizing committees would disapprove); appropriations, which must pass, thus may be held hostage.

Yet the appropriations process has been and is meaningful: Appropriations committees derived power from the special advantages granted to legislation on the floor; for many years, placement on the committee of members from fairly safe districts; and the influence of powerful chairmen, in the years when chairmen had great formal powers over committees (which lasted until the mid–1970s). Most important, the role of the committee was accepted both by its own members and by other members of each house. Since anybody could spend, committee members for many years found both virtue and power in limiting expenditure.

The appropriations committees exemplify the American practice of opposing ambition with ambition, of functioning under the checks and balances so eloquently justified in *The Federalist*. The ambition of those committees to restrain spending counters that of the authorizers to increase it; the results vary. In a wider sense, House, Senate, and president all check each other. When they were thought not to check each other enough, a new layer of committees, called budget committees, was added to help safeguard the treasury. Once that happened, something obvious but unexpected occurred: The appropriations committees withdrew from their previous positions as guardians of the Treasury. Support for committee norms gave way in part to self-expression by members. For some members, program advocacy became the main purpose. For others, still adhering to notions of helping improve the management of federal program efficiency remained important but holding down spending did not.

Despite these changes in ideology and perceived self-interest, the appropriations committees remain important. For one thing, the growth of government to over a trillion dollars a year means that the two-fifths going through the appropriations committees represents big money. Put another way, although the proportion of the whole passing through the appropriations process has declined, the absolute amount is still far larger than the total budget for all but the last two decades. For another thing, as social security has been placed politically out of reach and other entitlements get harder to decrease, appropriations become a large part of what is up for grabs in the short term. But we run ahead of our story.

The mutual checking of House and Senate is easily overlooked but hard to overemphasize. These bodies represent people in different ways; their members deal with different political facts (campaigning every six years instead of every two changes members' perspectives immensely); their budget committees are of different sizes (causing different patterns of division of labor, the Senate being less detail- and more debate-oriented). The leadership and members of the two bodies depend on each other very little, and neither will accept leadership from the other. Independent and different, the two houses frequently support different policies. In appropriations or tax bills, as on any other, disagreement must be resolved by bargaining on conference committees, in which delegates from each house work out a package of provisions that can be supported by both. What emerges from conference, if anything, may be quite different from what either house wanted. Members of the House, anticipating conference, build coalitions and take positions with one eye always on the Senate. Senators may vote for more defense spending than they really want, establishing a bargaining position to take to conference. House members may vote for a program that wins constituency support even if they dislike it, calculating that Senate nonsupport will allow dropping the proposal in conference. An interest group defeated in the House will work to prevail in the Senate and then in conference. So does the president.

The bicameral system complicates legislation, assuring that many votes will be taken before a final decision is made. It provides numerous opportunities for bargaining. Until a bill emerges from conference and gains final approval, not only its fate but its provisions may be uncertain. Because it is hard to distinguish between maneuver and preference, interpretation of congressional action is difficult. Even after a bill is passed, the president might veto it. Of course, if all the president gets a crack at is a single omnibus bill for the whole government, a continuing resolution, it is not easy to veto that.

THE PRESIDENT IS BOTH RIVAL AND PARTNER OF CONGRESS

The president has the first and last moves in the budget process. He can both check and use Congress, and it can both check and use him.

The last move is the veto—a bludgeon where a scalpel might be more apt. Rarely will a president dislike more than a small part of an appropriations bill, the bulk of which funds relatively uncontroversial and long-standing activities. Therefore, the veto of an appropriation act becomes part of a game of chicken; neither the president nor the act's supporters in Congress want to be blamed for shutting down federal activities in a dispute over details. The president—if only because members of his own party do not want to see him lose—usually can find enough support in at least one house to sustain the veto. He also holds the high ground in a public mudslinging contest with Congress: The president commands more media attention; as the only nationally elected official, he can claim to represent the national interest better than any set of congressional leaders; and Congress is less popular with voters than even the most unpopular president. For these reasons the president is likely to win a veto battle, with Congress having to pass a new bill that suits the chief executive.

Yet the relationship has its own dynamic. Members of Congress do not like a pattern of vetoes and may unite to defend their institutional power against a president who overdoes it. Presidents do not like to lose, especially because losses reduce the White House's credibility. Anticipated reaction—the side that expects to lose by giving in—is the usual rule. When the president fails to heed the signals, he can ask for less and end up having to spend more. In essence, both president and Congress have good reason to avoid a public veto fight, in which one or the other may be embarrassed, programs that each values be hurt, and much time be wasted. The veto, therefore, gives the president a loud voice in the bargaining over spending and tax legislation; its threat is more important than its use.

The Constitution, through the veto, gave the president a voice in bargaining; Congress gave the president the right to set many of the terms. The Budget and Accounting Act of 1921 created the Bureau of the Budget. The Bureau, in a couple of steps, became the Office of Management and Budget (OMB), located in the Executive Office of the president. OMB prepares, and the president submits to Congress, a budget for each fiscal year. (Each fiscal year runs from October 1 of the previous calendar year to September 30 of the same numbered calendar year; thus fiscal 1999 began October 1, 1998, and ended September 30, 1999.) The president's budget is submitted at the beginning of the congressional session at which appropriations for that fiscal year must be made (e.g., January of 1999 for fiscal 2000).

The president's budget is a combination of proposals for legislation and predictions of events. It suggests amounts of budget authority for various line items (e.g., salaries and expenses) for each agency, which will be considered by the appropriations committees. The president's budget estimates outlays both from last year's actual spending and from the combination of old and new budget authority. It predicts the performance of the economy and, from that, the revenues and expenditures that will be produced by current tax and entitlement law. Estimated interest rates (which, at times, are difficult to predict) determine estimates of the government's debt-service costs. These proposals and estimates are summed to a bottom line: surplus or deficit. The deficit, total spending, and revenues are the most publicized aspects of the president's proposal and must be justified both to himself and to others as good policy and good politics.

In the past, the only way to affect the totals was to affect the components. The budgetary process worked by adding together spending and revenues as they emerged in separate actions, though with informal understanding of what the totals would be. Recent formal and informal deficit reduction processes work the other way—from totals to parts. Outlays have to fit within prespecified deficit reduction targets.

In preparing his budget, the president faces the problem of matching preferences over programs with preferences about overall spending, taxing, and borrowing. In the past, since agencies limited their spending bids, the first step was to ask them what they needed or wanted. Budget examiners at OMB analyzed detailed agency submissions, searching for the best places to make cuts, if needed. Their judgments were based both on rules of thumb (cut new elements or reduce ineffective programs) and on a sense of the administration's attitude toward each program. While OMB was examining, the president's economic advisors—the Secretary of the Treasury, Chairman of the Council of Economic Advisers, Director of OMB, and others—prepared estimates of economic performance and arguments in support of particular tax and spending levels. But that was then. Nowadays, with presidential preferences starting out at much lower totals, the OMB sends out advice on the level of permissible spending. Sometimes this advice includes "give backs," that is, previously allowed funds that must be returned. This is not to say that the OMB previously existed only as a passive repository of departmental requests. The OMB did provide spending guidelines in the past, but the extent and focus of this involvement has changed dramatically.

Normally the totals suggested mean spending at a lower level than the total of the agency submissions to OMB. How the president resolves that mismatch depends on the economic situation, the president's own policy preferences and management style, and how other political actors such as commentators, Congress, and interest groups are expected to respond. Whatever politico-economic judgments are made, decisions on individual programs may be reconciled with preferred totals by:

1. Changing appropriations requests for the agencies either by presidential command through OMB or by placing supporters in charge of agencies. This method has a distinct advantage: Congress has to enact some appropriation and therefore must confront the president's proposal and justify different action.

2. Recommending changes in the laws governing entitlements. Congress need not act at all. Thus the president cannot force the Committee on Ways and Means to report out medicare changes. But Congress may choose to act by limiting eligibility, reducing payments, or limiting cost of living increases.

3. Recommending tax changes. Tax hikes are usually political poison; politicians do not want to be seen sponsoring them. Hikes, therefore, tend to be disguised as loophole closing, reform, "revenue enhancement," or are called "temporary" surcharges.

4. Changing the economic projections to make the tax and spending estimates come closer together. In the past, economic projections were made only by the White House. Now the House and Senate Budget Committees and the Congressional Budget Office join in the act. Any juggling of the numbers, if done too often or too blatantly, however, may cause Congress to ignore the president's budget altogether. But it has an advantage: The administration need not propose to hurt anyone. Since economic forecasting is a highly uncertain art, the economists in any event are quite probably wrong. Use of this tactic requires that the president care more about fiscal appearances than consequences. After all, the budget and the economy will be there again next year.

5. Deciding that the totals are not so bad after all. Ronald Reagan did that with his deficits, but so did Jimmy Carter and many other presidents. When Congress decided that the appearance of meeting the Gramm–Rudman–Hollings deficit reduction targets was better than the havoc caused by the necessary cuts, it was doing the same sort of thing. Problems are bad only if their solutions are not worse.

However the president defines his problem, his budget is issued with great fanfare. The budget documents include detailed justifications of his choices.

Agency heads are expected to argue for the president's proposals even if they had requested larger funds.

The obvious questions are: Why did Congress establish this procedure? How much effect does it have on what Congress does? The main advantage to Congress is that this procedure gives the president primary responsibility for proposing cuts. The president can impose his priorities on the executive branch in a way that is impossible for any part of Congress, since the executive is in principle (and, in part, in fact) a hierarchy; Congress is anything but. A president can create a package that the noncentralized appropriations committees would have a hard time doing. Congress can then respond to his package of programs, changing it where it differs too much from congressional priorities or where constituency pressures are great, and letting the president take the blame for other decisions. But in 1995 the primary benchmark for budget cutting was the program of the Republican majority, and the critical questions were whether the leadership could maintain its majority to achieve that program, and how the president would react to that initiative.

Often the price of power is blame; this gives both president and Congress reason to duck responsibility in budget politics. The process was once flexible enough for members of Congress to act if they felt it necessary. They could beat up on agencies in hearings, showing these agencies did not deserve increases. They could ask leading questions at appropriation hearings, enabling agency heads to establish for the record why higher spending might be justified. They could pick and choose among presidential requests, raising popular ones (the National Institutes of Health) and cutting unpopular ones (foreign aid). By cutting here and increasing there, appropriations committees could expand some programs while staying below the president's total. Members of Congress who disliked the committees' actions could blame them or fight for changes on the floor.

These partly cooperative and partly conflicting relationships existed within a general framework of informal understandings: The budget would be balanced, the level of taxing and spending would not grow rapidly, and agreements on the amount and distribution of public monies would be maintained. The understandings and agreements that underlay the old budgetary order, however, have been undermined, as I shall show, thus raising in a more acute form the question of which of the many promises that make up the budget will be maintained.

CONFLICTING PROMISES: THE MULTIPLE MEANINGS OF BUDGETARY CONTROL

Thus far I have sought to describe what is meant by the budget and to depict the various actors and procedures involved. Underlying the discussion has been the question of who is in control. As might be expected, the question of control raises a host of difficult issues.

The word "control" may usefully be considered a synonym for "cause" or "power": One controls events by making them come out as intended, against opposition. Budgetary control involves conflict among people who want different outcomes and who attempt to exert power in order to make the size and distribution of spending different than it might otherwise have been. To say that "the budget is out of control," therefore (to invoke the most common public statement), implies a whole series of failed relationships among participants that relate to intentions and outcomes. Inability to specify these relationships makes control (over what, by whom, under which circumstances) a murky subject. Consequently, the information content of most statements about budgetary control is near zero or even negative. Before readers delve into the history of budgeting, they may wish to consider various useful ways of thinking about common questions of control.

Who is to do the controlling? Is it the general population, interest groups, Congress as a whole, appropriations committees alone, the president, agency heads, political parties, or some combination of these? If it is the general public one has in mind, then certain considerations—well-known to students of democracy but rarely applied to the process of budgeting—must be taken into account. There may well be no general opinion on most matters of budgeting. Politics in general, let alone expenditure in particular, is far from being at the forefront of citizen consciousness; that is one good reason for electing representatives. Indeed, whatever opinion the citizenry holds may be but a shallow reflection of what they have learned from their politicians and parties. Even supposing there are definite opinions, these cannot be directly applied to the budget. For, in the absence of referenda, people vote for or try to influence their representatives. Now, since these representatives deal with many nonbudgetary matters, voting against a candidate solely on budgetary grounds may be unwise. Hence it is possible that citizens may actually vote for people whose budgetary preferences they oppose.[8]

The advent of public opinion polling, however, has made it possible to ask whether citizen preferences do or do not generally accord with those expressed in consecutive budgets. In a rough and ready way, government does not appear to have departed too far from the people. A good illustration would be the presidency of Ronald Reagan. The best evidence[9] suggests that most people thought welfare spending was too high and defense spending too low in 1980. Opinion on the level of taxation was mixed, but there was widespread sentiment that the tax code was biased in favor of those already well-off. The Reagan administration moved spending in the direction desired by the electorate and then some. By 1984, polls revealed that the general public wanted more welfare and less defense spending than Reagan. Congress followed these wishes. In the discussion of clever maneuvering around the budget, it is well to note that shifting political alignments, which come from elections, remain by far the largest determinant of outcomes. The ultimate power remains with the people. But if the people are divided, as we often are, and are too far away to exert direct control, that task belongs to officeholders.

Who has power over the budget does not tell us whether or not the budget is under control. That is to say, we need to develop criteria to judge the prospect of budget control or, for that matter, of knowing what it would mean to be in or out of control. Actually, two approaches are commonly proposed. The first of these is to look at the apparent agreement on, but failure to achieve, budget balance. Surely,

---

[8]See, by inference, Robert A. Dahl, *A Preface to Democratic Theory* (Chicago: The University of Chicago Press, 1956).

[9]See J. Merrill Shanks and Warren Miller, "Policy Direction and Performance Evaluation: Complementary Explanations of the Reagan Elections." Presented to the Annual Meeting of the American Political Science Association, New Orleans, Aug. 29–Sept 1, 1985.

it is said, the government budget must be out of control if Congress cannot keep its continuously reiterated commitment to budget balance. It is true that huge majorities in Congress say they want balance. It is probably true that they mean what they say. But that truth is not the only truth because reducing the deficit is not the only goal that is important to members of Congress. Some want to reduce welfare spending while others wish to raise taxes. Only a minority cares more about balance than about other policies. The majority supports balance but not to the extent of giving up other preferences.

A second criterion for viewing the budget as out of control is that appropriations committees no longer make annual decisions on anything like most of the budget. These "relatively uncontrollable" expenditures, to use government parlance, essentially are estimates of spending that cannot be changed without altering the statute that authorized the expenditure. As the General Accounting Office puts it:

> From the perspective of the Office of Management and Budget (OMB), the spending in any 1 year for a program that is determined by existing statute, contract, or other obligation is considered relatively uncontrollable and is so classified. OMB also treats the legislative and judicial budgets as uncontrollable; the Congress, on the other hand, regards these budgets as alterable. Under OMB's general rules, the President's budget, submitted on January 15, 1981, reported that about 76 percent of the budget is now relatively uncontrollable.[10]

Thus, relatively uncontrollable spending includes not only entitlements but also obligations incurred and contracts signed in prior years. There are also immutable or fixed costs, such as interest on the debt or a variety of loans to which the credit of the United States is pledged. Only an unthinkable default can alter these expenditures. Viewed another way, much of the rest of the budget is tied up in salaries for soldiers and civilians, operating expenses, data collection, and other items not easy or desirable to change at a moment's notice.

Is it true, then, that the budget becomes uncontrollable because the appropriations committees cannot cover most of it every year? I think not. Taxes generally continue in force until changed, yet few claim they are out of control; this is because Congress can alter them at any time. The same is true of entitlements.

There is some utility to the relatively controllable and relatively uncontrollable dichotomy. The observer is sensitized to certain important facts: The relative uncontrollables are growing, the portion passing through the appropriations committees is declining, most controllables are in the defense budget, and it may be more difficult to change a law than to alter an appropriation.

Yet to identify controllability with appropriations and uncontrollability with entitlements also can be misleading. The distinction between controllable and uncontrollable expenditures "indicates *how* budget items may be changed."[11] Appropriations are seen as easier targets for change because Congress must act on them annually, but they are not necessarily more flexible. Congress can cut the Coast

---

[10]Report to the Congress by the Comptroller General of the United States, "What Can Be Done To Check the Growth of Federal Entitlement and Indexed Spending?" p. 10.

[11]Lance LeLoup, "Discretion in National Budgeting: Controlling the Controllables," *Policy Analysis*, Vol. 4, No. 4 (Fall 1978), pp. 455–75; quote on p. 456, italics in original.

Guard, the Bureau of Labor Statistics, and the Federal Aviation Administration somewhat but not a great deal; after all, people need to be rescued, unemployment statistics are vital, and safety in the air is a legitimate concern. Since entitlements occupy a large budgetary space, moreover, they can actually offer more tempting targets—and these targets are hit every year, albeit not every one or to the same extent. The Omnibus Reconciliation Act of 1981, for instance, raised the level at which the states would start paying extended benefits for unemployment compensation. And states toughened eligibility requirements.[12] Further, since many appropriations are sacrosanct while most entitlements are frequently adjusted—through changes in eligibility, indexing against inflation, taxation of benefits, and a host of other devices—to speak of the former as controllable and the latter as uncontrollable is somewhat inaccurate.[13]

The truth of the matter is that the 75 percent figure for uncontrollables significantly underestimates the proportion of the budget that is politically subject to change at any one time.[14] As discussion of classical budgeting will make clear, a good 90 to 95 percent of total spending is locked in as a consequence of past commitments and present promises. Here, in commitments to others, lies the insight we have been seeking into the apparent decline of controllability.

Congress wants to keep more expensive promises to a more extensive body of people (a phenomenon that sometimes goes under the name of the welfare state) than it did in the past. Consequently, though Congress could renege on its promises all at once, it does not want to do so. Whether this reluctance stems from fear of retribution at the polls from those who lose a portion of social security payments, or from abandoning a moral commitment, as with kidney dialysis, or more likely, from some combination of motives, Congress is torn between two kinds of contradictory promises: to certain beneficiaries in particular, or to people in general, in regard to budget balance. This conflict is resolved in the usual way by backing and filling, that is, by doing something that seems to satisfy each promise. With rare exceptions, such as revenue sharing, Congress keeps most commitments while making marginal moves toward budget balance. Just as political parties under pressure from rival factions move first "left" and then "right," and just as appropriations members used to satisfy committee norms by cutting the president's budget and constituency demands, by granting more money than in the previous year, Congress keeps its promises by modifying them.

For good reasons, this policy flexibility has been rendered more difficult in recent years. Automatic protection of entitlement against price rises makes sense in many ways. Needy beneficiaries no longer have to chase declining purchasing power. Politicians are no longer tempted to make up for inflation by election year benefit increases. Promises to the sick and elderly are kept with a minimum of fuss. Idyllic, isn't it? Well, the trouble is that as government absorbs the shock of price increases, it also loses the flexibility to respond to other changes—such as

---

[12]Kent Weaver, "Controlling Entitlements," in John E. Chubb and Paul E. Peterson, eds., *The New Direction in American Politics* (Washington, D.C.: The Brookings Institute, 1985), p. 321.

[13]For an excellent discussion, see LeLoup, "Discretion in National Budgeting," op. cit.

[14]See Martha Derthick, *Uncontrollable Spending for Social Services Grants* (Washington, D.C.: The Brookings Institute, 1975).

huge deficits that themselves stem in part from another set of promises, to provide tax cuts and to protect people against facing higher tax brackets because of inflation. It is neither right for people to pay more taxes while their purchasing power remains the same and government collects more from inflation, nor for government to have to spend more through indexing entitlements while simultaneously collecting less from income taxes. A "right" for one side obviously makes a "wrong" for the other.

Promises today conflict in other ways unknown to practitioners of budgeting until after the Second World War. The Employment Act of 1946 made the federal government responsible for keeping people at work. That promise, in keeping with the principles of Keynesian economics, was deemed to require varying the deficit or (rarely) surplus to suit the needs of the economy. While fiscal policy called for varying the rate of spending, however, the promise of entitlement policy was to keep the value of benefits constant. If government often resembles a contortionist, this is because it promises, in effect, to move simultaneously in two opposite directions.

Thus far we have looked at conflicting promises as residing between governmental actors and between government and citizens. But there is a different dilemma that occurs in budgeting—the conflict between individual and collective rationality. What makes sense to pursue individually may appear undesirable when these individual actions are viewed from a more general perspective. We see this conflict in budgeting: A desire for more programs conflicts with spending control.

Often, it is revealed with a certain amount of cynicism that members of Congress will vote for spending increases for specific programs and then turn around and vote for deficit reduction measures. But to focus solely on Congress is to investigate only part of the issue. Polling data, for example, suggest that the public is similarly ambivalent. While a large majority of citizens favor a balanced budget, they do not want higher taxes and they support most programs most of the time.

In trying to understand this dilemma, it is important to examine both attitudes and the structure of opportunity. There is little doubt that increasing program expenditures is compelling for congressional participants and the electorate alike. Each of us has particular programs that benefit us or aid someone we know, or we may view particular governmental activities as essential to the community or the nation. But the structure of the political system does not permit us to choose which programs we want and discard the rest; rather the political system works toward the exchange of benefits. To get what we want necessitates our acceptance of programs other people want, programs to which we may be either indifferent or averse. Within Congress, this is exemplified by the bill that becomes laden with a multiplicity of programs designed to muster widespread support.

What we desire in particular (more programs) turns out not to be what we desire in general—less total spending and lower taxes. The trouble is that while incentives exist to expand programs, few incentives exist to control the totals. The voter is rarely presented with the choices spelled out and usually does not have the opportunity to place limits on totals (whether that be taxes or program expenditures). Members of Congress, while having the opportunity to see budget totals, do not have a corresponding incentive to control these totals. Whether because of a perception by members of Congress that cuts will alienate voters or because of an inability to agree on what programs should be cut, the fact remains that even with the new focus on totals (brought about by the Congressional Budget and Impoundment Control Act of 1974), the incentives to cut remain weak.

For government to keep its promises requires not only a will but a way. Agreement on budget policy satisfies only governmental actors; no internal agreements can guarantee that external forces—wars, the weather, what have you—won't interfere with the best-laid plans. Resilient response is made more difficult, however, because governmental resources are now dedicated in advance to so many good causes. Alice Rivlin, former head of the Congressional Budget Office, observed that

> Spending is no longer growing for the old pork barrel, log-rolling reasons. Prospective spending growth is concentrated in a small number of programs with very broad popular support (primarily defense, pensions, and medical benefits). . . This is not a procedural problem, it is simply a question of wanting more government services than there are revenues to pay for them and having to make some hard choices to bring the two sides of the budget closer together.[15]

I am not suggesting that controlling the budget implies that it must be balanced or that domestic and/or defense spending must be held down. Rather, control goes more to the roots of governmental will. For there to be control, there must be a conjuncture of purposes; the promises government makes to others must coincide with its own budgetary plans. As it now stands, the promise of balancing the budget conflicts with all the other commitments government makes and would like to keep.

We are more likely than our predecessors to suspect that "the budget is out of control" because there are so many more knowledgeable people around to tell us so. In olden times, reaching back through the 1950s, public officials and a few politicians on appropriations committees were the only budget experts. And they rarely quit their jobs or were removed from office. The monopoly of expertise and security of tenure that Max Weber listed as defining characteristics of modern bureaucracy applied to this tiny cadre of political administrators. No longer. Every area of public policy has layers of experts who once served in office or who soon expect to do so. They are in the think tanks, the universities, state and local governments, foundations, research centers, and the big consulting and accounting firms. In effect, there are rival teams out there in the hinterlands. Second guessing becomes a sophisticated art when there are so many informed people to do it. With the loss of their former near-monopoly of information, public officials find it increasingly difficult to keep deficits from being publicized. Whether we are talking about welfare or defense, super-fund or the trade deficit, very little can be kept from public scrutiny. More and more people now know where the dollars are buried.

The existence of a loyal opposition in parliamentary democracies guarantees a string of criticism against existing governmental policy. But such criticism tends to be quite general. The only people who know much are civil servants who now

---

[15]Alice M. Rivlin, "Reform of the Budget Process," *The American Economic Review*, Vol. 74, No. 2 (May 1984), pp. 133–37; quote on p. 137.

work for the other side or who are silenced by official secrets acts. The existence of rival teams of policy analysts in the United States, with no commitment to governing but with superior sources of information, by contrast, guarantees that there will be numerous and quite specific allegations of unwise or improper budgeting. Too much is being spent for X, not enough for Y. Error rates (the wrong people receiving welfare payments) or cost overruns (the wrong people profiting from defense) are exposed. Needy populations, the emergence of children as the largest category of poor people, or unmet technological needs that, if neglected, promise to ruin American competitiveness are heard of every day. Criticism has been institutionalized, but support has not. The remarkable devices used in the Omnibus Budget Reconciliation Act of 1990 to leave congressional appropriators free of fault if external circumstances make their budget plans go awry, have their roots in a criticism so constant that legislators despair of being thought to have acted wisely no matter what they do. The task of control, of coordinating commitments, is so difficult because of the many different meanings the budget has for different people, hence the conflicting criticisms leveled against a particular budget. In the past these variegated desires were held together by certain common concerns: a balanced budget, avoidance of rapidly rising spending or taxing, and a broad agreement on the distribution of expenditures. The collapse of these premises of the old budgetary order has loosened the strictures that constrained these many desires. Because the new order is being built on the scaffolding of the old—not so much replacing as adding to it—the next chapter begins with the historical origins of American budgeting, origins that still affect what is done today.

Chapter 2

Budgets as Struggles for Power: The Evolution of Classical Budgeting

F ew truisms of American political thought are more hoary than this: The power of the purse is the heart of legislative authority and thus an essential check on the executive branch. An executive establishment freed from dependence for funds upon the legislature (and hence the public) would be a law unto itself and ultimately a despotism. Those who made the American Revolution concluded from experience in Britain and the colonies that a free people had to keep its governors on a tight fiscal leash. From the earliest days of American government, budget decisions were treated as a struggle for power.

The evolution of federal budgeting thus reflects the political struggles of the nation, translated into the institutions of government. The early strictures of the colonists against the powers of the colonial government were quickly adapted to efforts by the Congress to constrain the president.[1] Various turning points—wars, the income tax, the executive budget process, and the Depression—cumulatively tilted the balance toward the executive branch. This development did not take place in a vacuum: Between the late eighteenth century and the mid-twentieth century, the United States moved from an agrarian to an industrial economy; its citizenry diversified to include former slaves and immigrants from totally different backgrounds; urban growth and revolutions in transportation transformed the lives of every person; and the nation assumed the powers and burdens of an international power. Governments acknowledged newer responsibilities and federal budgets grew, but with the exception of wars, expenditures were constrained. Until the beginning of the great budget battles of the 1960s, the politics of the federal budget process seemed oddly untouched by the developments around it, a

---

[1]For a more detailed study, see Carolyn Webber and Aaron Wildavsky, "Balanced Regimes, Balanced Budgets: Why America Was So Different," Chapter 7 in *A History of Taxation and Expenditure in the Western World* (New York: Simon and Schuster, 1986).

reflection of the political system as a whole. The compromises, balances, and understandings of the early years of the Republic, which restricted participants in the budget process and stamped institutions and budgets with a conservative view of the world, continued to hold fast, and to maintain a "classical" dance of dollars.

COLONIAL ORIGINS

Colonial expenditures were simple in nature. Care of the poor, insane, sick, or otherwise indigent was a local responsibility. Public works were few and scattered. Highways were short and rough, and courthouses, though sometimes gilded with a handsome facade, were small. Judges were few and did not require many helpers. No colonial navy existed and the army—except in the period of the great Indian wars, or during the war with France for control of the North American continent—was composed of local militia. Legislatures met only for short periods, and payment, if received, was small. Colonial executive departments were tiny, and officials were often paid by fees rather than from general revenues. Royal governors alone received substantial salaries.

The extraordinary effort of colonial legislatures to control executives by limiting their expenditures, the duration for which they could be paid, and the objects for which the money could be spent, gives this period its peculiar stamp. If the colonies belonged to England, and if the colonists were English subjects, then it was their duty to support royal governors. Since the colonists wanted British protection but not British rule, however, they freely used the English tradition of denying supply in order to force compliance with the legislative will.[2]

It was common colonial practice to vote salaries annually. Indirect taxes, excises, and import duties were often reenacted yearly. Royal governors were allowed no permanent sources of revenue that might make them "uppity."[3] And that was only the beginning: Appropriations were specified for object and amount; extremely long appropriation clauses prescribed exactly what could and what could not be done and for how much. The requirement that all unexpected balances revert immediately to the treasury added insult to injury.

Even so, it might be thought that once an appropriation was voted, a royal executive could proceed to spend the money for the purpose stipulated. Several colonies, however, went so far as to elect independent treasurers that precluded the governors from managing their own finances. Other legislatures insisted that no payment might be made without their specific consent, thus giving colonists control over the disbursement of public funds. And when an emergency arose that everyone felt should justify a special appropriation, colonial assemblies might well appoint special commissioners accountable to them rather than to the governor. Should such measures prove too loose, there were still others: Revenues were

---

[2]See Robert C. Tucker and David C. Hendrickson, *The Fall of the First British Empire: Origins of the War of American Independence* (Baltimore/London: Johns Hopkins University Press, 1982), pp. 152–59, 174–75, 406–10.

[3]Charles Bullock, "The Finances of the United States from 1775–1789 with Special Reference to the Budget," *Bulletin of the University of Wisconsin,* Vol. 1, 1894–1896, Frederick Turner, ed. (Madison: University of Wisconsin Press, 1897), pp. 217, 225.

segregated by voting taxes for exceedingly narrow purposes (such as the building of a fort or of a lighthouse or the salary of a governor), always with the added clause that once the purpose had been accomplished, that money could be spent for "no other use or purpose whatsoever."[4] Colonial assemblies also reduced the salaries of royal officials; they stipulated the precise name of the person who was to do the work and made these officials legally accountable for all funds expended.[5]

When it came to doing sums, everyone understood what was at stake: Royal governors and their supporters desperately wanted a civil list of appointments and perquisites independent of the funds supplied by legislatures; the colonists wanted to create uncertainty, parsimony, and narrowness so as to bend royal governors to their will. To the English, it seemed only reasonable for the colonists to pay for the support of the royal government. The Stamp Act, duties on tea, and other impositions on colonists were a parliamentary effort to provide independent sources of income for English officials in America. Power, not money, was the issue.

After the Revolution, Americans found that it was hard to run a government that lacked authority. If they wanted action, they had to give the executive leeway. The Constitutional Convention was called into being by those attempting to create a more energetic government than existed under the Articles of Confederation— one with direct coercive power over individuals. Nevertheless, the influence of supporters of legislative power helped weaken the executive. For Roger Sherman, as for many others, an independent executive was "the very essence of tyranny. . . ." The legislature was "the depository of the supreme will of the society."[6]

Alexander Hamilton also saw political power behind financial power. He believed it necessary to fund state debts incurred during the Revolutionary War not only to establish strong credit, but also as a means of attaching the people who would be paid to the purposes of government.[7] From the outset of his term as secretary of the Treasury, he wrote Congress that Americans had to learn "to distinguish between oppression and the necessary exercise of lawful authority."[8] Hamilton's interest in levying taxes other than tariffs and in enforcing the exercise of the taxing power in the case of an excise tax on whiskey had as much to do with his desire to strengthen government as it did with the need to raise money.

Immediately upon Hamilton's appointment there arose a clamor, unfathomable outside the United States, that a powerful secretary of the Treasury, by giving his opinion to Congress, might overawe or otherwise influence that body in an un- desirable manner.[9] The law establishing the Treasury Department merely said that the secretary was supposed to send departmental estimates to Congress; the law

---

[4]Ibid., pp. 216–19.

[5]Ibid., pp. 219–21.

[6]Leonard D. White, *The Federalists: A Study in Administrative History* (New York: Macmillan, 1961), p. 14.

[7]William J. Schultz and M. R. Caine, *Financial Development of the United States* (New York: Prentice-Hall, 1937), p. 100.

[8]Dall W. Forsythe, *Taxation and Political Change in the Young Nation 1781–1883* (New York: Columbia University Press, 1977), pp. 44–45.

[9]Schultz and Caine, *Financial Development,* pp. 93–94.

did not say that the secretary was to revise these estimates or, if he did, whether anybody had to pay attention. Over time, an informal understanding developed that though the secretary might interest himself in estimates, his sole duty was to collect them and send them, without comment, to Congress. Though there is evidence of a secretary questioning this or that estimate and of occasional intervention by a president, the trend was to make appropriations without participation of the president or the secretary of the Treasury.

Since the strong executive was part of their platform, the Federalist Party preferred "lump-sum" appropriations for each specified purpose—say, customs collection or a navy—which would give administrators as much leeway as possible. Favoring economic stringency and distrusting the executive—the one reinforcing the other—the Republican party sought specific, line-item appropriations—for personnel, maintenance, supplies, on and on—that would limit departmental heads to exactly what Congress had commanded.[10]

What could Congress do? Plenty. It could itemize appropriations in excruciating detail; it could seek to apportion funds by the month or quarter so that agencies did not run out of money before the end of the fiscal year—potential deficiencies that might lead to requests for supplementary funds to carry out essential functions; it could limit transfers from one line item to another and recapture unexpended funds, or at least it could try. Congress could and did specify the number of employees, their exact remuneration, and sometimes their names. One of the many budget reform acts forbade all departments, except State, to spend more than $100 on newspapers; denied funds for commissions of inquiry, except courts-martial; refused extra allowances and additional clerks; insisted upon detailed reporting about the expenditure of contingency funds; prohibited the purchase of engravings, pictures, books, or periodicals other than by written order of head of department; and set the maximum amount that could be paid to the Dragoman of Constantinople.[11]

Despite continuous legislative effort to narrow administrative leeway, Congress could not control everything. The army and the navy, insisting they could not be held to specific line items, did get their way.[12] The legislated sanctions against executive offices for overspending, unauthorized transfers, or other violations of the innumerable prohibitions were not invoked; no doubt enforcement was not possible.[13] Most departmental appropriations soon became regular and customary as to both content and amount. Whether or not a new annual appropriations bill was passed, Congress did renew allocations in more or less the same manner year after year; social stability had produced agreement on a budgetary base.

An easy way around specific appropriations was to transfer sums from one purpose to another. The Act of 1820 allowed the president to make only certain transfers; all others were forbidden. But when Congress became overburdened

---

[10]Ibid., p. 324.

[11]Leonard D. White, *The Jacksonians: A Study in Administrative History 1829–1861* (New York: Macmillan, 1954), pp. 126–27.

[12]Ibid., p. 131.

[13]Ibid., p. 141; and Albert S. Bolles, *A Financial History of the United States, 1774–89* (New York: Appleton, 1879), pp. 539–40.

with requests for change and discovered it could not monitor even a small proportion of transactions, it tried to legalize prevailing practices. Funds for forts could be moved from one stockade to another, as could appropriations for naval forces from branch to branch, and postal funds from here to there. Departments kept appropriated funds from lapsing by finding ways to spend at the end of the fiscal year. When, in 1842, department heads received authority to transfer surplus funds from one item to some other (always excepting, of course, funds for newspapers, which in those days were party organs), the battle against transfers had been lost.[14]

Even at this point, the great financial issues of the times—the tariff, federal public works, and the debt—reflected ideological divisions among those contending for power. The Federalists and their successors sought to promote social order through deficit finance, first by making internal improvements and second by the financial arrangements arising out of the resulting debt. They were supported by growing commercial interests, advocating high tariffs and expanded debt. Besides encouraging the growth of industry, the tariff provided surplus revenues to expand roads, canals, and other facilities.[15] The debt also increased money in circulation, thus aiding industry as well as tying its holders to the central government.

But these allied interests had to contend with supporters of Jeffersonian Democratic Republican thought, reflecting fear of strong centralized government.[16] Small agricultural communities with an educated electorate, not far from one another in economic status and geographical distance, could handle their affairs on a face-to-face basis. Jeffersonians believed personal liberties would be endangered if government were to grow too large and if substantial inequality of resources were to develop. The Jacksonians, two decades later, continued and embroidered on their distrust of government and debt.

Interests supporting social order, economic individualism, and the Jeffersonian-Jacksonian Democrats disagreed about the potential and purposes of government, and the nature and dangers of rule. But they found common ground in the belief that liberty and equality could be made compatible and in consensus on the small size of the federal government.[17]

The era before the Civil War remained a time of tiny government. Between 1800 and 1860, as Table 2.1 shows, federal expenditures rose from about $11 million to $63 million in total. More than half were military expenditures. The general category of "Civil & Miscellaneous" included a substantial amount for the postal deficit, thus covering everything except defense, pensions, Indians, and interest on the debt. Kimmel is correct in concluding "that federal expenditures made little or no contribution to the level of living. Only a minor portion of Civil and miscellaneous expenditures were for developmental purposes. . . ."[18]

---

[14]White, *The Jacksonians*, pp. 133–34.

[15]Leonard D. White, *The Jeffersonians: A Study in Administrative History 1801–1829* (New York: Macmillan, 1951), p. 483.

[16]Adrienne Koch and William Peder, *The Life and Selected Writings of Thomas Jefferson* (New York: Modern Library, 1944), p. 123.

[17]Lewis H. Kimmel, *Federal Budget and Fiscal Policy 1789–1958* (Washington, D.C.: The Brookings Institution, 1959), p. 19; and White, *The Jeffersonians*, p. 483.

[18]Kimmel, *Federal Budget and Fiscal Policy*, p. 57.

Table 2.1   Federal Expenditures, Fiscal Years 1800, 1825, 1850, and 1860

	(In Million of Dollars)			
	1800	1825	1850	1860
Civil and Miscellaneous	1.3	2.7	14.9	28.0*
War Department	2.6	3.7	9.4	16.4
Navy Department	3.4	3.1	7.9	11.5
Indians	—	0.7	1.6	2.9
Pensions	0.1	1.3	1.9	1.1
Interest	3.4	4.4	3.8	3.2

*Includes postal deficit of $9.9 million.

TURNING POINTS: CIVIL WAR THROUGH WORLD WAR I

The written law often follows from the law of necessity. Public officials who believe an act to be essential may undertake it without legislative warrant, appealing to Congress to approve their conduct retroactively. The strongest proponent of this view was undoubtedly Abraham Lincoln. As the nation split into irreconcilable factions, Lincoln took the position that whatever was required for national defense had to be approved. On grounds that there was then "no adequate and effective organization for the public defense," he justified ordering the Treasury to advance $2 million to a variety of private agents to provide requisitions for the military:

> Congress had indefinitely adjourned. There was not time to convene them. It became necessary for me to choose, whether, using only the existing means, agencies, and processes which Congress had provided, I should let the Government fall at once into ruin or whether availing myself on the broader powers conferred by the Constitution in cases of insurrection, I would make an effort to save it, with all its blessings, for the present age and for posterity. . . . The several Departments of the Government at that time contained so large a number of disloyal persons that it would have been impossible to provide safely through official agents only for the performance of the duties thus confided to citizens favorably known for their ability, loyalty, and patriotism.[19]

The higher law was one thing and low-down behavior another; investigations provided ample evidence of abuse of contract power during the war.[20]

Performance being more important than protocol during the war, Congress legally authorized all that it had been denying for the past century: lump-sum appropriations, spending in excess of authorizations and appropriations, transfers, revolving funds perpetuated by reimbursements, and more.[21]

---

[19]Lucius W. Wilmerding, Jr., *The Spending Power: A History of the Efforts of Congress to Central Expenditures* (New Haven, Conn.: Yale University Press, 1943), p. 14.

[20]Albert S. Bolles, *The Financial History of the United States from 1861 to 1885* (New York: Appleton, 1886), p. 231.

[21]Wilmerding, *Spending Power*, p. 154.

When funds were inadequate and transfers failed to produce necessary moneys, departments could and did resort to the tactic of the coercive deficiency. What could Congress do if the money for an essential service were to run out before the end of the fiscal year, other than to pass a supplemental appropriation? Deficiencies before the Civil War had already risen to something like 10 percent of total spending. Congress did demand to be informed of an emergency leading to a waiver of required apportionments, but by the time the waiver was reported there was no effective remedy.[22] From time to time, departments also used unexpended balances for purposes not previously contemplated in congressional statutes, following earlier instances of administrative discretion, particularly involving the building up of naval forces.

The Civil War thus acted as a catalyst for the president to wrest from Congress some discretion over spending. The war also resulted in a structural transformation of the congressional budgetary process. For the first 75 years of the republic (from 1789 to 1864), revenue and expenditure matters in the House of Representatives were handled by its Committee on Ways and Means (and in the Senate by the Finance Committee). Largely in response to the ways and means committee being overworked, the House in 1865 and the Senate in 1867 carved a committee on appropriations out of the old single committee. This dual committee system—one for taxes, the other for spending—lasted until 1885.[23]

The new Appropriations Committee "embodied a balance between the need for some financial expertise with the aversion to placing too many institutional resources in the hands of one individual."[24] The arrangement allowed for unified control of spending in one committee. Yet, it did not have authority to control all spending—the size of pensions and other permanent appropriations (together constituting over half the budget) were determined by other committees.[25]

By and large, members of Congress appeared content with the new arrangement. Collaboration occurred between the Ways and Means and the Appropriations Committees and there was consensus in Congress that Civil War spending and waste needed to be curtailed and that war profiteering had been widespread. Additionally, Congress was too preoccupied with Reconstruction to get caught up in other domestic issues.[26]

In the succeeding years, the House Appropriations Committee came under attack for amassing too much control over other committees' programs, primarily through Appropriations control over reporting bills out. As the smooth flow of patronage was threatened by the Appropriations Committee, members of

---

[22]Ibid., pp. 137–47.

[23]E. E. Naylor, *The Federal Budget System in Operation* (Washington: Hayworth Printing, 1941), pp. 20–21.

[24]Charles Haines Stewart III, *The Politics of Structural Reform: Reforming Budgetary Structure in the House, 1865–1921,* Dissertation, Stanford University, August 1985, p. 139.

[25]Ibid., pp. 139–40.

[26]Ibid., p. 140.

Congress reacted in 1885 by giving a number of spending bills to the substantive legislative committees made up of spending advocates. Congress first stripped Appropriations of constituency-oriented legislation (rivers and harbors spending, agriculture) and then moved to more general items (Army, Navy, diplomacy, post office, and Indian affairs). By these acts, more than half the total appropriations, including the most controversial items, were effectively removed from the appropriations committee's jurisdiction.[27]

These changes became "a symbol of dysfunctional fragmentation in Congress and of waste and mismanagement, and would serve as a rallying point in the creation of an executive budget focused around presidential leadership."[28] Actually, the escalation of spending after 1885 was less the result of decentralization (spending rates increased at fairly equal rates for bills outside appropriations control compared to bills under appropriations jurisdiction) and more the consequence of an acceleration of visible spending, including Army and Navy reform and the rebuilding of southern productive centers destroyed during the war, in response to two decades of neglect.[29]

The leading budget reformer before World War I, Frederick A. Cleveland, excoriated the chairmen of these spending committees as

> functionalized, bureaucratic, feudal lords [who] did not look to their titular superior, the leader chosen by and responsible to the nation, for powers and policies. They looked to irresponsible committees. And because of the independence that was thus given, each chief built around himself a bureaucratic wall that even the constitutional Chief Executive himself could not get over. . . .[30]

Cleveland's theme, bureaucratic feudalism, reveals the emergent pattern of budgeting. Close relationships were developing among chiefs of governmental bureaus, their clientele, and the chairmen and ranking members of the congressional appropriations committees.

It appears that administrative bureaus would advocate higher spending; their estimates would be cut by the House Appropriations Committee, but the Senate would then act as an appeals court to give the money back. The appropriations committee was slowly assuming its role as "watchdog of the Treasury" or defender of the public purse. "You may think my business is to make appropriations," said Joseph Cannon, a powerful former Speaker of the House and chairman of the appropriations committee, "but it is not. It is to prevent their being made."[31]

A further turning point came in 1894 when Congress passed and President Cleveland signed the first income tax bill. Its strongest proponents argued that this tax would be paid for by "wealth, not want"; the time had come to "put more tax

---

[27]Richard F. Fenno, *The Power of the Purse: Appropriations Politics in Congress* (Boston: Little, Brown, 1966), p. 43.

[28]Stewart, *Politics of Structural Reform*, p. 211.

[29]Ibid., p. 215.

[30]Frederick A. Cleveland, "Leadership and Criticism," *Proceedings of the Academy of Political Science*, Vol. 8 (1918–20), p. 31.

[31]Fenno, *Power of the Purse*, p. 99.

upon what men have, less on what they need."[32] Opponents argued that the income tax was a tax on "mind and energy," taking from the "thrifty and enterprising" to give to "the shiftless and the sluggard."[33] In the political conditions of the 1890s, the kind of taxation and its incidence were far more important than the amount.

The Supreme Court ruled the progressive aspects of income tax unconstitutional in *Pollock v. Farmers Loan and Trust Co.* (157 U.S., 429) in 1895. The federal government was in deficit 11 of the 21 years from 1894 through 1914. What to do? Faced with revenue shortfalls, Presidents Roosevelt (in his 1906 annual message) and Taft (accepting the Republican nomination in 1908) both endorsed the idea of an income tax. But the Supreme Court was a large barrier. In 1908 the Democrats called for a constitutional amendment to allow the tax, and in 1909, under substantial pressure, Taft agreed. The amendment sped through Congress with little debate in 1909[34] and was ratified in 1913. The income tax subsequently enacted was, however, extremely small. And any prospect that it could handle budget shortfalls was eliminated when America entered World War I. Income tax revenues were greatly expanded, but failed by a large amount to match wartime spending. In the three years from 1917 through 1919, federal debt grew from $1.2 billion to $25.5 billion.[35]

Coping with that massive debt, retrenching from wartime to peacetime expenditures, and responding to the new public awareness of budgetary issues resulting from a direct tax (rather than hidden taxes such as tariffs) posed a major challenge. As usually happens when problems arise, people were waiting with pet solutions. The appropriations committees wanted their power back. The president and a group of Progressive reformers wanted an executive budget. Congress moved to create an executive budget, but also to strengthen itself.

THE EXECUTIVE BUDGET MOVEMENT

Reformers are not radicals; those who left their imprint upon American budgeting between the Civil War and 1920 were not opposed to American social structure or to competitive markets, nor were they proponents of income redistribution. A political force unique in this most unusual of nations, reformers were the establishment's antiestablishment—critical of the fragmented way politicians did things— and also the anti-anti-market, who opposed threats by corporate trusts to limit competition. To lessen the "irresponsible power" of party bosses and chairmen of congressional standing committees, the budgetary reformers wanted a visible and democratically accountable Chief Executive served by experts dedicated to the public interest. The experts, whose ideas and attitudes matched the reformers', would be the instruments of change.

---

[32] Edwin R. A. Seligman, *The Income Tax* (New York: Macmillan, 1921), p. 497.

[33] Ibid., p. 500.

[34] Ibid., p. 590–96.

[35] Historical Statistics of the United States, Colonial Times to 1970, Part 2; U.S. Department of Commerce, Bureau of the Census, pp. 1104, 07–08, 14–15, 21–22, 24–25, 49.

The people of the United States had a deep attachment to the Constitution and to the separation between executive and legislative branches it embodied. Yet it was precisely this separation (or at least the form it took in America) that the reformers opposed.[36]

The budgetary practice to which the reformers most objected was the time-worn one of itemization of spending, known today as the line-item budget. Itemization was wasteful and, worst of all, did not allow for executive discretion. President Taft's Commission on Economy and Efficiency argued that because government did not trust its officers, "judgments which can be made wisely only at the time that a specific thing is to be done are attempted to be made by a Congress composed of hundreds of Members from six months to a year and a half beforehand on the recommendation of a committee which at most can have but a limited experience or fund of information as a basis for their thinking."[37] The principle of deference to expertise was thus twice denied by Congress, once to the Chief Executive and then again to his subordinates.

The piecemeal process by which budgets were put together—each committee recommending appropriations for the agencies and purposes under its control and the houses of Congress acting on them one at a time—was singled out for special condemnation. Because of this fragmentation, no formal attention was given to total spending.[38]

Reformers had no concept of informal coordination and never thought to ask whether all concerned might not have had a pretty good idea of where they were, and were likely to end up. It was chiefly the form of the budget, and what it represented, to which they objected: "no standard classifications . . . of expenditures according to their character and object . . . no uniform scheme of expenditure documents calling for the recording of expenditure data in accordance with any general information plan . . . no budgetary message, no proper scheme of summary, analytical and comparative tables. . . ." In short, nothing in the United States appropriations process remotely resembled budgeting in the executive-centered governments of Europe.[39]

So much for what the reformers were against, what were they for? Hierarchy, known to them as "executive leadership," is the best short answer. Leadership would purify politics. This was Woodrow Wilson's theory, and his practice as president.[40] Wilson was ready with both diagnosis and remedy: "This feature of disintegration of leadership runs . . . through all our legislation; but it is manifestly of much more serious consequence in financial administration than in the direction of other concerns of government." Budgets must be "under the management of a

---

[36]Nicholas M. Butler, "Executive Responsibility and a National Budget," *Proceedings of the Academy of Political Science*, Vol. 8 (1918–20), p. 46; Wilson, *Congressional Government*, p. 284.

[37]Quoted in Wilmerding, *Spending Power*, p. 150.

[38]Charles Wallace Collins, *The National Budget System* (New York: Macmillan, 1917), p. 3.

[39]William Franklin Willoughby, *The Problem of a National Budget* (New York: Appleton, 1918), pp. 56–57.

[40]Arthur Macmahon, "Woodrow Wilson: Political Leader and Administrator," in Earl Latham, ed., *The Philosophy and Policies of Woodrow Wilson* (Chicago: University of Chicago Press, 1958), pp. 100–22; reference is to page 113.

single body; only when all financial arrangements are based upon schemes prepared by a few men of trained minds and accordant principles, who can act with easy agreement and with perfect confidence in each other" will budgets make sense.[41] The major premise of executive leadership led also to its important corollary: executive discretion by reliance on experts. It is important to understand that the reformers believed their recommendations derived from scientific principles. Often they referred to "the science of budgetmaking,"[42] or said they were subjecting budgetary problems "to scientific analysis."[43] Their assumption was that the goals or objectives of budgeting were agreed so that only the details of administrative execution were left to be considered.

The policy-administration dichotomy—in which political choices are made through general legislative enactments, and administrative choices are limited to technical implementation of these larger and prior decisions—was an essential postulate of budget reformers. They held that if administrators also were to make large and therefore political choices, the principle of neutral competence—which justified civil-service reform and the important role reformers wished to give to experts—would be undermined. Their text was Frank J. Goodnow's *Politics and Administration.* Goodnow believed that the two primary functions of government were to determine the will of the people and to execute that will. Though, as Dwight Waldo observes, Goodnow was far from making the distinction exclusive (seeing better than his followers the interpretation of the two functions), when taken up by less sophisticated acolytes Goodnow's ideas generated the doctrine of a strict separation between the two.[44] This dichotomy legitimizes taking power from the legislature and giving it to the executive—and, ultimately, to the executive's expert administrators, the reformers themselves.

The reformers' recommendation to adopt business practices manifestly did not mean approval of bidding and bargaining among legislature and executive. Rather, they adopted from big business its internal organization, that is, its hierarchical structure, which served to solidify the distinction between policy and administration that the reformers wished to make.

The reformers' budgetary principle of principles was reiterated like a litany: "There must be established a national budget prepared and recommended by the Chief Executive."[45]

If the proposals were adopted, how did the reformers picture themselves (or people like them) as participants in the budgetary process? They had already been instrumental in staffing commissions to recommend the proposed reforms. These same men aimed to become part of the expert staff of the executive—mayor, governor, or president—whose task would be formulating the budget. As A. E. Buck said so succinctly, "budget-making requires special staff assistance . . . to . . .

---

[41]Wilson, *Congressional Government,* pp. 180–81.

[42]Charles Beard, "Prefatory Note," *Municipal Research,* No. 88 (August 1917) (New York: Bureau of Municipal Research), p. iii.

[43]Willoughby, *Problem of a National Budget,* p. 55.

[44]Dwight Waldo, *The Administrative State* (New York: Ronald Press, 1948), pp. 105–107.

[45]Butler, "Executive Responsibility," p. 49.

assist the executive. . . ."[46] By extending this function to other governmental purposes, budget experts could easily become a general administrative staff supporting the executive. When one recognizes that presidents of the United States up to Franklin D. Roosevelt's time were assisted at most by a few clerks, these were far-reaching proposals.

A simile—be like Britain—justified recommendations for budget hierarchy in the United States. The only way Parliament could alter the budget was to change the government. "If one looks for the secret of . . . the English system," Willoughby comments, "it must be found in . . . the clear distinction . . . between legislative and administrative powers. . . . No proposals for . . . expenditure . . . shall be made . . . except . . . by the cabinet acting as the custodian of the administrative powers of government. . . ."[47]

Because the British Chancellor of the Exchequer and Department of the Treasury were responsible for both expenditure and revenue, the reformers believed that these would be taken up at the same time and that, therefore, comprehensive and simultaneous consideration would be given to the relative desirability of spending versus taxing.[48] Whether this formal unity would make any difference, either to the totals or to the division of expenditures among departments, was not a subject for discussion by reformers who already knew the answer.

Agency personnel were to be completely subservient to budgetary decisions of the president. If agency heads could not support estimates changed by the president, they should be fired.[49] Apparently it never occurred to the reformers that heads of spending departments might speak privately with legislators or, if wide-ranging differences arose, that presidents might not be able to maintain dominance over the cabinet. In those days cabinet members represented party factions; asking a cabinet member to step down therefore had significant political costs.

The reformers insisted that, having gained executive approval, every spending proposal would ipso facto represent the national view, allowing no room for "logrolling" in Congress.[50] In the same manner, in Lewis Carroll's *Through the Looking Glass,* the Red Queen tells Alice that anything she says three times is true.

At the time, the reformers' position was effectively criticized by Edward A. Fitzpatrick in his *Budget Making in a Democracy* (1918). His views are interesting because they embody the stance of the expert administrator who does not aspire to be a staff assistant to the Chief Executive. Fitzpatrick looked at the political implications of the president amassing such budgetary power. "Are we to have a one-

---

[46]A. E. Buck, "The Development of the Budget Idea in the United States," *Annals of the American Academy of Political and Social Science,* Vol. 63 (May 1924), p. 36.

[47]Willoughby, *Problem of a National Budget,* pp. 59–60.

[48]Ibid., p. 405.

[49]Frederick A. Cleveland and Arthur E. Buck, *The Budget and Responsible Government* (New York: Macmillan, 1920), pp. xviii–xix.

[50]Collins, *National Budget System,* p. 41.

man government? That," Fitzpatrick told his readers, "is the fundamental question in back of the executive budget propaganda."[51]

As for the much-vaunted British example, cabinet government, he said, was not government by one person, but by a committee of the legislature, a parliament with the ultimate right to dismiss its cabinet.[52] *"Do those who are proposing the executive budget also propose the legislative recall of the executive?"*[53] This is what the British Parliament does and that is what a business board of directors does when it loses confidence in management. Fitzpatrick, however, insisted such action is impossible under presidential government with its fixed terms.[54] Reformers, Fitzpatrick contended acidly, should tell the people they want to make a fundamental change in the American form of government, and not camouflage the issues "under the name of 'executive budget.'"[55]

To promote the idea of a federal executive budget, President William Howard Taft set up a Commission on Economy and Efficiency. The commission's tone was set by its chairman, Frederick A. Cleveland, then director of the New York Bureau of Municipal Research, and by other noted budget reformers appointed with him, including Frank J. Goodnow and W. F. Willoughby.[56] The commission's basic task, accepted by Taft in its entirety, was that the president would submit spending estimates to Congress and would assume responsibility for them.[57] The commission's major report, "The Need for a National Budget," completed in 1912, was followed by "A Budget for the Fiscal Year 1914," in which President Taft, at the commission's instigation, submitted the kind of budget document he thought appropriate for the Chief Executive as top administrator.[58] It rejected the prevailing narrow view of economy—of spending merely the minimum. Instead, the President (like earlier advocates of internal improvements) stated that he wanted the government to operate economically in order to do more for the people with available resources.[59] Power for presidents and their advisors was sublimated under a rubric with which it was difficult to argue: efficiency.

Congress was of a different mind altogether. Expressing fear of the executive's usurpation of power (in language harking back to the early days of the republic), Congress passed a law requiring department heads charged with preparing estimates to do what they had always done: to send estimates directly to congressional appropriations committees.[60] And department heads responded

---

[51]Edward Augustus Fitzpatrick, *Budget Making in a Democracy* (New York: Macmillan, 1918), p. 55.

[52]Ibid., pp. 50–51, 59.

[53]Ibid., p. 54.

[54]Ibid., p. 5.

[55]Ibid., p. 292.

[56]Naylor, *Federal Budget System in Operation,* pp. 23–24.

[57]Cleveland, "Leadership and Criticism," p. 33.

[58]Naylor, *Federal Budget System in Operation,* p. 24.

[59]Wilmerding, *Spending Power,* p. 151; and Jesse Burkhead, *Government Budgeting* (New York: Wiley, 1956), p. 119.

[60]Naylor, *Federal Budget System in Operation,* pp. 24–25.

to these contradictory directives by preparing one set as Congress specified and another as directed by the president. As business conditions improved and passage of the Sixteenth Amendment in 1913 permitted a graduated income tax, thus raising revenue, pressures for change in the budget system diminished.

Nothing was done to establish an executive budget until after the First World War,[61] when the desire for fiscal prudence, both against the growing debt and for a balanced budget, reasserted itself with a vengeance. World War I had been fought largely on borrowed money. From 1914 to 1918, the government's role in directing economic activity expanded enormously. There was a new public concern that the profligate habits of wartime would carry over into peacetime civilian life,[62] which spurred renewed interest in a national executive budget; between 1918 and 1921, the reformers presented proposals to congressional committees. Once again reformers criticized the federal expenditure process: There was overlap among substantive committees, and hence duplication of effort; there was no comprehensive consideration of revenues and expenditures; the consequence of bureaucratic rivalry was waste.

In the name of managing the huge national debt, the Budget and Accounting Act of 1921 made the major changes budget reformers had long supported. Departments sent spending estimates to the president through a new institution, the Bureau of the Budget, and the Chief Executive had total control over the Bureau of the Budget.[63] Henceforth no appropriation could be considered unless first reviewed by the president and the two appropriations committees. "Review," however, was a far cry from the near-absolute control exercised by European cabinets.

No stronger statement of the spirit of legislative supremacy, or of its practical consequences, can be found than in the House report commenting on the Budget and Accounting Act of 1921. The only executive aspect of that act, the House insisted, was that the president would henceforth be held responsible for the agency estimates he submitted. After that, the budget was still legislative all the way. Members of Congress could still move his proposed numbers up, down, or sideways by ignoring them entirely. If anyone doubted that the president's budget was just his set of recommendations, the Committee Report sought to disabuse them:

> The President's responsibility ends when he has prepared the budget and transmitted it to Congress. . . . the proposed law does not change in the slightest degree the duty of Congress to make the minutest examination of the budget and to adopt the budget only to the extent that it is found to be economical. If the estimates contained in the President's budget are too large, it will be the duty of Congress to reduce them. If in the opinion of Congress the estimates of expenditures are not sufficient, it will be within the power of Congress to increase them. The bill does not in the slightest degree

---

[61]Burkhead, *Government Budgeting*, pp. 20–21.

[62]Kimmel, *Federal Budget and Fiscal Policy*, p. 88.

[63]Fritz Morstein Marx, "The Bureau of the Budget: Its Evolution and Present Role," *American Political Science Review*, Vol. 39, No. 4 (August 1945), pp. 653–84.

give the Executive any greater power than he now has over the consideration of appropriations by Congress.[64]

If Congress were to give the president the power to propose, it wanted also to ensure its power to dispose, and then to oversee the execution of its decisions. It created the Bureau of the Budget and the Executive Budget process, but checked the president in two ways. In 1920 the House, and the Senate in 1922, restored their former powers to the appropriations committees, thus providing an institutional counterweight to the centralized executive process. In addition, Congress removed from the Treasury the power to audit and account for expenditures (where it had resided since 1789) and lodged it in a General Accounting Office (GAO) outside of the president's control. The comptroller of the Treasury was replaced by a new official, the comptroller general of the United States. He had a single, 15-year term and could be replaced only by a joint resolution of both houses of Congress, signed by the president.

What remained to be decided was the function of the newly created Budget Bureau within the executive branch. Its first head, General Charles G. Dawes, a student and practitioner of administration, insisted that the offices not be in the Treasury building, but outside it, and near the White House (Dawes wanted to insulate the Bureau from interdepartmental squabbles).[65] He insisted on his right to call department heads into conference; President Warren Harding wisely suggested that such conferences be held in the White House Cabinet Room (instead of in the budget director's office), to emphasize the Chief Executive's commanding role in budget decisions.[66]

The 1920s witnessed a major assault on federal spending. Led by General Dawes, his successors, and businessmen whom Dawes brought into government (often working for "a dollar a year"), the Bureau zealously pursued efficiency. Its accomplishments provoked panegyrics. Martin Madden, chairman of the House Committee on Appropriations, wrote as if the promised land had been reached: "One noticeable feature has been the . . . self-sacrificing of local interests in favor of the common good. When one recalls the former days when appropriations were sought with avidity for local projects . . . it is appropriate to commend the change from local to national attitude."[67]

An economy mood prevailed. The reconstitution of the appropriations committees and the Budget and Accounting Act of 1921 reflected overwhelming agreement on a balanced budget at a restricted level of spending. That consensus enabled the system to work with little friction. Far from exceeding revenues, spending had to fit within them, and then some, to permit deficit reduction. The

---

[64]House Report No. 14, 67th Congress, 1st Session, 6–7 (1921), cited in Louis Fisher, "The Item Veto: The Risks of Emulating the States." Prepared for delivery at the Annual Meeting of the American Political Science Association, New Orleans, August 29–31, 1985, p. 6.

[65]See Charles G. Dawes, *The First Year of the Budget of the United States* (New York: Harper, 1923).

[66]Ibid., p. 29.

[67]Quoted in William Franklin Willoughby, *The National Budget System with Suggestions for Its Improvement* (Baltimore: Johns Hopkins, 1927), pp. 287–88.

debt was steadily reduced through the 1920s, conveniently a time of plenty when Congress was receiving few petitions for help anyway.

Then came the market crash of 1929, followed by the Great Depression of the 1930s. Federal revenues were cut in half (1930: $4.06 billion; 1932: $1.92 billion); state and local revenues plummeted; demands for relief soared. State and local funds ran out; people turned to Washington.

DISLOCATION AND CONTINUITY: DEPRESSION, WAR, AND THE POST-WAR INTERLUDE

At the beginning of the depression, consensus on balancing the federal budget continued. Both Presidents Hoover and Roosevelt stressed its priority. By the early 1930s, a number of Americans in the Democratic party began to seek a rationale for encouraging the government to expand public works and thus increase employment. They found it in the work of economist John Maynard Keynes and introduced his thought to key figures, including President Roosevelt.[68] Keynes argued that it was appropriate, in a deflationary period when vast economic resources went unused, for the government to create deficits as a means of expanding demand. When economic activity was slow, government should step in to speed it up; when the economy overheated and inflation resulted, government could decrease spending. In short, raising and lowering the deficit would become a prime means of economic control.

The New Deal in the United States was never a coherent set of measures. Rather it comprised ad hoc answers to immediate crises.[69] Accordingly, Roosevelt's program (presented to Congress in the famous first Hundred Days) aimed at relief, recovery, and reform: proposals to reestablish public confidence in the banking system, to achieve a balanced budget by cutting government spending, to revive agriculture through an increase in farm incomes, to assist industry by creating a system of price codes, and to institute a program of public works.

In response, the House of Representatives passed the Economy Bill, which halved the pensions of disabled war veterans, reduced congressional salaries as well as those of all federal employees, and curtailed other federal expenditures. The Economy Bill was designed to balance spending with revenue, which, since two-thirds of it was based on individual and corporate income taxes, had declined by nearly a half between 1930 and 1933. This bill increased hardships among pensioners and, by curtailing government expenditure, reduced individual purchasing power.

Clearly, Roosevelt was no believer in the desirability of deficits. Indeed, when Keynes conferred with Roosevelt in Washington in 1935, the two apparently did not agree. Roosevelt maintained his balanced budget preferences; throughout the 1930s, he viewed current spending as pump priming. After an overwhelming victory

---

[68]For Felix Frankfurter's efforts in this direction, see H. N. Hirsch, *The Enigma of Felix Frankfurter* (New York: Basic Books, 1981), p. 113.

[69]Jim Potter, *The American Economy between the World Wars* (New York: Wiley, 1974), p. 113.

in the 1936 election, Roosevelt tried to cut spending in 1937 to balance the budget, but a sharp upturn in unemployment in 1938 forced him to abandon this effort.[70]

A look at federal income and expenditure between 1929 and 1939 gives some sense of government's growth and its expanded role in the economy. In 1929, federal expenditure was $3.3 billion; in 1939, $8.9 billion. While federal spending increased by 170 percent, there was only a 25 percent increase in federal revenues (from $4.0 billion in 1929 to $5.0 billion in 1939). Federal expenditure as a percentage of gross national product (GNP), moreover, tripled (from 3.2 percent in 1929 to 9.7 percent in 1939) whereas federal revenue as a percent of GNP during the same period did not even double (from 3.9 to 5.5 percent).

The enduring legacy of the New Deal was acceptance by the American public of the doctrine that the federal government has ultimate responsibility for the economy. The struggle for power that marked the budget process since colonial times took on a new dimension: As government faced outward toward society—to alleviate poverty—its budgetary procedures, previously reflecting an orientation toward internal control, became more concerned with relating spending to revenue than with the substance of spending itself. Consensus as to governmental responsibility was joined to a decline of the balanced-budget norm.

Under Keynesian doctrine, as understood and practiced at the time, the idea was to balance the economy at full employment (accepting between 3 and 5 percent of "frictional" unemployment), not necessarily to balance the budget. To the extent that relationships between participants in budgeting depended on belief in balance—since revenue limits expenditure, no spending agency can grow faster than the economy without taking unfair advantage of the others—the pillars of spending control were severely shaken. So long as there was more for everyone, so good. If (or rather when, in view of historical experience) the rate of economic growth declined, however, the participants in budgeting would have to agree on their fair share of a more limited pie. Before we can understand how operating under conditions of ideological dissensus affects budgeting, we need to understand how ideological consensus, when it existed, moved budgeting along a more incremental path.

---

[70]Robert Lekachman, *The Age of Keynes* (New York: McGraw-Hill, 1966), pp. 122–23.

Chapter 3

The Dance of the Dollars: Classical Budgeting[1]

W ars are catalysts of change. The United States emerged from the Second World War determined not to reexperience the depression of the 1930s. Its federal government, being victorious, enjoyed an enhanced respect. The task assigned was to maintain prosperity by managing the economy, institutionalized in the Full Employment Act of 1946, which created the Council of Economic Advisers. How far government should go was a matter of controversy, but that it should act was accepted. Along with that consensus came an expanded importance for the Executive Office of the President, including the Bureau of the Budget (BOB).

Although there was a lot of doubt and soul searching about the place of the United States as a (perhaps the) major international power after the war, internationalism won out over isolationism. There was no turning back.

The budgetary consequences for postwar America were profound. War had accustomed the nation to hitherto unheard of levels of taxation; while these went down considerably, they never fell to prewar levels. Domestic spending rose not only for veterans (the G.I. Bill put many through school) but also to some degree for social purposes. After the roller coaster of rapid demobilization was followed by the buildup after the Korean War, the defense budget had stabilized at levels much higher than the prewar period. By 1955 defense constituted over two-fifths of total spending while social welfare programs, including social security, were about one-fifth. The economy began to grow. Keeping defense stable in constant dollars (adjusted for inflation and without raising tax rates) allowed domestic spending to rise in the late 1960s and early 1970s with the advent of new and expanded welfare programs such as medicare for the elderly and medicaid for the poor. Government

---

[1]This chapter is largely a summary of the sections on "Strategies and Calculation" in the 1964 edition of *The Politics of the Budgetary Process.*

grew painlessly. Though President Kennedy cut taxes to stimulate the economy in the early 1960s and President Johnson rejected the advice of the Council of Economic Advisers to raise them during the Vietnam War in the mid–1960s, revenue and expenditures remained close, with small, albeit growing, deficits. No great sacrifices—substantial tax increases or large spending cuts—were seen to be necessary. Incremental advance was the order of these times.

Yet the inherited practices and understandings of the budgetary process continued to be accepted. The Truman and Eisenhower administrations saw a balanced budget as economically desirable. Their position was supported by a conservative coalition in Congress: an alliance between conservative Republicans and conservative Democrats, mostly from the South. The coalition was held together by basic policy agreement on limited government and was facilitated by joint meetings among leaders. Throughout the 1940s and into the late 1950s, the conservative coalition was able to win at least 70 percent of the votes in both Houses.[2]

A growing economy and increasing federal revenues, however, made it simultaneously possible to accommodate advocates of defense spending, social spending, limited government, and balanced budgets. Adequate revenues within a framework of mutual expectations maintained the formal institutions of the budget process, and created a "classical" world of budgeting. It was a world bounded by its own horizons, in Allen Schick's words,

> shut off from the outside world. Its participants knew one another, maintained on-going contact, fought repeatedly, and always came to terms. They were budget and program officials in federal agencies, finance experts in the old Bureau of the Budget, and members and clerks of the appropriations committees. Many of these bonded together at annual retreats, swigging beer and trading war stories. Theirs was "the private government of public money" . . . It was a world in which the budget was a tightly guarded secret during months of preparation in the executive branch and a bewildering book of numbers after it was released to Congress. The insiders had a monopoly on budget information, and they did not share much with outsiders. In that world, budgets were made by government talking to itself; agencies to the bureau, the bureau back to the agencies, agencies to the appropriations committees, the committees to the agencies.[3]

Classical budgeting, we see in retrospect, was premised upon agreement on the size, scope, and distribution of expenditure. Conflict was confined to the margins, a little more here, a little less there.

Should we look at this period as an exception, a situation resulting from a peculiar set of circumstances at a particular time? Was classical budgeting simply the manifestation of a disappearing era in which an elite played out dying rituals even as it was undermined by the currents of history? Did those years in fact represent lost opportunities for forging more viable solutions for critical problems of American society, instead stretching the fabric of inherited institutions and accompanying compromises, deals, and evasions until it tore and collapsed? Was classical

---

[2]John F. Manley, "The Conservative Coalition in Congress," *American Behavioral Scientist,* Vol. 17, No. 2 (November/December 1973), p. 239.

[3]Allen Schick, "From the Old Politics of Budgeting to the New," in Naomi Caiden and Joseph White, eds., *Budgeting, Policy, Politics: An Appreciation of Aaron Wildavsky* (New Brunswick, N.J.: Transaction Publishers, 1995) p. 134.

budgeting merely an interlude, a pause before the storm to come, and a respite following the traumas of war and depression? In stressing the static elements of the postwar world to, say, the end of the 1960s, are we ignoring its more dynamic movements, which ultimately overwhelmed what might have been previously taken for granted as normal political life in a prosperous, stable superpower?

However legitimate these questions, and whatever their answers, it is worth pausing to examine the characteristics of classical budgeting. It provides a base, a point of contrast, for later transformations. Since reform of budget institutions is typically cumulative, much remains in place. While calculations and strategies may have changed to adapt to new constraints and opportunities, their necessity continues.

What follows is therefore often written in the present tense so as to retain a sense of immediacy. The Bureau of the Budget became the Office of Management and Budget in 1970, but in discussing classical budgeting it is referred to as the Budget Bureau for reasons of clarity. The reader should be aware, however, as the following chapters attest, that much of what follows belongs to a bygone era. Calculations remain complex but the roles and strategies of the participants and the budgetary process itself have been markedly altered.

CALCULATIONS

Participants in budgeting operate in an environment that imposes severe constraints on what they can do. Neither the opportunities they seize upon nor the disabilities they suffer are wholly, perhaps not even largely, within their control. Though perceptions of reality differ somewhat, and views of what is desirable differ more, budgetary actors accept certain elementary facts of life to which they must adjust.

Everyone is aware of the structural conditions of political life—such as the separation of powers, the division of labor within appropriations committees, and the customary separation between appropriations and substantive legislative committees. All participants face the usual overt political factors involving group pressures, relationships between members of Congress and their constituents, political party conflicts, executive-legislative cooperation and rivalry, interagency disputes, and the like. Participants soon come to know the rules of the budgetary game, which specify the roles they must play and the kinds of moves that are more or less permissible. It would be hard indeed to ignore the contemporary climate of opinion—a spending or cutting mood—as when a rise in defense spending becomes obvious after a provocation, or when a rise in unemployment demands creating jobs. Trends in the growth of national-welfare programs and increasing federal responsibility for a host of services are unlikely to be reversed. The participants take these conditions as "given" to a considerable extent and make calculations based on the way they perceive their environment. By "calculation" is meant the series of related factors (manifestly including perceptions of power relationships) that budgetary actors take into account in determining the choice of competing alternatives. Calculation involves a study of how problems arise and are identified, how they are broken down into manageable dimensions, how they relate to one another, how determinations are made of what is relevant, and how the actions of others are given consideration.

Complexity

One cannot hope to understand why people behave as they do unless one has some idea about how they make their calculations, and calculations are far from neutral. "Who gets what and how much" in politics depends on how calculations are made. Different methods of calculation often result in different decisions.

Budgeting is complex, both because there are many interrelated items and because these often pose technical difficulties. Suppose that you were interested in the leukemia research program and you wondered how the money was being spent. By looking at the National Cancer Institute's budgetary presentation you would discover that X amount is being spent on a project studying "factors and mechanics concerned in hemopoiesis," but that much less is being put into "a study of the relationship of neutralizing antibodies for the Rouse sarcoma virus to resistance and susceptibility for visceral lymphomatosis." Could you tell whether too much is being spent on one as compared to the other, or whether either project serves any useful purpose? It is not surprising, therefore, that members of Congress express dismay at the difficulties of understanding technical subjects. Representative Jensen has a granddaughter who is reputed by him to have read "all the stuff she can get on nuclear science. . . . And . . . she just stumps me. I say, 'Jennifer, for Heaven's sake. I can't answer that.' 'Well,' she says, 'You are on the Atomic Energy Commission Committee, Grandpa.' 'Yes,' he replies, 'but I am not schooled in the art.'"

Endless time and unlimited ability to calculate might help. But time is in short supply, the human mind can encompass just so much, and the number of budgetary items may be huge. "We might as well be frank," stated the chairman of the defense appropriations subcommittee, Representative George Mahon (D-Tex.), "no human being regardless of his position and . . . capacity could possibly be completely familiar with all the items of appropriations contained in this defense bill . . . ."

Aside from the complexity of individual budgetary programs, there remains the imposing problem of making comparisons among different programs—how much highways are worth as compared to recreation facilities, national defense, and schools—that have different values for different people. No common denominator among these functions has been developed. No matter how hard they try, therefore, officials discover that they cannot find an objective method of judging priorities among programs. How, then, do budget officials go about meeting their staggering burden of calculation?

Aids to Calculation

The ways in which the appropriations committees go about making budgetary calculations are affected by their central position in the congressional system. Their power to make budgetary decisions is in a sense rooted in their ability to help keep the system going by meeting the needs of other members of Congress. Appropriations must be voted each year if the government is to continue to function. To put together budgets running into the billions of dollars and involving innumerable different activities is a gargantuan task. But sheer effort is not enough. The committees must reduce the enormous burden of calculation involved in budgeting, in order to reach the necessary decisions. Otherwise, the necessity for decision might propel them into making random or wholly capricious choices that would throw governmental operations out of kilter. Nor could Congress as a whole shoulder the burden. Most members are busy with other things; they can hardly hope to become knowledgeable in more than a few areas of budgeting, if that. Unless they are to abdicate their powers, some way of reducing their information costs must be found. The way they have adapted is to accept the verdict of the appropriations committees most of the time and to intervene just often enough to keep the committees (roughly) in line.

Their mode of decision making might be characterized as incremental, enabling management of calculations and resolution of conflicts within the time frame of the budget. The various aspects of incrementalism reinforce each other in an informal system of coordination based on mutual expectations of participants pursuing their own agendas in a fragmented institution.

INCREMENTAL BUDGETING

The largest determining factor of this year's budget is last year's. Most of each budget is a product of previous decisions. The budget may be conceived of as an iceberg; by far the largest part lies below the surface, outside the control of anyone. Many items are standard, simply reenacted every year unless there is a special reason to challenge them. Long-range commitments have been made, and this year's share is scooped out of the total and included as part of the annual budget. The expenses of mandatory programs (entitlements), such as price supports or veterans' pensions, must be met. Some ongoing programs that appear to be satisfactory are no longer challenged. Agencies are going concerns and a minimum must be spent on housekeeping (though this item is particularly vulnerable to attack because it does not appear to involve a reduction in services or benefits). Powerful political support makes including other activities inevitable. At any one time, after past commitments are paid for, a rather small percentage—seldom larger than 30 percent, often smaller than 5—is within the realm of anybody's (including congressional and Budget Bureau) discretion as a practical matter.

Budgeting is incremental, not comprehensive. The beginning of wisdom about an agency budget is that it is almost never actively reviewed as a whole every year, in the sense of reconsidering the value of all existing programs as compared to all possible alternatives. Instead, it is based on last year's budget with special attention given to a narrow range of increases or decreases. General agreement on past budgetary decisions combined with years of accumulated experience and specialization allows those who make the budget to be concerned with relatively small increments to an existing base. Their attention is focused on a small number of items over which the budgetary battle is fought. Political reality, budget officials say, restricts attention to items they can do something about—a few new programs and possible cuts in old ones.

Budgeting Is Linked to Base and Fair Shares   Central to incrementalism is the concept of the base. The base is the general expectation that programs will be carried on at close to the going level of expenditures. Having a project included in the agency's base thus means more than just getting it in the budget for a particular year. It means the expectation that the expenditure will continue, that it is accepted as part of what will be done, and therefore that it will normally not be subjected to intensive scrutiny. (The word *base*, incidentally, is part of the common parlance of officials engaged in budgeting, and it would make no sense if experience led them to expect wide fluctuations from year to year, rather than additions to or subtractions from some relatively steady point.)

Linked to the concept of the base is the idea of "fair share." Fair share means not only the base an agency has established but also the expectation that the agency will receive some proportion of funds, if any, which are to be increased over or decreased below the base of the other governmental agencies. Fair share, then, reflects a convergence of expectations on roughly how much an agency is to receive in comparison to others.

The absence of a base, or an agreement on fair shares, makes it much harder to calculate what the agency or program should get. That happens when an agency or program is new or when rapid shifts of sentiment toward it take place. When times are tough, the base is subject to debate and adjustment. The base may be defined either as the "current estimate" (existing spending level of an agency) or next year's anticipated cost of maintaining programs at current levels of service (particularly important in inflationary times and usually referred to as a "base-line"). In any case there will be disagreement on what constitutes the base.

Budgeting Is Consensual   There must be agreement on the general direction of public policy, at least on most past policies, or Congress would be swamped with difficult choices. Past policies would have to be renegotiated every year, a time-consuming and enervating process. Simultaneously, new programs are sure to engender controversy; without agreement that keeps the past mostly out of contention, it becomes harder to deal with the present. Consensus on policies need not be total; conflict is ever-present. Yet if disagreement encompasses too many policies, aids to calculation will not work well.

Budgeting Is Historical   One way of dealing with a problem of huge magnitude is to make rough guesses while letting experience accumulate. When the consequences of various actions become apparent, it is then possible to make modifications to avoid the difficulties. Since members of Congress usually serve for several years before getting on appropriations committees, and since they are expected to serve an apprenticeship before making themselves heard, the more influential among them typically have long years of experience in dealing with their specialties. They have absorbed the meaning of many past moves and are prepared to apply the results of previous calculations to present circumstances. In this way the magnitude of any one decision at any one time is reduced, and with it the burden of calculation.

A line-item budgetary form facilitates this historical approach. Instead of focusing on various programs as a whole, the committees usually can concentrate on changes in various items—personnel, equipment, maintenance, specific activities—which make up the program. By keeping categories constant over a number of years, and by requiring that the previous and present year's figures be placed in adjacent columns, calculations made in the past need not be gone over again completely. And though members know that the agency is involved in various programs, the line-item form enables them to concentrate on the less divisive issue of how much for each item.

Yet the past is not a foolproof guide to the future. Because so many actions are being undertaken at the same time, it is hard to disentangle the effects of one particular action compared to others. Consequently, disputes may arise about the benefits of continued support for an item. Ultimately, reliance on a theory of cause and effect to provide guidance as to what is expected to happen becomes necessary.

Budgeting Is Fragmented   Budgets are made in fragments. Agencies develop budgetary requests based on their specialized needs. These requests are then channeled to any number of the multiple levels of specialization within Congress—the House and Senate Appropriations Committees, their subcommittees, the subject areas within these subcommittees, the Senate Appropriations Committee appeals procedure, the conference committee, and the authorizations functions of the substantive committees and their specialized subcommittees. Even the subcommittees do not deal with all items in the budget but will pay special attention to instances of increases or decreases over the previous year. In this way, it might be said, subcommittees deal with a fragment of a fragment of the whole.

Budgeting Is Simplified   Another way of handling complexity is to see how actions on simpler items can be indices for more complicated ones. Instead of dealing directly with the cost of a huge new installation, for example, decision makers may look at how personnel and administrative costs, or real estate transactions with which they have some familiarity, are handled. If these items are treated properly, then they may feel better able to trust administrators with the larger ones. Unable to handle the more complex problems, decision makers may retreat to the simpler ones.

Budgeting Is Social   Participants take clues from how others behave. They try to read character to reach programs. This method calls for looking at the administrative officials responsible rather than at the subject matter. To see if they are competent and reliable, officials can be questioned on a point here and there, a difficulty in this or that. One senior congressman reported that he followed an administrator's testimony to probe for weaknesses, looking for "strain in voice or manner," "covert glances," and so on.[4] Also, if an official can get people to go along, and if too many others do not complain too long and loud, then he may take the fact of agreement on something as his measure of success.

Budgeting Is "Satisficing"   Calculations may be simplified by lowering one's sights. Although they do not use Herbert Simon's vocabulary, budget officials do not try to maximize but, instead, they "satisfice" (satisfy and suffice).[5] Which is to

---

[4]L. Dwaine Marvick, *Congressional Appropriation Politics*, Ph.D. Dissertation, Columbia University, 1952, p. 297.

[5]Herbert Simon, *Models of Man* (New York: Wiley, 1957); see also Jerome S. Bruner, Jacqueline J. Goodnow, and George A. Austin, *A Study of Thinking* (New York: Wiley, 1956), for a fascinating discussion of strategies of concept attainment useful for dealing with the problem of complexity.

say that the budgeters do not try for the best of all possible worlds (whatever that might be) but, in their own words, try to "get by," to "come out all right," to "avoid trouble," to "avoid the worst." And since the budget comes up every year, and deals largely with piecemeal adjustment, this is one way to correct glaring weaknesses as they arise.

Budgeting Is Treated as If It Were Nonprogrammatic   This statement does not mean that people do not care about programs; they do. Nor does it mean that they do not fight for or against some programs; they do. What it does mean is that, given considerable agreement on policy, decision makers may see most of their work as marginal monetary adjustments to existing programs so that the question of the ultimate desirability of most programs arises only once in a while. "A disagreement on money isn't like a legislative program . . . ," one appropriations committee member said in a typical statement, "it's a matter of money rather than a difference in philosophy." An appropriations committee member explains how disagreements are handled in the markup session when members retire behind closed doors to work out their recommendations. (Nowadays many such sessions are open.) "If there's agreement, we go right along. If there's a lot of controversy we put the item aside and go on. Then, after a day or two, we may have a list of ten controversial items. We give and take and pound them down till we get agreement."[6] Obviously, they did not feel too strongly about each item or they could not agree so readily.

Budgeting Is Repetitive   Decision making in budgeting is carried on with the knowledge that few problems have to be "solved" once and for all. Everyone knows that a problem may be dealt with over and over again. Hence considerations that a member of Congress neglects one year may be taken up another year, or in a supplementary action during the same year. Problems are not so much solved as they are worn down by repeated attacks until they are no longer pressing or have been superseded by other problems. Problem succession, not problem solving, best describes what happens.

Budgeting Is Sequential   The appropriations committees do not try to handle every problem at once. On the contrary, they do not deal with many problems in a particular year, and those they do encounter are dealt with mostly in different places and at different times. Many decisions made in previous years are allowed to stand or to vary slightly without question. Then committees divide up subjects for more intensive inquiry among subcommittees and their specialists. Over the years, subcommittees center now on one and then on another problem. When budgetary decisions made by one subcommittee adversely affect those of another, the difficulty is handled by "fire truck tactics," that is, by dealing with each problem in turn in whatever jurisdiction it appears. Difficulties are overcome not so much by central coordination or planning as by

---

[6]Simon, *Models of Man.*

a cybernetic approach—attacking each manifestation in the different centers of decision in sequence.[7]

These aids ease the burden of calculations that are necessary for the development of a budget. Because attention is focused on the increment rather than on the relative value of a particular program compared to others, aids to calculation also serve to moderate conflict. The specialized and apparently nonprogrammatic character of decisions enhances the appearance of the budgetary process as technical. Since decisions are simplified and are made in different arenas at different times, the chance that severe conflicts will converge is reduced. In such a situation, the roles of participants—agencies, appropriations committees, and the Bureau of the Budget—were clearly defined.

ROLES AND PERSPECTIVES

The Agency

Agency people are expected to be advocates of increased appropriations. A classic statement of this role was made in 1939 by William A. Jump, a celebrated budget officer for the Department of Agriculture, who wrote that in budgeting

> . . . there inevitably are severe differences of judgment as to whether funds should be provided for a given purpose and, if so, in what amount. . . .

> It is at this stage that the departmental budget officer becomes an advocate or special pleader of the cause he represents. His position in representing the department then is analogous to that of an attorney for his client. In such circumstances, departmental budget officers put up the strongest and most effective fight of which they are capable to obtain . . . funds. . . . No apologies are offered for a vigorous position, or even an occasional showing of teeth, if circumstances seem to require it.[8]

Jump justified playing the advocate's role partly on the grounds that other participants had counterroles that necessitate a strong push from the departmental side.

Appropriations committee members tend to view budget officials as people with vested interests in raising appropriations. This position is generally accepted as natural and inevitable for administrators. As Assistant Chief Thayer of the Forest Service put it, "Mr. Chairman, you would not think that it would be proper for me to be in charge of this work and not be enthusiastic about it and not think that I ought to have a lot more money, would you? I have been in it for thirty years, and I believe in it." At times this attitude may lead to cynicism and perhaps annoyance on the part of House Appropriations Committee members. Yet if agencies

---

[7]The methods of calculation described here are similar to those attributed to social scientists by David Braybrooke and Charles E. Lindblom in their *A Strategy of Decision* (New York: Free Press, 1963), and to private firms by Richard Cyert and James March in their *A Behavioral Theory of the Firm* (Englewood Cliffs, N.J.: Prentice-Hall, 1963).

[8]W. A. Jump, "Budgetary and Financial Administration in an Operating Department of the Federal Government." Paper delivered at the conference of the Governmental Research Association, September 8, 1939, p. 5. See also the psychological portrait in Robert Walker, "William A. Jump: The Staff Officer as a Personality," *Public Administration Review*, Vol. 14 (Autumn 1954), pp. 233–46.

did not advocate, Congress would have a harder time figuring out what they needed and wanted.

Deciding How Much To Ask For   With appropriations always falling short of desires, how much of what they would like to get do agencies ask for? The simplest approach would be to add up the costs of all worthwhile projects and submit the total. This simple addition rarely is done, partly because everyone knows there would not be enough resources to go around. With revenues fixed in the short run, asking for a lot more would mean taking these sums from other agencies and programs; this would not be popular. Largely, however, the reason is strategic. If an agency continually submits requests far above what it actually gets, the Budget Bureau and the appropriations committees lose confidence in it and automatically cut large chunks before looking at the budget in detail.

It becomes much harder to justify even items with top priority because no one trusts an agency that repeatedly comes in too high. Yet it is unrealistic for an administrator not to make some allowance for the inevitable cut that others will make. Administrators realize that in predicting needs there is a reasonable range within which a decision can fall, and they just follow ordinary prudence in coming out with an estimate near the top.

Budgeting goes on in a world of reciprocal expectations that lead to self-fulfilling prophecies; agencies are expected to pad their requests to guard against cuts. As Representative Jamie Whitten (D-Miss.), Chairman of the Appropriations Subcommittee on Agriculture put it, "If you deal with the Department [of Agriculture] long enough and learn that they scale down each time, the bureau or agency can take that into consideration and build up the original figures." The Budget Bureau is expected to cut, partly because of its interest in protecting the president's program, and partly because it believes that agencies are likely to pad. Appropriations committees are expected to cut to fulfill their roles, and because they know the agency has already allowed for just this action. Cuts may be made in the House in the expectation that the Senate will replace them. Members of Congress get headlines for suggesting large cuts, but they often do not follow through for they know that the amounts will have to be restored by supplemental appropriations. Things may get to the point where members of the appropriations committees talk to agency officials off the record and ask where they can make a cut that will have to be restored later.

Whether disposed to pad or not, the agency finds that it must allow for cuts, and the cycle begins again as the prophecies confirm themselves. We have seen that an agency's budget is chiefly a product of past decisions. Beyond this is an area of discretion in which budget people want to get all they can, but cannot get all they want. Asking for too much may prejudice their chances, so it soon becomes apparent that the ability to estimate "what will go" (a phrase of budget officials) is a crucial aspect of budgeting.

Participants look out for, and receive, signals from the Executive Branch, Congress, clientele groups, and also their own organizations; in this way they arrive at a composite estimate of how much to ask for in the light of what they can expect to get. After an administration has been in office for a while, agency personnel have a background of actions and informal contacts to tell them how its various programs are regarded, especially for the preceding year. They also keep up with public announcements and private reports about how tough the president is going to be in regard to new expenditures. Formal word comes in the shape of a policy letter from the Budget Bureau, which usually has some statement on how closely this year's budget should resemble the last one. The impression made by this letter may be strengthened or weakened by reports or remarks made in cabinet meetings or by statements from those high up in the administration. If the president's science advisor speaks favorably of a particular program, his comments may offset tough remarks by the Director of the Budget. And, together, all these are seen in the light of the agency's experience in day-to-day dealings with the Budget Bureau staff, whose attitudes and nuances of behavior may speak more eloquently than any public statements as to administration intentions.

A major factor for agencies to consider is the interest of specialized publics in particular programs. Periodic reports from the field on the demand for services may serve as a general indicator. Top officials may travel and see firsthand just how enthusiastic the field personnel are about new programs. How detailed and concrete are their examples of public reaction? Agencies also may have advisory committees and use newspaper clipping services to provide information on the intentions of the interests concerned. The affected interests ordinarily lose no time in beating a path to the agency's door and presenting data about public support. When the agency begins to notice connections between the activities of supporting interests and calls from people in Congress, it has a pretty good idea of the support for a program.

Since there is much continuity of both agency and personnel and the committees and staffs in Congress, there is a rich history on which to base predictions. Agency officials are continuously engaged in "feeling the pulse" of Congress; likes and dislikes of influential members are well charted. Hearings on last year's budget are perused for indications of attitudes on specific programs, particularly on items that may get the agency into trouble. If the committee chair lets it be known that not enough is being done in a certain area, the agency knows that a program there will meet with sympathetic consideration. Overall congressional support may be indicated by debates on votes or amendments or new legislation. Finally, continuous contacts with appropriations committee staff leave agency people with definite feelings about what is likely to go over with the committee.

Last—but certainly not least—agencies also study the national political situation in deciding how much to try to get. Are there political reasons for increasing or decreasing spending? Is control over the national government split between the parties, with the result that there will be competition for support of particular programs or for holding the line? Do certain elements in Congress want to force presidential vetoes, or will the threat of veto result in program changes more favorable to the president?

From time to time agencies are affected by emergent problems, current events that no one could have predicted but that will radically alter budgetary prospects for particular programs. A change in missile technology, a drought, a new plant disease, or a social problem may drastically improve the prospects for some programs. The agency or interest group that can exploit the recognized needs arising from these events or generate such recognition is in an excellent position to expand support for its budget.

Deciding How Much To Spend   Deciding how much to ask for may be a big problem, but sometimes it is equally hard for an agency to figure out precisely how much to spend. If an agency has a substantial carryover, this may be taken as a sign that the agency does not need as much as it received and may cut off that amount in the future. The practice of penalizing carryovers leads to a last minute flurry of spending in the fourth quarter of the year despite apportionment of quarterly allotments. But you can't win. The agency that comes out exactly even is likely to be suspected of spending its limit without considering the need for economy. Coming out even seems just too neat to be true. The hapless agency that runs out of funds, on the other hand, may well be accused of using the tactic of coercive deficiency, or trying to compel Congress to appropriate more funds on the grounds that a vital activity will otherwise suffer. Most agency budget people try to end up with a little amount in reserve for most programs, but with an occasional deficit permitted in programs to which they are certain the funds will have to be restored.

Where agencies are likely to lose funds they carry over, however, their incentive is to spend up to the limit. Agencies are acutely aware that the reputation they have built up can help or hinder them greatly in matters of this kind. The agency with a reputation for economy may be praised for turning funds back and not get them cut the following year, whereas the agency deemed to be prodigal may get slashed on the grounds it must not have needed the money in the first place.

Department versus Bureau   The term *agency* has been used thus far to signify either a bureau or a department, and most of the considerations do apply with equal force to departments and bureaus. Now it will be useful to make a distinction between departments and their component units, the bureaus, in discussing the special problems that departments face in deciding how much to try to get for bureaus under their jurisdiction. Let us assume that the department secretary and her staff have managed to work out some notion of the secretary's policy preferences, and it so happens that these preferences run counter to those of a bureau. Problems of influence immediately arise. The most obvious is that some bureaus may have considerable support in Congress and can thus override departments. Still, the secretary and her staff might well decide to push their own preferences anyway, if that were all that had to be considered. One difficulty, however, is that a record of a department recommending far less than Congress appropriates (and a bureau wants) may lead to a general disregard of what the secretary proposed. Why pay attention if she is obviously a loser? Another difficulty is that if department officials need bureau support in other matters, they may find that hostility over deep cuts can interfere with the necessary good relations. So the department often finds it wise to temper its preferences with a strong dose of calculations as to what would be acceptable to the other participants.

Considerations such as these involve the various departments (whether they know it or not) in resolving a basic question of political theory: Shall each bureau ask for what it wants or shall priority go to the total departmental situation in making requests? (Put in a different way, the question might be phrased: Is it best for each interest to pursue its own advantage or shall each seek a solution it believes is in the interest of all?) Of course, if every bureau just shoots for the moon, the total reaches an astronomical figure and that is not much help. Except in years when there are exceedingly powerful reasons for keeping budget totals down, the approach preferred by most department officials is a modified version of "tell us what you really want."

The usual practice is for a high department official to lay the whole budget before the bureau heads to show them why they cannot get any more than their limited share, despite the fact that the programs are eminently deserving. Some budget officials are extremely talented at cutting without getting the blame.

The Bureau of the Budget

The dominant role of the Bureau of the Budget, in form and in fact, is to help the president carry out his purpose,[9] and its orientation, therefore, depends on that of the Chief Executive. His concerns about the relative priorities of domestic and foreign policy programs, his beliefs about the desirability of a balanced budget, and his preferences in various other areas determine a good deal of what the Bureau tries to do. Ideally, a meeting of the various executive policy decision streams—domestic and defense budgeting, and fiscal policy, represented by the president with advisors from the White House, National Security Council, Defense Department, Council of Economic Advisers, Treasury, and Budget Bureau—will produce a "target total" for outlays and promote a rough indication of domestic and military priorities. A decision on target total outlays serves as the basis for the Budget Bureau to develop agency ceilings. Thus the Bureau finds itself trying to get appropriations from Congress for presidential programs and, at times, prodding agencies to come in with new or enlarged programs to meet the president's desires. Yet the BOB is also responsible for establishing agency ceilings based on the target total outlays. Thus BOB ordinarily gives less weight to advocating presidential programs than to keeping them within bounds, particularly since everyone already expects the agencies to perform the functions of advocacy.

This top-down approach to budgeting (i.e, the establishment of boundaries by setting budgetary totals) contrasts with the bottom-up incremental development of budgetary totals reflected in congressional decision making.

There are, of course, always some people in the Budget Bureau who identify more closely with an agency or program than do others, or who develop policy preferences independent of the president. They have a creative urge. ("I don't like to think of myself as a red-pencil man.") They see themselves as doing the right thing by pursuing policies in the public interest, and they may convince themselves that the president would support them if only he had the time and inclination to go into

---

[9]See Fritz Morstein Marx, "The Bureau of the Budget: Its Evolution and Present Role, II," *American Political Science Review,* Vol. 39 (October 1945), pp. 869–98; Richard Neustadt, "Presidency and Legislation: The Growth of Central Clearance," *American Political Science Review,* Vol. 48 (September 1954) pp. 641–71; Arthur Maas, "In Accord with the Program of the President?" in Carl Friedrich and Kenneth Galbraith, eds., *Public Policy,* Vol. 4 (Cambridge, Mass.: Graduate School of Public Administration, 1954), pp. 77–93; Frederick J. Lawton, "Legislative-Executive Relationships in Budgeting as Viewed by the Executive," *Public Administration Review,* Vol. 13 (Summer 1953), pp. 169–76; and Aaron Wildavsky, *Dixon–Yates: A Study in Power Politics* (New Haven: Yale University Press, 1962), p. 64.

the matter as deeply as they had. They would rarely resist a direct presidential command, but these are few at any one time and ordinarily leave much room for interpretation. The role adopted by its budget examiners is important to an agency even if the general orientation of the Budget Bureau is different.

Even within the same administration, different budget directors can have an impact of their own on Budget Bureau decisions. Some directors have much better relationships with the president than others; they get in to see him more often and without going through subordinates; he backs them up more frequently on appeals from the agencies. In bargaining on recommendations, a budget director who is close to the president has an important advantage since he knows how much leeway he has within the Chief Executive's desires. Should the president turn down an appeal, the agency and its supporters may seek to discover how much of an increase they can get from Congress without risking a presidential veto or strong opposition.

Members of Congress are ambivalent about the Bureau of the Budget; essentially they regard it as a necessary evil. For example, the ambivalence comes through when a member of the House Appropriations Committee, with a trace of contempt, calls Bureau officials a bunch of bureaucrats who think they are making the budget, but on another occasion reviles them for not having done enough. Or, further, the Bureau may be regarded as a rival for control of appropriations. Representative Flood (talking as a member of the Defense Appropriations Subcommittee) dramatized this feeling when he said, "Mr. Secretary [of Defense] . . . you are a very important man in the Government . . . but you are a minor deity, believe me, compared to the Director of the Budget. He is the Poo-Bah of this town. . . . I feel so strongly about it and many members of the committee and Congress, that we think the Bureau of the Budget as it is now set up should be ripped out altogether."

Every agency, and its officials, has to decide what kind of relationship to maintain with the Budget Bureau and particularly with its examiners. Since no examiner can know everything, the agency may decide to provide only the data specifically requested. More and more, however, one sees a tendency actually to heap data on the examiners all the time, not merely when they ask. Why? First, abundant information helps the examiners to defend the agency's viewpoint competently at Budget Bureau meetings when agency personnel is not represented. Second, well-informed examiners may become converted into advocates of particular programs. Third, the examiners' knowledge can be turned to advantage by getting them to secure administration assistance in clearing up some difficulty. The associated disadvantage, of course, is that examiners "get to know where the bodies are buried this way," as one budget officer put it. "But," he continued in words echoed by many others, "you can't hide serious weaknesses for very long anyway, and so the advantages far outweigh the disadvantages."

Agency people agree that Budget Bureau support is worth having if you can get it without sacrificing too much in Congress. Given the congressional propensity to cut, what the Budget Bureau proposes for an agency is likely to be the upper limit. (What was true in the classical period, I remind the reader, is not necessarily true now.) In addition, there are multitudes of small items that Congress would not ordinarily investigate but that might have trouble getting funded if Bureau approval were lacking.

Agencies recognize two basic limitations on Budget Bureau influence. The most serious handicap under which the Budget Bureau labors is not so much that Congress may raise its proposed spending (though this is obviously important) but that the BOB cannot guarantee a cooperating agency will receive the amount it has recommended.[10] Agencies that could depend on receiving what the Budget Bureau recommended would have much greater incentive to cooperate.

A second limitation of the Bureau is that its actions are often constrained by its perceptions of how Congress will view agency requests. Everyone knows that agencies make end runs around the Bureau to gain support from Congress. Yet if agencies do so too often, the Budget Bureau finds that its own prestige has declined. Hence, the Bureau frequently accepts consistent congressional action as a guide. A close eye is kept on congressional action for the preceding year before the Bureau sets an agency's total for the next one. The Bureau must also be wary of particular programs favored by Congress. Suppose an agency must choose between two alternatives, one favored by Congress, another by the Budget Bureau. The strategy probably would be to side with Congress because its record with Congress determines how an agency is viewed and treated both by the Budget Bureau and the department.

The Appropriations Committees

One of the prevailing roles played by members of the House Appropriations Committee is guardian of the public purse. Committee members are expected to cast a skeptical eye on the blandishments of a bureaucracy ever anxious to increase its dominion by increasing its appropriations. The role of guardianship is reinforced by the House leadership, which deliberately chooses committee members from safe districts who can therefore afford to say "no."

This role, of course, is not the only one that guides all committee members in all situations. Some members identify completely with an agency or its programs. "To me forestry has become a religion . . . ," said Representative Walter Horan. In a profound violation of House Committee norms, he took his protest against his own appropriations subcommittee to the Senate hearings, declaring that "The items are totally inadequate and I do not care particularly which way *we* get them, but we do need funds" (emphasis supplied). At times, then, the feeling of having served a great cause may create a sense of identification with an agency or program that overwhelms other considerations. To get credit for cutting, by contrast, requires an institutional milieu in which people are honored for being negative.

In the case of local constituency interests, the deviation from guardianship of the budget is exceedingly powerful because it touches on the most basic relationship members of Congress may have—that with the people who elect them and might conceivably defeat them—and because representatives are prone to take on faith another of their roles as defender of constituency interests. Where their constituencies are affected, appropriations committee members use all the vast leverage over men and money their positions give them to secure favorable

---

[10]See the first edition, *The Politics of the Budgetary Process* (Boston: Little, Brown, 1964), p. 41.

outcomes. Representative John Rooney engaged in a royal battle to keep a Department of Commerce office in New York City so that his constituents would not lose their jobs. Then there was Representative Ivor Fenton's tenacious campaign to have an anthracite laboratory located in Schuylkill Haven instead of Hazleton, Penn. Fenton said that he got no action until he got on the appropriations committee. In another skirmish, a little arm-twisting was applied by Senator Lyndon Johnson in order to make certain that a prison was built in the right place. "I sure would hate to put in this money to build a prison in Congressman Grey's district and Senator Dirksen's state in Illinois and find out that they got it in X, Y, Z, somewhere."

Tough as they may be when cutting the budgets of their agencies, appropriations committee members, once having made a decision, generally defend the agencies against further cuts on the floor. In an exchange with a member of the appropriations committee, Representative Clarence Brown (R-Ohio) complained that when an amendment is offered "to reduce an appropriations item, the appropriations committee stands like a stone wall most of the time, saying 'No, you mustn't touch this.'"[11] This kind of action is in part self-interest. The power of appropriations subcommittees would be diminished if their recommendations were successfully challenged very often. Members believe that the House would "run wild" if "orderly procedure"—that is, acceptance of committee recommendations—were not followed. But the role of defender also has its roots in the respect for expertise and specialization in Congress, and in the ensuing belief that members who have not studied the subject should not exercise a deciding voice without the presence of overriding considerations. An appeal to the norm of specialization is usually sufficient to block an attempt to reduce appropriations.

A member of the Senate Appropriations Committee is likely to view himself as the responsible legislator who sees to it that the irrepressible lower House does not do too much damage either to constituency or to national interests. And though members of the House Appropriations Committee tend to view their opposite members in the Senate as frivolous spendthrifts of the public purse, senators reverse the compliment by regarding their brethren in the other chamber as stingy and jealous types who do not care what happens to "essential" programs so long as they can show that they have made cuts.

The senators are rather painfully aware of the House Committee's preeminence in the field of appropriations; they know they cannot hope to match the time and thoroughness that the House body devotes to screening requests. For this reason, Senate members put a high value on having agencies carry appeals to it. "We all know," said Senator Richard Russell (D-Ga.), chairman of the agriculture appropriations subcommittee, "that almost since the inception of the Government, the Senate Appropriations Committee has served as an appeal body and has heard requests . . . that deal principally with items that have been changed or reduced or eliminated by the House of Representatives." Senators value their ability to disagree on disputed items as a means of maintaining influence in crucial areas, while experiencing the least possible strain on their time and energy. This

---

[11]House Government Operations Subcommittee, *Improving Federal Budgeting and Appropriations,* 85th Congress, 1st Session, 1957, p. 139.

dominant Senate function as responsible appeals court depends upon agency advocacy and House committee guardianship.

STRATEGIES

Budgetary strategies are actions by governmental agencies intended to maintain or increase their available funds. Strategies are the links between the intentions and perceptions of budget officials, and the political system that both imposes restraints and creates opportunities for them.

Strategic moves take place in a rapidly changing environment in which no one is quite certain how things will turn out and in which new goals constantly emerge. In this context of uncertainty, choice among existing strategies must be based on intuition and hunch—on an "educated guess"—as well as on firm knowledge. Assuming a normal capacity to learn, however, experience should eventually provide a more reliable guide than sheer guesswork. While the strategies recounted here relate to a bygone era of Congress—one without budget committees, budget resolutions, and vastly changed rules—many are timeless and form part of participants' repertoires in a variety of situations.

Be a Good Politician

What really counts in helping an agency get the appropriations it desires? Long service in Washington has convinced many high agency officials that some things count a great deal and others only a little. Although they are well aware that it is desirable to have technical data to support requests, budget officials commonly derogate the importance of the formal aspects of their work. As several informants put it in almost identical words, "It's not what's in your estimates but how good a politician you are that matters."

Being a good politician, these officials say, requires essentially three things: cultivation of an active clientele, the development of confidence among other governmental officials, and skill in following strategies that exploit one's opportunities to the maximum. Doing good work is viewed as part of being a good politician.

Clientele

Find a Clientele   For most agencies, locating a clientele is no problem at all; the groups interested in their activities are all too present. But some agencies find this a difficult problem, demanding extraordinary measures to solve. Men and women incarcerated in federal prisons, for instance, are hardly an ideal clientele. And the rest of society cares only to the extent of keeping these people locked up. So the Bureau of Prisons tries to create special interest in its activities by inviting members of Congress to see what is going on. "I wish, Mr. Bow, you would come and visit us at one of these prison places when you have the time. . . . I am sure you would enjoy it." The United States Information Agency faced a similar problem—partly explaining its mendicant status—because its work is all abroad rather than directly benefiting people at home. Things got so bad that the USIA sought to organize our country's ambassadors to foreign nations into an interest group to vouch for the good job USIA said it was doing.

Serve Your Clientele   For an agency that has a large and strategically placed clientele, the most effective strategy is to serve those who are in a position to help the agency. "If we deliver this kind of service," an administrator declared, "other things are secondary and automatic." His agency made a point of organizing clientele groups in various locations, priming them to engage in approved projects, serving them well, and encouraging them to inform their representatives of their reaction. Informing one's clientele of the full extent of the benefits they receive may increase the intensity with which they support the agency's request.

Expand Your Clientele   In order to secure substantial funds from Congress for domestic purposes, it is ordinarily necessary to develop fairly wide interest in the program. This is what Representative Whitten did when he became a member of the Appropriations Committee and discovered that soil conservation in various watersheds had been authorized, but that little money had been forthcoming: "Living in the watersheds ... I began to check ... and I found that all these watersheds were in a particular region, which meant there was no general interest in the Congress in this type of program. . . . It led me to go before the Democratic platform committee in 1952 and urge them to write into the platform a plank on watershed protection. And they did." As a result, Whitten was able to call on more general support from Democrats as well as to increase appropriations for Soil Conservation Service watersheds.

Concentrate on Individual Constituencies   After the Census Bureau made an unsuccessful bid to establish a national housing survey, Representative Sidney Yates (D-Ill.) gave the bureau a useful hint. The proposed survey "is so general," Yates said, "as to be almost useless to the people of a particular community. . . . This would help someone like Armstrong Cork, who can sell its product anywhere in the country . . . but will it help the construction industry in a particular area to know whether or not it faces a shortage of customers?" Later, the Bureau submitted a new program that called for a detailed enumeration of metropolitan districts with a sample survey of other areas to get a national total. In another case, the National Science Foundation made headway with a program of summer mathematics institutes not only because the idea was excellent but also because the institutes were spread around the country, where they became part of a constituency interest members of Congress are supposed to protect.

Secure Feedback   Almost everybody claims that their projects are immensely popular and benefit lots of people. But how can elected officials find this out? Only by hearing from constituents. The agency can do a lot to ensure that its clientele responds by informing them that it is vital to contact their representatives and by telling them, if necessary, how to go about it. In fact, the agency may organize its clientele in the first place, and then offer to fulfill the demand it has helped to create. Policies create clients just as clients can create policies. Indeed, members of Congress often urge administrators to make a show of their clientele: Senator Wherry: "Do you have letters or evidence from small operators . . . that need your service that you can introduce into the record. . . . Is that not the test on how much demand there is for your services?" When feedback is absent or limited, members of Congress tend to assume no one cares and they need not bother with the appropriation.

End-runs   When political considerations attach to the idea of a balanced budget, an administration may seek appropriations policies that minimize the short-run impact on the budget, even though total expense may be greater over a period of years. In the Dixon–Yates case (1954–1956) a proposed TVA power plant was rejected partly because it involved large immediate capital outlays. The private power plant that was accepted was to involve much larger expenditures over a 25-year period, but this spending, spread out over time, would have had comparatively little impact.[12]

When clientele are absent or weak there are some techniques for making expenditures so that they either do not appear in the budget or appear much later on. The International Monetary Fund may be given a Treasury note to be used at some future date when IMF needs money. Buildings for public use may be constructed by private organizations so that the rent paid is, in the short run, much lower than an initial capital expenditure would have appeared. (In the 1980s the military tried to take that approach to its housing.) An agency and its supporters who fear hostile appropriations committee action may seek authorization to spend directly from the Treasury to avoid direct encounter with the normal budgetary process. This action is bitterly opposed as backdoor spending, especially in the House Appropriations Committee.

Confidence

The sheer mass of budgetary matters means that some people have got to trust others because only rarely can they check up on things. "It is impossible for any person to understand in detail the purposes for which $70 billion are requested," Senator Thomas declared in regard to the defense budget. "The committee [recall this is way back when] must take some things on faith." If we add to this the idea of budgeting by increments (where large areas of the budget are exempt from serious questions each year), committee members will treat an agency much better if they feel that its officials will not deceive them.

Administrative officials unanimously agree that they must, as a bare minimum, enjoy the confidence of appropriations committee members and their staff. "If you have the confidence of your subcommittee your life is much easier and you can do your department good; if you don't have confidence you can't accomplish much and you are always in trouble." How do agency personnel seek to establish this confidence?

Be What They Think They Are   Confidence is achieved by gearing one's behavior to fit the expectations of committee people. Essentially, the desired qualities will appear to be projections of the committee members' images of themselves. Bureaucrats are expected to be masters of detail—hardworking, frank, self-effacing

---

[12]See the author's *Dixon–Yates: A Study in Power Politics.*

people devoted to their work, who are tight with the taxpayer's money, recognize a political necessity when they see one, and keep Congress informed. To be considered aboveboard, a fair and square shooter, a frank person is highly desirable.

But if and when a subcommittee drops the most customary role and becomes an outright advocate of a program, as with the Polaris missile system, the budget official is expected to shoot for the moon; he will be criticized if he emphasizes petty economies instead of pushing his projects. It is not so much what administrators do but how they meet the particular subcommittee's or chairman's expectations that counts.

Play It Straight!   Everyone agrees that the most important requirement for confidence, at least in a negative sense, is to be aboveboard. A lie, a blatant attempt to cover up some misdeed, a tricky move of any kind, can lead to an irreparable loss of confidence. A typical comment by an administrator states, "It doesn't pay to try to put something over on them [committee members] because if you get caught, you might as well pack your bags and leave Washington." And the chances of getting caught are considerable because interested committees and their staffs have much experience and many sources of information.

A committee that feels that it has been misled can take endless punitive actions. Senator Carl Hayden (D-Ariz.), chairman of the Senate Appropriations Committee, spoke at one time when a bureau received a lump-sum appropriation as an experiment. "Next year . . . the committee felt outraged that certain actions had been taken, not indicated in the hearings before them. Then we proceeded to earmark the bill from one end to the other. We just tied it up in knots to show that it was the Congress, after all, that dictated policy."

Integrity   The positive side of the confidence relationship is to make it known that the agency official is a person of high integrity who can be trusted. He must not only give but must also appear to give reliable information. Agency people must keep confidences and not get members of Congress into trouble by what they say or do—willing to take blame (but never credit). Like a brand name, a budget official's reputation comes to be worth a good deal in negotiation.

An agency that enjoys good relations with subcommittee staff has an easier time in Congress than it might otherwise. The agency finds that more reliance is placed on its figures, more credence is given to its claims, and more opportunities are provided to secure its demands. Thus one budget officer who received information that a million-dollar item had been casually dropped from a bill was able to arrange with his source of information on the staff to have the item put back for reconsideration. On the other hand, asked if they would consider refusing to talk to committee staff, agency officials uniformly declared that such a stance would be tantamount to cutting their own throats. A staff person whose nose is out of joint can do harm to an agency by expressing distrust of its competence or integrity.

I'd Love To Help You But . . .   Where the administrator's notion of what is proper conflicts with that of a member of Congress with whom he or she needs to maintain friendly relations, there is no perfect way out of the difficulty. Most officials try to turn the member down by suggesting that their hands are tied, that something may be done in the future, or by stressing some other project on which they are agreed. After Representative William Natcher (D-Ky.) spoke for the second time of his desire for a project in his district, Don Williams of the Soil Conservation Service complimented him for his interest in watershed activity in Kentucky but was "sorry that some of the projects that were proposed would not qualify under the law . . . but . . . they are highly desirable."

Congressional Committee Hearings

Play the Game   The Bureau of the Budget lays down the rule that members of the Executive Branch are not to challenge the Executive Budget. But everyone knows that administrative officials want more for their agencies and—in league with supporting members of Congress—sometimes are in a position to get it. On such occasions the result is a ritual that any reader of appropriations hearings will recognize. The agency official is asked whether or not he supports the amounts in the president's budget and he says "yes" in such a way that it sounds like yes but that everyone realizes means "no." His manner may communicate a marked lack of enthusiasm or he may be just too enthusiastic to be true. A committee member will then ask how much the agency originally requested from the Budget Bureau. There follows an apparent refusal to answer, in the form of a protestation of loyalty to the Chief Executive. Under duress, however, and amidst reminders of congressional prerogatives, the agency official will cite the figures. Could he usefully spend the money, he is asked. Of course he could. The presumption that the agency would not have asked for more money if it did not need it is made explicit. Then comes another defense of the administration's position by the agency, which, however, puts up feeble opposition to congressional demands for increases.

It Works: The Problem of Effectiveness   Apart from overwhelming public support, there is nothing that succeeds better than tangible accomplishment. The Polaris does fire and hit a target with reasonable accuracy; a range-reseeding project does make the grass grow again. Congressional interpretation of accomplishments as being worthwhile depends on what criteria of effectiveness agencies use and on how tough Congress permits them to be. There is great temptation for agencies to devise a criterion that will enable a project's supporters to say that it works. At the same time, opponents of a project may unfairly propose criteria that cannot be met. And there are times when reasonable people disagree over criteria. We hope and pray to avoid nuclear war. But if it comes, what criteria should a civil-defense program have to meet? If one argues that it must save everyone, then no program can show results. Suppose, however, that one is willing to accept much less—say half or a third or a fifth of the population. Then everything would depend on estimates that surely could be improved upon, but which nobody can really claim to be reliable—as to likely levels of attack, patterns of wind and radiation, and a multitude of other factors.

Strategies Designed To Capitalize on the Fragmentation of Power in National Politics

The separation of powers and the internal divisions of labor within Congress and the Executive Branch present numerous opportunities for program advocates (including both agency personnel and members of Congress) to play one center of power off against another.

Compensation   Program supporters who have superior access to one house of Congress may seek to raise the program's grant in one house to allow for bargaining with the other. If they can get their way or arrange to split the difference in the Conference Committee, they are that much ahead. A member of Congress may ask the agency for the lowest addition that would make a project possible so as to know how far to go in conference. Thus Senator Pat McCarran (D-Nev.) told the Census Bureau that he "just wanted to see . . . how much we could lose in the conference, and still give some assistance to be of value." Although the presence of differing interests and degrees of confidence in House and Senate may give an agency room to maneuver, this may also subject it to a withering cross fire from which there is no immediate escape.

Both Ends Against the Middle   The separation between appropriations and substantive committees creates another opportunity to exploit differences between dual authorities. Appropriations committees often refuse funds for projects authorized by substantive committees. And substantive committees, with or without agency backing, sometimes seek to exert influence over appropriations committees. As the classical period ebbed, substantive committees greatly increased their use of annual rather than multiyear or permanent authorizations. A familiar tactic is the calling of hearings by substantive committees to dramatize the contention that an authorized program is being underfinanced or not financed at all. Knowing that the appropriations committees have the final say, substantive committees can afford to authorize any project they deem good without too much concern for its financial implications. Also, appropriations committees sometimes seek to write legislation into appropriations bills; this effort may lead to a conflict with the substantive committee that spills over onto the floor of the houses of Congress.

Agencies stand to gain by exploiting such conflicts to their advantage. They can try to use an authorization as a club over the head of the appropriations committees by pointing to a substantive committee as their source of commitment for funds. In seeking an increase for fishery research, for example, the Fish and Wildlife Service declared that it "came about through direction of a Congressional Committee. . . . The [substantive] committee directed that hereafter the department should include this item for their appropriations." This strategy does not create much difficulty in the Senate, where some members of the substantive committees are likely also to sit on the appropriations committee. But House members do not like it at all—though a member may from time to time brag about how he got through a pet appropriation without a real authorization—and they are quick to remind administrators of their prerogatives.

Cut Less Visible Items   Counterstrategies are available to legislators. Many members of Congress feel a need to cut an agency's requests somewhere. Yet the same member may be sympathetic to the agency's program or feel obliged to support it because people in his or her constituency are believed to want it. Where, then, can cuts be made? In those places that do not appear to directly involve program activities: The department office or general administrative expenses, for example, may be cut without appearing to affect any specific desirable program. This fits in well with a general suspicion current in society that bureaucrats are wasteful. Housekeeping activities may also suffer since it often appears that they can be put off another year and they do not seem directly connected with programs. Yet deferred maintenance may turn out to cost more in the end. But cutting here enables a representative to meet conflicting pressures for the time being.

All or Nothing   This tactic is to assert that if a cut is made the entire program will have to be scrapped. "Reducing the fund to $50,000 would reduce it too much for us to carry forward the work. We have to request the restoration . . . ," said the Bureau of Mines. The danger is that Congress may take the hint and cut out the whole program. So this strategy must be employed with care, and only in connection with a program that is most unlikely to be abolished.

Shift the Blame   A widespread strategy is to get the other party to make the difficult decisions of cutting down on requests, thus shifting the onus for the cuts. He who must take the blame may not be willing to make the cut. Everyone knows that many agencies raise their budgetary requests (among other reasons) in order to show their supporting interests that they are working hard but are being thwarted by the president. So the Budget Bureau is disposed to cut. The most frustrating aspect of this activity is that when an agency's budget is squeezed it is often not the "wasteful" things that come out; priorities within the agency and Congress vary greatly and some legendary, obsolete facility may survive long after more essential activities have disappeared. Thus the Budget Bureau may be caught between a desire to make the agency responsible for a cut and the need to insist that cuts be made in certain places rather than others.

They Made Me   Members of Congress have developed their own strategies for making cuts without taking full responsibility. Just as budget officials say that "circumstances" have compelled them to ask for increases, so do people in Congress assert that "outside forces"—a climate of opinion against spending strong views of influential colleagues, presidential opposition, attempts by the other party to make spending an issue, an overriding need to balance the budget—leave them with little choice. This strategy has a corollary: If a subcommittee is not sure what to cut but feels pressure, it may make the cut and let the agency's protests reveal what the agency is really unwilling to give up.

The Transfer   One way of moving ahead while appearing to stand still is to keep appropriations for particular categories constant so that no change seems to be made although various past expenditures, no longer being made, have been replaced with others. Items may be transferred from one category to another so that no particular one stands out as being too far out of line. If a committee or the Budget Bureau is concerned over increases in administrative expenses, ways may be found of transferring these expenditures to other items by including them as part of less suspect costs. Some agencies include administrative expenses under each program instead of under the administrative category.

The Camel's Nose   A large program may be started by an apparently insignificant sum. The agency then claims that (1) this has not become part of its base and that (2) it would be terrible to lose the money already spent by not going ahead and finishing the job. As Representative Rooney observed, "This may be only $250 but this is the camel's nose. These things never get out of a budget. They manage to stay and grow." Congress has tried to counter this strategy by passing legislation requiring a total estimate for a project before any part can be authorized. But estimates are subject to change and a small sum one year rarely seems imposing even if a large amount is postulated for the future.

In arguing against a change in accounting procedures, Representative Mahon sketched the strategic implications:

> I believe it was last year that we appropriated $1 million, just a little $1 million to start a public works project of the Army Engineers which is to cost $1 billion. Why, if I go to Congressman Kilgore and say, "Listen, Joe, we have been colleagues for a long time, can't you vote for this little $1 million for my area to help me and my people?"

> Well Joe, I am sure he would do whatever was right and proper, but it might be something tempting, particularly if I had voted for a million-dollar project for Joe on a former occasion, to vote for my proposal. But what if I go up to Joe and I say, "Listen, Joe, I want you to vote for this project, it costs a billion dollars over a period of years, and if you start it, it is going to be completed."[13]

A Foot in the Door   The desire of budget officials to keep items in the budget, even if they are small and underfinanced, is readily explained once it is understood that they may one day serve to launch full-blown programs when conditions are more favorable. Research projects are often not terminated when they have either proven successful or have failed; a small item concerning applicability of the research is retained in the budget so that if the agency wishes to resume it has a foot in the door.

Just for Now   "Is there anything more permanent than a temporary agency of the Government," Representative John Phillips (R-Calif.) wanted to know. His colleague, Mr. Thomas, spoke with some asperity of a temporary activity that had begun four years ago. "Of course, [the agency] said it would take them about two years to clear it up and then they would be off the payroll. Since then I think you have added 30 [people] to this group." A temporary adjustment to a passing situation results in an emergency appropriation for a fixed period, which then turns out to be a permanent expenditure.

---

[13]*Improving Federal Budget and Appropriations,* House Subcommittee on Government Operations, 85th Congress, 1st Session, pp. 132–33.

The Commitment   Although expenditures may rise and requests for money may increase, an agency can hardly be blamed if it had no choice. As one official put it, "The increases are in every case presented as either related to commitments . . . or other uncontrollable factors."

A favorite strategy is to lay down long-range goals for an existing program, which the agency can use to show that its requirements are not being met. The very statement that there are X acres not yet under soil conservation practices or so many Native American children who need schooling may serve to create an implied commitment to meet the demand. The NIH and its congressional allies go one step further by speaking of "moral obligations" for continuing projects mounting up to tens of millions of dollars.

It Pays for Itself; It Makes a Profit   An increase may not seem like one if it can be shown that the increase brings in revenue equal to or greater than the cost. Although government is presumably not conducted for profit, the delight members of Congress take in finding an activity that returns money to the Treasury is indicated by the frequency with which they use this fact to praise administrators and to support programs they prefer. Senator Dworshak told the Fish and Wildlife Service that "when you return money like that [$1 million from seal furs] back in, you should be proud of it and have the record show it." Not to be outdone, J. Edgar Hoover pointed out that the FBI had recovered $73 million more through its investigation activities over a 10-year period than it had received in appropriations.

The Crisis   There comes a time, however, when it is necessary to admit that a new program is in the offing or that substantial increases in existing ones are desired. This situation calls for a special campaign in which three techniques—the crisis, salesmanship, and advertising—are often called into play. The purpose is to generate extraordinary support so that the agency or program does not merely inch ahead but secures sizable new appropriations.

Events do not have meaning in themselves; they are given meaning by observers. The agency in a position to meet a crisis, as TVA was by supplying huge amounts of power to nuclear energy installations, can greatly increase its appropriations. And, soon after a jet plane had crashed because of contact with a flock of starlings, the Fish and Wildlife Service was able to obtain funds for research into the habits of these birds. There is also a borderline area of discretion in which crisis may be made to appear more critical. A number of agency officials are famous in budgetary circles for their ability to embellish or make use of crisis. By publicizing a situation, dramatizing it effectively, and perhaps asking for emergency appropriations, an agency may maneuver itself into a position of responsibility for large new programs.

Salesmanship runs the gamut from a cops-and-robbers' appeal—"agents of our [Narcotics Bureau]. . . engaged in a 45-minute gun battle with Mexican smugglers"—to the "agony sessions" at NIH hearings. Who could resist Senator Hill's plea:

> As we begin today's hearings on appropriations . . . we take notice of the passing of . . . John Foster Dulles [who] fell victim to the most dreaded killer of our time, cancer.

> Cancer, that most ancient and accursed scourge of mankind, has . . . robbed the U.S. Senate of some of its greatest leaders: Robert A. Taft, Arthur Vandenberg, Kenneth Wherry, Brian McMahon, and Matthew Neely. What more fitting . . . memorial . . . could there be than a high resolve . . . to redouble our research efforts against the monstrous killer which . . . will claim the lives of 250,000 more Americans before this year has ended? . . . We are very happy to have with us our colleague, Senator Neuberger. . . . [then dying of cancer]

Who would vote against appropriations for medical research after being subjected to this treatment?

In the classical era of American national budgeting, that quarter century between the end of World War II and the early 1970s, there was a recognizable budgetary process, almost a budgetary minuet. Conflict was routinized and confined by informal understandings. These understandings, supported by the aim of balance, reinforced by agreement on the general lines of public policy and an expansive economic climate, led to budgetary incrementalism. Since there was agreement on most programs, these constituted a base that was generally considered untouchable. For the most part, differences centered upon small departures from the base, rather than the program itself. By focusing upon remedial measures, by usually dealing with difficulties as they revealed themselves and by making repeated attacks upon problems in different forums—within agencies, between agencies and the OMB, in House and Senate subcommittees—those problems could be factored down into small and manageable components. Calculation was improved and conflict limited by this incremental, remedial, and serial approach.

Just enough central control had been grafted on to historical budgeting—the process remained focused on the legislature and fragmented within that—to create a semblance of order. Indeed, my first reaction to classical budgeting was a sense of wonder at how much coordination actually was achieved without a central coordinator. Revenue and expenditure were approximately equivalent. Decisions were made on time. Deference was shown to informed judgment. Evident political self-interest was both accommodated—representatives were expected to vote their district—and limited. The leadership populated appropriations committees with people from safe districts; the president could be expected to impound overspending by prearrangement; spending considered unwise could be voted for and then allowed to die. Though there were complaints about insufficient analysis, followed by efforts to introduce more systematic intelligence, moderation remained the order of the day. Improving analysis of choices on individual programs was the great hope; no one thought of directly deciding total revenue and expenditure. All this came to an end with the collapse of the underlying political consensus, and opening of the budget process to the hurricanes of change.

Chapter 4

The Collapse of Consensus

We're a very divided committee, with some very conservative Republicans and very liberal Democrats. I always had to find different members for each coalition.

—A Congressman

Any book that says the appropriations committee sees its job as to cut the President's budget would just be wrong. They may see their job as to rearrange priorities but to stay within the total. But on this subcommittee the pressure's all upward.

—A Committee Staffer

Shortly after the standard accounts of classical budgeting were published in the early 1960s—Richard Fenno's *The Power of the Purse* and the first edition of *The Politics of the Budgetary Process*—that process began to collapse. What Allen Schick in *Congress and Money* calls the "Seven Year Budget War" lasted from 1966 to 1973. It ended with what he calls "The Congressional Budget Treaty of 1974," which Congress called the Congressional Budget and Impoundment Control Act of 1974 (the Budget Act). The new act did not abolish the old process; it heaped new relationships and institutions atop, and also layered them among, the old ones.

In retrospect, the pattern is clear; Congress and presidents had trouble agreeing. More time was being spent on budgeting to less effect. The difficulties were attributed variously to recalcitrant personalities, hard economic times, or defects in the process. The personalities, the time, and the process changed but to no avail. What caused the budgetary process to become so unsatisfactory?

It is not always easy to separate cause from effect, reality from symptoms. The actors in the budgetary minuet—president, congressional committees, administrators—could not indefinitely insulate their own politics from those of the real world. The ferment of the 1960s reflected long-standing dissatisfactions of groups previously excluded from the political process: denial of voting rights and racial discrimination in a democracy, hunger in the midst of plenty, poverty in prosperity. No less divisive issues of war and environment also took their place on the political agenda.

Legislature, executive, and judiciary changed in response, and social and environmental policies were rapidly enacted during the 1960s and early 1970s. The implications for budgetary politics were far-reaching. As long as the economy yielded an adequate increment and mutual understandings prevented too rapid a rise of expenditures, the budget could accommodate the powerful new trends. It had in fact gradually been doing so for some time. Keynesian economics also permitted and even encouraged deficit financing, which could act as a kind of safety valve, allowing the fragmented self-balancing budget process to continue to operate even if it were out of balance.

But the simultaneous pressures on expenditures of social programs and the Vietnam War strained the budget. Faltering economic growth ended the fiscal dividend, and with it the politics of accommodation among advocates of social spending, defense spending, more or less balanced budgets, and tax reductions. The legacy of earlier policies—entitlements, indexing, tax cuts, Keynesian economics, federal credit—was now visible in the changed composition and dynamics of the federal budget. This budget was much less flexible, far more difficult to control, and extraordinarily vulnerable to breakdown as the consensus underlying the old order collapsed.

THE GROWTH OF ENTITLEMENTS

Entitlement spending grew swiftly from 1960 to 1974. In part, entitlements grew from the need to keep old promises; as more and more people reached retirement age, the promised social security or civil service retirement pensions cost the government more. Entitlements grew also from making new promises—medical care to the aged (medicare), nutrition to the impoverished (food stamps)—and by the increasing costs of big, old programs (social security).

New efforts to preserve old promises were particularly important. Benefits promised in specific dollar amounts, such as pensions based on earnings, lost as inflation devalued their dollar worth. As a result Congress had to raise pension benefits frequently. By the early 1970s—in part to keep the promises solid, and in part to prevent members from voting over-adjustments on highly popular programs—Congress began indexing major benefit systems.

Entitlement spending grew faster than did other spending. Thus an increasing portion of federal spending could not be determined by the appropriations process. By "uncontrollable," of course, OMB did not mean beyond human control. Congress could, at any time, reduce spending or cancel the entire program. It is just that entitlement spending could not be controlled through the appropriations process.

A lot more could (and should) be said about entitlements (see Chapter 8). They grew partly at the expense of defense, which remained relatively stable in constant dollars but declined greatly as a proportion of total spending (see Chapter 9). With defense and economic growth used up as a means of funding social welfare programs, one question was, Where else might the money come from? More was going on to raise spending in ways that did not appear directly or fully in the budget. One way was through loans and loan guarantees, which we will discuss later in the chapter. Meanwhile, as agreement about priorities diminished, attitudes toward budget totals also changed. Total revenue and expenditure became both more controversial and more important. To the old conflicts over marginally "how much?" was added the potentially more divisive question of "what for?"

ECONOMIC ACTIVISM

Until the mid–1960s, attitudes toward total spending could be summarized in a few simple statements:

1. Deficits are bad. Borrowing has to be paid for later, gives financiers too much power (if you are liberal), and diverts money from productive use in the private economy (if you are conservative). The public views debt as bad for the government in the same way as for the household: a burden for the future, an indicator of poor management, and a sign that the country is in trouble.
2. Spending helps people in need and is therefore good, except that it must be paid for. Of course, some spending is better than others.
3. Taxes are necessary but unpalatable. Responsibility for tax hikes is dangerous. Avoid across-the-board tax increases by the "silent tax" of bracket creep or by selective, marginal changes that are difficult to oppose. Hope that economic growth will create a dividend in enhanced revenues so that part can fund higher spending and part can keep income tax rates stable or even reduced.

These rather contradictory premises fit with a set of decision rules for Congress designed to make calculations simple, conflicts manageable, and public policy predictable:

1. Do what you did last year if that worked. Change only at the margins so you can easily change back again.
2. Budgets should be balanced, or if not, as close as possible, and should look like they are getting closer.
3. If you have room to increase spending, do not increase it to an extent that would require tax increases or borrowing.
4. If none of the previous is possible, something unpleasant must be done. To minimize political cost, make the president propose a solution first. If his solution is tolerable, adopt it and blame him for what unhappiness does result (representatives with different constituencies will blame him for different consequences). If a seemingly more popular solution can be found, adopt it and take the credit. Reaction to the president's proposal can be used to gauge the political pressures.

These premises and decision rules were challenged by the Keynesian revolution in macroeconomics. The simplified Keynesian premise is:

The goal of policy should be to balance not the budget, but the economy. The government should adopt the levels of spending, taxing, and borrowing that will produce acceptable levels of GNP, inflation, and unemployment.

Keynesianism was as much a political as an economic revolution. Keynes pointed to a theoretical way out of the strictures of classical economics (although through actual experimentation several European countries had arrived at Keynesian solutions without benefit of Keynes). No longer did government have to raise taxes and cut spending in times of recession. Politicians could finally justify what they had long desired to do, namely, do something (spend) to help people (and, in turn, benefit the economy) in a time of crisis. Thus Keynesianism destroys old premise 1, that deficits are bad. Sometimes deficits are necessary to stimulate the economy. In an obvious way, this makes budgeting much easier. Constraints are loosened, especially when the economy declines, which automatically reduces revenues and increases both entitlement costs and thus the deficit. Keynesian theory says that deficits are desired precisely when unemployment rises, which is certainly convenient, if not largely unavoidable. There are, however, hidden costs to the Keynesian perspective.

In most of Europe and the United States, after the initial fear of postwar depression proved unfounded, rapid economic growth in stable economies was expected to continue indefinitely. The Keynesian doctrine of economic stabilization by means of counter-cyclical spending triumphed everywhere. So powerful was this faith in the feasibility of economic fine-tuning and of its potential for sustaining economic stability that few if any mainstream advisors to governments in those days considered the possibility of having to make cuts in spending. The political difficulty of cutting was still recognized, but, expecting the expansion to go on indefinitely, no one worried much about reductions or how to implement them.

As Keynesianism developed through years of political use, old premises 2 and 3 also were revised. When times are good, according to Keynes, spending should be limited and taxation increased to keep the economy from overheating. Put in terms of political appearance, "Times are good so we should do less because citizens can afford to pay (their real income is rising) and they won't notice." Instructions to reduce benefits people are already enjoying, however, are not attractive. Consequently, in both good times and bad, despite Keynesian doctrine, spending kept going up.

Less obviously, the Keynesian perspective calls the first decision rule into question. What "worked," which means what was politically acceptable last year, cannot be assumed to work this year, since the perceived needs of the economy may have changed. When politicians assume responsibility for managing the economy, and the economy changes faster than party coalitions, the political task becomes complicated.

The president's role also becomes more troublesome to Congress, for budget totals become more important. Keynesian economics would see a tradeoff between unemployment and inflation; a healthy economy is defined in terms of some balance of the two evils (hopefully both at low levels). Unfortunately, politicians may not see eye to eye on the proper balance; some politicians (usually Democratic) are more worried by unemployment, others (usually Republican) are more fearful of inflation. The choice depends on whether one's constituents are labor unions (which can defend in their contracts against inflation but have trouble defending against unemployment) or stock or bond holders (who worry less about unemployment but can be clobbered by inflation). The tradeoff therefore hits at the fundamental difference between Democratic and Republican constituencies. When a Republican president must deal with a Democratic Congress, members of Congress, in allowing the president the first move, do not necessarily succeed in getting him to take the blame for going in the direction that Congress wishes; instead, the president could push them in a direction—say, choosing unemployment over inflation—where they would not choose to go. And at that particular time, before the Congressional Budget and Impoundment Control Act of 1974, the appropriations process gave Congress no way to articulate a coherent alternative.

When budget totals become a tool of economic policy, then those totals, not just the spending programs within them, become a subject of major constituency conflict. Politicians can be blamed if the economy runs into trouble, for proper fiscal policy would presumably have kept the economy healthy. This responsibility is dangerous enough if politicians are actually able to direct the economy. In the last half of the 1970s, acceptance of Keynesian premises did establish political responsibilities while the policy theory it represented turned out to be less useful than expected.

The stagflation of the 1970s, when unemployment and inflation rose together, could not be solved within the Keynesian framework. Perhaps the causes were outside the framework, or perhaps the fiscal tools available were too blunt for the job. Possibly, as Robert Eisner argues, failure to measure the proper level of deficits, due to inflation and the lack of a capital budget, gave the wrong signals.[1] The community of economists, business executives, and labor leaders, however, persisted in demanding the "proper" macroeconomic adjustments. Even the revolt against Keynesianism in the form of supply-side economics (basically, much lower marginal tax rates to increase incentives for economic activism) presumed that there was a proper economic policy that would save the country if misguided politicians would only see the light.

Yet the public never abandoned the old premises. Deficits remained unpopular, spending for programs appreciated, and taxes difficult to justify. Macroeconomic activism added a new layer of expectations and responsibilities to budgeting without eliminating the old concerns.

PRIORITIES

The division of roles among the president and Congress, OMB, and the appropriations committees was weakening simultaneously with the growth of entitlements. The system could work only so long as conflict about both totals and relative priorities was kept within negotiable bounds. In 1960 most government programs had either been around long enough for their existence and scope to be taken for granted (the New Deal ended 20 years earlier) or, if recent, had been endorsed by both Democratic and Republican administrations in the course of passage. Even though Congress was Democratic and the administration Republican, or vice versa, there was broad agreement about the existence or size of programs: Government was to limit itself to the existing tax take. During the 1960s, however,

---

[1]See Robert Eisner, *How Real Is the Federal Deficit?* (New York: Free Press, 1986).

and especially after the 1964 landslide election, Congress became more Democratic and northern liberals dominated the Democratic party. Lyndon Johnson's Great Society created many new programs and agencies. These changes in priorities reflected the opening up of Congress and changes in its procedures.

During the early 1970s, the norms of participatory democracy had their way in Congress. Power was dispersed from committee chairs (no longer guaranteed by seniority) to a proliferation of subcommittees (all committees had to have them) and new staff. Democrats did the most; under a subcommittee "bill of rights," the prerogative of determining the number, budget, size, and jurisdiction of subcommittees was transferred from the chairs of standing committees to the caucus of the majority party. The Democratic caucus also had the right to elect subcommittee chairs. From 1967 to 1980 the personal staffs of representatives rose from 4,051 to 7,376, an 82 percent increase, while in the Senate the increase was 114 percent (1,749 to 3,746). During the decade of the 1970s, Senate standing committee staff rose 88 percent (635 to 1,917).[2]

Whereas in earlier times subcommittee members might be chosen with an eye toward countering constituency influences, now they mostly selected themselves. "What we find," a staff member told Allen Schick, "is that the city and inner-city guys are all on Labor-HEW, all of the hawkish guys go to Defense, and the big (full) committee chairman no longer has the power to take a guy who has a defense interest and say, 'you serve on the Agriculture subcommittee and do the public some good.'"[3]

No wonder individual legislators had more clout. No longer under the thumb of seniority, loaded with staff, they could express many more preferences with less personal expertise than in the past. The tendency to behave as individual political entrepreneurs, often running against Congress as an institution, was strengthened by a greater ability to intervene in more areas of policy, and thus serve larger numbers of constituencies or by their own visions of desirable public policy. While Democratic chairs had more reason to stand close to their party cohorts, it was not just the Speaker and the whips but the entire caucus (which could not be expected to act very often) to whom they were beholden. Members could act with impunity on individual programs, providing their overall voting record was roughly in line.

With increasing rapidity, from the 1950s until the present time, permanent or multiyear spending authorizations gave way to the annual kind. (Before 1950, there were only two; three were passed in the 1950s, seven in the 1960s, sixteen in the 1970s, several more in the 1980s.)[4] One reason for this trend toward annual authorization was to exert better or more frequent control over administrative agencies; another was to increase influence over appropriations subcommittees. By and large authorizing committees want higher spending. While reducing authorizations is an effective way of cutting spending over the next few years, raising authorizations may be ineffective if the appropriations committees refuse to recommend

---

[2]John W. Ellwood, "The Great Exception: The Congressional Budget Process in an Age of Decentralization," in Lawrence Dodd and Bruce Oppenheimer, eds., *Congress Reconsidered*, 3rd ed. (Washington, D.C.: CQ Press, 1985), pp. 4–5 of typescript.

[3]Allen Schick, *Congress and Money* (Washington, D.C.: Urban Institute Press, 1980), p. 432.

[4]See Louis Fisher, "Annual Authorizations: Durable Roadblocks to Biennial Budgeting," typescript, n.d.

the necessary budget authority. By repeating those requests on an annual basis, authorizing committees create more numerous opportunities to lobby for them; this lobbying also serves as a means of influencing the actions of agencies. On the one hand, annual authorizations are a pain to administrators who have to keep testifying. On the other hand, since the result is more likely to be higher than lower future spending, there is some recompense for this inconvenience.

With two sets of hearings—appropriations and authorizations—scheduled each year in each house, the opportunities for interaction on spending between administrators and legislators, as well as among legislators, expand greatly. So do the opportunities for delay. The complexity of the joint authorizing-appropriations process, moreover, lends itself to further maneuver.[5]

Presidents, too, responded to change. Republican Richard Nixon was nothing if not flexible. In his first term (1968–1972) he approved or allowed large spending increases, especially, as in housing, where the costs did not show up immediately. When spending was popular, despite contrary rhetoric, he spent. Faced with the consequences of past commitments, including those of his own administration, buoyed by a large electoral victory in 1973, Nixon returned to his long-standing convictions, determined in his second term to rein in spending.

Northern liberals had created many new programs and agencies to heal social ills that ranged from inadequate medical care for the aged to poverty in the mountains of West Virginia. To most Democrats these programs, many of which included implicit promises of more to come, were the new base. To Richard Nixon, most Republicans, and many southern Democrats, these programs were bad ideas at worst or at best, nice sentiments that could not be afforded. These attitudes toward spending commitments were reversed when the spending was for the military. Particularly after Nixon took office and they were no longer constrained by loyalty to their Democratic president, congressional liberals thought the levels of spending generated by what they considered a stupid and immoral war in Vietnam could hardly be claimed as an inviolable "base." Conservatives thought new domestic welfare programs were equally illegitimate. The result was a series of debilitating battles over budget priorities. Richard Nixon used his budget powers to challenge congressional priorities. He proposed some funding levels far below what majorities in Congress expected. Then when the appropriations committees responded by raising the allocations, Nixon refused to spend the money. He impounded the funds.

IMPOUNDMENT

It had always been understood that if money were appropriated for a purpose that turned out to be unnecessary or if the funds could not be spent usefully and immediately, the executive did not have to spend it, so long as most concerned members of Congress concurred. Indeed, they might want the president to do what was

---

[5]Mark S. Kamlet and David C. Mowery, "Contradictions of Congressional Budget Reform: Problem of Congressional Emulation of Executive Branch," *Journal of Policy Analysis and Management,* Vol. 6, No. 3 (1987), pp. 365–84.

necessary when it was nonpolitic for members to do so. Thus impounding based on tacit consent was an informal safety valve for keeping spending under control. Congress would not have to vote to repeal the funding (since that was troublesome); the president, through OMB and the Treasury, would merely refuse to release the funds to the affected agency. And of course the decision would come too late for the agency to protest effectively. Nixon tried to change this tradition of informal understandings in special cases to a general presidential prerogative: He would spend only what he chose to. After other efforts to shape appropriations through vetoes and lobbying had failed, and after the 1972 election had, he claimed, given him a mandate, Nixon resorted to impoundment en masse. As Allen Schick wrote,

> Far from administrative routine, Nixon's impoundments in late 1972 and 1973 were designed to rewrite national policy at the expense of congressional power and intent. Rather than the deferment of expenses, Nixon's aim was the cancellation of unwanted programs. . . . When Nixon impounded for policy reasons, he in effect told Congress, "I don't care what you appropriate; I will decide what will be spent."[6]

The policy stakes in Nixon's impoundments may have been striking enough, but the political stakes were decisive. Save during a major war, no president had ever asserted his primacy over Congress so bluntly. If Nixon could get away with massive impoundments, what could he not do? If the power of the purse could be defied, what was left for Congress?

The power of the purse had to be protected in 1974 as in 1774—but in 1974 for the opposite reason. The world had been stood on its head. For two centuries Congress had defined the threat as an executive that wanted to spend too much. Since the days of royal governors and their civil lists, the legislature's problem had been to restrain the executive by limiting its funds. Now it faced a Chief Executive who wanted to spend too little, and who defied the legislature (or, as Congress saw it, the people) by refusing funds for the bureaucracy. The challenge to Congress was as great, but its meaning to the public and the possible remedies now had to be very different.

A division of labor and sharing of power in budgeting requires shared notions of what is accepted, and thus not subject to dispute—that is, controversy must be limited to the margins, and battles once settled must not be continually refought, lest the system collapse. Much of the legitimacy of OMB and the president depends on a belief that they too concur in Congress's base, that they merely adjust it by judging the technical aspects of programs and the management needs of agencies. If, instead, the president's preferences differ and if his budget becomes mainly an attack on programs he does not like, its use to Congress is drastically reduced. The appropriations committees' power similarly depends on their not going overboard and using that power to change policy beyond the will of Congress. If they overstep their bounds, Congress will revolt. If the appropriations committees had gone along with Nixon, they would have been overridden in their parent houses. When, instead, they conformed to congressional intent, Nixon, by impounding, tried to short circuit the entire appropriations process. Congress had

---

[6]Schick, *Congress and Money*, pp. 46, 48.

to respond and attempted to reassert its role in the Congressional Budget and Impoundment Act.

THE BUDGET ACT: MORE CHECKS, MORE BALANCES, BUT NOT MORE CONTROL

Another word is in order about that elusive concept called control. By itself it is a synonym for power. But power over people is not necessarily the same as power over events. Controlling the president is not necessarily the equivalent of control over the budget, and neither necessarily adds up to control over the economy. While Congress in general did want more power over presidents and did wish to relate expenditure more closely to revenue, it was not in agreement about whether expenditures per se were too high, or revenues were too low, or if so, which parts should be raised or lowered. The question of whether Congress could achieve self-control, at least making the budget come out as it wished, was solved at a formal level: It could command itself to do right. Whether Congress was sufficiently in agreement to obey its own command was the question. If Congress was agreed on the desirability of making big choices on total spending and taxing but disagreed about the content of these decisions—both "how much" and "what for"—Congress would get not control but stultification.

The old procedures were controlling neither spending nor the president. Yet new procedures would shift power within Congress and therefore would meet resistance. Decisions about totals would need to be converted into decisions on programs. The taxing and spending committees would have to be both coordinated and coerced. Any procedure that could do all that, however, would put great power in someone's hands. Historically members of Congress have been unwilling to give that power to any of their number.

The solution, of course, was compromise. Nothing was taken away (hence the need for chapters on historical, classical, and entitlement budgeting). Following the traditions of the American political system, Congress created new committees above and beside the appropriations and tax committees, adding to the system of checks and balances.

Impoundment Again

A new procedure was created that formalized the impoundment process. If the president wishes not to spend appropriated funds, he can propose a rescission; if he wishes only to delay spending, he must propose a deferral. Since 1983 the president may not use a deferral for policy purposes. For a rescission to take effect, both houses must pass a bill approving the change within 45 legislative days of its proposal. If they do not do so, the money must be spent as originally appropriated. A deferral takes effect automatically but cannot last longer than through the end of the fiscal year. Either house can reject the deferral with a vote specifically disapproving it. This procedure exploits the difficulty of congressional action. By requiring positive action in both houses, the more serious policy change (rescission) is made unlikely. The lesser change (deferral) is allowed to occur, but either house can choose by majority vote to enforce the appropriation legislation.

If the president fails to spend the money but does not report to Congress, the comptroller general (who, as head of the General Accounting Office, monitors the executive for Congress) reports the action himself. His report has the same legal effect as the president's proposal of a rescission or deferral. If presidents ignore congressional disapproval, the comptroller general can bring a civil action in the courts. Presidents can, of course, choose to provoke a constitutional crisis. Because they must live with Congress, they are unlikely to do so. Because they are increasingly at odds with Congress, presidents are tempted to take back with one hand (impoundment) what they cannot gain with the other (the congressional budget process).

Congressional Budget Office

The 1974 Act also created a new staff institution, the Congressional Budget Office (CBO), budget committees in each house, and new budget procedures.

The CBO was set up to provide a congressional counterpart to the OMB and the president's economic staff, the Council of Economic Advisers (CEA). Much of budgeting, such as projection of entitlement costs, involves technical analysis. It is fairly easy to rig the numbers, and members of Congress did not believe that the presidential staff would be above such activity. In fact, they did not even believe that congressional committee staffs would be much more reliable. The CBO was to provide a bastion of neutral analysis, loyal to the institution of Congress, rather than to committees or to parties. Its director, with extensive authority over the office, is appointed jointly by the Speaker of the House and Senate President Pro Tem for a four-year term.

In a development that reminds us that our institutions can work well, the CBO, under its first director, Dr. Alice Rivlin, won a reputation for both competence and neutrality. While its reports have not always been popular, its technical work has been credible. CBO became a modest actor in budgeting, greatly reducing congressional dependence upon the president's experts.

Because estimates of future spending cannot be made with certainty, there are bound to be errors. CBO, no more immune than anyone else, also may make overoptimistic or overpessimistic assumptions about economic growth, inflation, unemployment, and other matters—such as the value of the dollar or the price of oil or interest rates—that confound expectations. In its first few years, especially, CBO's estimates proved more accurate and OMB and agency estimators moved closer to CBO by prior consultation. In short, the existence of competition in estimation has led to modest improvements in accuracy. Evidence suggests that executive long-range economic forecasts tend to be more optimistic than CBO projections, though the accuracy of both forecasts is similar.[7]

CBO and impoundment control easily found their places in the congressional process. Budget committees, and the new budgeting schedule, however, were more problematic.

---

[7]Kamlet and Mowery, op. cit.

Senate Budget Committee and House Budget Committee

The Senate Budget Committee (SBC) was established in 1974 with 16 members, to be chosen by the party caucuses and to serve indefinitely. The House Budget Committee (HBC) was structured in an unusual manner. Five of its members were to come from the appropriations committee and five from ways and means. One was a member of the Democratic leadership and one from the Republican leadership. The other 13 members were appointed through the usual House procedures (this discussion is in the past tense because of changes in details, but not in the basic design, in later years). The committee is a mixture, therefore, of regular members and representatives of power centers within the House. In addition, membership is rotating, rather than permanent; no member could then serve on the budget committee for more than four years (now six) out of every ten. Rotation decreases the chance that budget members will become isolated or parochial in their viewpoints, and helps the committee to gain information from other committees. Rotation also ensures that power will not be hoarded by a small group of representatives.

Scheduling

The new schedule both added new steps and changed the timing of old ones. Previously, Congress convened in early January, the president submitted his budget in late January, and Congress had to adopt appropriations acts by July 1, when the next fiscal year began. Appropriation and authorization legislation created logjams; often an appropriation could not be made because some part of the act was annually authorized and the authorization had not yet passed (e.g., as in military procurement). Frequently, appropriations were delayed past July 1, forcing Congress to pass a continuing resolution (CR). A CR provides funding for agencies lacking appropriations for some short period of time at the rates authorized during the previous year. Its need was minimized for a short while, however, by changing the fiscal year's start to October 1. The calendar change gave Congress three extra months to perform all its old tasks and to pass the new budget resolutions.

Resolutions

These budget resolutions were the centerpiece of the new process. The first resolution, originally to be passed by May 15 (now April 15), was intended to set targets for other committees and for Congress as a whole to meet. It included recommended levels for budget authority, outlays, revenues, that year's deficit or surplus, and the resulting total public debt. The first resolution also recommended totals for spending divided into a small number of budget functions. These were the same categories of programs into which the president's budget is divided—such as Function 150, "International Affairs," or Function 350, "Agriculture." The resolution is a formal reply to the president's proposal. Budget committee staff and members tend to have rather detailed ideas of how the functional totals translate into committee jurisdictions and report those to the committees as required by Section 302. For much of this time there were 19 functions. These divisions match the president's budget, but not Congress's committee structure. Consequently, there arose the need to "crosswalk" between the

19 categories in the president's budget and those used by the 13 congressional subcommittees.

The first resolution was assembled on the basis of a wide range of information. HBC and SBC were to have available a Current Services Budget prepared by OMB to show the cost of continuing services at the current level (including changes in prices). The president's budget provided another basis for comparison, analysis, and argument. CBO analyzes the president's budget and its deviations from current policy. After submission of the president's budget, committees with jurisdiction over spending and/or taxing legislation were to submit to the budget committees views and estimates that told the budget committees what members on other committees would like to do.

The budget committees, meanwhile, would hold hearings to discuss the president's economic policy and projections, as well as other aspects of his budget. With the president's proposal, their colleagues' views and estimates, and much technical analysis in hand, HBC and SBC then craft their versions of the resolution. Procedures in passing that resolution are much like those for any other bill except that since the resolution is a rule for Congress, it does not need the president's signature. Neither does it have the force of law or appropriated funds. Disagreements between House and Senate must be resolved in conference.

As designed by the Budget Act, this resolution is more than, less than, but much like the president's budget. It resembles the president's budget in being only a recommendation, something to which action will be compared. It is less than the president's budget because it is less detailed; aggregated only at the functional level, it usually contains only very general guidance and standards for comparison. The resolution is more than the president's budget because it is the product of a lengthy process of discussion and accommodation within Congress; it is therefore more likely to reflect what Congress will actually do. And it is, again, much like the president's budget in being, in its estimates of revenue and debt and entitlement spending, dependent upon predictions of the future course of economy.

After passing the resolution, Congress is to go about its business of authorizing and appropriating. By the Monday after Labor Day, the regular authorizing and appropriating legislation—the laws that actually commit funds—should have passed. In late summer the budget committees would have held hearings to review the latest data about the economy and the actions taken or expected to be taken by the rest of Congress. In the original act this information was to be used to decide whether the targets from this first resolution needed adjustment. HBC and SBC then reported out versions of a second concurrent resolution on the budget. The second resolution had the same components as the first, except that the second resolution's total was supposed to be binding. Thus any legislation considered after passage of the second resolution, which would cause limits in that resolution to be breached, could be objected to and ruled out of order.

Reconciliation

If the limits in the first resolution could not be met due to unforeseen changes or new legislation, reconciliation instructions could be included in the second resolution. These instructions could direct one or more committees to report legislation in order to bring revenues or spending into conformity with that resolution. This process could apply to authorizations as well as appropriations. Reconciliation was to be packaged by the budget committees without change and enacted by September 25.

In fact, reconciliation was not used in this form: Until 1979 appropriations were simply packaged into the second resolution without conscious efforts to make them fit into preassigned (or any other) totals. The reasons were simple. At the very end of the process, after all the deals were made and the bargains struck, participants were in no mood to reopen the whole budget debate again. The potential of reconciliation was not discovered until the last year of the Carter presidency, or fully exploited until the Reagan administration used it as a unprecedented weapon of budgetary policy. It was then used in conjunction with the first resolution, which became the only resolution.

Complexity

The budget resolutions added a new layer of activity to what was already a complicated process. Appropriations already were conditioned by authorizations. Now both were to be based on budget resolutions, which in turn were derived from estimated authorizations and appropriations. All this instruction and advice among different parts of Congress were to be coordinated by provisions of the Budget Act. Authorization bills were to be reported by May 15, enabling the appropriations committees to work with both the reports and the first resolution as guidelines. No act making budgetary commitments—appropriating funds, creating a new entitlement, or changing taxes—could be considered on the floor before adoption of that resolution. Special procedures expanded both the appropriations committees' ability to question entitlement growth, and their control over various other types of "backdoor" spending. CBO reports, required by the act, provided information for decision making at specified times. These assorted provisions were meant to relate action on programs to action on the totals. The budget committees, presumably, were to do the coordinating. But could they?

A Congressional Budget, or Merely More Budgeting?

In form, therefore, the 1974 act created a budget: Congress would look at programs, think about totals, choose a relationship between spending and revenue, and bring the two together. Entitlement spending would be confronted while considering the totals. New entitlement spending would be analyzed by CBO and delayed by provisions in the schedule, thus getting a longer, harder look than it had before. Established entitlements might be adjusted during reconciliation. The budget resolutions would enable congressional majorities to respond directly to the president's budget, asserting their own functional priorities and fiscal goals. The process of adopting resolutions would focus attention on these questions—the relative sizes of revenue and expenditures and their effects on the economy—far more explicitly than had been done in the past; and voting would force members of Congress to take stands in a way not previously required. Hearings and CBO analyses would generate information; resolutions would occasion debate; debate would inform Congress and the public about the choices made. The procedures relating taxing and spending to the size of the budget would force members to take the totals seriously.

All that was possible; yet, instead of creating a budget, the new procedures might merely create more budgeting. Members would follow the budget act's rules only if they wanted to do so; they would want to do so only if they valued the process itself more than they valued what they would lose if they obeyed the act.

THE BUDGET PROCESS, 1975–1979: THE STRUGGLE TO RELATE TOTALS TO DETAIL

At stake was power and policy: power within Congress, the power of Congress in regard to the executive branch, and congressional power over programs. If Congress disagreed over policy, however, its members would find that power over one another had a different institutional significance than power vis-à-vis the presidency.

Members of the budget committees had a power stake in making the process work. Unless budget resolutions influenced taxing and spending action, HBC and SBC members would gain nothing from membership. Appropriations committee members objected to their loss of power, of course, but they also had reason to go along with the process. Before 1974, deficits were blamed on them; the new process made it possible to direct attention toward the authorizing, in particular the tax, committees. Members of these other committees were threatened by the Budget Act, which could undermine their committees' independence and ability to serve constituents. Because only a minority of representatives serve on budget and appropriations committees, enforcement of budget totals required either that they be satisfactory to other members of Congress and their roles as committee members, or that other roles and allegiances (to party, to a president, to a constituency, or to an ideology) override loyalties as committee members. The budget committees therefore tried both to create resolutions that stepped on very few toes and to mobilize those other loyalties to pass and enforce resolutions on the floor of their respective houses.

In the Senate, budget committee chairman Edmund Muskie (D-Maine) and ranking minority member Henry Bellmon (R-Okla.) worked to develop resolutions that could command substantial bipartisan support. They then united in defense of the recommendations on the floor. In the House, the resolutions became partisan documents. Republicans continually opposed them on the ground that taxing and spending were too high. Democrats were forced to seek resolutions that could carry without Republican votes. In mobilizing Democratic majorities, party leaders became key actors in that process. Only the Speaker and his lieutenants could (sometimes) muster the Democratic troops. The Democratic House resolutions and bipartisan Senate plans were often difficult to compromise in conference.

By 1980 budget process observers and participants were engaged in a running debate as to whether these resolutions and the entire process were having any, and if so, what, effect on spending and taxing policy. The views and estimates submitted by the committees to HBC and SBC on March 15 tended to turn into wish lists. Requests averaged about 10 percent higher for spending than actually were approved. Because the budget committees had so many alternative sources of information, they fortunately did not have to depend on the March 15 reports for technical data. Instead, both the formal reports and informal contacts among committee staffs made budget drafters aware of how much conflict might be expected in considering alternative spending levels. HBC and SBC therefore had enough information for their purposes. They had estimates of the program base—what was spent last year, which obligations existed, and how the expected performance of the economy would influence program costs. This information might not be accurate, for some of it was unknowable, but members would be as informed as anyone else. They also knew, normally, what kinds of changes would be proposed by various participants, such as the president and the authorizing committees, and could judge the political force of those proposals.

A far greater difficulty was the potential that the first resolution, however nicely calibrated, would be ignored at other steps of the process. First resolution totals for the functions—spending, taxing, etc.—were only targets, but, as it turned out, they were moving targets open to challenge.

The stakes and difficulty of such challenges were highlighted in the first year of the process (1975 for fiscal 1976). Senator Muskie, whose chairmanship of the Senate Budget Committee gave him the incentive to keep spending within the limits of his committee's resolution, challenged authorization legislation for both military procurement and the school lunch program, thereby showing he had no policy axe to grind. In each case he was able to force changes in the legislation, but in doing so he risked a backlash, which materialized a year later, from members whose policies were threatened by reduced spending.

Within this context of mutual uncertainty, HBC and SBC worked to accommodate other congressional actors, who also tried to avoid direct confrontations with budget committees. The terms of accommodation depended in part upon who was trying to change the status quo. The budgeters could more easily resist new legislation by publicizing its cost or nonconformance to the resolution than they could force the passage of a change that would cut spending or increase revenue. It is easier to stop people from acting than to make them do something, especially if the action is complicated, requires cooperation, and involves members of Congress. Proponents of legislation, who had strong incentives to avoid complications on the floor (delay can be deadly), tried to adapt bills to satisfy the budget committees. But the budget committees could do little to urge, say, Ways and Means to report out medicare reforms. In between these two extremes were legislative changes that seemed so pressing to so many members that, if budget committees got in the way of passage, they might be regarded as pests and brushed aside—as happened whenever they tried to reduce the rate of increase in social security. In general, if the first resolution assumed either legislative changes to programs or funding below what had been Congress's habit, the first resolution had to be adjusted upward.

ECONOMIC MANAGEMENT

One of the major aims of budget reform was to connect more closely attempts to manage the economy with the expenditure process. And it does appear that members of budget committees took the trouble to learn more about the relationship between levels of spending and the condition of the economy. One difficulty is that not much is known; another is that ability to apply what little is known is strictly limited.

Economic management (or fiscal policy, as it is called) requires a notion of what level of expenditure is appropriate either to stimulate or depress economic activity. Commitments of the past make up the largest part of the budget, however, and it is difficult, either legally or politically, to alter them drastically. Considerations of desirable defense and domestic expenditures compete of necessity with optimal fiscal policy, assuming anyone knows what that should be. Among the many constraints within which the makers of fiscal policy operate, the least understood are those imposed by time and by targeting.

For example, take time: There is a fallacy that assumes that fiscal policy goes into effect at the time it is made. If we are talking about expenditures, that assumption cannot be correct. The most important time, usually, for bringing fiscal considerations to bear on budgetary totals is during the spring preview conducted by OMB in April. Suppose this is done in April. The fiscal policy total is considered along with other matters, and OMB establishes and passes down a budgetary target to the spending agencies. For the moment, suppose that this total is not challenged by agencies nor revised by the president but goes directly into his budget in the winter. Even if these contrary-to-fact conditions are met, Congress will not finish acting on appropriations bills until almost a year later in the fall of the next calendar year. Spending agencies will take several months to act on this legislation; the impact of these expenditures, then, will not begin to be felt until the winter of the following year. Thus about two years elapse before the thoughts that went into fiscal policy are reflected in real budgetary behavior. By that time, to be sure, conditions may have markedly changed so that what seemed appropriate then is now inappropriate.

The two years can be shortened to 18 months by postponing or modifying fiscal policy decisions until November or December. This alternative, however, sacrifices the benefit of considering fiscal policy in the ceilings initially set by OMB. Renegotiating all the bargains of the prior six months in a few weeks in late November and December is an experience that most participants will try to avoid. By late fall, fiscal policy can be adjusted but the entire orchestral arrangement (insofar as budgetary totals are concerned) is likely to have been settled earlier or not at all. Fall fiscal policy is even tighter than what was already an extremely constrained situation the previous spring.

The existence of unprecedented rates of inflation in the mid–1970s, followed by extraordinarily high interest rates in the late 1970s, coming together with multi-hundred-billion-dollar deficits in the early 1980s, and topped off by the largest unemployment rate since the Great Depression highlighted congressional responsibilities for economic management. But no budget committee could do this alone. Reducing the deficit, for instance, would have required a package deal about taxation and domestic and defense spending that could have been achieved only by concerted action among congressional committees, backed up or led by the formal leadership and supported by the president. Without such agreement, the members of Congress would only end up fooling themselves: There are any number of innovative ways that Congress can circumvent its own will. Congressional efforts at economic management were stymied both because of doubt over effective policy and inability to act together to enforce whatever set of actions is deemed desirable.

DID THE BUDGETARY PROCESS HAVE A PRO-SPENDING BIAS?

The Budget Act of 1974 expressed Congress's desire to enhance its own power of the purse by granting it the ability to visibly relate revenue and expenditure. Since the broad coalition supporting the Act included both high and low spenders, however, the new process was not designed to favor either side. On the one hand, the mere existence of budget committees raised another possible impediment to higher spending; on the other hand, the need for these committees to maintain collegial relations with tax and spending committees, as well as to remain subject to the will of Congress, meant that budget committees had to subordinate themselves to the widespread desires for higher spending. The evidence from Allen Schick's *Congress and Money* is conclusive:

> In almost a hundred interviews with Members of Congress and staffers, no one expressed the view that the allocations in budget resolution [sic] had been knowingly set below legislative expectations. "We got all that we needed," one committee staff director exulted. The chief clerk of an Appropriations subcommittee complained, however, that the target figure in the resolution was too high: "We were faced with pressure to spend up to the full budget allocation. It's almost as if the Budget Committee bent over backwards to give Appropriations all that it wanted and then some."[8]

All internal incentives worked to raise expenditures. Who, for instance, would take the lead in reducing expenditures? Each sector of policy, including the people in Congress who cared most about it, naturally was concerned with its own internal development. Those who favored radical restructuring of programs soon discovered that this was exceeding difficult to do without sweetening the pot. More money made it easier to settle internal quarrels. The price of policy change was program expansion.[9] Like all others who wish to be influential, budget committees could afford to lose only a few times, for if it becomes obvious that budget committees are likely to lose, no one need pay attention to them.

To no one's surprise, the HBC's difficulties in enforcing reductions came from advocates of increased spending. But it was in the Senate that the clash between the Budget and Finance committees was most severe. Chairman Muskie of SBC was interested in the big picture. As he told the Senate, the budget committee "is not a line-item committee."[10] Tax preferences cause so much loss of revenue and, indeed, are so much an alternative form of accomplishing the same purpose as expenditures, Muskie felt, that to ignore them would be to nullify efforts at budget control. In colorful language, he raised and answered the rhetorical question:

---

[8]Schick, *Congress and Money*, p. 313.

[9]For example, see Aaron Wildavsky, *Speaking Truth to Power* (Boston: Little, Brown, 1979), Chapter 4, "Coordination Without a Coordinator," pp. 86–107.

[10]*National Journal*, September 25, 1976, pp. 1348–49.

Are we supposed to meet each March to propose a congressional budget and then retire to the cloakroom until the fall, when it is too late to advise the Senate of the implications of its tax and spending decisions? And then pop back out like some unwelcome jack-in-the-box each fall to shout, "Surprise! You've blown the budget."? Hardly.[11]

Not to be outdone, Senator Russell Long, chairman of the committee on finance, retorted, "The chairman of the Budget Committee cannot find anything small enough for the Finance Committee to decide anything about."[12] Back at the House, an HBC staff member expressed dismay at such direct confrontation, saying, "We're aware that we'll get killed if we take on other committees head to head. All we have to work with is the good will of other committees."[13]

The budget reform was designed to help Congress relate obligations to income by setting targets for total expenditures. Senator Muskie said of legislators' simultaneously voting for more spending and lower budget deficits, "We just can't make the system work with that kind of philosophy."[14] Yet Joel Havemann reported several instances of representatives engaging in this sort of behavior on the grounds, as one put it, "That's the beauty of the budget process. You can vote for all your favorite programs, and then vote against the deficit."[15] What, then happened to congressional efforts to engage in economic management?

To increase spending, no coordination is necessary; program advocates already want to do that. To decrease spending, coordination is essential. Without spending ceilings that require choice among programs, budgeting by addition rather than subtraction remains common practice, and participants will look for creative ways to evade attempts at control.

ON AGAIN, OFF AGAIN: FEDERAL CREDIT

Without doubt, credit is an important way to increase federal spending; it vastly expands the scope and extent of federal influence. Credit is also a flexible instrument that helps implement diverse public policies—from rural electrification to student loans to increasing the volume of exports. Given the desire to subsidize certain activities, the instruments used—loans, guarantees—may be an efficient mode of accomplishing that result.

Subsidization of such favored borrowers, however, may well decrease the growth of the economy by diverting resources from more to less productive uses. Loans and loan guarantees also make the desired activities budgetarily more attractive; either

---

[11]Ibid., p. 1347.

[12]Ibid., p. 1348.

[13]Ibid.

[14]See Aaron Wildavsky, "Ask Not What Budgeting Does to Society but What Society Does to Budgeting." Introduction to the second edition of *National Journal Reprints* (Washington, D.C., 1977), p. 4.

[15]Ibid. See Mark S. Kamlet, David Mowery, and Gregory Fischer, "Modelling Budgetary Tradeoffs: An Analysis of Congressional Macrobudgetary Priorities, the Impact of the Congressional Budget Act, and the Reagan Counterrevolution." Paper prepared for the Midwest Political Science Association Meetings, Chicago, Ill., April 22, 1983; and Louis Fisher, "In Dubious Battle? Congress and the Budget," *The Brookings Bulletin*, Vol. 17 (Spring 1981), pp. 6–10.

they do not show up in the budget at all or they appear at a much lower amount than they would if they came in the form of appropriations. By the same token, credit instrumentalities raise federal spending and its reach far beyond what would take place in their absence, partly by obfuscating accountability. Credit instruments make it difficult to determine how much is being spent by whom for what purpose and with what consequences.

Big changes often come from small beginnings. The authority of federal agencies to borrow money through the Treasury is not an ancient practice; it dates back only to 1932 when, after bills to create a Reconstruction Finance Corporation (RFC) were on the way to passage, the Treasury Department recommended that in addition to being able to borrow from the general public, RFC should also be able to borrow from the Treasury so as to avoid interfering with its own debt issues.[16] In the next few years, once the precedent had been set at a time when antidepression measures were paramount, borrowing from the Treasury was extended to housing authorities, the Tennessee Valley Authority, and the Commodity Credit Corporation.

These entities could thus borrow from the Treasury to lend the funds to their clientele for approved purposes. This kind of borrowing represented only a small amount compared with appropriations. But nearly all of it came directly from the Treasury. Whereas borrowing through the appropriations process was highly constrained, nonrevolving, available only in specified fiscal years and with fixed ceilings, borrowing through the Treasury could be of variable amounts and durations. These direct drafts came to be called treasury budgeting or, more popularly, backdoor financing, on the grounds that these sums had been obtained by bypassing the appropriations process.[17] Revolving funds could use repayments to sponsor still more borrowing ad infinitum.

From an institutional and partisan point of view, the backdoor method was favored by the more liberal Senate in the 1950s and early 1960s while the more conservative House, fearing invasion of its prized power of the purse, unsuccessfully resisted the device. Appropriations committee members disliked most the fact that the Senate would pass additional credit authorizations in what Appropriations considered violation of the constitutional provision requiring that money bills originate in the House. The granting of such "special favors," Chairman Clarence Cannon thundered, had made the Senate into "the dominant body of Congress."[18] Supporters would argue that programs would be more effective if funded by loans available over the long term, while opponents responded that all such matters should go through the appropriations process where, of course, requests were certain to be treated less generously. "The debate over 'backdoor spending,'" Sun Kim concluded, "is a contingent battle over the programs themselves."[19]

During the 1960s and early 1970s, federal credit offerings increased. By 1972 such issues appeared in financial markets three out of every five days, and by 1973

---

[16]Sun Kil Kim, "The Politics of a Congressional Budgetary Process 'Backdoor Spending,'" *Western Political Quarterly,* Vol. 21 (December 1968), pp. 606–23; especially pp. 607–09.

[17]Ibid., pp. 607–09.

[18]Ibid., pp. 617–18.

[19]Ibid., p. 622.

there were $43.9 billion outstanding in direct loans and $174.1 billion in loan guarantees.[20] By the time the Budget Act was passed, there was considerable concern about the efficiency of federal credit operations. Coming from everywhere, without order or expertise, federal credit offerings were often badly placed, wrongly sized, and poorly publicized, so that rates of interest were considerably higher than ordinary treasury securities. In order, it said, to reduce costs of administration and of interest, the Treasury Department proposed in 1973 (and in 1975 the government began) the Federal Financing Bank (FFB), a small unit within the Treasury that would centralize the issuance of federal securities, thereby eliminating underwriting fees and securing other such economies. That did happen. But Paul Volcker, the undersecretary for monetary affairs, promised that the FFB would not be "a device to remove programs from the federal budget. . . . The Bank would in no way affect the existing budget treatment of federal credit programs."[21] But that promise was not kept.

It has been well said in ecology that no act does only one thing. Nowhere is that more true than of the FFB. It did indeed cut the micro-costs of borrowing. Despite its small one-eighth of a percent loan fee, FFB brought in far more than it spent. Loan costs to agencies went down considerably. But as James Bickley put it, "The very success of the FFB's operation may have also contributed to the rapid growth of federal credit assistance."[22]

At the outset, it is important to understand that the size of the Bank's holdings were not limited by statute nor were its disbursements and receipts included within budget totals nor was there any limit on its outlays (that is, the excess of loans over receipts). Where agencies, whether on-budget or "off-budget" borrowed from the FFB instead of public financial markets, there was no change from the existing position except easier access and lower cost of funds. But when a loan was sold by an on-budget agency to the FFB, which was off-budget, the loan itself became off-budget, and was no longer recorded in the federal budget. The agency, which still retained title to the loan could then use these "loan assets" as, in effect, collateral for additional loans. A federal agency providing a guarantee, could also direct the FFB to issue a loan to a nonfederal borrower as a second party debt. Though the agency was responsible for any defaults, the loan was, with the speed of a single transaction, converted into off-budget status.[23]

It should come as no surprise, therefore, that from 1975 to 1984, FFB on-budget agency debt declined from 41.2 to 20.2 percent while loan assets went from 0.3 to 43.7 percent and its second party guaranteed debt rose from 16.6 to 35.3 percent.[24] Between 1974 and 1981, direct on-budget loans doubled from $46.1 billion to $91.3 billion; off-budget direct loans increased sixfold from $15.4 billion to $93.7 billion; and guaranteed loans rose from $180.4 billion to $309.1 billion.

---

[20]See Dennis S. Ippolito, *Hidden Spending: The Politics of Federal Credit Programs* (Chapel Hill: University of North Carolina Press, 1984).

[21]James M. Bickley, "The Federal Financing Bank: Assessments of Its Effectiveness and Budgetary Status," *Public Budgeting and Finance*, Vol. 5, No. 4 (Winter 1985), pp. 51–63; quote on p. 51.

[22]Ibid., p. 57.

[23]Ibid., pp. 54–55.

[24]Ibid., p. 55.

Table 4.1   Summary of Outstanding Federal and Federally Assisted Credit*

	Direct	Direct	Government		
	Loans	Loans	Guaranteed	Sponsored	
Year	On-budget	Off-budget	Loans	Enterprise Loans	Total
1974	$46.1	$15.4	$180.4	$ 43.8	$ 285.7
1975	49.8	24.4	189.0	43.5	306.7
1976	64.2	21.6	200.7	54.0	340.5
1977	68.2	32.7	214.5	71.8	387.2
1978	76.5	43.9	226.1	93.8	440.3
1979	83.0	57.5	264.6	123.0	528.1
1980	91.7	72.3	299.2	151.0	614.2
1981	91.3	93.7	309.1	182.3	676.4
1982	100.2	107.6	331.2	225.6	764.6
1983	105.0	118.0	363.8	261.2	848.0
1984 (est.)	103.7	128.8	393.6	301.0	927.1
1985 (est.)	101.5	139.3	428.1	343.9	1,012.8

*Table from Clifford M. Hardin and Arthur T. Denzau, "Closing the Back Door on Federal Spending: Better Management of Federal Credit," Formal Publication #64, September 1984, Center for the Study of American Business, Washington University, St. Louis. Table 10.1 provides additional information on federal credit in the 1990s.

Source: Special Analysis F., *Budget of the United States Government, FY1985,* and earlier special analyses; and *Mid-Session Review of the 1985 Budget.*

Meanwhile government sponsored enterprise loans grew from $43.8 billion to over $182 billion (see Table 4.1). While this debt did count toward whatever overall debt limit Congress established, it did not count in the federal deficit. And that—enabling agencies to borrow more on behalf of their clients while keeping the formal deficit down—was apparently the purpose of these transactions.

How much, we may ask, following the medieval philosophers, is a loan guarantee worth? Defaults are counted as outlays. But the difference between the cost in private markets and the rate at which the FFB-cum-Treasury could borrow was not. And that difference was real money amounting to billions over a large volume of transactions. Guaranteed loans get priority, which is also worth something. In 1982, for example, new direct loans of $44 billion and loan guarantees amounting to $78 billion were given by the federal government. Total cash disbursements were $15.3 billion, but only $4.8 billion was noted in budget accounts. It would not be excessive, though there was no agreement, to estimate the cost of the subsidy at over $20 billion, albeit not in one year.[25] Thus the size of the deficit was distorted in two ways, one by moving nearly 80 percent of loan transactions off-budget and the other by providing a substantial but unaccounted for interest rate subsidy. Whatever opportunity there might be, moreover, for comparing the relative desirability of different

---

[25]Marvin Phaup, "Accounting for Federal Credit: A Better Way," *Public Budgeting and Finance,* Vol. 5, No. 3 (Autumn 1985), pp. 29–39; figures from p. 30.

loans—say, Rural Electrification Administration versus Farmers' Home Administration versus the Foreign Military Sales Program, to mention three of the largest—or to evaluate them in the context of on-budget spending programs was lost or made more difficult.[26]

Why were all FFB loans not placed on-budget? "Right now we deal with Congress and FFB to finance our programs," the president of the National Rural Electric Cooperatives said. "If we are put on budget, we will also have to deal with OMB."[27] The Rural Electrification and Telephone Revolving Fund (RETRF) needed all the help it could get. Created in 1973 under a Republican administration, the funds provided loans for 35 years at 5 percent interest, 2 percent for hardship cases. Its $7.9 billion endowment funds were mostly composed of old loans bearing a 2 percent interest rate whose repayment (interest only until 1993, principal thereafter) was to go to the Treasury until the entire amount had been paid off. Since these payments amounted merely to $314 million while new disbursements were twice that sum, the rural fund made up the difference by reducing its cash on hand, borrowing short-term notes from the Treasury, and issuing Certificates of Beneficial Ownership to FFB, for which the rate was one-eighth percent plus the rate of long-term treasury debt, then around 13 percent. Clearly, with defaults on the rise, repayment would be difficult. So refinancing legislation was introduced that would, according to a CBO estimate, increase costs to the federal government by $10.4 billion over a quarter century.[28]

The 1980s saw several attempts by the federal government to control credit. OMB regularly provided an appendix to the president's budget that tried to account for all governmental credit. In fiscal year 1981, for the first time nonbinding targets for federal credit were made part of congressional budget resolutions. In the following two years these targets were disaggregated to functional levels, tied to the same appropriations subcommittees that consider regular spending. Where formerly the Defense Department used FFB to place guaranteed loans for arms purchases off-budget, Congress decided in 1984 that in the future such loans would appear on-budget. The Gramm–Rudman–Hollings bill of 1985 (GRH) included a section placing the FFB on-budget. Further comprehensive reform took place in 1990 (see Chapter 10).

POLARIZATION: CLASSICAL BUDGETING WITHERS WITHOUT QUITE DISAPPEARING

By the beginning of the 1980s, the practices of classical budgeting had been seriously undermined. Compromise more frequently gave way to confrontation that threatened the budget process altogether. Both Presidents Nixon and Reagan stepped beyond the conventional power of their office in pursuing their own policy

[26]Thomas J. DiLorenzo, "Putting Off-Budget Federal Spending Back on the Books," *The Backgrounder,* No. 406, Heritage Foundation, January 30, 1985, p. 3.

[27]Darwin G. Johnson, "Comments" on Robert Hartman, "Issues in Budget Accounting," in Gregory B. Mills and John L. Palmer, *Federal Budget Policy in the 1980s* (Washington, D.C.: Urban Institute Press, 1984), pp. 448–56; quote on p. 451.

[28]Phaup, "Accounting for Federal Credit," p. 33.

agendas. Increasingly it became clear that compromise on the budget would be difficult to obtain. The president wanted higher defense spending, much lower domestic spending, and no tax increases. The opposition wanted higher taxes, lower defense spending, and higher domestic spending than did the president. Each insisted that their preferred programs were not up for negotiation. The result was stalemate. From 1982 on, the budgetary process slowed down. Individual appropriations were delayed. Continuing resolutions came to replace the ordinary budget process. Dissensus was the order of the day.

The budget was no longer elastic. More for one meant less for someone else. In a sense the budget had been preempted, as entitlements and entrenched programs left less and less margin for new initiatives or even expansion of older programs. Budget management on Keynesian principles seemed less viable: While the theory came under attack, its practice seemed discredited by persistent (even if in retrospect not very large) deficits.

The major effort to regain control, the 1974 Congressional Budget Act, had mixed reviews. The legislation itself had been weakened by compromises, notably the inability of the budget committees to enforce ceilings on the other committees of Congress. Their attempts to assert authority ran counter to the committees' assumed prerogatives, and their own cautious sense of self-preservation. The proliferation of credit programs during the 1970s, and also later in the 1980s, attested to the upward pressures on spending.

Meanwhile the major players of the old budget process, the appropriations committees, no longer appeared capable of performing their old role. In the 1970s the appropriations committees had moved away from their role as guardians of the Treasury. A combination of appointing advocates to appropriations and the existence of budget committees did the trick. With more liberal Democratic members and more conservative Republicans, the policy distance among members grew, thereby reducing internal cohesion. And as budget committees were placed over appropriations committees, the spending committees tended to regard their recommendations not as likely to be final but rather as opening bids in a sequence of negotiations. Like the executive spending agencies, therefore, appropriations subcommittees tended to pad their favorite programs so as to leave room for cutting by budget committees and by action on the floor.

New patterns began to emerge. Neither the guardian norm nor spending control had totally disappeared. Indeed, spending control was what made appropriations decisions worth contesting. But appropriations politics became vastly more centralized—a contest not only among committees and agencies, but also among OMB and congressional leaders, whose differences were not so much about individual programs as about spending totals or about the largest possible divisions, domestic versus defense, within them.

Little in Congress is completely original; heirs to old practices tend to bear some resemblance to their parents. So it was with appropriations. Committees continued to write bills and party leaders within the committees still had important roles in bargaining and in floor maneuvers. Many programmatic differences (especially on defense) were worked out in committee. In small matters, the attention to district interests, which critics of all political persuasions find so unseemly, remained. So did the unusual nonpartisanship of House Appropriations staff, especially compared to the partisan rancor in the House Budget Committee. Most important, the appropriations committees still held the role of translating program preferences into the line-item language of appropriations acts. Therefore, they maintained a crucial position in the process of program funding.

But while much was still familiar in the 1980s, the relationships among all the parts of the process changed drastically as the broad sweep of partisan budget politics, reflecting deep division over public policy took primacy over the management of agencies and distribution of benefits through appropriations oversight. The new policy partisanship did not so much displace the old as subsume it.

Chapter 5

The Politics of Dissensus

The battles over the budget that were waged during the 1980s are remarkable. Neither in American history nor in contemporary budgeting in other industrial democracies do we see their like. Disagreement over the size or scope or content of budgets had been a frequent occurrence before and after the founding of the American republic, but not all of these at once. Never had budget battles been pursued for so long.

While the sources and manifestations of dissensus had been apparent for over a decade, the beginning of the Reagan administration in 1981 intensified polarization over policies. The Republican presidential victory was accompanied by a Republican majority in the Senate (though not the House). The presidency remained in Republican hands until 1992, though the Democrats regained the Senate in 1984. The Republican program was clearly enunciated—cut domestic programs, increase defense, and balance the budget. The ideological fervor with which this program was pursued not only provoked political opposition, but also brought about deliberate and unintended institutional consequences. Although congressional committees and executive agencies continued to operate according to the Congressional Budget Act, their roles and patterns of mutual expectations had been disrupted. Dissensus was reflected in budget processes, whose turmoil in turn intensified it.

WHY BUDGET DECISIONS BECAME SO DIFFICULT

From the end of the Second World War until the late 1960s, the budgetary process was stable. Though there were efforts to alter its form, such as program and performance budgeting, these were largely concerned with improving program efficiency and effectiveness. While efforts to improve efficiency continued, the Congressional Budget Act of 1974 focused attention on the substance of the budget—how much in total, how divided among major programs, who should pay. From the mid–1970s onward, the reformed process worked in a manner of speaking—decisions were made—but the procedures did not work in quite the same way in any two consecutive years. Sometimes the president's budget message provided the starting point, sometimes it didn't. Sometimes there were three budget resolutions, sometimes two, other times only one. The relative power of appropriations, finance, and budget committees varied markedly. And the coalitions in Congress that eventually made the crucial choices—so much for defense and domestic, so much in total, reallocation of tax burdens—could not be predicted from one year to the next. Nor could anyone say who (by position, role, or ideology) would take the lead in putting together the winning coalition. Uncertainty, delay, disarray, crisis, even fatalism (Why bother if each heroic effort had to be followed by another, or if interest rate increases wiped out the effects of months of struggle?) became hallmarks of budgeting. There was increasing complexity (the old appropriations and tax processes still operated but they were overlaid with the new resolutions, reconciliation procedures, presidential sequester orders, let alone credit and tax expenditure budgets) but there was not clarity. What did all this mean?

I recall hearing it said about a father of 11 children that he was always one child over being adequate. Perhaps the simplest explanation is that the demands made on Congress, together with its self-imposed requirements, always remained one step above congressional capacity to manage. But in the dramatic rise of government spending from the mid–1960s through the 1970s, there was nothing intrinsic that had to lead to overloading the budgetary process. Even the decline in economic growth, though it undoubtedly made decisions more difficult (there being less to go around), was no insuperable obstacle. Indeed, the Congressional Budget Act enabled Congress, were it so inclined, to relate revenue to expenditure—either raising taxes or reducing expenditures so as to arrive at totals it thought appropriate. And Congress did try. The rate of increase in spending did slow down. New entitlements, and other forms of spending that had hitherto escaped the appropriations process, were made more difficult to achieve. If rates were not raised, "bracket creep" increased the tax take in an inflationary period. While deficits continued, they did not represent as large a proportion of national product.

At the same time, however, Congress had placed itself in the position of having to take global positions unique in American budgetary history. It did have to establish total spending and revenue and divide these totals by major substantive categories. Whereas before, such choices were best described as outcomes—known only by adding up choices made on an item-by-item or program-by-program basis through a maze of semi-independent committees and subcommittees—now Congress had to operate as a collective body.

A notable accompaniment of the concentration on budget resolutions—total taxing and spending—was an increase in partisanship. After 1975, as Schick reminds us, "the two parties have been polarized on budget policy. Twenty resolutions [not every one passed] have wended their way through the House over the past decade; on every one of these, a majority of Democrats have been on one side and a majority of Republicans on the other."[1]

Why did partisanship over the budget increase so sharply? Ellwood suggests that

---

[1]Allen Schick, "The Evolution of Congressional Budgeting," in Allen Schick, ed., *Crisis in the Budget Process* (Washington, D.C.: American Enterprise Institute, 1986), p. 35.

the movement toward a coordinated, top-down decision making process is one explanation. In the appropriations process members are cross-pressured. They have an individual and party commitment to increases or decreases in expenditures, revenues and deficits; but they also want to serve their constituencies and interest groups. In such a situation they are more likely to abandon their ideological and party position.[2]

The difference in the type of issue—parts versus the whole budget—may well account for the higher scores on global issues but it does not serve to explain the general rise in partisanship.

Louis Fisher of the Congressional Research Service, an astute observer of budgeting, argues that changes in the form of budgeting were responsible for the rise not only in partisanship but also in the intensity of conflict. According to Fisher:

> Increasing the size of a legislative vehicle—from an appropriations bill to a budget resolution—magnifies the scope of legislative conflict and creates the need for additional concessions to Members. The likelihood is that it will cost more to build a majority. . . .

> Paradoxically, it appears that Members could redistribute budgetary priorities more easily under a fragmented system. They could trim the defense appropriations bill and add to the Labor-HEW appropriations bill, without ever taking money explicitly from one department and giving it to another. The budget process of 1974, Schick explains, may have complicated the congressional process because it focuses attention on budget priorities, especially by moving money from one functional category to another. Yet Members are reluctant to vote on amendments that transfer funds between categories. They prefer to do this implicitly and by indirection. The ironic result is that congress did more reordering of budgetary priorities "before it had a budget process than it has since."[3]

In this view, inserting centralized procedures into a decentralized institution had diminished Congress's capacity to cope with conflict.

Another sign (and further cause) of polarization was what Robert Reischauer has called "the fiscalization of the public policy debate." Few programs were considered solely on their substantive or political merits. Rather, it was asked, to what degree do programs contribute to the deficit? Do they fit within the latest congressional budget resolution or the president's budget? How fast would defense or welfare grow? The substantive question, however—What is being bought with the money?—increasingly was shunted aside.

Fiscalization of the policy debate is a crude but effective way of accounting for wins, losses, and ties. To the extent that bigger is deemed better for some and worse for others, more for welfare or less for defense, higher or lower tax rates, these sum up the political struggle. Where observers once thought that confining

---

[2]John W. Ellwood, "The Great Exception: The Congressional Budget Process in an Age of Decentralization," in Lawrence Dodd and Bruce Oppenheimer, eds., *Congress Reconsidered*, 3rd ed. (Washington, D.C.: CQ Press, 1985).

[3]Louis Fisher, "The Congressional Budget Act: Does It Have a Spending Bias?" Paper delivered at Conference on the Congressional Budget Process, Carl Albert Congressional Research and Studies Center, University of Oklahoma, Norman, February 12–13, 1982, pp. 21–22.

conflict to amounts would make it easier to reconcile differences as a matter of a little more or a little less, fiscalization came to have the opposite effect. By aggregating totals and converting them into signs of who is ahead or behind, budgeting became a conflict of principles that is difficult to resolve.

The End of Economic Management

One reason for emphasizing the aggregate amounts was that these are what matter for purposes of macroeconomic management. Efforts at economic management by the federal government, however, largely disappeared in fact, though not in form. The villainous "stagflation," that hitherto unheard of, simultaneous occurrence of inflation plus unemployment undermined congressional confidence in Keynesian methods of managing the economy. "Fine-tuning" was out. Instead of the widespread consensus based on positive postwar economic performance, doubt grew not only about whether deficits were desirable but also about whether there was any right way to proceed.

The broad agreement on economic management had not been total. Always there were market individualists—supporters of a smaller government that would intervene less in economic activity. What was new in the 1970s was that they had developed ideas—monetarism, supply-side economics—at variance with the by-then conventional Keynesian wisdom. Stagflation brought these ideas to the fore. Consequently, since there was disagreement over the causal relationships, the general public and political elites were disposed to try something new.

The doctrinal basis had gone. Automatic stabilizers, such as unemployment compensation, still operated. But President Reagan's policy was simply to reduce income tax rates as low as possible. When the economy did well, rates would be cut because they could be; and when the economy did badly, rates would be cut as a necessary stimulus. Presumably, tax cuts were good for all seasons.

Despite hard times, however, Democrats would have liked to increase taxes in order to reduce the deficit and prevent the compounding of interest on the debt that would force out future spending. In good times, taxes should be increased because the extra could be used to fund more programs. With the major parties committed politically to tax decreases or increases irrespective of economic circumstances, there was not much room for adjustment. Ideology replaced economic "fine-tuning" with Johnny one-note. And the reconversion of Democrats to budget balance made it even more difficult for them to use the Keynesian approach to the size of deficits in order to manage the economy.

Dominance of the Deficit

When Congress was better at resolving differences, it was also true that those differences were narrower. Conflict resolution took place in a climate of informal understandings about the tolerable limits of taxation and the extent of permissible spending; budget balance, that is, provided strong guidelines. Once that agreement collapsed, Congress and the president were left with the shell—balance the budget—but not with agreement to do it through higher taxes or lower spending, nor whether domestic or defense programs should bear the brunt.

"In the current environment," Robert Reischauer came closer to the problem, "the nation and its budget process may be capable of handling a fight over the relative distribution of spending benefits and tax burdens but they are not capable of taking on both fights at once."[4] The difficulty of reaching agreement was certainly multiplied by the intersection of these two global issues. But why were they considered part and parcel of the same conflict? Spending issues might be ameliorated, no doubt, if there were more ample revenues. And tax questions would be easier to answer if more revenue were not necessary. Yet how could revenue and expenditure ever be kept separate when each depended so vitally on the other? Only in America, as the saying goes, have the two sides of the budgetary coin historically been kept separate. The overriding reason revenue and expenditure did not meet up at the same time and the same place with the same set of officials is not that they could not have agreed but rather that they would have agreed too well. Revenue was limited by common consent which, except in wartime, changed only gradually. Expenditure was expected to (and mostly did) fit within that revenue. No formal instructions were needed. Now we needed such formal instructions because agreement was lacking—had not Congress voted any number of times to balance the budget? But rules in the midst of disagreement are very hard to enforce.

To the extent that taxing and spending were viewed as essentially the same, or as similar issues, disagreement was intensified. One set of issues then could not be resolved while the other remained open. The more comprehensive the agreement required (not only because there are global resolutions but because the issues are linked in the minds and hearts of participants), the harder it was to achieve.

Conservative Republicans insisted that the budget be moved toward balance by sharp reductions in domestic spending while defense was increased—and all without new taxes. Liberal Democrats agreed on balance but only by cutting defense while maintaining domestic programs, preferably aided by new taxes on business or high-income individuals. Conservative Democrats and moderate Republicans together insisted first and foremost on balance, the sooner the better, however it was arrived at; they contemplated defense and domestic cuts as well as tax increases. Everyone, it seems, was for balance but not on the same terms. No perspective commanded a majority. What to do?

The deficit became both an obsession and a weapon. Controlling the deficit became a "metaphor for governing."[5] On the political extremes, the deficit was a stick with which (take your pick) to beat liberals for excessive domestic spending or conservatives for excessive defense spending. Precisely because those at the extreme poles correctly suspected each other of insincerity and knew each other to be vulnerable, both types spoke as if possessed of the one true religion. How better to beat the other side than by spewing forth what former Supreme Court Justice Thomas Reed Powell called a "parade of horribles" about the catastrophic consequences of deficits? In this, extremists were gladly joined by the party of responsibility because this was the one belief (and weapon) that they genuinely shared. So the fiscal responsibles trotted out streams of the nation's economists

[4]Robert Reischauer, "Mickey Mouse or Superman? The Congressional Budget Process during the Reagan Administration." Paper presented to Association for Public Policy Analysis and Management, October 20–22, 1983, Philadelphia, p. 3.

[5]Symposium on Budget Balance: Do Deficits Matter? New York City, January 9–11, 1986, p. 161.

who swore that (even without actual hard evidence) it was in the nature of things, or plain common sense, that awful events—depression, inflation, higher interest rates, the fall of civilization as we know it—were just over the horizon. This might or might not be true in the long run. But it was certain that any adverse economic circumstances would be blamed on deficits, so whatever else happened, it was necessary to disassociate oneself from their contaminating influence. In sum, the deficit became a means of holding adversaries accountable for adversity without oneself being responsible, and polarized the parties.

Polarization of the Parties

A general rule is that to crosscut cleavages is to reduce the intensity of conflict. Legislators who oppose each other on some issues know they will need one another's support on a different type of issue. Therefore, they moderate their positions. Budgetary polarization may be explained (or at least described) by exactly the opposite phenomenon: self-reinforcing, hence ever-deepening, cleavages. The same people who opposed each other on one kind of issue now tended, more than before, to oppose each other on other issues as well.

Most of those who wished to maintain or add to welfare spending wished to decrease spending on defense—and vice versa. Nor was that all. The social issues—school prayer, abortion, women's rights, affirmative action, parental versus children's rights—tended to move in the same direction, with conservatives and liberals taking opposite positions. Of course, there were issues—the social safety net, equal pay for equal work—on which widespread agreement did exist. But those still left plenty of room for these three major cleavages (welfare, defense, and social issues) to reinforce one another.

At least on domestic issues, Republicans voted for less and Democrats for more.[6] My guess is that the movement of Republicans to the south and of southern conservatives to the Republican party made the major parties more internally cohesive. By the same token, however, this development drove the parties further apart on the budget. While everyone said, with self-satisfaction, that they favored a balanced budget, the parties differed dramatically on how this should be done. Balance at lower levels is quite different from balance of taxing and spending at high levels. The mix between defense and domestic, even the distribution between welfare and infrastructure are matters of controversy.

Enter Ronald Reagan. Attention has been focused on his efforts to reduce domestic spending. He and his administration were only modestly successful in their first term, although too little attention has been devoted to the important ways in which Reagan made it harder to budget in the old ways. Income tax cuts wiped out several years of resources otherwise available for incremental program increases and deficit reductions. Indexation of tax brackets took away revenue increases that would otherwise have come about without requiring legislative action. Increases in defense spending left less room for maintenance of domestic programs or deficit reduction. Taken together, these Reagan-inspired changes made hard choices by Congress more necessary but also more difficult. Such changes foreclosed the

---

[6]James L. Payne, "Why They Spend," typescript, 1986.

most important actions—quiet revenue and spending increases—that participants in budgeting might, in earlier times, have used to come to an accommodation.

The visible presence of Ronald Reagan brought to the surface a phenomenon that had been going on for at least two decades—an increasing polarization of elites. The conservative majority of the Republican party and the liberal majority of the Democratic party were further from each other in the 1980s than they had been in earlier decades. The main cleavage was over how far government should go in reducing social and economic inequalities in a time of diminishing fiscal resources, sizable defense increases, and cuts in many social programs.

Let us suppose that there was general agreement on budget balance. One way to proceed would be to raise revenues and/or reduce expenditures. But Democrats wanted to maintain or increase domestic spending while Republicans wished to cut taxes and increase defense spending. No room there. Another way would be to cut all spending (except interest on the debt) across the board, thus avoiding disputes over distributive issues. But if Democrats insisted on not cutting welfare programs and Republicans refused to touch defense, the scope for cuts would be small. When there are big things neither side will give up, the scope for compromise is greatly diminished.

Thus disagreement over the desired levels of spending and taxing became intertwined with differences over how benefits and burdens should be distributed. If decisions on taxing and spending could be disaggregated, it might be possible to find shifting majorities on this or that alternative. That is exactly how things were done from the mid–1970s through the early 1980s. But Congress increasingly denied itself that option. The result, consequently, of having to confront the issues—the size and composition of taxing and spending—all at once was the creeping stalemate that characterized budgeting in the 1980s and influenced the working of the Congressional Budget Act.

EVOLUTION OF THE CONGRESSIONAL BUDGET ACT

In form (and, occasionally, in fact) the budget process as reformed in 1974 does (or could) work. Congress could attack deficits and any other problem or priorities through its resolution and reconciliation procedures. Given a determined majority in favor of a particular policy, Congress has all the necessary tools to implement its desires. The trouble was the lack of majorities. Individual appropriations might pass with substantial majorities, but these majorities differed among the 13 appropriations bills, and the budget reductions that were designed to tie them together had even less support. Indeed, the fact that budget resolutions require a majority of majorities—a majority comprehensive enough to integrate all other majorities—stultified the process.

The lack of support for a central comprehensive approach to budgeting did not come from lack of opportunity. Budget resolutions operating through budget committees gave Congress an opportunity to work out a central solution. Party leadership and party caucuses were now routinely involved in budget negotiation. So was the president. What was missing was an agreement at the center on a solution that would be validated by legislative majorities, or even on an agreed starting point. The procedures of the 1974 Act evolved to accommodate the pressures of the conflicts, without being able to resolve them.

R and R: Resolution and Reconciliation

It used to be said of Latin America that what was needed was a law stating that all the other laws be enforced. In this respect, budget resolutions may be said to represent the Latin Americanization of federal budgeting. For these resolutions do indeed resolve to enforce all the other actions that Congress claims it is undertaking to balance the budget, control spending, or achieve some other worthy purpose.

The first victim of the pressures was the second resolution. The second resolution, as contemplated in the act of 1974, was the one that was supposed to be binding. The first resolution, to be passed in May, was to be tentative, setting the process in motion with a general sense of revenue and spending goals. The work of the tax and spending committees was to proceed until September when the second resolution would, if necessary, reconcile the whole to the parts. "The idea of waiting until September to make strategic budget decisions and still have time to translate them into detailed appropriations and tax laws before the first of October," Alice Rivlin insisted, "is patently absurd."[7] But why? Why couldn't Congress either ratify committee decisions or shape them at the margins during the month of September before the fiscal year begins on October 1? If there were informal understandings about the size and shape of the budget codified in the form of a first resolution, then committee recommendations would bear a family resemblance to that resolution. Only modest adjustments would then be required to arrive at the second and final resolution. In the early years after 1974, something like this did happen as the budget committees, by anticipation, made room for spending desires. Spending discipline was not evident, but then neither had it been before.

Two things happened to make the second resolution unsatisfactory. One was that it exerted too little control, the other that it exerted too much. Control was insufficient in that even when economic conditions changed and ideas about public policy moved toward lesser spending, such views were difficult to translate into practice. The concentration of benefits made potential losers far more aware and better organized than taxpayers whose costs were widely dispersed. Nor, since the first resolution was not binding, was it possible to apportion sacrifices, for reductions on the first resolution might well be made up on the second. By giving in advance, congressional program advocates got nothing except to watch others spend what had once been their money. Everyone learned quickly to open with higher bids. Unable to accommodate the totals to which the bids added up, the new budget process proved flawed. From 1979 on, the second resolution required either big cuts (in the $30 billion range) if it were to live up to the first, or admitting large deficits. After neglect for years, the second resolution fell into disuse.

The solution in essence was to strengthen the first resolution with the reconciliation procedure and other protection. Reconciliation procedures did not feature prominently in the Budget Act of 1974. Originally, reconciliation was to be

---

[7]Alice M. Rivlin, "The Political Economy of Budget Choices: A View from Congress." Paper presented at American Economic Association meeting, December 29, 1981.

applied to spending bills after they had passed in order to bring them within the budget resolution's totals. While under fire in fiscal 1981 for tolerating a deficit during rampaging inflation, the budget committees rediscovered their "elastic clause," a hitherto obscure provision of the budget act permitting them to install "any other procedure which is considered appropriate." By then, the necessity of using third resolutions to accommodate excesses in the second (necessary because of overages on the first) had persuaded budget committee members that they needed a device to make the first resolution stick. For this reason reconciliation was made part of the first resolution in the Carter administration.[8] A 1981 rule provided that if the second resolution had not been passed by October, the first resolution would become final, and the initiative of the Reagan administration made reconciliation the central machinery for unprecedented budget cuts, which included entitlements as well as budget authority and appropriations. The reconciliation acts, while less in amount, continued as an intrinsic part of the budget process and as a vehicle for critical legislation.

With their elastic clauses in hand, the budget committees, led by the Senate, expanded into trying multiyear controls. Spending targets, beginning in 1978, were to be made for five years at a time. Containing allotments for both revenue and spending, these budget resolutions propounded targets not only for the next fiscal year but for the two succeeding ones.

Deferral and Rescission Redux

Even as Congress modified its procedures for reconciliation and resolutions in an effort to impose centralization on its decentralized processes, the deep dissensus between the president and Congress led the president to impose his will unilaterally. The struggle over the impoundment of funds revealed presidential efforts to gain by executive action what Congress would not give through its budgetary process.

Presidents can try to act on their own. They can try to forbid agencies from making requests for programs presidents want eliminated or reduced. They can reorganize units and categories so as to make it more difficult for affected interests to figure out where their money is and, therefore, how much they are being cut.[9] Presidents can impose hiring freezes and otherwise try to reduce what they consider unnecessary personnel. Their most direct approach, however, is to refuse to spend funds Congress has appropriated.

In the past, impounding had been based on tacit consent; either the president's staff persuaded the committees involved, or committees indicated they would not mind too much if the money were not spent. When the Reagan administration found itself unable to persuade Congress, and as it failed to get approval for an item veto, it tried to achieve similar results by a delay or a refusal to spend. Then the courts entered the fray by calling the impounding procedure into question.

[8]Jean Peters, "Reconciliation 1982: What Happened?" *PS*, Vol. 14, No. 4 (Fall 1981), pp. 732–36. See also Allen Schick, *Reconciliation and the Congressional Budget Process* (Washington D.C.: American Enterprise Institute, 1981).

[9]See Irene Rubin, *Shrinking the Federal Government: The Effect of Cutbacks on Five Federal Agencies* (New York: Longman, 1985).

Under the 1974 Act designed to limit the president's powers, presidents can stop spending, provided that within 45 days *both* houses of Congress give their consent to this rescission. Alternatively, the president can delay spending to the end of the fiscal year, unless the Senate *or* the House voted to override the deferral. In 1983, however (*Immigration and Naturalization Service* v. *Chadha*), the Supreme Court declared a legislative veto by one house an unconstitutional violation of the separation of powers, thus negating the provision. In response, Congress disallowed presidential deferrals for policy reasons. They could only be employed to provide for contingencies or to achieve efficiency or other savings through changes in requirements.[10] The president could use impounding as a de facto item veto. He could wait, thus delaying spending; he could postpone until the end of the fiscal year when it might be too late for Congress to act; he could attempt to straddle the fiscal years, combining a future cut with a past deferral. When Reagan used deferrals in several programs that Congress had explicitly told him to continue, Congress responded with outrage. Although the administration suggested that the deferrals were no different than deferrals in prior years, Congress felt Reagan was attempting "to an unprecedented extent . . . to implement his controversial policy goals" through this method.[11] Efforts to distinguish between deferring spending for management efficiency and for policy impoundments foundered in a spate of accusations. Unless there is agreement on the frame of reference, technical (or management) deferrals cannot be distinguished from changes in policy. The only real distinction is between programs you approve of and the ones you don't.

There's the rub: Agreement on the broad outlines of the budget—how much, what for—facilitates compromise on the details. Knowing they are headed in the same direction, participants can talk about better ways to get there. Divided as they stand, however, disagreement over policy turns on itself in two directions: Technical management questions become policy disputes, and policy differences become converted into disputes about who has the authority to decide. While it is true that there can be no fast line between means and ends, techniques and objectives, converting every question of fact into one of value expands the scope and intensity of conflict. The same is true of the old policy-administration dichotomy. It is quite wrong to imagine that Congress makes only broad policy choices while the executive branch merely implements the legislative will. If there were no difference between policy and administration at all, however—that an administrative regulation is equivalent to a congressional statute—relationships between the branches of government would become chaotic. And that, just that, as the controversy over impoundment reveals, was beginning to happen to budgeting.

The Shifting Budgetary Base

There was dissensus at every stage of the budgetary process, disagreement over policy compounded by differences over process. Deals on appropriations totals had to stretch across a variety of bills and stages of the process. Each stage's agreement

---

[10]Allen Schick, *The Federal Budget: Politics, Policy, Process* (Washington D.C.: Brookings Institution, 1995), p. 173.

[11]*National Journal*, May 24, 1986, p. 1060.

required trust that all parties would perform as promised at the next stage. Of course if everybody really were reliable, they would have delivered on the spot. In fact, agreements on defense between the administration and parts of Congress kept unraveling, while at the same time antagonists ceaselessly looked for ways to make up lost ground on domestic spending. Every agreement between the Republican administration and the Democratic House eventually collapsed under charges that the legislators had not provided sufficient cuts in social programs or that the executive branch had spent too much on defense or that both had distorted the budgetary base.

In days of old, budgeting had far fewer participants. Though the rule was sometimes honored in the breach, the president's budget was the acknowledged starting point for congressional considerations. Most disputes about initial requests were resolved within the executive branch—albeit in anticipation of congressional action. Now differences that would have been resolved within the executive spilled over into Congress. Why?

It is easy to forget the obvious. The power of the purse belongs to Congress. Presidents have previously acknowledged that fact by the ancient rule of anticipated reactions; the presidential role was both to acknowledge and alter incrementally the prior year's congressional action. By this act of acquiescence, presidents provided a convenient starting point, not far from last year's congressional action, so as to maintain continuity in budgeting. When in President Reagan's time, however, the president's desires were far from congressional majorities on taxes, defense, and welfare, his budgets were routinely pronounced "dead on arrival." The president's base had become his own preferences.

On the congressional side also, the base and the agreements that underlay it were undermined. Reconciliation had introduced an important new dimension. It was now attached to the first resolution, and required separate negotiation of its own majority. Budget negotiations moved from the budget committees to extra-committee groups. "Members do not defer to the decisions of autonomous, well-integrated committees, as they would in a committee-centered budget system," John Ellwood tells us. "Instead, the policy decisions conveyed by budget resolutions are the result of direct negotiations among large numbers of members that produce a majority coalition in favor of a single budget policy."[12] Reconciliation had been transformed, Allen Schick informs us, "from a means of reviewing decisions made during the current year into a process of revising legislation (mostly entitlements and revenue laws) enacted in previous years."[13] Reconciliation, therefore, especially reconciliation of budget authority, represented a permanent institutional attack on the budgetary base.

The budget both reflects and justifies the existing political order. Its boundaries guard that order. This is the social significance of the budgetary base, the

---

[12]John W. Ellwood, "Providing Policy Analysis to U.S. Congress: The Case of the Congressional Budget Office." Paper prepared for 1984 Annual Meeting of the Association for Public Policy Analysis and Management, New Orleans, October 18–22, 1984.

[13]Allen Schick, "The Evolution of Congressional Budgeting," in Allen Schick, ed., *Crisis in the Budget Process* (Washington, D.C.: American Enterprise Institute, 1986), p. 13.

bulk of which is protected from serious scrutiny so it will remain unchallenged.[14] Inside the base, except for small additions or subtractions, all is protected; outside that base, everything is up for grabs. On the stability of the budgetary base, therefore, rests the stability of ongoing government programs. An across-the-board attack on the budgetary base is equivalent to a radical restructuring of spending priorities. Governments, therefore, seek to invest major items of expenditures with some sort of sanctity; "entitlement" is but a stronger method of guarding one's borders. Breaching the base is equivalent to opening up to renegotiation the boundaries of past political contracts. The fundamental priorities of the regime— who will receive how much for which purposes—are in danger of being turned upside down.

Way back when, the budgetary base—the residue of past agreements not normally opened up for reconsideration—was approximated by the amounts in the prior year's budget. Recommending small changes, depending on presidential desires for economic management as well as preferences on a few programs, the president's proposed budget was an acceptable further approximation of the base. Not now. Kamlet and Mowery pronounced the last rites:

> . . . agreement within Congress on the definition of the budgetary base no longer exists. Both the House and Senate Budget Committees frequently have employed a definition of the budgetary base that differs from the one utilized in the Appropriations Committees. This practice has created severe problems in the compatibility of budget resolutions and appropriations actions. Moreover, the House and Senate Budget Committees themselves frequently use different definitions of the budgetary base, with disastrous consequences for the conference committees charged with the development of a joint budget resolution.[15]

Whether or not the president's budget was pronounced unsuitable, unworthy of further use, a mere historical curiosity, or even if it was closer to certain congressional desires, it no longer served as the base. Instead, Congress, through its budget committees, used either the CBO's current-services budget or the House or Senate budget resolutions, or some combination thereof, depending on the programs in question.

Since playing the budgetary game in Congress now required a respectable deficit reduction number—deficit cuts, not the total deficit, were the focus of attention—obfuscation of the base might be a deliberate move to overestimate how much would be cut. Manipulating baselines enabled legislators to meet the twin imperatives of helping clients by saving programs and helping the economy by cutting deficits. According to Tomkin, sometimes everyone used the same baselines, but for different reasons: Republicans could pretend their budgets were really making savings while Democrats would not have to agree to deep program cuts. At other times, different baselines reflected different assumptions to serve

---

[14]See Aaron Wildavsky, *The Politics of the Budgetary Process*, 4th ed. (Boston: Little, Brown, 1984), pp. 16–18, 102–08, 231–33, for discussion of the budgetary base.

[15]Mark S. Kamlet and David C. Mowery, "The First Decade of the Congressional Budget Act: Legislative Imitation and Adaptation in Budgeting," *Policy Sciences*, Vol. 18, No. 4 (December 1985), p. 320.

different political goals.[16] "The baselines have an important political advantage," Schick tells us. "They depict rising expenditures as budget cutbacks. Between fiscal 1981 (when reconciliation was first applied) and fiscal 1986, medicare has climbed from $39 billion to an estimated $67 billion. Yet Congress has taken credit for almost $25 billion in medicare cutbacks during these years."[17] Like the youngster in my childhood experience who would save the candy store from being robbed by deciding not to do it, "savings" are not calculated as reductions from last year's outlay but from a hypothetical baseline—an estimation of what future spending would have been without the action in question. Baselines, therefore, are man-made, depending on predictions of price changes and participation rates. Suppose a $100 billion increase is projected; would a mere $80 billion increase lead to a $20 billion "saving"? Like the man who "saves" $50 by buying the $100 hat (that he didn't need) at a half-off sale?

The disappearance of an agreed base was both a symptom and a cause of disagreement over the amount and distribution of expenditures and revenues. It was a symptom because disagreement must be running deep if participants could not agree where to begin, no less than where to end. It was a cause of further disagreement because policy differences were exacerbated by quarreling over the proper place to start.

Continuing Omnibus Resolutions

Continuing Resolutions (CRs), which provide interim funding, are old hat. Where in the past they were exceptional, during the 1980s they became routine. What is more, CRs became longer; between 1975 and 1984 they grew from five pages to an average of 100 pages. Length grew with function. Where before CRs were applied only to a few programs or agencies, now they might cover most of them. Where before simple language would do—merely stating the agency would be funded at the lowest level passed by House or Senate, or a committee thereof—now entire appropriations bills were included.

"[T]he growth of continuing resolutions," Robert Keith and Edward Davis correctly conclude, "appears to be directly related to the growing inability to enact some regular appropriations bills on time or at all."[18] True, but not true enough. If time were the major difficulty, pushing back the fiscal year, together with abandoning the second resolution, should have alleviated it. If time mattered most, CRs would be shorter, not longer. On the contrary, the complexity of CRs was a strong indicator of dissensus; CRs carried on the struggle over spending in another guise. The overwhelming detail could only be meant to commit the parties to specified spending. Thus we learn that by incorporation CRs now commonly included references to authorizing legislation whose sponsors were otherwise unable to have

---

[16]Shelley Lynne Tomkin, *Inside OMB: Politics and Process in the President's Budget Office* (M.E. Sharpe: Armonk, N. Y., 1998), p. 158.

[17]Allen Schick, "Controlling the 'Uncontrollables': Budgeting for Health Care in an Age of Mega-Deficits." Paper prepared for Pew Fellows Conference, November 1985, pp. 25–26.

[18]Robert Keith and Edward Davis, "Congress and Continuing Appropriations: New Variations on an Old Theme," *Public Budgeting and Finance*, Vol. 5, No. 1 (Spring 1985).

them passed on their own merits. The more continuous Continuing Resolutions became, the more they testified to a breakdown of what had been ordinary modes of accommodation.

The culmination of the Continuing Resolution occurred in 1986. Instead of using a CR for only a few appropriations bills, the CR packaged all 13 bills in an Omnibus Appropriations Act. No, Congress wasn't kidding; the act included all regular appropriations bills and a lot more (from Pentagon procurement rules to transferring Washington's airports to local control). To vote "no" or to veto meant closing down government. To vote "yes" meant voting in ignorance. "Either vote is irresponsible," Representative Henry Hyde (R-Ill.) said.

When conflicts are of long standing, the CR is the ultimate weapon. It was now possible for the entire texts of appropriations bills that would otherwise face special difficulties on the floor to be folded into an omnibus CR. In this way foreign aid was partially protected from members of Congress who wanted to shift funds to domestic spending.

Continuing Resolutions also vitiated the veto power. While the president, through OMB, had ample opportunity to express his preferences, it was not easy for him, in effect, to veto the government. For instance, President Reagan vetoed a bill for several executive agencies in 1985 because it contained $900 million more spending than he wanted, but he signed a CR for only $115 million less. Meanwhile, the executive branch was also feeling the effects of change.

OMB IN AN ERA OF PERENNIAL BUDGETING

As governing and budgeting became equivalent in the late 1970s and the 1980s, the part played by the Office of Management and Budget (OMB) was bound to be more important than it had been. No matter who was the director of the budget, the rise of budget resolutions, continuous resolutions, reconciliation, the deficit, the strategic centrality of negotiations over the size and composition of taxing and spending, the ensuing stalemate (and hence the extraordinary degree to which budgeting crowds out other issues)—any, or all, of these would have made OMB more pivotal. David Stockman, a man of exceptional force and talent, and President Reagan's Director of the Budget from 1981 to 1985, speeded up the transformation of OMB from an agency-centered to a congressionally centered presidential adviser-cum-negotiator. Stockman also gave this change an enhanced centralized slant. But under circumstances in which the budget dominated policy making, no one could have prevented OMB from being a key player.

Since its establishment in 1921, when it was cutting small sums, to its revitalization in the late 1930s—and again after the Second World War as presidential staff agency with a cutting bias—OMB (then the Bureau of the Budget) has counted itself (and has been considered by others) to be powerful. Without money of its own, without authority except what the president lends it, and without a large staff, OMB has long been an elite unit. It is one of the best places to be. It is at the center of policy. Service there counts high for promotion elsewhere. The sense of service to the president, upon whose backing all depends, coupled with a belief that this central staff has a national (rather than parochial) viewpoint, has long created a strong *esprit de corps*.

OMB's primary role, as explained by Shelley Lynne Tomkin in her classic book on OMB, is "to offer advice and assistance that benefits from long-term knowledge and experience rooted in insititutional memory of federal government activities and programs."[19] Its functions include acting as a clearing house for legislative proposals, a reviewer of federal regulations (since 1981), supervision of financial and management reform initiatives, and apportionment of funds to agencies. But its most fundamental function is to assist the president in preparing his annual budget. During the 1980s, OMB was "an institution in flux," reflecting changes in both formal budget processes and informal understandings. Its activities shifted from emphasis on agency budget examination and an avowedly nonpolitical stance to top-down policy making, continuous oversight of the budget, much greater interaction with Congress, tracking, and scorekeeping. These institutional adaptations raised questions regarding politicization and the ability of OMB to maintain its primary role.

Up to the 1980s, OMB worked both from below and above. The usual practice was for OMB to conduct a Spring Preview in which likely spending demands (estimated by OMB staff) were compared to expected revenues; then both were manipulated to achieve desired effects on the economy. Agency spending bids, therefore, were made in a controlled context. Because agencies were told how high they could go, they could accurately translate administration intentions into a loose (ask for more) or tight (keep what you've got) budget request. Agencies could appeal to the president or make an end-run to Congress. Such attempts had to be limited not only because they might fail but also because, given limited time and attention, extra political efforts were better reserved for the most important issues. On run of the mill stuff, the guts of agency activities, OMB recommendations were likely to be final.

There was now a pronounced difference. During the 1980s, in Allen Schick's words, the formal Spring Preview "withered away, possibly because of OMB and White House preoccupation with congressional budget activity and possibly because they did not want to risk premature leaks of budget cuts."[20] Shelley Lynne Tomkin noted that the administration's clear budget priorities determined policies so that

> Policy and policy development in OMB became top-down as opposed to bottom-up, and policy guidance from OMB's political appointees became increasingly more specific. This change in OMB's communications dynamics was one of the most striking institutional reversals that I observed in my 1982 and 1983 interview data. The responses revealed that a trend had been set in motion for budget examiners to be used to justify or fill in details on decisions that had already been reached by political appointees, rather than to provide advice and information to support decision making in progress.[21]

Working largely top-down was not the same as working largely bottom-up. Once budget examiners used to examine; they went into detail on programs, made

---

[19]Shelley Lynne Tomkin, *Inside OMB: Politics and Process in the President's Budget Office,* p. 3.

[20]Allen Schick, *The Federal Budget Process,* p. 54.

[21]Shelley Lynne Tomkin, *Inside OMB: Politics and Process in the President's Budget Office,* p. 89.

final visits, and otherwise kept track of agency programs. Some still did; many did not. Now most examiners dealt with aggregates, with total agency spending. Within that total, agencies were freer to spend as they wished (subject, of course, to congressional constraints and clientele demands). The price of this enhanced discretion was increased uncertainty. There might be not only less money but its flow also might be interrupted by delay, deferrals, rescissions, the latest continuous round of negotiations, stalemate followed by continuing resolutions, on and on. Budgetary planning is not easy. The decline of the annual budget, early decisions good for a year, is but the other side of the coin of continuous budgeting.

Totals dominated all discussion. How much, not what for, was the first question. Escaping from macro-choices over total taxing and spending, moreover, was hardly possible when the 1974 Act required an annual resolution to do just that, a requirement reinforced by the establishment of congressional budget committees whose main assignment this was.

"The creation of the budget committees," Bruce Johnson writes, "gave the OMB its own committees to work through. OMB became a client of the budget committees—perhaps their chief client—like the Veterans Administration is a client of the Veterans committees. A similarity of purpose grew, and staff-to-staff contacts developed. The budget committees became a window through which the OMB could view and influence Congress."[22] The assumed role of the Senate Budget Committee (SBC) as spokesman for responsible finance—that is, deficit reduction through increased control over budget authority—made it a natural ally of OMB. OMB also became a window through which SBC could obtain information about executive office discussion, and thus leverage in trying to influence executive policies. When the Executive Office of the President reached out to external constituencies, by the same token, SBC reached in. What was going on in Congress then became a part of White House deliberation.

Partisanship and ideology also influence executive-legislative relationships. The informal cooperation between SBC and OMB depended in part on the fact that from 1981 to 1986 the Senate was Republican while the House was Democratic. As policy differences between moderate Senate Republicans and the more conservative Reagan administration deepened, moreover, it became more difficult for OMB and SBC to maintain informal cooperation. OMB and SBC became antagonists, but the early reasons for their cooperation remained.

The existence of the Congressional Budget Office (CBO) was the scene for another mixed-motive game. Unlike the old days, OMB no longer had carte blanche in manipulating agency estimates. Should events prove CBO's spending estimates more accurate in too many instances, OMB's reputation would suffer. Over time, therefore, the staffs of the two agencies came closer together. This regard was furthered by the substantial presence in both organizations of economists

---

[22]Bruce Johnson, "The Increasing Role of the Office of Management and Budget in the Congressional Budget Process." Paper prepared for the Fifth Annual Research Conference of Association for Public Policy Analysis and Management, Philadelphia, October 21–22, 1983, p. 6. See also Bruce Johnson, "OMB and the Budget Examiner: Changes in the Reagan Era," *Public Budgeting and Finance,* Vol. 8 (Winter 1988), pp. 3–21; and Bruce Johnson, "The OMB Budget Examiner and the Congressional Budget Process, *Public Budgeting and Finance,* Vol. 9 (Spring 1989), pp. 5–14.

with similar perspectives about how to value governmental programs. This does not mean that the two organizations harmoniously coexisted. Much of President Reagan's first term was marked by strenuous disagreement between the OMB and CBO over economic assumptions and deficit projections.

Changes in attention (the financial markets, other governments, and congressional budget committees observe total spending) and in process (continuous budgeting) made the central budget agency more important. Bruce Johnson had it just right:

> To respond immediately to changing financial market reactions to the Federal budget, the Executive branch has to be able to change the budget quickly. Only the OMB can perform this function for the Executive branch. The fine-tuning of fiscal policy is now occurring every 3 to 6 months when it used to be an annual affair.

> Not only is the Executive branch, under the guidance of the OMB, formally changing its budget requests to Congress more frequently, but implicit Administration budget policy is changing almost every month as a result of compromises struck with Congress. . . . Each time a new "bipartisan compromise" is announced by the President, the Administration's internal budget estimates change (although for public consumption they may just receive an asterisk to show they are out of date). Various deals are also struck with Congress as the appropriations bills wind their way through committee floor and conference action. OMB is the only Executive branch agency able to sum the totals of all the give and take of the Congressional process to see where the budget estimates are going. The importance of budget "scorekeeping"—keeping track of all these deals—has been increased by the emphasis on budget projections and their importance to the financial community. For this reason alone, the OMB has assumed a leading role in negotiating budget and fiscal policy adjustments with Congress.[23]

Had total spending not become all-important, neither would OMB. It was the concentration on totals combined with the requirement for annual budget resolutions, together with the possibility of invoking reconciliation, and later the necessity of avoiding or following Gramm–Rudman–Hollings sequestration procedure, that made the central budget agency so central. When one budgets all the time, budgeters may indeed get more tired, but also they become more important.

Differences in quantity, if they are large enough, may become differences in quality. BOB-OMB always had relations with Congress. There were always appropriations committees. Since these committees were even more important then than they are today (taking up a larger share of the budget), the director and his chief aides, including top civil servants specializing in public works and other matters of interest to these legislators, had frequent contact with appropriations committees. Failure to pass appropriations on time or the need for supplementals or raising the debt ceiling required OMB to arrange a policy position for the Executive Branch. The difference now lay in the increased frequency of contacts, the institutional arrangements facilitating them, and the character of the interactions.

Though any specific starting point must be arbitrary, the entry of OMB into congressional negotiations may be traced to the time of James T. McIntyre, Jr.,

---

[23]Ibid. pp. 7–8.

President Carter's budget director, who gradually recognized the need for stronger contact with Congress.[24] When, because of (what appears in retrospect a tiny) $16 billion deficit, Carter's last budget had to be withdrawn and resubmitted, McIntyre dealt directly with top party leaders instead of the committees (using for the first time the reconciliation procedure with the first resolution). OMB then took an active role in lobbying Congress for the president's preferences, and its influence grew. David Mathiasen, deputy assistant director for budget review at OMB, has noted that more important than the package of cuts in 1980 was "the way in which this revision took place. Traditionally the American budget has been developed by the executive and presented to the Congress and the public without formal discussions or negotiations. . . . In contrast, the 1981 budget revisions were literally negotiated between executive branch representatives (primarily the Office of Management and Budget and the White House) and the leadership in both houses of the Congress."[25]

Lobbying the administration budget through Congress came to take precedence over the examining and assembling of agency requests. "OMB career staff," related Tomkin,

> were now interacting with congressional staff at more points in this ever-changing congressional budget process. With Stockman's departure, the "potential" for the blurring of OMB staff analytic support roles with "negotiating and selling" roles was now greater than it had ever been before. Certain stages of the process created more ambiguous situations for career staff than others. OMB staff support during the highly politically charged reconciliation process was particularly problematic in this regard.[26]

Budget examiners spent far less time in the field getting to know their agencies. Instead, staff was dedicated to tracking budget action through the multiple stages of the congressional process—resolutions were tracked from budget committees to the floor and into conference, out again into appropriations subcommittee and full committee markups, to reappearance on the floor in a continuing resolution, then again in a regular appropriations bill, seemingly settled only to pop up again in markup on a supplemental. To facilitate this tracking, Stockman ordered the development of a computer system that aggregated budget items by both budget function categories and committee jurisdictions, allowing him to trace the spending implications of action at all levels. He also increased the size of the OMB unit that was tracking spending legislation through Congress. Stockman could afford to take this course because there was nothing that he really needed to know about the agencies. For at least a few years he could get by on previous analysis by OMB, the extensive literature produced by GAO, CBO, and the think tanks, and his own preferences about what government should and should not do. Ideology provided a substitute for information. The new OMB approach, Hale

---

[24]Jonathan Rauch, "Stockman's Quiet Revolution at OMB May Leave Indelible Mark on Agency," *National Journal,* Vol. 7, No. 21 (May 25, 1985), p. 1213.

[25]"Recent Developments in the Composition and Formulation of the United States Federal Budget," *Public Budgeting and Finance* (Autumn 1983), p. 107.

[26]Shelley Lynne Tomkin, *Inside OMB: Politics and Process in the President's Budget Office,* p. 96.

Champion commented, therefore "almost excluded cabinet departments and agencies from the formulation of the budget."[27]

Since the administration was interested in achieving a preferred set of cuts, not in using the budget to finance agencies, OMB also moved away from the norm of annual budgeting. The annual budget served many needs, but its primary purpose was to regularize the funding, and therefore functioning, of government agencies. Funded for a year in advance, an agency would be able to plan and coordinate its activities. Since in many cases the administration either did not care about these agency functions or was convinced it knew a better (and, not coincidentally, cheaper) way to do the job, in 1981 and 1982 Stockman discarded the norm of annual budgeting, proposing instead large rescissions—administratively imposed cuts of previously approved appropriations. Basically the budget was under continuous negotiation so that even a place in the formal budget did not guarantee funding at the once-agreed level. Federal agencies, therefore, were whipsawed back and forth, torn between hope and fear that their allocations would be changed during the year. Predictability of spending flows, and whatever short-term planning went with it, were lost.

OMB also gave up its role as protector of agencies against sudden and unreasonable reductions. The place of agencies in the new appropriations process was both precarious and peculiar. Both their budget authority and staffing levels (also partially controlled through that process) were unpredictable. Many agencies were running reduction-in-force (RIF) operations, which were designed to reduce employment while maintaining civil-service preferences and protection against political bias. RIFs and a twist called RIF exercises—in which procedures were war-gamed in a drill to determine who would land where in the game of civil-service musical chairs—were spreading fear and chaos in agencies far out of proportion to actual layoffs.

After the congressional elections of 1982 increased Democratic majorities in the House and discomfited the Republican majority in the Senate, reconciliation no longer seemed a viable option to the administration. Nor—considering the liberal Democratic majority in the House and the moderate Republican party Senate majority, which wanted higher taxes and lower defense spending—was Reagan likely to get acceptable budget resolutions. Therefore, Bruce Johnson explains,

> in the absence of a budget resolution acceptable to the president, the director of the OMB attempted to impose presidential budget targets on the various appropriation bills. Because of the implicit and sometimes explicit threat of a presidential veto, the OMB was successful in exerting such influence in an area of decision normally reserved for an agency and its appropriation subcommittees. Thus, although the process of budget resolution and reconciliation was near collapse in 1983, the OMB continued to be active in the appropriation process, attempting to sell pieces of the president's budget to Congress in that forum.[28]

---

[27]*Federal Budget Policy in the 1980s* (Washington D.C.: Urban Institute Press, 1984), p. 292. Also see Hugh Heclo, "Executive Budget Making," in Gregory B. Mills and John L. Palmer, eds., *Federal Budget Policy in the 1980s* (Washington, D.C.: Urban Institute Press, 1984).

[28]Bruce Johnson, "From Analyst to Negotiator: The OMB's New Role," *Journal of Policy Analysis and Management,* Vol. 3, No. 4 (1984), p. 504.

One might well say that OMB became the president's lobbyist in Congress.

Within OMB, the realization was growing that the budgetary game had undergone decisive changes. Resolutions did not carry enforcement powers; they could not be counted on to pass; if they did, they often were not enforced. Failing to agree meant only that the real play was in a continuing resolution. Besides, appropriations committees could work without a resolution. Authorizations matter for entitlements but big ones were unbudgeable and little ones didn't move much. Not much point in talking to authorizers when there are no new programs.

Discovering by 1984 that it could not get authorizations down far enough to bite, OMB concentrated almost entirely on discretionary appropriations and, within those, on the allocations under which appropriations committees divided the amount they received from budget committees. Like the old joke about the man who looks for his collar button under the street lamp rather than where he lost it—because the light is better there—OMB concentrated on the pieces of budget it could do something about. This focus on appropriations accounted for the bulk of time Director Stockman spent negotiating with committee members as well as tracking bills. Before deals could be struck on appropriations, it was necessary to estimate how much they were worth and where the bill was located in the process.

OMB expanded its handful of bill trackers to 13, one for each of the major committees. Trackers infiltrated hearings, got data whenever they could, and immediately prepared letters to all concerned on Capitol Hill about whether they thought savings were real or illusory. OMB's two-fold role involved it in tracking budgetary proposals through the increasingly convoluted congressional budgetary process and estimating their potential cost impact.[29]

As OMB improved its congressional intelligence, thus being able to intervene in the right subcommittees at the right time, it sought further to streamline its task by combining consideration of appropriations hitherto dealt with separately. The development of continuing resolutions, from stopgap funding to program changes with future spending implications, provided OMB with another point of entry.[30] OMB was monitoring spending not only in agencies but also in Congress. Would the role of salesman of spending cuts to Congress, the OMB staff wondered, interfere with its tradition of neutral competence and general repository of wisdom about the value of programs?

Hugh Heclo, for instance, was troubled "that the capacity for loyal independence . . . may have diminished over time."[31] There are, as usual, two sides to this story. Loss of agency supervision was compensated for by greater OMB influence with Congress. True, examiners whose predecessors had once spent the slow summer months nosing around agencies could no longer do so. Yet, if they were honest with themselves, they knew that the old ways had started to crumble with the new requirements of the 1974 budget reform. Phenomena like budget resolutions, running totals, even reconciliation, had not been invented, only intensified, by David Stockman. The Central Budget Management System, which records existing spending-decision and projects alternatives, was inevitable in that era of conflict over totals and panic over deficits.

---

[29]Shelley Lynne Tomkin, *Inside OMB: Politics and Process in the President's Budget Office*, p. 154–57.

[30]Johnson, "From Analyst to Negotiator," and "Increasing Role of the Office of Management and Budget."

[31]Interview quoted in Rauch, "Stockman's Quiet Revolution."

Depending on one's political philosophy, the politicization of OMB began either with its predecessors (BOB as linchpin of big government under Franklin Roosevelt) or with the Reorganization Plan Number 2 in 1970 under President Nixon, which established a new strata of four program associate directors who were political appointees.[32] President Carter's creation of a new executive associate director for budget to supervise the earlier four only intensified this practice. Politicization is bipartisan. Heclo is rightly interested in maintaining the ethos of OMB: "It was not a place to be just another bureaucrat. It was a place to work for the presidency broadly understood."[33] But if the presidency is no longer "broadly understood" in the sense of presidential preferences being widely agreed, the politicization of those who serve presidents may be unavoidable.

In a polarized political environment the significance of significance, as it were, also changes. Is it significant to understand the effects on programs of changes in funding? Surely. But it may be deemed more significant to understand the implications of different programs for the size of government.

OMB had changed from an institution that emphasized providing information and support in putting together a budget, to supporting policy choices already made, from a focus on budget choices and their justification to totals; from negotiating with agencies to negotiating with Congress; from advance budget preparation to continuous recalculation, tracking and scorekeeping as the budget metamorphasized through the multiple complex budgetary processes of Congress. Meanwhile, Congress was trying to work out its own adjustments.

DISSENSUS IN CONGRESS

The stable relationships of the past had been disrupted. Instead of their usual role as advocates, agencies found themselves defending the cuts mandated by the Republican administration. While something of the old relationships remained, appropriations committees and subcommittees in a Democratic House (and later Democratic Senate) took on a role of program advocate. Their hearings became a forum for policy disagreements, and a three-way conflict among authorizing and appropriations committees and the administration. The appropriations committees lost authority on the floor of the House, as budgeting grew both to displace and include other legislative activities. It was fertile ground for proliferation of budgetary gimmicks.

Role Reversal

With agencies under repeated attacks, appropriations committees had to come to their defense. Committee members of both parties objected to the repeated cuts on programmatic grounds but also because rescissions were presidential challenges to the power of Congress and to its appropriations committees. Yet the politically appointed heads of the agencies, and their immediate civil-service subordinates,

---

[32] Tomkin traces politicization of OMB to the Truman administration after World War II when BOB career staff began assisting the White House in drafting legislation, or to the Johnson administration's use of BOB staff to achieve politically motivated ends in the agencies. Shelley Lynne Tomkin, *Inside OMB: Politics and Process in the President's Budget Office*, p. 54.

[33] Rauch, op. cit.

formally supported most of these OMB decisions. In appropriations hearings, agency heads continually cited the need for budget restraint, or the administration's philosophy, as the reason for cuts. There were some cases in which the positions taken probably did reflect the views of the senior civil servants involved. But, generally, civil servants were testifying in obedience to the desires of their political superiors; they had to worry about the consequences for their careers of defying those superiors. This hierarchical control, as well as placement of ideological Reaganauts in policy-making positions, left agencies in the peculiar position of publicly endorsing their own suffering. The peculiarity was not that agencies had never been in such a position before—they surely had—but that saying "yes" and meaning "no" had become the standard position.

Although thus formally neutralized, civil servants could, of course, feed information secretly to the appropriations staffs. Then, in hearings, committee members would try to establish for the record that the justifications for many reductions were, in their view, insupportable. Members of Congress also used hearings to inform the administration that it was stirring up hornets' nests that were best left undisturbed. A good example of a number of these themes—skepticism about agency justifications, agency leaders squirming to justify reductions, members furious about the short life span of agreements with the administration, the adverse effects on agency operations, and the disregard for Congress—is provided by a Senate hearing on compensatory education and programs for special populations. In response to reductions in federal aid, Ms. Harrison, for the Department of Education, claimed that state and local governments could and would find cheaper ways to do things, or pick up the slack. In the circumstances of 1982 this argument won little support, since state and local governments themselves were slashing programs because of their own recessionary fiscal crisis. Mark Andrews (R-N. Dak.) was skeptical on principle:

> You know the impression you give us on the other side of the bench when you come up with a statement like that is that somehow or another you have found a magic way of doing exactly the same thing that has been done years ago for two-thirds of the cost. Have your people somehow or another found a way to spend in essence two-thirds of the money and have exactly the same amount of success?[34]

Clearly, Senator Andrews and his committee were not convinced. Shortly thereafter the majority whip, Senator Stevens (R-Alaska), and department representatives crossed swords over the use of rescissions. The agency argument that entitlement overruns required discretionary reductions did not win praise.

SENATOR STEVENS: I'm greatly concerned with the 1982 rescission concept. It seems to me that [the grant recipients] have been led to believe they had money for 1982, and now you come and say there is no money for 1982 . . . .

MS. HARRISON: I can only respond that this is consistent with our position in September 1981 relating to those programs. In fact, if you look at a program like the Follow Through program, that program has been proposed for phaseout and abolishment by successive administrations. These grantees are well aware of the fact that there has never been any guarantee of the money.

---

[34]Hearings before a Subcommittee of the Committee on Appropriations of the U.S. Senate on Departments of Labor, Health and Human Services, Education, and Related Agencies, Appropriations for FY1983, Part IV, pp. 100, 105.

SENATOR STEVENS: But successive Congresses have disagreed. So it looks like what you are telling us is that this year you are not going to spend the money in spite of the action of Congress last year. The President signed that bill last year.

MS. HARRISON: That's why we are proposing a rescission . . . .

SENATOR STEVENS: I think the Department is just buying itself a fight. . . . There is a de facto breaking of a commitment as far as the government is concerned to those people, because you are putting us in a position of fighting the fiscal year 1982 battle again, the battle that you lost last year.

MR. JONES: . . . In order to stay within our budget mark, we needed to stay with the President's budget request because of the nearly $1 billion supplemental request for the guaranteed student loan. So, if you subtract the supplemental from the rescission—

SENATOR STEVENS: . . . What you are saying is that you are going to take the increasing entitlements out of discretionary funding, which you can't. You people are not reading Congress correctly if you think you are going to get away with this.[35]

No, they would not. Far more important, the principle followed—the president's budgetary base was what he recommended last year, not what Congress voted and he signed—signaled a radical change in the president's role.

The Reagan administration's proposals were likely to put agency heads in a tough spot because people in Congress expected agencies to defend their own missions. Responses of bureaucrats and political appointees varied with their inclinations and their circumstances. But the observer of budgeting who overslept the 1970s, though possibly surprised by the intransigence, nevertheless would still recognize the classic motives. The voice might be the voice of Republican Senator Norris Cotton ("You will forgive me, but you will not forget the Norris Cotton Cancer Center up in Hanover, will you? That will be the only memorial I will leave after 28 years in Congress"[36]) but the body might be any one of a legion of legislators. An official of the National Cancer Institute, anxious like his predecessors to follow the strategy of "spend to save," contends that ". . . each annual cohort of patients brings into the national economy about $3 billion. Federal revenues from their earnings is in the range of $500 million a year. So in just a cost effectiveness consideration, the program has been very productive."[37]

The "all or nothing" strategy was also alive and well. While the head of the Federal Aviation Administration (FAA) joined the Reagan administration in rallying "around to help reduce the deficit" in 1985, he was careful to point out that his agency was "a carefully woven organization designed to function as a whole."[38] Everyone knows that seamless garments should not be cut.

---

[35]Ibid., pp. 142–43.

[36]Quoted in Scott Stofel, student paper on "Budgetary Strategies."

[37]Ibid.

[38]Clifton Von Kann, Testifying in Hearings before a Subcommittee on the Committee on Appropriations, Subcommittee on the Department of Transportation and Related Agencies, Appropriations, for FY1986, House of Representatives, 99th Congress, 1st Session, Part 5, April 3, 1985, p. 322.

Voices calling for "fair shares" could still be heard. Amtrak, the government owned and operated railroad, had its reputation damaged by studies showing that every passenger cost the government $35. Without quite denying the allegation, Amtrak insisted it was "misleading and unfair" because, taking into account tax expenditures, airline passengers were subsidized even more heavily.[39]

Although there might not be many differences in kind, there were considerable differences in degree. The future of many more programs was threatened by criticisms ranging from fraud and abuse to lack of evidence of performance. Unusual in the extreme in classical budgeting, but common during the Reagan administration, was to present cuts that looked less severe than they actually were. The Environmental Protection Agency's (EPA) press release stated that "When comparing EPA's 1981 operating and superfund budget of $1.43 billion and 10,621 work years, the President's proposal for next year represents a 2% reduction in spending." While the statement was true as far as it went, the EPA budget included $200 million for the superfund, an item that did not exist when the 1981 budget was adopted. If superfund spending was excluded, EPA's operating budget would have represented a cut of 12 percent in 1982.[40]

There were many more instances of appropriations committee members acting as program advocates than there used to be. Most often administrators showed quiet appreciation. If legislators insisted that the National Park Service acquire new space, using that to justify more money for maintenance, officials would play along with the "squeezed to the wall" strategy. Explaining why NPS could not "take a cut," an NPS official gave his "personal feeling . . . that the Park Service is stretched about as thin as it can be manpowerwise and financially, given the new areas and responsibilities that have been added in the last several years."[41]

So far, so much the same. As legislators rushed to protect programs, however, their administrators began to fear being crushed by a too-loving embrace. Asked in 1984 what was the biggest obstacle to the improvement of Amtrak's financial position, its chairman, Graham Claytor, Jr., claimed that "the single biggest threat is that Congress will legislate reversals of management decisions that we make not to run trains that are going to cost a lot of money, or not to do cost saving things that we have undertaken to do, or not to do re-routes because there's local opposition."[42] Between those who liked them too little and those who loved them too much, federal administrators were caught between a rock and a hard place.

Hearings turned into forums for attacks on the administration that had little to do with budgets, but a lot to do with disagreement over policy. Observers witnessed the strange spectacle of agency representatives and members of Congress trading barbs—hardly a model for how to get funds from guardians of the public purse. Appropriations hearings became the site of policy wars between the administration and House Democrats. Often members elicited information they could

[39]W. Graham Claytor, Jr., ibid., Part 8, May 2, 1985, pp. 284–85.

[40]Lawrence Mosher, "Will EPA's Budget Cuts Make It More Efficient or Less Efficient?" *National Journal*, No. 33 (August 15, 1981), p. 1468.

[41]House, Hearings Before the Appropriations Subcommittee for the Department of Interior and Related Agencies, 96th Congress, 2nd Session, p. 599.

[42]J61, A6, 98th Congress, #23, Part 5, House, AMTRAK, 3/29/84, p. 871.

use to justify their positions. In one case—personnel levels for the National Park Service—Representative Sidney Yates (D-Ill.) established that what was really at stake was an administration preference for "contracting out" federal personnel needs, thereby reducing direct federal employment:

MR. YATES: It is almost like a yo-yo, because last year you added 300 employees. What is it, the Secretary giveth and the Secretary taketh away, blessed be the name of the Secretary? [Secretary of the Interior Watt was known for his religiosity.] . . . Your figures . . . do show that rather than paying $5,732,400 in employee salaries, you are going to contract that work out. . . . Let me ask somebody who operates a park. What is the advantage: Is it better to have your employees on hand, or to contract the work out? Which would you rather do?

MR. DICKENSON: [Russell Dickenson, Director of the National Park Service]: I have to tell you in all candor that as an experienced manager there really is no substitute to having the flexibility that comes from Federal employees. But the thrust of the Administration right now is to move into the contractor field. Therefore, we are adhering to that instruction.

The defense subcommittees on appropriations and the substantive Armed Services Committees had self-selected members with a bias toward the military. But the full appropriations committee in the House was more liberal than its authorizing counterpart; hence it was concerned about leaving room for social programs. The late House subcommittee chairman Joseph Addabbo was a solid liberal whose committee staff was far more suspicious of the military than was its counterpart at Armed Services. As a result, House Appropriations and Addabbo were the military's most dangerous domestic adversaries, and their exchanges reflected that relationship. This excerpt from testimony on the FY82 supplemental captures the flavor of that antagonism:

MR. ADDABBO: My spies got a copy of a memorandum to the chief of Naval Operations written by the Chief of Navy Legislature Affairs dated July 9, 1981. It was stated that: "Appropriation members and their staffs are not as thoroughly briefed and informed as their authorization counterparts." How did the Navy arrive at that conclusion? [The Navy's man made a properly deferential denial.] . . . I think they meant our staff and the members of the Appropriations Committee are not [as] brainwashed as the authorizing committee members.

If liberals were watching defense to create room for domestic spending, the conservative Reagan administration, to be sure, was attempting its own end-runs around authorizing committees in the domestic policy arena. Thus the administration's FY82 education rescissions included legislation that changed the rules on guaranteed student loans. Though such legislation was clearly out of order in an appropriations bill, that route was still more promising than going through the House Education and Labor Committee. This zeroing out of programs was a slightly more formally acceptable way to legislate through appropriations, but only slightly.

MR. YATES: Tell me about the historic preservation fund. Has Congress repealed the basic legislation for which you are eliminating all funds?

MR. DICKENSON: No, sir, the Congress has not.
      MR. YATES: Why are you eliminating the funds then?

Budget fights took so much time that little was left for floor action on authorizations. Since the widely different positions of the administration and the authorizing committees made agreement on legislation difficult, the committees tried to hitch rides on the appropriations process, particularly the continuing resolutions, as well as to exploit reconciliation. Representative Silvio Conte expressed the appropriators' discomfort with the result. "Personally," he told the House, "I am not at all comfortable dealing with issues such as steel import licenses and the International Coffee Agreement. But," he added, "the facts of life are that when the legislative committees are not able, for whatever reason to resolve highly controversial issues, Congress will find some other way, which is usually appropriations bills."[43]

Rolled on the Floor

During the heyday of the House Appropriations Committee, its members prided themselves on the high (over 95 percent) proportion of recommendations that were accepted by the House. Being "rolled on the floor" was a mark of ineptitude or disgrace. It meant that members were out of touch, that they had not performed their political function of anticipating and, therefore, failed to ward off opposition before it occurred. If they were to get rolled often, the most knowledgeable and (more important) the most responsible members might lose control so that budgeting and chaos became equivalent terms.[44]

In the 20 years following 1963, the number of amendments offered annually to appropriations acts rose continuously, from 120 to 433. The average number of amendments per bill went up from 2.5 to 9.2. Where the number of amendments approved by the House (more accurately, the committee of the whole) remained at roughly 25 percent until the mid–1970s, by the end of the decade it had gone to 43.3, after 1980 rising to over 50 percent. Looking more precisely at the success rate of contested amendments, these went from a high of 30 percent in the 1960s to the 1980s average of just under half.[45] Evidently, as Stanley Bach concludes,

> Increases in the number of amendments proposed in recent years, and increases in the percentage of winning amendments, suggest that the Committee has had increasing difficulty in accommodating to the preferences of the House and in anticipating and settling potential controversies in advance. In turn, this may reflect decreasing sensitivity and acumen among Committee and subcommittee leaders, a decline in adher-

---

[43]cf. Richard F. Fenno, *The Power of the Purse: Appropriations Politics in Congress* (Boston: Little, Brown, 1966).

[44]*Congressional Record*, October 1, 1982, p. H8360.

[45]The data come from Stanley Bach, "Representatives and Committees on the Floor: Amendments to Appropriations Bills in the House of Representatives, 1963–1982." Paper prepared for 1985 Annual Meeting of the American Political Science Association, New Orleans, August 29–September 1, 1985.

ence to such norms as reciprocity and comity, or the increasing divisiveness and controversy within the House as a whole over spending policies and priorities.[46]

Incomplete explanations for the growth of victorious amendments to appropriation bills are easy to find. There were more subcommittees with more members. Access to meetings was far more open while interest in activities was more widely spread. After all, government had grown larger, programs had broader impacts (defense, housing, and unemployment programs occur almost everywhere), legislators had more staff, and they were more interested in making a name for themselves in a number of areas rather than just in one. Congressional centers of expertise, such as CRS and CBO, offered help in tracking the status and effects of appropriations, as did a generation of informed legislators. All this is persuasive. Members of Congress offered more amendments because there was more to amend, more interest in amending it, and more of a chance to be successful.

There were now fewer sanctions than in the past for stepping out of line by challenging committee recommendations. Chairmen were no longer powerful enough to control the outcomes. The growing partisanship over budgetary matters increased the likelihood that subcommittee members would visibly disagree; choosing among various majority and minority reports, consequently, was less a violation of the norms of reciprocity than it once would have been. Party leaders and committee chairs could do little to invoke sanctions. Assignments were difficult to deny, since now there were many more to go around. Staff was plentiful; so were subcommittee positions. Indeed, because members served on more subcommittees, they were less liable to assign overriding importance to a single amendment or to be challenged on one of their recommendations. Short of the ultimate sanction—reading a legislator out of the party, which is only a last resort—the publicity and perhaps even the power went to those who act and speak up.

Consideration of the merits might also lead legislators to try to overturn subcommittee judgments. Because there were many more programs and expertise was more widely shared, there was less reason to believe that subcommittees knew more than other members. Since turnover on subcommittees also had risen, there was less reason to defer to expertise.

Budgeting Penetrates Congress

Votes on budget resolutions and major spending items became more partisan even though members of appropriations and budget committees were not more partisan than the House as a whole.[47] The basic reason for this is that differences over the budget had increasingly come to define differences between the parties.

A good indicator of this noteworthy development was the growing importance of votes on budgeting in Congress. Before the Budget Act of 1974, votes on budgeting—taxes, appropriations, debt ceilings—represented less than one-third

---

[46]Ibid., pp. 24–25.

[47]On the House Budget Committee, see John W. Ellwood and James A. Thurber, "The New Congressional Budget Process: The Hows and Why of House-Senate Differences," in Lawrence Dodd and Bruce Oppenheimer, eds., *Congress Reconsidered* (New York: Praeger, 1977), pp. 163–92.

of votes on all matters. To add in votes on authorizations—including entitlements, the fastest growing portion of the budget, as well as the new budget resolutions and reconciliation—produces a startling result: Ellwood's account shows that from 1982 to 1984, half of floor votes in the House and two-thirds (!) in the Senate were concerned with budgeting.[48] It took some 30-odd roll calls for the Senate to pass its resolution in 1985. If one saw budgetary matters as irrelevant to political parties, there would be little left about which parties would be relevant.

An indirect indicator of the ever-growing importance of budgeting is the workload of the Congressional Budget Office. CBO produces estimates of the likely cost of almost every bill that requires expenditure. As the markup of legislation proceeds, it gives informal input on estimates. But that is not all. CBO is also required to issue periodic scorekeeping reports on the degree to which outlays and authorizations stay within the budget resolutions. So far, so simple—until it turned out that the Senate and House committees wanted different scores.[49]

All along the way, CBO alters its estimates to keep up with the president's budget, committee changes, budget resolutions, floor votes. The important consequence was not that CBO succeeded in keeping all this straight, which it did, but that Congress, as it decomposed itself into subcommittees, was dealing with different budgetary bases.

Because it took so much time in so many places, the budget displaced whatever else Congress would be doing. Not only were there more actors but each had to, in effect, negotiate with the others and with the president. In addition to more participants, there were also larger choices—annual budget resolutions, continuing resolutions, and reconciliations—that either were not made before or, if they were, were made far less frequently.

Whether one says "It is Congress, therefore it budgets," or, "It budgets, therefore it must be Congress," the conclusion is the same: Congress and budgeting were becoming synonymous.

One might think that with so much time and effort devoted to budgeting Congress would get better at it. In a sense, this was true. There was much more understanding of spending, taxing, and the relationship between them in Congress. But understanding does not agreement make. Indeed, the more that people fundamentally in disagreement know about the consequences of their actions, the better become their reasons for opposing one another. Disagreement spread not only to present policies but also to past policies; from an agreed base to what that base ought to be; from where the budget should go to where it was.

Gimmicks

When relations among participants in budgeting are relatively stable and trustworthy, based on long-term convergence over objectives, the use of gimmicks— appearances costumed as realities—has its amusing aspects. Taking a cut that is

---

[48]John W. Ellwood, "Providing Policy Analysis to U.S. Congress: The Case of the Congressional Budget Office." Paper prepared for 1984 Annual Meetings of the Association for Public Policy Analysis and Management, New Orleans, October 18–22, 1984, pp. 35–36.

[49]Ibid., p. 10.

actually an increase because an inappropriate base has been used, or because lost funds will have to be restored, the ancient Washington Monument ploy (named after impossible proposals to close down this American shrine) may be treated with wry amusement. Large-scale and repeated efforts to deceive would be treated by dismissal or demotion as the participants depend on trust to get their work done, it being impossible, even in those days up through the 1950s, to study most claims firsthand. Now that budgetary stringency became severe, as a consequence of deficits and a general attack on spending, however, the use of gimmicks reached major proportions. The difference was that gimmicks were now used by participants who once opposed them. As gimmickry became more the rule and less like the exception, it was no longer funny.

Cuts might be used as sanctions against legislators opposed to spending programs. Senator Pete Domenici, chair of the Senate Budget Committee until 1987, was compelled to vote for certain projects in his district so as to show that in this respect he was "one of the boys." When Senator James Buckley attempted to remove 44 public works projects at the committee stage, members of the Public Works Committee ostentatiously voted for 43, all except the one in his state.[50]

Congress might appear to meet targets in budget resolutions by voting only 11 months of funds, knowing the rest would have to be restored. The food stamp program received this treatment several times. Paydays might be moved forward or back so they didn't count toward the deficit for the fiscal year in question. A similar feat might be accomplished by failing to provide essential spending authority. The Commodity Credit Corporation is financed by authority to borrow in order to provide farm price supports. By refusing some hundreds of millions of CCC's request, thereby seemingly cutting the budget, Congress would fail to provide funds that would have to be restored later.[51]

Gimmicks were chosen for a purpose. Congress needed to meet a certain figure for reducing the deficit. One way to help accomplish this purpose, while still not savaging programs, was to do what consumers do, that is, "buy now and pay later." The deficit figure might be met by choosing the House outlay number for defense, which was lower, and the Senate authority, which was higher but could be paid out over a number of years.

"Hypocrisy," La Rochefoucauld observed, "is an homage vice pays to virtue." This maxim came to life in light of the budget quandary. There would be no reason to vote for a lower budget resolution and for higher individual expenditures if the appearance were not seen as serving virtue. "In effect," Senator Hatfield complained, "we're talking out of both sides of our mouth. We want everyone else's project reduced." No one wanted to make what have come to be mostly painful choices, although occasionally Congress resisted.

Fiddling with the fiscal year—either to put expenditure in an earlier or later accounting period, depending on which will help the most—is a pure (if that word may be used) gimmick. Defense salaries may be paid a day earlier or later, thus

---

[50]Reported in David Mayhew, *Congress: The Electoral Connection* (New Haven: Yale University Press, 1974), pp. 91–92, footnote 32.

[51]Jerome A. Miles, "The Congressional Budget and Impoundment Control Act: A Departmental Budget Officer's View," *The Bureaucrat,* Vol. 5, No. 4 (January 1977).

"saving" billions for the next fiscal year. Medicare miraculously lived an 11-month year in 1980 and a 13-month year in 1981.[52]

There are other unacceptable reasons for the use of gimmicks. One is the reverse gimmick, a real spending cut, but one that actually reduces quality while increasing future costs. In making across-the-board cuts, for example, the first things to go are such "nonessential" items as travel and staff training. These may be false economies, however, when the lack of necessary information or training produces poor performance, more expensive medical treatment, and the like. After the closing of public health hospitals, to take another example, the Indian Health Service had to dismiss a number of its lower-paid professionals in order to make room for higher-paid people from public health who had more seniority.[53]

What is gained by making genuine economies if the result is only further reductions? Padding the budget to leave room for OMB and Congress to cut makes sense in the face of formula cuts. Donna Shalala, a political scientist (then assistant secretary of the Department of Housing and Urban Development, now secretary of the Department of Health and Human Services) tells a familiar tale:

> If you want to maintain your budget in an agency at a certain level, there's no incentive for coming and suggesting ways of delivering those precise services in different ways. Cost-conscious budget managers for the President will take advantage of your initiative, and they'll simply take the rest of the money off to someone else who didn't show that ingenuity.
>
> I went to the Hill this year without an increase in my budget. . . . And I told the Secretary I didn't want an increase, and everybody yelled and screamed and jumped up and down and said, "You've got to take an increase the way everybody does, 'cause when you get to the Hill you've got to take a cut." The Hill paid no attention to the fact that I went up without an increase; they just gave me the same cut they gave everybody else. And I went up and I argued that I hadn't asked for an increase. And they said that was just dumb.[54]

Padding in the expectation of cuts is part of playing the game. As Senator James Abdnor argued, "While this figure [the 7.5 percent figure for real growth in defense spending] is entirely responsible and defensible in its own right, the truth of the matter, as we all realize, is that whatever numbers we settle on will be our starting point when we go to conference with the House. The House approved only a 2.3 percent increase." Similarly, Representative David Obey, desiring to ameliorate cuts in social programs, suggested that "I simply don't think you should lead with your bottom line. It's like selling your soul to the devil before you're tempted."[55] Later, Representative Obey let it all hang out: "The only kind of budget

[52]See Allen Schick, "Controlling the 'Uncontrollables': Budgeting for Health Care in an Age of Mega-Deficits." Paper prepared for AEI Pew Fellows Conference, November 1985, pp. 25–26.

[53]An article by Joseph S. Wholey contains examples of both true and false economies: "Executive Agency Retrenchment," in Mills and Palmer, *Federal Budget Policy in the 1980s* (Washington D.C.: Urban Institute Press, 1984), pp. 295–332.

[54]Quoted in David Broder, *Changing of the Guard: Power and Leadership in America* (New York: Simon and Schuster, 1980), p. 434.

[55]Robert Reischauer, "Mickey Mouse or Superman? The Congressional Budget Process During the Reagan Administration," Paper presented to Conference of Policy and Program Analysis and Management, Philadelphia, October 20–22, 1983.

resolution," said he sadly, "that can pass this place is a dishonest one. I think that degrades the entire congressional process."[56]

Gimmickry has spawned criticism of the post–1974 process inside and outside of Congress. Citing evidence that "the reconciliation process has run amok," for instance, Richard Cohen of the *National Journal* noted that the 1985 bill ran to 198 pages in small print and required 30 subconferences to negotiate Senate-House differences. Among a long list of matters, it included

- a requirement that the transportation secretary withhold 10 percent of highway funds starting in fiscal 1989 from states that have not set their minimum drinking age at 21;
- an instruction to build three highway bridges over the Ohio River between designated points in Ohio and Kentucky;
- a plan to allocate to Gulf Coast states billions of dollars from oil and gas drilling on the Outer Continental Shelf;
- extensive overhaul of medicare, including changes in the 1983 law that set up a new prospective reimbursement system for hospital fees to limit costs;
- extension of the right to social security benefits to children adopted by and living with their great-grandparents;
- eligibility of Connecticut state police for social security.[57]

Members of Congress themselves realized that gimmickry was institutionally destructive. Members could now ring all the changes on devices to make spending fit within resolutions or to have them appear lower than they actually were. Committees reported savings that actually were only temporary. Votes were forced on cuts so as to make it difficult to approve them. Payments for medicare were pushed into the next fiscal year. That is why SBC and OMB tried to get multiyear reconciliations for appropriations and authorizations.[58] The lack of connection between appearance in the resolution and reality in spending fooled no one but did contribute to low morale and self-doubt in Congress.

The politics of dissensus wrenched and distorted budgetary processes and institutions. Whereas agreement had for many years reinforced incremental decision making, stable expectations, and orderly processes, dissensus now seemed to create a looking-glass world in which nothing seemed to work the way it should. The loss of consensus might be traced to a number of causes: the need to confront budget totals as well as program amounts demanded by the 1974 Congressional Budget Act; the loss of confidence in economic doctrine; the lack of flexibility associated with deficit politics; and the deepening political cleavages between the political parties, intensified by the strategies and tactics of a crusading administration. The fabric of the Congressional Budget Act expanded and tore, as its elements for control—resolution, reconciliation, impoundment regulations, baselines, and continuing resolutions—became vehicles for political advantages. OMB was transformed from a budget building institution focusing

[56]Quoted in Richard E. Cohen, "House Braces for Showdown Over How It Should Package Its Annual Budget," *National Journal,* November 27, 1982, pp. 2024–26.

[57]Richard E. Cohen, "Unreconciled," *National Journal,* January 11, 1986, p. 110.

[58]Robert D. Reischauer, "The Congressional Budget Process," in Mills and Palmer, *Federal Budget Policy,* pp. 385–413, especially pp. 397–98.

primarily on the agencies of government and the details of estimates, to a policy negotiator, whose major emphases were budgetary totals, top-down budgeting, negotiation with congressional committees, advocacy, budget tracking, and continuous working and reworking of baselines and their consequences. In Congress, accepted roles of committees and agencies were reversed because a Republican administration wanted to cut agency budgets, while a Democratic Congress wished to increase them. Well-defined deferential relationships between Congress and its committees were disrupted, budgeting came to displace other legislative activities, and gimmicks designed to conceal, mislead, and obfuscate took the place of responsible norms of conduct.

Allen Schick has pointed out that "policy and process are two sides of the same budgetary coin. One should not expect the procedures to be in good working order if the substantive results are not."[59] Yet there were many who blamed the budgetary process for the inability of Congress to do the things it professed to want. The next step was to try to stuff the genie back into the bottle through process reforms to force Congress to do the right thing, to balance the budget. But gradually, also, there was a dawning realization that tinkering with processes could not substitute for confronting the realities of budget policy: a budget in which more for some meant less for others.

---

[59]Allen Schick, *The Capacity to Budget* (Washington D.C.: Urban Institute Press, 1990) p. 3.

Chapter 6

The Politics of Balancing Budgets

In theory, balancing budgets is easy. All that is needed is to raise revenues or cut expenditures, or both. In practice, balanced budgets are harder to attain. The experience of the early 1980s highlighted the problems in gaining balance by cutting spending (especially while cutting taxes and increasing defense expenditures simultaneously). Raising taxes seemed equally implausible, in view of the Reagan administration's policy to cut taxes, and his successor's pledge of "no more taxes" (although in fact taxes were raised, notably the social security payroll tax).

But virtually everyone wanted to balance the budget, whose annual deficits had not only reached unprecedented heights but were declared "structural" i.e., the deficit would not fix itself when economic times improved but would remain a steadily widening gap between income and outgo. Perhaps it was all a matter of will—politicians had to be forced to do the very things they said they wanted to do. The Gramm–Rudman–Hollings legislation of 1985 assumed that if the president and Congress were confronted with horrific consequences (across the board sequestrations), they would be forced to cooperate to meet deficit reduction targets until the deficit vanished.

One reason it didn't work was the nature of the budget itself. Budgets are future oriented: They represent intentions. It is only after the end of the fiscal year that we discover if those intentions have been realized. So it is quite possible to present or pass a plausibly balanced budget to find later that it is actually not balanced at all. Why might this happen? One possibility is deliberate and cynical manipulation of the initial figures. But even with the best of intentions, close interdependence of budget and economy makes prediction hazardous over even one year. Every budget has a section and table that explain the sensitivity of the federal budget to key economic indicators and their interactions—inflation, unemployment, economic growth, and interest rates. Hence, budget summits, such as those at the end of the 1980s, could wring as much as half a trillion worth of deficit reduction over five years, and the deficit would still grow.

So all the effort and pain of agreeing to program cuts might be negated by swings in key indicators of as little as one percent. Or to put it differently, efforts to cut appropriations were likely to be offset by increased entitlement spending or inaccurate revenue projections, even as the deficit fed off itself in mounting costs for interest.

The dependence of the budget on the economy was not the only discouragement to action on the deficit. If the size of the total pie remained the same, more for one meant less for another. No one wanted to cut his or her own preference, to see this generous offering eaten up by someone else's program. Defense advocates fought with the champions of domestic spending. It was in neither side's interests to make unilateral sacrifices.

The Budget Enforcement Act of 1990 found a solution in new rules. It solved the problem of the effects of the economy on the budget by ignoring it. It recognized the difficulties of budgeting for entitlements by requiring that policy changes requiring greater outlays should be paid for or "offset." And the same went for policy changes affecting revenues. As for appropriations, separate caps for defense and domestic spending would not only provide definite ceilings, but would set up a temporary "fire wall" between them so that savings in one, at least initially, would not contribute to increases in the other.

But the best of rules, even if scrupulously adhered to, could not solve the primary issues of budget balance. Everyone might want to balance the budget, but they all had different ideas about how to do it. The divisions and permutations were inexhaustible. There were of course the major fractures between those who wished to increase taxes and those who wanted to reduce spending; between those in favor of more defense spending and those who wanted to increase domestic expenditures. But the parties themselves had become less cohesive, so that attempts to craft a single proposal that could find a majority even in one party, let alone bipartisan agreement, splintered into a mass of complex detail. This was the fate of two major policy initiatives at the beginning of the 1990s—the Omnibus Budget Reconciliation Act of 1990 and President Clinton's first budget in 1993. Each gained passage, but their tortuous path to assent reflected the difficult relationship between leadership and party rank and file, and the tensions and divisions in both parties.

The early 1990s represented a kind of watershed period in the development of federal budget process and policy. It was marked by three significant developments. First were changes in process, in which the Gramm–Rudman–Hollings Act represented a stage in cumulative learning about what would not work, and the Budget Enforcement Act changed the rules of the game for at least the next decade. Second was the emergence of a framework for making budget policy. Formalized in the negotiations during the summit conference that led to the Budget Enforcement Act, critical budget relationships soon became an intuitive focus. This framework determined the major issues requiring decision, the processes through which each component of the budget was decided, and the terms on which revenues and expenditures were placed in competition, or separated. Construction of a budget required consideration of relationships between:

- the budget and the economy, reflected in economic assumptions and projections and their implications;
- revenues and expenditures, whose balance determined deficit or surplus;

- entitlements and discretionary spending;
- defense and domestic discretionary spending; and
- competition among domestic appropriations, structured along the groupings of the appropriations acts.

These categories quickly became the vocabulary of budget debate.

The third development was the emergence of high level negotiations to produce packages of revenue and expenditure changes aggregating very large sums over several years. This development was significant because it set a precedent for subsequent similar methods of handling the budget, results were achieved against strong opposition in both parties, and the decisions set in motion longer-term trends that had a decisive effect on budget outcomes.

GRAMM–RUDMAN–HOLLINGS

Why GRH Passed

The Gramm–Rudman–Hollings bill (formally known as the Balanced Budget and Deficit Reduction Act of 1985), which essentially required five annual sequestrations (across-the-board reductions) in federal spending until the deficit had been reduced to zero, was proof of mistrust. (Of course, these reductions were required only if prior agreement on reductions was not forthcoming.) Here we have a procedure that almost every member of Congress believed was foolish, if not stupid; that everyone who knew anything about it thought could be improved upon in five minutes; yet it received majority support in both houses of Congress and was signed by the president. The act, which dramatically affected the future of numerous government programs and congressional budget procedures, was passed without public hearings, without debate by any House or Senate standing committee, and without any substantive debate on the House floor. When everyone says that something is not right, and yet they keep doing it, there is a puzzle that should excite our interest.

Year after year Congress advertised its disabilities by taking longer and longer to reach agreement; few could remember the last year all appropriations bills were passed on time. Congress was tired of budgeting to no purpose, tired of budgeting, budgeting, and nothing but budgeting. Its members despaired sufficiently of reaching agreement to resort to a formula, all the while expecting, even hoping, that the balancing mechanism had been made so onerous (After all, who wants to reduce the number of aircraft controllers?) that it would collapse due to its own weight. Crash! This is no way to run a ship, especially not the ship of state, unless you regard the wreckage the lesser evil compared to giving in to the other side.

Gramm–Rudman–Hollings was as (or more) important for what it symbolized as for what it did. The imposition of a formula for replacing the power of the purse, the most important congressional power, was an abdication of power. Congress was saying that it was out of control. It could not help itself. Faced with difficult decisions, the one thing Congress knew was that it wouldn't be able to decide wisely. Therefore, guarding against its own worst tendencies in advance,

Congress anticipated its collective unwisdom by taking away its discretion. If Congress was so out of control, if it was in disrepute with its own members, then maybe they could not trust themselves. Why not, then, force themselves to do the right thing, namely, balance the budget in such a fashion that they could not reverse the process by playing the usual games?

Binding oneself against one's worst inclinations may appear strange, but it has precedent. Fearing continual scandal, Congress took away its power to appoint local postmasters. Observing as well the unfortunate consequences of the Smoot–Hawley Tariff, Congress also created a buffer, a tariff commission between it and temptation so that it could no longer, as an ordinary matter, set tariff rates on individual items. At least since Ulysses and the Sirens, attempting to protect oneself against self-destructive tendencies has been a well-known strategy. Why did Congress agree to limit its most important power, the power that humbled tyrants and brought about representative government, a power, moreover, on which other legislative powers depend?

The rise of the Gramm–Rudman–Hollings Act took place in an environment of disarray, dismay at the ever-rising deficits, and concern by legislators with their own inability to govern. The opportunity was ripe for an outsider, Phil Gramm of Texas (who, upon being read out of the Democratic party in the House, won a seat as a Republican senator), to ally himself with a Democratic outsider, Senator Fritz Hollings of South Carolina, and with a dedicated budget balancer, Republican Warren Rudman of New Hampshire. The three offered the radical proposal as a rider to the annual misery of raising the debt ceiling, this time to a previously unheard of level of $2 trillion. They believed, as did many other legislators, that unless Congress was faced with something much worse than business as usual, it would continue to avoid balancing the budget.

President Reagan felt (partly rightly, partly wrongly, but with conviction) that every time he compromised by raising taxes, he did not get in return promised cuts in domestic spending. Though he preferred tax reductions to lower deficits, he did want balance if (and only if) it could be achieved solely by spending cuts. The GRH formula looked like it might make that possible. The president did not want to cut defense, but that was happening anyway.[1] So he supported GRH.

But why did Democratic liberals, Republican moderates, and otherwise sane and sensible legislators (there were a few, such as Republican Senator Nancy Kassebaum and Democrat Pat Moynihan, who opposed GRH to the end) go along? Fearful of rising deficits, frustrated by inability to get agreement on taxing and spending, unwilling to say "no" to any plan for balance, realizing that they could change their minds later when the crunch came, they went along.

Liberals have another story to tell. They wanted to pin the deficit tag on Reagan and not allow him to do that to them. Led by Speaker O'Neill, they insisted on changes in the original conception where everything, except possibly social security, was subject to proportional cuts, and they succeeded in getting the most important entitlements for low-income and elderly people either excluded or

---

[1]This summary is taken from a book by Joseph White and Aaron Wildavsky entitled *The Deficit and the Public Interest: The Search for Responsible Budgeting in the 1980s* (Berkeley: University of California Press, 1990).

subject only to modest reductions of 1 to 2 percent. By doing this, congressional liberals hoped not only to protect the poor and elderly but also, by making defense bear a disproportionate share, encourage the president to compromise with them so as not to invoke the dreaded sequestration procedure.

Opinions understandably vary as to whether the Balanced Budget and Emergency Deficit Control Act of 1985 (Public Law 99–172) was meant to be workable. If (as in the phrase Senator Rudman made famous, "It's so bad it's good.") the idea was to scare legislators into reducing the deficit, the consequences would have to be horrendous. And, if followed for the full course, they would be, wiping out half of general government. Anticipating this havoc, legislators might be motivated to settle on a more variegated and hence more sensible deficit reduction package than across-the-board cuts. Unfortunately, being sensible requires being able to choose among the entire panoply of governmental programs. But the act exempted 48 percent of these (mostly entitlements and debt interest) from across-the-board cuts, with an additional 24 percent available only for very limited reductions. Only 27 percent of the budget, mostly in defense, was fully available for sequestration—that is, the withholding of budget authority up to the amount required to be cut to meet the deficit target. You cannot get 100 percent of the deficit reduction you need from 27 percent of the budget.

In this game of budgetary chicken, one side assumed that as automatic cuts were triggered, the Republicans would blink by raising taxes while the other hoped that as meat-ax cuts in domestic spending grew near, Democrats would blink by making the policy decisions needed for domestic reductions. Each side hoped to prevail by making the budgetary process unworkable. This political Ludditism did not bode well for the ability to govern.

How GRH Was Supposed To Work

The Gramm–Rudman–Hollings process was invoked if (and only if) the preexisting process failed to meet the annual deficit reduction targets—from $171.9 billion in 1986 to $144.0 billion in 1987 to zero in 1991 (See Table 6.1).

The president was required to submit a budget that did not exceed the annual target figure. Congressional budget resolutions also had to conform to the targets

Table 6.1 The Gramm–Rudman–Hollings Record

	(in billions of dollars)		
	Original Deficit Limits	Revised Deficit Limits	Actual Deficits
1986	171.9		221.2
1987	144.0		149.8
1988	108.0	144.0	155.2
1989	72.0	136.0	152.5
1990	36.0	100.0	221.4
1991	0	64.0	269.2
1992		28.0	290.4
1993		0	255.1

Source: Compiled from data released to the public record.

Table 6.2   Revised Budget and Deficit Reduction Process under
Gramm–Rudman–Hollings

Action	To be completed by
President submits budget	Monday after January 3
CBO report to Congress	February 15
Committees submit views and estimates to budget committees	February 25
Senate Budget Committee reports budget resolution	April 1
Congress passes budget resolution	April 15
House Appropriation Committee reports appropriations bills	June 10
Congress passes reconciliation bill	June 15
House passes all appropriations bills	June 30
Initial economic, revenue, outlay, and deficit projections made by OMB and CBO	August 15
OMB and CBO report tentative contents of sequester order to GAO	August 20
GAO issues deficit and sequester report to the president	August 25
President issues sequester order	September 1
Fiscal year begins and sequester order takes effect	October 1
OMB and CBO issue revised projections based on subsequent congressional action	October 5
GAO issues revised sequester report to president	October 10
Final sequester order becomes effective	October 15
GAO issues compliance report on sequester order	November 15

Source: Balanced Budget and Emergency Deficit Control Act of 1985.

for cutting the deficit. Snapshot day was August 15. (See Table 6.2 for timetable.) OMB and CBO were to issue a joint report estimating revenue, expenditures, and therefore, the gap between them at that moment in time for the fiscal year beginning October 1. This early warning was designed to alert all players to the fact that the rules of the budget game were about to be altered. The month that followed was supposed to be budgetary show-and-tell time. I say "supposed" because no piece of paper, even a law, can make Congress do what it doesn't want to do. Congress could still ignore GRH or make believe, by various gimmicks, that it had done what was required.

In addition to estimating the size of the deficit, GRH required OMB and CBO to estimate economic growth for each quarter of the preceding year. The purpose was to tell Congress whether there had been two consecutive quarters of negative growth, in which case sequestration procedures were suspended. Depression, though obviously undesirable, was one way out of the deficit reduction process.

Five days later, according to the original legislation, the directors of OMB and CBO had to submit a joint report, not to Congress or the president but to the Comptroller General. This CBO-OMB report estimated revenues and expenditures (income and outlays) for the fiscal year. After comparing the two figures, the report stated for the record whether the difference plus an allowable $10 billion was larger than the allowed deficit. If the amount was smaller, and the Comptroller General concurred, the GRH process stopped there. If the target figure had been breached, the joint report specified the reductions necessary to reach that level for each quarter of the existing year as well as for the last two quarters.

At this point, CBO and OMB recommended, and GAO was supposed to decide upon, a base from which sequestration was to occur. The calculation of this base was no simple matter. The spending budget itself is complex. Specific priorities were embedded within GRH, requiring numerous exceptions and adjustments. And congressional desire to limit presidential discretion, especially on defense, led to extraordinary arrangements. The president was not to achieve by sleight of calculation what he had not won by legislative majorities.

Step one reduced the base for sequestration by the total of exempt programs. Step two deducted from the base the cost of living increases in the rest of government. These available COLAs were divided in half and then subtracted from domestic and defense programs, respectively. The reason for this rather strange 50–50 split was that defense and domestic programs had come to be seen as competitors. Where defense lost out in step one (because it was eligible for sequestration while the bulk of domestic spending was not), it gained a bit back in the second stage: Though defense represented more than half the cutable base, some 60 percent, it took just half the hit. By strict proportionality, on the other hand, defense should have had credit for 60 percent of the sequestered COLAs. Such are the odd outcomes of political bargaining. The defense sequestration was designed not merely to lower spending but to make sure that, after the first year, the president had as little discretion as possible.

The president issued an initial sequestration report on September 1 telling Congress he had followed the rules. At the same time, the president was allowed to suggest an alternative budget quite outside these rules, providing it met the target. Presidential sequestration had to be by uniform percentage reductions in defense and domestic categories.

The immediate significance of this uniformity was that the president could not, on his own, eliminate programs or make transfers among categories. He could not move to protect programs he deemed vital or to advantage new ones with small bases compared to large ones with large bases that could better withstand cuts.

On September 5 the president submitted a list of proposed changes in contracts to the armed services and appropriations committees. At the end of that month, GAO certified that the savings stemming from sequestration of contracts were correct. Starting in mid-August, Congress and the president had the chance to come up with an alternative to sequestration. If they did not, sequestration took place automatically on October 15.

In 1986, a lawsuit was brought by Representative Michael L. Synar (D-Okla.) and other members of Congress, joined by the Public Citizen Litigation Group affiliated with activist Ralph Nader. They argued that "Gramm–Rudman tried to insulate congress from the hard choices our Founding Fathers gave us and expected us to make."[2] The Supreme Court held it was unconstitutional to give final authority for making cuts to the comptroller general, who could conceivably be dismissed by joint resolution of Congress, since Congress could play no direct role in the execution of the laws.

---

[2]"Supreme Court's Gramm–Rudman Opinion," *Congressional Quarterly Weekly Report,* July 12, 1986, p. 1581.

Under a backup provision, the procedure was changed. The CBO-OMB joint report of the budget snapshot was now sent to a temporary joint committee on deficit reduction, made up of the entire membership of the House and Senate Budget Committees. Within five days the temporary joint committee was supposed to report to both houses a joint resolution of sequester based on the arithmetic average of the OMB and CBO reports. The full House and Senate had five days to act on the joint resolution. Debate was limited to two hours—easily done by special rule in the House, but requiring unanimous consent in the Senate.

Yet the institutional problem was not the major impediment to achieving GRH's objectives. Within two years, it was clear the original targets were impractical. There were three sets of sequestrations, but even these failed to bring actual spending in line with actual revenues. Though deficits dropped between 1986 and 1989, by 1990 the deficit was again approaching the $200 billion mark.

While it might be possible year by year to meet GRH's formal conditions, compliance was achieved by gimmicks. Revenues could be estimated higher and expenditures lower than realistic; payments could be changed from one fiscal year to another; asset sales could make up gaps. Overlooking gimmicks was widely believed preferable to damaging many desirable programs. Between the rock of sequestration and the hard place of reductions in the deficit, all that was left was appearances.

The most acute comment came from Representative Leon Panetta (later to become director of OMB and then White House Chief of Staff under President Clinton): "This place is reflective of the American people: they don't want taxes, they don't want cuts, and they don't want a deficit."[3]

The best that congressional leaders could do was to use humor to ward off depression. Among the kindest was Senator William Armstrong's (R-Colo.) "A package of golden gimmicks, a package of smoke and mirrors." Harsher was Senator James Exon's (D-Nebr.) characterization of the measure as "perverted, phony, unrealistic." Responding to Senate consideration of this purported deficit reduction, Senator Lawton Chiles (D-Fla.) bespoke the common understanding: "It's midway between the best we could do and the worst that could happen." Others, like Representative Martin Leath (D-Tex.), a member of the House Budget Committee, said, "We're about to pull the ultimate scam, and everybody's included."[4] The main lesson of the Gramm–Rudman–Hollings process may well be that while total trust is hard to come by, total mistrust makes budgeting impossible.

Why Didn't GRH Work?

Following regular budget procedure, failure to make changes merely sustains the status quo. The deficit might rise or fall because of external events, such as the condition of the economy, but not by deliberate governmental action. In order to bring the deficit center stage, the Gramm–Rudman–Hollings Act transformed inaction into a form of action: When Congress and the president did not work together to reach annual deficit reduction targets, GRH would mandate spending cuts.

While GRH established a fast track for the regular budget decisions, no one had reason to play along with them unless and until they knew whether their fa-

---

[3]New York Times, September 23, 1986, p. B8.

[4]New York Times, September 20, 1986, pp. 1 and 50; Oakland Tribune, September 10, 1986.

vorite programs would do better or worse in negotiation than in sequestration. The incentives all worked to promote delay. The speeded-up schedule provided in the act was not adhered to because no one wanted to bargain without knowing what the terms were. Would you?

The very same severity of GRH that was supposed to spur negotiation is bound to raise doubts about its workability. If all the consequences are so catastrophic, maybe no one will want to play. Each year the amount needed to meet the deficit reduction level became greater and greater, until finally in 1990 the whole effort was abandoned.

Despite its apparently mindless across-the-board cuts, GRH reflected a very strong sense of national policy priorities. That which could not be touched was holy— social security, Unemployment Compensation, WIC (Women, Infants and Children), child nutrition, medicaid, veterans' pensions and compensation, food stamps, and AFDC (Aid to Families with Dependent Children). Programs from which large numbers of people receive cash or equivalent value were exempt from cuts. Children, pregnant women, and veterans were favored. And programs, such as payments to doctors and other providers under medicare, under sequestration could be cut no more than 1 percent the first year or 2 percent over the remaining four years.

The trouble was that negative agreement on what could not be cut overwhelmed positive agreement on what could be cut. Getting all cuts essentially out of defense and general government (a category that goes by the bloodless title of "nondefense discretionary") was too tough and too foolhardy. Given the technical difference between fast-spending and slow-spending accounts of budget authority, moreover, a difference that has nothing to do with the desirability of programs, an awful lot of budget authority would have had to be sequestered to meet GRH's outlay targets. Reduction is one thing; destruction is another.

Apparent agreement on Gramm–Rudman–Hollings obscured the built-in disagreement that it embodied. What had happened was that growing polarization among political elites had produced agreement on extremism, that is, that Congress should make fundamental choices on total spending and revenues every year. But these self-same elites disagreed over what these levels should be, or how burdens and benefits should be divided. On the one hand, there was agreement that we should stand up like men and women and say our piece: "Yes, this is what the size of the budget should be, this is what the level of taxes should be, this is how spending and taxing burdens and benefits should be divided." The only problem was that while each of us could make a wonderful budget alone, together we cannot agree on how to make a budget for the rest of us. Thus, there is agreement over the desirability of having budget resolutions, but disagreement about their contents. The ability to govern depends ultimately on the capacity to agree; if Gramm–Rudman–Hollings has taught us anything, it is that no formula can substitute for political consensus.

THE ORIGINS OF THE 1990 BUDGET ENFORCEMENT ACT

The journey from GRH to the Budget Enforcement Act (BEA) evokes the grand themes of budgeting in our time—ideological dissensus so deep the opposing sides make minute measurements of outcomes, a deficit octopus so entangling that its grip can be loosened but not cut through, and a temporary truce based on the common desire of politicians to create a process that will not automatically stigmatize them as failures. Thus they moved from budget balance, which they could not achieve, to expenditure control, which they had a fighting chance to attain. But the deadlock over the budgetary base—the levels of revenue and expenditure and, within them, different proportions for different programs and taxpayers—remained.

The process of gaining agreement was tortuous and complex. As the deficit seemed increasingly out of control, and GRH targets, even with gimmicks, more and more implausible, a budget summit meeting took place between high level Republican administration officials and the Democratic congressional leadership. The 1990 summit, which followed a similar meeting in 1988, produced an agreement to cut $500 billion from the budgetary baseline deficit over the next five years. This agreement was rejected by a bipartisan majority in Congress, which replaced it with its own. As the difficult negotiations unfolded, it seemed increasingly clear that progress on the deficit would require direct action on substantive policy, not more formulas.

The hope was that if the prospect of a balanced budget were dangled before the American electorate by an agreement from on high, the bane of tax increases and spending cuts would be overawed by the glow of a leadership willing to sacrifice itself for the public interest. How could the president and his advisers believe this fairy tale? How could they not when every source of responsible opinion kept telling them that all that was required to make big dents in the deficit was political courage.

During the negotiations, the administration proposed and negotiators accepted a framework for dealing with the budget. This framework distinguished impacts of the economy on the budget from policy changes, left the gap between revenues and expenditures to determine itself, initiated different "tracks" for entitlement and discretionary spending, and explicitly separated defense and domestic discretionary spending. It has proven a useful way to discuss budgetary issues, and has been influential ever since.

The first issue was the budget outlook and the impact of the economy on the budget. In its 1991 budget, the administration had finessed the deficit with optimistic assumptions. As these assumptions started to look even less plausible, and President Bush came under increasing pressure internationally to do something about the deficit, forecasts were drastically revised upward. A huge sequester, enough to devastate the government, would be unavoidable without agreement. As negotiations dragged on, the numbers became more political. The more participants concentrated on deficit reduction, the less attention they seemed to pay to the baselines from which deficit reduction would need to take place. The baselines for future revenues and expenditures were of course critical, but once the target for savings was set, they receded as it were into the future, and perturbations such as oil price increases and probable future military expenditures were ignored.

The crucial question was less the real size of future deficits than the political feasibility of the size of deficit reduction. How much deficit reduction was enough? For the short term, the extreme-moderate view that $100 billion was the only deficit reduction worth making quickly went out of the window. Very early on,

CBO was asked how much of a hit in higher taxes and lower spending the economy could take in 1991 without going into a recession; the organization came up with a ballpark figure that would have been agreed to by most economists of around $50 billion. So for five years, with some further savings from saved interest and so on, a round figure of $500 billion seemed plausible.

Picking a target was only the beginning. Achieving that target would involve cutting expenditures or raising taxes or both, issues on which there was bitter division. But there was reason for hope that budget balance was within reach. Those who argue against the more excitable that tough issues should be postponed have one thing in their favor: sometimes conditions actually change. The incredibly swift collapse of communism in Eastern Europe and the Soviet Union opened up possibilities of greater reductions in the defense budget. At the same time the election of George Bush as president signified the replacement of a hard-nosed ideologue, Ronald Reagan, with a flexible and more moderate conservative who had, however, pledged not to raise taxes.

Previous tax policy had centered on reducing rates across the board, in an implicit social contract set in legislation in 1986 in which the lower rates were traded for fewer and/or lower tax preferences, the famous "loopholes" that enabled some taxpayers to greatly reduce their burdens. By contrast, President Bush sought to lower capital gains rates, mostly favoring the better off, so that the Democrats were able to raise the rich-versus-poor issue of tax equity. The agreement of 1986 had been breached, so that Democrats were now free to attack the rates themselves, and demand that the president rescind his no tax pledge: Either he would have to increase taxes or face an impossibly large sequester. The president gave in and agreed to support revenue increases, provided they were accompanied by expenditure reductions and reform of the entitlement expenditure processes.

The leading members of the Bush administration believed that the deficit was a great blight on the country because it showed that government could not control itself. Responsibility, to them, meant supporting governmental institutions by showing that they worked. Part of their view of the deficit problem, shared by any number of business people and editorialists, was that the American people were consuming too much and producing too little. They bought the economic argument that, other things not intervening too much, a lesser rate of savings would mean a lower rate of investment. If the people's representatives were unwilling to reduce expenditure to the lower level desired by the Bush administration, the people would have to support their government at the level to which it had, for better or worse, become accustomed: with new taxes.

The Republican negotiators' ideal agreement would be one that taxed consumption most heavily, especially consumption of undesirable commodities such as liquor and tobacco. They wanted to charge the elderly more for consumption of health services. In return for the unpalatability of taxes in general, the administration wanted to reduce the taxes on business by cutting capital gains substantially and subsidizing small businesses. Their hope was that a large increase in consumption taxes would pave the way for easier credit, higher exports, and capital spending, and thus not dampen economic activity, a position in accord with that of many economists.

Early on, Ways and Means Committee staff devised a format for the Budget Summit, and CBO and Joint Committee on Taxation staff provided support so that congressional participants could cost out, overnight, any proposals and, for the Democratic party members at least, the distributional consequences of revenue measures among richer, poorer, and middle-class individuals. Estimates came back quickly, as faxes arrived from Andrews Air Force Base where the later stages of the Summit were held (to avoid, so they said, the distractions of Washington and to keep the meetings down to size). This was a gain in calculating ability but not necessarily in agreement. Allegations that certain parts of the proposed package were unfair (i.e., inegalitarian) brought heated denials on the Republican side. Nevertheless, equality was an important value from beginning to end, institutionalized, as it was, in Democratic demand and available formulas.

What happened? No agreement could be reached at all on capital gains or the infamous income tax "bubble," but both sides compromised on excise taxes on tobacco, alcohol, gasoline, and luxury goods, to some extent offset by some income tax changes, clearly a regressive package. Where was the rest of the deficit reduction to come from?

What about entitlement cuts? It was agreed to cut unemployment benefits, farm support, and medicare (health care for the elderly). Location of these cuts tells us that budgeters were looking both for big cuts and for programs that were vulnerable for specific reasons. These cuts were augmented by increases in user fees, which after some hesitation were counted as mandatory expenditures rather than revenues, thus benefiting Democrats (leaving less to cut in programs they wanted to defend) and discomfiting Republicans (who wanted to boost the revenue hit with relatively noncontroversial items).

Next was the issue of discretionary programs, both defense and nondefense. Both sides assumed big cuts in defense would be possible because of the end of the Cold War, but agreement stopped there. Republican negotiators wanted fewer cuts in defense spending, but some wanted cuts in discretionary domestic spending. The Democrats, especially the appropriators, wanted increases. They argued that the domestic sector under the appropriations process had been paying for deficit reduction for years; that vital national needs had been neglected; and that small increases for domestic programs were practically nothing compared to getting a fair contribution from entitlements. In this they had a quiet ally in Budget Director Darman. The administration had lots of initiatives, such as space exploration and other scientific research—all of them discretionary. The appropriators' goal could be viewed as paying for those initiatives (which the committees might otherwise deep-six) by cuts in entitlements. That doesn't sound so bad. Darman told the appropriators he would give them their increases, but in order to avoid flack from his right, they would have to let him manipulate the baselines so it would look as if there were no growth, which he did. In fact, the Summit deal allowed at least a 4 percent and perhaps as much as a 6 percent real increase in outlays for the next two years.

The real disagreement was whether the Democrats could try for bigger domestic increases by cutting defense even more. Democrats wanted "caps" for discretionary spending in total; to protect its priorities, the administration wanted separate figures for defense, international affairs, and domestic spending. In the Summit agreement, as well as the final package, they compromised on separate caps for 1990–1992 and combined caps for 1993–1994. The reason for this division was to give whoever won the 1992 presidential election a chance to make changes.

In the end, after cuts in interest payments had been assumed, discretionary programs were reduced the most, about $180 billion, tax increases accounted for about $134 billion, and entitlement cuts looked after the rest, about $119 billion.

When the agreed-on deficit reduction plan was presented in the House of Representatives early in October 1990, the unexpected result was instantaneous and total defeat. Economic conservatives vehemently rejected the plan. Led by Minority Whip Newt Gingrich of Georgia (who became Speaker of the House in 1995), they felt left out of the whole process, alone and set adrift to face likely defeat in the midterm elections. They had not yet reconciled themselves to the president's abandonment of his no new tax pledge. Besides, a lot of Republicans had no more interest than Democrats in a plan that would get $30 billion in medicare savings from the pockets of the most powerful group in America, the elderly. Their reaction makes it easier to understand that one lawmaker's budget savings may be a lot of citizens' higher spending.

Once Republicans would not provide the minimum level of support, Democrats felt free to vote against the plan as well. On the theories that anything was better than Gramm–Rudman and that some agreement was necessary to show they could govern, the Democratic leadership had accepted a package far less progressive, particularly due to gasoline taxes, than their troops could buy, in the hope that if talks broke down, an alternative more progressive plan might prove attractive to voters.

Since all concerned recognized that deficit reduction, or at least Gramm–Rudman avoidance, still remained a task to be accomplished, negotiations continued. Defeat of the Summit agreement had been a double disaster for the president. Not only was it embarrassing, it also put him on the defensive in the next round of negotiations. And it put the conservative (mostly House) Republicans on the outside looking in. Consequently, he would have to rely mostly on Democratic votes to get it passed. As a result the new package would be more "Democratic" than the defeated agreement, with more egalitarian tax provisions. From the moment the Summit package was defeated, the issue was not whether, but how and by how much the next package would be more progressive.

The final agreement was contained in the Omnibus Budget Reconciliation Act of 1990. Reconciliation does not have to take place every year, but it is a powerful mechanism to gain and enforce agreement on two major elements of the budget—entitlements and taxes. The 1990 reconciliation act demonstrated just how complex these categories are, and also how once packages are opened up, all kinds of extraneous items make their way into them. Beyond the large changes, such as those in the tax code there were other little itty-bitty changes, barely noticeable except to those directly involved, but that summed to a substantial amount. They altered what was taxable (the unemployment insurance surtax), or who was taxable (extending social security taxes to state and local employees without other pension coverage), or how much was taxable (upping interest rates for late corporate tax payments), or changing the rules (such as insurance company amortization) so that more income was taxable. Amid a very simple political battle over distribution, tax policy remains as complicated as ever.

But even as efforts were made to revise revenues, others, amounting to as much as the income tax increases, were deliberately designed to reduce them. Some of these were barely known to the general public, such as credits for orphan drugs. There were also credits for children, as part of an unannounced children-oriented family policy, and similar provisions for credit for health insurance for low-income families.

Tax changes blurred into entitlement changes. Expenditure cuts and revenue enhancements are interchangeable but they affect different groups of people—the former impact providers, while the latter come in higher charges for beneficiaries. The largest entitlement target was medicare: Congress not only radically scaled down the total amount of medicare savings, but also shifted its emphasis from charges to beneficiaries to cuts in payments to providers. But given the proven ability of providers to shift costs to beneficiaries or to withold services, however, the distinction might not be maintained. Similar attempts to gain painless savings from medicaid (health care for the poor), such as getting discounts on pharmaceuticals, might also prove illusory. Meanwhile, medicaid was expanded through coverage of the most vulnerable elements in the population—children, the mentally ill, and the frail elderly. And medicare added payments for mammography screening, which might produce savings in the future.

Tax changes, entitlement changes, baseline changes—all suggested that as the agreement on deficit reduction wended its way through the Summit and congressional budget processes there was stronger egalitarian sentiment. But would the agreement hold? Enter the Budget Enforcement Act (BEA) of 1990, Title XIII of OBRA.

THE BUDGET ENFORCEMENT ACT OF 1990

Before new procedures can take place, it is necessary to do something about the old way. The first thing done by the BEA, therefore, was to raise the fiscal year 1991 GRH deficit target (actual 1990) way up to $327 billion (and these figures were adjusted upward in fiscal 1991 by the Bush administration, as the law allows). Why were these targets so large? The short answer is (a) recession, (b) the savings and loans bailout, and (c) surpluses in the social security trust funds would no longer count toward reducing the deficit. We know that recessions increase deficits by lowering revenues and increasing spending, but why do something voluntarily to make the deficit look much larger?

Proponents of balance believe that Congress and the president (the politicians) will not do enough unless they feel threatened. The larger the deficit, presumably, the greater the threat. This antipolitician sentiment also explains why they refuse to publicize the deficit in terms of proportions of GNP but insist on absolute numbers. Some $200+ billion is enough to frighten anyone, whereas under 3 percent of GNP sounds (and, in my opinion, is) a modest amount. The politicians also wanted to reassure retirees that social security was safe from budget cuts.

As a matter of economics, there are two currently popular ways to analyze the budget. The first economic approach emphasizes aggregate demand. By borrowing and spending the proceeds, the government increases demand for goods, thereby raising employment (good) or prices (bad). The second approach emphasizes savings: Government borrowing reduces total national savings, leaving less money to be invested; if we borrowed less we could invest more, the theory is, and hence the economy would grow more.

Neither approach would count the savings and loans (S&L) bailout, which would supposedly cost more than $100 billion in 1991.[5] The bailout, much as we may resent it, was necessary to preserve our financial system. Not spending the money would hardly increase savings because bank failures don't increase investment. Spending the money doesn't increase demand; instead it preserves the values people already have in their accounts. The S&L bailout, prayerfully, was a one-time thing. According to figures in the Fiscal Year 1996 budget, deposit insurance cost $2.4 billion in 1992, $28 billion in 1993, and $7.6 billion in 1994.[6] Usual accounting practice, as followed in regard to sending United States forces into the Persian Gulf in 1990 (following the Iraqi invasion of Kuwait), is to keep these off-budget. Since money was to be returned in part to the federal government in later years, deficits would be artificially diminished in return for making deficits artificially larger in the first few years.

Over the next five years, it was estimated that social security would spend $1.5 trillion and collect $300 billion in surplus taxes. Demand managers say the social security surplus has an immediate economic effect, and should not be ignored. Those who focus on savings, however, want to increase the social security surplus. They say we should treat the surplus not as income this year, but as savings for later social security expenses, when the baby boom generation retires.

If Congress and the president had adopted the demand managers' perspective, they would have kept savings and loans out and social security surpluses in the totals. Then, even with a more plausible (lower) economic forecast, the deficit would fall to around 1 percent of GNP, comparable to that of Germany or Japan, by 1994. It would indeed balance by 1996 if not before. But they adopted the savers' perspective on social security, taking its surpluses out, while keeping the S&L bailout in the deficit calculation. The S&L costs ballooned immediate deficits, on top of which the social security decision raised the 1994 deficit by $87 billion.[7] At baseball games, the hawkers say you can't tell the players without a scorecard. How much more true this is for the deficit!

This paroxysm of accounting "responsibility" created two problems. First, opponents of removing social security from the deficit feared that it would create an inviting target for those who wish to appropriate social security surpluses for their own preferred policy purposes. The House and Senate, therefore, adopted an array of provisions to try to prevent such raids.

---

[5] House Budget Committee Summary, October 27, 1990, p. 52. At the end of the 1990s, there were widespread failures of savings and loans banks, exceeding the capacity of the federal insurance agency and requiring a huge bailout action by the federal government.

[6] *United States Budget Fiscal Year 1996*, Analytical Perspectives, Table 1.6: Adjusted Structural Deficit, p. 7.

[7] These comments are adapted from Joseph White, "Better News Than They Think," published in the *San Diego Union* on October 7, 1990.

As things worked out, the S&L costs became relatively small and their impact on the deficit was slight. As for the social security issue, Allen Schick comments:

> Because social security is so large, excluding it from the deficit impairs the budget's utility as a measure of fiscal impact. How can the budget impact on the economy be assessed when one-fifth of the government's revenues and outlays are excluded? In fact, social security is almost always included in both government and news references to the budget. By law, social security is excluded; in practice, it is included.[8]

More important, negotiators had to find some way around the optimistic economic forecast, which they had adopted to make up for their social security score-keeping but which, by not coming true, would put them right back in sequester land. For both Bush and congressional leaders, 1990's pain would be worthless if it did not at least result in peace through the 1992 election.

Therefore the president was legally required to alter the hoped-for deficit target each year in order to account for changes in the economy, changes in budgetary terms, and changes in estimates of the cost of federal credit programs. That is, the deficit reduction targets were not really targets—thereby abolishing, at least for 1990–1992, the deficit sequester.

In reality, the old Gramm–Rudman sequester, designed to force action to reduce the deficit, was replaced by two much more sensible sequesters designed (a) to keep Congress from increasing the deficit, thereby enforcing the new package, and (b) to maintain the status quo by making proposers pay for spending increases and revenue decreases. Separate limits were set out for budget authority and outlays for defense, the international arena, and for domestic discretionary spending for the years between 1990 and 1992, after which these merged to a single category called total discretionary spending. Should expenditures within the relevant category be deemed, after the end of session, to exceed their target, the accounts for that category in the following fiscal year would be reduced across the board to make up the difference. There were further complications, but that was the basic idea: The offending category pays the fine.

The second new sequester applied to decreases in revenue or increases in entitlement expenditure enacted into law. This idea of "offsets" had a precedent in the "Byrd rule" in the Senate, according to which, spending or revenue measures might not be passed that would increase future deficits.[9] This PAYASYOUGO (later known as PAYGO) sequestration had to occur within 15 calendar days of congressional adjournment and on the same day as enforcement of limits on discretionary spending and overall deficit targets. Thus there was one sequestration for deficit targets, another for discretionary spending, and a third for new entitlement spending or revenue reduction. All of these provisions were further buttressed by elaborating on previous Gramm–Rudman points of order, designed to prevent offending legislation from being passed in the first place. It should also be noted that the entitlement sequester followed the GRH pattern in that the exemptions from sequestration for poor people's programs were still in place.

---

[8]Allen Schick, *The Federal Budget: Politics, Policy, Process* (Washington, D.C.: Brookings Institution, 1995), p. 28.

[9]Schick, *The Federal Budget*, p. 85.

As part of a long process of change, the Budget Enforcement Act contained provisions on federal credit reform. It not only called on the federal government to state the cost of loans and loan guarantees but required that, except for entitlements and the credit programs of agricultural price supports, there had to be appropriations to cover outlays defined as "the long-term costs . . . on the net present value basis. . . ."[10] This required calculating the cost to the federal government of borrowing to acquire the funds that were being lent in guaranteed loans in relation to the amount the borrower pays back. This is a positive and important change.

Government sponsored enterprises (GSEs), which are established by the federal government but operated and owned by private individuals, have long been the object of suspicion. Such entities include the Federal Home Loan Bank system, the Student Loan Marketing Association, the Farm Credit system, the Federal National Mortgage Association, and the Federal Home Loan Mortgage Corporation. By the end of April 1991, the Treasury Department and CBO were required to report to Congress on the GSEs' financial soundness. The savings and loan debacle had made everyone more cautious, thus giving force to concern over the last several decades about the exposure of federal finances to failures of GSEs. The BEA required reports on GSEs and federal credit activities in the president's budget.

These substantive changes in the budgetary process, partially eliminating but mostly adding new procedures on top of old, as has become customary, were the product of experience under GRH. This experience had made its impact on observers as well as on members of the executive and legislative branches. Believing that general sequesters do not work, both because these tend to be too large and because the penalty does not fit the crime, they had made them more numerous, more precise, and more responsible.

The BEA restored budgeting's long-term focus and substituted real policy change for Gramm–Rudman's hostage game. It used, rather than fought against, our political system's designed difficulty of action. It tried to limit scorekeeping games, and extended oversight to areas such as credit and GSEs.

What the BEA did not do is prevent the economy from destabilizing the budget. Entitlement spending that rises because of changes in the economy, or because of aging of the population or other demographic reasons, or for anything and everything outside of legislative enactment was not covered. Subjecting any change in entitlements to PAYASYOUGO principles would be much more powerful. But this would mean that entitlements would not be total entitlements but only quasi-entitlements, in that full payment could not be guaranteed.

On the political level there was not so much compromise as unspoken agreement to resolve the main charge against all politicians—that they cannot govern because they cannot balance the budget—in the two ways intractable problems are usually solved: (1) by doing something about them, that is, reducing the deficit and (2) by redefining them so they become solvable. Essentially the politicians moved away from a deficit reduction enforcement process to a spending control enforcement process. Inasmuch as objectives may be inferred from legislation, the goal of the budgetary process was to keep spending down to current policy, liberally defined, rather than to specific dollar limits. The BEA switched from deficit to expenditure control.

---

[10]Joseph White, "Better News Than They Think," p. 8.

Perhaps the BEA should be called the revenge of the appropriators. It gave them at least in the short term fairly generous spending caps, and protected these against all comers, whether external (e.g., the economy) or internal (e.g., direct spending). As much of the budget total as possible was put under preset, automatic controls. Like the economic stabilizers that kick in when unemployment grows large, these protections for appropriations were designed to create lulls in the budget battles so that the appropriators would not have to refight the same battles over and over and over again. The onus was against changing priorities by saying so through direct legislation.

Other informed observers expressed amazement that a Democratic Congress allowed OMB to gain so much power over the budget by deciding such seemingly arcane but vital matters as what item of expenditure fit under which spending cap, or how much program costs had risen due to factors out of Congress's control.[11] As we know, this power was granted because it is essential to budgetary control and the courts have ruled that only an executive agency can perform this function. And the Democratic budget professionals were not, in private, concerned.[12]

Both the House and Senate Budget Committees issued long descriptions and analyses of the process changes. The rules had changed so much and so often that making them had become part of budgeting. To get the feeling, here is one such process change.

> *Estimating adjustments.* There is a very small BA allowance and a larger outlay allowance provided on an "as used" basis. They differ from the other "as used" adjustments in that they are not intended to be used under congressional scorekeeping. . . . Imagine that appropriation bills meet their caps using congressional scorekeeping but breach them using OMB scorekeeping; if the breach is within the allowance, there would be no sequester.[13]

Technicalities include a series of "estimating adjustments" to bridge the inevitable small differences between congressional and OMB scorekeeping. Note also that while Senate and House do not follow precisely the same rules, the thrust of the major proposals in the BEA, especially the three sequesters, was expected to compel similar behavior.

THE PARTS VERSUS THE WHOLE

Through the thicket of budget provisions, piled helter-skelter atop one another, there comes the recognizable outline of disputes that have pitted institutions in the budgetary process against each other as far back as anyone can remember. If

---

[11]Susan F. Rasky, "Substantial Power on Spending Is Shifted from Congress to Bush," *The New York Times,* National Edition, October 30, 1990, pp. A1, A13.

[12]Joe White, Conversations with Appropriations, Ways and Means, and Budget staff.

[13]Richard Kogan, "The Budget Enforcement Act of 1990: A Technical Explanation," November 1, 1990, typescript, pp. 6–7. Senate Budget's typescript on the "Budget Enforcement Act of 1990" is supplemented by CRS Report 90–520 GOV: "Budget Enforcement Act of 1990: Brief Summary," by Edward Davis and Robert Keith, November 5, 1990.

one were to ask the members and chairs of the House and Senate Appropriations Committees how they felt about their part in the budgetary process, they would undoubtedly answer "Hard done by." Why? Because, they would reply in classical tones, their authority was not commensurate with their responsibility, especially because presidents had gone too far away to share responsibility and budget committees had come too close for the appropriators to exercise what they feel is their rightful autonomy. The budgetary process had come into deserved disrepute. In the classical process of the 1950s and earlier decades, presidents submitted budgets that accorded with their policy preferences, adding a gaming factor to allow the House Appropriations Committee, through its subcommittees, to cut at the margins, knowing full well the Senate Appropriations Committee would act as an appeals court, making selective additions so that in the end almost all the players got most of what they wanted. That is, the appropriators were second-guessers, marking up or down the bids proposed by the president and the authorizing committees. However, this budget minuet depended on the participants being close enough to begin with so they could play their appointed roles: There cannot be a second guess without a first.

In an age of budgetary dissensus, by contrast, presidents have maintained responsibility to their party and their own preferences but have behaved irresponsibly, as appropriators in both parties see it, by presenting budgets so far from what is likely to pass muster in Congress that they are pronounced (as we know) dead on arrival. Understanding as well the sense of the medieval dictum that one prince nearby is worse than many princes far away, the appropriators have not taken kindly to the efforts of budget committees to control their operations. Members of appropriations committees would rather be constrained, if they must, by a president concerned mostly with the size of spending than by many representatives and senators with detailed changes they wish to enforce. Little as the appropriators liked to observe the outlays of entitlement programs grow ever larger ("Look ma, no hands!"), they liked even less being told by budget committees through reconciliation orders (yes, instructions are orders) that they must make up for out of control entitlements by cutting their own appropriations authority far more than they thought desirable. Nor were the appropriators enthralled to observe deeply divisive ideological debates over budget resolutions, which may have sounded fine to those who like abstract discussions, but which, in their view, brought Congress into disrepute by forbidding the bargains and compromises that might have added up to the appearance of responsible budgeting.

The BEA tried to change all of this. While it could not create ideological and policy agreement where it did not exist, it did take away the necessity of making believe there is such agreement, thereby demonstrating once more that Congress is not what it was never supposed to be, a unified body. To begin with, presidents were now required to submit a budget within the ballpark of existing past agreements as memorialized in multiyear instructions about levels of taxing and spending. Therefore, for the subsequent five years the appropriators could look forward to the ancient pleasure of working off presidential budgets, marking them up here, marking them down there, as they used to do in what they think of as better days. Moreover, the appropriators succeeded in getting an additional $37 billion to spread around their part of the budget so as to lubricate the joints and ease the pain of making adjustments as they were wont to do in days of old. Nor could budget committees tell appropriators what to do. For one thing, the appropriators themselves had worked out agreements on what they are supposed to do, thus usurping the place taken in the bad old days by budget resolutions. For another, problems that arise from shortfalls in revenue or overages in entitlements would be dealt with where they occurred; only where appropriations themselves departed from agreed-on guidelines would there be points of order and sequestration provisions to restrain them by passing out the pain within their bailiwick, a principle they could accept provided it is accepted by others. Oh yes, this nonsense about meeting some artificial deficit target regardless of whether the world is at war or at peace and the economy is booming or busting has been done away with. In the future, the appropriators devoutly hoped, each part of the process would be held responsible for what it does or does not do and the rest of the world will have to take care of itself.

In order to make them play their assigned parts, presidents, through the OMB, were given stronger procedural powers. It is they who must submit a certain kind of budget according to their own calculations, alter their budget proposals according to the state of the economy, and whose findings must or must not trigger sequestrations of various kinds. This is a lot of procedural clout. It could be that some far-seeing budget director will attempt to use these procedural powers to bargain with the appropriations committees at every stage of the process, not just the stage of formulating the budget or of certifying sequestration. But Congress has the means, namely the power of the purse, to compel OMB (and through it the president) to back down. In following the thrust and maneuver of budgeting, it is all too easy to imagine that skill is all (or most) that matters. Skill counts but votes count more, especially in an age of ideological dissensus.

The BEA also relieved the president and Congress of the necessity of responding to external events that cause downward perturbations in revenue or upward alterations in expenditure, thus bringing the budget way out of balance. Held more tightly responsible for the effects they cause directly, the appropriators were relieved from responsibility for what they could not help immediately. If we assume that the balance of political responsibility has been shifted too far toward government and not enough toward the citizenry, holding government harmless is a good idea. If we think that government should bear its burden of the cost of change, or that everyone has to deal with forces they cannot control, then these hold-harmless provisions are a bad idea.

THE CLINTON BUDGET OF 1993

The election of Bill Clinton in 1992 meant that both executive and legislature were in Democratic hands. It might be thought that since a Democratic president was working with a Democratic majority in Congress, there would no longer be an adversarial relationship and the president would be able to count on support for his choices. Not so. The Democratic party was by no means cohesive. It was split between those who hold to a fiscally conservative philosophy, whose primary agenda is to cut spending to bring down the deficit, and those supporting a socially liberal philosophy to roll back the Reagan revolution and increase public spending to deal with the country's social ills.[14] Even within this group there was a split between "old-style" Democrats, primarily concerned with social equity, and "new" Democrats, who put priority on a stronger economy, greater efficiency, and reform of public programs. In addition, members of Congress had their own interests stemming from their constituencies, running the gamut from the unabashed pork of public works projects to protection and promotion of state and local economies. Superimposed on these concerns was Clinton's own agenda, which included an industrial policy of sorts, scientific and educational investment, and health care reform.

On taking office President Clinton was keen to rekindle economic growth, as a necessity to achieve his agenda for human investment. He therefore proposed an economic stimulus package as a supplementary to the Fiscal Year 1993 budget. But the package was defeated in Congress. The prospect of huge deficits could not be ignored. In January 1993, CBO was predicting a current year deficit of $310 billion and the administration forecast was even higher (see Table 6.3). The deficit had to take priority.

The budget had not been a central element in Clinton's campaign, which had emphasized change, political reform, economic growth and job creation, investment in human resources, and health care reform.[15] In his State of the Union address, Clinton declared there was nothing intrinsically good about deficit reduction alone, though it was necessary to reverse the trend toward a government that was unable to act because the burden of debt servicing prevented development of programs to help people. But he could not ignore the deficit. As Allen Schick explains

> With the budget awash in red ink, Clinton was barred by both the politics and the rules of budgeting from proposing actions that would add to the deficit. It was not tenable for him to insist that coveted initiatives be funded despite the budget's dire condition. Nor could he wish away the deficit the way Ronald Reagan did—with rosy economic

Table 6.3   Congressional Budget Office Deficit Projections

	1990	1991	1992	1993	1994	1995	1996	1997	1998	1999	2000
January 1992	220	269	352	327	260	194	178	226			
Summer 1992				331	268	244	254	290			
January 1993		270	290	310	291	284	287	319	357		
September 1993					253	196	190	198	200		
January 1994			290	255	223	171	166	182	180	204	
August 1994					202	162	176	193	197	231	
January 1995					203	176	207	224	222	253	
April 1995						177	211	232	231	256	276

(in billions of dollars)

Source: Congressional Budget Office, *The Economic and Budget Outlook,* 1992 to 1995, and Update for April 1995. The actual deficit for Fiscal Year 1995 was later assessed at $164 billion.

---

[14]John Brummett, *Highwire: The Education of Bill Clinton* (New York: Hyperion, 1994), pp. 92–93.

[15]*Congressional Quarterly Weekly Report,* November 14, 1992, p. 3631.

forecasts that overestimated future revenue and underestimated the program cuts or tax increases needed to close the budget gap. . . .

He could not risk discrediting his new administration by pretending that the deficit would go away by itself. And he could not assume that journalists who had become increasingly skeptical about budget promises and more knowledgeable about the budget's arithmetic than they had been when Reagan came to Washington, would ignore bad news.[16]

The immediate outlook for the deficit was gloomy. For Fiscal Year 1992 the deficit had set a record at $290 billion, although this was far below the January 1992 projections of the Bush administration ($400 billion) and CBO ($357 billion). On going out of office Bush had predicted a deficit of $327 billion for Fiscal Year 1993, and while CBO's estimate was less at $310 billion, the figure was still daunting. For Fiscal Year 1994, CBO estimated only a slight fall, to $291 billion, and believed that forecast improvements in the economy would reduce this figure only marginally.[17](See Table 6.4.)

Clinton responded first by trying to raise revenues. Top tax rates would rise from 31 percent to 36 percent, and those with incomes over $250,000 would pay a 10 percent surcharge. There were also increases in corporate taxes and increased taxes on high-income social security recipients. According to Allen Schick, increased taxes on business and high-income recipients would account for more than five-sixths of additional revenues sought by the president, whose election campaign had ruled out increased taxes for the middle classes.[18] In addition, the president proposed a broad-based energy tax (BTU), initially estimated to bring in $80.6 billion.[19] But to bring down the budget deficit from an estimated 4.1 percent of GDP in Fiscal Year 1993 to about 3.2 percent in Fiscal Year 1998, against a baseline taking into account inflation and expected growth in entitlements, would require $447 billion in deficit reduction. Tax increases were not enough.

Table 6.4   The Gap Between Revenues and Expenditures, 1985–1994

			(in billions of dollars)			
	Receipts	Percentage GDP	Outlays	Percentage GDP	Deficit	Percentage GDP
1985	734.1	18.5	946.4	23.9	212.3	5.4
1990	1,031.3	18.8	1,252.7	22.9	221.4	4.0
1991	1,054.3	18.6	1,323.4	23.3	269.2	4.7
1992	1,090.5	18.4	1,380.9	23.3	290.4	4.9
1993	1,153.5	18.4	1,408.7	22.5	255.1	4.1
1994	1,257.7	19.0	1,460.9	22.0	203.2	3.1

Source: United Stated Budget, Fiscal Year 1996, Historical Tables: Table 1.4, *Receipts, Outlays and Surpluses or Deficits by Fund Group, 1934–2000,* pp. 19–20. Numbers have been rounded.

[16]Schick, *The Federal Budget,* p. 3.

[17]Congressional Budget Office, January 1993.

[18]Schick, *The Federal Budget,* p. 6.

[19]Karl O'Lessker, "The Clinton Budget for Fiscal Year 1994: Taking Aim at the Deficit," *Public Budgeting and Finance,* Vol. 13, No. 2, Summer 1993, p. 13.

In 1985, mandatory (entitlement) and discretionary spending had been almost even as proportions of the federal budget. By 1993, mandatory spending took up half the budget, while discretionary spending had dropped to 38.5 percent. The trend was unmistakable: By the year 2000, it was estimated that entitlements would take up well over half the budget, while discretionary expenditures would be less than 29 percent. Entitlements, it seemed, were eating up the budget.(see Table 6.5)

Why were entitlement programs growing so rapidly? The fastest growth was occurring in three of the largest programs: social security, medicare, and medicaid (see Table 6.6). When Bill Clinton took office, he was facing, according to CBO baselines, mandatory outlays of $816 billion, of which $319 were for social security, $167 billion for medicare, and $92 billion for medicaid.[20] In the medium term baseline budget projections, these figures swelled to a total of over $1 trillion.

Table 6.5   Discretionary and Mandatory Expenditures, 1985–1994

	(in billions of dollars)					
	Discretionary			Mandatory		
	Total Outlays	Percentage Budget	Percentage GDP	Total Outlays	Percentage Budget	Percentage GDP
1985	416.2	44.0	10.5	433.4	45.8	10.9
1990	501.7	40.1	9.2	603.5	48.2	11.0
1991	534.8	40.4	9.4	633.5	47.9	11.2
1992	535.9	38.8	9.1	684.8	49.6	11.6
1993	542.5	38.5	8.7	704.8	50.0	11.3
1994	545.6	37.3	8.2	750.2	51.3	11.3

Source: United States Budget, Fiscal Year 1996, Historical Tables: Table 8.1, *Outlays by Budget Enforcement Act Category, 1962–2000,* p. 95; Table 8.3, *Percentage Distribution of Outlays by Budget Enforcement Act Category, 1962–2000;* and Table 8.4, *Outlays by Budget Enforcement Act Category as Percentages of GDP, 1962–2000,* p. 98.

Table 6.6   Fastest Growing Mandatory Expenditures, 1985–1994

	(in billions of dollars)				
	Social Security	Medicare	Medicaid	Income Security	Veterans
1985	186.4	64.1	22.7	109.1	15.9
1990	246.5	95.8	41.1	123.6	15.9
1991	266.8	102.0	52.5	144.6	17.3
1992	285.2	116.2	67.8	168.8	18.5
1993	302.0	127.8	75.8	176.0	19.3
1994	316.9	141.8	82.0	178.4	20.3

Source: United Stated Budget, Fiscal Year 1996, Historical Tables: Table 8.5, *Outlays for Mandatory and Related Programs, 1962–2000,* pp. 99–103.

[20]Ibid., pp. 46, 49.

Even if discretionary expenditures were kept below the caps, such expenditures would result in a deficit of nearly $300 billion in the coming year.

The Clinton budget lowered mandatory expenditures through both revenue and expenditure measures. By repealing the medicare tax cap and increasing the taxable portion of social security benefits, he gained nearly $45 billion in deficit reduction; reductions in medicare growth would amount to nearly $56 billion, and in other entitlements to a further $35 or so billion. Altogether the mandatory portion of the budget would have yielded nearly one-third of the deficit reduction over five years.

Discretionary expenditures continued to be constrained within the BEA caps (see Table 6.7). For the first three years, there were separate caps for defense, international, and discretionary expenditures. These caps were adhered to, although some adjustments were made in accordance with the provisions of the BEA.[21] In 1993, the three caps were replaced by a single cap on discretionary expenditures that was extended an additional three years (from 1995 to 1998). The single cap placed defense and domestic expenditures in direct competition.

Could the president fund his priorities by cutting defense? By the passage of the BEA in 1990, defense expenditures were already declining in terms of their share in the budget (from a peak of about 28 percent in 1987 to about 24 percent). After a brief increase in 1991, defense spending had continued to drop in nominal terms. By 1993, defense made up about one-fifth of the budget. On the other hand, domestic expenditures whose share in the budget had dropped during the 1980s increased after 1990 and by 1993 were about 16 percent. Clinton continued this trend, cutting defense outlays and increasing domestic spending. The five-year figures showed that by 1998, defense and domestic discretionary spending would be about even (see Table 6.8).

But only so much could be taken from defense, and in any case the president had his own priorities he wished to forward. It would, therefore, be necessary to make adjustments within domestic discretionary spending. The president was working within a zero sum game.[22] CBO analyses had shown that if full adjustment of programs were made for inflation, the caps would be exceeded.[23] The administration had initiated a wide-ranging survey of federal expenditures, "Reinventing Government" or "The National Performance Review," including a decision to eliminate over a quarter of a million federal employees. Accordingly, Clinton's Fiscal Year 1994 budget made room for program additions in the areas of crime prevention and education and training through off-setting cuts in over one hundred domestic programs.

The initial Clinton budget represented an amalgam of competing proposals that nonetheless added up to a fairly moderate program. The deficit would be reduced as a percentage of GDP, though not eliminated; taxes would be increased but primarily for high income taxpayers; the rates of the fastest growing entitlements would be slowed; the spending caps would be extended and tightened to

---

[21]See Dale Oak, "An Overview of Adjustments to the Budget Enforcement Act Discretionary Spending Caps, *Public Budgeting and Finance*, Vol. 15, Fall 1995, pp. 35–37, for an overview of the caps and explanation of the adjustment provisions.

[22]Lance LeLoup and Patrick Taylor, "The Policy Constraints of Deficit Reduction: President Clinton's 1995 Budget," *Public Budgeting and Finance*, Vol. 14, Summer 1994 p. 6.

[23]See Congressional Budget Office, January 1993.

Table 6.7 Discretionary Spending Limits as Originally Enacted

(in millions of dollars)

| | | Budget Enforcement Act of 1990 | | | | | Omnibus Budget Reconciliation Act of 1993 | | |
| | | Fiscal Year | | | | | | | |
		1991	1992	1993	1994	1995	1996	1997	1998
Total discretionary	BA	491,718	503,443	511,485	510,800	517,700	519,142	528,079	530,639
	Outlays	514,360	524,944	533,986	534,800	540,800	547,263	547,346	547,870
Discretionary categories									
Domestic	BA	182,700	191,300	198,300					
	Outlays	198,100	210,100	221,700					
International	BA	20,100	20,500	21,400					
	Outlays	18,600	19,100	19,600					
Defense	BA	288,918	291,643	291,785					
	Outlays	297,660	295,744	292,686					

Sources: Section 13111 of the Budget Enforcement Act of 1990, and section 12(b)(1) of House Concurrent Resolution 64 (One Hundred Third Congress). Reproduced in Dale P. Oak, *An Overview of Adjustment to the Budget Enforcement Act Discretionary Spending Caps, Public Budgeting and Finance,* Vol. 15, Summer 1995, pp. 35–37.

Table 6.8 Outlays For Discretionary Programs, 1985–1994

	Defense		International		Domestic	
(in billions of dollars)						
	Current	Constant	Current	Constant	Current	Constant
1985	253.1	261.5	17.4	18.2	145.7	154.1
1990	300.1	273.3	19.1	16.9	182.5	161.8
1991	319.7	281.4	19.7	16.8	195.4	166.2
1992	302.6	253.3	19.2	16.0	214.2	178.4
1993	292.4	238.2	21.6	17.6	228.5	185.5
1994	282.2	221.1	20.8	16.3	242.6	191.1

Source: United States Budget, Fiscal Year 1996, Historical Statistics: Table 8.7, *Outlays for Discretionary Programs, 1962–2000*, pp. 109–13; *Outlays for Discretionary Programs in Constant (Fiscal Year 1987) Dollars, 1962–2000*, pp. 114–18.

freeze the rate of discretionary spending; defense cuts would once again pay for expansions in certain domestic programs; the president would gain at least some of his own human investment agenda; and the environmentalists would support conservation through the broad-based energy tax. Even if some of the assumptions and projections turned out to be doubtful (e.g., revenue estimates, health cost savings, lower debt costs), the president's budget for Fiscal Year 1994 was a coherent proposal based on credible assumptions.

But the test of a budget is not in its reasonableness in the eyes of its framers, but whether it can be passed. There was little possibility of Republican support. What about the Democrats? The critical measure was the reconciliation bill, which incorporated the tax increases and entitlement reductions. The bill passed the House of Representatives by a vote of 219–213, but only because last minute promises of more spending cuts were made to moderate and conservative Southern Democrats.[24] Even so, 38 Democrats voted with the Republicans. In the Senate, the bill passed only by a hair's breadth, 50–49, on the vote of Vice President Gore. Finally in the conference committee vote to reconcile differences between House and Senate, Gore once again had to cast a tie-breaking vote, 50–49.[25] During the process it had been necessary for the president to woo individual members of Congress for their votes, to replace the BTU tax with a small energy tax, to make the income tax increase retroactive to the beginning of the year, to expand the earned income tax credit, and to include empowerment zones. As for appropriations, the president was able to gain only about 70 percent of his requests.

The budget seemed for the moment fairly settled. The economy might be expected to remain fairly stable with modest growth, inflation, and unemployment kept in check by the monetary policies of the Federal Reserve. The deficit would be kept somewhere in the 2 percent of GDP range. Mandatory expenditures would be allowed to rise with occasional readjustments as crises appeared (i.e) trust

---

[24]Brummett, p. 136.

[25]Ibid., p. 185.

funds were seen to be running out of money). Taxes would gradually rise. After an initial rise, discretionary expenditures would be squeezed and priorities readjusted, at first to diminish and later stabilize defense spending, and to satisfy certain domestic agendas while cutting others. Interest payments, (which by now rivaled those of social security) could take their own course (see Table 6.9), and the diminishing deficit could yield savings.

But the sources of budgetary dissensus had not disappeared, and the Republican victory in the 1994 congressional elections signaled even greater conflict.

Table 6.9   Net Interest Payments, 1985–1994

	$ Billion	% Share of Budget	% Share of GDP
1985	129.5	13.7	3.3
1990	184.2	14.7	3.4
1991	194.5	14.7	3.4
1992	199.4	14.4	3.4
1993	198.8	14.1	3.2
1994	203.0	13.9	3.1

Source: United States Budget, *Fiscal Year* 1996, Historical Statistics: Table 8.1, *Outlays by Budget Enforcement Act Category, 1962–2000*, p. 95; Table 8.3, *Percentage Distribution of Outlays by Budget Enforcement Act Category, 1962–2000*, p. 97; and Table 8.4, *Outlays by Budget Enforcement Act Category as Percentage of GDP*, p. 98.

Chapter 7

The Politics of Radical Reversal

W hy was 1995 different from all other years? At the end of 1994, the Republican party gained majorities in both houses of Congress, with a program to balance the budget, boost defense, and diminish the role of the federal government. Nothing so remarkable about that, you might say. Although Democrats had controlled Congress for over 40 years, party succession in democratic countries is to be expected. The Republican agenda seemed to differ little from the conservative program of Ronald Reagan when *he* came into office in 1981. Yet 1995 *was* different. While the program might be the same, the fervor and determination with which it was advanced were not. And while the formal institutions and processes of Congress were no different from before, the new majority set out to use the budget of a single year as the primary vehicle for accomplishing radical and irreversible change for many years to come. Let's see what happened.

THE POLITICS OF RADICAL REVERSAL

The Republican agenda might be seen in a number of ways. For some it was merely the latest phase of a cyclical movement that swung in one period in favor of government action and in another, against. For others, it was part of a more generalized attack on the public sector, made up in equal parts of distaste for bureaucracy and regulation, and resentment of taxation against a background of sluggish economic growth and stagnant incomes. Many, including bright young economists, saw the dismantling of government controls, reduction of taxation, and the liberalization of the economy as the key to future prosperity and a reinvention of the way in which the public's business was conducted. Still others regarded the Republican program as the beginning of a moral crusade to regain lost values and reassert individual responsibility (even though these might sometimes be in conflict). Yet another element saw the Republican victory as the opportunity for pressing pro-business policies. From the opposite perspective, the package of tax cuts, program cuts, and entitlement cuts would balance the budget on the backs of the poor, take a punitive approach to social problems, reverse measures protecting the environment, and restore the distribution of income that existed prior to the Depression.

Much of the Republican agenda was expressed in the House Republicans' manifesto, the *Contract With America*.[1] It stressed a balanced budget, including a constitutional amendment to ensure that it happened, as well as a presidential line-item veto. It outlined measures to change welfare, cut taxes, boost defense, crack down on crime, reinforce parental responsibility, carry out certain legal reforms, and impose term limits on members of Congress. The jumble of often quite specific proposals of the Contract represented a broader program, which used the rhetoric of a balanced budget to promote much more fundamental change. The devolution to state governments of primary responsibility for large areas of governmental activity would mark the ending of the federal initiative and commitment in social matters that had begun with the Depression. Its significance lay not only in the changed constitutional balance but in the lesser financial capacity and political will of the states to fund social policy, and the disparities among them. Devolution, tax cuts, and program cuts would enhance the private sector in relation to the public sector and strengthen market forces. They would reduce the role of government in providing a social safety net, redistributing income, offsetting dysfunctions of the economy, and providing goods and services not forthcoming from the market. These core ideas, augmented with other agendas, and translated into various policy arenas, constituted the package to which the Republican majority committed itself to put into action.

Who were the Republicans? Republican members of Congress represented over 36 million voters; they had attracted over 9 million more votes than they had in 1990. They won more House votes than Democrats in every region, completely reversing the previous position. The impact of the new majority in Congress was accentuated by turnover. More than half the current members in the House were elected in 1990 or later, and so were 29 of the 100 Senators, representing a generational transformation.[2]

The shock troops of the Republican majority were the younger, single-minded, hard-edged members of the House. Imbued with the rightness of their cause, they felt the end justified the means, and their majority not only entitled them to push through their agenda, but also represented a mandate from the American people.

The Republican strategy was to use the budget process of a single year to set in motion and commit the nation to its program. But to cut taxes, increase defense, *and* balance the budget turned out not to be so easy. Even with favorable economic assumptions, these objectives could not be achieved within the present terms. Cuts in domestic discretionary spending would not be enough. It would be necessary to confront the fast-growing entitlement programs—an item not on the original agenda.

The discipline and cohesion of the Republican majority enabled them to write their program into the budget resolution and reconciliation instructions. Polarization seemed complete and the level of rhetoric and vituperation reached

---

[1]*Congressional Quarterly Weekly Report*, November 12, 1994, pp. 3216–19.

[2]*Los Angeles Times*, February 14, 1995, p. A6.

new heights. It appeared that only the countervailing power of the presidency could block the radical agenda of the congressional majority. By the end of the year, the politics of radical reversal seemed to have turned into a raw power conflict determined by majority dominance, opportunistic leverage, threats, and deadlock.

While the surface fervor continued unabated, however, political and institutional realities worked toward compromise and middle ground between the two sides. The details of authorizations, appropriations, and reconciliation blurred the clean lines of ideological division. In the approach to the next election, neither side wished to be seen as beyond reason, intransigent, or responsible for breakdown.

Yet as the long saga of the budget unwound during the year, the basic assumptions that had governed previous budget policy gradually changed. Debate came to focus not on *whether* there should be cuts, but on how much; not *whether* budget balance was desirable, but how it should be achieved; not *whether* taxes should be reduced, but which ones; not *whether* social provision should be diminished, but how reforms should be carried out. There was still much room for disagreement, but the terms of the discussion had shifted. How did this happen?

The Republican majority was not totally united on all issues. The most troublesome were those that on their face were not really related to the budget at all, such as abortion and the environment, but proved significant issues in the budget debates. Members also varied in the degree of their radicalism, and the extent to which they wished to depart from the status quo, and especially to sign on to proposals originating on the far right. The standards of economic purity and moral rectitude might take second place to regional or constituency considerations, or to a genuine sense of what was politically possible or decently equitable. There were also legitimate questions of who or what the Republican majority actually stood for. Little evidence of whole-hearted public embrace of the Contract existed, and Senate Republicans had not endorsed it. As the Republican program evolved, became more specific, and broadened to include entitlements, polls showed increasing public uneasiness with legislative proposals.

Neither were the Democrats completely united in their opposition. The Democratic party was split between social liberals who wanted to increase social spending to deal with social ills, and fiscal conservatives who wished to cut spending and reduce the deficit. "Old-style," "liberal" Democrats leaned toward economic nationalism, opposing broad trade agreements such as NAFTA, demanding greater sharing of profits and power by corporations, linking social problems to underlying economic injustice, and maintaining or expanding existing federal policies on welfare, income redistribution, and crime. The "new" Democrats advocated strategies to adapt to economic globalization, opening overseas markets, and retraining American workers, while rethinking liberal approaches on crime, welfare, and family breakdown to emphasize greater individual responsibility.[3] Each of these positions offered potential allies for the Republicans, the former supporting growing isolationism and protection, and the latter working for modification of social programs. While most votes were along party lines, both individuals and significant

[3]John Brummett, *Highwire: The Education of Bill Clinton* (New York: Hyperion, 1994), pp. 92–93.

blocks of Democrats repeatedly voted for Republican measures, and there were a few outright defections. One block of Democrats, the Coalition, consistently sought a middle ground, and by the end of the year had attracted further support. As "Blue Dogs," they emerged as a significant force in the movement toward compromise in the deadlocks on continuing resolutions and the reconciliation bill.

As budget legislation moved through Congress, the president had to make difficult choices. If he opposed the Republican agenda in its entirety, he might be seen as unreasonable and obstructive. To cooperate completely would risk losing his own party and undercut initiatives he had endorsed in the past. He could veto, but could not be sure if he could sustain his veto in Congress, although the Republican majority was less than two-thirds in either House.

Gradually the president adopted a centrist strategy, which incorporated many of the elements of the Republican agenda—a balanced budget, increased defense expenditures, cuts in medicare and increases in premiums, a "middle class" tax cut, welfare reform, and acceptance of rejections of his spending proposals. Increasingly, differences were being defined by amounts rather than principles. The gulf still existed: On the Republican side, the zealots insisted their program was not negotiable—program cuts, entitlement cuts, balanced budget, and tax cuts. As the polls indicated the growing unpopularity of that program, the president strengthened his stance as protector of social programs, the middle class, and the environment. But the gulf itself was not quite as wide as it once seemed.

In any case, the budget process discourages radical positions. It diffuses power and sets up numerous opportunities for the advance or defense of numerous agendas. Budget committees, authorizing committees, appropriations committees and their subcommittees, and tax committees demand not one majority, but multiple majorities on multiple issues. And the committees are only one part of a story that involves House and Senate, conference deliberations, and floor votes. Institutional fragmentation strengthens partial perspectives against the whole, pits moderate against radical, and encourages regional and economic interests. To attempt radical change is to run the gauntlet of a process that repeatedly tests every issue, and requires every fight to take place again and again.

The budget drama plays out before an audience of public opinion. Each side has to weigh its objectives against the perception of its ability to govern responsibly in the eyes of the voters. In its reluctance to assume the blame for the ultimate disaster—no budget at all—each side has to consider what it is willing to compromise and on what it is worth taking a stand. Right from the beginning of the process, the participants responded to their perceptions of public acceptability, exemplified in the debates on the balanced budget constitutional amendment and the rescissions bill.

PROLOGUE: CONSTITUTIONAL AMENDMENT AND RESCISSION

The constitutional amendment to balance the budget and the rescissions bill, debated at the very beginning of the congressional session, were very different measures. The constitutional amendment was largely symbolic and was defeated, while the rescissions bill was a very specific and substantive measure and was successful. But each measure in its way prefigured the themes of the budget debate to come: the power and limitations of the majority, and redefinition of the common ground between the parties.

The details of the constitutional amendment are described in Chapter 10. Both the overwhelming support for the amendment in the House from both parties (the vote was 300 to 125) and the narrow loss in the Senate indicated a measure of agreement. In fact, the amendment would probably have received the necessary two-thirds majority in the Senate had it not been for the issue of social security. The unwillingness of the Republican leadership to provide sufficient safeguards to protect social security from any future budget balancing exercise cost the votes of several supporters. From this point on social security was absent from the budget debates. And, as an echo and foretaste of business as usual, the proposal contained a specific exemption for the Tennessee Valley Authority, inserted on the initiative of (guess who?) the Republican senator from Tennessee.

The rescissions bill made clearer the divisions between the parties and the ability of the majority to get its way. What, you may ask, is a rescissions bill? Tucked away toward the end of the President's Budget for Fiscal Year 1996 was Table S–11, Summary of Supplemental and Rescission Proposals.[4] It listed additions and subtractions for the current year's (Fiscal Year 1995) budget authority for selected agencies, netting out to just over $8 billion. There were no accompanying explanations, but the list included emergency supplementals for international aid (to eliminate Jordan's debts following the Jordan-Israel peace treaty), defense (partly to cover the Haiti peacekeeping expedition), and more disaster aid (particularly for California earthquake assistance).

Supplemental appropriations bills were not unusual, and President Reagan had successfully gained rescissions from the current year's budget in 1981. But this supplemental bill was turned around to enable the Republican majority to transform it into a rescissions bill of its own, and to propose $17 billion worth of cuts to the current year's budget. In a stunning display of majority power, the House bill cut a wide range of social and environmental programs and added amendments to prevent abortion funding under medicaid, increase timber harvesting on federal land, and block certain air pollution rules.[5] Some of the more controversial provisions were modified in the Senate and other changes were made in conference, but the rescissions bill passed Congress more or less on party lines.

The president, affronted by the conference's additional cuts in education and youth programs as well as community development banks and WIC, vetoed the bill,[6] but six weeks later after some compromises signed it. It still included cuts in job training, low income housing and energy assistance, education, energy research, foreign aid, and national parks.[7]

---

[4]United States Budget, *Fiscal Year 1996,* p. 207.

[5]*Congressional Quarterly Weekly Report,* March 4, 1995, p. 676 and March 18, 1995, p. 797.

[6]Ibid., May 20, 1995.

[7]Ibid., July 22, 1995, p. 2157.

This guerrilla raid on the budget exemplified the budget debates to come. It illustrated the primary dividing line between the parties—Democrats for social spending and Republicans against—but it also demonstrated the potential for compromise, as Democrats traded their support for some concessions, in effect redefining the center. Thus, David Obey, ranking Democrat on the House Appropriations Committee, remarked "The Senate demonstrated that you do not have to go to the extremes the House went to in cutting programs for children and the elderly."[8]

The bill also demonstrated the extent to which the majority party was able to use leverage to achieve its program, and the potential for deadlock in the system. The Republicans used "must pass" legislation to force confrontation with the president, and the president used a veto threat to try to gain changes. On both sides these tactics would be employed repeatedly during the budget process. A division between House and Senate was apparent, as the Senate, while remaining committed to general principle, defined its own somewhat less radical and confrontational approach. Finally, the bill took over five months to pass, during which, detailed provisions were inserted, removed, reinserted, and modified in a mind-numbing journey toward its conclusion. By the time the bill was finally signed in July, it was only a sideshow to the budget debates that had been in full swing for some time.

BUDGETS AND COUNTERBUDGETS: THE PRESIDENT'S BUDGET AND THE CONGRESSIONAL RESOLUTION

Nineteen ninety-five was a year of many budgets. At the beginning there was the president's budget, quickly set aside by the resolution and reconciliation instructions of the congressional Republicans, which became the authoritative budget framework. Belatedly, the president offered another budget in response. Later, appropriations bills and the reconciliation bill would constitute yet more budgets, to be followed by continuing resolutions and yet another presidential proposal. (The chart on p. 159 provides a guide to the process.) Let us begin with the efforts to shape the budget framework, and see how they both polarized the parties and yet brought them together.

In the "old" budget compromise, mandatory expenditures were allowed to grow more or less unchecked; discretionary expenditures were virtually frozen at 1993 levels by the caps, with changes in priorities funded either from juggling domestic discretionary programs or using defense to finance domestic initiatives; and the deficit was slowly diminishing as the result of the spending caps, tax increases, and a more favorable economy. This position was no longer viable.

Balancing Revenues and Expenditures

Initially there was little argument about economic assumptions, and the president's budget and the congressional resolution used similar figures.[9]

---

[8]Ibid., May 6, 1995, p. 1231.

[9]Congressional Budget Office, *An Analysis of the President's Budgetary Proposals for Fiscal Year 1996*, April 1995, p. 9; George Hager, "The Arduous Budget Talks of 1990 May Offer a Map to the Road Ahead," *Congressional Quarterly Weekly Report*, January 3, 1995, p. 1565.

The Budget Process

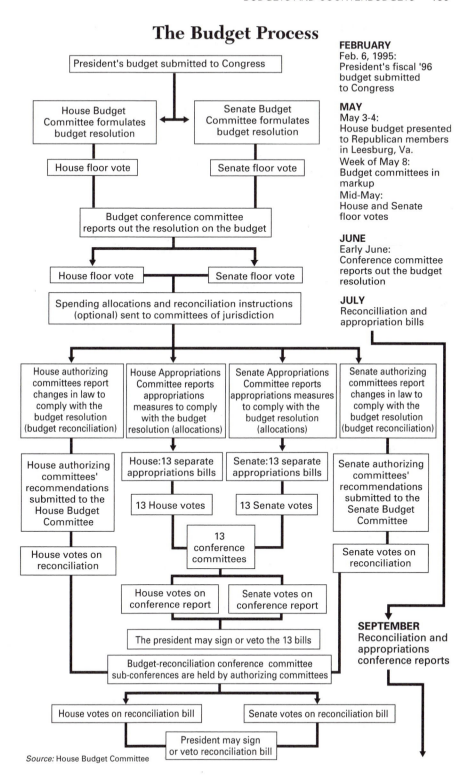

FEBRUARY
Feb. 6, 1995:
President's fiscal '96
budget submitted
to Congress

MAY
May 3-4:
House budget presented
to Republican members
in Leesburg, Va.
Week of May 8:
Budget committees in
markup
Mid-May:
House and Senate
floor votes

JUNE
Early June:
Conference committee
reports out the budget
resolution

JULY
Reconcilliation and
appropriation bills

SEPTEMBER
Reconciliation and
appropriations
conference reports

The president did not attempt to balance his budget, but instead stabilized the deficit at about $200 billion to the year 2000, when it would stand at about 2 percent of GDP, an enviable figure for many European countries and the lowest level since 1979.[10] In contrast, Congress set out a path to balance the budget by the year 2002. To make things harder, the House included over $350 billion in tax cuts and a large increase for defense. In the Senate resolution, where the ardor of tax cut advocates was met with caution, a new procedure was established: A tax cut would only be allowed if reconciliation instructions were consistent with the resolution to ensure a balanced budget by 2002.[11] The final resolution included $245 billion in tax cuts, after certification from CBO was duly obtained.

The budget resolution, which was followed by reconciliation instructions, invoked an extraordinary amount in deficit reduction, $894 billion measured against a freeze in 1995 spending levels, and about $1.25 trillion against the CBO estimated deficit baseline. It also made the task more difficult by adding in over $300 billion in tax cuts and defense increases. On the other hand, the task was facilitated when CBO "found" a $170 billion windfall in presumed savings from a presumed drop in interest rates and economic growth over seven years.[12]

The debates and votes on the resolution sharply divided the parties. The Republicans took a lofty tone. In the House, the Majority Whip, Tom DeLay, pronounced "Today we make a historic decision. We can protect the status quo or we can make a courageous stand for America."[13] In an impassioned speech, Budget Committee Chairman John Kasich said "What our vision is for the twenty-first century is a vision of taking power and money and control and influence from this city and giving it back to men and women all across this country."[14] In response, Minority Leader Richard Gephardt denounced the plan as a heartless attack on the poor and elderly, and Senator Edward Kennedy said the resolution was a "direct attack on senior citizens, children, families and veterans."[15]

But the ground was already slipping away. Even in the midst of his attack, Gephardt said "All of us believe our budget must be brought into balance. It's a question of how you do it."[16] At least two Democratic budget balancing alternative plans were put forward that attracted some Democratic, but no Republican, support. Finally the president jumped into the fray, ignoring his original budget, with a new plan to balance the budget in 10 years, requiring $1.1 trillion in deficit reduction, and including over $100 billion in tax cuts

---

[10]United States Budget, *Fiscal Year 1996,* Table 2.1, p. 40.

[11]The provision is reproduced in Congressional Budget Office, *The Economic and Budget Outlook: An Update,* August 1995, p. 40.

[12]Congressional Budget Office, *The Economic and Budget Outlook: An Update*, August 1995, p. 34.

[13]Janet Hook, "House Adopts GOP Plan To Balance Budget by 2002," *Los Angeles Times,* May 19, 1995, p. A17.

[14]Ibid., p. A1.

[15]*Los Angeles Times,* June 30, 1995, p. A28.

[16]Ibid., May 19, 1995, p. A17.

Table 7.1   Balancing the Budget Over Seven Years

House and Senate Versions of the Resolution Compared With
the Final Congressional Resolution and the President's Plan

(in billions of dollars)

	House	Senate	President	Congress
Deficit Reduction	1.04 trillion	958	520*	894†
Savings from				
Lower Interest	256	184	155	(170)
Tax Cuts	353	0	105	245
			($174 conditional)	
Medicare Savings	288	256	128	270
Medicaid Savings	187	175	54	182
		(offset by $24 expansion)		
Defense Increases	68	0	3	58
Nondefense				
Discretionary Savings	192†	190†	197	190†
Other Mandatory Savings	219	209	38	175

*The Clinton proposal balanced the budget over 10 years, requiring $1.1 trillion. The comparisons are for seven years.

† Measured against the 1995 enacted level (not the inflation adjusted baseline).

Source: Figures were revised several times. The figures in this table are taken from *Congressional Quarterly Weekly Report,* July 1, 1995, p. 1905, and do not add because of conceptual inconsistencies.

(see Table 7.1). Although not all the Democratic party endorsed the position, budget balance and tax cuts were now an integral part of the budget equation.

Mandatory and Discretionary Spending

The decisions on budget balance and tax cuts drove further decisions on mandatory spending. The president's budget had allowed entitlements to rise, constrained only by previous cuts. But now it would be necessary to cut them to attain the new totals. As part of the new consensus, social security remained untouched; other entitlements would meet two-thirds of the needed deficit reduction. The congressional resolution, the compromise between House and Senate plans, cut the rates of growth of medicare ($247 billion in cuts) and medicaid ($182 billion) spending by more than half over the next seven years. Cuts in antipoverty programs (including AFDC, food programs, supplemental social insurance, and the earned income tax credit) were scheduled to yield over $100 billion in savings. A further $75 billion would be cut from federal retirement, farm subsidies, unemployment benefits, and student loans. Details would follow in the reconciliation bill. Meanwhile, the Clinton plan also announced entitlement cuts. Once again, the center had moved.

Defense and Domestic Spending

The president's budget had continued the trend in defense spending, cutting defense by 3.8 percent as part of a plan to reduce military spending until 1998, when it would start to rise again. But the House had other ideas, and while the

Senate was content with the president's allocation, the resolution increased military spending by about $35 billion over seven years, although this would constrain spending to 17 percent below the baseline.[17] In response, the president added $25 billion to his figure (See Chapter 9). Yet again, the sides were coming closer.

Domestic Discretionary Spending

The president's budget worked within the totals imposed by the caps, making marginal adjustments in favor of his priorities of education, research and training, the environment, and anticrime programs. It cut international aid, agriculture, and transportation, and proposed more "reinventing government" reorganizations and consolidations. In contrast, the resolution proposed about $190 billion in cuts in nondefense discretionary payments, nearly half the total, compared with enacted 1995 levels. If measured against a baseline allowing for inflation, the cut would be about $390 billion, or 30 percent.[18]

Both House and Senate made specific recommendations. The House proposed eliminating the Departments of Commerce, Education, and Energy, another 13 agencies, 69 boards, commissions, and authorities, and 284 federal programs, while the Senate would also recommend abolishing the Commerce Department and eliminate over 100 federal programs. The conference report imposed new caps on discretionary spending from Fiscal Year 1996 through Fiscal Year 2002, separating defense and nondefense spending through 1998.[19] (See Table 7.2.) The president responded with a proposal for domestic spending cuts of $197 billion against the baseline, to be achieved by across-the-board cuts.

Table 7.2   New Discretionary Spending Caps in the Congressional Budget Resolution

	1996	1997	1998	1999	2000	2001	2002
Defense							
Budget Authority	265.4	268.0	269.7	—	—	—	—
Outlays	264.0	265.7	264.5	—	—	—	—
Nondefense							
Budget Authority	219.7	214.5	221.0	—	—	—	—
Outlays	267.7	254.6	248.1	—	—	—	—
Total Discretionary							
Budget Authority	485.1	482.4	490.7	482.2	489.4	496.6	498.8
Outlays	531.8	520.3	512.6	510.5	514.2	516.4	515.1

Source: Fiscal Year 1996 Budget Resolution (H Con Res 67—HRept 104–5), *Congressional Quarterly Weekly Report,* July 15, 1995, p. 2044..

---

[17]Congressional Budget Office, *An Update,* p. 37.

[18]George Hager, "Today's Appropriators Preside over a Shrinking Empire," *Congressional Quarterly Weekly Report,* May 20, 1995, p. 1365.

[19]George Hager, "Furor over First Spending Bills Promises Stormy Summer," *Congressional Quarterly Weekly Report,* July 15, 1995, p. 2044.

Substance Versus Rhetoric

Why was it that an objective previously regarded as unattainable suddenly appeared feasible? Could Congress really look such large cuts in the eye and not blink? As CBO put it, with characteristic understatement, "Balancing the budget over the next seven years will require many hard decisions about taxing and spending policies."[20]

The resolution and reconciliation instructions, passed almost entirely on party lines, were only the first step. The "hard decisions" would have to be taken in the complexities of the budget process, which framed the issues and revisited them again and again. Would congressional Republicans continue to vote together on the substantive expenditure cuts, especially where extraneous issues were brought into the vote? Could they successfully present social program cuts in terms of the need to balance the budget, the devolution of government, and the spirit of necessary sacrifice for a greater common goal? Or would these issues be seen as rich versus poor, big business versus working people, profits versus the general interest, and benefits for some at the expense of burdens for others? Would ideological commitment triumph over business as usual?

INCREMENTALISM IN MIRROR IMAGE: APPROPRIATIONS

The politics of subtraction in 1995 was not the simple reversal of incrementalism, but rather its mirror image. The appropriations committees were charged with cutting domestic discretionary spending, which made up 17 percent of the budget by some $10 billion below the 1995 level to meet the 1996 targets.[21] Cutting, not increasing, the base in this way meant losers not winners, raising the potential for conflict. Partisanship replaced consensus; debates focused on policy and ideology; and pressure from the leadership strove to enforce totals. But the majorities were not always cohesive, and the multiple, repetitive decision process still encouraged bargaining, modifications of hard-line positions, and more varied agendas.

The appropriations committees were critical to the success of a large part of the Republican agenda not only to balance the budget but to roll back the activities of the federal government, particularly in view of the slow progress of the legislative program. The Speaker had appointed the House Appropriations chair and demanded letters of loyalty from the top Republicans on the committee.[22] In a closed-door meeting with the appropriations committee chair and subcommittee chairs, Gingrich reminded them "You are going to be in the forefront of the revolution. You have the toughest jobs in the House. If you don't want to do it, tell me."[23] First in the rescissions bill and later in the congressional resolution, the budget committees provided not only overall totals, but also detail about the cuts they wanted.

---

[20]Congressional Budget Office, *The Economic and Budget Outlook: An Update,* August 1995, p. 37.

[21]George Hager, "Furor over First Spending Bills Promises Stormy Summer," *Congressional Quarterly Wealthy Report,* July 15, 1995, p. 2401.

[22]David Rogers, "Budget Round II," *Wall Street Journal,* May 19, 1995, p. A4.

[23]*Washington Post,* August 13, 1995, p. A6.

But the appropriations committees had their own prerogatives and their own way of doing business. Traditionally, they subordinated partisanship to the work of producing appropriations bills, working "congenially to advance spending they mutually agreed on and [resisting] partisan agendas, whether Democratic or Republican."[24] Bipartisan, pragmatic, and quiet, their style contrasted with House Speaker Gingrich's partisan, media-savvy, and abrasive attitude.[25] Theirs was a culture of building and trading favors, and also of a determined independence. "[The budget] becomes real when our bills pass," said House Appropriations Committee Chairman, Robert Livingston. Another subcommittee chairman declared "I don't think we care about the cuts he [Gingrich] wants. . . . He may have to live with the cuts we give him."[26]

Appropriations committees also differed from budget committees in their concerns. The budget committees had set out a seven-year plan; the appropriations committees were concerned about next year's budget, a traditional, year-at-a-time approach to budgeting. The budget committees viewed the budget as a whole and in large blocks; the appropriations committees, because of the way their jurisdictions were defined, had to trade one interest against another, below tight limits. More for the space program would mean less for housing programs and urban development. Anticrime measures had to compete head-on with economic development.[27] Support for one program automatically involved members in cutting others, quite the reverse of the traditional vote trading process.

Ideology and older interests played out their agendas in the rhetoric of budget cutting, changing priorities, and festooning appropriations bills with riders. Complex coalitions and pork barrel politics set prices for agreement. Some programs were targeted for elimination and others for preservation, unrelated to their budgetary impact. Attempts were made to swallow whole agencies. And in social and environmental policy areas, a slash-and-burn strategy attempted to implement, through the budget, the politics of radical reversal. The scope and detail of the debates defies easy summary. What follows is a brief description of the sometimes changed, sometimes perennial, and often inconsistent way of doing business.

Complex Coalitions

The case of agriculture illustrates how the juxtaposition of different interests and the multiple steps of the budget process complicated decision making, blurred lines of jurisdiction among the committees, and brought together strange bedfellows in complex coalitions. The agriculture appropriations bill contained two elements of contention: nutrition programs (making up two-thirds) and subsidies to farmers. As entitlements, these were also under the jurisdiction of the agriculture committees, which in 1995 had to reauthorize the farm bill after five years. In the past, rural conservatives in support of farm subsidies and urban liberals in support

---

[24]*Congressional Quarterly Weekly Report*, March 4, 1995, p. 677.

[25]Rogers, p. 1.

[26]Ibid.

[27]Ibid., p. A4.

of nutrition programs joined together on the House Appropriations Subcommittee to support the status quo. The Republican attack on food stamps and nutrition programs might encourage urban liberals to vote against farm programs to preserve programs for the poor.

The message to all concerned at the beginning was loud and clear: Cut the budget, and in particular, cut and even eventually eliminate the system of price supports and subsidies to farmers. House and Senate leadership, conservative think tanks, free market conservatives, environmentalists, food manufacturers, consumer advocates, and even the chairman of the Senate Agriculture Committee endorsed this position. They argued that agriculture would gain from increased competition, improved market conditions, and increased crop diversification; that the subsidies were "corporate welfare;" that they drove up commodity prices and undercut American exports; and that they supported undesirable environmental practices and represented "staggering waste."

But the Republicans were by no means unanimous in their hostility to farm programs. Although rural congressional districts formed a minority (only 76–100, depending on who did the counting, out of 435 House seats), they were in the Midwest and South where farmers depended heavily on subsidies. Many of these seats had been won in the last election by relatively narrow margins, and in the 1985 election, loss of the Senate Republican majority had been attributed to the loss of those seats following reauthorization of the farm bill. Freshmen Republicans and others, including Senate Majority Leader Dole and Senate Minority Leader Daschle, argued that farm programs stimulated the economy and guaranteed inexpensive food. Support programs worked well, and their sudden elimination would lead to devastation of rural America as well as undermining current agricultural stability and a large export industry. In any case, farm subsidies had fallen over the past decade from $26 billion to about $10 billion. All governments subsidize agriculture, and removing of subsidies and price supports would result in a flood of subsidized commodities entering the country to threaten the livelihood of the farmers and all those dependent on the food industry, directly and indirectly, for employment.

The Clinton administration, while supporting more crop variety, program reform, and some program cuts, also generally supported farm interests and opposed radical change: Agriculture Secretary Glickman saw himself as an "advocate for agriculture."[28] Farm lobby groups were active on the Hill and had made substantial contributions to 1994 candidates.

After initial skirmishing on the agriculture committees and budget committees that left subsidy programs more or less intact, the focus shifted to the House Appropriations Agriculture Subcommittee. With the Republicans split on the issue of subsidies versus budget cutting, it was necessary to maintain bipartisan support for the bill. The nutrition programs retained their position with only minor cuts. Subsidies were reduced, but through a favorable market situation, not expenditure cuts. The brunt of the cuts fell on agricultural research and extension projects, rural development, conservation, and export programs.

---

[28]*Wall Street Journal,* March 22, 1995, p. A8; *Congressional Quarterly Weekly Report,* May 13, 1995, p. 1316; *Congressional Quarterly Weekly Report,* June 24, 1995.

The House Appropriations Committee approved the bill and rejected amendments to end tobacco subsidies, cut the peanut program, and eliminate subsidies for wealthy farmers. Debate centered not on the funding choices, but on the administration proposal for tougher food inspections, which was postponed. When the bill came to the floor of the House, efforts to cap the number of participants in the WIC program and to bar use of funds for tobacco crop insurance failed.

The Senate Appropriations Committee, with an eye to presidential priorities, softened the cuts in rural housing and development programs. To do so, it had to find savings in other programs, infringing on the authorizing committees' territory. This move was not unusual, but in 1995 it was resorted to more frequently and illustrates the complex trading among different agendas. For example, the business-supported export promotion program was capped at $800 million, though not eliminated (but in a blow to the minks, the committee struck out a House provision that would have barred use of export promotion funds for the Mink Export Development Council). A $41 million disaster aid provision for cotton farmers, which had been inserted by Republican Thad Cochran of Mississippi and funded by an acreage freeze on the Conservation Reserve Program, was also a target for Democrats seeking to restore rural housing financing.[29]

The haggling continued until the bill finally emerged from conference nearly $6 billion below the Fiscal Year 1995 figure, but the major conflict over subsidies and nutrition programs was deferred to the agriculture committees and the reconciliation bill. The debates illustrate the difficulties of cutting budgets and pursuing ideologies in the face of conflicted politics. The resilience of local interests was attested to by the survival of pork.

The Survival of Pork

The survival of special research grants at the same time that university research was being sacrificed to the budget ax in the Agriculture Appropriations Subcommittee exemplifies the survival of the age-sanctioned practice of pork: the placing of projects in members' districts. Allen Schick has sensibly pointed out that the actual amount of such earmarking in the budget is quite small, and that even complete elimination of pork would not make much of a contribution to budget balance.[30] Perhaps this is just as well, since it was not difficult to find examples of pork, despite the pledge of the House Appropriations Committee: "We're not going to just stop projects in Democrats' districts. We're going to stop projects across the board. We're going to slow down the pork barrel. There's no doubt about it."[31]

Examples abound. For instance, the allocation for the Army Corps of Engineers was 6 percent below 1995 spending, but still included almost $20 million in funding for about 20 new construction projects, including three in the

[29]David Rogers, "Senate Panel Softens House-Passed Cuts in Rural Programs To Try To Avoid Veto," *Wall Street Journal*, September 15, 1995, p. A18.

[30]Allen Schick, *The Federal Budget: Politics, Policy, Process* (Washington, D.C.: Brookings Institution, 1995), p. 141.

[31]Jackie Koszczuk, "Lord of the Long Knives," *Congressional Quarterly Weekly Report*, May 20, 1995, p. 1366.

subcommittee chairman's home state of Indiana.[32] In the Transportation Appropriations Subcommittee's markup, no money was allowed for highway "demonstration" projects, a traditional pork barrel category, but the bill contained mass transit funds for high occupancy vehicle lane designations in Utah; hundreds of millions of dollars for previously authorized projects in the 1991 surface transportation law; and subsidies for rural airports.[33] The Senate Appropriations Committee also wrote in an exemption from the cap on highway construction to the tune of $23 million for roads in Indian reservations, at the request of Pete Domenici, the chairman of the Senate Budget Committee and senator from New Mexico.[34]

The House Appropriations Committee preserved the Appalachian Regional Commission against the recommendation of the House Budget Committee, as well as the Botanic Garden, a facility supported by Chairman Livingston's wife. But the Botanic Garden was later killed in the Senate.[35] The final version of the energy bill added $55 million to the administration's proposal for water projects, "including several written into the legislation on behalf of senior Republicans in both chambers."[36] As the appropriations process continued, it was clear that appropriators were "still ready and willing and able to finance projects that benefit members or districts."[37]

Why does pork survive in an era of tight fiscal limits? For the same reasons it always has. Additionally, the Republican leadership was often reluctant to control the details of spending as long as the totals were met, and were aware of their need to gather votes where they could and to maintain the momentum of the appropriations process. Ideological purity gave way to pragmatism, and many Republicans, including Speaker Gingrich, supported federal government participation in infrastructure. As a freshman member of the House Appropriations Committee, George Nethercutt put it (presumably with a straight face), "I don't think we can assume just because a special project is funded, that project is not meritorious."[38]

Balancing Acts

Because totally disparate functions and agencies may be grouped together in a single appropriation, when the appropriations committees divided up the total allowances of the budget resolution among their subcommittees to shape the appropriations bills, programs jostled one another. For example, a vote for stepped-up law enforcement translated into less for foreign aid and commerce

---

[32]*Congressional Quarterly Weekly Report,* June 24, 1995, p. 1833.

[33]Ibid., p. 1831.

[34]Ibid., August 5, 1995, p. 2357.

[35]Ibid., July 22, 1995, p. 2143.

[36]David Rogers, "Congress Approves $37.45 Billion Bill for Transportation," *Wall Street Journal,* November 1, 1995, p. A3.

[37]*Congressional Quarterly Weekly Report,* July 8, 1995, p. 1190.

[38]Ibid., p. 1991.

in the appropriations bill for Commerce, Justice, and State. Some programs were hurt simply because they were grouped together with others of higher priority.[39]

In the transportation appropriations bill, funding had to be balanced among highways, airports, and mass transit. In the House version of the bill, total spending would be nearly $1 billion less than in 1995, but programs would not be cut evenly. The winners would be the federal aid highway program and the airport improvement program, each of which would receive increases from the cuts in mass transit and Amtrak (which would lose one quarter of its subsidies). In the Senate, however, the Appropriations Committee cut budget authority about 10 percent more than the House, and approved a freeze on spending on highway construction, cutting deeply into airport construction, Amtrak, and mass transit operating subsidies, which were slashed by nearly half with the biggest cuts coming in cities over 200,000 in population.[40]

Economy and Ideology

Budget cutting was not the only agenda. The appropriations process provided multiple opportunities to assert political positions that really had little to do with money issues. With time short, appropriations seemed a fast track way to gain legislative changes, normally the province of the authorizing committees, and became a major vehicle for legislative action. Mused Allen Schick, "The paradox of 1995 is that in some ways, the appropriations committees are weaker in money matters and stronger in legislative matters, which is exactly the opposite of what it's supposed to be."[41] The following are only a few of myriad examples that might be cited.

The issues were contentious. The House bill funding the Environmental Protection Agency prevented the agency from enforcing regulations affecting wetlands protection, automobile emissions inspections, and drinking water standards. Money for enforcement of statutes, such as the Clean Air Act and Clean Water Act, would be withheld until Congress had voted to reauthorize them.[42] But the riders were ultimately defeated in the House by a coalition of Democrats and 65 moderate Republicans, largely from the Northeast and Midwest, although 29 Democrats voted to retain them.[43] The bill still emerged from conference including riders allowing logging in the Tongass National Forest, and allowing the sale of mining rights on federal land for as little as $250 an acre.[44] There were many other riders attacking environmental policies, including a moratorium on

---

[39]Ibid., July 29, 1995, p. 2272.

[40]Ibid., August 5, 1995.

[41]George Hager, "As They Cut, Appropriators Add a Stiff Dose of Policy," *Congressional Quarterly Weekly Report,* July 29, 1995, p. 2247.

[42]*New York Times,* July 19, 1995, p. A10; *Los Angeles Times,* July 29, 1995.

[43]James Gerstenzang, "House, Reversing Itself, Drops Bid To Limit EPA Powers," *Los Angeles Times,* November 13, 1995, pp. A1, A23.

[44]James Gerstenzang, "White House Threatens Veto of Environmental Measures," *Los Angeles Times,* September 23, 1995, p. A3.

listing new wildlife and plants under the Endangered Species Act, and reversing a ban on issuing low-cost "patents" allowing mining claims on federal lands.[45]

Many of the riders were highly provocative and were eventually dropped. They included a prohibition on the federal government doing business with companies that replaced striking workers with permanent employees;[46] reversal of the ban on offshore drilling for oil and gas;[47] prohibition of organizations receiving federal funds engaging in lobbying and other political activities;[48] and a prohibition on federal contracts being awarded on the basis of reverse discrimination.[49]

The issues ranged up and down the whole gamut of federal government activities. The Senate Appropriations Committee acted to block a new Agriculture Department rule to ban labeling of frozen poultry as "fresh," a move upheld on the Senate floor.[50] The committee also responded to pressures by roofing and house-building industries to limit enforcement of new OSHA safety rules,[51] and there was language written into the bill to change its direction from rule enforcement to voluntary compliance.[52] The House version of the appropriations bill for Commerce, Justice, and State contained provisions blocking funds to normalize relations with Vietnam and to support peacekeeping operations involving U. S. troops operating under foreign command.[53]

The biggest ideological fights were over abortion, an issue that crossed party lines and appeared in several appropriations bills. For example, the House and Senate versions of the Treasury, Postal appropriations bill included a ban on abortions for women enrolled in taxpayer-subsidized federal employee health care plans, though the Senate version contained exceptions for rape, incest, or health concerns.[54] The House Appropriations bill for Labor Health and Human Services included dozens of amendments, which were freely admitted as paybacks to the Christian Coalition and other antiabortion groups. Republicans joined Democrats to defeat efforts to transfer funding for Title X, the administration's main family-planning program, to locally controlled programs with no mandate for family planning. But a provision was approved to bar the use of federal medicaid funds to pay for abortion in case of rape or incest: 52 Republicans voted against the provision, and 40 Democrats for it.[55]

---

[45]*Congressional Quarterly Weekly Reports* June 24, 1995.

[46]*New York Times,* September 29, 1995.

[47]*Congressional Quarterly Weekly Report,* June 24, 1995.

[48]David Wessel and Jackie Calmes, "No Progress Made on Shutdown," *Wall Street Journal,* November 16, 1995, p. A22; Jennifer Corbett, "House Votes To Curb Activity of Non-Profit Groups," *Los Angeles Times,* September 5, 1995, p. A20.

[49]*Congressional Quarterly Weekly Report,* July 22, 1995, p. 2144.

[50]*Wall Street Journal,* September 15, 1995, p. A18; *Wall Street Journal,* September 20, 1995, p. A6.

[51]*Wall Street Journal,* September 15, 1995, p. A18.

[52]*Los Angeles Times,* July 29, 1995.

[53]*Congressional Quarterly Weekly Report,* July 29, 1995, p. 2272.

[54]Andrew Taylor, "Treasury-Postal Bill Passes After Abortion Debate," *Congressional Quarterly Weekly Report,* September 12, 1995, p. 2439.

[55]*New York Times,* August 4, 1995, pp. A1, A24.

An interesting situation arose in the House consideration of the transportation appropriations bill. The House Appropriations Committee, which had passed a measure to repeal labor protection provisions over Democratic opposition, asked for a rule from the Rules Committee to protect its action from procedural challenges on the House floor. The rule would also have protected 15 unauthorized mass transit projects included in the bill. The chairman of the House Transportation and Infrastructure Committee was so outraged by the attempt to circumvent his committee on this latter issue that he joined the Democrats in asking the House Rules Committee not to allow the waiver. When the Rules Committee complied, the House Republican leadership forced the two committee chairs into a compromise, which required the House to pass an authorization for the disputed transit projects, but which also protected the repeal of the labor protection provisions. But all this maneuvering came to nothing as an unexpected bipartisan coalition, in which 44 Republicans joined with a unanimous Democratic vote, defeated the repeal on the floor of the House, claiming that it would cause thousands of blue-collar transit workers to lose collective bargaining rights. All of which goes to show that the Republican leadership could not always count on getting its own way, and that surprises do happen.[56]

Targeting Programs

Further fissures were opened in party unity through efforts to eliminate or save specific programs. In many cases the amount of funding involved was relatively small, so the motivation for cutting was not primarily economy, while programs might be saved even where the party leadership was in favor of termination.

For example, the Corporation for Public Broadcasting had already lost funding in the rescissions bill. It was attacked by a solid Republican coalition composed of fiscal conservatives (who wanted to save money), free market advocates (who saw it as a program for the rich and wished to privatize it), and ideological conservatives (against its alleged liberal programming bias). Against this position were arguments that it was not a program for the rich, that the federal contribution was only 14 percent of expenditures and represented seed money, and that it would not be possible to fill the federal funding gap.[57] An attempt to eliminate the agency failed on the floor of the House because some Republicans supported it, but funding was cut by nearly a quarter.[58]

The National Endowments for Arts and Humanities were also targets. The House Appropriations Committee voted for a three-year phaseout of the agencies, giving rise to contentious debates on the floor of the House: New York Republicans actually supported further funding of the NEA, but right-wing Republicans attempted to gain its immediate demise. In the end, the House voted to abolish NEA in two years and NEH in three years, and to cut spending by 40 percent.[59]

---

[56]*Congressional Quarterly Weekly Report*, July 22, 1995, p. 2170; *Congressional Quarterly Weekly Report*, July 29, 1995.

[57]*Los Angeles Times*, January 31, 1995, p. A10.

[58]*New York Times*, August 4, 1995.

[59]*Los Angeles Times*, July 19, 1995.

Many other examples may be related of programs targeted for elimination. Sometimes this occurred in a roundabout way. For example, the East Mojave National Park had been created in 1992 amidst considerable controversy, as it had previously been administered by the Bureau of Land Management as a multiuse area. The Interior Appropriations Subcommittee voted the National Park Service $1 for its administration, effectively giving it back to the BLM.[60] About two dozen energy conservation programs were targeted for extinction, as well as the Strategic Petroleum Reserve, the Yucca Mountain high-level nuclear waste depository, the Institute of American Indian and Alaska Native Culture and Arts Development, the Advisory Council on Historic Preservation, and the Congressional Office for Technology Assessment.

The survival of the space station also illustrates the complex dynamics of program rescue. Despite a bipartisan effort to cancel the space station by freshmen members, the House Science Committee reauthorized the program for seven years. It appeared that opposition had been augmented by Democrats, who actually supported the station but wanted an increase in funding for the space agency (NASA) in the Veterans Affairs–Housing and Urban Development (VA-HUD) appropriations bill, in opposition to the cut proposed by the House Budget Committee. In the end, NASA sustained only a modest cut compared to the budget committees' recommendation, and funding was retained for the space station.

Sometimes the recommendations of the budget committees were modified or overturned by determined subcommittee chairs or bipartisan coalitions, whose choices in turn might be upset by supporters or detractors of specific programs on the floor of the House or Senate. For example, President Clinton had requested $62 million for domestic violence programs in the Department of Health and Human Services, but the draft appropriations bill in the House funded them at $400,000. However, the House Commerce, Justice, and State Appropriations Subcommittee agreed to transfer $40 million in crime trust funds to the Labor, Health and Human Services, and Education Subcommittee, which then voted $73 million for the program. Similarly, many House Republicans and most Democrats sustained funding for the Economic Development Administration, slated for elimination in the House budget resolution.[61] On the other hand, the Corporation for National and Community Service, a priority of the president, was terminated.[62]

The appropriators also targeted programs with a weak constituency, like the gas turbine modular helium reactor. The rationale was cogently argued by David Minge, a Democrat from Minnesota—"I ask my colleagues: Do you think your constituents would approve of throwing more money into a black hole of waste? I think not." But when it came to another big project, the advanced light water reactor backed by powerful large companies, or the advanced spallation neutron source facility, no coalition in favor of termination appeared.[63]

[60]*Los Angeles Times*, September 23, 1995, p. A3.

[61]*Congressional Quarterly Weekly Report*, July 22, 1995, p. 2196.

[62]Ibid., July 15, 1995, p. 2069.

[63]Ibid., p. 2052.

Sometimes a regional program would attract bipartisan support to avoid the budget ax. A broad coalition of Republicans and Democrats, including many from states in the region, voted against abolishing the Appalachian Regional Commission, although its funding was cut in half, and the Tennessee Valley Authority also survived with funding cut by about a third. In general, fiscal conservatives were unable to muster coalitions in favor of radical budget cutting against shifting interests favoring a variety of water and energy projects.[64]

Swallowing Whole Departments

Republican party rhetoric and the budget resolutions set their sights not only on specific programs, but also on whole departments, such as the Departments of Commerce, Education, and Energy. This proved harder than it first appeared.

For example, the initiative of Republican freshmen to eliminate the Energy Department was backed by the Republican leadership. Said John Kasich, House Budget Committee chair, "We don't want this department at the end of the day."[65] But the Department also represented an array of programs, dealt with by a variety of committees, which could not simply be eliminated or placed elsewhere overnight. The House Government Reform and Oversight Committee was reluctant to move in the face of an already crowded agenda. The House Science Subcommittee on Energy and Environment approved authorization for research and development programs, focusing on cutting, not eliminating the Department. The Energy and Water Development Appropriations Subcommittee followed its lead, concentrating on reorienting priorities within the Department and cutting the overall appropriation. Similarly, the Commerce Department involved the jurisdictions of no fewer than 11 authorizing committees.[66] But the Department's funding did not emerge unscathed.

Critical Issues

What did all the sound and fury signify? Was it true, as Democrats contended, that federal programs were gutted by the actions of 1995, and as Republicans contended, that 1995 was an epochal year in changing the entire direction of the federal government? Or was Herbert Stein nearer the mark when he said that really all that divided the two sides were relatively minor money matters?[67] The critical issues were environmental and social programs contained in three large appropriations bills: Veterans Affairs—Housing and Urban Development (VA-HUD), Interior, and Labor, Health and Human Services, and Education.

---

[64]Allan Freedman, "Department Likely To Survive as Focus Moves to Cutbacks," *Congressional Quarterly Weekly Report*, June 10, 1995, p. 1633.

[65]*Congressional Quarterly Weekly Report*, June 17, 1995, p. 1736; *Congressional Quarterly Weekly Report*, July 15, 1995.

[66]Donna Cassata, "Freshmen 'Have To Get' Commerce," *Congressional Quarterly Weekly Report*, June 29, 1995, p. 2273. See also Ben Wildavsky, "On the Block," *National Journal*, July 22, 1995, pp. 1880–84.

[67]Interview with Herbert Stein on *The News Hour with Jim Lehrer*, November 22, 1995.

Despite skillful work by the Speaker in urging through the Republican program, involving greater centralization than had been seen in the House for decades, the sheer range of issues and disputes over them hindered speedy passage.[68] In the Senate, where the Republican majority was much smaller, the pace was even slower. In both houses, passage of appropriations bills was delayed by disputes, often over policy rather than money, and disagreements between the House and Senate further delayed matters. By the beginning of the fiscal year, only two bills had been sent to the president, and while 10 others had passed both House and Senate, conferences and final votes were still outstanding.

The VA-HUD spending bill was particularly contentious, since it contained funding for the Environmental Protection Agency (EPA), housing programs, and the president's national service program. The House version of the bill cut EPA funding by over a third.[69] When the bill reached the Senate, some of the EPA funding was restored and the legislative riders deleted, but superfund funding was cut even further, and money for the revolving funds and research and development deleted altogether. In House-Senate negotiations, the agency's enforcement budget was still cut by 22 percent.[70]

The House bill cut the appropriation for the Department of Housing and Urban Development by one quarter. Several programs were cut by as much as a half or a third, but funds were increased for housing vouchers and family subsidies.[71] Although moderate Republicans restored some funding (e.g., preventing rent increases in public housing), and the HUD secretary was able to blunt the cuts by other savings, the proposed HUD appropriation was still down by about one-fifth from the 1995 level.

Conflict dragged on over Interior appropriations. Compromise between House and Senate resulted in an overall cut of about 10 percent from the previous year. But the bill, which contained a variety of riders relating to mining royalties, logging in the Tongass National Forest, the Mojave Desert, and the Endangered Species Act, was rejected in the House in a surprise vote when 48 Republicans voted with the Senate majority, and the bill was recommitted to conference.

Major issues were at stake in the Labor, Health and Human Services, and Education bill, and the House leadership stressed its importance. Democrats had little success in attempting to reshape the bill, which cut discretionary spending roughly 10 percent from 1995 levels. Nearly 200 programs were cut or eliminated.[72] Eighteen Republicans voted against the bill and six Democrats voted for it. Some of these cuts received some partial replacement in the Senate Appropriations Subcommittee debate.[73] But the House debate was blurred by the riders concerned

---

[68]See Michael Weisskopf and David Maraniss, "In a Moment of Crisis, the Speaker Persuades," *Washington Post*, September 13, 1995, p. A8.

[69]*Congressional Quarterly Weekly Report*, August 5, 1995, p. 2366.

[70]David Rogers, "Congressional Republicans Use Spending Bills as Bargaining Chips over the Budget," *Wall Street Journal*, November 17, 1995, p. A16.

[71]*Congressional Quarterly Weekly Report*, July 29, 1995, p. 2270.

[72]*Congressional Quarterly Weekly Report*, October 7, 1995, p. 3071.

[73]David Rogers, "Gap Between House, Senate Republicans Reflects Conflict within the Party Itself," *Wall Street Journal*, September 14, 1995, p. A20.

with use of federal funds for abortion, and although many moderate Republicans wavered in their support for the bill, they rallied to urgent appeals by the leadership to maintain the momentum toward budget balance. At the end of 1995, the bill had still not passed Congress.

By the beginning of the fiscal year, only two appropriations bills had been signed by the president. While reductions in appropriations averaged 5 percent below 1995 levels, the overall figures masked much deeper cuts in certain programs, which the president sometimes accepted, perhaps for concessions in other areas. For example, in agriculture, rural development aid was cut by 10 percent and rural housing preservation grants by half. In transportation, a shift in priorities was represented by the 43 percent cut in operating assistance for mass transit and a 25 percent cut in Amtrak subsidy, while highway construction funds (a traditional pork barrel category) were increased. The energy and water bill retained many local projects, but cut solar and fission research. Whether large or small, these and similar cuts represented changes in priorities, and cuts in programs and services. And domestic appropriations in future years would have to shrink even further if the president approved the extension of the domestic spending caps attached to the reconciliation bill passed by Congress.[74] But at the end of the fiscal year, attention focused on the lack of appropriations for most of the federal government, necessitating a continuing resolution.

CONFRONTATION: CONTINUING RESOLUTIONS AND THE DEBT LIMIT

Continuing resolutions, because Congress had not passed some or all of the appropriations bills by the beginning of the fiscal year, were not unusual. Even interruptions in federal government operations were not so exceptional—there had been nine since 1981, though none since 1990. The crisis of 1995 was different because of its length (the first shutdown was for six days, and the second for nineteen), and because Congress tried to use the leverage of the essential continuing resolution, and its approval of a raise in the debt limit, to gain advance commitment by the president to important elements in its forthcoming reconciliation bill. The reconciliation bill would contain the entitlement and taxation proposals on which a future balanced budget depended, as well as a number of other measures. It was a key part of the Republican program.

Congress and the president had agreed with little problem to a continuing resolution to keep government running until mid-November, even though the temporary funding it enacted was below the levels so far agreed to in appropriations bills still going through Congress.[75] But by mid-November, the president had signed only the bills for agriculture and military construction, and vetoed the appropriation for the legislative branch (on the grounds it would be unfair to vote

---

[74]Janet Hook, "Republicans Win Early Budget Battles," *Los Angeles Times,* November 26, 1995, p. A28.

[75]David Rogers, "GOP Proposes Stopgap Spending Bill Imposing a Deeper Cut than Its Budget," *Wall Street Journal,* September 21, 1995.

funds for Congress while denying them to other federal employees). Of the ten bills outstanding, Clinton had threatened to veto at least five, as well as the reconciliation bill. Meanwhile, the federal government had reached the debt limit ($4.9 trillion), requiring Congress to raise it.

The sense of crisis had been building for a month. At the beginning of September, Treasury Secretary Rubin had warned that "even the appearance that the government will default on its debts would roil the financial markets and cause severe economic problems." Unless the limit was raised before the end of October, the government would be unable to borrow money to pay its debts. The Republicans were unimpressed, suggesting the government could function on a cash flow basis, and called on President Clinton to prevent a crisis by balancing the budget over seven years.[76]

A month later, the Treasury began to cut back its short-term borrowing and again called on Congress to raise the debt limit. White House Chief of Staff Panetta reiterated the president's determination to veto any balanced budget bill that contained unacceptable spending reductions, and blamed congressional Republicans for creating an "atmosphere of instability."[77] There was a brief interlude when it appeared Speaker Gingrich was willing to increase the debt ceiling temporarily, but in apparent deference to radical elements, backed down.[78]

Attitudes hardened as a showdown neared. On November 13, the continuing resolution would expire, and on November 15 the Treasury Department would owe nearly $25 billion in interest payments. As Congress prepared a new continuing resolution and bill to raise the debt limit with conditions attached, a senior Treasury Department official remarked, "The bus is near the edge of the cliff."[79] The twin possibilities of simultaneous federal government shutdown and financial default seemed imminent.

What were the issues? The immediate concerns were the conditions set out by Congress to resolve the short-term spending and borrowing crisis and their unacceptability to the president. Some of the most objectionable clauses (abolition of the Commerce Department; ban on lobbying by organizations receiving federal money) had been removed during the debates in Congress. What remained was a short-term spending bill, which sharply cut funding and eliminated a scheduled medicare premium reduction, and a temporary raising of the debt ceiling until December 12 when it would drop to below the existing level. The debt limit bill would also prevent the Treasury from using cash from trust funds to avoid the limit, and confirm Congress's intent not to raise it again until legislation eliminating the deficit in 2002 was signed. Both bills would commit the president to balancing the budget by 2002; would require federal agencies to weigh the projected

[76]Jack Nelson, "Rubin Urges Congress To Raise Debt Ceiling," Los Angeles Times, September 8, 1995, p. A33.

[77]Jonathan Peterson, "Treasury To Scale Back on Borrowing To Avert Debt Crisis," Los Angeles Times, October 18, 1995, pp. A1, A21.

[78]Wall Street Journal, October 19, 1995, pp. A23, A13.

[79]Jonathan Peterson, "Default Scenario Looms Larger as Budget War Rages," Los Angeles Times, November 9, 1995, p. A26.

costs of regulations against their expected benefits and allow Congress to kill new regulations; and would limit appeals by death row prisoners.[80]

The Republican strategy was to use the leverage of the two measures to force the president to pass the reconciliation bill. They wanted to deliver on the promises they had made on election to Congress and to balance the budget in seven years. If the president acceded to their demands they would triumph, and if he did not, they would be able to blame him for the consequent breakdown. Declared Majority Leader Robert Dole, "If the government shuts down, his fingerprints are going to be all over it."[81]

The administration for their side labeled the Republican tactics "a form of terrorism."[82] Buoyed by recent polls that showed public opinion swinging in his favor, the president reiterated his intention to veto the bills, on the grounds that they were attempts to impose policy and should be legislated separately. The president, having so far taken a mostly passive role in the budget debate, now needed to show he would "stand firm," and to "draw a line in the sand," even if this involved the possibility of a stopgap bill right through to the election in November 1996. In this stalemate, a senior White House official said, "Voters would ultimately see him as the leader who saved Medicare from excessive spending curtailment, preserved the environment, and headed off tax cuts that give too much to the rich."[83] At a meeting with the congressional leadership on November 1, both administration and Republicans appeared to realize the limitations on compromise on both sides and the necessity for each to work out proposals acceptable to their own parties.

It was in the interest of both sides to come to an agreement. It was also in their interest to show how hard it was and to magnify the crisis—the Republican leadership to impress on the party's radical wing that they risked gaining nothing if they did not give in on something, and the president to impress on the Democratic liberal wing that certain concessions were necessary if anything was to be preserved at all. Both sides had to convince the voters that they were the responsible party of government, and so could not afford blame for a prolonged shutdown. "They will blame all of us," said Speaker Gingrich.[84] But each side saw its electoral appeal differently, and an imminent disaster as demonstrating its serious commitment to the cause. Senate Budget Committee Chairman Pete Domenici said, "The issue is whether we're going to get a real balanced budget—after all the effort we've put into it—or not."[85] And the

[80]Eric Pianin and Ann Devroy, "Clinton and GOP Push Fiscal Standoff to Brink," *Washington Post*, November 11, 1995, p. A1.

[81]Helen Dewar and John E. Young, "Political Stakes Are High as Each Side Cries Foul in Budget Showdown," *Washington Post*, November 10, 1995, p. A10.

[82]Paul Richter and Jonathan Peterson, "Federal Shutdown Nears Despite GOP Budget Action," *Los Angeles Times*, November 10, 1995, p. A32; Eric Pianin and Ann Devroy, "Clinton and GOP Push Fiscal Stand Off to Brink," *Washington Post*, November 11, 1995, p. A1.

[83]Jack Nelson, "Clinton Draws Line in the Sand on Budget," *Los Angeles Times*, November 10, 1995, p. A34.

[84]Janet Hook, "Showdown: High Stakes Game for Both Parties," *Los Angeles Times*, November 14, 1995, p. A14.

[85]Ibid., p. A15.

president, "I've worked hard for 25 years on these issues [education, welfare, health care reform, and other social issues]. I care deeply about them. I don't care if I go to 5 percent in the polls. I think your bill is bad for America and I'm not going to sign it."[86]

The president vetoed the continuing resolution and the debt limit bill. The federal government closed down, except for essential activities, and the Treasury secretary carried out a maneuver to "disinvest" in two federal trust funds as a technical way to lower federal debt and allow fresh borrowing under the debt limit so that the federal government would not default.[87]

The negotiations were at an impasse. The president denounced the Republicans for using "the threat of a government shutdown to force America to accept their cuts in education and technology and the environment." The continuing resolution would have required "a level of cuts in Medicare and Medicaid, in education, in the environment and a tax increase on working people, all of which I find highly objectionable."[88] For their part, Republicans contended that Clinton distorted their proposed budget cuts and blamed him for precipitating the crisis by not making a realistic effort to balance the budget.[89]

Given the rhetoric on both sides, the end to the impasse came relatively quickly and enabled both sides to claim advantage. Congress passed a new version of the continuing resolution, allowing normal government operation with only one condition—that the president should agree to balance the budget in seven years, using CBO assumptions, while dropping the medicare premium increase. Again the president promised to veto it, but the tide was running against both parties. The Republicans' position in the polls was lagging, and in Congress nearly 50 House Democrats and 7 Senate Democrats voted for the latest version of the continuing resolution.

The final compromise achieved both sides' bottom lines. It stated that Congress and the president "shall enact" a balanced budget by the year 2002, based on the projections of the CBO "following a thorough consultation and review with OMB and other government and private experts." One up for the Republicans. On the other hand, the agreement stipulated that the balanced budget must "protect future generations, ensure Medicare solvency, reform welfare and provide adequate funding for Medicaid, education, agriculture, national defense, veterans and the environment." Further, "the balanced budget shall adopt tax policies to help working families and to stimulate future growth.[90] One up for the Democrats.

---

[86]Edward Chen, "Sharp Edges and Blunt Talk as Two Sides Meet," *Los Angeles Times*, November 15, 1995, p. A16.

[87]What the Secretary did was to cancel $61.3 billion in securities held by two federal retirement funds, thus freeing the government to sell more debt to the public without violating the limit. This action would carry the government through to the end of December, and other options could carry it through to mid-February or March 1996. Alan Murray, "Debt Limit Crisis Is Not Over Yet," *Wall Street Journal*, November 27, 1995, A1.

[88]Jerry Gray, "Feuding Goes on as GOP Presents Its Budget Plan," *New York Times*, November 17, 1995, p. A14.

[89]Paul Richter and Janet Hook, "800,000 Federal Workers Idled in Budget Impasse," *Los Angeles Times*, November 15, 1995, p. A1.

[90]Alan Miller, "Budget Deal Reached To End Government Shutdown," *Los Angeles Times*, November 20, 1995, p. A6.

House Speaker Gingrich hailed the accord as

one of the great historic achievements in modern America. And I think every family is going to have a better Thanksgiving because we really are now looking out for the children of America, and we really are providing them a chance to have a future in which they're not going to be crushed by debt and taxation and high interest rates.[91]

But the president appeared to have reserved his right to block any budget plan that did not meet his priorities: "The real winners tonight are the American people because now we can have an open honest discussion about how best to balance the budget. . . . Nothing will be agreed to unless all elements are agreed to."[92]

The question of whose deficit projections would be used was critical. In July, the administration had updated its forecasts; its figures for economic growth and inflation diverged slightly from those of CBO. The CBO March forecast, relied on by Congress, had seen real growth at 2.3 percent, while the new administration figure was 2.5 percent, the CBO figure for inflation was 3.1 percent, and the administration figure was 3.2 percent. Together with other assumptions about the growth of profits, and calculations of the Consumer Price Index and GDP Inflator, which measure inflation, the differences were responsible for a discrepancy of over $400 billion in deficit projection![93]

The Republicans made a great deal of the need for "honest numbers," but as Felix Rohatyn has pointed out, seven years is a long time, and projections are notoriously uncertain. There was no process established to keep the movement toward the balanced budget on track.[94] And President Clinton's big "concession" to agree to balance the budget in seven years seemed less impressive, as Herbert Stein skeptically remarked, in the light of virtually every president's pledge to balance the budget.[95] The agreement to use revised projections satisfied both sides for the moment and maintained the pretense that absolutely accurate forecasts really did exist.

Much then seemed to have been left unresolved. Nothing had been decided on the debt limit, which had come to be seen as symbolic by the far right.[96] The president still vowed to veto the reconciliation bill, and the outstanding appropriations bills were problematic. The president signed four more bills immediately

[91]John Broder and James Gerstenzang, "Accord Doesn't Signal the End of Budget Fight," *Los Angeles Times*, November 20, 1995, p. A6.

[92]Todd S. Purdum, "President and GOP Agree To End Federal Shutdown and Negotiate a Budget," *New York Times*, November 20, 1995, p. A1.

[93]David Wessel, "The Art of Tweaking: White House's Altered Forecast on Economy Underlies Capitol Hill Budget Deal," *Wall Street Journal*, November 3, 1995, p. A16.

[94]Felix Rohatyn, "The Budget: Whom Can You Believe," *New York Review of Books*, August 10, 1995, pp. 48–49. See also Robert Eisner, "The Deficit Is Budget Battle's Red Herring," *Wall Street Journal*, November 28, 1995, p. A13.

[95]Interview with Herbert Stein, *The News Hour with Jim Lehrer*, November 22, 1995.

[96]It was doubtful that it would be possible to continue to use the civil service retirement fund to enable the federal government to borrow the $160 billion it would need up to the November 1996 election, even though the fund held over $300 billion. It appeared that legally access was limited to the amount of one year retirement benefits in any one year. Alan Murray, "Debt Limit Crisis Is Not Over Yet," *Wall Street Journal*, November 27, 1995, p. A1.

after the agreement, despite disagreement with some of their contents. Meanwhile, the major conflict over the reconciliation bill assumed urgency.

RECONCILIATION AND INTRANSIGENCE

The reconciliation bill packaged together the work that had been carried out for months by the various committees of Congress to rewrite legislation on revenues and entitlements. (It also included a variety of measures that had been attached because this seemed a good way to get them passed, e.g., opening up the Arctic Wildlife Reserve to oil development.) The aim was to pass measures that would conform to the spending and savings limits set out in the reconciliation instructions attached to the congressional resolution. The resulting bill, over 1700 pages long, was subject to only 20 hours of debate in each House, and required a single vote—yes or no. Separate versions were passed by House and Senate, reconciled in conference, and an agreed measure finally passed in each House, almost entirely along party lines. The president immediately stated he would veto it. Polarization seemed complete.

The reconciliation bill was seen as the key to budget balance. But the primary goal of budget balance was brought into question by the Republican insistence on a tax cut of $245 billion, which of course made the task much harder. Among other proposals, the tax cuts included child tax credits, reductions in the capital gains tax, reduction in the rate of corporate tax, and creation of new forms of Individual Retirement Accounts. They also included several allowances for post-secondary education, adoption, and elderly care, as well as several business-friendly tax concessions, such as continuation of ethanol subsidies,[97] windfall tax savings for thrift institutions,[98] and extension of the business research credit.[99] These tax cuts were offset by $33 billion in increased revenues from restricting the eligibility criteria for the Earned Income Tax Credit, which had reduced taxes for the working poor. *The Economist,* not usually noted for its charitable approach, characterized the tax measures as "unnecessary, badly targeted and over-favorable to the rich."[100]

The other side of the equation was spending cuts. The reconciliation bill set out new caps that would reduce domestic discretionary expenditures to 30 percent below the baseline.

The scale of change in the entitlements programs was unprecedented. They encompassed over half a trillion dollars in cuts from medicare, medicaid, welfare, agricultural subsidies, and student loans, as well as smaller programs. The cut in medicare of $270 billion was well in excess of the $130 billion the administration estimated as sufficient to secure the viability of the trust funds, and the legislation

---

[97]James Bovard, "Dole, Gingrich and the Big Ethanol Boondoggle," *Wall Street Journal,* November 2, 1995, p. A14.

[98]John R. Wilke, "Thrifts May Reap Windfall with Budget Bill Measure," *Wall Street Journal,* November 27, 1995, pp. A4, A6.

[99]Christina Duff, "Friendly Footwork in Congress Spells Special Tax Breaks for Some Businesses," *Wall Street Journal,* November 27, 1995, p. A5.

[100]"Right Size, Wrong Contents," *The Economist,* November 11, 1995, p. 16.

involved substantial restructuring of the program. Whether these changes would actually produce the savings targeted was unclear, but if they did not, a "look back" clause would impose further cuts. Medicaid, cut by $163 billion, ceased to be an entitlement, and the federal commitment was replaced by lump sum grants to the states. The $82 billion cut in programs loosely grouped together as welfare also ended federal entitlement status and involved reductions in cash welfare, food stamps, nutrition aid, and supplemental security income for the disabled. The proposal turned the programs over to the states and allowed them to deny cash benefits to unmarried mothers under 18 and those who had more children while on welfare. Agricultural subsidies were replaced by capped and shrinking payments to farmers, and other changes added up to $13 billion in savings. The student loan program was cut by an estimated $5 billion, and an entire program was eliminated.[101]

The reconciliation bill, on one reading, represented in the words of Martin Olav Sabo, a House Democrat from Minnesota, "two very different visions of America's future. I call on my colleagues to reject a vision of America that seeks to reward those who have already prospered in our economy while imposing burdens on those who have not." Added Representative John Dingell, the dean of the House, "This is one of the worst pieces of legislation I've seen in my 40 years in Congress."[102] Understandably, Republicans saw things differently.

The division between the sides was underscored by the choice of more stringent proposals over more moderate ones: larger cuts from food stamps ($37 billion instead of the Senate proposal for $28 billion); rejection of more lenient Senate work requirements for welfare and cut in child care provision; erasing Senate retention of elderly nursing home standards and commitment to aid all disabled poor under medicaid; and deeper cuts in services to legal immigrants.[103]

For his part, the president said, "I am not prepared to discuss the destruction of Medicare and Medicaid, the gutting of our commitment to education, the ravaging of our environment, or raising taxes on working people."[104] In response to a request from the Republicans for specific proposals, at the end of November, the administration set out nine principles: high quality medical care for the elderly under medicare, adequate funding for medicaid, tax fairness, maintenance of real funding in education, sustain progress in environmental protection, provide adequate resources to move people from welfare to work, preserve the strength of America's farms, provide enough military spending to meet the nation's needs, and continue providing veterans with the benefits to which they are entitled.[105]

---

[101]*Wall Street Journal*, November 17, 1995, p. A4.

[102]Jackie Calmes and Christopher Georges, "Senate, House Close to Votes on Budget, Taxes," *Wall Street Journal*, October 27, 1995, p. A2.

[103]Christopher Georges, "Budget Bill Dismisses Moderates' Input," *Wall Street Journal*, November 20, 1995, p. A14.

[104]Hilary Stout, "Clinton, After His Veto, Will Have Tricky Job of Trying To Strike a Budget Deal on His Terms," *Wall Street Journal*, October 30, 1995, p. A20.

[105]*Los Angeles Times*, November 25, 1995, p. A25.

UNFINISHED BUSINESS

The euphoria of the November agreement did not last long, as cracks inevitably appeared in the glossed-over disagreements. The president's declared agenda was to protect health, social, environmental, and education programs, even within a balanced budget framework. The Republicans were determined to ensure a balanced budget in the next seven years, to reverse the role of the federal government, and to implement large tax cuts.

Neither side sustained its position completely. The president repeatedly revised his figures. The Republicans discovered that closing the federal government, though within the grand tradition of refusing supply to an intransigent executive, extorted too high a political price, and revised their strategy to provide a series of continuing resolutions for partial government funding. They also made some concessions on tax reductions and expenditure cuts. Even the debt limit, the apparent ultimate and invincible weapon to force budget choices on the executive, might turn out to be the equivalent of a nuclear warhead whose fallout would destroy victor and vanquished alike.

The budget seemed to have evaporated into a few appropriations and piece-meal continuing resolutions. Neither side appeared to see electoral advantage in agreement on a funding plan, at least for the coming year, although the main indicators were not so far apart. Both sides seemed to have lost. The Republicans, by refusing to compromise, had failed to realize their dream of a balanced budget, tax cuts, and determination of the course of budgetary policy for the next seven years. The president, by acceding to demands for a balanced budget, large expenditure cuts, and tax reductions, had adopted much of the Republican program. But the Republican loss was not the president's gain, since funding by continuing resolution in fact meant funding well below existing levels. How did all this happen?

In early December 1995, budget talks collapsed and the president vetoed the reconciliation bill, providing a 50-page fact sheet on the reasons why. However, he did offer a new budget proposal, his third in 1995. This proposal balanced the budget in seven years and incorporated about $140 billion more savings than his previous plan in June 1995. About a quarter ($36 billion) came from recalculation of the Consumer Price Index, and almost as much from sale of assets, notably auction of space on the broadcasting spectrum. Medicare, medicaid, and tax reductions would be unchanged from the June proposal, but an additional $15 billion would be taken from welfare spending and a further $64 billion from unspecified cuts in domestic discretionary programs, about 5 percent below current levels or 20 percent from the baseline.

The Republicans rejected the plan and found further justification in the new CBO forecast a few days later. The CBO projected that there would be an additional $135 billion in deficit reduction over the next seven years, but that the president's latest proposal would result in a $115 billion deficit in 2002, and over the whole period savings would fall short by $350 billion. The Republicans reconfigured some of the major indicators of their budget, and talks resumed to try to avert a new federal government shutdown on December 15. Congress passed three appropriations bills (Interior; Veterans Affairs, Housing and Urban Development; and Commerce, Justice, and State) which the president promptly vetoed. The budget talks collapsed.

The Republicans contended that the president refused to present a new "good faith" plan to conform to CBO figures, and the president insisted he was being pressured to make unacceptable cuts in the health programs.

This time the federal shutdown lasted 19 days and involved furloughs of 260,000 to 280,000 federal employees, compared with 800,000 in November, since only six appropriations bills were now still in contention. Although many government services continued, such as issue of social security checks and medicare payments, protection of public health and safety, and the post office, the crisis was more severe. Within a week, Congress approved a stopgap law to fund temporary benefits for veterans and welfare recipients. But the effects of the shutdown were still noticeable as passports and visas were unobtainable, federally funded unemployment offices closed, tourists found national parks, museums, and monuments closed, and funds for programs as diverse as Head Start, FEMA, medicaid, courts, and services to the elderly began to run out. Regulatory functions relating to immigrants, the environment, and health were impeded. As federal employees went unpaid, the ripple effects spread and public opinion grew more adverse to the Republicans and more favorable to the president.

The stakes for both sides were high, and each blamed the other for the shutdown. The continued popularity of the seven-year balanced budget was attested by a largely symbolic vote in the House of Representatives (December 19), won by 351 votes to 40, with 133 Democrats voting for it. But neither side seemed prepared to budge on what it saw as advantage. In addition to vetoing the three appropriations bills, the president vetoed the defense authorization bill, and when the House passed a welfare reform bill, he said he would veto that also. Various plans to end the shutdown were blocked by Republicans who believed that, in Speaker Gingrich's words, "giving up on balancing the budget would be a tragedy that would haunt us for the rest of our lives."[106] Even though the leadership might be willing to compromise, many of the rank and file saw the budget fight as the moral equivalent of war, and believed they could win if only they stood firm.

By the beginning of January 1996, it seemed clear that the Republican strategy to shut down government to force the president's hand had failed. It only made them appear extreme and willing to use over a quarter of a million federal employees as pawns. The tactic to use the debt ceiling as leverage had also been foiled by Treasury Secretary Rubin's tactics, and although the position would be dire by the beginning of March if nothing were done, blame for the consequences of a federal default was a daunting prospect.

The Republican leadership, therefore, changed course. The House, which had earlier rejected a short-term continuing resolution passed by the Senate, now acceded to leadership proposals for a new strategy of selective funding. The president, after initial hesitation, agreed to a continuing resolution to fund the government until January 26, 1996, on condition he submit a new balanced budget proposal using congressional figures. Congress also passed a "targeted appropriation," restoring funds for the rest of the fiscal year for 17 high-profile agencies, including law enforcement, medicare, medicaid, National Institutes for Health, Centers for Disease Control, black lung benefits, and some Native American programs. This

[106]*Los Angeles Times,* December 19, 1995, p. A16.

strategy allowed Congress to pick and choose and, in effect, make policy through continuing resolution. Thus they fully funded a deaf school in Washington but not Head Start; federal mortgages for single-family homes but not housing subsidies for the poor; meals on wheels but not elderly transportation programs.

Meanwhile, the two sides had actually moved closer together. On January 7, the president endorsed a Senate Democratic plan, which would achieve a total of $605 billion in savings by 2002, and which was certified as resulting in a balanced budget by CBO. But although the dollar amounts were closer, neither side wanted to appear to have given in. Negotiations broke off on January 9, 1996, and only briefly resumed on January 17. The outlook for an agreement appeared bleak.

A week later, agreement was reached on another continuing resolution to fund the government until mid-March, 1996, and to raise the debt limit. Each side made a few concessions. The continuing resolution covered unresolved appropriations bills Clinton had vetoed as unacceptable: Veterans Administration, Housing and Urban Development, Interior, and Commerce, Justice, and State; the Labor, Health, and Human Services bill had not yet cleared the Senate. Both sides were tired of the conflict: The reconciliation bill was dead and the impasse over a seven year balanced budget seemed unlikely to be resolved; state governors were lobbying for welfare reform, yet another contentious issue; the need to reauthorize the five year Agriculture Bill, a further source of ideological conflict over farmers' subsidies, was pressing; and both sides wanted to devote their energies to the 1996 elections.

On April 25, after several weeks of negotiations, Congress passed an omnibus appropriations bill that was signed by the president the next day. It covered the final five outstanding contentious appropriations bills, and provided a remarkably bipartisan ending to the bitter disputes that had characterized the previous year. Compromise was the order of the day: In the words of the chairman of the Senate Appropriations Committee, "Everybody got something, everybody gave something."[107]

Several of the more draconian cuts and program eliminations in the earlier bills were scaled back. For example, EPA ended with about a 10 percent cut instead of a third; HHS suffered about a 4 percent cut in discretionary spending instead of about 10 percent; the Department of Education lost about 6 percent compared with 1995 funding, but this was about 7 percent more than the House approved; and the Department of Labor ended with about a 5 percent cut below its 1995 funding but 11 percent more than the House sought. On the other hand, HUD still suffered a cut of about 23 percent, little better than on the initial bill, and the Interior Department funding was similar to the previously vetoed bill.

Several programs slated for elimination were rescued, though their funding was cut. These included several education programs favored by the president such as Goals 2000 and Americorps. A school-to-work program and Drug Free Schools received nearly double the amount the House had voted, and programs for AIDS and Head Start also received increases above the previous year's funding.

Beyond the funding issues were considerations of policy. The House Republicans had quite deliberately used the budget process to further their social

[107]George Hager, "Congress, Clinton Yield Enough To Close the Book on Fiscal '96," *Congressional Quarterly Weekly Report*, April 27, 1996, p. 1155.

and environmental goals, through the addition of controversial riders to appropriations bills. In particular, they had targeted the Mojave Natural Preserve in California, expansion of logging in the Alaskan Tongass National Forest, and the EPA's veto over permits to develop wetlands. As the budget negotiations dragged on, the environmental issues began to refocus the budget agenda to the Democrats' advantage as defenders of the environment. In the end, the environmental riders were either dropped or the president was given authority to waive them, which he promptly did.

It is easy either to overemphasize or to dismiss the effects of the events of 1995. A congressional majority was not sufficient to ensure the passage of a radical program of change or definitively to change the future. Its agenda was thwarted not only by a president of the opposing party, but also by its own lack of cohesion and by the complex mechanisms of the budgetary process, which allowed multiple opportunities for diverse agendas, demanded the repeated making and remaking of different coalitions, and diffused power into numerous centers, any one of which could exercise a veto or press a cause on its own account. The president's successful veto of the reconciliation bill spelled the end of the attempt to force through large tax and entitlement cuts, so that the sole channel for change was domestic appropriations, or 16 percent of the budget. The net cuts achieved in this area were only about 9 percent, well below the 14 percent achieved by Reagan in 1981.[108] The president was able to protect his priorities, such as education, job training, and the environment. A constitutional amendment to balance the budget failed passage, and the apparently powerful weapons of refusing to raise the debt limit or pass continuing resolutions backfired and became political liabilities. Efforts to use the budget process to enact policy through riders to appropriations also for the most part failed.

But the budget saga of 1995 is more than a cautionary tale about the limits of the politics of the budgetary process. The cuts in appropriations, though less than their proponents had sought, were nonetheless significant. The cuts were made not from a baseline, i.e. a projection of next year's spending, but from the previous year's expenditures. The net sums marked much larger cuts in some individual programs. The final amounts also usually were considerably less than the administration's requests. And although domestic appropriations were only 16 percent of the federal budget, they represented most of federal government activities, what it actually *does*, excepting defense and entitlement payments.

Perhaps even more important, the conflicts of 1995 had altered the terms of the debate. The president combated much of the Republican program by seizing the central ground, but this was not the same center as it was the year before. There had been a change in assumptions. A balanced budget, tax reductions, entitlement overhaul, and welfare reform were all now a part of the budgetary rhetoric, symbolized by the president's State of the Union message at the beginning of 1996: The era of big government was over.

The events of 1995 reflected not only the immediate political situation, but a more general crisis and response, evident in other industrialized countries. In Europe, the requirements of the Maastricht Treaty creating a European Monetary Union demanded a reduction of national government deficits to 3 percent of GDP and government debt to 60 percent of GDP, bringing into question the long-standing

---

[108]Hager, op. cit., *Congressional Quarterly Weekly Report,* April 27, 1996, p. 1155.

policies of the welfare state. The prolonged and serious strike in France at the end of 1995 indicated public reaction to measures to slash public expenditures and retract pension and health benefits. Moreover, demands to cut the role of government were being made in the face of high unemployment, growing crime, large-scale immigration, environmental degradation, and the diffuse impacts of the difficulties of the "transitional economies" of Russia and Eastern Europe.

Beyond the pressing current issues lay compelling demographic trends. In several countries, it was estimated that persons over 65 would constitute over one quarter of the population early in the twenty-first century. At issue was the sustaining of the health and pension benefits of the elderly, while maintaining and improving the standard of living (through private and collective provisions) of the working population and their children. The politics of radical reversal was pitting old against young in a zero sum game.

In the United States, the budget battles of 1995 framed these issues in terms of individualism and reliance on the market against government intervention in the general interest and coping with social problems. But, as we have seen, the lines were not clear-cut. Other disputes centered on the division between rich and poor, on business advantage through public largesse, on arguments about moral rectitude and standards of behavior, as well as the conflict between children and the elderly.

How did the budget process cope with these conflicts? From one perspective, the budget process might be seen as an impediment to the legitimate realization of the will of the majority. The Republican leadership (particularly the Speaker of the House) coordinated and streamlined a coherent program and shepherded it through Congress in an unprecedented display of power and persuasion. In a parliamentary system, where the executive is drawn from and dependent on a legislative majority, its policies would have become law. But the existence of an independent executive forced the congressional majority into confrontation, a confrontation they were unable to win through crude tactics of refusal of supply.

Yet, perhaps the process really did work the way it was intended. The fragmentation of congressional procedures and sharing of power between executive and legislature prevented any single group from forcing through a highly contentious and far-reaching program, and required compromise to maintain the working of the system. The budget process reflected the pluralist nature of American politics in which issues splinter along a series of fault lines, rather than a single ideological front.

The American system of shared powers deals uneasily with absolute, unshakable positions. Either side may insist on its prerogative and maintain its cause is so right that it can in no way be modified. Congress may legitimately hold government hostage, preventing it from expending funds or borrowing, as a weapon in the holy war for a balanced budget, tax cuts, and radical change. The president may legitimately veto appropriations bills. But the price of obstinacy is often deadlock, with political consequences that may be unsustainable.

The 1995 budget process was thus not entirely a unique episode or a vehicle for radical change. It was a drama, illustrating the interplay of personalities, the limitations of political power, the realities of institutional checks and balances, the cut and thrust of debate and negotiation. But it also represented a development in the debates about the role of the federal government, which still continue and which provide the inevitable backdrop for the budget dramas of subsequent years.

Chapter 8

The Politics of the Entitlement Process

T he "old Politics" remains a good description of less than 20 percent of the budget. Aside from defense (which now makes up about 16 percent of the total) and the 13 percent devoted to interest on the debt, some 57 percent—more than half the budget—is devoted to entitlements, mostly payments to individuals, leaving that catchall category—nondefense discretionary—to cover most of what we think of as domestic government—the Weather Bureau, the Forest Service, the State Department, the Labor and Commerce departments, and the rest.[1]

Entitlements are legal obligations created through legislation that require the payment of benefits to any person or unit of government that meets the eligibility requirements established by law. Budget authority for such payments may be, but is not necessarily, provided in advance. Thus some entitlement legislation, such as food stamps, requires the subsequent enactment of appropriations. Examples of entitlements are social security, medicare, and unemployment compensation. Entitlements comprise the largest single part of the budget. Obviously any contemporary account of budgeting cannot only be about the appropriations process, but must also cover the politics of the entitlement process.[2]

Why is there concern over entitlements? Because entitlements are growing faster than the rest of the budget (see Table 8.1). According to the Congressional Budget Office, mandatory spending increased its budget share from 32 percent in 1962 to over 55 percent in 1998. Projections are for entitlements to continue to grow faster than other spending, and to reach 63 percent of the budget in 2002 (double the share of discretionary outlays) and nearly 75 percent in 2009.[3]

[1]Congressional Budget Office, *The Economic and Budget Outlook: Fiscal Years 2000–2009,* January 1999, pp. 66–78. Figures do not add due to rounding.

[2]R. Kent Weaver, "Controlling Entitlements," in John E. Chubb and Paul E. Peterson, eds., *The New Direction in American Politics* (Washington, D.C.: Brookings, 1985). For general discussion of entitlements, see John C. Weicher, *Entitlement Issues in the Domestic Budget* (Washington, D.C.: American Enterprise Institute, 1985).

[3]Congressional Budget Office, *The Economic and Budget Outlook 2002–2009,* January 1999, p. 68.

Table 8.1 Growth in Discretionary and Entitlement Spending 1975–1998

	Entitlement			Discretionary			Total		
	Outlays ($ billions)	Percentage of outlays	Percentage of GDP	Outlays ($ billions)	Percentage of outlays	Percentage of GDP	Outlays ($ billions)	Percentage of outlays	Percentage of GDP
1975	164.9	49.6	10.6	157.8	47.5	10.2	332.3	100.0	21.4
1985	434.0	45.9	10.6	415.7	43.9	10.1	946.4	100.0	23.1
1995	782.5	51.7	10.9	545.1	36.0	7.6	1,515.7	100.0	21.1
est. 1998	918.8	55.1	11.0	552.7	33.1	6.6	1,667.8	100.0	20.0

Source: Budget of the United States Government, Fiscal Year 1999, Historical Tables, Tables 8.1–8.4, pp 117–20.

Consequently, conservatives fear much higher taxes and/or deficits; liberals fear that entitlements will squeeze out other programs.

Entitlements cover a wide variety of programs in which individuals gain benefits because of their circumstances. Only about one-quarter of total spending goes to "poor people's" programs, often known as "means tested" programs. The largest share goes to programs for the elderly (including social security, medicare, and retirement), (see Table 8.2). Not all social programs are entitlements, and not all entitlements go to needy people. Nor do all entitlement programs grow at the same rate, though growth does characterize many of the largest entitlements. Before we look at the dynamics of entitlement spending, however, we need to look at what all entitlement programs have in common: the explicit benefit they confer on a specific group of people who fit the requirements of legal eligibility.

THE "OUGHT" AND "IS" OF ENTITLEMENTS

There are legitimate policy reasons—of efficiency, or the political difficulty of alternatives, or the desire to keep promises—for entitlement funding. Entitlements increase stability and security, and represent community provision for the routine hazards of life in an uncertain market economy. But there are also good policy reasons for protecting government from adversity by enabling it to limit demands on its resources. When good reasons conflict, difficult choices are necessary.

Moral power—the shared beliefs about who is entitled to what in society—is a necessary though not a sufficient condition for an entitlement program not only to exist on a minimal level, but to grow. In the beginning of the American republic, the concept of entitlement did not exist and there were no such programs. After the Civil War, pensions were provided for veterans and their widows. The era of modern entitlements began with railroad retirement in 1934, a combination of influence and grievance no more easy to disentangle than the general question of where moral norms begin and political power ends.

Table 8.2   Growth in Entitlement Spending: 1975–1997 Selected Programs

| | (in billions of dollars) | | | | |
	1975	1985	1990	1994	1997
Social security and related programs	63.6	186.4	246.5	317.0	362.3
Medicare	12.2	64.1	95.8	141.8	187.4
Medicaid	6.8	22.7	41.1	82.0	95.5
Federal employee retirement	13.2	38.5	51.9	62.4	71.3
Food and nutrition assistance	6.6	16.7	21.3	33.0	31.6
Unemployment	12.8	15.8	17.1	26.4	20.6
Public assistance	9.4	19.0	28.1	52.0	55.0
Veterans benefits	12.5	15.9	16.1	20.8	20.7
Education, training, etc.	3.1	7.6	11.1	9.0	13.7
Agriculture	2.0	23.5	9.3	10.6	5.0

Source: United States Budget, Fiscal Year 1999, Historical Statistics: Table 8.5 Outlays for Mandatory and Related Programs pp. 121–25

The moral force of entitlements has varied with the degree to which beneficiaries are deemed responsible for their condition. The more the individual is considered responsible for poverty, for instance, the less likely is governmental
provision. The more government or society is held responsible, the more appropriate an entitlement would be. Two views on civil service retirement illustrate the
difference. The conservative position, emphasizing individual responsibility and
fearful of government "handouts," was expressed in a 1956 hearing by Tom
Murray, chairman of the House Committee on Post Office and Civil Service:

> In this day and time you never hear of the philosophy of saving for a rainy day or prac-
> ticing thrift; it looks like everybody wants to depend, or so many want to be dependent,
> on the Government to keep on supporting them for the rest of their lives after they re-
> tire. I cannot go along with that philosophy. I am interested in getting a retirement bill,
> but I want a sound actuarial fund. [4]

The liberal position, emphasizing adequacy, won out, as is expressed in a
House report in 1969:

> Federal staff retirement systems represent a mixture of insurance and humanitarian
> principles. In the matter of adjusting annuities after retirement, insurance practice
> would guarantee that whatever annuity an employee had earned at the time of retire-
> ment should be preserved without change. On the other hand, humanitarian consider-
> ations would argue that the welfare of the retired person is the major concern, and that
> annuities should be adjusted to changing needs. The latter theory has prevailed
> through congressional action. [5]

Differences of opinion on who is responsible for poverty, and therefore entitled to
what, remain great. [6] As entitlements rose, the balance swung away from individual
and toward social (i.e., governmental) responsibility.

A crucial factor in arguments about entitlements, therefore, is the socially
constructed definition of equity or fairness. Should employees get what they paid
for? Get what (somehow comparable) employees get? Not lose (to inflation)?
Keep pace with society (retiree gets increases in line with increases in the standard
of living)? Be guaranteed some "adequate" level of benefit? Any of these may legitimate an increase, but a package that reduces benefits overall can be justified on
the grounds that beneficiaries are already doing better than they should.

Even the prevailing sense of fairness—people should not be deprived of benefits—has variations. Is it fair to change the benefits for someone already retired,
that is, reduce benefits currently received? If that is unfair, what about a change in
benefits promised to those already working? Is it more fair to change the promise
to younger employees than to older? The notion is that certain obligations are
more obligating than others, in part because the ability of recipients to compen-

---

[4] House Committee on Post Office and Civil Service, *Hearings on S.2875 and Related Matters*, June 18,
19, 21, 26 and July 3, 10, 12, 1956, p. 78.

[5] House Committee on Post Office and Civil Service, U.S. House of Representatives Report 91–158,
Civil Service Retirement Financing and Benefits, p. 14.

[6] See Sidney Verba and Gary R. Orren, *Equality in America: The View from the Top* (Cambridge, Mass.:
Harvard University Press, 1985), p. 74.

sate for changes and the degree to which they may have relied on the old system varies.

Only the naive think that political power plays no role in entitlements; only the foolish think that politicians' perceptions of who is deserving play no part in determining who receives entitlements. Indeed, the two conceptions are related: Perception that a clientele is powerful makes it easier to think they are deserving and belief that a clientele is worthy makes it easier to justify mobilizing resources on their behalf. Widespread belief that a class of citizens ought to be helped makes it harder to deny them entitlements just as the opposite belief in their unworthiness makes it harder to keep giving them priority claim on our collective resources. In the nature of human affairs where mixed motives prevail, it is difficult to disentangle them; yet we can still recognize reciprocal influence between the "is" and "ought" of entitlements.

Anyone affected by a program may be among its clientele. This clientele includes not only the direct beneficiaries—wheat growers or schoolchildren who also eat subsidized lunches—but also the service providers—fertilizer and tractor companies, cooks and bottle washers, administrators, and interest groups—who live off the recipients. Also included are the politicians and publicists who claim credit or bask in the glow of having not only done well but good. Clients comprise, to use Hugh Heclo's term, the issue networks of people not only in the federal but at all levels of government who are regularly concerned with operating, defending, criticizing, and altering entitlements.

The conditions for constituency influence are well known: The broader based the group, the larger its numbers, the wider its geographic spread, the more intense its feelings (a joint product of the perceived importance of the benefits and beliefs about their rightness—for example, I have fought for my country or worked all my life), the better its organization, the more resources (votes, money, intelligence, ability to appeal to shared values) it can mobilize, the more politically powerful it will be. So far so obvious. The size of a constituency depends not only on those affected now but those who expect to be affected later, not only on those directly involved but on those who care about them. The political potency of social security depends, to be sure, on the many millions of retired people. But it also is a consequence of those who contribute now and hope to benefit later, their families who will have to provide less support, and providers, like nursing homes, who service them.

The size of the direct beneficiaries is not a given factor, out there in nature like a fruit waiting to be plucked, but rather is socially and politically constructed. Who is or is not physically or mentally handicapped to what degree, requiring what sort of assistance, changes with the standards of the time.[7] While the extremes are usually clear enough, programs can be altered to include more or fewer people. Major efforts may be made, as with food stamps, to actively encourage more people to apply. Here social mores figure prominently: Whether programs are seen as stigmatizing or whether recipients are exercising a too-long delayed right makes a considerable difference in "take-up" rates and hence in costs.

---

[7]See Deborah Stone, *The Disabled State* (Philadelphia: Temple University Press, 1984).

Potential recipients have both to know about the availability of benefits and to feel the moral desirability of applying before their numbers will rise.

While it is true that political forces create and alter entitlements, it is also true that entitlements help create political forces. Whether or not interest groups are influential in creating entitlements—often they are not—the very existence of these benefits creates incentives for interest groups to organize.[8]

Since size is such an important resource in obtaining political support, strong clients with weak claims, to use David Stockman's apt phrase,[9] or with insufficient influence are motivated to form coalitions. The survival of price supports in Congress is largely due to coalition building: Representatives from farm states, already advantaged by the rule that gives states with sparse population equal representation in the Senate, trade votes with each other; cotton is added to wheat and other commodities, farm and urban representatives trade votes on price supports in return for food stamps, nutrition programs, and so on. "It was the height of cynicism," so Robert Bauman, Republican from Maryland, said, "to marry the food stamp program to the agricultural bill . . . it was done for purposes of political logrolling to gain votes for both bills."[10]

But how, if changing values matter, the reader may wonder, did tobacco supports survive? By compromise and by craft. The bad name given to smoking by the massive evidence of its connection to lung cancer, emphysema, heart disease, and other health dangers has naturally raised questions about why government should subsidize the production of the noxious weed. Then, again, counterbalancing this concern was the plight of the family farmer in the South. On one side, this clash of values led to compromise: Without going into the very technical details, a complex scheme was devised through which it could be said that tobacco farmers were paying for their own support. On the other side, strategies were followed making it difficult to single out tobacco for special (and, therefore, hostile) treatment. At various times, under the aegis of Senator Jesse Helms, Republican of North Carolina, tobacco supports were combined with wheat and dairy programs or held hostage by southern senators to other dearly desired programs. By reducing the visible budgetary cost and by making opposition politically expensive, tobacco support was maintained, albeit at a reduced level.

"Entitled to" may suggest "deserving of." Without touching on questions the courts have sought to avoid—namely, whether entitlements constitute what Charles Reich called "the new property"[11]—one's picture of the just society may include a view of what individuals are entitled to, of what they should give to others, and of what part government should play in making such provisions. Who should give or take how much from whom is a fundamental political question. For entitlements are not only benefits to some people, but also represent costs to others. Transfers of income from taxpayers to recipients require moral justification as

---

[8]See Aaron Wildavsky, *Speaking Truth to Power* (Boston: Little, Crown, 1979), Chapter 3, "Policy as Its Own Cause," pp. 62–85.

[9]David Stockman, "The Social Pork Barrel," *The Public Interest*, No. 39 (Spring 1975), pp. 3–30.

[10]John A. Ferejohn, "Logrolling in an Institutional Context: A Case Study of Food Stamps Legislation," *Working Papers in Political Science*, P–5–85 (Palo Alto, Calif.: Hoover Institute, October 1985), p. 19.

[11]Charles Reich, "The New Property," *Yale Law Journal*, Vol. 73 (April 1964), pp. 733–87.

well as political clout. Should poverty be the criterion? What about the well-off elderly? Should the criterion be financial loss? If there is an entitlement for beekeepers (yes, there was, read on), why not for anyone else in danger of losing income or going out of business? Why are certain farmers who raise particular crops given price supports, but not others? Should anyone who is already a farmer or anyone who wishes to become one be entitled? Actually, it is not so much who is entitled, important though this question is, but rather the priority given to entitlement over nearly all other claims that has caused the most controversy.

The status of entitlements is both accepted (no one expects much change in the largest ones) and disputed, due to the budgetary bind into which their cumulative impact has led government. Because entitlements stand as prior claims that must be paid before others, they achieve certainty at the expense of all other residual claimants on government. It is the "nonentitled" who must change. When revenues rise as fast or faster than expenditures, this conflict among classes of claimants—the entitled versus general government programs (justice, information, regulation, etc.) and defense—is muted. When deficits rise, however, and spending levels are considered too high while entitlements have risen to half or more of the total, the desirability of entitlements does come into question.

When the dollars individuals receive from entitlements are tied to a measure of price changes, such as the Consumer Price Index (CPI), the benefit is said to be "indexed." At set intervals, a change in the price index beyond a specified degree triggers a change in the dollars received by beneficiaries. The Congressional Budget Office has estimated that automatic increases in benefits account for over one-third of the growth in entitlement programs. All the major retirement programs are automatically indexed to the cost of living, and two other major entitlements, food stamps and medicare, are annually adjusted for price changes. In 1999, outlays for programs with cost of living adjustments constituted nearly one-third of the budget.[12]

Hard as it may be to believe, indexation was once adopted as a way to save the government money. In 1972, buoyed by false predictions of future surpluses and perhaps by hopes of electoral rewards, Congress voted to raise social security benefits by 20 percent while raising taxes hardly at all. In 1973, to prevent a recurrence of this episode, Congress, in an act designed to "take Social Security out of politics," adopted automatic indexation. Retirees would not have to wait to catch up with inflation and politicians would have less reason to provide their regular election-time increase. Tax rates were set on the assumption that wages would grow at the rate for the Consumer Price Index (CPI) plus an additional amount of productivity. The plan backfired; although in the past price increases had lagged behind wage growth, starting in the 1970s, inflation began to outstrip wages.

But it is hard to outguess the future. A friend of social security, economist James Tobin, tells us what went wrong:

> In retrospect it is easy to see that indexation by the CPI is not a good idea, even in less turbulent economic times than the 1970s. Such indexation immunizes the favored group from inescapable national losses—in 1973/74 and 1979/80 the big rise in the

---

[12]Congressional Budget Office, *The Economic and Budget Outlook 2000–2009*, p. 73.

cost of imported oil—and throws their costs onto unprotected fellow-citizens. Likewise indexation in effect exempts its beneficiaries from paying increased taxes embodied in the prices that compose the index; others must bear the burdens of the public programs financed by those taxes.[13]

When only a favored few are indexed, little harm is done. The selected few may well need more protection than the rest of us. But when indexation covers tens of millions of people, the few begin to protect the many and the social contract of mutual support in society is weakened.

ENTITLEMENTS AND BUDGETING

Entitlements represent a protean subject: At the edges, it is not easy to say exactly what is in or out; and one can say virtually nothing that is true of everything. The reason is that entitlements are a product of history, not logic—of evolution, not design. The features one wishes to stress depend on the kind of analysis one wishes to make. Some entitlements, like social security, are permanent (sometimes called "no-year") and run on in perpetuity unless changed. Others, like commodity credit-price supports and food stamps, receive annual appropriations, though, in effect, they are treated as full entitlements because shortfalls are made up by supplemental appropriations. Some entitlements, such as medicaid for the poor, are means-tested; that is, eligibility depends on income and other assets. By contrast, unemployment compensation has no means test at the entry stage, but benefits are subject to taxation above a specified level of income. Retirement programs (for civilian and military federal employees but also for others) are financed in part by trust funds based on employer and employee contributions. Some entitlements serve narrow clienteles (e.g., black lung, student loans) while others (e.g., medicare) are broadly based. Railroad retirement and veterans' pensions are tied (or indexed) to the consumer price index (so as to protect recipients against inflation), while the kidney dialysis entitlement is not. Merely to describe the characteristics of these programs would be like reading the telephone directory—helpful when you need a bit of data, but not recommended reading. As students of budgeting, what we want to know is how entitlements grow compared to one another and to appropriations and why. How does the struggle over entitlements differ, if at all, from the conflict over appropriations? And what does the rise of entitlements portend for the ability of our political institutions to make effective budgets?

Budgeting and entitlement are incompatible concepts. Budgeting refers (or used to refer) to the allocation of limited resources for financing competing purposes. But if budgeting is supposed to be resource allocation, then entitlement is mandatory resource segregation. Nothing can be taken away; every person or entity who qualifies for payment—by meeting conditions for unemployment compensation, for agricultural subsidies, and so on—is entitled to receive the amount stipulated by the formulas in the authorizing statutes, no matter what is happening elsewhere or to other people. Basically, entitlements are about budgeting by

---

[13] Tobin, "the Future of Social Security: One Economist's Assessment." Working Paper No. 4, Project on the Federal Social Role, National Conference on Social Welfare, Washington, D.C., 1985, p. 10.

addition—each sum for every program added to the others—not budgeting by subtraction, in which programs are eliminated or reduced, or where more for one means less for another.

Entitlement is, well, entitlement; these programs shall not be moved. For if the sums provided are seen to be not merely a matter of judgment of comparative merits, but also of singular moral virtue (this must be provided because a class of people is entitled to receive it), then allocation, priorities, and similarly relative terms are inappropriate when absolute judgments must be made. So where budgets are understood to be integrative, relating one part to another, entitlements forbid comparisons, allowing consideration only of the program or activity in and of itself. Budgeting is about balancing commitments; if something is an "entitlement" then it is not to be compared to anything else. While it is true, of course, that relating parts of the budget to the whole was an aspiration not an accomplishment, it was universally considered proper conduct.

Entitlements completely change the direction of budgeting. Classical budgeting was concerned largely with internal relationships between central recommenders and allocators (president and Congress), and spenders (the executive agencies). To control spending, the central units sought to control agencies. Nowadays that control apparatus is obsolete because agencies (bureaus and departments) no longer do most of the spending. In the past, most government spending activity was composed of its own purchases of goods and performance of services; now, the era of entitlements has changed all that. Today government spends most of its money by writing checks to individuals. Whereas in earlier times government faced inward, doing and controlling its own programs, in our time government faces outward to the people it must support. Aiding pregnant women to eat nutritious foods, or the elderly to put aside money for retirement, or the poor to use medical services are but a few examples of governmental efforts to alter citizen behavior.

If one asks a grand question about political life—Who will bear the costs of change?—entitlements provide a markedly new answer. The old one—"we the people"—has been changed to "all of us except the entitled." When the entitled are few in number and their entitlements are relatively small, the vast majority pays for a small minority. But when entitlements grow large (covering not only poor but rich, not only the elderly but the young), the budgetary system becomes loaded with many constants and few variables. Put plainly, the prevalence of entitlements means that but a minority of programs and agencies remain to absorb the vast majority of cuts. Resource allocation becomes a lot harder when you have to take three-fifths of total spending (entitlements plus interest) off the table. Bottom-up budgeting (by adding programs together) works just fine for entitlements, but it does not suit budgeting from above (trying to fit spending within a given total) because the cuts that have to be apportioned over the remainder of the budget are necessarily severe.

Where classical budgeting is mostly about modifications of the budgetary base (increments up or down), entitlements guarantee a permanent base, thus foregoing flexibility. The entitlement is the base, and a base that can go only one way—up—unless a deliberate and difficult decision is made to alter the natural course of spending. This resistance is not only a matter of keeping old conflicts closed, but of a shared sense of justice. The base becomes the politically shared belief about "who is entitled to what" and is therefore bolstered by arguments about equity and fairness. Moreover, entitlements hold the size of the base hostage to external events—to price increases (if payments are indexed to inflation), to demographic changes (if the entitled group increases in size,) to the weather, to the economy, and more.

The external focus that entitlements have imparted to budgeting has profound implications for the political lives of participants in the budgetary process. The lives of the beneficiaries may become more stable but relationships among budgeters become more hostile as agreement on what constitutes "fair shares" breaks down. Once the program base is guaranteed, with additions to it coming from formulas tied to external events, no one can say how much is too much. Internal conflict over budgeting rises.

Congressional control of public policy was thus under challenge. In pursuing entitlement programs, Congress subjected itself and the budget to great uncertainty. With other programs, legislators would give an agency some money for a project and, if it cost a little more than expected, Congress had a real choice about what to do next: build a smaller building, change some schedules, allocate more money, or just tell the agency to do its best with the funds it had. If the agency incorrectly estimated a project, it could be forced to give up some other part of its budget (e.g., travel expenses). Relations were largely between members of Congress and the agency, and Congress could displace a lot of the burden of error onto bureaucrats. If Congress misestimated entitlement costs, by contrast, it had no opportunity for second thoughts; the money just poured out from the Treasury.

Entitlements squeezed the old budget process directly by increasing spending and indirectly by siphoning off revenues from other programs. The guaranteed certainty of entitlement funding creates so much uncertainty for budgeters that it reduces the capacity of public officials to govern. Entitlements place a sizable burden on budgetary actors: They must find a way to support large numbers of individuals while still helping manage the economy and control the deficit, all this with most of the budget "committed" or essential. Government must be simultaneously firm (for entitlements) and flexible (for appropriations) while still trying to govern. It is as if government were a giant centipede on its back out in space with innumerable little feet holding up innumerable little people, with scant attention being paid to what holds up the creature who holds everyone else up. More tax money or fewer entitlements—either would solve the problem. But our legislators and presidents so far have not been able to see eye to eye. They agree that entitlements make a big difference, but not on what to do about them.

For the present, the place to begin is with the protection given to a program by virtue of the fact that it stands as an entitlement and, therefore, is not subject to the pressures of the annual appropriations process. It is not easy for Congress to consider reneging on obligations it already has incurred, or intervening to deprive beneficiaries of something to which the law says they are entitled. Entitlement means not having to say you're sorry because the money has run out.

Like other decision-making bodies, Congress does not necessarily spend its time on what is most important but rather on what it can change. Often this means neglecting the much larger entitlements in favor of the much smaller but more readily changeable appropriations. In this way entitlements alter the prevailing conception of the budgetary base. From a concept formerly tied to individual programs, the base emerges here as a function of the type of financing: Entitlements become the base that is expected to continue much as before while appropriations become the increments that are subject to dispute and negotiation. While the expansion of entitlements has not eliminated legislators' interest in distributing projects geographically, the public works pork barrel has nonetheless been dwarfed by payments to individuals.

As entitlements come to dominate much of public spending, they act so as to place the budget on automatic pilot. Far more than before, the budget is determined by prior authorizations. And, as what might be termed "maximal entitlements" (universal, no-year, fully indexed, financed in part by their own trust funds) come to take up a larger share of the total, the scope for change is reduced still further.

Yet entitlements are not monolithic. Every entitlement program has its own dynamic, its own clientele, and its own constituency. Each has been created in a specific set of circumstances, where its advocates have been able to convince a wider and receptive audience as to the merit of its claims. Entitlements have been designed in different ways and grown at different rates. While some have grown unimpeded, there have been a number of efforts to curb others.

WHY DO ENTITLEMENTS START?

The beginning of modern entitlements may be found in "the revolutionary response to the New Deal to the problems of poverty and unemployment that plagued the United States during the Great Depression."[14] The Social Security Act of 1935 was a seminal event that marked the beginning of several new social programs including social security, unemployment insurance, and aid to dependent children. A few years later, President Roosevelt proclaimed a second Bill of Rights as a new basis for security and prosperity. Roosevelt stopped short of saying those rights should emanate from government, but the philosophy of entitlement was clear and impelled a broad movement in favor of social provision. Later entitlements followed from the same logic of collective provision for circumstances felt to be beyond individual control and financial resources. But the movement was neither inevitable nor planned: Each entitlement arose out of a special urgency and was initiated and shaped by the politics of the moment.

Some programs start slowly. The enactment of medicaid, a federal-state means-tested program to provide medical services to poor people, was an outgrowth of a slow but orderly involvement of government in health care spanning decades. As early as 1798, the federal government funded the delivery of medical services to merchant seamen in special hospitals.[15] Later, the federal government provided hospitalization and other types of medical care for members of the armed forces, veterans, Indians, and certain other groups. The Federal Emergency Relief Act of 1933 constituted the first federal legislation to provide

---

[14]Gary Bryner, *Politics and Public Morality* (New York: Norton, 1998) p. 2.

[15]Anthony Jong, *Dental Public Health and Community Dentistry* (St. Louis: C.V. Mosby, 1981).

health care for the needy. Under this act, the Federal Emergency Relief Administration (FERA) was set up to make funds available to states for paying medical care costs of the unemployed needy.

The FERA program lasted only two-and-a-half years. Although it was not uniform throughout all the states, did not cover some essential services, and had many serious shortcomings, the program did exercise great influence on subsequent medical care programs. FERA, for example, emphasized the role of governmental agencies as purchasers of medical care in contrast with previous reliance on volunteer services of physicians and hospitals, and set a precedent for increased participation of the federal and state governments in financing medical care for the indigent.[16]

Sometimes an entitlement results from crisis to benefit a specific group arousing public sympathy. Black lung disability payments to miners were the outcome of a nationwide outcry over working conditions in coal mines following an explosion in 1968 in Farmington, W. V., that killed 78 miners.

Black lung disease (or pneumoconiosis) refers to the pathological process of inhaled coal dust lining the airways of the lungs.[17] The disease, to a very significant degree, increasingly restricts the person's activities. In extreme cases, fibrotic changes can be so overwhelming as to inhibit blood flow from the heart to the lungs, resulting in heart failure and eventual death. But for the great majority of pneumoconiosis cases, even in coal miners, the result is dust retention with no visible pathology.

The black lung issue became a passion when, by early 1969, spontaneous walkouts at various mines exploded into a series of "black lung strikes" involving over 45,000 miners in West Virginia, Pennsylvania, and Ohio. In West Virginia, a bill was passed that established black lung as a compensable occupational illness with liberal criteria for disability.[18]

The West Virginia law established a black lung entitlement framework that miners took to be a central tenet of their health care interests, and its definitions and criteria carried over into federal policy. The fervent demonstration of militancy by the miners, furthermore, instilled a popular notion of moral obligation by the federal government to ensure safety and compensation. The public image of the miner as an economic instrument of the coal companies put that industry, and the expenditure-control groups in Congress, on the defensive for the coming decade.

Soon Congress crafted the landmark Federal Coal Mine Health and Safety Act of 1969, the forerunner to the Occupational Safety and Health Act (OSHA) of 1970. Title IV of the act, entitled "Black Lung Benefits," mandated that the disease be compensable with general revenue funds. The black lung provisions entitled totally disabled coal miners and their widows to benefits linked to federal civil service disability levels that increased as federal salaries were adjusted.[19] It was in-

---

[16]See Margaret Greenfield, *Medicare and Medicaid: The 1965 and 1967 Social Security Amendments* (Westport, Conn.: Greenwood, 1968).

[17]This section is based on a paper by Jack Chow.

[18]Alan Derickson, "The Origins of the Black Lung Insurgency," *Journal of Public Health Policy*, Vol. 4, No. 1 (March 1983), pp. 32–33.

[19]Bernard Popick, "The Social Security Disability Program. The Black Lung Benefits – an Administrative Case Study," *Journal of Occupational Medicine*, Vol. 13, No.7, (July 1971), p. 335.

tended that federal participation would be temporary and limited in scope and that once the states and mining companies had negotiated compensation the federal government could withdraw.

An entitlement might grow out of another program. The entitlement for end-stage renal disease (ESRD) grew out of a small program established for veterans in 1963. ESRD describes the kidney in its dying moments, unable to filter and process the body's metabolic wastes and allowing the waste to accumulate to fatal levels in the blood. Only intervention through hemodialysis and transplantation can save the person's life.

As early as 1963, the federal government had established a small ESRD entitlement program for veterans eligible for medical benefits. In 1967, a group of experts set up by BOB and the Office of Science and Technology endorsed the VA program, urged the use of home dialysis (a much cheaper mode of treatment), and recommended patient care financing through medicare.[20]

The appropriations committees moved cautiously by providing only limited support to the first 14 community dialysis centers administered by the Public Health Service (PHS). The Senate Appropriations Committee in 1964 explicitly limited the PHS's use of appropriated monies in renal treatment to "demonstration and training programs" and not toward patient care financing. The overriding concern was cost:

> The Federal government has borne the cost of treatment for its legal beneficiaries and shared these treatment costs when it has been in connection with research investigation or demonstration. Traditionally, payment for illness has been the responsibility of the patient or the local community. If the Federal government were to share the full costs of lifetime treatment for all who suffer from these chronic diseases and conditions, the financial burden would be excessive.[21]

If this was the voice of the classic budgeter, new budgeters were more concerned with alleviating individual suffering and less with collective financial burdens.

A number of factors favored entitlement status: Influential politicians became convinced of the need for financial help for ESRD patients; the plight of patients became highly publicized; the community based dialysis centers were transferred from PHS with its restrictive research orientation to the more patient-oriented Regional Medical Programs Service; with the improved efficacy of treatment, the number of clinically oriented renal physicians was growing; and the VA benefits provided an existing entitlement framework.

Alan Schick tells the story

> On the next to last day of its 1972 session, Congress completed action on an omnibus social security bill that (among its many provisions) entitled victims of kidney failure to medicare benefits. The provision was added to the bill by a Senate floor amendment, without prior committee hearings or review and without any consideration of the issue in the House. When it adopted the amendment by an overwhelming margin, the

---

[20] The ensuing discussion is taken from R.A. Rettig, "The Policy Debate on Patient Care Financing for Victims of End-Stage Renal Disease," *Law and Contemporary Problems,* Vol. 40, No.4 (Autumn 1976), pp. 217–18.

[21] Ibid., pp. 203–04.

Senate had no reliable cost estimates and only a fuzzy notion of how expanded medicare coverage would affect future budgets. During brief floor debate, Senator Vance Harke, the amendment's sponsor, implored the Senate to put health care ahead of budgetary concerns: "How do we explain," he asked, "that the difference between life and death is a matter of dollars."[22]

The entitlement provided eligibility to persons with ESRD who were disabled, had worked under the social security or railroad retirement systems, or were the spouse or dependent child of an employee with enough social security or railroad retirement credits. In 1978 age considerations were eliminated, creating a nearly universal entitlement covering 93 percent of persons with ESRD, and the program was placed under the new Health Care Financing Authority within the Department of Health and Human Services.

Various industries have gained subsidies related to their perceived special needs. The honey subsidy was a case in point. The rationing of sugar and the need for beeswax to waterproof ammunition in World War II led to an increase in the production of honey. Prices dropped after the war, so the industry requested assistance. The Agricultural Act of 1949 required the Secretary of Agriculture to support the price of honey. The rationale given was that bees are essential in pollinating a number of crops and that this service either would be insufficient due to a shortage of bees or, in any event, farmers could not afford to pay. Naturally, like the World War II buildings that still dot our college campuses, the honey price support was supposed to be temporary. As usual, it was the government that got stung.

A price support level for honey was set. Beekeepers then obtained loans using honey stored with the government as collateral. If the market price rose, the keepers sold the honey and paid the government the principal plus a low rate of interest. If the market price declined, producers might default on their loans (without paying interest), leaving the government holding bags of honey.

Sweet stuff can lull you to sleep. From 1970 to 1979, no loans were in default. Then the usual combination of life (external forces) and government (internal legislation specifying conditions for entitlements) took hold. The inflation of the mid–70s, tied to an index for farm products, doubled the support price. At the same time, foreign suppliers increased production and the world price of honey dropped. The rising value of the dollar, which made foreign goods cheaper, led imports to double between 1979 and 1984.

The combination of high support and low market prices had the expected results: Honey loans increased almost three times, honey left to the government increased twenty times, and the defaults and administrative costs quickly came to a bill for $160 million. Essentially, honey was being produced to serve as collateral on which beekeepers could default. A little more than half of all honey produced in the United States was defaulted to the government. In 1993, the honey support program was finally discontinued, and later efforts to raise quotas and tariffs against cheap Chinese imported honey were unsuccessful.[23]

---

[22]Schick, "Controlling the 'Uncontrollables,'" p. 1.

[23]The final fate of the honey subsidy is based on a research paper by Tom Donahue, a graduate student in the Department of Political Science, California State University, Los Angeles, 1999.

WHY DO ENTITLEMENTS GROW?

There is no particular mystery why entitlements grow. One reason is that more people become eligible to participate. According to the Congressional Budget Office, mounting case loads on average produce more than one-fifth of total expenditure growth, but they are expected to be responsible for 15 percent of future growth in social security, medicare, and medicaid, reflecting continued expansion in the numbers of the elderly, disabled, and poor. Another third of the growth occurs because of automatic increases in benefits, which apply to all the major retirement programs, as well as food stamps and medicare. The remainder may be traced to rising costs, particularly in the health areas, as well as other factors, such as the higher earnings base for calculation of social security benefits.[24] But none of this explains why some entitlements gain ground while others lose. To understand these fluctuations in fortune, we need a more detailed knowledge of their history.

All entitlements are not created equal. Some have grown quickly, some have stayed about the same (allowing for inflation), and some have been terminated or declined significantly (see Table 8.2). Among the latter have been the GI Bill after World War II and the Korean War, Social Services Grants, and General Revenue Sharing. These, however, are the exception, and as entitlements have assumed their dominant role in the federal budget, attention has focused on the large, fast-growing health and security programs on which so many people depend. Their growth has been determined by a mixture of factors, including indexing for inflation, demographic changes, expansion in eligibility, federalism, the interests of government agencies and providers, and the political support of large constituency groups.

Maintaining Commitment: Social Security

Old age, survivors, and disability insurance—social security—has been a stable program that has grown as its original commitment has been fulfilled. Begun in 1935 during the Depression as part of the New Deal, its aims were, and remain, basic protection against the economic hazards of old age or death.[25] Social security is a compulsory and contributory scheme, independently financed, whose benefits are based (with some bias toward lower paid wage earners) on past earnings and are not means-tested.

There have been relatively few changes in the program, most of which have simply been to extend benefits to achieve near universality and a level of benefit consistent with the original intent. The major changes occurred in 1956, with the extension of insurance to disability as well as old age, and in 1972, when automatic indexing was enacted to replace ad hoc increases in benefits. Both these changes followed the logic of enabling workers to plan for their protection against circumstances that might otherwise force them into poverty and destitution.

---

[24]Congressional Budget Office, *The Economic and Budget Outlook: Fiscal Years 2000–2009*, p. 73.

[25]Robert E. Ball, "The Original Understanding on Social Security: Implications for Later Developments," in Theodore Marmur and Jerry Mashaw, *Social Security: Beyond the Rhetoric of Crisis* (Princeton, N.J.: Princeton University Press, 1988), p. 18.

Social security is a success story. As beneficiaries have gradually qualified, the program has come to cover 90 percent of people over 65, and to protect 95 percent of mothers and children through survivors' insurance and 80 percent of wage earners under disability provisions. Thirty years ago, the poverty rate for the elderly was double that for the general population; now it is about 12 percent.[26]

Social security expenditures have grown an average of 6 percent a year over the past decade, but they have been stable at about 4.5 percent of gross domestic product, and are projected to stay at that level for the next decade.[27] The growth has been relatively predictable (somewhat less so for disability insurance), based on growth of the elderly population, wage changes, and the rate of inflation.

Concern about the program stems from its very predictability, and also from past policy decisions. First—the demographics. In 1940, hard as this is to believe now, only 7 percent of the population were elderly; in 1996, this figure had grown to 13 percent. As the "baby boom" generation reaches retirement age, the numbers will swell so that by 2050, the elderly are projected to reach 20 percent. Clearly expenditures will rise. What about revenues?

Social security was conceived as a pay-as-you-go system: As money came in, it would be immediately paid out in a rough balance between inflow and outflow. In 1983, alarm that expenditures would outstrip financing led to the Greenspan Commission, whose recommendations for increased contributions resulted in large surpluses in the social security trust fund. It is now estimated that in 2013 the trust fund will begin paying out more than it takes in; in 2018, reserves will reach their peak at $2.9 trillion, and in 2032, the reserves will be exhausted and current revenues (at present rates of contribution) will only be sufficient to support 75 percent of projected required benefits.

This alarmist scenario seems a classic entitlement situation. One generation worked for the next and paid for their retirement to find nothing in the kitty when they came along. The budget is being gobbled up by greedy old codgers, with nothing left for the needs of young folks. The income of the elderly is protected against inflation through indexing, while the working element struggles to maintain living standards against the steady erosion of their salaries.

But all this would belie the popularity of social security. Its constituency stretches well beyond the immediate beneficiaries to their families, who are relieved of the primary burden of support, and to providers who derive their own income from services for them. The elderly, moreover, are not a separate class, but (assuming we survive) ourselves in a few decades' time; interests of young and elderly are thus, if not entirely identical, at least congruent. Finally, social security is a redistributive program in the sense that it skews benefits toward the more needy, a certain corrective to a market economy in which disparities between rich and poor continue to grow.

Yet the apprehension is not unfounded and is intensified by the nature of the current debates about the "social security surplus." The unified budget created in

---

[26]United States General Accounting Office, *Social Security: Restoring Long-Term Solvency Will Require Difficult Choices*, Statement of Jane L. Ross before the Special Committee on Aging, United States Senate, February 10, 1998, p. 4 (GAO/T-HEHS–98–95)

[27]Congressional Budget Office, *The Economic and Budget Outlook: Fiscal Years 2000–2009*, January 1999, p. 71.

1967 lumped together social security and the remainder of the budget: Since then, the social security trust fund surpluses have routinely offset the federal deficit, making it appear smaller (see Table 8.3). Even when social security was separated from the budget in the mid–1980s, in practice the surplus was counted against the deficit.[28] As the projections for the long-term depletion of the surplus became common political currency, the issue of social security reform hit the agenda—but not quite, because no one really wanted to embark on real reform: raising premiums and retirement ages or cutting benefits. But everyone did want to be seen as protecting social security for future generations. Hence the rhetoric of the trust fund and the social security surplus, which promised that from now on, social security money would be kept inviolate from the predations of irresponsible politicians.

Table 8.3   Social Security Trust Funds And The Budget 1985–1997

	(in millions of dollars)				
	1985	1990	1993	1994	1997
OASI	10,673	55,125	49,364	60,691	67,916
DI	−1,310	3,091	−2,576	−3,935	13,399
On budget deficit/surplus	−221,698	−227,974	−300,487	−258,823	−103,307
Off-budget deficit/surplus	9,363	56,590	45,347	55,654	81,364
Total	−212,334	−221,381	−255,140	−203,169	−21,943

The problem with this scenario was that the trust fund does not really exist: It is only an accounting device. Excess revenues are used by the federal government to buy Treasury bonds that pay interest, and are then redeemed as needed for current uses—whether payments to beneficiaries or other purposes.[29] It makes no difference to the health of the trust fund what the funds are used for, although a good argument might be made for using them to pay down the national debt (reducing the interest burden that is currently as much as the defense budget), rather than, say, a tax cut benefiting the better-off part of the population. Meanwhile the rhetoric of "protection" obscures the debate on measures that if undertaken incrementally now might help the financial future of the program.[30] And politicians display their virtue through gimmickry, which pretends that they have financed the federal budget without the aid of even one cent of the social security surplus—although everyone knows this is not true.[31]

---

[28]See Allen Schick, *The Federal Budget: Politics, Policy, Process* (Washington, D.C.: Brookings Institution, 1995), p. 28.

[29]See General Accounting Office, *Budget Issues: Trust Funds in the Budget, 1999*, p. 3 (GAO/T-AIMD/RCED–99–110); General Accounting Office, *Social Security and Surpluses: GAO's Perspective on the President's Proposals*, Statement of David Walker, Comptroller General of the United States before the Committee on the Budget, United States Senate, February 23, 1999, p. 3 (GAO/T-AIMD/HEHS–99–95).

[30]Art Pine, "Rhetoric Aside, Clinton, Congress Fell Short of Fixing Social Security," *Los Angeles Times*, November 14, 1999, p. A32.

[31]"Beyond Do-Nothing," *Washington Post National Weekly Edition*, November 4, 1999, p. 24.

Demography and Costs: Medicare

Medicare, the health care program for the elderly, was enacted in 1965 as a logical extension of social security. At that time only just over half the elderly had hospital insurance, and clearly their incomes were highly vulnerable to medical exigencies.[32] Medicare was controversial: Liberals saw it as an incremental step toward universal health insurance, while conservatives and particularly the medical establishment opposed it as an extension of government control over medical practice. The result was a program design that divided hospital insurance from outpatient medical insurance, as did the major insurance for health at the time. The former, Part A, would be financed by a trust fund, paid for by a compulsory payroll tax on employers and employees, while the latter, Part B, would be supported by voluntary premiums supplemented by the federal government to cover the full cost.

Since its inception there has been very little change in the medicare program, except for expansion of services for disability and end stage renal disease in 1972, and home health services in 1989. But although the eligibility pool is the same as that for social security, there are important differences. Medicare allows for an open-ended benefit; with certain provisions for deductibles and copayments, beneficiaries may choose to use the entitlement as much or as little as they like. Since the original scheme also embraced the norm for the time—fee-for-service reimbursement—health service providers (hospitals, doctors, and others) were in a determining position regarding costs, while the government was only a third party. Medicare is also unique among health plans internationally as it covers only one group, notably the least healthy and most expensive one, rather than pooling the costs of the elderly with those of the younger and less expensive population.

These differences presaged rapid growth. In its first five years, outlays for medicare more than doubled, and then roughly doubled again in the next five. During the 1980s, the rate of growth slackened somewhat, but by the end of the decade, expenditures had still more than doubled from just over $41 billion to over $107 billion. The 1990s registered 10 percent increases each year to reach $213.6 billion in 1998 although in 1999 spending dropped by 1 percent. Differently viewed, medicare's expenditures had grown from 0.7 percent of GDP in 1969 to 2.5 percent a decade later.[33]

Why did spending grow so fast? Medicare has a strong political base. Aside from the 39 million people currently eligible for payments, medicare also draws support from family members who are protected against possible financial responsibility for the illness of a parent or relative, and of active members of the work force who are current contributors and future beneficiaries of the trust fund. Since medical care for the elderly has come to be recognized by society as the morally correct course to follow, politicians talk about cutting medicare only at the risk of sounding uncaring toward the aged.

---

[32] Theodore R. Marmor, "Coping with a Creeping Crisis: Medicare at Twenty," in Theodore Marmor and Jerry L. Mashaw (eds.), *Social Security: Beyond the Rhetoric of Crisis* (Princeton N.J.: Princeton University Press, 1988), p. 177.

[33] Congressional Budget Office, *The Economic and Budget Outlook: Fiscal Years 2000–2009,* January 1999, pp. 136–37 and p. 72. *Los Angeles Times,* November 15, 1999, p A15.

A second reason has been legislated price increases. There is little incentive to control costs. Until recently, at least, medicare's primary goal was to improve access. Consequently, rather than designing cost-sharing schedules to ensure that beneficiaries don't overuse services, schedules have been designed to ensure that no one who needs services hesitates to seek help merely because of cost-sharing arrangements. Another is that both providers and intermediaries have strong incentives not to control costs. For providers, like hospitals, lower costs would mean lower revenues. For intermediaries, such as insurance companies, the interest is to promote good relationships with providers, for insurers have to deal with providers to process their own claims. They have no incentive to lower costs, since the government is paying the bills.

It has been estimated that growth in the number of enrollees and legislated price increases account for about 60 percent of growth. What about the other 40 percent? According to CBO, historically increases above enrollment and price increases derive from a number of varying factors, including the enrollment mix (inclusion of young-elderly and old-elderly), program changes, billing behavior, changes in technology, and practice patterns.[34] Roughly translated, these amount to usage: If benefits are available, those in need will use them, professionals will prescribe them, and private enterprise will take advantage of them.

A recent case in point is home health services. In 1989, the guidelines governing medicare's home health benefit from a program covering short-term post-hospitalization needs were changed. As a result of a court case, the criteria for coverage of home health visits were liberalized to serve chronic long-term patients. Between 1989 and 1993, the number of beneficiaries receiving home health services increased from 1.7 million to 2.8 million (although this was still less than 10 percent of the medicare population).[35] Between 1989 and 1996, expenditures increased from $2.5 billion to $18.1 billion, an average annual increase of 33 percent. The growth in expenditures resulted less from increases in payments than from heavier usage: The majority of visits in 1996 were for the 15 percent of users who received 150 visits or more, while the remainder received less than 50 visits a year. The number of home health agencies grew from nearly 6,000 in 1989 to nearly 10,000 in 1996, and most of this growth was in for-profit agencies.[36] Since then, growth in expenditures has slowed markedly, partly in response to measures to cap services and freeze payments per visit in the 1997 Balanced Budget Act.[37] It is a measure of the strength of this constituency that in 1999, Congress voted to restore many of the 1997 cuts, including payments to teaching hospitals, skilled

---

[34]Ibid., p. 72.

[35]General Accounting Office, *Medicare: Home Health Utilization Expands While Program Controls Deteriorate,* Report to the Chairman, Special Committee on Aging, United States Senate, March 1996, pp. 3–7 (GAO/HEHS–96–16).

[36]General Acounting Office, *Medicare: Interim Payment System for Home Health Agencies,* Statement of William Scanlon, Director Health Financing and Systems Issues, Testimony before the Subcommittee on Health, Committee on Ways and Means, House of Representatives, August 6, 1998, p. 3 (GAO/T-HEHS–98–234).

[37]General Accounting Office, *Medicare Home Health Benefit: Impact of Interim Payment System and Agency Closures on Access to Services,* September 1998, p. 5 (GAO/HEHS–98–238).

nursing facilities, and managed care plans, while delaying the scheduled reduction in home health services.[38]

Another source of growth in medicare spending has been fraud. The Health Care Financing Administration (HCFA), which oversees medicare (and medicaid), processes over 900 million claims for the program every year, and it is only possible to examine closely about 10 percent of them.[39] In 1997, the General Accounting Office estimated over $20 billion or 11 percent of medicare fee-for-service payments were improper.[40] Congress enacted legislation in 1996 to attack health care fraud and abuse, and the error rate for Fiscal Year 1998 was down to about 7 percent, still an estimated $12.6 billion in overpaid claims.[41]

Medicare is widely believed to be a program in crisis. Over the next 10 years, beneficiaries were projected to increase from 39 million to 45 million. In 1997, it was forecast that the Part A Trust Fund would run dry by 2001.[42] Between 1998 and 2002, prices for the fee-for-service sector would grow on average 2.7 percent a year, and accelerate over 3 percent after that.[43] Between 1995 and 2005, costs per beneficiary were projected to grow by nearly 7 percent a year.[44] By 2007, medicare expenditure might constitute as much as 4 percent of GDP.[45]

The long-term projections were even scarier. As the baby boomers reached retirement, around the year 2030, according to the Bipartisan Medicare Commission, beneficiaries would reach 22 percent of the population and costs would reach two to three trillion dollars a year.[46] By midcentury, it was estimated that medicare would consume 8 percent of GDP.[47]

Is the medicare program really endangered? Joseph White, in an insightful paper, has challenged the conventional view.[48] To begin with, projections are notoriously subject to error. While demographics will undoubtedly determine an increase in medicare spending in line with the growth in beneficiaries, population growth has only been responsible for about half of expenditure growth. It is the re-

---

[38]Shailagh Murray, "House Passes Bill To Help Reverse Cuts to Medicare," *Wall Street Journal*, November 8, 1999, p. A8.

[39]Sue Kirchhoff and Mary Agnes Carey, "Purse Strings and Heartstrings: The Home Health Dilemma," *Congressional Quarterly Weekly Report*, September 26, 1998, p. 2556.

[40]General Accounting Office, *Medicare: Health Care Fraud and Abuse Control Program Financial Report for Fiscal Year 1997*, June 1998, p. 4 (GAO/AIMD–98–157).

[41]Congressional Quarterly Weekly Report, February 13, 1999, p. 399.

[42]David Cutler, "Restructuring Medicare for the Future," in Robert D. Reischauer (ed.), *Setting National Priorities: Budget Choices for the Next Century*, (Washington, D.C.: Brookings Institution, 1997), p. 199.

[43]Congressional Budget Office, January 1999, p. 72, op. cit.

[44]Joseph R. Antos, "Preparing for the Retirement of the Baby Boomers," in Robert Reischauer, Stuart Butler, and Judith Lave, *Medicare: Preparing for the Challenges of the 21ˢᵗ Century* (Washington, D.C.: National Academy of Social Insurance, 1997), p. 46.

[45]Cutler, op. cit., p. 203.

[46]Joseph White, "'Saving' Medicare—From What?" Paper for the Annual Meeting of the American Political Science Association, Committee on Health Politics, Boston, September 3–6, 1998, p. 6 and p. 11.

[47]Cutler, op. cit., p. 203.

[48]White, op. cit.

mainder of the growth that is hard to predict, as this will depend on external events (e.g. medical breakthroughs) and policies, in turn based on public opinion, which up to now has been accepting of costs and has rejected medical cuts.

Expanding Eligibility: Medicaid

Medicaid was initiated in 1965 as a means of helping the poor elderly cover costs and services not included in medicare. It consolidated federal efforts to provide medical assistance to the poor and extended benefits to families with children, the blind, and disabled.[49] Each state designs its own program, which is federally approved for compliance with federal laws that mandate eligibility and benefit requirements. The program is jointly financed by state and federal governments, with state payments matched by federal outlays based on a formula determined by each state's average per capital income, without any upper limit on federal spending.

Since its inception, medicaid was always a fast growing program. In 1966, combined state and federal costs were $1.7 billion; by 1980, they had grown to $25.8 billion. This growth amounted to 17 percent a year, largely due to health cost inflation, although there were some program expansions such as increased child health benefits and optional programs for the mentally retarded.

Efforts during the early Reagan years slowed growth in federal outlays to about 7 percent a year. Reforms included tightened cost controls, options to allow states to implement cost-cutting measures, across the board cuts in federal payments, limitations on hospital reimbursements, and a prospective payment system that set out a schedule of allowable charges for different services.[50]

However, in 1984 eligibility began to expand, particularly targeting pregnant women and children, both mandating and allowing the states options to extend benefits.[51] Between 1984 and 1987, total state and federal expenditures grew nearly 10 percent a year; enrollees increased by nearly 2 percent a year, and per capita spending by 5.6 percent a year. In only four years, expenditures rose from less than $36 billion to over $54 billion.[52]

In the late 1980s and early 1990s, further inclusions of pregnant women and children resulted in a virtual explosion in eligibility and expenditures.[53] In 1989, program spending increased 13 percent, in 1990 19 percent, and in 1991, 26 percent. Between 1989 and 1991, beneficiaries grew from 23.5 million to 28.3 million.[54] By 1995 there were 33 million children, poor adults, and disabled people

---

[49]Congressional Quarterly Weekly Report, June 10, 1995, p. 1638.

[50]See Allen Schick, "Controlling the "Uncontrollables," Paper prepared for the American Enterprise Institute Pew Fellows Conference, November 1985, p. 4.

[51]General Accounting Office, *Medicaid Spending Pressures Drive States Toward Program Reinvention*, Report to the Chairman, Committee on the Budget, House of Representatives, April 1995, pp. 56–59 (GAO/HEHS–95–122).

[52]John Holahan, Teresa Coughlin, Leighton Ku, David Heslam, and Collin Winterbottom, "Understanding the Recent Growth in Medicaid Spending," in Diane Rowland, Judith Feder, and Alina Salganicoff (eds.), *Medicaid Financing Crisis: Balancing Responsibilities, Priorities, and Dollars* (AAAS Press, 1994), p. 24.

[53]For details see General Accounting Office, 1995, op. cit. and Holahan et al, p. 28, op. cit.

[54]Stephen H. Long, "Causes of Soaring Medicaid Spending 1988–1991," in Rowland, Feder, and Salganicoff, op. cit., p. 9.

depending on medicaid, and the program was costing state and federal governments $131 billion.[55]

In the late 1990s, growth slowed as the result of state cost containment efforts, but in 1998 program costs again began to increase. Without further policy changes, it is likely that growth will continue at about 8 or 9 percent annually. Federal outlays are projected to rise from $101 billion in 1998 to $245 billion in 2009.[56]

What accounts for the high growth of spending in medicaid in the early 1990s, and for the projections for continued program growth in the future? An obvious answer is broadened access to medicaid, both through changes in eligibility and administration. State efforts, particularly in the South, stemming from concern about high infant mortality rates, spurred options to liberalize eligibility, options that later became mandates. In such states, where previous provision for medical services for the poor had been niggardly, expansion was correspondingly large and matching rates for federal reimbursement were high. The new legislation changed the nature of medicaid from a welfare program to one linked to income level, and as Gary Clarke put it, "the art of the possible suddenly became more wide open in Congress."[57] From the federal point of view, policy expansion might be seen as more feasible because the states were picking up nearly half the bill; from the state perspective, federal reimbursement was an attractive incentive.

But the inclusion of more women and children in the program did not really account for the growth in spending. According to one analysis, only just over one-third of the expenditure growth between 1981 and 1992 came from expanded enrollment. Most of the remainder might be attributed to price inflation (26 percent) and service use and reimbursement (33 percent).[58] Although women and children are 60 percent of beneficiaries, in fact they make up a relatively small component of costs.

Medicaid has become a key support for the elderly, as it covers over half the cost of nursing homes and part of medicare costs.[59] By the late 1990s, long-term care of the elderly accounted for about 40 percent of medicaid expenditures, and was responsible for much of the growth in costs. "These are not the stereotypical recipients of welfare," said Stephen O'Connell of the Alzheimer's Association. "They are middle class working families who have spent all their money [on care] and now turn to Medicaid."[60]

But the growth of expenditures on the elderly was exceeded by the rapidly rising bill for hospital care: 20 percent in 1990, 42 percent in 1991, and 41 percent in 1992, accounting for half of total expenditure growth in 1991 and 1992.[61] At least part of the reason for this out-of-line growth in hospital expenditures appears to lie

---

[55]General Accounting Office, 1995, op. cit.

[56]Congressional Budget Office, op. cit, p. 69.

[57]Gary Clarke, "Medicaid Fiscal Stresses and the States: A Medical Director's Perspective," in Rowland, Feder, and Salganicoff, op. cit., p. 156.

[58]"Medicaid Spending and Enrollment Trends 1981–1992," ibid., p. 22.

[59]General Accounting Office, "Medicaid: Restructuring Approaches Leave Many Questions," April 1995, (GAO/HEHS–95–103).

[60]Jonathan Peterson, "Given Facts, Cause of Slash Medicaid Not So Clear-Cut," *Los Angeles Times*, May 10, 1995, p. A13.

[61]Ibid., p. A17.

in creative financing by the states to leverage additional federal dollars. States were able to collect special taxes or donations from hospitals, use them to collect federal matching reimbursements, and then return the original contributions to their source. These were hospitals that served a disproportionate share of medicaid and low income patients and generated matching federal dollars. The states were in a position either to pay these federal reimbursements to the hospitals or to use them to finance other medicaid beneficiaries. This practice was ended in 1993.

It seems unlikely that medicaid costs can be seriously constrained in the future. Despite the expanded coverage of the previous decade, it has been calculated that the program only reaches about 60 percent of those now eligible. Current efforts are to increase children's health coverage, to maintain medicaid benefits for those leaving the welfare rolls, and to provide them for the disabled who are able and willing to work.[62]

The medicaid population includes those with highly expensive medical needs, particularly the disabled and the frail elderly. Moreover, medicaid does not exist in a vacuum—to the extent that medicare benefits are cut back and medicare recipients' costs rise, medicaid's expenditures will grow. The same is true for private insurance that raises premiums, copayments and deductibles each year while providing diminished benefits. While managed care, and particularly health maintenance organizations (HMOs) appear to offer a way to cost containment, these too are finding it more difficult to remain profitable, as governments cut fees and the full costs of serving patients with expensive needs are realized. Finally, since medicaid covers prescription drugs, medical equipment, and supplies, inflation in these items also contributes to the growth in spending, as does widespread fraud.[63]

Provider Pressures: End Stage Renal Disease[64]

One of the fastest growing entitlements in recent years is one serving a relatively small number of people, the part of medicare that pays benefits to patients with End Stage Renal Disease (ESRD). The story of how ESRD became an entitlement has already been related (see pp. 199–200) In 1973 there were 11,000 beneficiaries; by 1997 there were 304,000. Although annual enrollment growth slowed during the 1990s, patient population might be expected to double every 12 years.[65]

Costs exploded. In 1974 the program cost $283 million. By 1996, about a quarter of a million ESRD beneficiaries accounted for nearly $10 billion in medicare payments, although they were less than one percent of medicare beneficiaries. The average annual cost per person was $38,574, compared with the average cost for other medicare beneficiaries of only $5,253. Even the highest cost groups, those who died and those who stayed in a hospital cost only $17,862 and

[62]Sue Kirchhoff, "Breaking Down Barriers for the Working Disabled," *Congressional Quarterly Weekly Report,* November 28, 1998, pp. 3209–10.

[63]Virginia Ellis, "$40 million in Medi-Cal Fraud Alleged," *Los Angeles Times,* November 3, 1999, p. A21.

[64]This section draws on a research paper by Thomas Donahue, a graduate student at California State University, Los Angeles.

[65]United States Renal Data System, *USRDS 1999 Annual Data Report* (National Institute of Health, National Institute of Diabetes and Digestive and Kidney Disease, Bethesda, MD: April 1999), pp. xvii–xviii.

$18,985 respectively.[66] A year later, costs had swelled to nearly $12 billion, the number of patients had risen to over 304,000, and each was costing on average nearly $45,000 a year.

How did this happen? A leading cause has been demographic change within the ESRD population: As Tom Donahue explains, they are like other Americans "living longer, growing older, and getting sicker."[67] In particular, diabetes in older populations has meant older people contracting ESRD, with multiple health problems and needs for more difficult and expensive treatment.[68] It also appears that physicians have been willing to prescribe dialysis for elderly patients, most of whom would not previously have been treated.[69]

Advances in medicine, particularly expensive drugs, have improved patients' lives without preventing the need for dialysis, and have greatly added to program costs. Just one drug, recombinant human erythropoietin (rttn EPO), currently costs medicare about $1 billion a year, nearly one-tenth of the ESRD program costs.[70]

But demographics and medical advances do not fully explain why such high costs have been incurred for a relatively small group of individuals. While entitlements are generally thought of as benefits conferred upon individuals or families who meet certain eligibility criteria, the reimbursement mechanism of payment to enterprises and institutions that secure the promised benefit becomes a form of entitlement for the providers. In ESRD, as long as they deliver treatment to the designated beneficiaries, the providers are guaranteed reimbursement for their services. Often more vocal in promoting the entitlement than the beneficiaries, providers themselves then become a vested interest group.

An example of their strength might be seen in the failure to take advantage of the possibility of home dialysis, a much cheaper mode of treatment than dialysis at a hospital or proprietary clinic. The ESRD provisions did not provide economic incentives (such as coverage for medical supplies, supportive services, or reimbursement for supervisory facilities) for home dialysis, so patients continued to depend on hospital or proprietary center dialysis. An attempt to provide incentives for home self-dialysis in 1978 was opposed by the major groups involved, and the final bill gave hospitals and centers differential reimbursement rates that boosted their profits.[71] Other efforts to encourage home dialysis offered insuffient incentive to encourage large-scale use.

On the other hand, ESRD treatment through national and international corporations has become a highly lucrative and fast growing industry. After the enact-

---

[66]"High-Cost Users of Medicare Services," *Health Care Financing Review*, 1998 Statistical Supplement, Washington D.C., 1998, p. 42.

[67]Donahue, op. cit., p. 6.

[68]See U.S. Renal Data System, op. cit., p. 75.

[69]"End Stage Renal Disease Services," *The Green Book* (Washington, D.C.: U.S. Government Printing Office, November 4, 1996), pp. 197–98.

[70]Allen R. Nissenson and Richard A. Rettig, "Medicare's End-Stage Renal Disease Program: Current Status and Future Prospectis," *Health Affairs*, January-February 1999, Vol. 18, No. 1, pp. 167–68.

[71]L. E. Demkovich, "Kidney Dialysis Payments May Be Test of Reagan's Commitment to Competition," *National Journal*, (December 5, 1981), pp. 2162–63.

ment of the ESRD entitlement, the National Medical Care Corporation (NMC) grew phenomenally. By keeping its costs low and opening centers in populous areas, NMC was able to reap substantial profits with government reimbursements. By the 1980s NMC was treating nearly one-fifth of the nation's dialysis patients and had become a potent lobbying force.[72]

NMC was followed by other large corporations. In 1992, there were 2,086 dialysis-only centers, but by 1998 there were 3,470.[73] During the 1990s a wave of consolidations occurred as large international and national corporations bought each other up and snatched up small single dialysis center operations. Large chains now dominate the market and have been able to reap substantial profits on activities financed primarily through the public sector to the benefit of a small number of patients. These corporations and their investors have become stakeholders interested in maintaining the current program and its continued survival.

Doctors and professionals who derive their living from ESRD patients also have a vested interest in the program. Finally, the government agencies involved have an interest in terms of resources and influence in the continuance of the ESRD program. These agencies include not only the Health Care Financing Administration, but also the ESRD Networks created in 1978 to collect and exchange information and to provide oversight, as well as the United States Renal Data System, which in addition to making more information available also has helped build and legitimize the program.

All these elements—demographics, medical advances, program design, and the interests of the private sector, professionals, and government agencies—have contributed to the high growth in expenditures for the ESRD program. Efforts to control costs through payment caps, bundling of services (as opposed to separate billing), waiting periods for benefits, and restrictions of drug use may have slowed expenditures, but the trend is still up.

HOW HAVE ENTITLEMENTS BEEN CONTROLLED?

Entitlements seem to carry with them a sense of fatalism, of inexorable growth beyond our powers to control or influence. But entitlements, like any other kind of expenditures, are shaped by more than economic and social conditions. They are the outcome of political decisions about program design. Such decisions are not made or maintained in a vacuum, but in response to pressures and influences—from groups seeking advantage, from conceptions of the public interest, from crises of the moment, from bureaucrats and committees. True, costs may be deliberately underestimated, decisions may be taken without regard to the picture as a whole, forecasts of the future may be inaccurate or biased, but all this is a far cry from saying that entitlements cannot be controlled.

Mechanisms to control federal entitlements are certainly available. At any time the president and Congress may pass legislation affecting entitlements. Each entitlement is subject to specific authorizing committees in the House and the

---

[72]G. B. Kolata, "NMC Thrives Selling Dialysis," *Science,*Vol. 208 (April 25, 1980), pp. 380–381.

[73]U.S. Renal Data System, op. cit., p. 165; Nissenson and Rettig, op. cit., p. 172.

Senate. Special commissions may be set up to recommend reforms. The reconciliation provisions of the congressional budget process are well-tailored to package legislative changes in eligibility, payments, benefits, or contributions. Further, limitations in the Congressional Budget Act of 1974 severely limited new entitlements, and the 1990 Budget Enforcement Act's PAYGO provisions discouraged expansions (see pp. 138–142).

Still, entitlement reform is not easy. Beneficiaries mobilize to defend their rights. One conception of public interest wars against another. Witness, for example, this exchange between members on the bipartisan commission to reform medicare, which failed to reach agreement in 1999. Senator Kerrey's argument was about affordability and discipline: "The baby boomers have a claim on Social Security and Medicare we can't afford—it is too large . . . [the commission and Congress] can't demonstrate the will to restrain this program [sic] in the future." In response, Representative John Dingell (whose father helped write the original medicare bill in 1965) declared that medicare "was one of the triumphs of the century"; it had been "an enormous success in improving the quality of life for elderly Americans" and its benefits had to be protected for the baby boomers.[74]

The splits that polarize Congress spill over into entitlement debates and cannot be disentangled from them. Where tax cuts are on the table, the proponents of entitlement reform are attacked as paying for tax benefits for the rich by cutting back entitlements for the poor. The debates themselves become increasingly difficult to follow as different measures are used to amplify or reduce the measure under discussion—at one moment the basis is nominal dollars, the next inflation-adjusted figures; sometimes projected cuts are from the budget of a specific year, sometimes they relate to a future baseline and are billed as only a "slowdown" in the rate of spending.

Yet to portray entitlements as static or entirely inflexible would be misleading. Changes do take place, and space is too restricted here to encompass the volumes that have been written on reforms of the large entitlement programs such as social security and medicare, or the detailed program changes that have taken place in various pieces of legislation. In general, sweeping radical reforms affecting the distant future have been the exception; politicians have preferred to chip at the details. They have also avoided attacking the status quo of current beneficiaries, instead altering the rights of future claimants. The most direct ways of cutting current or future benefits, or increasing beneficiaries' contributions, or restricting eligibility have been less popular than efforts to reach some kind of painless fix. In recent years this approach has often involved some kind of privatization. Sometimes, however, a program terminates or diminishes either by design or because there is no further need for it.

Declining Need: Black Lung Disease[75]

The black lung entitlement is a program in a state of gradual decline because of healthier working conditions and a decline in the recipient population. (For a discussion of the origins of the program, see pp. 198–199) Yet it was a program whose

---

[74]Robert A. Rosenblatt, "Medicare Panel Fails To Adopt Rescue Plan," *Los Angeles Times*, March 17, 1999, p. A11.

[75]This section is drawn from a paper by Thomas Donahue, a graduate student in the Department of Political Science, California State University, Los Angeles.

design presaged future growth. The definitions of the disease and disability rested on presumptive evidence (linked to time spent in the mine). The coal mine operators' responsibility to reimburse the government in particular cases could only be recovered through a lengthy appeals process in the courts. Benefits were later liberalized to include dust-induced bronchitis and emphysema.

By the late 1970s, concern about the program led to the end of automatic eligibility (though standards for disability were relaxed) and the establishment of a new Black Lung Disability Trust Fund, financed through a federal excise tax on coal. Benefits were paid for claims filed before 1973 by the Social Security Administration (SSA); for claims since then, by coal mine operators through workers' compensation or a self-insurance program; and through the trust fund.

Payments to miners for black lung disease reached their peak in 1981. The SSA benefits grew from $112 million in 1970 to over $1 billion in 1981.[76] The Black Lung Trust Fund, which was meant to be self-supporting from coal operators' payments, was affected by lagging coal sales. Since a key provision of the legislation committed the Treasury to cover trust fund deficits, the government was required to pay out large sums. In one year, between 1979 and 1980, the number of cases transferred to the trust fund nearly doubled, and in 1981, the government spent about $1.5 billion.

The Reagan administration attempted to rein in the program. There was a sharp reversal in benefit and eligibility standards, in exchange for transferring 10,200 more unresolved cases to the trust fund (which more than offset the savings from benefits changes for the next five years). It became more difficult to establish eligibility, the coal tax was doubled, and benefits were reduced for those with earnings above the social security level.

These measures were secondary to other reasons for declining program expenditures. First, regulation enforcement, technology, and education have reduced exposure to coal dust in the mines, and several studies in recent years have concluded that fewer miners are afflicted with black lung disease.[77]

The second reason for the decline has been the decreasing number of beneficiaries. At its peak in 1974, the SSA was paying benefits to nearly half a million beneficiaries; in 1997 the number had dropped to about 119,000. This population is aging, and as fewer new cases arise, costs will continue to decline. The Black Lung Trust Fund beneficiaries are also fewer, dropping from 138,000 in 1980 to 58,320 in 1998. New claims have declined from 10,530 in 1994 to 6,115 in 1998.[78]

However, although the trust fund has been paying out less to beneficiaries, its debt to the Treasury to cover its deficits means that every year it pays out large amounts in interest. The debt continues to grow: in 1981 it was $1.5 billion; in 1995,

---

[76]"Black Lung Benefits: Currently Payable to Miners, Widows, and Dependents, 1970–97," *Social Security Bulletin,* 1998 Annual Statistical Supplement, Washington, 1998, Table 9 D1.

[77]Brandy Fisher, "Between a Rock and a Healthy Place," *Environmental Health Perspectives,* November 1998, Vol. 106, No. 11, p. A545; Susan Goodwin and Michael Attfield, "Temporal Trends in Coal Workers' Pneumoconiosis Prevalence: Validating the National Coal Study Results," *Journal of Occupational and Environmental Medicine,* December 1998, Vol. 40, No. 12, pp. 1065–71.

[78]L. E. Kerr, "Black Lung," *Journal of Public Health Policy,* March 1980, Vol. 1, No. 1, p. 59; United States Budget, Fiscal Years 1996 and 2000.

$3.1 billion; and in 1998, $5.9 billion. The revenues the trust fund receives from the coal operators still do not cover its outlays, and it is now paying out more in administrative and interest costs than it is paying to the black lung beneficiaries. Even though costs are likely to decline in the future, because of the decline in the number of beneficiaries, the trust fund is likely to continue paying interest costs well into the next century. New regulations were passed in 1998 (despite strong opposition by the coal and insurance industries) to improve and speed up the claim filing process, which will probably expand slightly the number of new beneficiaries. Even so, the program is in decline, with 10,000 beneficiaries leaving it each year.

Cutting Provider Payments: Medicare

How is it possible to make cuts in a popular program with a large constituency? Why should anyone do so? In 1995, the Republican majority in Congress attempted a huge cut in medicare as part of its program to cut government and taxes. Its comprehensive reconciliation bill was vetoed by the president. Two years later, the 1997 Balanced Budget Agreement succeeded in cutting medicare growth by $115 billion over five years, allegedly extending the life of the Part A trust fund to 2008. This was done in the traditional way—primarily by cutting payments to medical care providers. The cuts would take effect over a number of years, as would an increase in Part B premiums. There were also some sweeteners such as free or assisted screenings for some diseases, as well as enhanced "choices" for beneficiaries ("medical savings accounts," health maintenance organizations, and some other plans).[79]

In the euphoria over balancing the budget, and the relief of organizations representing seniors that worse had not befallen them, there was little critique of the detailed proposals. Two years later, as their ramifications became more evident, the difficulties of controlling entitlements in patchwork fashion became evident.

Cutting payments to providers has the advantages of not affecting beneficiaries directly, and also attacking directly the causes of cost inflation. In the past, this strategy might have been criticized as ineffective in controlling costs; the 1997 cuts seem to have been all too effective. Hard evidence is lacking, but medicare spending slowed beyond projections. According to the Congressional Budget Office, spending for the first seven months of Fiscal Year 1999 was $3 billion less than for the previous year.[80]

What had the 1997 changes done? Among their major provisions were lowered reimbursement rates for nursing homes. Previously, costs had been reimbursed; now rates were set by the federal government according to average industry costs for different types of care. Second, payments for physical, speech,

---

[79]"The Medicare Puzzle," *Los Angeles Times*, November 10, 1998, p. A24; "Proposal Leaves Seniors Relieved," *Los Angeles Times*, May 4, 1998, p. A23.

[80]Amy Goldstein, "Is the Remedy To Retreat?" *Washington Post National Weekly Edition*, May 17,1999, p. 19.

and occupational therapy were capped. Third, home health care agencies' payments were cut by 15 percent (beginning October 2000). Fourth, payments to teaching hospitals and health maintenance organizations were cut.

Evidence of harm from the cuts has been both fragmentary and contradictory. Examples abound of services denied, patients refused entry to nursing homes, bankruptcies of HMOs and nursing homes, and deleterious and expensive impacts of loss of therapy. What has been clear is the reaction of every segment of the health care industry, which has been feverishly lobbying to gain restoration of at least some of the cuts. The National Association for Home Health Care, the National Rural Health Association, and the American Hospital Association, among others, have all decried the effects of the cuts and warned of impending harm. Their efforts have found considerable sympathy in Congress, with the chairs of the Senate Finance Committee and health subcommittee of the House Ways and Means Committee drafting proposals to reinstate a small portion of the cuts.

The difficulties in cutting medicare incrementally underscore the political problems facing control of entitlements. Not only has it proven difficult to justify cuts in services to the oldest and sickest members of society, who have undoubtedly benefited in length and quality of life from them, but it has also been hard to come to any agreement on how to restructure medicare in a more comprehensive way, or to avoid further claims to meet felt needs, for example, expansion of coverage to prescription drugs. Should one part of the health system be expanded, while another, the estimated 44 billion people without any health insurance at all, be neglected? There is no mechanism for confronting such a choice.

Ending an Entitlement: Welfare

On August 22, 1996, President Clinton signed the Personal Responsibility and Work Opportunity Reconciliation Act of 1996 (HR 3734-PL104-193) ending a 60-year-old federal entitlement. The legislation replaced Aid to Families with Dependent Children (AFDC) with a federal block grant to states, giving states almost complete control over eligibility and benefits. How did this change take place? The immediate causes lay in the political environment of the mid–1990s, but the end of the entitlement was foreshadowed in the development of the program and changes in public opinion.

AFDC began, as Daniel P. Moynihan writes, "almost as an afterthought."[81] It was tacked onto higher priority components of the Social Security Act and the need for it was expected to fade out. As with many Depression-Era programs, AFDC was not designed for the poorest of the poor but rather for the temporarily submerged working and middle classes, such as the wife and children of a factory worker killed on the job. The legislative record indicates Congress's expectation that the program would wither away as the economy improved and as such programs as social security became established.[82]

---

[81]Daniel P. Moynihan, *The Politics of Guaranteed Income* (New York: Random House, 1973), p. 42.

[82]Ibid., p. 197.

By the early 1960s, it was clear that AFDC was serving a different constituency—the broken families of blacks and whites who had migrated out of agriculture into urban areas. And despite the fact that the economy was steadily
improving, the AFDC rolls were steadily growing. By the mid–1970s, AFDC cases
stood at 3.7 million, over three times the number in 1960, and the bill for all antipoverty programs also tripled. Although spending growth was slower over the
next decade, the proportion of the population in poverty traced a less optimistic
path. Over the 1960s and early 1970s, it fell more or less steadily, reaching about
11 percent in 1973. It then remained constant through 1979 when it began rising
again, and by 1983 it exceeded 15 percent. This contradiction—a rising poverty
rate in the face of rising antipoverty expenditures—led to the argument that the
expenditures themselves had caused poverty by fostering dependence.[83] As chairman of the Ways and Means Committee, Wilbur Mills asked, "Is it in the public interest for welfare to become a way of life?"[84]

AFDC was under serious attack, as it had been for some time. Neither party
was comfortable with the program. In 1988, in recognition of the change in its
clientele from widows whose needs would eventually be met by social security to
"a new class of dependent families," the Family Support Act redefined AFDC as
"a form of temporary assistance, with a wholly new emphasis on getting a job and
becoming self-supporting." The states were encouraged to experiment, innovate,
evaluate.[85] Further efforts continued to try to push welfare recipients into the
workforce, but the initiative of the Clinton administration in 1994 to "end welfare
as we know it" could not elicit sufficient agreement to restructure the program.

Welfare reform was high on the Republican agenda in 1995, but the consensus that something had to be done went little beyond the hoped for contribution of
expenditure reductions to budget balance. In some sense welfare reform was not
really about money. The AFDC program cost the federal government only $17 bil-
lion a year, despite growth in AFDC recipients from nearly 11 million in 1989 to
over 14 million in 1994, and it was sensitive to economic fluctuations. Between
1970 and 1994, AFDC benefits in real terms declined by nearly 50 percent.[86] The
welfare debate was a debate about morals. Its budgetary aspect was about the influence of federal expenditures on behavior i.e., the behavior of the poor or the
"underclass," rather than the actual dollars themselves. The ideological issues
were up front. "Although" as Timothy Conlan explains, "the idea of "reforming
welfare" was immensely popular, putting the concept into practice raised so many
complicated issues and encountered so many policy "traps" between conflicting
objectives that legislation failed in the legislative arena, "time after time."[87]

For example, should teenage unwed mothers be denied welfare payments?
Should mothers already on welfare be denied welfare payments for additional

---

[83]Charles Murray, *Losing Ground: American Social Policy, 1950–1980* (New York: Basic Books, 1984).

[84]Cited in Angela Browne, "Welfare Legislation," *Congress and the Nation, 1965–1968*, p. 772.

[85]Daniel Patrick Moynihan, "The Devolution Revolution," *New York Times,* May 6, 1995, p. E15.

[86]Bryner, op. cit., p. 20.

[87] Timothy Conlan, *From New Federalism to Devolution: Twenty-five Years of Intergovernmental Reform* (Washington D.C.: Brookings Institution, 1998), p. 273.

children? It was argued that welfare payments to unwed teenage mothers and mothers already on welfare were incentives for family disintegration, dependency, and out-of-wedlock births, and that their denial would reverse these trends. Evidence on both these propositions was scanty and ambiguous, and questions were raised whether the denial of benefits would encourage a higher abortion rate. In fact, only 8 percent of welfare mothers were teenagers, and less than 3 percent of poor families were headed by women younger than 19.[88]

The funding issue was also critical to the issue of federal-state relations and the nature of entitlement. Properly speaking, welfare was not an individual entitlement but a federal guarantee of assistance to all eligible low-income mothers and children to match state spending. Much of the initiative for welfare reform came from the states.

In 1995, the general attack of the Republicans on social spending came to a halt with President Clinton's veto of its major reconciliation bill. The following year he vetoed another welfare reform bill, but he signed the third effort. The debates along the way had been extraordinarily detailed, but the general outline of the final compromise was clear. The previous entitlement which guaranteed payments to all eligible low-income mothers and children was eliminated. Block grants gave states almost complete control of eligibility and benefits. Recipients of aid would be required to work within two years and there was a five year lifetime limit for benefits. Additional restrictions were made to the food stamp program, and various benefits were denied to legal immigrants. The savings from the bill (about $54 billion over five years) came primarily from these provisions rather than the change in AFDC.

What made it possible for such a change to pass? Welfare reform had been on the agenda of virtually every president since Richard Nixon.[89] Despite its longevity, the program had little support: A 1996 survey concluded that "an overwhelming percentage of Americans believe welfare is badly flawed and in need of overhaul."[90] AFDC recipients, despite their numbers, were a weak constituency—they comprised the poorest segment of society, single mothers, and nearly 10 million were children. Though reality did not support welfare stereotypes of large proportions of teenage mothers, large families, and a preponderance of minorities, these misconceptions persisted and fueled antagonism toward the program. There was sufficient truth in the growth of the number of out-of-wedlock births, single-headed families, and a cycle of welfare dependency to enable people to accuse the welfare system as being their cause. At the same time, another constituency, the working poor, were attracting attention, and their claims for benefits in some measure competed with those of the welfare population.

The immediate political situation favored reform. President Clinton's 1992 campaign included a pledge for welfare reform, which became an issue that demarcated "new" Democrats from "old" Democrats. Emphasis was on the work

---

[88]Eliza Newlin Corney, "Taking Over," *National Journal*, June 10, 1995, p. 1382–87.

[89]Conlan, op. cit. p. 272.

[90]Bryner, op. cit., p. 32.

ethic and opportunity in a restructured economy with some assistance from government, rather than the old guarantees for mothers and children. Clinton was too distracted by other issues to make good on his pledge, but welfare reform was a central theme in the Republican "Contract with America." The lack of success of their first two efforts to achieve welfare reform might be attributed to an excess of ambition. The first reconciliation bill's broad-based attack on the welfare state was not popular and Clinton's veto could not be overruled; the second attempt coupled welfare with medicaid reform, a program with a much broader constituency, and again ended in presidential veto. The final bill moderated many of the more radical proposals and isolated welfare as a single issue. It obtained the critical support of the National Governors' Association: States wanted control of their own welfare programs both to control expenditures and in many cases for ideological reasons. Given the choice of vetoing welfare reform and being open to accusations in the forthcoming election of reneging on his promise, or assenting to it and depriving the opposition of an issue, Clinton signed the bill. Republicans in Congress were willing to compromise on some issues to show they had achieved at least something during the 104th Congress. A large number of Democrats followed the president in voting for the bill, with a similar rationale.

Perhaps we should turn the question around and ask how it was that the AFDC entitlement had lasted so long, and by extension, other "means-tested" entitlements, such as food stamps and public assistance programs. Since 1996, enrollments for these programs have been declining, but most of the decline has been attributed not to the reforms, but to the improved economy.[91] Perhaps, this tells us that in an unforgiving economy, people know instinctively that good times do not last forever and that changing circumstances may all too easily jeopardize everything they have. Possible, compassion may still triumph over self-interest to maintain a standard of decency below which no one should fall.

THE CORNERS OF THE FIELD[92]

Every society makes some provision for those who cannot look after themselves: the old, the sick, the disabled, the destitute, and children. Historically this role has been undertaken by the family, predominantly by women, supplemented by charity. But as far back as the Bible, farmers were exhorted to leave the crops in the corners of their fields for the poor. In the twentieth century, with the development of modern industrial economies, governments have increasingly stepped in to shoulder the risks arising from economic uncertainties, to provide security in old age and sickness, and to ensure at least a minimum standard of living to those unable to cope on their own. In communist countries, where there was no private sector, these benefits were related to the workplace.[93] In Western Europe, with considerable variations, they formed a comprehensive system of rights and guar-

---

[91]Bryner, op. cit., pp. 6–8.

[92]"And when ye reap the harvest of your land, thou shalt not wholly reap the corner of thy field, neither shalt thou gather the gleaning of thy harvest; thou shalt leave them for the poor, and for the stranger." Lev. 23:22. (J. H. Hertz (ed.) *Pentateuch and Haftorahs,* (London: Soncino Press, 1972), p. 522.

[93]See Naomi Caiden, "The Roads to Transformation: Budgeting Issues in the Czech and Slovak Federal Republic 1989–1992," *Public Budgeting and Finance,* Vol. 13, No. 4, Winter 1993, pp. 57–71.

antees enshrined in the cradle-to-grave policy of the welfare state.[94] In the United States, a patchwork of provision evolved, providing benefits in various ways to differing groups of eligible beneficiaries. By the end of the twentieth century, all these arrangements were showing strain. The collapse of communism in the Soviet Union and Eastern Europe disrupted the system of rights and benefits tied to it. In Western industrialized countries, what is sometimes grandly called "the social contract" is being rethought. In the United States, there are persistent proposals to reform the major entitlements.

While individual entitlements form the backbone of public social provision, it would be misleading to draw a sharp distinction between them and the remainder of the budget. Rather they form a major element in a blurred continuum of measures creating rights and conveying benefits, including individual entitlements, subsidy programs, tax expenditures, trust funds, credit programs (loans and loan guarantees), intergovernmental formula grants, and appropriations.

Among these mechanisms, entitlements are distinguished by a number of characteristics. First, they are clearly demarcated by the title "federal entitlement." Second, they are not subject to changes through the appropriations committees. Third, the amount of their funding is determined by the number of eligible claimants and the law setting out the rates at which they are paid. Fourth, decision making for entitlements rests with different committees in Congress.[95]

Other characteristics of entitlements are also seen in other programs. An obvious feature has been explosive growth, which has been tied not only to long-term demographics, but to program design. A single change, such as eligibility for home health care, has enormous implications, not only because it is a sought after benefit and an opportunity for income for providers, but simply because of the huge numbers involved. By 1990, it was estimated that nearly half of all families in the United States were receiving benefits from one or more of 11 major entitlement programs, averaging $10,000 each.[96] Even the smallest entitlement has a constituency that spreads out from the immediate beneficiaries to their families, providers, suppliers, government agencies, and future cohorts who expect to take advantage of the same benefits in the next generation. Other social programs share this complexity of constituency, which quickly mobilizes to resist cuts and ensure continued program growth. Since not all programs benefit poor or unfortunate people, or even the middle classes, the same characteristic applies to a variety of subsidies and tax breaks that are often referred to as corporate welfare.[97] All these represent benefits that accrue to individuals or groups because of some kind of definition of their eligibility, and which are quickly interpreted as rights.

---

[94]Gerald Caiden and Naomi Caiden, "Brothers' Keepers," *Society*, Vol. 32, No. 6, September/October 1995, pp. 16–22.

[95]See Joseph White, "Entitlement Budgeting vs. Bureau Budgeting," *Public Administration Review*, Vol, 58, No. 6, November/December, 1998, pp. 510–21.

[96]Congressional Budget Office, *Reducing Entitlement Spending* (Washington, D.C.: Congressional Budget Office, September 1994), p. xi.

[97]The Cato Institute has estimated that the federal budget contains over $60 billion in subsidies to business, not counting special tax breaks. (See *Congressional Quarterly Weekly Report,* January 17, 1998, pp. 121–22).

Entitlements have also been characterized by their stability, but this does not mean they have been either impervious to change or responsive to it. Observers have noted that incrementalism has not been confined to appropriations.[98] In some cases changes have been deliberate, for example expansions in eligibility, but other entitlements have adapted beyond their original intentions to fulfill needs and demands. For example, medicaid expanded to pay for nursing home care for the elderly, and AFDC came to support never-married mothers. Conversely, there are allegations that entitlement programs have moved too slowly to keep up with changed circumstances; for example, medicare provision emphasizes payments for hospital stays, not prescription drugs or long-term care, failing to take account of changes in modes of medical treatment or changes in clientele.

Entitlements may change much as other parts of the budget do: through piecemeal, repeated noncomprehensive actions. Even smaller entitlements share with other government programs an incredible complexity of detail, which makes it extraordinarily difficult to follow, let alone reproduce, eligibility formulas, reimbursement provisions, payments schedules, subsidy arrangements, and so on. But such detail facilitates incremental change, which can focus on them without bringing into question the existence of the program itself.

Finally entitlement spending is dominated by baselines—the projection of where spending would be in the future without deliberate policy changes, given inflation, cost of living adjustments, and estimates of increased eligibility. These baselines are an active component of entitlement budgeting: They impart a future-oriented focus to decision making, as proposals for this or that are costed out for the years ahead. But the baselines also degrade budget debate. Their projections rest on assumptions that may be unrealistic or untenable or both. Baselines are essentially imaginary figures whose credence depends on their provenance (what is the record of the issuing agency?) and credulousness of their audience (whose figures do you want to believe and for what purpose?). Conservatives like baselines because they can show that their cuts are only of program "growth," that horrors lie ahead if nothing is done, and how certain favored areas (e.g. defense) have lost ground in relation to the baseline. Liberals like baselines because they magnify cuts (even an increase may be a cut), because they show the magnitude of future needs, and how certain favored areas (e.g. social and environmental programs) have lost ground in relation to the baseline.

These characteristics of entitlements—widespread, entrenched constituencies with perceived rights to benefits; adaptation through piecemeal, intentional and unintentional incremental changes; complex detailed provisions; and the im-

---

[98]See Maureen Berner, "Incrementalism, Congressional Power Structures and Budget Deals—What Really Matters to Budget Policy? Insights from a Behavioral Analysis of the U.S. Federal Budget from 1962–1995," Paper prepared for the 1999 Annual Meeting of the Midwest Political Service Association, April 9, 1999; Eric M. Patashnik, "Ideas, Inheritances and the Dynamics of Budgetary Change," *Governance*, Vol. 12, No. 2, April 1999, pp. 147–74; James L. True, "Attention, Inertia and Equity in the Social Security Program," *Journal of Public Administration Research and Theory*, Vol. 9, No. 4, October 1999, pp. 571–96; Joseph White, "(Almost) Nothing New Under the Sun: Why the Work of Budgeting Remains Incremental," in Naomi Caiden and Joseph White (eds.), *Budgeting, Policy, Politics: An Appreciation of Aaron Wildavsky* (New Brunswick, N.J.: Transaction, Inc., 1995), pp. 111–32.

portance of baselines—are also evident in a variety of other measures that confer benefits. This chapter would not be complete without a brief discussion of some of these "quasi-entitlements."

Appropriations: Head Start and WIC

Head Start is a highly popular program for poor preschool children begun in 1965. Like an entitlement, its beneficiaries qualify through eligibility criteria, but despite its bipartisan support it failed to become an entitlement. Its original funding derived from unspent Office of Equal Opportunity appropriations, and it seems the opportunity for entitlement status was lost.[99] The program is reauthorized every five years through the Labor and Human Resources Committee in the Senate and the Committee on Education and the Work Force in the House. It requires appropriation every year.

Head Start has grown steadily since its beginning. In 1965 it served over half a million children at a cost of $96.4 million. By its last reauthorization, enrollment was up to 830,000 and expenditures were nearly $4.5 billion. President Clinton declared the aim of participation by 1 million children by the year 2000. Head Start covers only a minority of children eligible (probably only about a quarter), and questions have arisen about its effectiveness and quality.[100] But it is highly unlikely that the program will be cut, let alone eliminated. It shares the stability of entitlement programs in the face of change, as well as a constituency not only of clientele (who are not exactly influential), but of a network of nonprofit organizations, policy professionals, and government agencies.

The Women, Infants and Children's program (WIC) is a supplemental feeding program that provides individuals earning less than 185 percent of the federal poverty level with temporary nutrition assistance through vouchers worth about $30 a month. It is aimed at high risk pregnant women, mothers, and young children. The program is federally funded, but administered by state departments of health, which distribute funds to local public and nonprofit agencies, which provide vouchers and other services to clients. WIC is dependent on periodic authorization, which falls under the jurisdiction of the House Education and Workforce Subcommittee on Early Childhood, Youth and Families and the Senate Agriculture Committee. It is also subject to annual appropriation. The program costs about $4 billion a year, and was sufficiently popular with both parties to fight off cuts in the Reagan era. Although it is funded by appropriations that set annual limits to funding, it is routine for shortfalls to be made up by supplementals.

WIC has a widespread constituency of support. It serves half of infants in the United States. Its congressional support has been strengthened by reports extolling its effectiveness in reducing potential health care costs. Nonprofit organizations and antipoverty advocates also lobby for the program. But some of WIC's

---

[99]See Edward Zigler and Jeanette Valentine, eds., *Project Head Start: A Legacy of the War on Poverty* (New York: Free Press, 1979).

[100]Sue Kirchhoff, "Head Start Is Growing But Is It Improving?" *Congressional Quarterly Weekly Report,* June 27, 1998, p. 1743–46.

most ardent supporters are in the food industry, particularly the producers of cereals and infant formula. Just one company, General Mills, derives about 3 percent of its annual cereal sales from WIC, while half of infant formula is bought with WIC vouchers.[101]

WIC looks very much like an entitlement program. Those eligible may claim benefits, it has a widespread influential constituency, and it has been a stable program. Even in the arduous budgetary climate of 1995, House and Senate agreed to a slight increase over the previous year's funding to allow maintenance of the current caseload. The 1998 reauthorization, while instituting measures to combat rampant fraud, also expanded nutrition programs by such measures as providing afternoon snacks for teenagers in low income areas, extending the summer meals program, and allowing a five state free breakfast pilot program.[102]

Tax Expenditures: Earned Income Tax Credit (EITC)

Tax expenditures are revenue losses due to the preferential provisions of the federal tax laws, such as special exclusions, exemptions, deductions, credits, deferrals, or tax rates.[103] They are listed in the annual budget, together with estimates of their cost in foregone revenues. Only two tax expenditures actually return money to beneficiaries if tax liability is less than the legal credit. One of them is the Earned Income Tax Credit (EITC). It was created in 1975 as an incentive to people with low incomes to work, and it aimed to offset payments for social security and medicare, as well as other tax liabilities, to enable them to stay above the poverty line. It is a refundable tax credit: If the credit is in excess of taxes, taxpayers receive the credit as a cash grant.

Like an entitlement, beneficiaries qualify according to eligibility i.e., income and number of dependents. Like an entitlement, the program grew explosively after the mid–1980s, faster than any other program helping the poor. From $2 billion in 1985, expenditures grew to over $21 billion in 1997, with a further $6 billion or so of costs in foregone revenues. Direct expenditures were expected to rise to over $27 billion in Fiscal Year 2000, with additional revenue loss of about $5 billion.[104]

The EITC has no real concerted constituency, but it has bipartisan support from both Republicans and Democrats because of its incentives for working people, and because of its warm endorsement from economists as a "negative income tax." It was expanded three times, in 1986, 1990, and 1993. All the same, the EITC came under attack from Republicans in 1995, but like other entitlements remained when the president vetoed the reconciliation bill. The extent of its support may be gauged from another attack in 1999, when the

---

[101]Sue Kirchhoff, "Nutrition Program's Tempest in a Cereal Bowl," *Congressional Quarterly Weekly Report*, May 16, 1998, p. 1276.

[102]Sue Kirchhoff, "House Clears Reauthorization of Nutrition Programs," *Congressional Quarterly Weekly Report*, October 10, 1998, p. 2745.

[103]United States Budget, *Analytical Perspectives*, Fiscal Year 1999, p. 89.

[104]United States Budget, Fiscal Year 1999, *Historical Tables: Table 8.5 Outlays for Mandatory and Related Programs 1962–2003*, p. 125; *Analytical Perspectives, Table 5.1, Total Revenue Loss Estimates for Tax Expenditures in the Income Tax*, p. 93.

Republicans attempted to spread out payments to beneficiaries over a year instead of giving a lump sum payment, as a gimmick to balance the budget. This move resulted in such an outcry, including a condemnation from the Republican contender for the president, George Bush, Jr., that the proposal was quickly withdrawn.

Formula Grants to States: Adoption Assistance Program, Individuals With Disabilities Education Act, and the Ryan White Care Act

To describe the world of federal grants to states is to enter a labyrinth of detailed provisions for eligibility and funding. Three examples illustrate the complexity of these programs, and their resemblance and differences from entitlements.

The Adoption Assistance Program (Title IV-E of the Social Security Act) was enacted in 1980 to assist states in moving children, particularly those difficult to place, from foster care to permanent adoption.[105] For every child who is removed from his or her home, the federal government will reimburse from 50–80 percent of the state's adoption assistance and foster care maintenance costs. This grant is an open-ended entitlement whose annual funding does not depend on annual appropriation. During the 1990s, federal expenditures for the program grew from $171 million in 1991 to $700 million in 1998, and are estimated to exceed $900 million in 2000. In 1997, the president declared a goal of doubling the number of children in foster care who are adopted or otherwise permanently placed in homes, by 2002. Over half a million children were in foster care, many for two years or more.[106] In 1998, the Adoption and Safe Families Act was passed, which among other provisions, gave the states $4,000 for each adoption from foster care that exceeded their previous annual level, and an extra $2,000 for a child with disabilities. Unlike the earlier legislation, these incentive adoptions were authorized for $20 million each for five years. The bill received bipartisan support. The ASF Act shares with the earlier adoption assistance program its general aim, its eligibility provisions, and its reliance on states for implementation. The two parts of the program complement each other, but one is an entitlement, and the other an authorized appropriation.

Another entitlement-like program for children is the Individuals with Disabilities Education Act (IDEA), which served nearly 5.5 million children in 1993–94. IDEA was enacted in 1975 to bolster an earlier statute after several court rulings required equal access to public education for disabled children. At the time, 2.5 million disabled children were receiving a substandard education and 1.75 million no education at all. IDEA permanently authorized funds to help states cover the extra educational costs for school-age children. In 1990, the program was extended to preschoolers, and in 1990, eligibility was considerably

---

[105] This description is based on a paper by Rowena Lauretta Holt, a graduate student in the Department of Political Science, California State University, Los Angeles.

[106] Jeffrey Katz, "President Expected To Sign Foster Care Adoption Bill," *Congressional Quarterly Weekly Report*, November 15, 1997, p. 2858.

broadened. By 1996, IDEA encompassed three formula grant programs (permanently authorized) and fourteen discretionary programs. For each disabled student, states are authorized to receive up to 40 percent of the national average cost of educating a student, but in fact grants have been below 12 percent.[107] IDEA guarantees the rights of disabled children to free education and to placement in "the least restrictive" environment. It rests on strong support in Congress, as well as a general coalition of groups representing disabled children and the general education community.[108] At about $3 billion a year, it covers only a relatively small proportion of the costs of special education, but it is still the second largest source of federal aid to schools. Like an entitlement it rests on a formula that in turn depends on definitions of eligibility and is open to revision, it incorporates ideas about rights and it draws for support on a large constituency. However, funding requires annual appropriation and has remained well below the authorized level for each child.

The Ryan White CARE Act was named for a teenager who contracted AIDS and became an active public educator on the disease before he died.[109] Enacted in 1990, the Ryan White legislation marked the entry of the federal government into the area of care and treatment for HIV/AIDS. Previously the federal government had supported research, but direct assistance to the victims had been left to state and local governments. As costs mounted, these could no longer cope with the huge health cost burden, and there was a fear that without federal intervention, costs would be even higher.

The four titles of the Act provide federal funding, chief of which is a Title 1 Formula grant that provides funds to eligible metropolitan areas disproportionately affected by the HIV epidemic. These areas are eligible for funds if they have reported more than 2,000 AIDS cases in the preceding five years and if they have a population of more than 500,000. Administration is in the hands of planning councils that represent specific groups such as health care agencies and providers. The Act provided for reauthorization every five years, and has proven controversial. Appropriations in the early years were well below the $4.5 billion authorized under the Act, but qualifying cities rose from 16 in 1991 to 49 in 1998. Since 1991 nearly $5 billion has been expended under the Act. The formula grants share with entitlements both issues of eligibility and the expectation of funding as a right.

These examples are only a few of the kinds of quasi-entitlements that have grown up to fill specific needs and respond to particular groups. With one exception (the Adoption Assistance Program), they are not true entitlements, and, except for the AAP and the EITC, require appropriations for funding. But they do represent, together with trust funds, loans, and loan guarantees and subsidies, parts of the budget to which recipients feel they have an enduring claim. Hence, for example, the demand that programs should be fully funded up to their autho-

---

[107]Christopher Swope, "How Aid for Disabled Children Works," *Congressional Quarterly Weekly Report*, May 11, 1996.

[108]Jeffrey Katz, "Panel Oks IDEA Revisions Despite Controversies," *Congressional Quarterly Weekly Report*, June 1, 1996, p. 1532.

[109]This section is based on a paper by Maricella Rodriguez, a graduate student in the Department of Political Science, California State University Los Angeles.

rization limit, or that trust funds, such as those for transportation, should expend all their annual income.[110]

Comparison between entitlements and other measures in the federal budget is interesting, but subordinate to other issues. In asking why some kinds of provision are funded at one end of the entitlement continuum and others at the other end, why some provisions are directly funded and administered by the federal government and others through grants to states and localities, why some groups, diseases, or needs have become protected, we are really questioning the patchwork of social provision. Does it represent a mere reflection of relative strengths of different claimants, a culture of entitlement in which existing recipients enjoy and retain entrenched benefits unshared by the rest of us? Or are we looking at a complex interwoven system, infinitely adaptable through incrementalism, reflecting compromises between liberals and conservatives and a common consent on what is right and reasonable? Or do the fragmented arrangements that should constitute a social safety net defy effective policy making and provide no institutional framework for setting priorities in any meaningful way?

---

[110]See United States General Accounting Office, Testimony by Susan J. Irving, *Budget Issues: Trust Funds in the Budget,* before the Subcommittee on Transportation and Related Agencies, Committee on Appropriations, House of Representatives, March 9, 1999, (GAO/T-AIMD/REC-99-110).

Chapter 9

Budgeting for Defense

Understanding defense budgeting, even at a relatively simple level, is a lot like finding your way through a maze blindfolded. Defense is huge and complex; its procurement alone could qualify as the largest business in the world. But budgeting for defense is really just budgeting writ large: Its problems are those of financing and managing any public organization, though they take on a scale and urgency that set them apart.

Budgeting for defense highlights the question of whether policy can be determined without reference to resources. It may be argued that where national interest is at stake, only needs should be considered, and debates should not be tainted by the question "Can we afford it?" But even at the highest level, defense is subject to economics—it competes against other goals. Objectives cannot be realistically defined without reference to some constraint—otherwise why should we not spend all our resources on defense? In any case, people have different ideas about the extent of risks, the need for preparedness, the scale of current or future threats—all of which are weighed against the different amounts they are willing to invest in them. At a lower, strategic level, resource questions are more directly addressed. Should we have more of this or less of that? What would give us the best return on our resources? So budgeting is not just about costing out and fulfilling financial commitments for aims and strategies already decided. It is about choosing policies and making decisions in the light of available resources, and deciding what resources should be available in the light of feasible and desirable policies. Ends and means, as always, cannot be separated.

Like other budgets, defense budgets focus on the year ahead, but plans are long term. Planning is essential to make realistic policies that take account of change and prepare for the future. Budgeting for defense involves making long-term commitments for expensive weapons development and deployment, maintenance of facilities and equipment, and training and readiness of military forces. The difficulty, then, is dealing with changes. Not only may the defense establishment be locked into long-term contracts and sunk costs, but it is hard for so large and complex an organization (which of necessity depends on much routinization) to turn on a dime, to scrap and renew its weaponry and infrastructure, retrain its personnel, and deploy anew its resources. No wonder the military in all countries is so often accused of fighting the last war.

All public organizations face contingencies and have headaches in finding the resources to deal with them. In the uneasy world of the turn of the century, surprises for defense policy makers come fast, and they have to respond quickly and effectively. But because they have already planned their use of resources, they may lack flexibility for fast and expensive response. Clearly, flexibility is needed, but how much flexibility is a democracy willing to allow its armed forces? What resources, or redundancy, may a military organization move (reprogram) from one purpose to another as it thinks fit without prior authorization? What amount should be available for unforeseen contingencies, making it possible for defense to improvise its own policies or commit the country to unauthorized actions? Or should we just allow defense units to scramble for what they need, patching resources together from various budgets, and make things up afterwards?

In any case, where do strategy and objectives merge? Even where goals are prescribed, what freedom should defense organizations have to deploy resources to meet those goals? If resources are cut back, who decides where those reductions should be made? For example, recent years have seen a persistent competition between "modernization" and "readiness," with charges that each has gained to the detriment of the other. The budget process, at all levels, is deeply involved in the shifting balance between them.

Public budgeting is characterized by transparency of its processes and results. Many public organizations try to shield certain information, justifiably or not. Because of its close relationship to national security, defense budgeting is particularly sensitive. There is a contradiction between the public's right to know and the need for much about national security to be kept secret. Delineating what should be public—and therefore legitimate for budget debate—and what should be secret, is an important issue. And who should decide how much should be budgeted for secret activities?

Budgeting goes beyond transacting wish lists to assessing the efficiency and effectiveness of agencies. Traditional budgeting focuses on inputs, but for nearly a century reformers at all levels of government have tried to change the emphasis to performance, productivity, and effectiveness. Defense poses an especially difficult problem in measuring outcomes, particularly in the absence of conflicts. Yet the Department of Defense (DOD) was a pioneer in budget techniques for Planning, Programming, Budgeting (PPB) systems, and retains them in its budget processes. To what degree are such techniques appropriate, and how may the conceptual and practical problems be met?

Budgeting for defense, like other budgeting, raises the issue of where politics ends and administration begins. The concept of politicians setting clear lines of policy, and defense administrators simply carrying them out, falters on the difficulties in establishing just where that line should be. Congress, for a variety of reasons, is not prepared to give up power in such matters as appropriate weapons and equipment, location of facilities, mix of resources at quite detailed levels. From one point of view, this is congressional oversight; from another, micro-management.

Finally, budgeting involves control and accountability. In defense, these issues take on urgency because of the size and complexity of operations, their enormous geographical spread, the opportunities for fraud, waste and abuse, and the serious consequences of carelessness, errors, corruption, misdirection of funds, delays, or sloppiness.

All these themes are present in the following discussion of how budgeting for defense is conducted. Following a brief analysis of the size and scope of the defense budget in recent years, the focus is on how recent mission and strategies have been aligned with financing, including the impact of cuts on modernization and readiness, funding for new activities, and problems in finding new funding and savings. The next section describes internal processes, particularly how PPB has been applied in the Department of Defense, and problems of control and reform. The final section explains the dynamics of congressional control and decision making.

DIMENSIONS OF DEFENSE

The Department of Defense (DOD) employs almost 1.5 million active uniformed-service personnel, and nearly another million civilian employees.[1] More than 80 percent of federal employees work for DOD or on defense projects. At least 1.2 million private sector jobs (some say over 2 million) are created directly by DOD procurement, contract projects, and overseas military bases.[2]

The defense budget represents an enormous amount of resources. In 1989, outlays passed the $300 billion mark. Ten years later, they were estimated at $271 billion, and the United States was still spending almost as much on defense as the rest of the world combined. Despite the end of the Cold War, defense expenditures remained at about 85 percent of the average level of those years and actually higher in real terms than under Eisenhower or Nixon.[3]

The pattern of defense budgeting has been one of peaks and valleys, which encourages Defense Department officials and defense advocates to get as much as they can as fast as they can as long as they can. Between World War II and the Reagan buildup, the longest period of real annual increases for defense was three years. Between 1963 and 1969, the combination of a missile buildup and the Vietnam War led to a 23 percent increase in real purchasing power; between 1970 and 1979, because of the end of the war in Vietnam and concentration on domestic policy, defense spending declined by 25 percent in real terms. President Reagan entered office with two years of real military growth created by the Carter administration. He was able to extend that increase for four more years.

---

[1]William W. Kaufmann, *A Reasonable Defense* (Washington, D.C.: Brookings Institution, 1986), p. 42.

[2]Lawrence J. Korb, "The Process and Problems of Linking Policy and Force Structure through the Defense Budget Process," in Robert Harkavy and Edward Kolodziej, eds., *American Security Policy and Policy Making* (Lexington KY: Lexington Books, 1980), p. 186.

[3]Lawrence W. Korb, "The Republicans Up in Arms," *Washington Post,* January 31, 1995.

In 1985, the defense roller coaster reached its peak, and despite continued growth in nominal terms until 1991, dropped 9 percent by 1998. However, it is estimated that in "real" terms, adjusted for inflation, defense budget authority declined by 36 percent.[4] Defense spending had slipped both as a percentage of gross domestic product (from 6.2 percent to 3.2 percent) and as a proportion of total federal spending (from 26.7 percent to 15.8 percent). By 1999, military personnel had declined to about 1.4 million, while defense related employment had shrunk from an estimated 7 million workers in 1987 to 4.8 million in 1995.[5] (See Table 9.1.) Yet, as Table 9.2 shows, throughout the 1990s the United States was still spending more on defense than on all domestic discretionary programs, and the amount in nominal dollars was still huge.

Further cuts in defense (as well as domestic) spending were planned. But toward the end of 1998, bipartisan consensus grew that the decline in defense spending had gone far enough, and that it was time to begin to rebuild military capacity. Thus the president's budget for Fiscal Year 2000 budgeted about $12 billion more than for the previous year, and by the end of the budget process, the defense allocation had grown by $17 billion. The president scheduled more than $110 billion in increases over the next six years, although the combined services believed it would take nearly $150 billion for defense to fulfill its authorized mission.[6]

Table 9.1   National Defense Outlays Compared to Payments to Individuals

	Defense		Percentage GDP		Percentage Outlays	
	Current Outlays ($ billion)	Constant Outlays ($ billion 1992)	Defense	Payments to Individuals	Defense	Payments to Individuals
1950	13.7	113.5	5.2	5.0	32.2	32.1
1955	42.7	275.0	10.8	3.6	62.4	20.9
1960	48.1	260.3	9.3	4.7	52.2	26.2
1965	50.6	248.9	7.4	4.8	42.8	28.0
1970	81.7	315.4	8.1	6.4	41.8	33.1
1975	86.5	394.7	5.6	9.9	26.0	46.3
1980	134.0	229.4	4.9	10.2	22.7	47.1
1985	252.7	306.1	6.2	10.4	26.7	45.1
1990	299.3	324.6	5.3	10.3	23.9	46.6
1995	272.1	256.4	3.8	12.2	17.9	57.7
1996	265.7	240.3	3.5	12.1	17.0	58.3
1997	270.5	239.3	3.4	11.9	16.9	59.3
1998 est.	264.1	229.3	3.2	11.9	15.8	59.4

Source: United States Budget Fiscal Year 1999: Historical Tables: Table 6.1, Composition of Outlays 1940–2003, pp 103–09.

---

[4]Mary T. Tyszkiewicz and Stephen Daggett, *A Defense Budget Primer*, Congressional Research Service, December 9, 1998, p. 12; General Accounting Office, *Defense Sector: Trends in Employment and Spending*, April 1995, p. 10 (GAO/NSIAD-95-105BR).

[5]Ibid., p. 13.

[6]Pat Towell and Chuck McCutcheon, "Right-Face on Defense Policy," *Congressional Quarterly Weekly Report*, January 23, 1999, p. 181.

Table 9.2   Defense and Domestic Discretionary Outlays Compared 1962–1997

	Defense Outlays ($ billion)	Domestic Discretionary Outlays ($ billion)	International Outlays ($ billion)	Total Discretionary ($ billion)
1962	52.6	14.0	5.5	72.1
1970	81.9	34.3	4.0	120.2
1980	134.6	128.7	12.8	276.1
1985	253.1	145.2	17.4	415.7
1990	300.1	181.1	19.1	500.3
1991	319.7	193.6	19.7	533.0
1992	302.6	212.3	19.2	534.0
1993	292.4	226.4	21.6	540.4
1994	282.3	240.2	20.8	543.3
1995	273.6	251.4	20.1	545.1
1996	266.0	249.5	18.3	533.8
1997	271.9	256.9	19.8	548.5

Source: Congressional Budget Office, Economic and Budget Outlook Fiscal Year 1999–2008, Table E-10 Discretionary Outlays, Fiscal Years 1962–1997, p. 118.

What exactly is the defense budget? In the president's budget, defense spending is a function called "National Defense," which comprises not only the military activities of the Department of Defense, but also national security functions of the Department of Energy, and certain other defense-related activities. Other defense-related activities are not included in this function—such as military construction, veterans affairs, international military assistance, the civilian projects of the Army Corps of Engineers, and retirement payments to military retirees.[7] Whether these items should be included in a determination of budgetary resources or accounting for them is debatable, but straightforward. In any case, most primary defense activities are included under the Department of Defense.

More complex is the relationship of the budget function to the category used by Congress, which is appropriations or budgetary authority, and the relationship of budget authority to outlays (or money actually spent). This distinction is the same in the rest of the budget, but the complexity of defense budgeting is reflected in a concept unique to the Department of Defense, total obligational authority. The primary reason for this concept is that defense budgeting involves spending requirements that last beyond one year, so that each year it is necessary to add amounts for previous year's budget authority, while subtracting budget authority granted that will not be spent in the current fiscal year.[8] The result is a lack of uniformity in figures which confuses discussion.

Further discrepancies arise from the base from which additions or subtractions are counted. When the defense budget was still growing, DOD tried to select the

[7] Tyszkiewicz and Daggett, op. cit., p. 3.

[8] Tyszkiewicz and Daggett state that "total obligational authority is equivalent to the sum of all budget authority granted by Congress, plus amounts from other sources authorized to be credited to certain accounts, plus unobligated balances of funds from prior years which remain available for obligation." op. cit., p. 6.

highest base it could find from which to maximize additions, such as the prior year's presidential proposal rather than what Congress actually provided the previous year. The decline in real defense spending after the mid-80s changed assumptions about the base and increased dissensus and confusion about what it should be. Since 1990, the caps for discretionary spending set in place by the Budget Enforcement Act and their later renewals effectively set the baselines for defense spending.

These baselines had a number of implications. First, together with optimism about the end of the Cold War, they encouraged expectations of a huge amount of resources—a "peace dividend"—that would become available from scaling down defense, although it was doubtful that such a large reduction could be achieved. Second, the caps were in nominal dollar figures, so that really there were two baselines—one based on the caps that forced defense spending down each year below that of the previous year, and another based on an inflation factor, which widened the gap between actual spending and the spending that would have taken place had the peak been maintained in real terms. Third, there were really two sets of caps, one for budget authority and one for outlays. While constraints on budget authority eventually translate into reduced outlays, there is a distinct lag as earlier budget authority appears in current spending; conversely, resources apparently available within the budget authority cap may disappear because of the more stringent outlay caps.[9] Finally, the caps varied, sometimes covering both domestic and defense discretionary expenditures, and sometimes setting "fire walls" between them. When a single cap was in operation, the conflict between the two was open. Domestic and defense policies became two sides of the same coin, as more for one meant less for the other; human resources were pitted against military hardware. And where the two were merged, who could tell in advance where the baseline lay?

The concept of an agreed base or starting point lends certainty and stability to budgeting. While budgets are growing, the base may be easy to ascertain, if not always to accept. When the process is in reverse, and budgets decline from year to year, the base becomes confused. Instead of one base, there are many: actual spending, "real" spending, extrapolations of past spending adjusted for inflation, various plans for the future, spending limitations, and ideas about "needs." The base is no longer an accepted beginning figure against which to measure policy proposals, but a bid for resources, adding to conflict rather than reducing it. Choice of base presages choice of argument. Multiple baselines produce multiple estimates of savings, but the instability is not restricted to totals. Reductions are not achieved smoothly or automatically: They require changes in priorities, which translate into specific and critical issues in the budget process.

MISSION AND STRATEGY

What should national defense do, and what resources does it need for the purpose? Once upon a time, the answers were self-evident. In the early 1960s, defense budgeting began with estimates of all the military might that would be

---

[9]Congressional Budget Office, *The Economic and Budget Outlook: Fiscal Years 1995–1999*, (Washington, D.C.: January 1994), p. 39.

necessary to defend against the worst imaginable threat. President Kennedy and his defense secretary, Robert McNamara, believed that whatever was required should be provided, and this assumption apparently continued into the 1990s.[10] But the end of the Cold War together with the domestic war against the deficit imposed constraints on defense budgeting and a decline in real funding. Now the mission of the armed forces came into question, as the Soviet threat could no longer justify unrestricted demands for resources. In September 1993, the Clinton administration set out its defense program in a "Bottom-Up Review," a comprehensive assessment of defense strategy and the resources required to carry it out.[11] The guiding assumption was the capability of the United States to fight two major regional conflicts concurrently, as well as to support peacemaking activities. The subsequent budget projections called for reductions of $104 billion over the next five years, below the previous administration's baselines.[12]

The Quadrennial Defense Review (QDR) in May 1997 essentially reaffirmed this mission, while recognizing the need for defense to cope with regional conflicts, terrorism, peacekeeping, chemical and biological warfare, and domestic and international emergencies. But would the resources allocated for the plan be sufficient to accomplish it? Secretary of Defense William Cohen was reassuring: The QDR had provided the Department of Defense with "a comprehensive strategy for striking the delicate and difficult balance between America's present security needs and the needs of the future."[13] Resources would be sufficient, as long as scheduled savings were made through efficiencies, privatization, and base closures. Similarly, the chairman of the Joint Chiefs of Staff assured the Senate Armed Services Committee, "We are within an acceptable band of readiness and risks."[14]

Others were not so sure. The Center for Strategic Resources charged it would be impossible to fulfill the mission outlined in the QDR with the reduced resources it projected, at least in part because of the inclusion of high cost weapons systems that were no longer appropriate in the post-Cold War era.[15] Critics doubted both the realism of the QDR mission, and the proposed economies and efficiencies expected to make it feasible. A Defense Review Panel, mandated by Congress and appointed by the secretary of defense warned the two-war scenario was counterproductive in the long run, since it emphasized traditional weapons buildup rather than the nonconventional threats

[10]Meyers, op. cit.; L. R. Jones, "Policy Development, Planning and Resource Allocation in the Department of Defense," *Public Budgeting and Finance*, Vol. 11, No. 3, Fall 1991, p. 18.

[11]Les Aspin, *National Security in the Post-Cold War World* (Washington, D.C.: Office of the Secretary of Defense, September 1993).

[12]Andrew F. Krepinevich, *The Bottom-Up Review: An Assessment* (Washington, D.C.: Defense Budget Project, 1994), pp. 8–9.

[13]William S. Cohen, "Defense: Getting Down to Basics," *Washington Post National Weekly Edition*, April 27, 1998, p. 27.

[14]Pat Towell, "Strain Is Showing as Military Tries To Do More with Less," *Congressional Quarterly Weekly Report*. April 25, 1998, p. 1081.

[15]Center for Strategic and Budgetary Assessments, "Cost of Defense Plan Could Exceed Available Funding by $26 Billion a Year over Long Run," *Backgrounder*, April 2, 1998, p. 1.

likely to be faced in the future.[16] Lawrence Korb, an assistant secretary of defense in the early 1980s, queried the need for outspending allies and competitors, the duplication between the forces, and the need for a second simultaneous war capability.[17]

Meanwhile, each year Congress was adding substantial amounts to Pentagon requests—nearly $7 billion in Fiscal Year 1996, $10.5 billion in 1997, $2.6 billion in Fiscal Year 1998, and at least $4 billion in a Fiscal Year 1999 supplemental appropriation that had not been requested.[18] The administration itself had begun adding to defense budgets even before the QDR, to try to meet the gap that was appearing between mission and financing, although its trend for defense spending was still down.[19] The turning point came in September 1998, when the chairman of the Joint Chiefs of Staff testified before Congress that forces were "showing increased signs of wear."[20] His speech marked the beginning of a bipartisan consensus on a necessity to rebuild defense.

The consensus was not complete. Defense policy could not be made in isolation. The tightened caps set out as part of the 1997 Balanced Budget Agreement placed defense and domestic discretionary budgets under a single ceiling. A dollar more for defense was another dollar that had to be cut from domestic budgets. Defense budgets also have a highly symbolic value. The amount of spending for defense is believed by some observers to be an indicator to foreign countries, and to the home front, of American resolve to assert our national interests. In this sense, budgeting for defense is making foreign policy, signaling the stance and view of the world of the United States. Why should the United States, now the only superpower, pour more billions into armaments and build up its military forces at the expense of other pressing priorities and in the absence of any plausible overwhelming threat? But justifications favoring military interventions seemed more compelling, whether in defense of Moslems in Kosovo, peacekeeping in Bosnia, democracy in East Timor, threats from North Korea, new nuclear capabilities in South Asia, Iraqi intransigence, a crumbling Soviet empire, an uneasy relationship with China, and terrorism everywhere. The world seemed a very dangerous and insecure place, and the Clinton administration announced a plan for "the first, sustained, long-term increase in defense spending in a decade."[21]

---

[16]Pat Towell, "Commission Urges Pentagon To Think Futuristically," *Congressional Quarterly Weekly Report*. December 6, 1997, p. 3036.

[17]Lawrence Korb, "Start with Logic To Put the Pentagon on a Businesslike Footing," *Los Angeles Times*, November 25, 1997, p. B7.

[18]Mary Tyszkiewicz and Stephen Daggett, *A Defense Budget Primer*, Congressional Research Service, December 9, 1998, p. 47.

[19]Steven M. Kosiak, *Analysis of the Fiscal Year 1996 Defense Budget Request* (Washington D.C.: Defense Budget Project, March 1995), p. 12; David Morrison, "Defense Deadlock," *National Journal*, February 4, 1995, p. 276.

[20]Eric Pianin, "A Meeting of Minds on Defense," *Washington Post National Weekly Edition,* June 7, 1999.

[21]Pat Towell, "Clinton's Defense Budget Increase Falls Short," *Congressional Quarterly Weekly Report,* January 9, 1999, p. 71.

The primary justification for increasing defense budgets lay in a perceived plan-budget gap. The mission of the armed forces had expanded and changed, while its real budget allocations had declined. The most visible evidence of the gap lay in the area of readiness. "Readiness" is "the collective capability of the elements of the force to deliver outputs for which they were designed."[22] In the contemporary context, readiness meant the capacity of defense forces to meet the highly varied and complex tasks demanded of them, which particularly required fast and flexible response, well-trained personnel able to operate in unfamiliar situations, sophisticated communications, and accessible backup resources of material and people.

By the mid-1990s, the Pentagon had already disclosed that five of the Army's twelve divisions had suffered a significant decline in military preparedness.[23] Readiness became the touchstone for defense planning.[24] Reports were surfacing of serious deficiencies: ships putting to sea without adequate crew complements;[25] difficulties in recruiting and retaining high quality personnel (or even anyone at all); inadequate backup for more frequent and longer-term overseas missions, disrupting regular units and deployments.[26] As the armed forces dropped from their Cold War peak of 2.1 million to 1.4 million, missions, bases, and command structures were not reduced commensurately, leaving skeletal forces, deficiencies in specialized occupations, inadequate training, as well as unsatisfactory conditions of work, pay, housing, and pensions.[27]

There were, however, a number of difficulties in remedying the lack of readiness. For a start it is a difficult concept to quantify. For another, there is no single budget category for readiness. Readiness has tended to be identified with O and M funding, although this is not the same thing, since it includes much that is not related to readiness (e.g. environmental cleanup) and excludes much that is (e.g. spare parts and training ammunition, which are part of procurement, and force structure and sustainability, which are separate categories).[28] While total budget authority for defense declined in real terms between 1985 and 1998 by 36 percent, O and M funding dropped only 17 percent, making it harder to sustain an argument for increases. The argument is even further confused by the question of whether a fixation on near-term readiness might actually undermine future long-term readiness or capacity.[29]

[22]Tyszkiewicz and Daggett, op. cit., p. 22.

[23]*Los Angeles Times*, November 16, 1994, p. A18.

[24]David Morrison, "Ready for What?" *National Journal*, May 20, 1995, p. 1219.

[25]Steven Lee Myers, "It's All Too Few Hands on Deck for the Navy," *New York Times*, February 2, 1999, pp. A1, A17.

[26]Pat Towell, *Congressional Quarterly Weekly Report*, May 25, 1998, op. cit., p. 1082.

[27]Martin Fritz, "A Gradual Erosion of U.S. Force," *Los Angeles Times*, November 11, 1998, pp. A1, A20. Paul Richter, "Fewer Troops, More Missions Strain Military," *Los Angeles Times*, January 10, 2000, pp. A1, A15.

[28]Tyszkiewicz and Daggett, op. cit., p. 23.

[29]See Richard Betts, *Military Readiness: Concepts, Choices, Consequences* (Washington, D.C.: Brookings Institution, 1995).

An obvious problem in improving readiness is that increases in pay, improved conditions of work, equipment, and so on are expensive. Can the armed forces work more efficiently? Efficiency would mean not only changing age-old labor-intensive drudgery or using technology intelligently to streamline or eliminate tasks, but also realigning resources to match changed missions. Throughout the 1990s, there were persistent complaints about the excessive number of military bases throughout the United States, that, it was alleged, were expensive to run and often served little useful purpose. But base closings throw thousands of people out of work, and will obviously be fought by those in Congress whose states and districts would be affected.[30] Congress, therefore, devised a special procedure. The 1990 Defense Base Closure and Realignment Act authorized base closures in 1991, 1993, and 1995, according to a set process. Services and defense agencies submitted their candidates for closure and realignment to the secretary of defense for his review, after which he submitted his recommendations to an independent Base Closure and Realignment Commission (BRAC). All bases had to be compared equally against selection criteria and the current force structure plan. These criteria, developed by DOD, included military value, return on investment (i.e., savings), and economic and environmental impacts. The BRAC could add, delete, or modify the secretary's requirements, and then submitted its proposed list to the president, who could either accept or reject them. If he accepted them, the list was forwarded to Congress and became final unless Congress enacted a resolution rejecting the whole list.[31]

The first three rounds of base closures resulted in 70 full or partial closures of major bases and scores of others. They represented a reduction of 14 percent of major domestic bases, and a net present value savings over 20 years of over $17 billion, with annual recurring savings of $1.8 billion. The cumulative effect of the four rounds of base closings was expected to result in a total of about $6 billion in recurring annual savings. The 1995 round was expected to result in 33 closures of major bases, 26 major realignments, and 27 modifications of previous decisions, affecting 146 installations nationwide.[32]

At this point, the program hit a hitch. Faced with a list of closures that included two large bases in California and Texas, the president instead proposed privatizing their functions. Whatever the merits of this proposal, the political furor his action provoked provided the excuse or rationale for Congress to refuse further base closures. Despite an estimate of a recurring annual savings of nearly $6 billion from completed base closures, and claims for an additional $3 billion a year if two more rounds were implemented, the mood had changed.[33]

---

[30]For analysis and critique of the base closing issues, see Fred Thompson and L. R. Jones, *Reinventing the Pentagon* (San Francisco: Jossey Bass, 1994), pp. 194–205, 210–15.

[31]General Accounting Office, *Military Bases: Analysis of DOD's 1995 Process and Recommendations for Closure and Realignment*, Report to the Congress and the Chairman, Defense Base Closure and Realignment Commission, p. 19 (GAO/NSIAD-95-133).

[32]Statement of Frank Conahan, *Defense Programs and Spending: Need for Reforms*, Testimony before the Committee on the Budget, House of Representatives, April 27, 1995, p. 4 (GAO/T-NSIAD/95-149).

[33]William Cohen, "Defense: Getting Down to Basics," *Washington Post National Weekly Edition*, April 27, 1998, p. 27; Elizabeth Becker, "Senate Rejects Closing More Military Bases," *New York Times*, May 27, 1999.

Even if the anticipated savings had been realized, they would not have provided the amounts of resources now contemplated to meet the apparent gap. Readiness competes against modernization, defined as the "technical sophistication of all the elements of the force," but translated as procurement, or buying things.[34] During the great defense budget decline, procurement spending had diminished by over 60 percent, and so an argument could be made that it was time to embark on renewed expenditures on weapons systems. It was also no coincidence that claims for new weaponry were pressed at a time of an emerging budget surplus. Justifications lay in the need to maintain a technological edge over regional aggressors, who could buy off-the-shelf sophisticated gadgetry, and the maintenance of large land armies by certain hostile countries. Plans are therefore under way for development and production of highly expensive items such as the F-22 fighter aircraft, Crusader artillery systems, and new attack submarines and antiarmor weapons.[35]

Even those who accept the need for increasing defense spending have paused in contemplating these demands. For example, Jerry Lewis, the Republican chair of the House Defense Appropriations Subcommittee sought to halt production of the F-22 fighter.[36] Was this back to business as usual, the funding of Cold War weaponry that was not only inappropriate for the most likely kinds of emerging threats, but whose funding would cut into readiness initiatives that it had been agreed were of critical importance? The primary justification for increased defense funding—a need for greater capability to meet a changed mission—was being used to fund a different purpose, which, according to many critics, did not appear to contribute to and would probably detract from that mission. It seemed that decisions were in the grip of a momentum that resisted change, even as lip service was paid for the need for change.

This momentum might be seen in what may turn out to be one of the most significant funding decisions in the new century. Between 1983 and 1995, over $36 billion had been spent on ballistic missile defenses, with questionable results. The Clinton administration drastically scaled back and reorganized the missile defense plan,[37] but there was strong Republican pressure to move ahead with a full-scale program. In 1995, Congress added a large amount for deployment of a national missile defense to Clinton's request. After the president had vetoed the defense authorization bill because of its inclusion of funding for a national antimissile program, a compromise was reached that took out the requirement for deployment by 2001 but still left $3.5 billion for ballistic missile programs for the coming year, over half a billion more than the administration had requested. But in mid-February 1996, the administration announced cuts of $2.5 billion in these programs, slowing down development of long-range missiles in favor of short-range cruise missiles.[38]

[34] Tyszkiewicz and Daggett, op. cit., p. 22.

[35] Bradley Graham, "The Pentagon's Budget Battle," *Washington Post National Weekly Edition*, September 6, 1999, p. 6.

[36] *Los Angeles Times*, September 30, 1999, p. A11.

[37] Pat Towell, "Senate Bill Boosts ABM Effort," *Congressional Quarterly Weekly Report*, July 29, 1995, p. 2288.

[38] Pat Towell and Donna Cassatta, "Senate Backs Nuclear Tests, Anti-Missile Program," *Congressional Quarterly Weekly Report*, August 5, 1995, p. 2380; *Los Angeles Times*, February 17, 1996, p. A6.

By 1999, the situation had changed. Pentagon officials, citing the threat of missile attacks from North Korea, Iran, and possibly other sources, fully backed construction and deployment of an antimissile shield early in the next century.[39] The defense secretary asked for $6 billion over the next six years. The Senate was almost unanimous in voting for development and deployment of the missile defense system.[40] Despite criticisms that note that there is no real evidence that the system really would work, and its probable infringement of the ABM (antiballistic missile) treaty with Russia, it seems that massive spending for an antiballistic missile system will be a reality.

No one in the budget process seems to be talking about defense budget cutting any more, and no one is discussing mission either. Few people seem willing to ask the hard questions—efficiency for what, modernization for what, readiness for what? "What new threats will we face in the future? What do we need to meet those challenges? Is there still fat in the Pentagon budget we can cut?"[41] To these might be added another question: How do the processes of making defense budgets contribute, in William Kaufmann's felicitous phrase, to "a reasonable defense?"[42]

THE INTERNAL BUDGET PROCESS

To construct and implement an annual budget for so large and complex an area as defense is a formidable task. Producing a budget for the Department of Defense (DOD) requires an effort by a large number of participants stretching over some 26–27 months. Since 1961, the process has been organized according to a Planning, Programming, Budgeting system (PPB), which divides the budget into different programs, sequences the process into different phases, and seeks to integrate long- and medium-term planning with programming and budgeting over the immediate budget period. (Between 1987 and 1999, DOD produced a biennial budget, in which the second year of the cycle amended the budget of the first, but after initial deference, Congress has worked essentially with one-year budgets, and DOD has asked to be relieved of the burden of the two-year cycle.)

Planning, Programming, Budgeting

The distinctive characteristic of PPB is classification of the budget according to programs. The internal process of DOD uses "program elements," which group together weapons, manpower, and support equipment, and which cut across the

---

[39]*Los Angeles Times*, January 21, 1999, p. A18.

[40]Mary McGrory, "Hit-and-Missile Politics," *Washington Post National Weekly Edition*, March 29, 1999, p. 23; Eric Schmitt, "By a Wide Margin, Senate Approves Missile Defense System," *Los Angeles Times*, March 18, 1999, p. A18.

[41]Stan Crock, "Before We Throw More Money at Defense," *Washington Post National Weekly Edition*, February 2, 1999, p. 22.

[42]William W. Kaufmann, *A Reasonable Defense*, (Washington, D.C.: Brookings Institution, 1986).

line-item format used by Congress in appropriations. These program elements are aggregated into 11 "Major Force Programs:"[43]

Program 1: Strategic Forces
Program 2: General Purpose Forces
Program 3: Command, Control, Communications, Intelligence, and Space
Program 4: Mobility Forces
Program 5: Guard and Reserve Forces
Program 6: Research and Development
Program 7: Central Supply and Maintenance
Program 8: Training, Medical and Other General Personnel Activities
Program 9: Administration and Associated Activities
Program 10: Support of Other Nations
Program 11: Special Operations Forces

This program emphasis is modified (some might say vitiated) by the rivalry among the different services: Army versus Navy versus Air Force. Competition among agencies within a department for resources and prestige is commonplace in all bureaucratic institutions. No other federal department has the intensity of competition or the stakes as high as in the DOD budget. Former Chairman of the Joint Chiefs of Staff (JCS) General David Jones described the defense budget as an "intramural scramble for resources."[44]

Each service is a separate organizational entity. There is no such thing as a "military officer." Individuals are members of the Army, Air Force, Navy, or Marines. The services maintain separate facilities, training programs, and budgets. Each service has its own distinct traditions, service academies, and uniforms, and even its own agencies for funding scientific research.[45] Organizational boundaries are clearly marked and well understood by all participants. A particular service is the source of individual identification and serves "as the predominant source of sanctions, rewards, and focus of organizational loyalty."[46]

Competition is a mixed bag; on the downside, there is plenty of evidence for lack of essential battlefield coordination. Advocacy takes the place of analysis, efficiency, or logic. Services may seek programs because the programs are beneficial to the particular branch—its size, importance, promotions—while claiming (or believing) the programs are good for the nation.[47] The Navy fought the Polaris missile submarine program because it believed Polaris was "not a traditional navy mission and therefore should not be financed out of the navy's share of the defense budget."[48] The Air Force was not enthusiastic about the A-10 ground attack aircraft because it saw ground targets as a job for the Army; Air Force officers like supersonic

---

[43]See Tyszkiewicz and Daggett, op. cit., pp. 17–20.

[44]Glenn Pascall, *The Trillion Dollar Budget* (Seattle: University of Washington Press, 1985), p. 6.

[45]Allyn Jackson, "Declining Mathematics Funding at DOD," *Notices of the American Mathematics Society,* Vol. 47, No. 1, January 2000, pp. 42–45.

[46]Arnold Kanter, *Defense Politics* (Chicago: University of Chicago Press, 1975), p. 17.

[47]See Mark Rovner, *Defense Dollars and Sense* (Washington, D.C.: Common Cause, 1983), p. 36.

[48]Alain C. Enthoven and Wayne K. Smith, *How Much Is Enough?* (New York: Harper & Row, 1971), p. 17.

aircraft with state-of-the-art technology. Defense analyst William W. Kaufmann described the situation in the mid-1980s.

> . . . all three services are trying simultaneously to expand their capabilities, upgrade older weapons, and replace them as rapidly as possible with new and more costly models. Furthermore, [each service] is investing in weapons that will enable it to operate independently of the others. The Army is buying expensive attack helicopters and air defense weapons because it does not expect to be given the necessary support by the Air Force. The Air Force, which could acquire more close air support aircraft and short-range air defense interceptors, prefers to invest in long-range fighter-attack aircraft that can attack targets deep in the enemy's rear and conduct an interdiction campaign in the hope of winning the war regardless of what happens to the Army. The Navy, asserting its independence of everyone else, prepares to fight its own small wars with amphibious forces and carrier-based tactical aircraft, more than half the cost of which goes into protecting this power-projection capability.[49]

On the upside of service independence, all innovation requires advocates. A fine study of naval aviation, for instance, shows that the success of the United States and Japan and the failure of Britain before the Second World War were due to the institutionalization of advocacy. Britain turned naval aviation over to central command, which always had other priorities. It never came up with enough money or promotions to create a cadre of people able to push the cause against other competitors.[50] Yet, it has been estimated that the relative budget allocations among the services have hardly changed over the past 25 years, and that the rigidity caused by the service structure may impede necessary changes in deployment of resources.[51]

In 1986, in an effort to improve coordination among the services, Congress passed the Goldwater-Nichols Reorganization Act. The act, according to Thompson and Jones, "corrected some of the more pathological administrative shortcomings of the defense department." In particular it clarified the role of the Joint Chiefs of Staff and strengthened the position of its chair.[52]

Formal preparation of the defense budget is divided into three phases. The *planning phase,* which begins more than two years before the fiscal year in which funds will be spent initially, establishes defense objectives and indicates the resources needed to meet these objectives. The *programming phase* centers on the development of programs to meet these goals. In the *budgeting phase,* program cost and efficacy are reviewed, and defense spending is combined with the rest of the federal budget for submission to Congress.[53]

---

[49]Kaufmann, *A Reasonable Defense,* pp. 101–02.

[50]Thomas C. Hove and Mark D. Mandeles, "Interwar Innovation in Three Navies: USN, RN, IJN," sponsored by the Office of Net Assessment, DOD, 1982.

[51]Richard J. Sherlock, "New Realities, Old Pentagon Thinking," *Wall Street Journal,* April 24, 1997.

[52]Thompson and Jones, *Reinventing the Pentagon,* p. 78.

[53]This description is based on Fred Thompson and L. R. Jones, *Reinventing the Pentagon: How the New Public Management Can Bring Institutional Renewal* (San Francisco: Jossey Bass, 1994); L. R. Jones and Glenn Bixler, *Mission Financing to Realign National Defense* (Greenwich, Conn.: JAI Press, 1992); and Tyszkiewicz and Daggett, op. cit. These accounts do not always coincide on the details of the formal PPB process.

The planning part of the budgetary process is of course constrained by the policy directions from both the executive and legislative branches of government. Within DOD, the main planning instrument is the Defense Planning Guidance (DPG), which sets out policy, outlining missions, strategies, ongoing plans and programs, and projected resources. It draws on the reviews and comments of civilian and military officials in each of the services and the Joint Staff. The Joint Chiefs of Staff prepare a separate Joint Strategic Planning Document, which provides a detailed program element analysis in a formal recommendation to the secretary of defense. The DPG, which is prepared in the office of the under secretary of defense for policy, is translated into the six-year Future Year Defense Program (FYDP), which aggregates all the program elements into "a summary of requirements and alternatives for achieving force structure, readiness, sustainability and modernization objectives."[54] Up to this point, there has been little concern with resources.[55]

The programming phase uses the FYDP to produce a two-year resource plan. It is begun by the military services, each of which aggregates its requests into a Program Objective Memorandum (POM). They develop and prepare programs to meet the objectives of the DPG within the financial limits set by the secretary of defense and in line with the view of the Joint Chiefs of Staff on risks and capability. After analysis by OSD staff, the POMs are reviewed by the Defense Resource Planning Board, an executive budget committee chaired by the deputy secretary of defense and including representatives from the Joint Chiefs and organizations within the office of the secretary of defense. This body makes final decisions on the budget framework, which is set out in Program Decision Memoranda (PDMs).

The PDMs serve as the basis for cost estimates, which are submitted by the military departments as requests to the DOD comptroller to implement their own priorities.[56] The comptroller, with other OSD staffs and the OMB review the budget for accuracy in cost estimates, feasibility, scheduling, and consistency with established priorities.

Here the exceptional role of OMB should be noted. Instead of providing an independent review, as with other agencies, OMB works as a part of a DOD team to come up with a joint recommendation to the president.[57] Under presidents Kennedy and Johnson, it became a matter of tradition that the budget director would have to appeal budgetary decisions of the secretary of defense to the president—a direct reversal of the relationship between the other department heads and the budget director. OMB scorekeepers on appropriations action also send a letter detailing objections to each action on a domestic bill in subcommittee vote, full committee, etc. But on defense, one reported, "We just say 'it's too little; the Pentagon will send the details later.'" It may be that growing congressional

---

[54] Jones and Bixler, op. cit., p. 23.

[55] Tyszkiewicz and Daggett, op. cit., p. 56.

[56] Jones and Bixler, op. cit., p. 26.

[57] L.R. Jones, "Policy Development, Planning, and Resource Allocation in the Department of Defense," *Public Budgeting and Finance* Vol. 11, Fall 1991, p. 20. See also Gordon Adams, *The Role of Defense Budgets in Civil Military Relations* (Washington, D.C.: Defense Budget Project, 1992), p. 14.

intervention in defense budgeting is partly related to OMB's abandonment of its adversary position.

The comptroller then develops a "final" budget, which restructures the budget format from the program elements of the internal process to the appropriations format used by Congress. Unresolved issues between the OSD and the OMB are discussed, and the latest economic assumptions are incorporated into the budget estimates (usually causing adjustments in hundreds of budget items). The budget is submitted to the president for approval. After this, the OMB incorporates the defense budget with the rest of the federal budget for submission to Congress.

No budget system is perfect, and there is no ideal to which any specific system should be compared. There is also probably no public sector organization in the world that has been able to implement a "pure" PPBS system. The DOD reforms grew out of the inefficiencies, piecemeal short-sightedness, and service rivalries of the post-World War II period.[58] The aims of PPB as implemented by Secretary of Defense McNamara in the 1960s were to increase the authority of the office of the secretary of defense, and to use the budget system to make policy along functional lines, which would then flow down to the departments.[59] Was this purpose fulfilled? Was it, and is it, relevant to the budgeting needs of DOD today?

The programming process and the program classification were certainly implemented, but in the period up to the 1990s, it seems doubtful that the substantive purposes of the PPB reforms were achieved. DOD maintained an input orientation, focusing on objects of expenditure and allowing no discretion at the operating level to relate resources to tasks.[60] The budget system also did little to ensure real consideration of purposes; the earlier reforms divorced responsibility (of commanders for carrying out missions) from administration (the military departments that actually received the funding); McNamara's reforms focused control on functional constructs, which separated control from responsibility.[61]

According to Thompson and Jones, the budget process intended to help the office of the secretary of defense establish its strategic priorities and allocate resources between major programs did not do so until 1991, when the base force proposal of the Bush administration made the first comprehensive alteration in force structure since 1961. They conclude: "This means that the elaborate mechanisms of the PPBS process were used throughout the entire Cold War merely to grind out updated tables of organization and equipment and to fill them with new weaponry and trained personnel—rarely has process so completely triumphed over purpose."[62] But Jones suggests that PPB does provide a framework for decisions and analysis for making the marginal choices that ultimately determine defense budget decisions (except for the obvious "pork" considerations). While it

---

[58]Thompson and Jones, op. cit., pp. 25–6.

[59]Ibid., p. 54.

[60]Ibid., p. 63.

[61]Ibid., p. 69.

[62]Ibid.

may be clumsy, it also provides the primary opportunity for the military to participate in defense budgeting, aside from the JCS level.[63]

The PPB reforms, even as they centralized budgeting, were also intended
to change budgeting to a results-oriented system that would direct funding to
mission centers, whose needs would drive budget allocations and gain accountability for the use of resources in actually accomplishing tasks. This reform
would require organizational changes to restructure DOD along combat mission lines, and to relate support activities to the missions. This was not done.[64] A
joint DOD-GAO working group at the beginning of the 1980s found difficulties
in relating support activities to missions, and inadequate linkages between
funding and outcomes.[65]

Even those programs that could be related to missions suffer from inadequate
linkages between funding and outcomes. In a separate study, the General
Accounting Office (GAO) "found no accountability systems linking military capability and rising or falling program funding levels. . . . Since funding is not linked
to intermediate outputs, such as increased proficiency or mission capable weapon
systems, or to ultimate outputs, such as increased readiness, there is no way of determining if the services could achieve the same goals with fewer dollars."[66] In the
end as at the beginning, the Joint Study Group was preoccupied with the same
subject: "the difficulty in relating the output orientation of decision making, so
necessary for broad policy making at the national level, to the input orientation
used for purposes of management and control at the budget level."[67]

In 1993, the Gore Report[68] pursued the same theme, recommending mission-
driven, results-oriented budgets, which would include performance measures and
relate performance to budgeting. The 1993 Government Performance and Results
Act required DOD, like other federal agencies, to prepare an annual performance
plan, performance measures, reports on performance, and alignment of budgets
with performance categories.

DOD's performance plan for Fiscal Year 2000 was assessed by GAO.[69] GAO
reported that the plan included a clear discussion of corporate-level annual performance goals, a general discussion of strategies and resources, and output-
oriented measures and indicators related to most management challenges. Among

---

[63]See L. R. Jones, "Policy Development, Planning, and Resource Allocation in the Department of
Defense," op.cit. pp. 15–27.

[64]See Joint DOD-GAO Working Group, "The Department of Defense's Planning, Programming and
Budgeting System," September 1983, pp. 119–20 GAO/DOD-84-5.

[65]Ibid., p. 121.

[66]*Report to the Congress by the Comptroller General of the United States,* "The Defense Budget: A
Look at Budgetary Resources, Accomplishments, and Problems," April 21, 1983, p. 24 GAO/PLRD-
83-62.

[67]Ibid., p. 113.

[68]*Reinventing Government: From Red Tape to Results: Creating a Government That Works Better and
Costs Less. Report on the National Performance Review* (New York: Times Books, 1993).

[69]General Accounting Office, *Managing for Results: Opportunities for Continued Improvements in
Agencies' Performance Plans,* July 1999, pp. 61–63. (GAO/GGD/AIMD-99-215). Complete observations and DOD's comments are available at http://www.gao/gov/corresp/ns99178r.pdf.

other criticisms, GAO faulted DOD because it did not relate budget program activities to performance goals, and because while performance goals were clearly stated, there was no explanation about how key outputs (such as Army divisions) were related to the outcomes. DOD responded that both output and outcome of DOD's annual budget were "a specified military force ready to go to war," and the performance plan set out the performance goals in a measurable path to achieve it.[70] GAO wanted more: a qualitative assessment of the conduct of military missions and of the investment in technology to improve weapons' capabilities. Which brings us to the issue of acquisitions.

Acquisitions

The acquisition of equipment, vehicles, and weapons is a large part of defense budgeting. The services constantly strive for greater performance from military hardware. The search for superior performance requires expensive research into new fields at the cutting edge of science and engineering. The services promote the production of sophisticated, and therefore costly, weapons systems.

The drive to acquire the most sophisticated weaponry available is dramatically revealed in cost differences for weapons between the Carter and Reagan administrations. According to a Congressional Budget Office study, in his first term, Reagan bought 6.4 percent more missiles than Carter, but it cost 91.2 percent more in constant dollars. Reagan funded 30 percent more tanks, but paid 147.4 percent more for them;[71] 8.8 percent more aircraft cost 75.4 percent more; and 36.1 percent more ships were acquired at a cost that was 53 percent higher.[72] By 1995, costs had escalated further: A single Sea Wolf submarine would cost $1.5 billion, while a C-17 long-range cargo jet aircraft had a tab of $2.4 billion and a single LHD helicopter cost $1.3 billion.[73] In the year 2000, the Army is planning to buy more than 1000 Crusader artillery systems for about $17 million each; the Navy plans a $2 billion fleet of new attack submarines; while nine new antiarmor weapons will cost $3.5 billion.[74]

All soldiers understandably want the best weapons they can get. As General Tooey Spatz said, "A second-best airplane is like a second-best poker hand. No damn good."[75] Weapons development takes years and cannot easily be quickened. Since each service only gets a new generation of weapons every 10 years or so, each seeks to incorporate all conceivable capabilities in every upgrade. The services know from experience that in times of war or heightened tension Congress will make available the funds to expand forces and increase production of weapons.

[70]Ibid., p. 63.

[71]Jacques S. Gansler, "How To Improve the Acquisition of Weapons," in Robert J. Art et al, eds., *Reorganizing America's Defense* (Washington, D.C.: Pergamon Brassey, 1985), p. 384.

[72]Kaufmann, *A Reasonable Defense*, p. 43.

[73]*Congressional Quarterly Weekly Report,* June 29, 1995, p. 2288.

[74]Bradley Graham, "The Pentagon's Budget Battle," *Washington Post National Weekly Edition*, September 6, 1999, p. 6.

[75]Robert J. Art, "Restructuring the Military-Industrial Complex: Arms Control in an Institutional Perspective," *Public Policy,* Vol. 30, No. 4, Fall 1974, pp. 429–30.

However, congressional action cannot instantly create the advanced technology the services believe will be needed.

It might be thought that the funding of long-term purchases would be an integral part of the PPB process. Instead, according to Jones and Bixler, "Budget alternatives and decisions for the acquisition of major capital assets by DOD such as missiles, weapons systems, ships, aircraft, tanks and so forth, are reviewed and analyzed in a budget process that operates semi-autonomously from the defense operating budget process."[76] Moreover, because of security considerations, much of what we know of the acquisition process is anecdotal in nature.

Criticisms of acquisition decisions have been persistent, but there are certain intrinsic difficulties involved in the defense acquisition process. A detailed description of acquisition and contracting processes is beyond the scope of this chapter, that can only touch on significant aspects that affect defense budgeting more generally.[77]

While the armed forces buy all kinds of things, large and small, many purchases are not only very expensive, but take years to develop. Armaments, aircraft, rockets, ships, tanks, and so on are technically complex, and often the technical problems cannot be adequately foreseen in advance. Many of the requirements of the military are highly specific, and have to be custom made. Often the defense department is the only buyer, and companies contracting with it are dependent on the defense contracts, without which they would go out of business. Conversely, the defense department has an interest in keeping such firms in business, so that it does not compromise its specialized sources of supply. With the downsizing of acquisitions over the past decade, there are now fewer firms in a position to fulfill military requirements. Since many contracts require high up-front costs in research and development, companies are reluctant to embark on projects where they will later have to compete for the production phase. Finally, the sheer size of acquisitions poses a challenge in control and accountability.

The long-term nature of research and development in large-scale military hardware is at least partially responsible for one of the most visible problems in the acquisitions process: cost overruns. The history of weapons procurement cost overruns is long and inglorious. On March 27, 1794, Congress approved the creation of a sea-going navy by appropriating funds to build six frigates. The work was contracted to six private shipyards geographically spread in order to distribute the benefits of federal spending and to garner political support for the program. War in Europe prevented the purchase of necessary supplies and the keels were not laid until the end of 1795. Shortly thereafter, due to mismanagement, delays, and cost overruns, the number of frigates to be purchased was cut to three.[78]

On average, weapons systems' costs (including inflation) have been estimated to increase 100 percent over the initial cost estimate given to Congress by the services for the first appropriation.[79] An example of this problem occurred with the B-1

---

[76]Jones and Bixler, op. cit., p. 26.

[77]For detailed description and analysis of the acquisition and contracting processes, see Jones and Bixler, op. cit., and Thompson and Jones, op. cit.

[78]Charles Hitch, *Decision-Making for Defense* (Berkeley: University of California Press, 1970), p. 6.

[79]Rovner, *Defense Dollars and Sense*, p. 42.

bomber. The initial cost for 100 aircraft was estimated by Rockwell International, the prime contractor, as $11.9 billion in 1981 dollars. This estimate was given to the House Appropriations Subcommittee in January of 1981. Fifteen months later the Air Force estimated the cost at $25 billion (excluding inflation).[80] No doubt there are reasons (redesign, reductions in quantities, etc.), but the result is the same. Roy Meyers reports that underreporting total expected costs for weapons was "a way of life in the Defense Department for decades."[81]

At the end of 1992, the General Accounting Office reported that "Despite the laws and regulations, overpricing of defense contracts remains significant and widespread, costing the taxpayer billions of dollars more than necessary for the goods and services purchased."[82] Three years later, the situation did not seem to have changed much. A GAO official testified before Congress:

> DOD weapons acquisitions frequently experience cost overruns, schedule delays, and performance shortfalls. For example, we have reported that cost increases of 20 to 40 percent have been common for major weapons programs and that numerous programs have experienced increases greater than that. Despite past and current efforts to reform the acquisition system, wasteful practices still add billions of dollars to defense acquisition costs. Many new weapons cost more, are less capable than anticipated and experience schedule delays. Moreover, the need for some of these costly weapons is questionable, particularly since the collapse of the Soviet Union. These problems are typical of DOD's history of inadequate requirements determination for weapons systems; projecting unrealistic cost, schedule, and performance estimates; developing and producing weapons concurrently; and committing weapons systems to production before adequate testing has been completed.[83]

Costs can be underestimated any number of ways. An unrealistically low inflation rate may be used. Particular resource costs may not be fully accounted for. Additionally, necessary components may not be included in the estimate, either deliberately or because of changes in specifications or the addition of features.

As military hardware and software have become more technically complex, particularly with the revolution in computers and communications, uncertainty in the acquisitions process has grown. For example, in late 1999, DOD was consolidating its radio acquisition programs into the Joint Tactical Radio System (JTRS), which would replace all of its current radio inventory, avionics upgrades, appropriate satellite terminals, and personal communications systems. This would potentially entail replacing over 750,000 existing units, including about 200 types of radio. The total cost, currently unknown, could be billions of dollars. Similar uncertainties affect development of high-tech weapons, which do not rely on already developed technology.[84]

---

[80]Ibid., p. 44.

[81]Roy Meyers, *Strategic Budgeting* (Ann Arbor, Mich.: University of Michigan Press, 1994), p. 95.

[82]General Accounting Office, *Defense Contract Pricing*, December 1992, p. 7 (GAO/HR-93-8).

[83]Statement of Frank Conahan, *Defense Programs and Spending: Need for Reforms*, Testimony before the Committee on the Budget, House of Representatives, April 27, 1995, p. 4 (GAO/T-NSIAD/95-149).

[84]General Accounting Office, *Defense Acquisitions: Challenges Associated with Implementing the Joint Tactical Radio System*, Report to the Chairman, Subcommittee on Defense, Committee on Appropriations, House of Representatives, September 1999, (GAO/NSIAD-99-179).

Because of DOD's specialized requirements, there is a tendency for the Pentagon (also motivated by congressional micro-management as well as bureaucratic tendency), to spell out detailed specifications not only for major procurements but for everyday items. It hopes to avoid blame by proceeding according to the rules. The need for a whistle resulted in 16 pages of military specifications, including the requirement that the item should "make an audible characteristic sound when blown by the mouth with medium or high pressure." There are similarly thorough specifications for taco shells and fruitcakes.[85]

The result has been accounts of outrageous costs paid for everyday items, in which the Defense Department has been depicted as composed of bumbling bureaucrats being ripped off by dishonest contractors. Stories circulated about the Pentagon paying $91 for a 3-cent screw, $110 for a 4-cent diode, and $9,609 for a 12-cent Allen wrench. These stories may be true, though it is not easy for an outsider to tell.[86]

Despite the implications of reports on waste, the Defense Department does review equipment costs. When a contractor submits designs for spare parts for the original weapon, for example, a Defense Department contracting officer will review the designs and make suggestions about substituting common-use for custom-designed parts where appropriate. An independent evaluation by DOD value engineers is undertaken at a later stage to analyze whether custom-designed items are necessary. In the case of the $9,609 Allen wrench, the system worked. Value engineers in the DOD found that an ordinary wrench should be substituted for a proposed custom-designed one.[87] DOD project managers are now encouraged to buy products "off the shelf" where available and appropriate.

There are problems in buying "off the shelf" products. To the extent that the cheapest components may be manufactured overseas, there are issues of security and reliability. There is also the question of whether the commercial marketplace is sufficiently developed to provide competitively priced products that meet DOD requirements. For example, the JTRS project is relying on commercially produced products to provide hardware and software, but GAO reports that recent studies indicate that current commercial technology might not be available to support fully either replacement or future requirements.[88]

It would be easy if it were clear from the outset just what should be bought, and who could supply it at a given price. Where long-term, complex, and technical projects are concerned, all these are problematical and require decisions in which the interests of supplier and consumer are not necessarily identical. Jones and

---

[85]"In Wake of Foul-Ups, the Pentagon Is Pressured To Shop Around for Bargains on Everyday Goods," *Wall Street Journal,* October 3, 1986, p. 50.

[86]Steve Kellman argues that many of the stories were exaggerated. The $91 screw and the $110 diode were not indicative of waste, he says, but of accounting procedures. Often contractors will allocate overhead on an "item" basis rather than a "value" basis. For example, if there is an overhead total of $1 million to be allotted over 10,000 parts, some contractors will allocate $100 to each item regardless of its proportionate cost. Thus a $15,000 item will appear at a cost of $15,100 and a 4-cent item as $100.04 [Steve Kellman, "The Grace Commission: How Much Waste in Government?" *The Public Interest,* No. 78, Winter 1985, p. 64]. Unfortunately, it is not certain that such procedures exist.

[87]Ibid., p. 65.

[88]General Accounting Office, September 1999, op. cit., p. 7.

Bixler have explored the accommodation of uncertainty in the defense systems acquisition process through different stages. It would be in the interest of the company undertaking the research and development phase, either to be able to market the concept it has developed later in the production phase, or to be assured of the contract for production. DOD is unwilling to grant either proprietary rights to the concept or to assure a single source contract for later development.[89] Thus the JTRS is being developed in three phases: In the first phase, contracts were awarded to three consortia to define the level and mode of development of the JTRS architecture; in the second, there are plans for a competition for a single award to develop the architecture and demonstrate it in a laboratory environment; and the third phase will be a detailed acquisition strategy of service procurement actions to implement the project.[90]

Part of the problem of acquisition in defense is that the Department of Defense may be the only consumer of certain products. In turn, this may mean that it needs to keep firms in business to maintain capacity, and also that competition is too limited for it to shop around. As the boom in defense spending in the 1980s came to an end, there was a corresponding decline in the military-industrial complex. While there had been 50 or so major companies in the mid-1980s, by 1998, there were only five. For example, the custom-built computer screens for M-1 tanks were made by only one company, which, since it was losing $2 million a year, decided to go out of business at the beginning of 1999. The problem was solved by a small company that bought commercially available screens from Japan and modified them.[91]

The lack of competition highlights the dilemma of the DOD. Should it conduct acquisitions through fixed or flexible price contracts? In the former case, where competitive bidding results in awarding a contract to the lowest bidder, or even if there is a single source, there is a risk that an initially low bid may be unrealistic. Low bids also favor the armed services, which might want to fund as many programs as possible, even though they may not receive adequate resources for all of them. It is more difficult to launch a program than to keep it going once it is started. It is also easier to launch an inexpensive program than an expensive one. In such circumstances, the services have strong incentives to accept the most optimistic cost estimate. But, according to Jones and Bixler, in most cases contracts leave price unspecified, and "defense contracts typically establish a process by which prices are to be determined—often fully distributed average costs plus an allowance for profit."[92]

The sheer size of the defense budget makes mismanagement and waste more likely. Every year the Department of Defense spends over $80 billion to research, develop, and procure weapons systems. In 1993, DOD overpaid contractors $1.3 billion more than it should have done, and the Pentagon was unable to match $19.1 billion worth of disbursements to specific requirements in acqui-

---

[89]See Jones and Bixler, op. cit., 178–82.

[90]General Accounting Office, September 1999, op. cit., pp. 5–6.

[91]Pat Towell, "Does Security Suffer as Pentagon Shops in the Global Marketplace?" *Congressional Quarterly Weekly Report*, February 13, 1999, p. 401–02.

[92]Jones and Bixler, p. 175.

sition contracts.[93] About a year later, GAO reported that "DOD's records contained at least $24.8 billion of problem disbursements as of June 1994. As of February 1995, the amount of problem disbursement transactions had increased to $33 billion."[94] In 1991, when a centralized Defense Finance and Accounting Service was initiated, there were 66 major financial systems and 162 major accounting systems in operation.

Inventories have been another problem. What should be the balance between readiness, which means having things on hand when you need them, and streamlining inventories so as not to tie up resources? During the defense buildup in the 1980s, it appears that inventories in certain areas were increased above needs, so that in some cases literally thousands of items—compressor rotor blades, engine case assemblies, duct segments, fuel control, and other spare parts—worth millions of dollars were lying around and probably would never be used.[95]

It is easy to find examples of waste and abuse in any large program. In the Defense Department, which signs 52,000 contract actions every working day, even if a 99.9 percent purity in contract actions were achieved, 15,000 actions would still be defective.

Recent years have seen increased efforts to improve the defense acquisitions process. Since the passage of the Defense Acquisition Workforce Improvement Act (DAWIA), DOD has made a great effort to try to improve acquisition management expertise through increased education and training.[96] Efforts to improve and modernize financial administration are being made under a Senior Financial Management Oversight Council, working with a chief financial officer and steering committee under the Chief Financial Officers Act.[97] In 1997, the DOD initiated a Defense Reform Initiative as a major effort to reduce infrastructure costs and improve business operations, and several additional initiatives have since been added, including acquisition, financial management, and logistics reform.[98]

The combination of secrecy and complexity surrounding weapons systems, the immense detail involved, the networks of relationships within the services and between the branches and their contractors, and the communities in which they are located make defense budgeting exceedingly difficult to comprehend. Distinguishing between self-serving arguments and defense achievements is difficult for civilian and military defense personnel alike. No one can be certain of the threats that will be faced, or how their choices of weapons and personnel policies will turn out. Mix vast uncertainty with immense complexity and it is not clear that anyone, no matter what position is taken, can have but a small grip on the future.

---

[93]Conahan, p. 9.

[94]Ibid.

[95]General Accounting Office, *Defense Inventory: Growth in Air Force and Navy Unrequired Aircraft Parts,* pp. 16–22; General Accounting Office, *Defense Inventory: Changes in DOD's Inventory,* 1989–93, August 1994, pp. 4–5 (GAO/NSIAD-94-235).

[96]Communication from L. R. Jones.

[97]David C. Morrison, "Green-Eyeshade Blues," *National Journal,* December 10, 1994, pp. 2898–2901.

[98]General Accounting Office, *Defense Infrastructure: Improved Performance Measures Would Enhance Defense Reform Initiative,* Report to the Chairman, Committee on Armed Services, House of Representatives, August 1999, pp. 1–2. (GAO/NSIAD-99-169).

THE CONGRESSIONAL BUDGET PROCESS

The defense budget process in Congress is essentially the same as for the rest of the budget. The building blocks of the budget—authorizations, appropriations, and outlays are the same, and the budget passes through authorizing committees (primarily the Senate Armed Services Committee and the House National Security Committee) and appropriations subcommittees (defense subcommittee of the Senate Appropriations Committee and the national security subcommittee of the House Appropriations Committee) as well as the Senate and House Appropriations Committees. The differences in handling the defense budget rest not so much on structure as on the extensive and growing control Congress has attempted to exert over the defense budget even as power in Congress has become more dispersed.

The congressional politics of defense budgeting changed, in the words of James Lindsay, from the "inside game" in the 1960s to the "outside game" in the 1980s and 1990s. During the 1960s, as previously, the defense committees were dominated by autocratic chairs who ran them as "their personal baronies."[99] During the 1970s, reforms in Congress strengthened the positions of subcommittees and their chairs by stripping committee chairmen of their power to make subcommittee assignments. Power was wielded less autocratically, although influence remained primarily within the defense committees. In the 1980s, the locus of discussion shifted from the committees to the much broader community of interested members. The change was exemplified in increasing amendments to committee recommendations on the floor, and the very large House-Senate conferences on defense authorizations and appropriations to resolve differences, on which committee members might even be a minority.

This dispersal of influence over defense budgeting was accompanied by the growth of a dual system of decision making. Until 1959, most of the defense budget was permanently authorized; by the mid-1980s, virtually all defense programs required annual authorizations.[100] Theoretically, the defense authorizing committees would exercise broad policy control and oversight, while the appropriating committees would be concerned with the funding of authorized programs. In practice, the jurisdictions of the two kinds of committees became almost identical, and rivalry between them reached pandemic proportions. As one observer noted, "The Defense Appropriations Subcommittees are doing more legislating; the Armed Services Committees are doing more 'budgeteering'"[101]

The duplication of defense budget review prolongs and further complicates the process, increasing its uncertainties. Authorizations should precede and act as a template for appropriations, and thanks to tough authorization committee

---

[99]James M. Lindsay, "Congress and Defense Policy: 1961 to 1986," *Armed Forces & Society*, Vol. 13, No. 3, Spring 1987, p. 377.

[100]Les Aspin, "Congress vs. Department of Defense," in Thomas M. Franck, *The Tethered Presidency* (New York: New York University Press, 1981), p. 251; Rovner, *Defense Dollars and Sense*, p. 28; Jones and Bixler, op. cit., p. 48; Tyszkiewicz and Daggett, op. cit., p. 35.

[101]Robert J. Art, "Congress and the Defense Budget: Enhancing Policy Oversight," *Political Science Quarterly*, Vol. 100, No. 2, Summer 1985, p. 228.

chairs, have usually done so, but in at least two recent years (1996 and 1998) defense authorizations have been held up, and appropriations have gone ahead. Appropriations have often provided amounts above and for activities not included in the authorizing legislation. Because of the level of generality, disputes have not required legal action, but have had to be resolved by consultation and informal compromises. Discrepancies between the two sets of figures are also confusing, as defense authorizations include funding for activities financed in several appropriations bills, such as military construction, or the defense-related activities carried out by the Department of Energy.[102]

The four major defense committees represent the main decision-making focus for the defense budget, but there are plenty of other fingers in the pie. The Budget Committees have influence through the budget resolution, although they do not specify allocations among specific programs and allow for flexibility even in the level of defense spending.[103] Ten Senate committees and 11 House committees have formal jurisdiction over one aspect or another of defense policy. And other committees without formal jurisdiction hold hearings on particular defense matters.[104]

The most important mechanism for control of the DOD budget is defense appropriations. The annual appropriations process is the opportunity for comprehensive investigation of budgetary requirements and financial operations. "The testimony of hearings that enable such investigations extend in some instances to thousands of pages and furnish extensive evidence of how the agencies spend the resources enacted by Congress."[105] The growth in the control of detail is evidenced by the growth in the number of pages in defense authorization and appropriations bills. In 1970, the defense bill had 10 pages and the appropriations bill, 19. By 1991, the authorization bill had grown to 371 pages, and the appropriations bill to 59.[106] Committee staffs have also grown, increasing the capacity of the committees to gain information.

It appears that in recent years, there has been a greater reliance on lump sum, as opposed to detailed line-item funding in the defense appropriations bills. Tyszkiewicz and Daggett report that

> Congress does not formally specify in the language of the appropriations acts themselves levels of funding for every item in the defense budget. Instead for the most part, defense appropriations acts appropriate a "lump sum" for all the programs funded in a given appropriations account, although specific amounts may be appropriated for individual programs of particular concern to Congress.[107]

But this does not mean that Congress has given up detailed control of the defense budget. Appropriations acts are accompanied by the reports of the committees,

---

[102]See Tyszkiewicz and Daggett, pp. 40–45.

[103]Ibid., p. 33.

[104]Jones and Bixler, op. cit., p. 94.

[105]Ibid., p. 46.

[106]Ibid., p. 47.

[107]Tyskiewicz and Daggett, op. cit., p. 39.

which specify levels of funding at the line-item level. These reports have become longer and more detailed in recent years. Budget submissions are also presented with detailed justifications, and if no change is made, it is assumed that funds will be spent accordingly. Hearings and testimony before the committees have proliferated, and debates on the floor of Congress each year add large numbers of amendments to the defense budget.

The defense budget process in Congress is thus porous, allowing multiple opportunities for intervention. Members of Congress are free to amend the president's requests, and in the late 1990s have deliberately sought out "unfunded priorities" from representatives of the armed services. For example, in 1999, each of the services came to the Hill with "shopping lists" that added billions of dollars to the DOD budget: the Army asked for 47 items, whose top 10 priorities were for operations and maintenance accounts; the Navy wanted 53 items, of which about half were for base operations and maintenance gear. But there were also equipment requests, such as night vision equipment and communications gear for the Army, a Navy-wide computer intranet, and two tanker planes and two Osprey troop aircraft for the Marines.[108]

Because defense is by far the largest purchaser of goods and services, Congress is also concerned with defense as a continuation of constituency policy. Where military bases are located, what DOD buys from whom, according to which criteria, subjects defense to all sorts of social, economic, and ultimately political judgments. Now that most domestic spending is in the form of payments to individuals (entitlements), the defense budget becomes a candidate for the "new pork barrel." Of course it is more than that—the debate over defense spending is still largely concerned with national security—but a lot of money still remains to aid localities and many other worthies.

There are numerous instances of projects being forced on DOD in order to maintain local employment. Unlike the 1960s, when it could only be acquired by cultivating support of committee members (a lengthy and uncertain process), "pork" has now been democratized. The barrel has been placed out in the street. Now everyone, junior committee members as well as other legislators, has a chance to use defense to benefit their constituents. As the New York state delegation fought to maintain funds for the T-46 jet trainer, which the Air Force wanted to cancel because of poor performance, for instance, the ranking Republican on the House Armed Services Committee, William M. Dickinson of Alabama, told his colleagues off: "Many of the very people who voted to cut the defense budget Friday led the fight to stuff the T-46 into the budget Monday. The T-46 is a $3 billion program of airborne pork . . . a program that wasn't even included in the $320 billion budget request these same people call bloated."[109] Most members agree with Representative Jim Courter of New Jersey: "We can't reform the Pentagon until we've reformed ourselves."[110]

---

[108] Pat Towell, "Spence Faces Reluctant Leaders in His Quest for $8.7 Billion More in Defense Budget Authority," *Congressional Quarterly Weekly Report*, March 6, 1999, p. 564.

[109] David Morrison, "Chaos on Capital Hill," *National Journal*, September 17, 1986, p. 2305.

[110] Ibid., p. 2302.

Defense budget additions usually take place in committees "with members quietly inserting their projects in reports."[111] Some of these projects have a defense-related purpose (e.g. a $1.5 billion ship in Mississippi, home state of Senate Majority Leader Trent Lott); other have little apparent connection (e.g. a plan to keep the brown tree snake out of Hawaii, sponsored by Senator Daniel Inouye from Hawaii).[112] Often these earmarks and add-ons appear late in the process in the fine print of conference reports or omnibus spending bills with little scrutiny or debate. Charles Babcock explains how it works:

> "Members seeking late favors have to appeal for backing to a colleague on the appro-priations sub-committee. These members then ask the committee leadership to insert special provisions. Usually the items require no formal vote but are handled in private conferences and then included as line items in the final appropriations report."[113]

Since the defense budget is considered "must pass legislation" and usually "veto proof," the temptation to attach unrelated legislation (called "riders") has grown as well. Moreover, as numbers of congressional players in defense rise, it has become more difficult to tell what is, or is not, germane to national defense. The great increase in legislative staff is helping to make this interest more than cursory. "The downside," Gordon Adams, then director of the Defense Budget Project in Washington, added, "is that you do get this phenomenon of everybody looking for their issues and having the staff to exploit it: a combination of micro-management and flag-waving."[114]

There are so many changes—over 1,800 in 1985 alone, together with 458 re-quired studies—that it is difficult for defense officials to know where they are.[115] "If I am going to be responsible to make certain that I have done a good job trying to prioritize defense systems," Donald A. Hicks, then defense undersecretary for research and engineering, admonished the Senate Appropriations Subcommittee on Defense in 1985, "I can hardly be held responsible if in one-third of my pro-grams I am told by Congress what to do, not to kill a program or to add this or sub-tract that."[116]

The complaint of the Packard Commission was that late in the calendar year, as DOD is trying to firm up its budget proposal for the coming year, the previous year's budget is still being debated. Whenever Congress acts on the past year, at the last minute DOD has to revamp its submission for the coming year.[117] "Unfailingly," Frank Carlucci reports from personal experience, despite the joint

[111]Charles R. Babcock, "A Slice of Pork for the Pentagon," *Washington Post National Weekly Edition,* August 24, 1998, p. 28.

[112]Ibid.

[113]Charles R. Babcock, "Some Last-Minute Pork to Chew On," *Washington Post National Weekly Edition,* October 19, 1998, p. 32.

[114]David Morrison, "Chaos on Capital Hill," *National Journal,* September 17, 1986, p. 2305.

[115]Report to the President by the President's Blue Ribbon Commission on Defense Management, "National Security Planning and Budgeting," June 1986, pp. 15–16.

[116]Morrison, "Chaos on Capital Hill," p. 2303.

[117]President's Blue Ribbon Commission, "National Security Planning and Budgeting," p. 16.

DOD–OMB review, "after you have put the budget together, OMB will make a run on Christmas Day [the ghost of Stockman past?], and then you have to redo it overnight." Can this be true? Carlucci claims that there are as many as 900 late line-item changes. "As late as December, based on issues raised by the OMB review," the Packard Commission revealed, "the President has directed changes to the Secretary's budget plan that have affected thousands of line items and that have required major revisions to the Five-Year Defense Program." Obviously, DOD does not have much time to calculate the consequences of these changes or to appeal for reconsideration (a "reclama") by the president. Since DOD, like other departments operating under OMB's quarterly apportionment rules, is not allowed to spend more than 20 percent of its funds in the last quarter, it has to do a lot of guessing on its huge (say, $90 billion) procurement budget. Afterwards, DOD has to go back to Congress if it wishes to reprogram its funds.[118] While the executive branch is changing the defense budget as it is being made, Congress, for added emphasis, is doing the same. Continuing resolutions in recent years have created additional uncertainty.

Such additions and amendments, of course, divert resources, represent haphazard incursions into the defense budget, and evade discussions of the overall direction of military spending, a task that arguably would be a more fruitful use of congressional resources. Intervention in defense authorizations and appropriations may also make serious policy changes and change priorities. An example already discussed was funding for the antimissile defense system. Another was the B-2 bomber, whose production had been capped by the Bush administration at 20 aircraft at a cost of nearly $45 billion. In 1995 the Clinton administration sought to finish the program, but proponents succeeded, with bipartisan support from members of states affected, in appropriating funds for components to build future B-2s. It was a classic case of the camel's nose. Not only did it make commitments to a project not sought by the military and not included in their budget, but its expense took resources away from priorities that the armed forces emphasized and still had to fill.

The control of Congress over the details of the defense budget does not end with its passage. For purposes of flexibility (changes in needs, inadequately funded pay increases, unplanned operations, cost overruns), DOD may wish to shift funds from congressionally approved purposes through transfers or reprogramming.

Reprogramming

"Reprogramming," to use the GAO definition, "is the use of funds for purposes other than those originally contemplated at the time of appropriation."[119] In the five years from 1981 to 1986, requests to use defense funds already appropriated

---

[118]Frank Carlucci, "A Private Sector and National Perspective," The State of American Public Service, Occasional Papers, National Academy of Public Administration, sixth in a series of reports on American government, p. 7.

[119]General Accounting Office, "Budget Reprogramming: Department of Defense Process for Reprogramming Funds." Briefing Report to the Honorable David Pryor, United States Senate, July 1986, p. 1. GAO/NSIAD-86-164BR. The following description is drawn from this report.

for other purposes came to some $29 billion or 2.7 percent of the total. A small proportion of a huge amount can still be pretty big.

Reprogramming is not the same as the *transfer of funds.* Transfers move money from one appropriations account to another; reprogramming moves money from one item to another within the same account. Transfers can be undertaken only with specific formal authority while reprogramming is based on informal understandings. Taking money from maintenance to give to personnel, for instance, is a transfer, while providing more money for certain items and less for others within the maintenance account constitutes reprogramming.

Always there are exceptions. When defense appropriations accounts are very large and very controversial, and when Congress has created statutory subdivisions—as with Army missile procurement and Navy shipbuilding and conversion—the rules for transfer apply. And while reprogramming ordinarily takes place at the request of the military services, Congress may decide to fund certain items by directing that they be taken from others, such as a pay raise subtracted from Air Force procurement. This tactic leaves the military unhappy but not as unhappy as if they had to determine where what are called "undistributed adjustments" will come from. For if Congress says to find the money within the defense budget but does not specify where, the services struggle over whose hide it will come from.

There are four types of reprogramming. Congressional Prior Approval Reprogramming occurs when it is known that the legislature is especially interested, when the DOD uses its general transfer authority (you can do it, apparently, but you have to ask), and when there is increased procurement for an item already approved. When the agreed-upon dollar amounts in the appropriation law are exceeded, or new programs or items are undertaken that would lead to continuing costs, congressional Notification Reprogrammings are supposed to take place. Both Prior Approval and Notification Reprogramming require approval by the secretary or assistant secretary of defense. Internal Reprogramming, which has to be approved by the DOD comptroller, involves accounting changes that reclassify dollar amounts between and within appropriations accounts. The purpose is to leave an audit trail so Congress can see what went where. Finally, Below-Threshold Reprogramming, as its name implies, does not require prior approval but can be handled within a service. Nevertheless, a semiannual report of cumulative changes in line items goes to Congress so it can maintain its oversight responsibilities. In case of doubt, say a new program begun by a small amount, Congress expects advance notification by mail.

How large is large enough to require that Congress be notified? It depends. Criteria vary between $4 million to add a line item in procurement and $10 million to increase an existing procurement line item or a budget activity in military personnel.[120]

The objectives of reprogramming are to prevent DOD from undertaking new programs or items under the guise of old activities, while permitting flexibility where merited. Four congressional committees—the House and Senate Appropriations Subcommittees on Defense and the armed services committees

---

[120] Ibid., p. 10; Tyszkiewicz and Daggett, op. cit., p. 49.

(secret matters bring in the two intelligence committees)—decide what is merited. Since all this oversight is carried on without a statutory basis, reprogramming requirements are not legally binding, but are rather, as GAO says, a matter of "keeping faith." Since all four committees must approve a request for Prior Approval, any one can turn it down. The result is negotiation and differentiation. The subcommittee on defense of the Senate Appropriations Committee turns Notification Reprogrammings into Prior Approval Reprogrammings by demanding that it give approval.

Reprogramming reviews are carried out a bit differently by the various committees. Upon receipt of a request for reprogramming, the staff of the Senate Armed Services Committee sends copies to the legislative assistants of all members and to the professional staff members. All professional staff must sign off. If, in 10 days, no objection is received, a favorable response for submission to DOD is prepared. This draft response is then circulated to the committee general counsel and the party majority and minority staff directors for approval. A single senatorial objection is sufficient to deny reprogramming, though this could be overridden by a vote of the full committee.

The staff of the Senate Appropriations Subcommittee reviews the requests, shows them to the chair and ranking minority members and anyone else especially interested, and prepares a letter containing a decision. The staff may request a subcommittee vote in five to seven days. Though formal hearings are not usually held, reprogramming may be discussed at other hearings or at sessions where appropriations bills are being marked up prior to decision. Whether or not Congress is in session, the committee expects DOD to wait for a response letter before proceeding with reprogramming.

In the House Committee on Armed Services, Prior Approval Reprogramming is given a full-dress discussion during regular business meetings. Notifications of reprogramming are sent only to staff who take up objections with the chair. A letter of objection stops the reprogramming.

Following its receipt of reprogramming request forms, the subcommittee on defense of the House Appropriations Committee holds hearings at which the comptrollers of the services testify. Committee action is taken at markup sessions. The subcommittee is especially interested in anything it sees as new; it responds by phone or letter and has procedures for expediting decisions. Even internal reprogramming may be brought up if the staff or a member wishes to intervene.

DOD waits for a written affirmative response before proceeding with certain reprogramming actions. OMB, as in almost all budgetary matters, is involved in establishing the criteria for reprogramming and in approval of transfers. Most matters are routine, but if dissatisfied, OMB can hold up a request.

With all these fingers in the budget pie, the question has naturally arisen as to whether the reprogramming process might be a wee bit too cumbersome. If managers in business were thought to require such close supervision, they would more likely be fired.[121] The unique aura of the governmental milieu comes across as committee staff uniformly respond that "cumbersome is desirable" because it assures that only high priority requests will be brought up.

---

[121]For more on micro-management by Congress, see Jones and Bixler, Chapters 1, 4, and 5.

The whole elaborate process of reprogramming exemplifies the anxiety of Congress to maintain control over defense budgeting. Some of its concern, to be sure, is the inevitable members' interest in programs for their own districts. But Congress is always running to catch up. It is supposed to be in charge of this huge budget and to make critical and technical decisions on such complex matters as force levels, equipment, weapons, aircraft, and ships in a highly dangerous area. Size and detail alone are daunting; secrecy is often a problem; cuts are difficult to make because of long-term commitments; and contingencies (after all, the armed forced do sometimes go to war) disrupt planned budgets.

Secrecy

Secret activities appear (or don't appear) in the budget process either as generally appropriated funds with undisclosed purposes (confidential funds) or as completely covert funds where everything, including the appropriations, is kept secret (secret funds). Sometimes the activities funded by secret or confidential funds are called "black programs." Secret funds have been with us since the early days of our republic.[122] In 1811, Congress secretly provided President Madison with $100,000 to take temporary possession of some territory south of Georgia out of fear that the land would pass from Spain to another foreign power. During World War II, $1.6 billion was secretly provided to fund the development of the atomic bomb.[123]

Billions of secret funds are expended on weapons systems. While there is little doubt among legislators that "black" budget programs are necessary for national security, Congress has become increasingly concerned with the significant rise of such requests from an estimated $5.5 billion in fiscal 1981 to a commonly accepted figure of $28 billion in 1994.[124] What concerns Congress is that the Defense Department has a tendency, according to the House Armed Services Committee's ranking Republican, William Dickinson (R-Ala.), "to put things into the black unnecessarily or to prolong them in the black world unnecessarily, probably because it is easiest to do work without somebody looking over your shoulder."[125] As Roy Meyers, remarked, "There is overwhelming evidence that programs were classified black to protect them from budgetary controls, for even advocates for defense spending publicly voiced this belief." He concluded: "The best example of stealth technology is where the Air Force hid the money."[126]

Acknowledging the occasional need for secrecy, annual appropriations acts for defense, following the provisions of 10, United States Code 140, give authority to the services to use their operations and maintenance money for Emergency and Extraordinary (E&E) expenses. These come in two categories: one for extending official courtesies to guests of the United States (hardly an emergency), and the

---

[122]Louis Fisher, *Constitutional Conflicts between Congress and the President* (Princeton N.J.: Princeton University Press, 1985), pp. 244–47.

[123]Louis Fisher, *Presidential Spending Power* (Princeton N.J.: Princeton University Press, 1975), p. 214.

[124]David Morrison, *National Journal,* April 1, 1987, p. 867.

[125]Ibid.

[126]Roy Meyers, *Strategic Budgeting,* p. 60.

other "when the use of normal funding channels would compromise the security of operations, jeopardize the safety of personnel and sources involved, or result in losing an investigative or intelligence opportunity."[127] The amounts are tiny, coming to about $25 million a year.[128] Their importance is that, subject to DOD regulation, they can be used for any purpose the secretary of defense or the service secretaries deem proper.

Can E&E funds be used to violate the law? Executive Order 12333 on United States Intelligence Activity asserts that the collection of information must be in accord with the Constitution and must not involve assassinations and unauthorized electronic eavesdropping. Otherwise, the field of legality and illegality is muddy. A GAO report states that

> We asked Defense officials whether E&E funds could be used in violation of law and found that their views varied. An OSD general counsel official would not say whether the funds could be used illegally, but told us that the purpose of the emergency and extraordinary authority was to make funds available for uses which would otherwise be unauthorized. An Army general counsel official advised us that he interpreted the OSD view to be that the funds could be used for any purpose unless specifically prohibited by statute. The official explained that if a statute does not specifically state that E&E funds cannot be used, then these funds could be used in contravention of that statute.[129]

Presumably then, diverting funds from one purpose to another might be legal unless specifically prohibited in the authorizing statute.

Cuts

Theoretically, the annual appropriations process should give Congress the opportunity and power to cut defense programs at will. Recent years have also seen strict caps on defense outlays. But because of "full funding" of much defense procurement, appropriations overlap from year to year. As much as a third of defense outlays in any one year result from budget authority of previous years.[130] Accounts "spend out" at different rates: changes in pay or benefits or Operations and Maintenance (O and M) accounts impact outlays immediately, while weapons procurement changes may take several years. Congress has a major concern with balancing budget authority and outlays.[131] (See Table 9.3 for spend-out rates.)

When Congress must make cuts, they are made along the path of least resistance. Traditionally, this means that when defense is cut the burden falls on the readiness and manpower accounts of the services. Both the services and Congress

---

[127]GAO, "Internal Controls: Defense's Use of Emergency and Extraordinary Funds," Report to the Chairman Legislation and National Security Subcommittee, Committee on Government Operations, House of Representatives, June 1986, p. 2 GAO/AFMD-86-44.

[128]Ibid. "E&E expenses in fiscal years 1984 and 1985 were about $24 million and $25 million respectively. In both fiscal years, approximately 86 percent of the E&E expenses were for confidential purposes."

[129]GAO, "Internal Controls," p. 4.

[130]Tyszkiewicz and Daggett, op. cit., p. 8.

[131]Ibid., op. cit., p. 9.

Table 9.3   Spend-Out Rates for Different Accounts in the Department of Defense: Estimated Outlay Rates for Fiscal Year 1999 Appropriations by Title

Title	(outlays as percentage of budget authority)					
	Fiscal Year 1999	Fiscal Year 2000	Fiscal Year 2001	Fiscal Year 2002	Fiscal Year 2003	Fiscal Year 2004
Military Personnel	94.4	4.8	0.4	0.1		
Operation and Maintenance	75.5	18.9	3.1	1.1	0.4	0.1
Procurement	22.3	30.4	23.6	11.3	5.7	3.5
Research, Development, Test and Evaluation	51.3	36.6	7.7	2.2	0.9	0.4
Military Construction	13.5	36.1	26.3	14.1	6.2	1.7
Family Housing	54.0	28.7	9.8	3.9	2.0	0.8
Revolving and Management Funds	44.5	24.6	17.0	4.4	4.1	

Source: Mary T. Tyszkiewicz and Stephen Daggett, *A Defense Budget Primer,* Congressional Research Service, 1998.

have incentives to cut (more accurately to "cap") these accounts first. Congress prefers manpower caps because the effects are not concentrated in any one district. Additionally, as Table 9.3 indicates, manpower and readiness cuts are "quick" money, resulting in an immediate decrease in outlays. Outlay rates for procurements, on the other hand, are distributed over several years, so an identical cut in procurement budget authority would result in a much smaller annual decrease in outlays. When Congress is looking for an immediate way to cut a budget, these fast spend-out accounts produce quick results. In the environment of defense budgeting, famine is expected to follow feast. When the famine hits, defense will most likely cut readiness and manpower, knowing that funds for these categories are easiest to restore and quicker to rebuild than major procurements. Manpower and readiness cuts thus spare procurement contracts. As a bonus to Congress and the military, manpower and readiness cuts can be spread to preserve the force structure.

While members of Congress wish to influence the defense budget, they often do not want to take responsibility for specific decisions terminating programs. According to Representative Les Aspin, chair of the House Armed Services Committee, "Congress almost never cuts a major weapons procurement request from the Administration's defense budget. It usually approves those systems requested though not always the amount sought."[132]

---

[132]Art, "Restructuring the Military-Industrial Complex," pp. 429–30.

One reason for the unwillingness to eliminate defense programs lies in the development of entrenched interests. Large defense contractors gather congressional support for purchasing their products by distributing production facilities and subcontracts over a wide geographic area, thereby maximizing the number of representatives having constituents with a direct economic interest in securing a contract for a weapons system. North American Rockwell exercised this strategy close to the absolute limit in producing the controversial B-1 bomber. Parts of the B-1 were made in 48 states and 400 congressional districts.[133] The services and DOD civilians attempt to cultivate political support by creating programs with large and dispersed constituencies. Presidents can cancel programs that would bust the budget or are no longer militarily useful due to changing conditions. President Jimmy Carter campaigned on a pledge to cancel the B-1 bomber, arguing it was too expensive, Soviet air defenses had grown too dangerous, and the cruise missile had rendered the B-1 obsolete. Despite a House and Senate controlled by his own party, Carter barely killed the program in the House with a majority of three votes.[134] Ronald Reagan picked it up.

Once a service, contractors, Congress, and labor groups have committed themselves to a program, it is difficult to stop procurement and deployment. Representative Michael Harrington, former member of the House Armed Services Committee, described this situation:

> By the time a weapons program reaches the stage at which it becomes a prominent issue of debate, the battle is lost. The defense department's near monopoly on relevant information together with the vested bureaucratic and economic interests which propel the high-budget high-prestige weapons programs conspire to give such programs an unstoppable momentum.[135]

Were this often-expressed view the only truth—programs get in but never out—the defense budget would be larger than the gross national product. The truth is programs are canceled or underfunded, leading to eventual abandonment or "stretching out." Thus, in its Fiscal Year 1996 budget proposal, the Clinton administration sought to achieve reductions in its procurement budget by stretching out or deferring six major weapons programs.[136]

Other reasons help to explain this reluctance to eliminate defense programs. Members of Congress may not feel qualified and they may not wish to take the heat if whatever they advocate turns out badly or if something they eliminate turns out to have been necessary. They are well aware that, in the event of actual hostilities, public opinion may shift from thinking too much has been done for defense to not enough was done to give the fighting forces the best of everything, especially if opponents have something advanced that the United States lacks.

---

[133]Pascall, *Trillion Dollar Budget,* p. 104.

[134]Norman J. Ornstein and Shirley Elder, "The B–1 Bomber: Organizing at the Grassroots," in Eston White, *Studies in Defense* (Washington, D.C.: National Defense University Press, 1983), p. 46.

[135]Michael Harrington, "Building Arms Control into the National Security Process," *Arms Control Today,* February 1975, p. 4.

[136]Steven M. Kosiak, *Analysis of the Fiscal Year 1996 Defense Budget Request* (Washington, D.C.: Defense Budget Project, March 1995), p. 12.

Congress also will often make cuts in general but not in particular or make additions without stating specifically what programs are to be reduced. DOD may be told to absorb part of the annual pay raise when that supplemental comes up late in the fiscal year. Budget requests may be cut with DOD being told to make up for them by "undistributed adjustments."[137] In the fiscal 1985 budget, for example, Congress cut the president's request by $20.5 billion, yet only half a billion, or 2 percent, involved termination of procurement or cancellation of programs. The rest was made up by stretching out procurement, reducing the level of effort, and accounting changes.[138] So what? "Large annual contracts may be deobligated and renegotiated monthly," the joint DOD-GAO Study Group observed, "resulting in higher costs and severe disruption to those programs involved. Delays in contract awards for combat readiness and other initiatives and delay or cancellation of combat training exercises are common."[139] Once weapons procurement or combat readiness is stretched out, moreover, the unit costs of these endeavors change, resulting in "reconsidering previously discarded alternatives that a stretch-out now makes cost effective."[140] Instability feeds on itself.

Contingencies

One of the most interesting points about defense budgeting is that the defense budget actually makes no provision for fighting wars—these are, so to speak, extra. Funds for peacekeeping and peace-enforcement operations have been covered through drawdown of operations and personnel accounts, contingency funds, other emergency or special funds, reprogramming, and budget transfers. According to Banks and Straussman, "In 1991 incremental costs of the Defense Department for international peace keeping commitments was $346.5 million; by 1996 spending for peace commitments was $3.35 billion."[141] After the event, the outlays have needed to be made up by supplementary requests from the president to Congress. There has usually been little problem in Congress acceding to these requests—in the case of the Kosovo/Serbia operation in 1999, Congress provided nearly double what was asked for.

There are a number of problems in budgeting for wars after the event. First, the immediate diversion of funds for the contingency deployments is disruptive to other areas of the budget, such as O and M and research, making holes in the forces and equipment of other units. Second, not having to request funds in advance gives the commander in chief and the armed forces a high degree of freedom in deciding military interventions anywhere in the world: Whatever other controls might operate, budgetary control is negated. Third, Congress loses control of the size of the defense budget, to the extent that it automatically provides

---

[137] Joint DOD-GAO Working Group on PPBS, p. 73.

[138] President's Blue Ribbon Commission, "National Security Planning and Budgeting," p. 16.

[139] Joint DOD-GAO Working Group on PPBS, p. 85.

[140] Ibid., p. 47.

[141] William Banks and Jeffrey Straussman, "Defense Contingency Budgeting in the Post-Cold-War World," *Public Administration Review*, March/April 1999, Vol. 59, No. 2, p. 137.

increases to make up outlays already incurred. Fourth, where supplementaries are not offset by cuts elsewhere in the defense budget or in other parts of the budget, they are counted as emergency spending. This means they are not counted against the BEA defense spending or discretionary spending caps, and thus effectively negate the intention of the caps. Yet this is real money, either increasing the deficit or cutting into spending elsewhere in the budget.

The United States is the only nation, as far as I know, that budgets for defense on an annual basis. This is said to be too short and too frequent. The annual appropriations and authorization process has been blamed for what the previous Senate leader on defense, Democratic Senator Sam Nunn of Georgia, often referred to as "the trivialization of Congress' responsibilities for oversight . . . and excessive micromanagement." I think this criticism puts the cart of stability before the horse of policy and hence political agreement. What Nunn desired, discussions of broad defense issues, presumes basic consensus about the amount of resources that should be committed to the military and the types of weapons systems that should be pursued.

If one has to choose between the old days when DOD had much freer rein (Pentagon witnesses routinely used to submit questions in advance at hearings until in 1969 "a committee member read both the prepared question and its answer"[142]) and the present adversarial climate, chaos is preferable to order. No doubt it would be better if skepticism were saved for larger questions of defense policy. If the political leadership cannot agree on the largest questions—the "how muches" and "what fors"—either DOD will get to choose by default or no one will be able to make intelligent choices.

This account of defense budgeting may seem overcomplicated, because it is. Does this make the subject one for only the experts? No. Wearying as the complexities are, they provide an insight into how decisions are made about a large chunk of the federal budget. As it appears that defense is likely to receive a larger share of national resources, an understanding of how they are budgeted is critical to asking questions that need to be asked, and evaluating answers that should be supplied.

---

[142]D. Ronald Fox, *Arming America: How the U.S. Buys Weapons* (Cambridge, Mass.: Harvard University Press, 1974), quoted in Morrison, "Chaos on Capital Hill," p. 2303.

Chapter **10**

Reform

There's nothing wrong with the process, it's those who are in the process.

—Senator Phil Gramm

That process has gone all to hell.

—Representative Leon Panetta

I can't imagine anybody wanting to go back to a time when we had no budget process, to inform you as to what the situation is and . . . what the choices are.

—Representative Anthony Beilenson

Budgeting has become the major issue of American political life because it brings to a head questions about what kind of a government we will have and, therefore, what kind of a people we will be.

This chapter is about how people have tried to improve the process, and how the original norms of budgeting have evolved and been augmented. It is not always easy to remember that the budget itself constituted a reform. As the role of government changed, principles of budgeting have changed too, reflecting not, perhaps as we would expect, technical advances or the increased speed of modern life, but political transformations and the budgetary responses to political problems. Later changes and proposed reforms in budgetary arithmetic (how do you count?), time span, and decision-making criteria were not neutral but political. The budget process still swings uneasily between centralization and decentralization, within both executive and legislature, and the tension and compromises they involve have important results for outcomes. Process reforms, seen as ways to solve political problems, continue to be advocated while thinking little of the changes they would probably bring about in the nature and level of revenues and spending. Is the process broken, or are we disappointed in the tenor of political life? Meanwhile quieter reforms in credit budgeting and financial management may have been important in improving control and transparency. This chapter ends with reconsideration of budgetary norms, and their place in a time of limits.

This seems like (and is) a lot. If, when readers think "reform," they also think about changes in "what kind of government" and "what kind of people," they will be on the right track.

NORMS OF BUDGETARY BEHAVIOR

There is no better way to understand what has happened to budgeting in our time than to consider the radical changes in the norms of desirable behavior that used to guide budgeters. Budgets emerged at the beginning of the nineteenth century as the result of reforms, which replaced centuries of muddle and mismanagement with expenditure control based on norms of annularity, comprehensiveness, legislative appropriation, audit, and balance. While lip service is still paid to these norms, their assumptions—accepted limits on taxes and spending, predictability for a year, and departmental control of spending—no longer hold. Federal budgets today are evaluated against their long-term implications; they consist of many different kinds of spending; they are unbalanced, uncertain, and dependent on circumstances beyond their control.

The norm of balance established an equilibrium between spending and taxing. Strong feelings about the limits of taxation (modified at the margin by raising or lowering tax rates) established effective ceilings for government spending. Everyone concerned, consequently, had a pretty good idea of allowable spending for years to come. Bids by departments to increase their shares beyond the level of expected increases, if any, would be resisted by other departments and program advocates who knew that much more for some department meant much less for others. Spending thus was inhibited at the source; bids to "break the bank" were not put in because everyone knew that would also mean breaking social solidarity among departments. The interests entrusted to the care of these spending departments would expect to suffer. Along with budget balance, then, went the widely shared assumption that requests for funds would be made in the context of fairly firm spending limits. Budgets would not merely bubble up from below but would be shaped by pressure from above, pressure that affected the perception of departments about what was reasonable to ask for as well as what they might get. This budget restraint reflected a political system dominated by "insiders," whose wishes to keep taxes low were matched by their ability to do so in a situation of highly unequal distribution of resources and power.

Balance as a desirable norm, however, began to be weakened by near-universal acceptance of Keynesian economic precepts: Don't balance the budget, dummy, balance the economy at some hypothetical equilibrium point that would bring full employment. But as faith in Keynesian economics receded, as "full" employment was reinterpreted as a variable and not a constant at a good deal less than full employment, and as "fine tuning" the economy gave way to consistent deficit spending, the idea of the budget as a means to maintaining economic growth, stable prices, and full employment also faded. A budget in the grip of economic uncertainty would itself be an expression of uncertainty, without clear criteria for decision making. For these drifting budgets, without agreements on the basic issues of the levels of taxing and spending, the norm of balance has eroded even further; it lacks operational guidance. One side wants higher taxing and spending; the other, the reverse. So both swear fealty to the idea of balance while clinging to their opposite preferences as to the level and distribution of taxing and spending.

The norm of comprehensiveness stipulated the ideal that all revenues go to the central Treasury and that all expenditures be made within a comprehensive set of accounts. Although there were some special funds, the vast bulk of revenue did go to the Treasury. Today no one needs to be told that direct loans, loan guarantees, tax preferences, off-budget corporations, regulations that increase costs in the private sector, open-ended entitlements, and other such devices have made a hash out of comprehensiveness.

Comprehensive accounting once meant accounting by departments; governmental expenditure, except for a special fund here and there, meant department expenditure. If you controlled departments, the understanding was that you controlled expenditure. Today, when spending by departments on goods and services in industrial democracies accounts for only a third of spending, the inescapable conclusion is that traditional norms do not cover the bulk of expenditure. Most money is spent to affect citizen behavior rather than to support direct government actions. Since most spending is done by individuals who receive payments or loans, and by subnational governments, the irrelevance of department control is clear.[1]

Control of spending declined along with the norm of comprehensiveness because one cannot simultaneously maximize in opposing directions. Varying the level of spending to help modulate swings in the economy is not compatible with keeping departmental spending constant. The more interest a government has in influencing citizen behavior, say by encouraging use of medical facilities, the less such a government is able to control its own spending.

Nor can it be said, following the norm of comprehensiveness, that there is a house of budgeting whose conceptual rooms are comparable. Accounting is in shambles. Because there is no common budgetary currency, it is not possible to reallocate resources from loans to tax preferences to entitlements to departmental spending to government corporations (not, at least, in the sense of being intended).

A phenomenon that used to be confined to poor countries—repetitive budgeting, remaking the budget several times a year[2]—has now become standard practice in relatively rich nations as well. Whether the budget is formally redrawn or not, its underlying premises, financial assumptions, and actual allocations are subject to rapid change measured in months rather than years. Because governments cannot control large proportions of their budgets, they lack the reserves to cope with short-run economic fluctuations. Therefore, they reconfigure allowable spending several times a year. Annularity, the one budgetary norm thought to be unassailable (because so simple and so uncontroversial), has been gravely weakened.

---

[1]See the important paper by Allen Schick, "Off-Budget Expenditure: An Economic and Political Framework." Paper prepared for the Organisation for Economic Co-operation and Development, Paris, August 1981.

[2]Naomi Caiden and Aaron Wildavsky, *Planning and Budgeting in Poor Countries* (New Brunswick, N.J. Transaction, Inc., 1980).

So what? Does it matter if some old-fashioned norms—derived from an era in which industrialization had hardly begun—have outlived their usefulness? Not necessarily, a prudent person would reply, providing such norms have been replaced by something better or, at least not noticeably worse. For, if one set of norms no longer applies and another is not yet in sight, budgeting is adrift, without rudder or compass. This means that the main governmental process for reconciling differences and setting directions—for consent and for steering—creates problems instead of solutions.

Why did the norms erode? The answer lies in changes in the scope and nature of public spending. Over half the budget came to consist of stable commitments in the form of various kinds of entitlements, and to these might be added multiyear contracts and interest payments. It has been some time since these were labeled "backdoor" spending, an indication of their acceptance and legitimation. In effect, government took on many of the risks of individuals, particularly those of old age, disability, destitution, and the instability and uncertainties of markets. From a strictly budgetary (as opposed to an economic or social perspective) point of view, this transfer of risk involved governments in massive transfers of resources and the assumption of high uncertainty. The swings in projections of budget deficits during the 1990s give some idea of the uncertainty now involved in budgeting. It is hardly surprising that annularity is less a serious decision-making principle than a pause for a single year in a steadily marching series of assumptions about where the budget is headed next.

The coexistence of entitlements and appropriations in the same budget affects not only predictability but comprehensiveness. Because the appropriations process was insufficiently elastic to accommodate pressures for spending, and annual decisions would impose unacceptable uncertainty, entitlement spending could escape appropriations control. Complete comprehensiveness was probably always something of an illusion—budgets tend to fragment as central controls are found too restrictive and uncertain. Loans and loan guarantees, off-budget entities, special funds, earmarked taxes, tax expenditures, and preferences in the tax code[3] all impair the ideal of comprehensiveness. Regulations, too, are a form of spending, as private parties must bear the cost even though these amounts do not appear in agency budgets. Comparison of all these different kinds of expenditures becomes impossible.

The decline of comprehensiveness weakens budget control, as transactions take place outside the scope of the budget. There is, it seems, a constant centrifugal force operating on budgets, as efforts are made to escape their boundaries and corresponding efforts are made to regain unity. If the budget does not express the whole of government spending, the idea of balance too is less feasible—just what is it that is to be balanced?

The norms of annularity, comprehensiveness, and balance conjure up a time when the budget process "worked"—a time of gentlemanly accepted "limits," of budgetary stability and incremental change. There is some doubt whether or when

---

[3]See John F. Witte, "Tax Philosophy and Income Equity," in Robert A. Solo and Charles Anderson, eds., *Value Judgment and Income Distribution* (New York: Praeger, 1981), pp. 340–78; and Ronald King, "Tax Expenditures and Systematic Public Policy." Paper prepared for delivery at the Annual Meeting of the American Political Science Association, Denver, Colo., September 2–5, 1982.

this period of "classical" budgeting actually existed.[4] If and when it did, these norms represented budgetary values that might be set against other values—such as winning wars, greater individual security, and less inequality of wealth, tasks beyond the capability of the private sector to accomplish. If a budget process based on the traditional budgetary norms prevented the emergence of these values, then it would have to be transformed.

Yet no one, it seems, was really happy with the result: There was too much disagreement on how much spending there should be and on what, and on how much taxes should be and who should pay. There was a constant nagging refrain that the budget was out of control, though few could articulate just what this meant.

Central control makes most sense against a historical background of agreement, so that only small proportions of the budget remain in dispute. The old *Politics of the Budgetary Process* could focus on incremental differences because the base was largely agreed. When there is disagreement about the starting point as well as the desirable outcome of budgetary negotiation, incremental change is in trouble.

Another explanation for the demise of the traditional budget process lies in economic growth—its presence from the end of World War II until the mid–1970s and its lessening or absence thereafter. It is easy to reach agreements, the growth theory holds, when everyone is getting more. Incrementalism, Schick says, is based on the expectation of continued plenty. When prosperity declined, incrementalism went with it.[5] Will the return of "good times" in the second half of the 1990s mark the return of incrementalism, too?

Which came first, the change in budgetary norms, or the change in spending practices? Did the practices change the norms or vice versa? My view is that both changed together. The purpose of norms is to justify practices. When there is a strong desire to change behavior, as in the New Deal America of the 1930s in regard to government spending, there is also a search for new norms to rationalize that conduct. There is a struggle over theory as well as over practice; each influences the other so that one cannot say which came first but only that ideas and actions go together.

The importance of budgetary norms can be seen indirectly in new practices and proposals for reform that are meant to make up for what used to be. Constitutional spending limits, the presidential item veto, and strategic planning, which we will discuss in this chapter, are all efforts to do by law what once was done by custom—namely, provide accepted premises under which conflict over the budget could be negotiated so as to resolve disagreements while still imparting stability to government. Once, the norms of balance, annularity, and comprehensiveness performed that task. Let us, by reviewing different proposals, appraise to what extent the genie of agreement might be put back into the bottle of budgeting.

---

[4]See critique in Roy T. Meyers, *Strategic Budgeting* (Ann Arbor, Mich.: University of Michigan Press, 1994), Chapter 1.

[5]Allen Schick, "The Politics of Budgeting: Can Incrementalism Survive in a Decremental Age?" Paper prepared for the 1982 Annual Meeting of the American Political Science Association, Denver, Colo., September 2–5, 1982.

FORMS OF BUDGETING[6]

So far as I know, existing forms of budgeting have never been compared systematically, characteristic for characteristic, with the leading alternatives.[7] By doing so, we can see better which characteristics of budgetary processes suit different purposes under a variety of conditions.

What purpose should any form of budgeting be expected to serve? Control over public money and accountability to public authority were among the earliest purposes. Predictability and planning—knowing what there will be to spend over time—were not far behind. From the beginning, relating expenditure to revenue was of prime importance. In our day we have added macroeconomic management, intended to moderate inflation and unemployment. Spending is supposed to be varied to suit the economy. In time, the need for money came to be used as a lever to enhance the efficiency or effectiveness of policies. Here we have it: Budgeting is supposed to contribute to continuity (for planning), to change (for policy evaluation), to flexibility (for the economy), to rigidity (for limiting spending), and to openness (for accountability).

These different and (to some extent) opposed purposes contain a clue to the perennial dissatisfaction with budgeting. Obviously no single form can simultaneously provide continuity and change, rigidity and flexibility. And no one should be surprised that those who concentrate on one purpose or the other should find budgeting unsatisfactory; or that, as purposes change, these criticisms should become constant.

The ability of a budgetary form to score high on one criterion may increase the likelihood of its scoring low on another. Planning requires predictability, and economic management requires reversibility. Thus, there may well be no ideal model of budgeting. If so, this is the question: Do we compromise by choosing a budgetary process that does splendidly on one criterion but terribly on others? Or, do we opt for a process that satisfies all these demands even though it does not score brilliantly on any single one?

A public-sector budget is supposed to ensure accountability. By associating government publicly with certain expenditures, opponents can ask questions or contribute criticisms. Here the clarity of the budget presentation—linking expenditures to activities and to responsible officials—is crucial. As a purpose, accountability is closely followed by control: Are the authorized and appropriated funds being spend for the designated activities? Control (or its antonym "out of control") can be used in several senses: Are expenditures within the limits (1) stipulated or (2) desired? While a budget (or item) might be "out of control" to a critic who desires it to be different, in this nomenclature control is lacking only when limits are stipulated and exceeded.

Budgets may be mechanisms of efficiency—doing whatever is done at least cost, or getting the most out of a given level of expenditure—and/or of effectiveness—achieving certain results in public policy, such as improving child health or reducing crime. An efficient program may still be ineffective.

---

[6]This section is a revised version of "A Budget for All Seasons? Why the Tradional Budget Lasts," in *Public Administration Review*, (November/December 1978), pp. 501–09.

[7]But, for a beginning, see Allen Schick, "The Road to PPB: The Stages of Budget Reform," in *Public Administration Review* (December 1966), pp. 243–58.

In modern times, budgeting also has become an instrument of economic management and of planning. With the advent of Keynesian economics, efforts have been made to vary the rate of spending so as to increase employment in slack times or to reduce inflation when prices are deemed to be rising too quickly. Here (leaving aside alternative tax policies) the ability to increase and decrease spending in the short run is of paramount importance. For budgeting to serve planning, however, predictability (not variability) is critical. The ability to maintain a course of behavior over time is essential.

Budgeting is not only an economic but also a political instrument. Since inability to implement decisions nullifies them, the ability to mobilize support is as important as making the right choice. So, too, is the capacity to figure out what to do, that is, to make choices. Thus the effect of budgeting on conflict and calculation—the capacity to make and support decisions—must also be considered. When conflict overwhelms calculation (that is, when there is dissensus), subterfuge, either to permit some sort of agreement or to carry on the struggle, may overwhelm the more desirable qualities of budgeting.

REFORM WITHOUT CONFLICT

A large part of the literature on budgeting in the United States is concerned with reform. The goals of proposed reforms are couched in similar language—economy, efficiency, improvement, or just better budgeting. The president, the Congress and its committees, administrative agencies, even the interested citizenry all stand to gain by some change in the way the budget is formulated, presented, or evaluated. For a long time there was little or no realization among the reformers that effective change in budgetary relationships must necessarily alter the outcomes of the budgetary process. Today this is widely recognized. Far from being a neutral matter of "better budgeting," proposed reforms inevitably contain important implications for the political system, that is, for the "who gets what" and the "who ought to get," and even the "who ought to decide what is worth getting" of governmental decisions. What are some of the major political implications of budgetary reform? I begin with the noblest vision of reform: development of a normative theory of budgeting (stating what ought to be) that would provide the basis for allocating funds among competing activities.

In 1940, in what is still the best discussion of the subject, V. O. Key lamented "The Lack of a Budgetary Theory." He called for a theory that would help answer the basic question of budgeting on the expenditure side: "On what basis shall it be decided to allocate X dollars to Activity A instead of Activity B?"[8] Although several attempts have been made to meet this challenge,[9] not one has come close to succeeding—and for an excellent reason: The task, as posed, is impossible to fulfill.

---

[8] V. O. Key, Jr., "The Lack of a Budgetary Theory," *The American Political Science Review,* Vol. 34 (December 1940), pp. 1137–44.

[9] Verne B. Lewis, "Toward a Theory of Budgeting," *Public Administration Review,* Vol. 12 (Winter 1952), pp. 42–54; "Symposium on Budget Theory," *Public Administration Review,* Vol. 10 (Winter 1950), pp. 20–31; Arthur Smithies, *The Budgetary Process in the United States* (New York: McGraw-Hill, 1955).

For a normative theory of budgeting to be more than an exercise, to have any practical effect, it must actually guide the making of governmental decisions. Expenditures that are passed by Congress, enacted into law, and spent must in large measure conform to the theory, which is tantamount to prescribing that virtually all government activities be carried on accordingly.

The budget (for whatever the government does must be paid for from public funds) is the financial reflection of what the government does or intends to do. A theory that contains criteria for determining what ought to be in the budget, therefore, is nothing less than a theory stating what government ought to do. If we substitute the words "what the government ought to do" for the words "ought to be in the budget," it becomes clear that a normative theory of budgeting would be a comprehensive and specific political theory detailing what the government's activities ought to be at a particular time. Given that the budget represents the outcome of political struggle, a normative theory of budgeting suggests the elimination of any such conflict over the government's role in society. Such a theory, therefore, is utopian in the fullest sense of the word: Its creation and acceptance would mean the end of politics.

By suppressing dissent, dictatorial regimes do enforce their normative theories of budgeting on others. Presumably, we reject this solution to the problem of conflict in society and insist on democratic procedures. How then arrive at a theory of budgeting that is something more than one person's preferences?

Two crucial aspects of budgeting are "how much?" and "what for?" The problem is not only "How shall budgetary benefits be maximized?" as if it made no difference who received or paid for them, but also "Who shall pay for and who shall receive how much in the way of budgetary benefits?" One may purport to solve the problem of budgeting by proposing a normative theory that specifies a method for maximizing returns for budgetary expenditures. If it is impossible to impose a set of preferred policies on others, however, this solution breaks down. It amounts to no more than saying that if you can persuade others to agree with you, then you will have achieved agreement. Yet such a state of universal agreement hardly has arisen.

Another approach is to treat society as a single organism with a consistent set of desires. Instead of revenue being raised and the budget being spent by and for many individuals who no doubt have varied preferences, these processes would be regarded, in effect, as if only a single individual were concerned. This approach sidesteps the central problem of social conflict, of the need somehow to aggregate different preferences so that a decision may emerge. (After all, the grave difficulties we experience in agreeing on annual budgets today are not a result of individual incapacity; any number of representatives and presidents could make a coherent budget; it is gaining the consent of others that is difficult.) How can we compare the worth of expenditures for irrigation to certain farmers with that of widening a highway to motorists, or weigh the desirability of aiding old people to pay medical bills against the degree of safety provided by an expanded defense program?

In the real world, the process Americans have developed for dealing with interpersonal comparisons in government is not economic but political. Conflicts are resolved (under agreed-upon rules) through the political system by translating different preferences into units called votes or into such types of authority as veto power. There need not be (and there is not) full agreement on goals or the preferential weights to be accorded to different goals. Participants directly threaten, compromise, and trade favors in regard to policies in which values are implicitly weighted, and then agree to register the results according to the rules for tallying votes.

Bargaining takes place among many dispersed centers of influence, and favors are swapped as in the case of logrolling public-works appropriations. Since no single group can impose its preferences upon others within the American political system, special coalitions are formed to support or oppose specific policies. In this system of fragmented power, support is sought at numerous centers of influence—congressional committees, congressional leadership, the president, the Office of Management and Budget, interdepartmental committees, departments, bureaus, private groups, on and on. Nowhere does a single authority have power to determine what is going to be in the budget.

THE POLITICS IN BUDGET REFORM

The seeming irrationalities of a political system that does not provide for formal consideration of the budget as a whole (except by the president, who cannot control the final result) have led to many attacks and proposals for reform. But such reforms are aimed at the wrong target. If the present budgetary process rightly or wrongly is deemed unsatisfactory, then one must alter in some respect the political system of which the budget is but an expression. It makes no sense to speak as if one could make drastic changes in budgeting without also altering the distribution of influence. This task, however, is inevitably so formidable that most reformers prefer to speak only of changing the budgetary process (as with the Congressional Budget and Control Act of 1974 or Gramm–Rudman–Hollings), as if by some subtle alchemy the intractable political element also could be transformed into a more malleable substance.

In actuality, it is the other way around. The budget is inextricably linked to the political system; by far the most significant way of influencing the budget, therefore, would be to introduce basic political changes. Give presidents powers enabling them to control the votes of their party in Congress; enable a small group of members to command a majority of votes on all occasions so they can push their program through (now that would be a budget committee!); then, you will have exerted a profound influence on the content of the budget.

Further, no significant change can be made in the budgetary process without also affecting the political process. There would be no point in tinkering with the budgetary machinery if, at the end, the pattern of outcomes was precisely the same as before. On the contrary, budget reform has little justification unless it results in different kinds of decisions and, when and if this has been accomplished, the play of political forces has necessarily been altered.

Since the budget represents conflicts over whose preferences shall prevail, moreover, one cannot speak of "better budgeting" without considering who benefits and who loses or by demonstrating that no one loses. Just as the supposedly objective criterion of "efficiency" has been shown to have normative implications,[10]

---

[10]Dwight Waldo, *The Administrative State* (New York: Ronald Press, 1948); Herbert A. Simon, "The Criterion of Efficiency," in *Administrative Behavior,* 2nd ed. (New York: Macmillian, 1957), pp. 172–97.

so a "better budget" may well be a cloak for someone's hidden policy preferences. To propose that the president be given an item veto, for example, is an attempt to increase the influence of those particular interests that have superior access to the Chief Executive (rather than, say, to the Congress).

Unit of Measurement: Cash or Volume

Budgeting can be done not only in terms of cash but also in terms of volume. Instead of promising to pay so much over the next year or years, the commitment can be made in terms of operations to be performed or services to be provided. The usual way of guaranteeing a volume of activity is indexing the program against inflation so its purchasing power is kept constant. Why might someone want to budget in terms of volume (or in currency held constant as to purchasing power)? To aid planning: If public agencies know they can count not on variable currency but rather on what that currency actually can buy (i.e., on a volume of activity), they can plan ahead as far as the budget runs. Indeed, if one wishes to make decisions now instead of at future periods, so as to help assure consistency over time, then estimates based on stability in the unit of effort (so many applications processed or such a level of services provided) are the very way to go about it.

So long as purchasing power remains constant, the distinction between budgeting in cash or by volume makes no difference. But should the value of money fluctuate (and, in our time, this has meant inflation), the public budget must expand available funds so as to provide the designated volume of activity. Budgeters then lose control of money because they have to supply whatever is needed. Given large and unexpected changes in prices, the size of budgets in cash terms obviously would fluctuate wildly. But it is equally obvious that no government could permit itself to be so far out of control. Hence, the very type of stable environment that budgeting by volume is designed to achieve turns out to be its major unarticulated premise.

Given an irreducible amount of uncertainty in the system, not every element can be stabilized at the same time. Who, then, will enjoy stability? And who will bear the costs of change? The private sector and the central budget office pay the price for budgeting by volume. What budgeting by volume says, in effect, is that the public sector will be protected against inflation by getting its agreed level of services before other needs are met. The real resources necessary to make up the gap between projected and current prices must come from the private sector in the form of taxation or borrowing. In other words, for the public sector, volume budgeting is a form of indexing against inflation.

By the mid-1990s, the idea of volume budgeting had been firmly institutionalized in baseline budgeting. Budget decisions were increasingly discussed in terms of a future baseline: This year's budget for an agency might be above what it received in the previous year, but if it were below the baseline, it would count as a cut. This strategy, which Allen Schick calls "cutting back and spending more,"

> assumes that existing programs will continue without policy change. It adapts projected expenditures for estimated inflation and mandated workload change.[11]

---

[11]Allen Schick, *The Capacity to Budget* (Washington, D.C.: Urban Institute, 1990), p. 145.

As baselines are projected into the future, the cuts in terms of constant dollars may appear alarming. Yet baselines are indispensable in forecasting the future, and have become an essential element in the vocabulary of budgeting and in the politics of what is or is not feasible.

Time Span: Months, One Year, Many Years

Multiyear budgeting, that is, viewing resource allocation in a long-term perspective, has long been proposed as a reform to enhance rational choice. Considering one year at a time, it has been argued, leads to short-sightedness (only next year's expenditures are reviewed), overspending (because huge future disbursements are hidden), conservatism (incremental changes do not open up larger future vistas), and parochialism (programs tend to be viewed in isolation rather than by comparison to future costs in relation to expected revenue). Extending the budget time span to two, three, or even five years, it is argued, would enable long-range planning to overtake short-term reaction, and to substitute financial planning for merely muddling through. The old tactic of the camel's nose—beginning with small expenditures while hiding larger ones that will arise later on—is rendered more difficult. Moreover, the practice of stepped-up spending to use up resources before the end of the budgetary year would decline in frequency.

One of the reforms suggested by the National Performance Review in its 1993 Report *From Red Tape to Results: Creating a Government That Works Better and Costs Less* (Gore Report) was a biennial budget, and previously quite detailed bills had been put forward to implement the idea.[12] A two-year budget would not change much. There is no reason to believe it would facilitate agreement or encourage better understanding, but it might be approved as a sort of budget officers' humane act. Instead of working 80 hours a week every year, participants in budgeting might get a breather every other year. Being less tired, they just might decide more wisely. In any event, no great harm is likely to be done and a bit of good might be accomplished.

A multiyear budget would work well for certain parts of the budget, like military procurements, which take years to complete. But benefit, salary, and operating expense categories are ill-suited to long-term budgeting. The size of these items is significantly influenced by external factors, such as inflation, that are difficult to predict. The problem of prediction appears more formidable when it is recalled that preparation of the budget begins almost a year before the budget is implemented. A two-year budget cycle, consequently, would have to forecast economic changes almost three years into the future. The result may be that budgeters would "spend more time tinkering with the assumptions over the 33-month period and, even assuming good faith, making some decisions on longer-term assumptions that would have to be altered even more dramatically later on."[13]

Much depends, to be sure, on how many budgetary commitments last. The seemingly arcane question of whether budgeting should be done on a cash or volume basis has assumed importance because of the increasing habit of multiyear

---

[12]See Naomi Caiden, "The New Rules of the Budget Game," *Public Administration Review*, Vol. 44, No. 2 (March–April 1984), pp. 109–17.

[13]Symposium on Budget Balance, p. IV–30.

budget agreements. The longer the term of the budget, the more significant becomes inflation. To the extent that price changes are automatically absorbed into budgets (volume budgeting), a certain amount of activity is guaranteed. But to the extent that agencies must absorb inflation, the real scope of activity will decline. Multiyear budgeting in cash terms, without indexing, diminishes the relative size of the public sector and leaves the private sector larger. Not always up front in discussing the time span of the budget, but very important, is the debate over the relative shares of the public and private sectors—which sector will be asked to absorb inflation and which will be allowed to expand into the other.

A similar issue of relative shares is created within government by proposals to budget in some sectors for several years, and in others, for only one year. Entitlements, for example, can be perpetual. To operate in different time spans poses the question of which sectors of policy are to be exposed to the vicissitudes of life in the short term and which are to be protected from them. Like any other device, multiyear budgeting is not neutral but distributes indulgences differently among the affected interests. Although being treated as an entitlement, until basic legislation changes, is no guarantee of future success; it is better for beneficiaries. But entitlements, if they grow large, are not necessarily better for government because they reduce legislative discretion.

Another potential downside to multiyear budgeting is the increased permanence of programs. Just as some programs may have a more difficult time getting into the budget, so "hard in" often implies an even "harder out." Once an expenditure gets included in a multiyear projection, it is likely to remain because it has become part of an interrelated set of proposals that might be expensive to disrupt. Thus control in a single year may have to be sacrificed to the maintenance of limits over the multiyear period. And, should there be a call for cuts, promised reductions in future years (which are always "iffy") are easily traded for maintenance of spending in the all-important present.

Suppose, however, that it were deemed desirable to reduce some expenditures significantly in order to increase others. Due to the built-in pressure of continuing commitments, what could be done in a single year is extremely limited. But making arrangements over a two-to-five-year period would permit larger changes in spending to be affected in a more orderly way. This is true; other things, however—prices, priorities, politics—seldom remain equal. At a time when maintaining the annual budget has become problematic, so that the budget may have to be remade several times a year, lengthening the cycle possibly will just compound uncertainty. As Robert Hartman put it, "There is no absolutely right way to devise a long-run budget strategy."[14]

Calculation: Incremental or Comprehensive

Just as the annual budget on a cash basis is integral to the traditional process, so also is the budgetary base; normally, only small increases or decreases to the existing base are considered in any one period. If such budgetary practices may be described as

---

[14]Robert A. Hartman, "Multiyear Budget Planning," in Joseph A. Pechman, ed., *Setting National Priorities: The 1979 Budget* (Washington, D.C.: The Brookings Institution, 1978), p. 312.

incremental, the main alternative to the traditional budget is one that emphasizes comprehensive calculation. The main modern forms of the latter are planning, programming, and budgeting (PPB) and zero-base budgeting (ZBB).

Think of PPB as embodying horizontal comprehensiveness—comparing alternative expenditure packages to decide which of them best contributes to large programmatic objectives. ZBB, by contrast, might be thought of as manifesting vertical comprehensiveness: Every year alternative expenditures from base zero are considered, with all governmental activities or objectives being treated as discrete entities. In short, PPB compares programs, while ZBB compares alternative funding levels for the same program.

The strength of PPB lies in its emphasis on policy analysis to increase effectiveness: Programs are evaluated, found wanting, and presumably replaced by alternatives designed to produce superior results. Unfortunately, PPB engenders a conflict between error recognition and error correction. For an error to be altered, it must be relatively easy to correct; but PPB makes this hard. The "systems" in PPB are characterized by their proponents as highly differentiated and tightly linked. The rationale for program budgeting lies in its connectedness: Like groups are grouped together. Program structures are meant to replace the confused concatenations of line items with clearly differentiated, nonoverlapping boundaries—that is, only one set of programs to a structure. Hence a change in one element or structure necessarily reverberates throughout every element in the same system.

Budgeting by programs, precisely because money flows to objectives, makes it difficult to abandon objectives without also abandoning the very organization that gets its money for those activities. The cutting edge of dealing with competition among programs lies in postulating a range of policy objectives small enough to be encompassed and large enough to overlap so that there can be choices (tradeoffs) among them. Instead, PPB tends to generate a tendency either toward only a few generalized objectives (so anything and everything can fit under them), or such a multitude of objectives that each organizational unit has its own home and does not have to compete with any other.[15] Participants learn how to play any game.

The ideal ahistorical information system is zero-base budgeting. The past, as reflected in the budgetary base, is explicitly rejected: There is no yesterday; nothing will be taken for granted; everything at every period is subject to searching scrutiny. As a result, calculations become unmanageable.

To say that a budgetary process is ahistorical is to conclude that the sources of error multiply while the chances of correcting mistakes decrease: If history is abolished, nothing is ever settled. Old quarrels resurface as new conflicts. Both calculation and conflict increase exponentially, the former complicating selection and the latter obstructing error correction. As mistrust grows with conflict, willingness to admit (and hence to correct) error diminishes. Doing without history is a little like abolishing memory—momentarily convenient, perhaps, but ultimately embarrassing.

---

[15]See Jeanne Nienaber and Aaron Wildavsky, *The Budgeting and Evaluation of Federal Recreation Programs, or Money Doesn't Grow on Trees* (New York: Basic Books, 1973).

Nowhere does a true zero-based budget practice exist. Everywhere the "zero" is ignored and the base gets larger, amounting in the end to 80 to 90 percent of the prior year; this, of course, is a reversion to incremental budgeting. What is worse, ZBB cannot give expression to the main reason for most activities, namely, to support some other activity. By building the budget entirely from the bottom up, the justification for expenditures is divorced from their connections to other activities and purposes. This does not make sense.[16] It does explain why ZBB has declined in use. But why do people keep resurrecting it? Because ZBB holds out the hope of liberation from restraints of the past, as if they could be willed away.

ZBB and PPB share an emphasis on the virtue of objectives. Program budgeting seeks to relate larger to smaller objectives among different programs, and zero-base budgeting promises to do the same within a single program. The policy implications of these budgeting methods, which distinguish them from existing approaches, derive from their overwhelming, shared concern with ranking objectives. Thinking about objectives is one thing, however; making budget categories out of them is quite another. Of course, if one wants the objectives of today to be the objectives of tomorrow, if one wants no change, then it is a brilliant idea to build the budget around objectives. Conversely, if one wishes to alter existing objectives radically, it may be appropriate to highlight the struggle over them. But if one desires flexibility (sometimes known as learning from experience), it must be possible to change objectives without simultaneously destroying the organization by withdrawing financial support.

Both PPB and ZBB are expressions of a view in which ranking objectives is rendered tantamount to reason. Alas! An efficient mode of presenting results in research papers—find objectives, order them, choose the highest valued—has been confused with proper processes of social inquiry. For purposes of resource allocation, which is what budgeting is about, it is irrational to rank objectives without considering resources. The question cannot be "What do you want?"—as if there were no limits—but should be "What do you want compared to what you can get?" After all, an agency with a billion dollars would not only do more than it would with a million but might well wish to do something quite different. Resources affect objectives and vice versa. Budgeting should not separate what reason tells us belongs together.

There is a critical difference between the financial form in which the budget is voted in the legislature and the different ways of thinking about budgeting. It is possible to analyze expenditures in terms of programs, over long periods of time, and in many other ways, without requiring that the form of analysis be the same as the form of appropriation. All this can be summarized: The more neutral the form of presenting appropriations, the easier to translate other changes—in program, direction, organizational structure—into the desired amount without increasing the rigidity in categories, and thus erecting barriers to future changes.

---

[16]See Thomas H. Hammond and Jack H. Knott, *A Zero-Based Look at Zero-Base Budgeting* (New Brunswick, N.J.: Transaction, Inc., 1979).

MANAGEMENT REFORMS

Performance and Budgeting

The forms of budgeting that once occupied center stage (PPB, ZBB, and similar reforms) have lost their allure, but the impetus toward a more analytical focus for budgeting has not diminished. In 1993, the Government Performance and Results Act (GPRA) was passed with the aim of improving federal program effectiveness and public accountability, improving public service delivery, providing more objective information to Congress on the achievement of statutory objectives and on the relative efficiency and effectiveness of programs and spending, and to improve internal management. By systematically holding federal agencies accountable for achieving program results, the Act would "improve the confidence of the American people in the capability of the Federal Government."[17]

The reasoning is common sense: From a budget point of view, we ought to know what purpose funds are expected to serve, and whether they do so. Despite all previous reform efforts, it seemed that this was not the case. According to GAO testimony in 1995, "many federal agencies" had not even gone beyond the first step and "lacked consensus in their mission and the outcomes sought."[18] Most had no systematic process "to identify and and address critical issues affecting their ability to meet their mission and achieve their desired results," nor did they collect the information necessary for them to do so.[19] The GPRA was designed to fill this gap. Within a framework of long-term and annual performance plans and reports, federal agencies were to engage in a process of setting goals, measuring performance against them, and reporting on progress.

What was required was

> the adoption of a results orientation—a clear sense of what results the agency wants to achieve, how the organization is aligned to achieve results, how it will measure progress toward those results, how those results will be achieved, what data will be gathered to support decisionmaking, and what incentives and accountability mechanisms will be used to help ensure success.[20]

The GPRA was in the tradition of the earlier budget reform efforts, but had absorbed some lessons from them. It required consultation between the executive and legislature to determine programs and objectives; it used existing budget classifications; and while emphasizing outcome measures, also took account of a wider range of measures. The Act also allowed for extensive preparation.

The processes of performance measurement and program evaluation were not only for purposes of information, they were expected to result in managerial and

---

[17]Government Performance and Results Act, p. 1.

[18]Statement of Johnny C. Finch and Gene L. Dodaro before the Subcommittee on Government Management Information and Technology, Committee on Government Reform and Oversight, House of Representatives, May 9, 1995, p.1 (GAO/T-GGD/AIMD-95-15-158).

[19]Ibid.

[20]General Accounting Office, *Major Management Challenges and Program Risks: A Governmental Perspective*, January 1999, pp. 33–34, (GAO/OCG-99-1).

financial improvements through reengineering and better information technology, and to allow greater management flexibility by holding managers to results rather than conformity to detailed processes. All this was expected to contribute to a smaller, more efficient government in line with current fashionable trends in reorienting the role of government, restoring public confidence in public institutions, and modernizing operations in the information age. The focus of management and accountability was to shift from "what federal agencies are doing to what they are accomplishing through "results-oriented management reforms."[21] The aim of reform was therefore not simply to provide information but to transform thinking about how the tasks of government agencies were carried out, and to change the organizational culture.

The GPRA was not enacted in isolation. It followed a number of similar reforms in other Western industrialized countries such as Australia, New Zealand, and Canada, as part of a concerted effort to improve financial management, development of information technology, and human resources administration. All these countries cited a similar rationale for reform: inflexibility, disincentives to efficiency, over-reliance on centralization and rules, and significantly, the adverse effects of political priorities on planning and productivity. The 1993 National Performance Review followed similar lines of argument.[22]

The Act envisaged a formal process of performance plans, which specified strategic, results-oriented goals, measures for determining whether these would be attained, systematic gathering of information, and reports to Congress on the extent of their attainment each year. There was no lack of advice for agencies to follow. The General Accounting Office issued a series of reports, under the general title *Managing for Results*, as well as an assessment guide to help Congress determine whether the agencies were doing their job correctly.[23]

The task, apparently, has not been easy. A primary problem lay in actually specifying results-oriented goals, which "should define an objective, quantifiable, and measurable target level of performance for each program activity," although OMB was empowered to allow modifications or exemptions from this standard. Where possible, the emphasis was to be on *outcome,* and many agencies, including those involved in regulatory activities or those primarily carried out by other levels of government, had difficulties in defining results-oriented goals. In developing measurements, there was a problem of responsiveness to competing demands such as cost, service quality, customer satisfaction, and other stakeholder concerns. A third problem arose in relating long-term goals to annual goals. And in any case, who was to say whether improved results (e.g. declines in crime statistics) were due to success of government programs or to something else?

---

[21]General Accounting Office, *Managing for Results: Experiences Abroad Suggest Insights for Federal Management Reforms,* May 1995, p. 12 (GAO/GGD-95-120).

[22]*From Red Tape to Results: Creating a Government That Works Better and Costs Less, Report of the National Performance Review,* Vice President Al Gore, 1993.

[23]General Accounting Office, *Agencies' Annual Performance Plans under the Results Act: An Assessment Guide To Facilitate Congressional Decisionmaking,* February 1998, (GAO/GGD/AIMD-10.1.18).

Assuming all these problems might, with persistence, good will, and expert advice, be overcome, there still remained the question of the budget. Generation of information may be a good thing in itself, but the best of information is of little help if no one is paying attention. The framers of the Act were not content with purely managerial concerns: self-evaluation, strategic planning, tinkering with reengineering, narrow efficiency gains, or changing organizational concerns. If anything real was going to happen, it had to involve two elements: money and Congress. Decades of attempts to improve general oversight of agencies had demonstrated Congress's disinterest, while budgetary conflicts filled the congressional agenda. The difficulty was getting the politicians in Congress to use performance information in actually making decisions about expanding, cutting, or eliminating program funding through the budget processes.

The Act, to a large extent, sidestepped the issue of the relationship between politics and administration, and confined its focus to trying to gain some alignment between program information and budget information. The agency plans were expected to "provide a means of showing how budgetary resources will be used to achieve goals."[24] Program activities and budget accounts diverged from one another so that

> some of the program activities that are currently used in an agency's budget request may be either too detailed or too general or they may lack a clear relationship to the programs that are useful for measuring agencies' performance.[25]

One could push or pull programs until they fitted into the procrustean budget classification, or one could change budget structures to conform to annual performance planning categories.[26] At the end of it all, Congress for its part should be helped to understand and assess the relationship between an agency's resources and results, while agencies, for theirs, should consider how "they can best deploy these critical resources to create a synergy that effectively and efficiently achieves performance goals."[27]

Can we leave it at that? According to the GAO's *Assessment Guide*, a performance plan is expected to demonstrate that an agency has the necessary strategies and resources to achieve its performance goals. But suppose they aren't. First, while strategies may be assumed to be within the sphere of an agency's control, goals and resources probably are not. The *Guide* discusses the relationship between strategies and reasonable goals and how an agency *should* adjust each; but when it comes to resources, the language is entirely descriptive, confined to showing how capital, human, financial, and other resources *are* being applied to achieve goals. But goals and resources are interdependent, variable things. With more resources, you can get more; with fewer resources, you can get less. Of course, we can simply tell agencies that resources are fixed, and their job is to

---

[24]Ibid., p. 12.

[25]Ibid., p. 13. See also, General Accounting Office, *Performance Budgeting: Past Initiatives Offer Insights for GPRA Implementation*, March 1997, (GAO/AIMD-97-46).

[26]General Accounting Office, *Managing for Results: An Agenda to Improve the Usefulness of Agencies' Annual Performance Plans*, September 1998, 17–22 (GAO/GGD/AIMD 98-228).

[27]Ibid., p. 16.

stretch whatever they are allotted from on high to the purpose they have been instructed to achieve. This is in fact the approach adopted and made famous by countries such as Britain and New Zealand, where a determined effort has been made to divide decisively politics from administration. It is a good case for efficiency, where goals are firm, clear, and extraneously set, and a reasonable stab can be had at what is required to fulfill them. But the framers of the GPRA aimed to go beyond efficiency to a consideration of what public organizations were doing and if they were, in fact, achieving results.

Why should it be so difficult for federal agencies to explain to Congress or the public what it is they were set up for or are trying to do? Why do so many federal agencies lack consensus on their mission and the outcomes they are trying to achieve? Where questions are raised, for example, regarding the effectiveness of the federal government's 62 programs promoting employment assistance to the economically disadvantaged, we might ask not just for "better data," but how those 62 programs came into being and have been sustained.[28]

The porousness of the federal budget process deliberately allows for the interjection of interests into the financing of public programs, and therefore into the determination of public purposes. The convoluted budget process embraces a dynamic imbalance of constituency politics, states' rights, ideological agendas, the whole and the parts, and institutional prerogatives, as well as administrative values (e.g. efficiency, effectiveness, economy, productivity, planning), and substantive interests (e.g. environment, poverty, industry, trade, foreign aid, defense). In this fermenting brew, no one ingredient entirely predominates, and efforts to assert one set of values are not likely to be successful.

Yet there is no reason why, given appropriate circumstances, managerial values should not find their place in the mix, particularly greater transparency. The uneasiness of the GPRA with budgeting signifies the limitations of its core assumptions. Purposes and resources are interdependent. Agencies are not simply implementing machines, but advocates. Where they have problems in figuring out their objectives, it is because their programs are a jigsaw puzzle of compromises, conflicts, strategies, loyalties, responses, and happenstances. Why, in any case, should they be determining those objectives in the first place? Shouldn't this be a function for the political leadership? That they are called upon to do so, says much about the complicated, fractured nature of United States politics today.

Recent reports indicate the difficulties in achieving GPRA objectives. A recent GAO report that reviewed the 1999 annual performance plans of 24 major agencies accounting for 98 percent of federal net outlays revealed major weaknesses that it believes undermined their usefulness.[29] The Act required agencies to link performance goals and budgetary resources.[30] More specifically, they needed to identify

---

[28] Finch and Dodaro, op cit., p. 2.

[29] General Accounting Office, *Managing for Results: An Agenda To Improve the Usefulness of Agencies' Annual Performance Plans*, September 1998, p. 3 (GAO/GGD/AIMD-98-228). *Managing for Results: Opportunities for Continued Improvements in Agencies' Performance Plans*, July 1999, p. 3. (GAO/GGD/AIMD-99-215).

[30] General Accounting Office, *Performance Budgeting: Initial Experiences under the Results Act in Linking Plans With Budgets*, Report to the Chairman, Committee on Governmental Affairs, United States Senate, April 1999, p. 1 (GAO/AIMD/GGD-99-67).

proposed funding levels required to get to the goals set out in the plans, and explain how that funding had been derived from program activities in their budget requests.[31] The plans should show by program activity the funding level being used to achieve performance goals, that is, how amounts in the budget request would be allocated to performance goals in the plan. Ideally, agencies would be able to show how different levels of funding would be related to different levels of performance, and OMB was mandated to set up pilot projects for fiscal years 1998 and 1999 in selected agencies to do this. This effort was postponed, "due to agencies' difficulties in developing performance measurement and cost accounting systems."[32] A study by the General Accounting Office for fiscal year 2000 showed that of 35 agencies only 15 were able to allocate program activity funding to performance goals.[33] It concluded that more agencies were indicating the budgetary implications of their performance plans and some progress was being made.

Centralization and Decentralization: The Role of OMB

A pervasive theme in the process of assembling and implementing budgets has been the tension between the center and periphery. Should budgeting be "top down" or "bottom up"? Should budget requests "bubble up" from agencies and programs, to be simply aggregated or sorted out at the end of the process by budget examiners in a central agency? Or should the whole process be guided and informed by an initial preconceived framework setting out guidelines and priorities, or even target spending? During the 1980s governments of industrialized democracies at all levels reviewed and revised their budget processes in favor of a more "top-down" approach as a pragmatic response to budget constraints and ideological agendas to reduce government. Meanwhile, a more persuasive theoretical argument that sought to unite both approaches was finding its way into the mainstream of budget and government reform literature.

The ideas behind the paradigm were not really new. They drew together concepts of managerial autonomy, criticisms of the rigidity and perverse effects of bureaucracy, alarm at loss of confidence in governments, desire for efficiency, effectiveness, and responsiveness in the public sector, admiration for business methods, and ideological and pragmatic concerns regarding the role of public programs and how they were carried out. "Reinventing Government," the title of a popular text and a federal government report of a task force chaired by Vice President Gore, promised a government that "worked better and cost less."[34] The primary idea was simple: Managers of government agencies should be given flexibility to work out the

---

[31]General Accounting Office, *Performance Budgeting: Initial Agency Experiences Provide a Foundation to Assess Future Directions*, Statement of Paul Posner, director, Budget Issues, Accounting and Information Management Division, and Christopher Mihm, associate director, Federal Management and Workforce Issues, General Government Division, July 1999, p. 9 (GAO/T-AIMD/GGD-99-216).

[32]Ibid., p. 3.

[33]Ibid.

[34]Albert Gore, *Reinventing Government: From Red Tape to Results: Creating a Government That Works Better and Costs Less. Report on the National Performance Review* (New York: Times Books, 1993).

most efficient and most effective ways to carry out their functions, according to policies and resources established for them by the political branch of government, and should be held accountable for the results they produced.

The National Performance Review castigated the existing "bottom-up" federal budget process, and advocated a mission-driven, results oriented budgeting approach, which stressed performance-based budgeting and greater flexibility."[35] At the beginning of the 1990s, it appears that there was relatively little policy guidance from the president and OMB at the beginning of the process, and the emphasis on detail and inputs was intensified by the fragmentation of the budget among the committees of Congress. Centralized intervention in the budget process tended to come at the end, rather than the beginning, when the president and OMB resolved outstanding matters, and options previously left open were closed.[36]

The NPR was therefore a critique of OMB, which might be seen as performing neither its traditional analytical functions of detailed budget examination, nor acting as a high-level, policy-setting agency for the budget. The NPR envisaged more of a top-down process, in which instructions at the beginning would guide the process, and agencies would have greater flexibility. The strategic planning focus and emphasis on results envisaged in the GPRA fitted within this approach. But reforms without institutional underpinning are unlikely to be successful. Who would be responsible for implementing and institutionalizing such a reformed budget process?

One possibility might be to implement a "Cabinet" style reform, in which instructions and policies emanated directly from the president and his advisers, but this approach would ignore comparative experience, which indicated the need for a strong central agency to maintain cohesion, such as the British Treasury or the Canadian Treasury Board. On the other hand, OMB was regarded with some suspicion, partly because of its perceived political identification with the administration in power, and partly because of a reputation for micro-management in the agencies.[37]

For this reason, responsibility for the new initiative was split: a National Economic Council (which included the OMB director as well as certain Cabinet secretaries and other high policy-making officials) was set up to take charge of economic policy making and supervising its implementation; and the National Performance Review was to implement the "Reinventing Government" reforms. Clearly these functions would impinge budgetary decisions quite directly in terms of tradeoffs among agencies necessary to make aggregate economic decisions and cutbacks required by "streamlining" the machinery of government.[38] The creation of competing policy-making centers was further complicated by the change in government after

[35]*Mission-Driven Results-Oriented Budgeting*, Accompanying Report of the *National Performance Review*, Office of the Vice President (Washington, D.C.: U.S. Government Printing Office, September 1993).

[36]Allen Schick, *The Federal Budget: Politics, Policy, Process* (Washington, D.C.: Brookings Institution, 1995) p. 55.

[37]Shelley Lynne Tomkin, *Inside OMB: Politics and Process in the President's Budget Office* (Armonk, N.Y.: M.E. Sharpe, 1998), p. 218.

[38]Ibid., p.219–20.

12 years, which now pitted a prime agent of the previous administration's policies against the advocates of programs that had suffered from them at that time.

These institutional problems reflected a certain paradox in the reform agenda. To reform and maintain the reformed budget process required a strong institution with top level support. But an integral part of that reform was the devising and enforcement of viable and agreed to policies at the top. Theoretically the two aspects could be separated: one was management and one was politics. In practice they could not. Policies are not made in a vacuum: They require advice, in turn based on analysis and knowledge of macroeconomic conditions and program details. In the peculiar circumstances of the separation of powers (and frequent party divisions between the executive and the legislative) policy making through the budget is not an executive prerogative, but, as recent years have shown, has required the executive to track, score-keep, provide information about, and even persuade throughout the tortuous processes of the budget through Congress.

The more the central agency identifies with the politics of the administration it serves, the less useful it might be in providing unbiased information and maintaining the cooperative and collegial relationship necessary to maintain cooperation with program agencies (as well as other bodies) in a decentralized budget situation. The institutional problem is significant because it reflects the difficulties of a major premise of the "reinventing government" paradigm—that politics may be separated from administration, or policies from management.

OMB was forced to perform "a delicate balancing act" between responding to the administration's political needs as well as supplying objective information and analysis.[39] Whatever the strains on the institution, OMB worked to meet the challenge. In 1994 it began to reinstate a "top-down" budget process, in cooperation with the White House and its other economic and Cabinet advisers, in a "decision-making environment that involved many more high level 'power centers' than had characterized preparation of presidential budgets in recent years."[40] At the same time, some agencies were given "a much expanded role in determining the specifics of 'who'" in the agencies would "get what, when, and how," and this trend toward greater agency flexibility continued.[41]

The following year, a similar effort to instill high level political guidance was carried out with considerable budget prepreparation consisting of a series of high level meetings, papers analyzing agency plans, and guidance to agencies with specific targets. These were followed by an iterative process involving OMB and agencies, reviews by the director of OMB, and a final presidential review through a series of meetings between the president and other high officials. But after final decisions at this level, the specific instructions "directing funding to the program or project level that the agencies had generally received in the past had been replaced by more "flexible" OMB guidance which agencies were not bound to follow"[42] except in certain presidential priority areas. In

---

[39]Ibid., p. 290.

[40]Ibid., p. 224–26.

[41]Ibid., p. 226.

[42]Ibid., p. 238–39.

1995, the "Spring Review" process was reinstated, and the decisions reached were communicated to the agencies in "Strategic Guidance" letters "directed toward giving the agencies detailed programmatic guidance to be used in preparing their 1997 budget proposals."[43] This guidance was then used to evaluate agency requests in the fall.

Even while it was implementing changes in the budget process, OMB was involved in further responsibilities relating to the budget. It already had assumed government-wide responsibilities in regulatory review and financial management. Now it was playing a key role in implementing the NPR and the GPRA. It designed pilot projects, reviewed outcomes, and worked on a performance plan for the executive branch. OMB was also heavily involved in implementation of the 1996 Cohen-Clinger Act (information technology management), the 1994 Government Management Reform Act (government financial statements), and the 1995 reauthorized Paperwork Reduction Act. All these potentially strengthened the hand of OMB in the budget process . . . if it had the capacity to take advantage of them.

As the result of a self-study in 1993, OMB embarked on a reorganization under the title OMB 2000. The reform addressed an old issue, the rivalry between management and program functions, in which it was contended that the program divisions had in recent years lost ground. Now both divisions would be merged into Resource Management Offices (RMOs), which would divide the areas of the budget. These RMOs were to be responsible for budget formulation and extension, "program effectiveness and efficiency," policy and program analysis, program evaluation, and implementation of government-wide management policy.[44] The rationale was the need for long-range analytic capability, a holistic view of budget formulation, attention to program details in the face of funding constraints, a collegial rather than adversarial relationship with agencies, and some alignment of OMB structure with that of the committees of Congress.[45] OMB's role should integrate budget analysis, management review, and policy development. Its staff would be policy analysts, who would make recommendations on existing and new policy implementation, provide information to Congress on the resource requirements of policy proposals, and ensure management initiatives were implemented. At the same time, the instructions and schedules for agency budget preparation would be revised to require an integrated management and budget process, including performance measures.

To try to integrate budget policy, crosscutting themes would be identified early in the budget process and communicated to agencies so they could be addressed, and the president's budget organized around them. Ad hoc staff teams would conduct multiyear budget planning, try to foresee future problems, and undertake program analyses. OMB would expect to improve its working relationship with the agencies by greater cooperation and information sharing. Strategic thinking would be enhanced by budget review of the areas of jurisdiction of the com-

---

[43]Ibid., p. 264.

[44]Ibid., p. 244.

[45]Ibid., p. 245.

mittees and subcommittees of Congress to gain a better understanding of policy tradeoffs likely to occur.

Credit Reform

The scope and complexity of federal spending is demonstrated perhaps most sharply in its credit programs. The federal government extends loans, or guarantees loans from the private sector to a wide variety of borrowers, including rural residents, students, exporters, homeowners, veterans, and small businesses. Direct loans, offered at lower than market interest rates are offered to those who would not be able to afford credit on the private market. Loan guarantees guarantee private loans and absorb the cost of defaults where private financial institutions would be unwilling to grant credit because of high risks.

Prior to 1990, credit programs were a significant loophole in budgetary control. In 1990, the Federal Credit Reform Act changed the basis for accounting for credit transactions in the budget. Previously the federal budget accounted for all credit transactions on a cash basis, which recognized transactions only as money was paid out or received.[46] Not only did this practice give a misleading idea of total credit (because of netting out of offsetting repayments), but it also failed to take into account the real costs of credit, and biased decisions in favor of loan guarantees, which appeared as costless—unless and until default took place.[47]

The aim was for policy makers to be able to compare credit programs with others in making budgetary decisions. The objectives of the Act were to measure more accurately the cost of federal credit programs, to reveal their costs in a way comparable to other programs, to encourage delivery of benefits in the most appropriate form, and to improve allocation of resources. Decision makers should know the full costs of credit for the year in which the programs made or guaranteed the loans so that they could make informed choices about the programs. Recording the subsidy costs provides Congress with a tool to control this form of expenditure, because cutting the amount of the loan subsidy cuts the amount that may be loaned. The Act required that subsidy costs should be calculated, expressed in terms of net present value, and included in outlays at the time the credit transaction was made. It also established new sets of accounts for separating the subsidized costs and the nonsubsidized cash flows. Implementation and oversight are in the hands of OMB, which is required to track, control, record, classify, and account for all credit transactions.

Additional reforms were made through the Debt Collection Improvement Act of 1996 (DCIA), which strengthened the existing 1982 Debt Collection Act. Agencies are now required to report on their debt collection activities to the secretary of the

---

[46] Congressional Budget Office, *Budgeting for Administrative Costs under Credit Reform,* January 1992, p. ix.

[47] For further information on the shaping of federal credit reform, see James M. Bickley, "The Bush Administration's Proposal for Credit Reform," *Public Budgeting and Finance,* Vol. 11, No. 1 (Spring 1991), pp. 50–65; Thomas J. Cuny, "Federal Credit Reform," *Public Budgeting and Finance,* Vol. 11, No. 2 (Summer 1991), pp. 19–32; and David B. Pariser, "Implementing Federal Credit Reform: Challenges Facing Public Sector Financial Managers," *Public Budgeting and Finance,* Vol. 12, No. 4 (Winter 1992), pp. 19–34.

Treasury, who is responsible for reporting on them annually to Congress. Agencies providing credit are also covered by the GPRA, and efforts have been made to work out common performance measures for credit programs.[48]

In 1998, the federal government was still the largest credit institution in the United States, with over $6 trillion in outstanding direct loans, loan guarantees, and insurance (See Table 10.1). If government-sponsored enterprise credit were included, the total reached $7.9 trillion, and if deposit insurance were also counted, the federal government assisted directly or indirectly over 35 percent of private domestic borrowing in the United States. For 1999, the subsidy authorized in the budget was $1,310 million for direct loans and $1,991 million for loan guarantees.[49]

Table 10.1 Summary of Outstanding Federal and Federally Assisted Credit

(in billions of dollars)

Year	Direct Loans	Guaranteed Loans	Government-Sponsored Enterprise Loans	Total
1974	61	180	44	286
1984	233	394	301	927
1991	160	723	1105	1988
1992	156	704	1225	2085
1993	151	693	1105	1949
1994	151	699	1502	2352
1997	181	822	1703	2733

Note: For earlier totals, see Table 4.1.

Source: Budgets of the United States Government, 1974–1998.

Credit programs are thus still a large part of federal expenditures, but problems of control remain. The General Accounting Office has reported that many agencies still do not have adequate or accurate information, in particular, for subsidy rates.

Financial management

Frank Hodsoll, on becoming chief financial officer for the federal government, recalls his shock on taking office "to discover that many programs didn't know the results of their outlays, the location and value of their inventories, the wear and tear on their buildings, the aging of their receivables, and the souring of their loan and guarantee portfolios."[50] Without effective financial management, all the budgeting strategies, policies, skills, and expertise would fall short of their objectives. Financial management is necessary to know whether money allocated has been used for the purposes intended and whether monies have been duly collected, as

---

[48]General Accounting Office, *Managing for Results: Experiences of Selected Credit Programs*, February 1998, p.7 GAO/GGD-98-41.

[49]*US Budget for Fiscal Year 1999, Analytical Perspectives*, p. 188–89

[50]Frank Hodsoll, "Facing the Facts of the CFO Act," *Public Budgeting and Finance*, Vol. 12, No. 4 (Winter 1992), p. 72.

well as provide information about commitments, savings, tradeoffs, policy and program outcomes, and savings.

The 1990 Chief Financial Officers Act was designed to address weaknesses in federal financial management that had been documented for some time.[51] It aimed to strengthen financial operations by two main measures. First, chief financial officers have been appointed in major departments and agencies, and OMB has oversight of financial management through a chief financial officer for the whole of the federal government. In this way, a structure was put in place specifically to establish, implement, and monitor financial management policies for the system as a whole. In the agencies, the chief financial officers report to agency heads, oversee all financial management activities, develop integrated agency and financial management and accounting systems, and take responsibility for financial management personnel, as well as monitor the financial execution of the budget. The intent is to consolidate accounting, budgeting, and other financial functions under the CFO, and five-year plans were required to show how this would be done.

Second, agencies are required to produce annual audited financial statements and management reports. These reports will include a statement of financial position, a statement of operations, a cash flow statement, and a statement of reconciliation to the budget. Further efforts to improve accounting concepts and standards are being made on an ongoing basis by the Federal Accounting Standards Advisory Board.[52] There has also been a large amount of additional recent legislation directed at improving financial management.

The first financial report by the U.S. government, together with reports for the 24 major agencies, appeared in 1998. However, according to the General Accounting Office,

> The majority of federal agencies' financial management systems do not meet systems requirements and cannot provide reliable financial information for managing day-to-day government operations and holding managers accountable.[53]

Major problems in 1998 included the federal government's inability to "adequately safeguard assets, properly record transactions, and comply with selected provisions of laws and regulations related to financial reporting."[54]

Nevertheless, the financial report is still an interesting document, bringing together and summarizing a variety of information about the operations of the federal government. This is not the place for a detailed commentary, but certain questions are in order. First, what is the significance of the figures explaining the financial position of the federal government? What should we understand, for example, from the deterioration of the federal government's position by over

---

[51]For background to the Act, see L. R. Jones and Jerry L. McCaffery, *Public Budgeting and Finance*, Vol. 12, No. 4 (Winter 1992), pp. 75–86.

[52]See Robert Bramlett and Frank Rexford, "The Federal Accounting Standards Advisory Board: A View of Its Role One Year Later," *Public Budgeting and Finance*, Vol. 12, No. 4, (Winter 1992), pp. 87–101.

[53]General Accounting Office, *Financial Audit: 1998 Financial Report of the United States Government*, March 1999, (GAO/AIMD-99-130) p. 33.

[54]Ibid., p. 20.

$100 billion from the beginning of Fiscal Year 1998 to its end? Should this situation be discussed in Congress as part of the budget process?

Second, the figures set out in the financial statement do not always coincide with those in budget documents. For example, in Fiscal Year 1998, there was a reported unified budget surplus of $69 billion, but the financial report recorded a $134 billion excess of net cost over revenue. Some of this difference occurred because of the different accounting bases used for the budget and the financial report: the former uses a cash basis and the latter uses accrual accounting concepts. But apparently the discrepancy still cannot be fully reconciled in this way.[55]

Finally, in order to cope with the unique position of the federal government, large portions of national assets and liabilities are excluded from the balance sheet and reported separately as national defense assets, stewardship land, and heritage assets. The large entitlement programs are included in the balance sheet, but only as "benefits due and payable," that is, those benefits owed to program recipients or medical providers at the end of the fiscal year that have not yet been paid. Other notes deal with longer term commitments of the trust funds.

From an accounting point of view, all this may be less than satisfactory, the best conceptual compromise that can be made, or a start to be improved on in the future. From the budget point of view, it raises questions about the accuracy of budget data, the appropriateness of accounting concepts to budget decisions, and the place of financial statements in the budgetary process. In general, however, the efforts to tighten up and control financial management in the federal government appear a necessary foundation for honest and effective budgeting.[56]

But to view the often arcane details of financial management as inhabiting a zone exclusively populated by experts would be to ignore an important aspect of the politics of the budgetary process. Figures matter: more for one is less for someone else, and the accuracy and classification of figures have political implications. A case in point is capital budgeting.

CAPITAL BUDGETING

For at least a quarter of a century a repetitive and inconclusive debate has dragged on as to whether the federal government should have a capital budget separate from its operating budget. State and local governments, it is argued, have capital budgets, why should the federal government be different? This contention is buttressed by a variety of other managerial-type arguments relating to the need for better planning of capital acquisitions and their maintenance. Their importance is, after all, indicated by their magnitude. In 1995, GAO estimated that direct federal spending for "non-defense physical assets" was $19.5 billion, a figure that has been

---

[55]Ibid., p. 28.

[56]For details, see General Accounting Office, *Executive Guide: Creating Value Through World-Class Financial Management, Exposure Draft*, August 1999, (GAO/AIMD-99-45).

roughly constant as a proportion of the federal spending and GDP since 1970.[57] The president's budget request for Fiscal Year 1999 was for a little over $18 billion, but the request for the Defense Department was over $50 billion.[58] This is a hefty chunk of annual spending to accumulate year in and year out, and on any grounds would seem to merit attention.

But budgeting is about more than accounting or even oversight: It is about making decisions about spending money—now and in the future. And this is why the debate about capital budgets is politically charged, and decisions are seriously affected by the decision rules of financial management. First, we need a definition: For purposes of the federal budget, capital has been defined by the GAO as "tangible assets owned by the federal government and primarily used in delivery of federal services."[59] Law and practice demand that these items should be "fully funded," or that right at the start of a program or project resources should be allocated *up front* to cover its total cost. This situation is not mere happenstance, but is a legal stipulation stemming from the 1861 Adequacy of Appropriations Act and the 1870 Anti-Deficiency Act, and endorsed by the 1967 Report of the President's Commission on Budget Concepts. Its rationale is straightforward: Congress does not want to embark on projects without a guarantee that money is available to finish them. In this way Congress maintains control; it knows the costs of projects and that their costs have been provided for, and also guarantees payments to contractors. In times of budget stringency or changes in priorities, Congress has the flexibility to change direction, without concern for unfunded obligations for unfinished projects.

The curious thing about these sensible arguments is that they have actually been opposed by advocates of capital budgeting, who contend that full funding practices bias the budget process against needed capital expenditures, enforce a short-term focus on capital planning, and make capital projects (and maintenance) compete directly against other expenditures. The result, it is contended, is the poor condition and inadequate planning of capital spending. Because capital projects are typically long term and very expensive by definition, agencies would prefer to fund them incrementally. In this way they would avoid "spikes" in their annual budgets that eat up resources they want to use for other purposes. Private businessmen typically stretch out the costs of their capital investment in this way, and so in the past have certain federal agencies, such as the Army Corps of Engineers and the Bureau of Reclamation. Thus the need for government-wide control is pitted against perceived agencies' (and their advocates') needs. The practical effect of this tension was evident for many years as agencies sought to avoid full-funding rules by lease-purchase contracts rather than outright purchases. The former might be more expensive, but showed up as cheaper in budgets because budget authority and outlays were scored over the period of the lease

---

[57]General Accounting Office, *Budget Issues: Budgeting for Federal Capital, Report to the Chairman, Committee on Government Reform and Oversight, House of Representatives* November 1996, p. 23 (GAO/AIMD-97-5).

[58]US Government, *Budget of the US Government for Fiscal Year 1999, Analytical Perspectives*, p.135.

[59]General Accounting Office *Budget Issues*, p. 20.

in an amount equal to annual payments.[60] The 1990 Budget Enforcement Act changed the rules to prevent this preferential treatment of leases.

Since 1994, efforts have been made to reconcile full-funding requirements with the programming needs of the agencies, and also to incorporate stronger planning and oversight into capital spending processes. The Federal Acquisition Streamlining Act of 1994 required agencies to institute a performance-based planning, budgeting, and management approach to the acquisitions of capital assets. In the same year, OMB began an effort to identify issues related to planning and budgeting for fixed assets. Its Bulletin 94–08, "Planning and Budgeting for the Acquisition of Fixed Assets" emphasized the importance of effective fixed asset management in an era of declining resources. It required agencies to prepare and justify five-year capital spending plans and to review funding mechanisms. They were also to present a narrative summary and a three-year table of fixed assets acquisitions for the Fiscal Year 1996 budget. OMB then conducted its first director's review of fixed assets. The following year a second Bulletin (95–03) broadened the definition of fixed assets, and led to a second director's review, which, like the first, focused on up-front funding.

In 1996, OMB replaced its previous bulletins with the authoritative Circular A-11 Part 3, which required five-year capital spending plans, encouraged agencies to consider use of flexible funding mechanisms, required full funding for the "stand alone" phases of all ongoing and new fixed asset acquisitions, and outlined broad principles for planning and monitoring. In accordance with GPRA, agencies also had to relate capital acquisition decisions to their mission and goals and link them with their strategic and performance plans.[61] OMB also issued a *Capital Programming Guide.*[62]

The president's budget for Fiscal Year 1999 presented a detailed discussion of capital budgeting practices and the efforts to improve them, as well as an appendix entitled "Principles of Budgeting for Capital Asset Acquisition."[63] A new table listed proposed spending to fully fund selected capital acquisitions in seven departments and five agencies, as well as brief narratives listing aggregate requests for capital acquisition and rehabilitation together with some detail about what the spending was used for.[64] The issue of how to budget for capital appears to have been firmly resolved in favor of full or up-front funding, but agencies are encouraged to identify "stand alone" phases of projects that could be individually funded.

So far, all well and good. The requests and analyses in the *Analytical Perspective* do not constitute a capital budget; decisions on fixed assets are folded into appropriations and do not constitute a separate funding or decision-making category in Congress. The recent developments in capital management have also not affected budget processes and institutions in Congress, so that capital funding is still subject to the competitive pressure and committee conflicts that affect

---

[60] General Accounting Office, *Budget Issues*, p. 29.

[61] US Government, *Budget of the US Government for Fiscal Year 1999, Analytical Perspectives.* General Accounting Office, p. 132–45; General Accounting Office, *Budget Issues*, p. 72–79.

[62] General Accounting Office, *Executive Guide: Leading Practices in Capital Decision-Making*, December 1998, (GAO/AIMD-99-32).

[63] US Government, *Budget of the US Government for Fiscal Year 1999, Analytical Perspectives*, pp. 140–450.

[64] Ibid., p.137–39

other spending.[65] Should capital spending ever be isolated, with its own spending allocation, this would change the rules of budgetary politics, effectively giving capital requirements a preference, tantamount to earmarking. A similar proposal has been advocated to provide a separate allocation or investment targets for federal long-term investments analogous to the spending caps under the Budget Enforcement Act. But whereas the BEA caps are ceilings on expenditure, targets intended to encourage investment would act as floors.[66]

All these reform possibilities have generally been couched in neutral language invoking efficiency and effectiveness of expenditures. Most recent reforms have been tied to the concept of strategic planning within the executive branch, which carries within it the idea of choice of direction, and by implication, potential change of direction. Yet the reforms are but loosely related to the budget process, and Congress is concerned with far more than managerial criteria in making resource allocation decisions.

LIMITS

The idea of budgeting from above—either by limiting revenue and requiring expenditure to fit within it, or limiting spending and forbidding revenue to exceed that level—would revolutionize resource mobilization and resource allocation. Budgeting by addition would no longer be possible; adding requests together would not work because exceeding a prearranged total would be ruled out. More for one program or agency, consequently, would mean less for another. Budgeting by subtraction—tradeoffs among good things that could not all be funded—would usher in a new budgetary order.

Attempts to gain passage of a constitutional amendment to enforce a balanced budget go back to at least 1936, and the movement has gained momentum in the last few years. Since 1990, four versions of the amendment have been proposed, but each has been defeated in Congress. In order to amend the Constitution, it is necessary to gain agreement of two-thirds majority in each chamber of Congress and ratification of three-fourths of the state legislatures. Alternatively, two-thirds of the states may petition a constitutional convention.

The Republican "Contract With America" contained a proposal for a constitutional balanced budget amendment, which would have compelled the president to present a budget to Congress in which total outlays were no greater than total receipts. Excess spending or increases in taxes would require a three-fifths majority in each house, and the amount of the national public debt would be capped, with increase in the limit only possible with a three-fifths majority of Congress. The amendment could be waived only in the event of a declaration of war or an imminent and serious threat to national security.[67]

---

[65]See General Accounting Office Report, p. 64.

[66]General Accounting Office, *Budget Trends: Federal Investment Outlays, Fiscal Years 1981–2003*, June 1998, (GAO/AIMD-98-184); *Report to Congressional Registers*, p. 3.

[67]Sandra J. Nixon, "Budget Amendments: An Idea . . . That Never Goes Out of Style," *Congressional Quarterly Weekly Report*, (January 14, 1995), p. 143.

This amendment did not specify the level at which the budget should be balanced, but it would have effectively pushed down and frozen spending because of the probable inability to gain super-majorities for tax increases or debt. This version of a balanced budget amendment differs from a more elastic proposal in which government expenditures would be related to the level of economic growth and allowed to rise each year by a specified percentage of GDP.

The political result of such a limitation, according to its advocates, would be to increase cooperation in society and conflict within government. As things stand, so the limitation's supporters contend, program advocates within government, by increasing their total share of national income, have every incentive to raise their spending while reducing their internal differences. Why fight among their public selves if private persons will pay? Thus conflict is transferred from government to society.

The amendment's advocates believe that once limits are enacted, however, the direction of incentives would be reversed: There would be increasing cooperation in society and rising conflict in government. Citizens in society would have a common interest whereas the sectors of policy—housing, welfare, environment, defense—would be plunged into conflict. Organizations interested in income redistribution to favor poorer people would come to understand that the greater the increase in real national income, the more there would be for government to spend on their purposes. Instead of acting as if it didn't matter where the money came from, such groups would have to consider how they might contribute to enhanced productivity. Management and labor, majorities and minorities, would be thinking about common objectives, about how to get more out of one another rather than about how to take more from each other.

But the idea of a limitation of this kind has never reached Congress, whereas the simpler balanced budget amendment seems to have an irresistible appeal despite many quite sensible arguments against it. By the end of the century, with the emergence of federal budget surpluses, the issue became moot, but another popular reform gained passage.

THE LINE-ITEM VETO[68]

Just occasionally, a cherished dream is realized, but like many long-deferred fantasies, the reality is disappointing. The Line-Item Veto Act of 1996 was the culmination of sustained advocacy, whose roots may be traced back over a century. The Act in practice lasted little more than a year, between the beginning of January 1997, when it came into effect, and April 1998, when the Supreme Court began hearing two cases challenging it. Two months later, the Court found the line-item veto unconstitutional because of its infringement of the separation of powers between the

---

[68] This section draws from a class paper by Renee Brandt, "No Big Deal: Measuring the Line-Item Veto Act of 1996," California State University, Los Angeles, Department of Political Science, November, 1998. An early assessment of the line-item veto may be found in Philip G. Joyce and Robert D. Reischauer, "The Federal Line-Item Veto: What Is It and What Will It Do?" *Public Administration Review*, Vol. 57, No. 2 (March/April 1997), pp. 95–104.

president and Congress. The experience, though short, was instructive because it illustrated some of the consequences of substituting process reforms for policy changes, overstating benefits, ignoring political realities, and glossing over critical practicalities.

The idea behind a federal line-item veto is simple and, on its surface, appealing. The U.S. Constitution gives the president power to review bills passed by Congress, and he may either sign or veto them in their entirety.[69] A line-item veto would allow the president to cancel particular items *within* legislation, specifically within the 13 appropriations acts and other financial legislation.

The line-item veto fits well with the reforms proposed by Progressive reformers at the beginning of the twentieth century, which favored strengthening the executive as a means of gaining rationality and efficiency in the conduct of government. Its origin in the United States goes even further back to the Constitution of the Confederate States. The rationale then was avowedly to bring some of the advantages of the British way. As we know, this hypothesis was never put to the test because the political system in which it was embedded was overthrown. But the idea remained. According to Lord Bryce, writing at the end of the nineteenth century, the line-item veto was one of those practices that "is desired by enlightened opinion." It would strengthen the executive and more clearly identify and locate responsibility in a centralized place.[70]

The line-item veto evokes an image of wise executives deterring profligate legislatures. The argument draws support from its alleged effective use in state government, where 43 governors have power to cut items from budgets passed by legislatures. On the surface, it does appear that in some states under certain governors, such as Ronald Reagan in California, the item veto eliminated 1 or 2 percent of spending, which if cumulated over a number of years could add up to significant reductions. But on the whole, what evidence is available from the states does not suggest a particularly impressive record, and the results are mixed. In one of the larger studies, Catherine Reese analyzed over 4,000 line-item vetoes cast by 63 governors in 10 Southern states between 1973 and 1992. She found that the annual average of state appropriations affected by line-item vetoes varied from .01 percent to 1.15 percent, with an average over the time period of .31 percent—hardly sufficient to control general expenditures or balance the budget. These findings were consistent with those of other studies, which found the line-item veto to have had a relatively small effect on appropriations totals. Moreover, her analysis indicated that the governors used their line-item veto power for partisan or policy reasons, rather than for fiscal purposes.[71] Other reports, for example by recent governors of Wisconsin and Michigan, suggest aggressive use of the line-item veto, but even in these cases the overall efficiency of

---

[69]Article 1, Section 7.

[70]House Resolution No. 1879, 49th Congress, 1st Session, 3. Quoted in John F. Wolf, "The Item Veto in the American Constitutional System," *Georgetown Law Journal*, Vol. 25 (1936), p.113.

[71]Catherine Reese, "The Line-Item Veto in Practice in Ten Southern States," *Public Administration Review*, Vol. 7, No. 6 (November-December 1997); pp. 510–16; See also, David Hosansky, "Can States Give Washington a Lesson in Veto Politics?" *Congressional Quarterly Weekly Report*, August 9 1997, pp. 1922–23.

the measure is unclear without consideration of a variety of contextual factors including appropriations politics, the degree of budget itemization, or the existence of balanced budget requirements.

A recent wide-ranging study by Louis Fisher has detailed the procedural and political constraints surrounding the line-item veto in the states, and has suggested that in many ways legislatures have been able to nullify its exercise through evasive tactics and court rulings.[72] Nevertheless, in the context of the deficit-ridden decades of the 1980s and 1990s, the federal line-item veto took on symbolic significance in the minds of Democrats as well as Republicans, political leaders as well as rank and file. The line-item veto was praised as "a weapon against wasteful, 'pork barrel' spending"[73]; "a tool to reduce federal spending and help bring the budget to balance"[74]; and a way to preserve "the integrity of federal spending"[75] (whatever that was). When Republicans gained control of Congress in 1995, the "Contract With America" endorsed by the House Republicans mandated in its first paragraph passage of a line-item veto.

It took Congress some time even so to put rhetoric into action and to come up with an acceptable version. To presidents, the line-item veto had an obvious appeal, but why would Congress be so anxious to deliver up to the executive branch a weapon that, in the words of Louis Fisher, clearly favors executive spending priorities over legislative spending priorities?[76] The fact of a Democratic president facing a Republican majority in Congress (later strengthened by reelection to a second term) surely gave some pause to ideologues, who must have been aware of the danger that the veto power might be used to promote priorities other than those they had in mind.

After some discussion of the form a line-item veto should take, Congress passed a bill that was enthusiastically signed into law at the end of March, 1996 by President Clinton, who stated that the Act would "permit presidents to better represent the public interest by cutting waste, protecting tax payers and balancing the budget."[77]

The Line-Item Veto Act of 1996 allowed the president during a period of five days *after* signing a bill into law, to cancel "(1) any dollar amount of discretionary budget authority", (2) any item of direct spending, and (3) certain limited tax benefits.[78] He was required to send a message to Congress detailing the need for and impact of the proposed deletions. He also had to determine that the cancellations

---

[72] Louis Fisher, "Line-Item Veto of 1996: Heads-up from the States," *Public Budgeting and Finance*, Vol. 17, No. 2 Summer 1997, pp. 3–17.

[73] Andrew Taylor, "Line-Item Veto Struck Down Again," *Congressional Quarterly Weekly Report*, February 19, 1998, p. 381.

[74] Hosansky, 1997, p.1922.

[75] Andrew Taylor, "Judge Voids Line-Item Veto Law," *Congressional Quarterly Weekly Report*, April 12, 1997, p. 833.

[76] Fisher, *op. cit.*

[77] Andrew Taylor, "Line-Item Veto Bill Becomes Law," *Congressional Quarterly Weekly Report*, April 13, 1996, p. 984.

[78] Louis Fisher and Virginia McMurtay "The Line-Item Veto Act," *Congressional Research Service*, April 23, 1998, p. 2.

would reduce the federal budget deficit, not impair any essential government functions, and not impair the national interest. All savings would be automatically earmarked for deficit reduction, and no equivalent sum could be voted for other purposes in their stead, that is, existing provisions capping discretionary spending and requiring offsets for increases in mandatory expenditures or cuts in taxation would remain in force. The president's powers were further augmented by authority to delete items in associated reports and memoranda, which meant that the large and aggregated items of the federal budget would not, as anticipated previously by critics, present an obstacle to deleting specific projects.

Congress could overturn a line-item veto by a simple majority in a disapproval bill passed within 30 days. If the president then vetoed this bill, Congress could override him by a two-thirds majority in each House. The Act was scheduled to come into force in January, 1997 and to lapse in 2004.

It was easy to see that the Act favored the president. In order to check his actions, and preserve items he had deleted, Congress had to take deliberate initiative. In order to prevent an override, the president needed only one-third of congressional votes. From the presidential perspective, the line-item veto could be a potentially powerful weapon to ensure "responsibility" in federal budgeting (on one reading), and, (on another) to gain his own priorities. From the congressional perspective, it seemed an admission of impotence to control their own irresponsible impulses, and an unprecedented transfer of powers.

The constitutionality of the Act was challenged soon after it came into effect, but the cases were rejected on the grounds that the plaintiffs lacked standing. It was nearly nine months before President Clinton actually used the veto, first on two projects in the Taxpayer Relief Act of 1997 and one provision in the Balanced Budget Act of 1997. During the 1997 appropriations cycle, he deleted or attempted to delete 80 projects or provisions from nine appropriations acts, amounting to a total savings of $1.95 billion over five years. Given an annual budget of over $1.5 trillion, and an estimated deficit for the year of over $100 billion, the line-item veto scarcely met proponents' claims for its efficacy as a weapon to balance the budget, erase waste, or roll back the tide of federal spending.

Brief consideration of the nature of the federal budget in 1997 demonstrates the inappropriateness of the line-item veto for such tasks. Even granting proponents the best of their possible worlds, a president in the White House ready to throttle the expenditure machine would have only a relatively small part of the budget on which to try the item veto. We might assume a Republican president would be unwilling to cut defense, which amounts to around 16 percent of the budget. It would be politically difficult to cut the large universal middle class entitlements, such as social security, and in practice entitlements of any kind do not easily lend themselves to reductions through line-item veto, since these would require eligibility changes rather than outright cancellations, that is, they are not divisible.

Together such programs amount to over half of federal expenditures. Allowing approximately 13 percent for interest on the national debt, this would leave little more than the relatively small 16 percent of domestic discretionary spending available for the line-item veto.

Still, this "small" slice of the budget in 1997 amounted to $276 billion, a by no means negligible sum. To this might be added the possibility of vetoing special interest tax expenditures and President Clinton was also willing to use the veto power in defense appropriations. Although the line-item veto might not be the solution to either federal deficits or overwhelming federal spending, it could offer considerable scope to a determined president to weed out wasteful projects and cut out pork barrel spending if he was so inclined. If he could not save the American people from the larger evil, he could perhaps inflict some smaller victories for morality.

But where to start? Pork and wasteful spending do not come labeled as such. Should the president delete all such items, or go after only the most egregious? What should be the criteria for the ax? The Act gave very little guidance—any deletion would presumably reduce the deficit; anything could be considered in the national interest; and who was to say what was essential or not essential?

To do a consistent job, was the president to go through the thousands of appropriation items, *and* memoranda, *and* tax provisions? The product of hours of committee wrangling, staff consultations, bargaining and tradeoffs, and repeated voting was now to be reconsidered, reanalyzed, and thought out? So large a task would surely elicit a parallel bureaucracy in the White House itself—in effect duplicating the work of Congress. And in such a short time frame.

Certain criteria did become apparent from the Clinton Administration's listing of its reasons for vetoing items. These included items

> not included in the President's budget request, not requested or appropriate for the agency, not far enough along to begin construction in 1998, not going to substantially improve the quality of life of military personnel and their families, or not agreed to in negotiations with Congress.[79]

But it seemed difficult to apply these often vague criteria consistently. The first appropriations bill on which Clinton tried his new veto power was for military construction. It included 129 projects not requested by Clinton, but only 38 were vetoed.[80] In the Defense Appropriations Act, Congress had added 750 projects at a cost of $11 billion, but only 13 items were cancelled, for a savings of $144 million.[81] Obviously not every project inserted by Congress was vetoed.

But the difficulties in setting out and applying consistent criteria were not the real reason why the line-item veto did not, and could not, work as those who gave it lip service envisaged. The veto assumed that the President would be some kind of a neutral arbiter, above politics, a kind of Lone Ranger outsider whose interests were purely in economy, efficiency, and advancing the good of the nation. These sentiments are virtually identical to those expressed by the early twentieth century reformers who advocated the federal executive budget. Of course institutional reforms may be useful, and they may vastly improve on previous practice. But their utility lies not in their supra-political or nonpolitical nature, but in their efficacy in

---

[79]Brandt, p.7.

[80]Andrew Taylor, "Line-Item Boosters Reconsider as Clinton Vetoes Hit Home," *Congressional Quarterly Weekly Report,* October 11, 1997, p. 2459.

[81]Donna Cassata, "President Uses a Delicate Touch in Vetoing Military Spending," *Congressional Quarterly Weekly Report,* October 11, 1997, p. 2557.

providing a positive framework of accepted rules and processes within which politics takes place.[82]

The fallacy of the line-item veto lay in pretending that the president—any president—had no political preferences and was uninterested in the exercise of power. The line-item veto did not supersede the politics of the budgetary process, but merely recast them, providing, as it were, a new battleground, a new set of opportunities and constraints for all the players. A president's use of the line-item veto would not take place in a vacuum but within the context of his relationship with Congress. A line-item veto could conceivably increase spending, if a president threatened to veto projects favored in Congress whenever Congress failed to fund his priorities, in a kind of quid pro quo budgeting.[83]

Whose preferences are to prevail? One person's pork and waste is another's essential project, and, except for broad national programs, most projects are local. "What have you done for me lately?" is a time-honored question in American politics, and it is asked of presidents who need votes in Congress as well as politicians who need votes in their constituencies.

The president had to pick and choose, and evenhandedness might not be seen as such by sponsors of what they perceived as useful projects. For example, Clinton cancelled funds for relocating the Army Reserve maintenance shop in Utah from the Military Construction Bill. Because the vacated land was to be used for a dormitory for athletes at the 2002 Olympic Games, Senator Robert Bennett (R-Utah), a sponsor of the project, was reported as saying he doubted the administration realized the potential consequences to the Olympics.[84] On the other hand, Clinton let stand an allocation for development of two cruise ships for a company serving the Hawaiian Islands in the defense appropriations bill, presumably benefiting Senator Daniel Inouye (D-Hawaii), the influential ranking Democrat on the defense appropriations subcommittee.[85]

The broader issue of course is policy. While a Republican president might be expected to use the line-item veto to cut domestic spending while leaving defense expenditures unscathed, a Democratic one might have no such inhibitions. After Clinton had tried out his new toy on tax provisions in the 1997 Taxpayer Relief and Balanced Budget Acts of 1997 (more later), and the deletions survived an attempted disapproval bill, he was sufficiently emboldened to veto 38 military construction projects amounting to $287 million out of the $9.2 billion act. Of course, his stance was avowedly nonpartisan: "The projects I have cancelled are all over the country, in the districts of lawmakers of both parties."[86] There was, predictably, outrage in Congress, which reinstated all the projects, overriding Clinton's veto of

[82] Naomi Caiden, "Paradox, Ambiguity and Enigma: The Strange Case of the Executive Budget and the United States Constitution," *Public Administration Review*, Vol. 47 (January/ February 1987), pp. 84–92.

[83] Hosansky, 1997, p.1923, quoting Louis Fisher.

[84] Andrew Taylor, "Line-Item Boosters Reconsider as Clinton Vetoes Hit Home," *Congressional Quarterly Weekly Report*, October 11, 1997, p. 2463.

[85] Cassata, op. cit.

[86] "Clinton Outlines Reasons for Defense Veto Items," *Congressional Quarterly Weekly Report*, October 18, 1997, p. 2562.

its disapproval bill. After this, it seemed the president was more circumspect, and fewer items were cancelled in the remaining appropriations bills. Clinton actually stated, after canceling eight projects in the Energy and Water Development Appropriations Act, "I tried to show deference to Congress' role in the appropriations process."[87]

But this did not prevent him from deleting 13 projects amounting to $144 million from defense allocations, a flea bite in the nearly $248 billion defense appropriations bill, but nonetheless a precedent. Taken together, the defense and military construction deletions totaled $431 million, compared with $47.3 million in domestic spending.[88] The scope of deletions varied in amounts from a project for $30 million for a SR-71 Blackbird spy plane in the Defense Appropriations Act to an item for $15,000 for a police training complex in Arab, Ala., in the VA-HUD Appropriations Act.

The line-item veto was declared unconstitutional in the Supreme Court, in the combined cases of the *City of New York* v. *Clinton* and *Snake River Potato Growers, Inc.* v. *Rubin*. New York City challenged deletion of a section in the Balanced Budget Act of 1997, which would have allowed it to count certain payments to be permissible taxes eligible for federal matching funds under medicaid. The Snake River farm cooperative challenged deletion of a section in the same act that would have allowed companies selling agricultural processing plants to form cooperatives to defer capital gains tax. In both cases, the plaintiffs could prove they had suffered a loss as a result of Clinton's action, and so had standing to sue. The majority in the Supreme Court held that by canceling provisions in enacted laws, the president was unilaterally amending legislation, contrary to the Constitution.

None of the deletions, worthy or unworthy, really would have fulfilled the possible desire of line-item veto proponents who perhaps thought that the president would use it to eliminate or reduce politically important expenditures on which there has long been a negative professional consensus, for example agricultural and maritime subsidies, way-below-market prices for grazing rights on federal land, water for irrigation in the West, all sorts of river and harbor projects, and the like. In any event, there was not enough to make a big difference in the area of domestic discretionary spending, which has over the past two decades been already heavily pruned.

The short experience of the line-item veto in 1997 demonstrated its insufficiency as even a selective solution. Its image of presidents valiantly trying to stem the tide of spending but, for the want of this one weapon, being overwhelmed by hordes of congressional spenders, is a fantasy. Presidents, no less than Congress, are in the forefront of spending, and are no less interested in pressing their own political interests. The line-item veto is a weak instrument, compared with those already available.

---

[87] Johathan Weisman, "Energy and Water Lawyers Line-Item Veto," *Congressional Quarterly Weekly Report,* October 18, 1997, p. 2552.

[88] Note that this does not include five-year savings gained from deleting the tax provisions of the 1997 legislation or the disallowance of a provision in the Treasury and General Government Act that would have allowed some employees to switch pension plans.

OVERLOADING BUDGETING

In the period of classical budgeting, there was an effective, albeit informal, ceiling beyond which spending could not go. Nowadays there are basic disagreements about the size and composition of the public sector. Bringing back the good old ways implies something that can no longer be achieved, namely, summoning up agreement on the underlying beliefs that once made them work.

Indeed, budget resolutions, automatic spending reductions to achieve balance, item vetoes, balanced budget amendments, and offsets are all formal substitutes for what used to be done informally. If (and when) congressional majorities do wish to control spending, we have seen that spending ceilings safeguarded by requiring that additions be balanced by subtractions (or by new revenues) work powerfully well. There's a way if there's a will. Suppose, however, that not one, but several wills are incompatible? Then perhaps the contemporary budgetary stalemate may be seen not as an aberration but as a sign of continuing dissensus. What, then, can be hoped for from budgeting?

The budgetary process is an arena in which the struggle for power over public policy is worked out. Budgeting is a forum for the exercise of political power, not a substitute for that power. By itself, budgeting cannot form majorities and enforce their will. While the rules for voting on spending and taxing may make agreement marginally easier or harder, they cannot close unbridgeable gaps. It is more reasonable to suppose that general political processes shape budgeting than that budgeting determines political alignments.

Chapter **11**

Deficits and Surpluses

Why do students of American budgeting need to understand the federal deficit? Although budgetary politics were dominated by high and seemingly intractable deficits for about 30 years, the end of the twentieth century appeared to herald a new era of surpluses as far as the eye could see. So should we drop study of the causes and consequences of deficits from our agenda?

A number of reasons are paramount. First, the surpluses may be more apparent than real: Much depends on budget arithmetic. Second, if the deficit dragon has indeed been slain, we need to know how this happened in order to complete the story. Third, the deficit was the defining issue of a political era. As Joseph White and Aaron Wildavsky put it,

> Political time is counted not in years but in issues; a political era is defined by the concerns that dominate debate and action, so that about other issues we ask: How does that affect? . . . The budget has been to our era what civil rights, communism, the depression, industrialization, and slavery were at other times.[1]

So central an issue should not be ignored. Fourth, a surplus, despite the different political dynamics it sets up, is only the mirror image of a deficit: They frame the debate about the same issues: the balances between taxpayers and recipients, public and private sectors, present and future generations, investment and consumption. Fifth, the surpluses of today are the deficits of tomorrow. Future economic conditions, demographic pressures, and negative attitudes toward taxation make it unlikely that deficits will be banished forever from the Earth. Any realistic study of budgeting, therefore, needs to analyze the origins of the massive federal deficits of the 1980s and 1990s, their nature and consequences, and how they seemed at least for the moment to have been conquered.

---

[1]Joseph White and Aaron Wildavsky, *The Deficit and the Public Interest* (Berkeley: University of California Press, 1990), pp. xv–xvi.

WHO DONE IT?[2]

Deficits had been a feature of post-war federal budgeting, reaching what were considered serious proportions in the 1970s, and then expanding to triple digit figures in the early 1980s. In February 1983 the Congressional Budget Office (CBO) projected $200 billion deficits far into the future. It explained that "to a great extent" the 1983 and 1984

> deficits are attributable to the economic recession, which has reduced federal revenues and increased federal outlays for unemployment compensation and other income maintenance programs. But even as these cyclical crises wither as economic recovery proceeds, the proposed deficits remain . . . high. . . . This indicates a long-term mismatch between federal spending and taxing.[3]

This long-term mismatch was what economists called the "structural deficit." This structural deficit amounted to 3.6 percent of GNP difference between income and outgo.

One obvious cause of the 1980s deficits was tax cuts and defense buildup at the beginning of the Reagan administration in 1981, but there were longer-term forces also at work to force apart revenues and spending. The first problem lay in tax levels. The trend in federal government tax burdens from 1961 to 1981 showed that taxes at 20.9%, including higher income taxes, were a lot higher than had been customary, or desired. If a "normal" level of revenue is about 19 percent,[4] it would be unlikely that either deliberately raising taxes, or allowing them to grow with inflation (through bracket creep) could be a viable way of solving or preventing the structural deficits. Even before tax cuts took place, expenditures were growing faster than revenues.

On the spending side, outlay growth during the first half of the 1980s could be entirely explained by increases in defense, social security, medicare, and debt interest. There were significant reductions made in domestic discretionary programs and means-tested entitlements during this period. At least some of the deficit might be attributed to recessionary conditions in the late 1970s and early 1980s. Social security, in particular, suffered from slowing production and revenues, while the number of program recipients and cost of living adjustments (COLAs) caused benefits to outstrip either the economy or contributions to the social security fund. Meanwhile, medicare expenditures also grew, mainly because of tremendous cost inflation in the medical business, a trend Congress had been wrestling with for years.[5] As deficits ballooned, governments had to borrow more, and borrowing and interest began to feed off each other, generating higher deficits

---

[2]Except for the last section, this chapter is a revised version of work done with Joseph White, *The Deficit and the Public Interest* (Berkeley: University of California Press, 1990); and "How to Fix the Deficit—Really," *The Public Interest,* No. 94 (Winter 1989), pp. 3–24.

[3]Congressional Budget Office, "Reducing the Deficit: Spending and Revenue Options," A Report to the Senate and House Committees on the Budget—Part III, February 1983, p. 1.

[4]Gregory B. Mills and John L. Palmer, *The Deficit Dilemma* (Washington, D.C.: Urban Institute, 1983) pp. 8–10, give a short summary of the tax increases. See also Allen Schick, *The Federal Budget: Politics, Policy, Process* (Washington, D.C.: Brookings Institution, 1995), p. 4.

[5]See Congressional Budget Office, "Reducing the Deficit," pp. 98–99

and more borrowing, at a time when an economy with both high inflation and high unemployment was generating high interest rates. Finally, the defense buildup, begun under a Democratic presidency, significantly increased outlays.[6]

Given difficult economic conditions, norms about the levels of taxation, and determination to increase defense spending, deficits might have been difficult to avoid. Spending grew because of past decisions made about entitlements for the elderly: They grew because the eligible population grew—people were living longer, and more and more of them were fully vested in the social security system; there were also big, multiple legislated hikes in social security in the 1969–1972 period with the support of Republican President Richard Nixon. In 1962, the Old Age and Disability funds had 16.8 million beneficiaries; in 1972, 25.2 million; in 1982, 31.9 million.[7] Spending grew in medicare because virtually nobody anticipated the costs of coverage; Congress began struggling with medical inflation soon after the program began. Costs grew, finally, because politicians kept benefits in line with rising prosperity (but out of line with contributions by recipients), eager to please a powerful group of voters and confident that continuing economic growth would enable current workers to pay the bill. The last big increase in social security coverage in 1972 tells both sides of the story: Democrats and Republicans competed to woo the elderly; the resulting increase "was financed largely by a change in actuarial assumptions" that politicians had little reason to reject.[8] But the economy did not behave as expected, and almost everybody was asking the wrong question.

With the first OPEC oil shock in 1973, the economy went into a "quiet depression,"[9] and social security got into deep trouble. Revenues for the trust fund would not cover the outlays. Social security had to be "rescued" twice. Whether social security's taxes could fund the system's expenses was important. But throughout the program's history, no one asked a second question: *If social security taxes increased, would those be new taxes or replace old ones?* (Tax aficionados speak of "fiscal cannibalism" where one tax eats up another.) Government raised the social security payroll tax from 3.1 percent of GNP in 1962 to 6.6 percent in 1982.[10] And it was scheduled by legislation to go higher. When new taxes took effect, the government usually cut other taxes to compensate. This strategy could work because either the economy would grow so strongly that other programs could live with a smaller share, or because spending (and thus revenues) was diverted from the shrinking defense budget to domestic (mostly welfare) programs. But it never had to make that choice—higher taxes on social security in addition to or in subtraction from income and other taxes—in advance. The repetition of what appears to be a truism—social security is self-financing—by Ronald Reagan, his

---

[6]See Congressional Budget Office, "The Economic and Budget Outlook," p. 153.

[7]Committee on Ways and Means, U.S. House of Representatives, *Background Material and Data on Programs Within the Jurisdiction of the Committee on Ways and Means,* Committee Print, 99th Congress, 1st Session, 99-2, February 22, 1985 (U.S. Government Printing Office), pp. 55–56.

[8]Martha Derthick, *Policymaking for Social Security* (Washington, D.C.: Brookings Institution, 1979) p. 357.

[9]The term is Frank Levy's. See his *Dollars and Dreams: The Changing American Income Distribution* (New York: Russell Sage Foundation, 1987).

[10]Congressional Budget Office, "The Economic and Budget Outlook," p. 162.

congressional opponents, and spokesmen for the elderly, though true as far as it goes, left the profoundly mistaken impression that by far the biggest domestic program did not affect the rest of government. Nonsense. Individuals and businesses feel taxation from all sources, so government eventually had to face the consequences of social security expansion either in deficits, higher taxes, or lower spending later on other things.

Here's the catch: Maybe the government could not have chosen in advance. No one could foresee the size of future problems; perhaps they would be small, for economic growth heals many ills. Perhaps it was for people in the future to choose whether they wanted higher taxes or fewer programs, or even (gasp!) higher deficits. Even if politicians in 1962 had decided that other programs would have to be cut by the same amount by 1972, for instance, how could they have done so? All right, one might say: If you can't plan, don't make the commitment. Don't have a national retirement plan, or policies with long-term, increasing costs. Toss out civil service pensions and medicare while you're at it. But that inaction would be intolerable. People in real life make long-term commitments like buying a house (even with an adjustable-rate mortgage). They marry, have children, plan to send them to college; they will figure out later what to sacrifice to that end. The government, with heavy public support, committed itself to social security. There is little evidence that people, on the whole, dispute that commitment or its necessity. Some problems come with the territory.

Is there, then, no room for choice? Yes, there is; one can always exercise prudence. Increases in payments to recipients, for example, could have been smaller. Many provisions, such as early retirement, could have been less generous. When bad times come, the nation must decide who will bear the costs of change. But choice is politically circumscribed by the difficulty of breaking promises on which millions have planned their lives. Because old commitments did not match the new economy, huge deficits would probably have occurred even without the policy choices of the early 1980s.

A reasonable conclusion would be that all who govern now and in the past half century share some of the blame for the deficit, some more than others, but few guiltless. Hardly anyone anticipated the relatively poor economic performance of the 1970s. Much of this slowdown might have been due to international oil increases, vast numbers of new entrants (especially women) into the labor market, the emergence of new economic powers on the world scene, too high taxes, insufficient demand, or too little saving, some of which government could affect and much of which it could not.[11]

It has been alleged that Reagan engineered the large deficit in order to keep down domestic spending. Not so.[12] He hoped that his policies would be successful; that is, the nation would avoid a recession and lower tax rates would bring in higher revenues. Once faced with a big deficit, however, he did choose to accept it rather than raise income taxes substantially.

---

[11]See Frank Levy, *Dollars and Dreams* (New York: Russell Sage Foundation, 1987), for a splendid analysis of how demographic changes affect spending outcomes.

[12]This judgment is based on numerous interviews and a perusal of virtually all of the documentary record. See White and Wildavsky, *The Deficit and the Public Interest.*

THE DEFICIT PANIC

The most obvious result of both President Reagan's choices and the policies he inherited, however, was the deficit panic of the 1980s. The deficit became the dominant policy problem, an issue that shaped consideration of all other issues. It was blamed for every economic ill, from inflation to unemployment to high interest rates to the large trade imbalance, from the strong dollar to the weak dollar. Strife over the deficit spilled over from policy into procedure, hogging the congressional agenda, encouraging paralyzing legislation, such as Gramm–Rudman, frustrating legislators, and stalemating the government. Otherwise, it was benign.

All political factions, hamstrung by the deficit, increased the pressure on themselves by using the deficit to attack each other. Liberals, blocked from responding to their definition of social needs by a lack of money, claimed prosperity under Ronald Reagan was bought on the credit card, to be charged to our grandchildren. Conservatives blamed ills like high taxes on the legacy of liberal overspending. Centrists, hating the deficit for its own sake as a sign of the government's inability to control itself, accused everyone, including themselves, of cowering before "special interests." Moderates, exemplified by people like Pete Peterson, former head of Lehman Brothers investment house and former secretary of commerce, excoriated the existing political system for failing to balance the budget. Whereas the economic conservatives wanted liberty and growth and the egalitarian liberals wanted equality and growth, these social conservatives wanted balanced growth. Their Cassandra cries were heard on radio, television, newspapers, magazines, wherever people listen. And they invoked the public interest over and over as if there was only a single interest and they were the only ones who knew exactly what it was.

Propagated by so many factions for so many different reasons, the antideficit clamor persisted for so long that it took on a life of its own. The deficit became a self-fulfilling crisis. The deficit is a difficulty, I contend, but it is not a disaster next to which all else is insignificant.

When the deficit panic began in 1980, it was supposedly due to the deficit's inflationary effect. Jimmy Carter was excoriated for a proposed deficit of $15.6 billion! When the deficit burgeoned and inflation shrank, however, the panic did not decline accordingly. As Herbert Stein expressed the common syllogism, budget deficits cause bad things, so whatever bad things were happening to us were blamed on deficits. The evolution of its supposed evils, from inflation to recession to strong dollar to weak dollar, and more, suggests that the massive disapproval of deficits was supported by no consistent logic of cause and effect. The cause is constant but the supposed effects keep changing.

Economic arguments about the deficit have been inconsistent. By economic arguments I mean those made in the public sphere of policy debate. When *Time* and *Newsweek* do a cover article on the deficit, or report that a market crash requires deficit reduction, it is part of the process of political debate that shapes notions of how to manage the economy. Since that debate is a process of persuasion, even otherwise trustworthy economists sometimes shade their arguments for effect in order to push the policy they desire. Excessive condemnation of the deficit proceeded, in part, from such experts putting matters too strongly for fear of otherwise being ignored by politicians, or in order to counter the minority of economists who dismissed the deficit's importance. Where the press presents majority economic wisdom, the schools of economists make arguments that fit into wider politico-economic agendas.

Skepticism on the effects of deficits is well-expressed in Guess and Koford's study of Organisation of Economic Co-operation and Development (OECD) countries:

> The U.S. results, taken by themselves, imply that deficits do not cause, but are themselves caused by inflation and reduced national product. If the United States continues to enjoy rapid economic growth and reduced inflation, we expect that the budget deficits should shrink from current projections. However, the broader seventeen-country results show that any definite relationship is difficult to pinpoint. We conclude that the macroeconomic harmfulness of budget deficits has not been shown, certainly for deficits within historical experience."[13]

Although the deficit need not cause inflation or recession, a weak dollar or a strong dollar, reasons for concern remain. A deficit feeds the interest costs of the federal government. More and more of the federal dollar goes to debt service. From an economically conservative point of view, this may be desirable. From an economically liberal view, this restriction is doubly undesirable: Debt creates economic opportunities for the well-off and limits new social programs for poor people. Many Democrats have been concerned that the deficit crowds out social program initiatives, now and in the future. Giving up programs now, however, for programs they might not get later surely seems to them like a bad bargain. Their ideal is higher revenues without reductions in their favored domestic programs.

A second argument says the budget must be balanced, or more, so as to increase national savings. Productivity has grown slowly; more productivity requires more investment; investment requires more savings; the United States saves less than its major competitors, particularly Japan; government deficits, by definition, reduce national savings; since our growth was too slow even before the era of big deficits, we therefore have to raise savings above the level of that time. Therefore, the federal government needs to bring its budget into balance or even surplus.

This savings argument has become the major reason academic economists object to the deficit. Savings, surely, is a Good Thing (though at other times it has appeared too much of a Good Thing), but I have a few questions. If investment is so strongly related to productivity growth, why did growth decrease steadily through the 1970s, while investment remained steady? Growth is a long-term problem, not a short-term crisis: Why is it to be treated as requiring immediate drastic changes in the entire federal government rather than a slow movement toward less consumption and more investment throughout our economy? That would require attention to the composition of outlays, the type of taxes, and many other complicated matters. Would it be morally right for government to force individuals to save more? The counterargument goes that it is precisely because we

---

[13]George Guess and Kenneth Koford, "Inflation, Recession and the Federal Budget Deficit (or, Blaming Economic Problems on a Statistical Mirage)," *Policy Sciences,* Vol. 17 (1984), pp. 385–402; quote on p. 400.

seem unable to shift the long-term pattern of individual saving that the net dis-saving of the federal government (that is, the deficit) becomes so important. Could a fall-off in savings be due to other factors, such as changes in the life cycle (e.g., baby boomers spending more on education, housing, and children, there-fore temporarily saving less)? Could it be that Americans only appear to be saving less because equity in mortgages and a significant part of pensions are not counted as savings?

It bothers some people to discover foreigners are taking up the slack and in-vesting more in the United States. I consider that an act of confidence. Now if there were capital flight, that would be a reason to worry. Why does it matter to us where the money comes from? In the nineteenth century, a great deal of develop-ment in the United States took place with foreign money. Why shouldn't they share our risks?

Even if all other things are not quite equal, I would like the nation's invest-ment to increase. That is a very long-term concern; it makes little difference whether the budget reaches some desired state in five or eight or ten years. The savings argument therefore does not justify a demand that the federal budget be balanced soon. It does argue for lower deficits, while telling us little about how much lower, how quickly.

The argument that the deficit must be reduced to guarantee market confi-dence is ubiquitous. Yet it presumes falsely that we can both know and influence what the financial markets "expect." Certainly we cannot assume that markets think (if they do) like an economist. For example, the dollar's steady increase in Reagan's first term cannot simply be ascribed to high U.S. interest rates. The United States was running high trade deficits, exchanging paper for goods, which ought to produce a countervailing trend for the paper (the dollar) to depreciate. If large budget and trade deficits increase the value of a currency, the dollar should have been riding high, which it was not. Perhaps investors put their money where they trust the government. They fled the franc when Socialist François Mitterand was elected president of France, then bought dollars when America was governed by the hypercapitalist Reagan. This may be rational, but has nothing to do with in-flation, interest rates, or other measurable variables.

Nobody knows why markets, whether in stocks or bonds or currencies or hog bellies, go in any particular direction, at any time. If they did, they would be rich. There are tendencies and explanations that look obvious in retrospect, but markets are panicky, neurotic, swayed by a million forces we don't understand, and thus unpredictable. And they don't behave the way their "experts" claim.

Market gurus told the politicians in 1980 that a $15 billion deficit would cre-ate hyperinflation; then when the government ran deficits of more than that per month, the markets threw a massive party (the stock market boom), but kept claiming the deficit was terrible. Would you have much confidence in such ex-perts' judgment?

Economists are hardly alone in thinking politicians have not done enough about the deficit. In giving talks on the deficit, I ask the audience whether they be-lieve Congress and the president have done a little, a fair amount, or a lot to re-duce the deficit. In every instance an overwhelming proportion signifies that the politicians have done very little. The audience mistakes the apparent lack of progress in reducing the deficit, especially to balance the budget, for failure to take corrective action. Not true.

As Rodney Dangerfield gets no respect, politicians neither get nor give themselves credit. From 1982 on, Congress gored a series of special interests, ranging from doctors to defense contractors. You don't take on the American Medical Association (freezing physician payments on medicare), or Wall Street (many of the provisions of the 1984 tax bill), or the armed services and arms makers (cutting defense in the past six years), unless you really care about the deficit. Through 1986, according to the most careful analysis of policy changes, the politicians had reduced the fiscal year 1986 deficit by an estimated $162 billion, or 3.9 percent of gross national product, from what it would have been if past policies had been left in place.[14] Why, then, did these efforts not show up in absolutely smaller deficits?

Perhaps these analyses give Congress a bit too much credit. Policy in 1981 included a projected defense buildup of 7 percent real growth per year. You can save a lot of money by scaling down such an increase; it hurts less than cutting from what people already have. Yet the defense buildup was stopped because moderate Republicans and conservative Democrats who supported it in 1980 and 1981 decided that reducing the deficit was more important. (No one then imagined that the cold war would be won, thus allowing even bigger cuts in 1990.) Nevertheless, despite persistent and positive congressional efforts, the deficit did not decline.

Unfortunately for our politicians, the deficit problem was too big, always bigger than it seemed. Going back through summaries of each year's efforts, we can see Congress swimming upstream. Each year's policy change was balanced by revisions in the economic assumptions, namely, worse than projected, so the deficit kept ending up around $200 billion. Since they were not getting anywhere, politicians came to believe they were not doing anything.

Dealing with the huge budget shortfall was made even more difficult by political dissensus. Many of us can think of ways to reduce the deficit substantially. So could any legislator. Yet the problem of budgeting is not for any one of us to create a budget alone but to do it together. Assembling a majority behind any scheme is difficult because anything substantial we do will change the size, shape, and role in society of our government. You might say that the participants in budgeting agree on everything except how much revenue should be raised and who should pay, how much should be spent and on which programs. The budget is about the future shape of government and society, not just balance; balance at low or high levels of spending would make a difference for our future.

Politicians could not balance the budget because the policy costs of doing so would have been huge. Before the costs of the savings and loan bailout ballooned, making the task obviously impossible, Joseph White and I asked what kind of deficit reduction in the first year of a new government, elected in 1988, would give a balanced budget, as Gramm–Rudman promised, by fiscal year 1992? Allowing for complexities of implementation, we estimated that the new government could

---

[14]Joseph J. Minarik and Rudolph G. Penner, "Fiscal Choices," in Isabel V. Sawhill, ed., *Challenge to Leadership* (Washington, D.C.: Urban Institute, 1988), pp. 279–316; John Palmer did his calculations for "Should We Worry About the Deficit?" by John Palmer and Stephanie Gould, *The Washington Monthly,* May 1986, pp. 43–46.

meet the Gramm–Rudman target if it changed policy by $100 billion on taking office. How much is that in policy terms?

One hundred billion dollars roughly equals the U.S. Navy. Not a smaller Navy but no Navy. One hundred billion dollars is larger than medicaid, the Department of Education, National Institutes of Health (including cancer and AIDS research), Department of Justice, Department of State, and Federal Highway Administration combined. That is the scale of policy change—no Navy or any six domestic departments of your choice—required to eliminate the deficit through spending cuts.

How could we have found over $100 billion from taxes? Individual income taxes would have to be raised by 21 percent, almost completely reversing the 1981 tax cut. Or we could have raised individual income taxes by 10 percent, corporate taxes by 20 percent, and doubled excise taxes. Even the most dedicated fan of the public sector can imagine the political difficulty of such tax hikes. Instead one might try a "balanced" package, say raising income taxes by 10 percent, cutting the Navy 20 percent (pick a fleet!), and abolishing medicaid. That sounds no easier.

Even more narrow options for deficit reduction had difficulties: Small does not mean harmless. For example, determining eligibility or benefit levels for Aid to Dependent Children and food stamps by counting as income payments under the Low-Income Home Energy Assistance program (LIHEAP) would have saved $225 million in Fiscal Year 1990. It would have eliminated duplication as well as a situation in which some recipients of LIHEAP were better off monetarily than non-recipients who actually earned more. But the change would have penalized families whose energy bills were particularly high, exactly the large families the program was supposed to help. What were they to do, shower in the dark? Move south?

These examples should put common calls for "tough choices" in perspective. Choices are tough because the consequences either way are unpalatable. Often people hide these choices by talking about cutting the deficit in stages: $30 billion one year, $20 billion the next year, and so on. It may well be desirable to cut spending incrementally, but that does not change the huge amounts of reductions required to approach a balanced budget. Cutting in stages doesn't change the policy stakes. Indeed, what you would have to do if you did it all at once is the smallest measure of the stakes, for that approach would maximize the savings from lower interest payments. There is no "free lunch" of harmless deficit reductions. Politicians who do not want to slash medicaid or education or infrastructure or defense, or raise income taxes by more than they have ever been raised in peacetime are not showing a lack of courage; they are making a reasonable choice about the national interest.

Budgeting is a process of discovering and enforcing preferences. The most basic difficulty is matching preferences about programs and totals. In the 1980s, panic about the deficit led both elites and the public to claim a breakdown of governance, because the total, the deficit, was too big. Yet it is fair to argue that, facing tough choices, Congress and the president have bargained responsibly, balancing the costs and benefits of both lower deficits and the policy choices to get there. The macroeconomic logic of balancing the budget is, at best, confused; balancing the budget would have serious policy costs. These costs are not simply "politics" or "special interests." Social security is in the special interest of the elderly; the Navy is in the special interest of the people who serve in and sell to it. They are also policies that define the nation; a nation that at least tries to guarantee to all citizens a financially decent old age, and one that is served by cutting such programs to eliminate the deficit is an open question. Politics is about debating such questions, not assuming they have only one answer.

Looking at the deficit as a policy problem like any other, the following conclusions seem reasonable:

1. There is no economic necessity to balance a budget. Mainstream economics provides no reason why deficits of 2–3 percent of GNP should cause panic, and smaller deficits, say 1 percent of GNP, are surely acceptable.[15]

2. Deficits persist not because of a lack of political "courage" but because politicians and the public judge, correctly, that serious efforts to reduce them—whether tax hikes or cuts in domestic or defense spending—themselves have serious consequences for the general welfare.

If citizens were to look at the federal government's actual accomplishments in holding down the size of the deficit, they might be optimistic about further progress. Were these same citizens to look at the ideological divisions over how to reduce the deficit, they might well be more pessimistic. But by the mid-1990s, the fervor to balance the budget had reached fever heights, and balancing the budget became a vehicle for an agenda to reverse the role of the federal government.

In April 1994, a group of experts on the federal budget gathered at the University of Virginia to discuss the current budgetary situation. Although the deficit naturally figured prominently in their discussions, there was virtually no hint of the imminence of radical and concerted action to balance the budget.[16] Yet warning signals had been apparent for some time. Nearly two years earlier, the comptroller general of the United States had testified on the necessity of prompt action to balance the budget, preferably by 2001, or to create a budget surplus by 2005. He predicted "an explosion of federal spending" related to demographic trends and the continuation of current policies, projecting deficits of as much as 20 percent of GDP by 2020 if no action were taken. [17]

Similarly, the deficit was not central to Bill Clinton's electoral campaign in 1992, but he quickly felt the pressure for deficit reduction. In his State of the Union address, Clinton declared that while there was nothing intrinsically good about deficit reduction alone, it was necessary to reverse the trend toward a government that was unable to act because the burden of debt servicing prevented development of programs to help people.[18] Backed by the deficit hawks in his ad-

---

[15]See James Savage, "Deficits and the Economy: The Case of the Clinton Administration and Interest Rates," in Naomi Caiden and Joseph White, eds., *Budgeting, Policy, Politics: An Appreciation of Aaron Wildavsky* (New Brunswick N.J.: Transaction, Inc., 1995), p. 97.

[16]James Savage, ed., "Symposium: President Clinton's Budget and Fiscal Policy: An Evaluation Two Budgets Later," *Public Budgeting and Finance,* Vol. 14, No. 3 (Fall 1994), pp. 3–40.

[17]Statement of Charles A. Bowsher, "Budget Policy: Long-Term Implications of the Deficit," Testimony before the Subcommittee on Deficits, Debt Management, and International Debt of the Senate Finance Committee, June 5 1992, p. 1 (GAO/T-OCG-92-4).

[18]Pat Towell, "Clinton Outlines His Priorities, Economy Chief Among Them," *Congressional Quarterly Weekly Report,* November 14, 1992, p. 3631.

ministration, though with less than wholehearted support from the Democratic party, Clinton's first budget focused on deficit reduction. But his narrow victory for nearly half a trillion in deficit reduction over five years was already being overshadowed by much more radical calls for action.

The founding of the Concorde Coalition by Paul Tsongas (previously a contender for the Democratic presidential nomination) and Walter Rudman (of Gramm–Rudman–Hollings) marked the beginning of a concerted campaign for an agenda—in which budget balance would provide the driving power for cutting federal domestic expenditures, returning power to the states, dismantling business and environmental regulations, cutting taxes, and reforming welfare programs. The movement culminated in the Contract With America, whose first provision was "to restore fiscal responsibility to an out-of-control Congress, requiring them to live under the same budget constraints as families and businesses." The Contract would "require the federal budget to be balanced by 2002 or seven years after enactment, whichever is later."[19]

The Republican victory in the November 1994 elections was widely interpreted as a mandate for the Contract program, although polls showed only about a quarter of the electorate had even heard of it let alone read it.[20] But the polls also showed that a majority of Americans felt that balancing the budget was an important, and maybe the most important, thing to do. Why?

In times of confusion and rapid transformation, people feel threatened by changes they do not understand and often do not like. The federal deficit seemed a symbol of all that was wrong, and something had to be done. The title of Peter Peterson's book, *Facing Up: How To Rescue the Economy from Crushing Debt and Restore the American Dream*, captured the mood of the times.[21]

The picture seemed gloomy. In January 1992, Congressional Budget Office (CBO) and Office of Management and Budget (OMB) were forecasting unprecedented annual deficits between $350 billion and $400 billion for the foreseeable future. The Fiscal Year 1992 deficit peaked at $290 billion,[22] and critics pointed to long-term projections that showed rising deficits toward the turn of the century, if nothing were done. The comptroller and auditor general, for example, reiterated that "Left unchecked through 2025, growing deficits would result in collapsing investment, a declining capital stock, and, inevitably, a declining economy."[23] Armageddon, it seemed, was just around the corner.

But between 1992 and 1995, the deficit, belying predictions, actually *declined* from over 4 percent of GDP to 2.7 percent, and was projected to drop to 2 percent

---

[19] "Republicans' Initial Promise: 100-Day Debate on Contract," *Congressional Quarterly Weekly Report*, November 12, 1994, p. 3216.

[20] "Results of the 1994 Congressional Elections," *Government in America Newsletter*, Harper Collins, Spring 1995, p. 4.

[21] Peter Peterson, *Facing Up: How To Rescue the Economy from Crushing Debt and Rescue the American Dream* (New York: Simon and Schuster, 1993).

[22] Roy Meyers, "Federal Budgeting and Finance in 1991: The Future is Now," *Public Budgeting and Finance*, Vol. 12, No.2 (Summer 1992), pp. 4–5; Congressional Budget Office, *The Economic and Budget Outlook: Fiscal Years 1993–1997*, 1992, p. xv.

[23] General Accounting Office, *The Deficit and the Economy: An Update of Long-Term Simulations*, April 1995, p. 41 (GAO/AIMD/OCE-95-119).

by 2000 (see Table 6.3 and Table 6.4). By the beginning of 1994, according to OECD figures, the U.S. deficit was the smallest of the major industrial economies.[24] Clinton's 1996 budget endorsed the position that budget deficits of 3 percent or less were sustainable, setting deficits at about 2 percent for the rest of the century. Further, the doomsday scenario rested on the assumption "if nothing were done"; it was unlikely that nothing would be done. There was little reason to believe that the budget, if not balanced, was out of control, and an immediate and future threat to economic well-being, as the conventional wisdom had rapidly come to accept.

Nonetheless, the move to balance the budget had become irresistible. While the Contract With America provided no specifics on how to balance the budget, a much blunter message was expressed in a fiscal manifesto set out by the Heritage Foundation, which claimed credit for key elements of the Republican program. In "Rolling Back Government: A Budget Plan to Rebuild America," budget balancing was the motive force for a radical overhaul of federal government policy in accordance with a coherent philosophy, reflecting faith in market economics and individual choice.[25] A threefold strategy embraced tax cuts, privatization of federal government activities, and devolution of functions to the states. To these were added defense buildup and anticrime policies as well as deregulation.

"If wishes were horses," says the old proverb, "then beggars would ride." The horse of budget balance was carrying a good deal of baggage. Balancing the budget appealed to many parts of the political spectrum—witness the close votes on a constitutional amendment to do just that. The issue was whether the budget balancing agenda would carry along with it the ideological agenda, or whether those supporting budget balance even realized it was being used to further ideological purposes.

As the race horse of budget balance slowed in the 1995 budget process, it came to resemble more a carthorse dragging along a much less coherent load. (See Chapter 7.) Ideological items were piled on top of those with real budgetary significance; programs were slashed or retained according to political, rather than economic criteria; and in an effort to make budget balance feasible, it was necessary to add in the major categories of medicare and medicaid. But the direction of the route was not in doubt: As the means for budget balance became more and more restricted (no tax increases, no change in social security, more untouchable areas of the budget), what remained was essentially those programs that served the weakest members of society.

Yet somehow, budget balance and even budget surpluses were achieved, in a relatively short time and with remarkably little trauma. What happened to achieve what only a short time ago was considered impossible, and why?

THE DISAPPEARING DEFICIT

Deficits had become such an enduring feature of federal budgeting that the sudden emergence of surpluses was at first difficult to grasp. As late as March 1997, the CBO was predicting high deficits as far as the eye could see (see Table 11.1).

---

[24]*The Economist,* February 12, 1994, p. 73.

[25]*Los Angeles Times,* April 28, 1995, p. A17.

Table 11.1   Surpluses into the Future

	Forecasts for Deficits and Surpluses 1995–1999								
	1996	1997	1998	1999	2000	2001	2002	2005	2009
December 1995	172	182	183	195	204	211	228	294	
March 1996	144	165	175	182	191	194	210	265	
May 1996	144	171	194	219	244	259	285	376	
January 1997	107	124	120	147	171	167	188	254	
March 1997		115	122	149	172	167	188	255	
September 1997		34	57	52	48	36	+32	+36	
January 1998			5	2	3	+14	+69	+75	
August 1998				+80	+79	+86	+139	+170	
January 1999				+107	+131	+151	+209	+256	
April 1999				+111	+133	+156	+212	+263	+383
July 1999				+120	+161	+193	+246	+286	+413

Source: Congressional Budget Office, *Economic and Budget Outlook, 1995–1999.*

Barely nine months later, the dragon, it seemed, had been slain, and in July 1999, CBO was projecting "a sustained period of rising surpluses"[26] in time for the new millennium.

What happened and why? The surplus first showed up in the actual figures for 1998 at about $70 billion; it was expected to double the following year. Table 11.1 shows how quickly the situation changed: in 1995, CBO was predicting the Fiscal Year 1998 deficit at $183 billion; by the beginning of 1998, its deficit projection was down to $5 billion. Even in the same fiscal year, it did not predict the emerging surplus. But from August 1998 on, the figures were all on the plus side. Even in the short period between January and July 1999, CBO was revising its figures upward—by $10 billion for 1999 and $30 billion a year after that.[27] The July 1999 estimates predicted a $413 billion surplus for 2009, so that cumulative surpluses for the decade (if the predictions were correct) would aggregate to over $3 trillion.

Nearly two-thirds of the projected deficit reduction was attributed to increases in revenues,[28] which consistently outstripped predictions. Between 1992 and 1996, revenues grew 33 percent, from 17.7 percent of GDP to 19.4 percent.[29] Two years later, they had risen to 20.5 percent and were expected to stay at that level, or somewhat below, for at least the next decade. This high and persistent growth derived primarily from the economic boom of the 1990s, but also from changes in the tax code: Taxes had been increased in 1993, and the 1997 tax cuts were largely offset by other revenue increases. Rapid growth in capital gains realizations from a booming stock market and increases in taxable income pushed up individual income tax and corporate tax receipts.[30] Tax revenue growth outstripped economic growth for five years running, to reach an unprecedented and unexpected level.

---

[26]Congressional Budget Office, *The Economic and Budgetary Outlook: An Update.* July 1999, p. 1.

[27]Congressional Budget Office, *The Economic and Budget Outlook: An Update*, July 1999, p. 2.

[28]Congressional Budget Outlook, *Economic and Budget Outlook, 1998–2008*, January 1998, p. 38.

[29]Congressional Budget Office, *Economic and Budget Outlook 1998–2007*, January 1997, p. 33.

[30]Ibid.

On the other side of the budget, outlays for 1999 were projected at 19.2 percent of GDP, while revenues would be at a post-World War II high of 20.6 percent: that 1.4 percent of GDP represented the surplus. Whereas revenues, if no further action were taken, would remain high, outlays were projected to decline to nearly 17 percent, so that the gap would widen. As time went on, a beneficent spiral would appear, as the bill for net interest (which had been about $200 billion at the beginning of the 1990s and forecast to increase[31]) would steadily decline from about 3 percent of GDP in 1997 to only 1.5 percent of GDP. Debt held by the public would decline from over 47 percent of GDP to less than 25 percent in 2008.[32]

Where did the outlay savings come from? One possibility was entitlements. The beginning of the decade had been marked by explosive growth in major entitlements, which doubled between 1986 and 1996, exceeding economic growth and inflation. Rising case loads, automatic increases through indexed cost of living adjustments, higher beneficiary utilization, excessive inflation in medical prices, higher income levels pushing benefits higher for social security benefits, and state actions to increase federal reimbursements all contributed to the rise.[33] At its peak years (1990–1992), medicaid was growing at 20–30 percent a year. By 1997, mandatory spending, which had been only about 6 percent of GDP in 1962, was over 11 percent,[34] and made up over half of federal budget outlays.[35] There was alarm that if current trends persisted, mandatory expenditures, particularly medicare and medicaid, would place unacceptable pressures on the budget even in the next few years. In the longer outlook, there was much talk of crisis, particularly in social security and the health programs. The 1997 Budget Agreement, like earlier summits in 1990 and 1993, tried to rein in entitlements by cutting provider payments and encouraging managed care solutions.

Meanwhile, earlier dire projections were not fulfilled. The previous explosive growth in medicare and medicaid (48 percent and 36 percent respectively from 1992–1996) had not been matched by other programs, which had grown on average only 2.5 percent.[36] In 1996, medicaid grew only 3 percent and in 1997, 4 percent; medicare grew 8 percent in 1996 and 9 percent in 1997; social security and food stamps payments actually dropped in those years.[37] In consequence, projections for entitlements were revised downward, cutting expected future expenditures.

The remainder would have to come from discretionary spending. The 1997 Balanced Budget Act extended existing caps on discretionary spending up to 2002, which would require expenditures to be at 10 percent less than projected inflation or to grow by only $3 billion over the period. Discretionary spending had

[31]Congressional Budget Office, *Economic and Budget Outlook, 1997–2006,* January 1996, p. 51.

[32]Congressional Budget Office, *Economic and Budget Outlook, 1999–2008,* January 1998, p. 43.

[33]Congressional Budget Office, *Economic and Budget Outlook 1997–2006,* January 1996, p. 47.

[34]Congressional Budget Office, *Economic and Budget Outlook, 1998–2007,* January 1997, p. xxi.

[35]Congressional Budget Office, *Economic and Budget Outlook, 1998–2008,* January 1998, p. 69.

[36]Congressional Budget Office, *Economic and Budget Outlook, 1998–2007,* January 1997, p. 33.

[37]Ibid., pp. 25–6.

been squeezed for several years. In 1966, it represented 12 percent of GDP; 20 years later it had dropped to 10 percent; and in 1997 it was just below 7 percent.[38] Deficit reduction has concentrated on discretionary spending. According to Robert Reischauer, the deficit reduction packages of 1990 and 1993 took 45 percent and 18 percent of their savings from discretionary expenditures respectively.[39] Between 1991 and 1998, total discretionary outlays rose only 4 percent, a decline of 13 percent in real terms.[40] Increases in domestic spending were offset by cuts in defense: defense dropped in "real" (inflation-adjusted) terms by 28 percent from 1990 to 1996, while the domestic discretionary part of the budget actually grew by 15 percent.[41] These results were achieved by caps on discretionary spending that set overall limits at near freeze, forcing decisions on cuts in annual appropriations.

It was estimated that the current caps would require a 20 percent decrease in discretionary spending in real terms over the next 10 years,[42] or a nearly $600 billion reduction below the baseline.[43] If, as is likely, defense expenditures rise, the cuts in domestic discretionary expenditures would need to be even more.

The projected surpluses, of course, are purely a construct of models that simulate the dynamic interactions of macroeconomic variables such as economic growth, inflation, employment, incomes, profits, and interest rates in the future. The predictions are highly uncertain and reflect assumptions about the future behavior of a global economy and its impact upon the United States as well as the cumulative results of millions of decisions made by individuals, corporations, government bodies of all kinds, and nonprofit entities. The projections also do not take into account possible wars, disasters, effects of global weather changes, mass movements of population, changes of regime, or technological breakthroughs. We have already seen how quickly the doom and gloom of deficit forecasts were transformed into the sunny optimism of surplus expectations.

The validity of the models and forecasts is open to question, but beyond the scope of the present discussion.[44] After all, some prophecies do sometimes come true, even if others turn out to be science fiction. What is important here is that people want the surplus scenario to be plausible and thus "the surplus" has already taken on a life of its own. "The surplus" is no longer just an immediate reality but

---

[38]Congressional Budget Office, *Economic and Budget Outlook 1999–2008*, January 1998, p. xxi.

[39]Robert D. Reischauer, "The Unfulfillable Promise: Cutting Nondefense Discretionary Spending," in Robert Reischauer ed., *Setting National Priorities*, (Washington, D.C.: Brookings Institution, 1997) p. 123.

[40]Congressional Budget Office, *Economic and Budget Outlook 2000–2009*, January 1999, p. 32.

[41]Ibid., p. 124.

[42]"The Surplus Illusion," *Washington Post National Weekly Edition*, July 12, 1999, p. 24.

[43]General Accounting Office, *Federal Budget: The President's Midsession Review, Observations of David M. Walker, Comptroller General of the United States,* (undated) (GAO/OCG/-99-29).

[44]Relatively cautious optimism has been expressed by such noted experts as Henry Aaron (*Washington Post National Weekly Edition*, March 23, 1998, p. 19), Herbert Stein (*Wall Street Journal*, May 19, 1998), Alan Blinder (*The NewRepublic*, August 9, 1999, p. 26), and Robert Samuelson, (*Washington Post National Weekly Edition*, February 1, 1999, p. 26). However, they all warn of the notorious unreliability of long-term forecasts.

an enduring assumption of budgeting. The surplus, no less than the previous deficit, furnishes the vocabulary, justifications, and issues of the time. The new paradigm is compelling because it opens up a cornucopia to a public weary of constant exhortations to thrift and warnings of a dire future. That huge budget surplus stands as an affirmation of the ultimate strength and security of the United States in a troubled and unpredictable world.

It might have been thought that with the deficit vanquished, all might be peace and tranquillity as politicians, economists, and others enjoyed the new experience of debating what to do with the surplus. In fact, the levels of conflict and vituperation rose to new heights, although (as in professional wrestling) much of the action was to make an impression on the audience, rather than serious stuff. The politics of the surplus seemed no less difficult than the politics of the deficit. Why?

To begin with, the surplus apparently was not what it seemed. Dissected, it revealed two elements: an "on-budget" surplus and an "off-budget" surplus. Taken together, they formed the unified budget surplus, but as Table 11.2 shows, the majority of that figure was made up by the "off-budget" surplus, that is, mostly social security. Once the surplus on the social security account was deducted, the estimate for the immediate surplus, say for the year 2000, shrank to a mere $14 billion. However, over the next decade, the cumulative "on-budget" surpluses were expected to amount to nearly $1 trillion (compared with over $2 trillion for the "off-budget" surplus).[45] So why should this matter?

Again, things matter because people want them to matter. In what Henry Aaron has called "the great budget Kabuki play,"[46] budget makers on both sides of

Table 11.2   The Disappearance of the Deficit

	Federal Deficits and Surpluses 1992–1998 With Estimates for 1999–2009		
	On-Budget Deficit/Surplus	Social Security Surplus	Total Deficit/Surplus
1992	–340.5	50.7	–290.4
1993	–300.4	46.8	–255.1
1994	–258.8	56.8	–203.1
1995	–226.3	60.4	–163.9
1996	–174.0	66.4	–107.4
1997	–103.3	81.3	–22.0
1998	–29.2	99.0	+69.0
1999	–4.0	125.0	+120.0
2000	–14.0	147.0	+161.0
2009	+178	235.0	+413.0

Note: Both the social security and the post office balances are added into the total deficit figures, but the post office figure is very slight and so has been omitted.

Sources: Congressional Budget Office, Economic and Budget Outlook, 2000–2009, January 1999 p. 28 and Update July 1999 p. 14.

---

[45]Congressional Budget Office, Economic and Budget Outlook: An Update, July 1999, p. 2.

[46]Henry Aaron, "Great Pretenders," Washington Post National Weekly Edition, November 15, 1999, p. 26.

the political arena took a righteous pledge not to count "the social security surplus" in their calculations. President Clinton's vow to "save social security first" (through a convoluted scheme that defied comprehension) was quickly followed by the Republican leadership, which not to be outdone, swore it would "stop the raids on social security." All this, despite decades of offsetting deficits against social security trust fund surpluses. Economists, too, have repeatedly assured us that spending these surpluses now would have absolutely no bearing on the state of the fund in the future (although it is hard to understand why that should be so). (See Chapter 8.)

Before we ask why politicians thought it necessary to rework the arithmetic of budgeting in this way, we need to look at the implications. The short-term effect was to shave the surplus razor thin (see Table 11.2), which made its existence almost entirely dependent on the continued enforcement of the caps set out in the 1997 Balanced Budget Act. On one estimate, domestic discretionary expenditures would need to be cut by a quarter between 1998 and 2002 if the caps were maintained and defense spending rose.[47] But if the surplus depends on the caps, and the caps are unrealistic in the cuts they require in domestic discretionary spending, one of two things is likely to happen. First, the surplus will be maintained only at the cost of enormous pressure on domestic discretionary spending. Or second, a variety of gimmicks and charades will be used to disguise the breach in the caps. Why should anyone practice austerity in a time of alleged affluence?

Why, anyway, should politicians be so keen to minimize the surplus (at least in the short term) and actually precipitate cuts in discretionary spending that they don't really want? Why act as though there is a deficit when there is a surplus? Both parties want to show they are responsible, and to "protect" social security, without actually doing anything about it (for example, raising revenues or cutting benefits). Republicans wanted the projected surpluses so they could justify big tax cuts, meanwhile using the caps to keep down government spending. Put this way, cuts in discretionary domestic spending would pay for the tax cuts. Democrats were willing to play some of this game because they too had to provide some tax cuts, and wanted to avoid the label of tax and spend and to preserve the balanced budget agreement.

All this shadow boxing and finger pointing, of course, avoids the real issues. Robert Samuelson has done the math. The current cost of social security, medicare, and medicaid is about 8 percent of GDP, other programs cost about 9 percent, while net interest totals to another 3 percent, adding up to a total bill of about 20 percent. By 2020, the three big entitlements are projected to take up 13 percent of GDP, an increase of 5 percent. Even allowing for some unreliability in predictions, where will this come from? Either "other programs" will need to be cut as much as 50 percent or there would need to be an increase in federal taxation of about 25 percent.[48]

Suddenly, the optimistic scenario seems less optimistic, or rather less straightforward. Does the surplus really exist? There is undoubtedly a current surplus in the social security trust fund, and there are long-term estimates of how long that

---

[47]Robert Reischauer, "The Phantom Surplus," *New York Times*, January 28, 2000, p. A27.

[48]Robert Samuelson, "Surpluses in the Sky," *Washington Post National Weekly Edition*, February 1, 1999, p. 26.

will last if no policy action is taken (see Chapter 8). At issue is the "on-budget" surplus, estimated at $1 trillion over the next 10 years. The problem of accuracy in even short-term projections has already been discussed. Even a small change in figures, the Congressional Budget Office warns, can change budget projections by as much as $100 billion in one year.[49] If taxes and spending were mispredicted by only 2 percent each in different directions, these tiny mistakes would result in a $70 billion change in budget balance.[50] Predictions for 10 or 15 years ahead, particularly where these are cumulated into a single figure, would seem a very fragile basis for making long-term and expensive decisions.

Whereas the deficit was regarded as "structural" in nature, we do not know if the same is true of the surplus. If the current boom is not maintained, revenues would again fall and expenditures rise. The structural elements that we know about—such as the retirement of the baby boomers and the adverse dependency ratio, the widening gap between rich and poor—are far less favorable. It may also be unrealistic to view the United States as an island of prosperity floating in a sea of increasingly troubled and volatile economies from which it is mysteriously isolated. A recent headline, "Overseas Revival Could Threaten US Economy," succinctly and ironically emphasized the vulnerability of present expectations.[51]

There is also the question of the surplus itself. To Republicans that trillion dollars represents an opportunity for a tax cut, on the argument that taxes now stand at an unprecedented high level. For over 25 years, revenues had usually been about 18 percent of GDP, and exceptions (such as the Vietnam War and inflationary period at the beginning of the 1980s) had been short-lived.[52] The extra 2 percent or so of revenues was an irresistible attraction, even though economists warned that proposals were regressive (since the rich paid more taxes they would get most of the returns), that they would overstimulate the economy (and so result in higher interest rates—a poor tradeoff), and that they could not easily be corrected if the surplus projections turned out wrong. On the other side, there was no lack of proposals to spend the surplus—to increase medicare benefits, to extend health insurance, to improve education, increase defense, and a variety of other good things. Nor were the party lines clear-cut: Both tax cuts and spending were on the agendas of the major candidates in the 2000 election.[53]

Any of these proposals might reduce or eliminate the surplus. The problem is not that wicked politicians scenting a surplus will not rest until it is consumed, or the much maligned and lamented influence of pork barrel spending, but that the realistic long-term costs of government will probably exceed its prospective revenues.[54] These costs were designated in the 1997 Balanced Budget Agreement to

---

[49]Congressional Budget Office, *The Economic and Budget Outlook: An Update,* July 1999, p. 5.

[50]Robert J. Samuelson, "Surpluses in the Sky," *Washington Post National Weekly Edition,* February 1, 1999, p. 26.

[51]*Los Angeles Times,* August 19, 1999, p. A1.

[52]In earlier analysis this figure had been cited at 19 percent; statistical revision accounts for the lower figure, which is used consistently from here on.

[53]"Surplus: Candidates Detail Plans," *Los Angeles Times,* December 13, 1999, pp. A1, 23, 24.

[54]"Spending the Surplus," *Washington Post National Weekly Edition,* January 18, 1999.

decline by about 20 percent in real terms, and this intention was built into subsequent budget assumptions. Given that the current mood is to rebuild some of the previous cuts in defense, domestic appropriations would bear the brunt of the tightened caps and should one category (e.g., highways or agriculture) gain, it would be at the expense of other government operations.[55] There are already signs that such cuts would be unacceptable, and that the caps on discretionary spending, already breached in 1998, will not hold against claims for all kinds of groups and purposes.[56] If keeping discretionary expenditures within the tight limits assumed in the projections for the surplus turns out not to be realistic, and if entitlement predictions are also unreliable, the surplus may very well be an illusion.

There was one other option, which received greater approval from economists, which was to use the surplus (or whatever was left of it) to pay down the national debt. At the beginning of 1999, the debt was $3.7 trillion, equal to about 45 percent of GDP. Paying down the debt would allegedly increase savings and investment, create more jobs, and improve productivity and economic growth.[57] This would also be a way, as the trust fund is currently set up, of somewhat improving the long-term prospects for social security. More practically and less speculatively, debt reduction would mean considerable savings on interest payments. By the end of the year, moreover, the political stalemate, which had frustrated many schemes for disposing of the surplus, by default had made debt reduction the least contentious option—at least for the moment. Yet even this apparently neutral solution involves political choices, relating to current versus future needs.

The lessons of the surplus are not very different from the lessons of the deficit. First, all is not as it seems, and causes and consequences may be more problematic than they initially appear. Second, deficits and surpluses are more than just facts, or even problems, in themselves: They represent opportunities and rationalizations for political agendas on both ends of the spectrum. Third, neither deficits nor surpluses are totally within our control, and may appear and disappear with disconcerting suddenness.

---

[55]"The Surplus Illusion," *Washington Post National Weekly Edition*, July 12, 1999, p. 24.

[56]"A Disintegrating Budget," *Washington Post National Weekly Edition*, August 9, 1999, p. 24.

[57]Richard Stevenson, "The Deficit's Gone, but Not the National Debt," *New York Times*, January 31, 1999, Section 4, p. 4.

Chapter 12

A Budget of Opposites

The end of the twentieth century was a time of opposites. While a minority of the world's population enjoyed unbelievable affluence, millions lived in abysmal poverty. The assets of just 358 billionaires exceeded the combined annual incomes of countries with 45 percent of the world's population—2.3 billion people.[1] Extraordinary technical achievements coexisted with primitive and backbreaking drudgery. The end of the Cold War brought peace, but a peace rent with savage ethnic conflicts. And while democracy flourished as never before, in many places it was undermined by corruption, ignorance, and failure to deliver on promises of better living standards for masses of people.

In the United States, the longest peacetime economic boom in history, together with increased life expectancy, decreasing crime, lower unemployment figures, and improved social indicators, was accompanied by a growing gap between rich and poor.[2] The federal budget process reflected unease, uncertainty, and lack of agreement on what direction to follow. The prospect of huge surpluses danced before the eyes of politicians, yet they were scrabbling for money. Budget processes were powerful enough to direct billions of dollars, as well as control the smallest programs, yet they seemed close to breakdown. Possibly the most democratic and participatory budget process in the world was incomprehensible to the ordinary citizen. The issues seemed clearly defined, yet the parties' positions were blurred by internal divisions and shifting of ground, until the party of spending (Democrats) seemed the party of fiscal responsibility, and the party of conservatism (Republicans) appeared the party of profligacy.

Why these paradoxes? They reflected difficulties in gaining agreement on basic policy issues, arguments taking place on both moral and economic grounds. Primary among them was the relationship between the individual and the collective. Conservatives argued for the moral responsibility of persons for their own

---

[1] Bernardo Kliksberg, "Rethinking the State for Social Development," Paper delivered at the 13th Meeting of Experts, United Nations, 1997 (New York: United Nations, 1997, p. 5 ST/SG/AC.6/1997/L.8).

[2] See George Hager, "While the Rich Get Richer," *Washington Post National Weekly Edition*, September 13, 1999, p. 19.

and their families' lives, as well as for maximum investment in an unfettered economy, whose consequent growth would cure social ills. Liberals argued that left alone the market would not provide adequately for social needs, and that government action was necessary to ensure at least minimum standards of living and equality of opportunity. These positions were manifest in continuing conflicts over the level and distribution of taxation, conflicts that spilled over into policy concerns about intergenerational equity with the graying of the baby boom generation. Further disagreements centered on what might broadly be considered the negative externalities of the market: the extent of environmental protection, limitations on individual and corporate autonomy, protection of domestic markets, federally underwritten research, and education. And defense and foreign policy formed yet another contentious arena in which different views of the role of the United States in a post-Cold War world were fought out.

These conflicts could not be ignored in making decisions about federal budgets. More accurately, the federal budget process has become the institution of choice for policy making about fundamental questions confronting the American people. Because so much of what government does needs revenues, because revenue raising is entangled with questions of distribution of income and the scope of government, because issues of health and old age touch everyone's lives, and because everything competes with everything else, policy making and budgeting seem synonymous.

But budgeting is *not* identical with policy making: It is a particular kind of decision making that imposes its own rules, biases, and institutional constraints on participants. We have become used to making policy through budget processes, at least in part because of the inadequacy of other mechanisms. Many issues end up in the government arena because markets and civil society (voluntary and nonprofit organizations) cannot satisfactorily deal with them. Once these are seen as matters of public concern, many of them gravitate to the budget cycle, rather than regular judicial, legislative, or bureaucratic decision processes.

Obviously, most things that need doing or interests that need satisfying require money, and resources cannot realistically be separated from purposes. Budget processes have other advantages. The basic conflicts that crisscross the budget debates arouse such strong feelings, they are such political hot potatoes, that once-and-for-all resolution is out of the question. The annual reiterations of the budget process allow repeated "bites" at insuperable problems. Such classic incrementalism facilitates compromises, growth of confidence, and gradual adjustment in complex policy areas. The budget process is a learning process in which definitive victory is elusive and the defeated live to fight another day. Changes may also take place almost imperceptibly over a number of years, as certain areas grow at the expense of others, or automatic mechanisms (indexing) or "fiscal dividends" provide "no-hands budgeting" without anyone having to make conscious decisions.

In addition, multiple opportunities for participation and intervention make it relatively easy for issues to reach the policy agenda. Look at all that voting—budget resolutions, authorizations, subappropriations, appropriations, Senate decisions, House decisions, conference reports, floor votes, continuing resolutions, omnibus this-that-and-the-other! In his revealing study of the making of the 1997 budget agreement, Daniel Palazzolo saw budget processes as "a series of adjustments in which individuals and factions in both parties constantly push the boundaries and alter the terms of the original agreement in order to achieve their policy objectives and political goals."[3] What better vehicle for those wishing to influence policies and achieve their agendas?

Conversely, Barbara Sinclair in her insightful book, *Unorthodox Lawmaking*, viewed the budget process as useful because it was a more restricted means of passing measures through Congress, reducing the number of deals that need to be struck, battles that have to be won, and coalitions that have to be built. House and Senate rules limit amendments and debate, while the deadlines of the budget process exert a pressure to action.[4]

But where public policy making is channeled through the budget process, participants have to accept its constraints. Budgetary decision making is bounded by formal procedures that operate within a framework of interacting roles and relationships. As Allen Schick has explained, "What distinguishes budgeting is that resources are claimed and rationed according to rules and procedures established for this purpose. Budgeting is the process that prescribes how, when and by whom, claims are made and resources rationed."[5] There are rules of the game to be mastered, deference to be paid, strategies and tactics to be weighed. Claimants contend with rationers, and in the fierce competition for resources, roles become confused and claimants battle each other—all of this within the compressed time schedule of the annual budget cycle. Even where commitments, especially those for entitlements, are multiyear in nature, discourse is annual: The budget equation must be solved—even though temporarily, unsatisfactorily, or late—within the annual cycle.

Using the budget process to make policy thus exerts a cost. Beyond the constraints of process, policy makers accept the framing of issues in budget terms. The substance of the issue becomes the substance of the budget and is drawn into the eternal competition for scarce resources. Budgetary norms of balance, control, planning, transparency, and comprehensive decision making confront other agreed or contended values such as defense, health, education, equity, or security. (Of course, there are exceptions where totally extraneous "riders" are attached to budget measures, and money issues are not involved at all.) The results are policies made piecemeal, fragmented by budgetary pressures, mere stopping places in the ongoing struggle for resources.

It would be surprising if budget processes and institutions had remained unchanged by the policy agendas thrust upon them—to eliminate the deficit, to cut taxes, to "save" social security, to rein in health programs, to "reinvent" government. This book has chronicled the development of the federal budget process as processes and policies have interacted and institutions have adapted. Now it is time to take stock and to ask how the federal budget stands.

---

[3]Daniel J. Palazzolo, *Done Deal? The Politics of the 1997 Budget Agreement,* (New York: Chatham House, 1999), p. 10.

[4]Barbara Sinclair, *Unorthodox Lawmaking: New Legislative Processes in the U.S. Congress* (Washington D.C.: CQ Press, 1997), pp. 151–52.

[5]Allen Schick, *The Capacity to Budget,* (Washington, D.C.: Urban Institute Press, 1990), p. 10.

THE BUDGET PROCESS

The budget process at the end of the 1990s presented to the ordinary citizen a seemingly impenetrable tangle of rules and procedures. Yet the process in outline is not difficult to follow, and the reader seeking a definitive guide need look no further than Allen Schick's *The Federal Budget: Politics, Policy, Process*.[6] This brief explanation of how the budget process has fared in the past five years does not attempt to substitute for that work or others like it, but to summarize the roles of the primary budget institutions and processes and how they fit together.

Any account of the formal budget process would be incomplete and misleading without an understanding of budgetary politics. In the budget battles of 1995, partisanship had reached a peak, and confrontations between the Republican Congress and Democratic president continued. The conflicts had also intensified divisions within the parties. There was a deep split between moderate Republicans concerned with balancing the budget, avoiding damaging confrontations, and reassuring the electorate on the retention of popular programs, and those who were determined to continue the revolutionary program by whatever means necessary. Democrats were split between liberals who saw public spending as the remedy for poverty and social problems, and deficit hawks who wanted a balanced budget and control of entitlements, as well as a third group who wanted a growth agenda including tax reductions. [7]

On both sides, the leadership task was to gain workable coalitions within their own party while gaining maximum concessions and preventing critical damage to their agendas from the other side. Institutional conflicts further complicated their strategies: congressional Democrats not infrequently ambivalent about presidential priorities; House Republicans at odds with their Senate counterparts; appropriations committees and subcommittees unhappy with the Republican leadership.

These divisions extended and strained the budget process. The Republican plan was to consolidate what had been gained the previous year and to press ahead to balance the budget by the year 2000. Battles erupted on all fronts, yet the leadership of both sides knew they had to work together if they wished to avoid blame for breakdown and if they were to accomplish anything at all. Bipartisan support in 1996 resulted in modest tax cuts, an increase in the minimum wage, welfare reform, and an omnibus appropriations bill. That year the reelection of the president and the Republicans' losses in the House were widely interpreted as a mandate for bipartisan cooperation.[8] Both mainstream Democrats and Republicans saw it in their own interests to compromise and cooperate to gain their priorities—Republicans wanted tax cuts; Democrats wanted domestic spending; both wanted to balance the budget. The processes and institutions of the budget formed the arena for simultaneous conflict and cooperation exemplified in the 1997 Balanced Budget Agreement.

---

[6]Allen Schick, *The Federal Budget: Politics, Policy, Process* (Washington, D.C.: Brookings, 1995.)

[7]Alissa Rubin, "Democrats Contemplate Formula for Growth, *Congressional Quarterly Weekly Report*, (June 1, 1996), p. 1518.

[8]Palazzolo, *op.cit.*, p. 41.

The budget process might be thought of most easily in terms of frameworks—president's budget, congressional resolution, reconciliation bill—and the measures that "fill them in"—authorizations and appropriations. Another way of viewing the budget would be to distinguish between "grand" politics and "program" politics, or between efforts for cohesion, planning and centralization against decentralized decision making and the pursuit of special interests. Of course these distinctions are not exact, but they work well enough to provide a useful perspective. The extent of the overlapping among them, and the divergences between the institutions and their expected purposes, indicate the stresses stemming from recent conflicts.

The President's Budget

The original idea of the president's budget was that it should be an authoritative plan, that coordinated government funding for the year based on an analysis of the administration's needs. By 1999, with a Democratic president and a Republican Congress, the president's budget had become a kind of opening bid. That year's budget is a good example of both the potential and limitations of the institution. The administration admitted it was unlikely that the president's proposals would survive in their present form. Said Jacob Lew, White House budget director: "First of all, the President has not said this should be the end of the discussion. This is the beginning of the discussion."[9] The realm of the president's budget is the realm of "grand politics." The Fiscal Year 2000 budget was intended to chart a path for the future well beyond the fiscal year. It was, in the words of Richard Stevenson, "really a political agenda, in spreadsheet form, for a new fiscal era."[10] The president's budget took the initiative in making decisions about the trillions of dollars in surpluses promised by his advisers for the next 15 years. In reserving two-thirds of the surplus for social security, the president laid out basic ground rules, which were adopted and extended by the Republican majority in Congress.

The president's budget also has to be more than just a political statement. It has to have integrity—the assumptions on which it is based have to be believable, and its elements have to be coherent. There was little question about the president's long-term forecasts or economic assumptions, which in the end turned out to be conservative—the initial estimate was surpassed six months later. But the relationship of the surplus to social security and debt reduction was far from clear, and Herbert Stein suggested, "The president's budget seems to have been written with a purpose to obscure."[11]

Perhaps no one really cared: The president's policy was to set the rules of the game by showing that he could fund the programs he wanted within the confines of existing rules, for example, PAYGO and the caps. The president's budget is not just about the framework of grand politics, but about the details of policies. The president proposed no less than 81 tax increases and 37 tax cuts. He proposed narrowly targeted tax credits designed for special constituencies, such as long-term

[9]*New York Times*, February 2, 1999, p. A17.

[10]Richard Stevenson, "Seeking the High Ground in Spending Surpluses," *New York Times*, February 2, 1999, p. A17.

[11]Herbert Stein, "Clinton's Budgetary Legerdemain," *Wall Street Journal*, March 3, 1999, p. A1.

care, child care and stay-home parents. He proposed expanding the age of eligibility for medicare, increasing the defense budget, and adding money for education, energy, and environmental programs.

All this added up to excess spending above the caps of about $18 billion, which was accounted for in all kinds of offsets—cutting medicare payments even further, closing tax loopholes, and (as before) revenues from increased cigarette taxes and the tobacco settlement. The president described the budget as a balance between fiscal discipline and responsible government: "It charts a progressive but prudent path to our future; a balanced budget that makes vital investments."[12] Others saw it as sleight of hand. But it was still only the president's program.

Yet even in a hostile political environment, the president was able to set the ground rules for use of the surplus and to gain general acceptance of the economic assumptions on which the budget was built. He was also able to use the budget to emphasize his priorities, and to appeal to political constituencies across a wide spectrum. But the budget lacked credibility, and in the hostile congressional environment, its influence was limited. Its program proposals could only become serious when the end of the process yielded a stalemate allowing the president leverage.

The Congressional Budget Resolution

The congressional budget resolution was designed as a counter-poise to the president's budget, a means for Congress to set out a framework for its later work and to coordinate its priorities and limits. Emanating from the budget committees, it sets out aggregate totals for the coming and subsequent years, as well as the totals for the functions set out in the president's budget. Like the president's budget, it is not a law; unlike the president's budget, it is not based on detailed agency and program analysis.

Once the budget committee in each House has come up with a draft resolution, each House has to approve it, divergences have to be reconciled by a conference committee, and then each House has to assent. The resolution should not only provide a coherent framework for subsequent committee actions, but should play an active part in determining the two streams of federal spending and revenues, through its allocations to the appropriations committees for discretionary spending and through reconciliation governing entitlements and taxation. But in recent years the level of conflict and turbulence has made it difficult to pass a resolution, and although its potential remains, there is some question regarding its ability to influence the budget process.

The experience of 1996 was instructive. In the aftermath of the previous year's turbulence, other more centrist plans competed with the resolution in both House and Senate, though neither could command a majority coalition. The budget committees delayed marking up the resolution because of the political uncertainty, and in the end the House Budget Committee's plan provided the basis for the House Appropriations Committee to begin to divide up spending allocations for its subcommittees. By the time the plan passed the House, with a near revolt by fiscal

---

hardliners, tax and spending measures were already under way without the authoritative framework of a resolution. The domestic discretionary allocations of the plan provoked an immediate backlash from the appropriations subcommittee chairs who (though good Republicans), saw the limits as too tight for them to satisfy their own agendas.

Following the 1997 agreement, (see pages 327-329) the budget resolution to implement it passed both House and Senate on bipartisan lines, though with some serious dissension. The next year, an attempt to use the resolution to further the Republican revolution could not find sufficient support; no resolution was passed, and the appropriations committees divided up their spending allocations among their subcommittees according to the discretionary spending caps. In 1999, the resolution set out spending totals according to the caps, but because it increased defense spending, it made deep cuts in domestic expenditures—an estimated 11 percent below current levels. The appropriations committee chairs insisted they could not pass viable appropriations bills within that limit.

The congressional budget resolution, as things now stand, seems to have lost influence over the budget. The existence of the caps means that decisions on the general level of discretionary spending have been preempted, and the division of spending under the caps either reflects one party's political preferences (as opposed to a coherent plan) or is irrelevant where the level of conflict is so high that the resolution is passed too late or maybe not at all. The inclusion in the resolution of quite detailed program decisions also means that conflicts are moved further forward in the process, that they will be repeated over again later on, and that the resolution moves further away from its original purpose as a cohesive framework or definitive medium-term plan.[13]

Reconciliation

Reconciliation has evolved as the means by which Congress may make major decisions about entitlements and revenues as part of a comprehensive package. Totals set out in the budget resolution are accompanied by instructions to the authorizing committees of Congress to make stipulated savings through legislative changes in entitlements or revenues. The committee actions are then packaged into a reconciliation bill, which after passage through Congress as a single measure, may be signed or vetoed by the president.

Reconciliation is an extraordinarily powerful tool. This is the arena of grand politics—moving large blocks of revenue and spending over a number of years. The 1997 Balanced Budget Act, packaged into two reconciliation bills, one for entitlements and one for taxes, demonstrates how influential reconciliation can be, as well as its limitations.

It was really amazing that agreement could be reached at all. At the beginning of 1997, budgetary politics were marked by distrust, division, and uncertainty. The

---

[13]A recent proposal for reform, H.R. 853 proposed a joint resolution that would be signed by the president and so become law. (See Statement of Susan J. Irving, Associate Director Budget Issues, United States General Accounting Office, before the Rules Committee of the House of Representatives, May 12, 1999, GAO/T-AIMD-99-188).

agreement to balance the budget by 2002 was a product of secret negotiations between the Republican leadership and the president.

The details of the agreement represented less an area of common ground than a deal in which each side had gained as much as it thought it could, conceded as little as possible, deferred the difficult decisions for the future, and added a certain amount of wishful thinking to make the numbers come out right. The primary utility of reconciliation is its ability to make changes in revenues and entitlements. Politically, each side had to find enough incentive for acceptance of each other's priorities. Thus, tax cuts and cuts in medicare and medicaid were balanced against restoration of benefits to legal immigrants (cut in the 1996 welfare reform), a variety of grants and savings schemes for students, and expansion of health care insurance for poor children. (See Table 12.1.)

Table 12.1   The 1997 Balanced Budget Act in Outline

	Impact over Five Years	
	Increases Deficit (billion $)	Decreases Deficit (billion $)
Tax Cuts	$85	
Medicare		$112
Medicaid		$ 7
Cigarette Tax Increases		$ 5
Other Saving and Taxes		$ 15
Children's Health Insurance	$20	
Restoration of 1996 Welfare Cuts	$13	
Electrogmagnetic Spectrum Auctions		$ 21
Increased Estimates of Tax Revenues by CBO		$225

Source: Based on summary "What the Budget Bill Does," Congressional Quarterly Weekly Report, December 13, 1997, p. 3082–91.

The agreement also limited discretionary expenditures by extending the Budget Enforcement Act caps on budget authority and outlays. Defense and domestic expenditures would have separate caps for the next two years, after which there would be a single cap. Discretionary expenditure in total would be cut below the level of inflation to result in about $135 billion in savings, somewhat over half coming from defense. After a slight rise for domestic expenditures in the first year, the caps would require a 12 percent cut in domestic expenditures between 1997 and 2002, more than had been achieved in the previous seven years.[14] It was the single cap for discretionary expenditure that was to prove so important in the 1999 budgetary process when increases in defense required concomitantly larger cuts in domestic spending—even though there were estimates of large surpluses.

Finally, to make the figures balance, more deficit reduction was found in auction of the broadcast spectrum, changes in federal employees' pensions, and veterans' programs. It was assumed that the Bureau of Labor Statistics would make technical changes to the calculations for the Consumer Price Index, to reduce en-

---

[14]Robert Reischauer, "Scrap the Budget Caps," Washington Post National Weekly Review, June 14, 1999, p. 26.

titlement spending. And providentially, CBO announced there would be nearly a quarter of a trillion dollars in deficit reduction due to technical reestimates and revised projections.

Reconciliation in 1997 also highlighted the limitations of the process. First, the measure is only as good as its content. Although the agreement comprised a comprehensive goal, balancing the budget in five years, and a strategy for meeting it, the numbers were still speculative, and since they referred to a future well beyond the terms of the current Congress and president, why should anyone care? Similarly, there was a regrettable tendency to push the hard decisions into the future, notably the tight multiyear caps on discretionary expenditures, looking good now, but postponing conflicts until later. Notably, the agreement omitted any attempt to deal with the long-term problems of social security or health programs.

Second, reconciliation is a centralizing mechanism that depends on committees acting within the framework of the instructions on savings they receive. Negotiations had been held in secret and then the agreement had to be steered through the complex maze of the budget process. Passage was not easy. Significant minorities on both sides had been left out of the negotiations, and had voted against what they believed were betrayals of basic principles. Given the change in circumstances, there was no reason for them to consider the case closed. The leadership on both sides could not rely on permanent majorities, and on any issue there was a danger that either extremist wing could summon enough other votes to block or pass measures violating the agreement, or that they might make common cause together. Party leaders, too, wanted to distinguish their position from the opposition, and so to sharpen rather than blur their differences. The story, told in detail by Daniel Palazzolo, relates a zigzag process of proposals put in and taken out again, efforts by individuals to further their own agendas, and attempts to change provisions of the agreement.[15]

Third, committees might not take kindly to the reconciliation instructions they were supposed to fulfill. Palazzolo concluded that the passage of the reconciliation bill for entitlements resulted in significant violations of key elements of the agreement shifting them in a conservative direction.[16] In the end, closed door negotiations between the Republican leadership and the president were necessary to restore the original agreement more or less, which to some degree cast doubt on the reality of the debates in Congress.

Fourth, through its provisions for restricted debate and single packaged votes, reconciliation by intention allows no room for individual agendas. But any "must pass" legislation inevitably attracts detailed proposals. For example, the 1997 reconciliation instructions included $700 million for the acquisition of land including two specific properties in California and Montana. This provision became highly contentious later in the process, involving not only appropriations subcommittees, but also authorizing committees in the House and Senate that imposed conditions on the purchases.[17] The inclusion of details of this kind confuses and complicates the process.

---

[15]Palazzolo, *op.cit.*

[16]Palazzolo, *op cit.*, p. 138.

[17]Allan Freedman, "Land Purchases Threaten Interior Spending Bill," *Congressional Quarterly Weekly Report*, October 4, 1997, p. 2395; Allan Freedman, "House Breaks Deadlock, Passes Interior Bill," *Congressional Quarterly Weekly Report*, October 25, 1997, p. 2600.

Finally, reconciliation is an occasional thing, which does not have to take place every year, or even at all. Between 1997 and 1999 there was no attempt at reconciliation. Like any other bill, it may be vetoed by the president. And the existence of reconciliation does not mean that free-standing legislation on revenues, expenditures, or entitlements may not take place. For example, in 1996, the Veterans Administration-Housing and Urban Development appropriations bill included a new entitlement for children with spinal bifida, one of whose parents had been exposed to Agent Orange in Vietnam.[18] Thus, reconciliation is not a routine process for regular consideration of either entitlements or taxation, though it enables changes on an ad hoc periodic basis, when party leadership feels justified in initiating them.

Authorizations

Authorizations are the legislative measures that are required prior to appropriation of funds: first there should be a program, and then funding for it. Programs are authorized for varying numbers of years, but if they are viewed as separate controlling elements of the budget process, their usefulness too may be regarded as limited.

The first problem has been that authorizations have frequently been bypassed. By the late 1990s, it had become increasingly difficult to pass major legislation through the authorizing committees. For example, authorizations lapsed on housing, foreign aid, and the entire Energy, State, and Justice Departments.[19] Instead, legislators turned to the appropriations process to maintain programs from year to year, and to make legislative changes through nonfinancial riders. In this way it is possible to pass single provisions without consideration of the whole. Officially of course this is against the rules, since appropriations must have authorizations and should not include legislative language. Thus appropriations committees have come to make policy, and the authorizing committees have become less relevant. The results are encouragement of piecemeal solutions, avoidance of difficult choices, and sometimes little debate where powerful appropriations subcommittee chairs can push through proposals even where there is substantial opposition.

Conversely, powerful authorizing committee chairs may use periodic legislative reauthorization to preempt appropriations decisions through the authorizing process, partly through overall spending totals in the bills and partly through "earmarks" for specific projects. A case in point was the 1998 reauthorization of the six-year Intermodal Surface Transportation Efficiency Act (ISTEA). As the bill progressed through House and Senate, proposals snowballed. The Act would increase spending for highways and mass transit by over 40 percent in the next six years, making it the biggest investment in highway spending since the 1950s. It included over 1,500 earmarks, more than ever before, and it was nearly $30 billion more than the amount allowed in the 1997 budget agreement.[20] Even the

---

[18]Jon Healey, "VA-HUD Spending Bill Clears With Bipartisan Support," *Congressional Quarterly Weekly Report,* September 28, 1996, p. 2762.

[19]Andrew Taylor and Lori Nitschke, *Congressional Quarterly Weekly Report,* May 30, 1998, p. 1453.

[20]Eric Pianin and Charles Babcock, "Piling up the Pork," *Washington Post National Weekly Edition,* April 6, 1998, p. 32.

most ardent of budget cutters joined in and every region of the country benefited. But to preempt spending in this way demanded offsets in other parts of the
budget: Increases in transportation were being pitted against social programs.
After bids to make reductions in medicaid and food stamps were bitterly opposed, final negotiations found offsets in veterans' disability payments and the social services block grant. ISTEA, in the president's words, was "disembodied from
the budget . . . [without] any relationship with all the other pieces in the budget."[21] But he signed it just the same. In addition, future highway spending would
be tied directly to the previous year's gasoline tax receipts so they could not be diverted to deficit reduction, and would be protected by a separate spending cap.[22]

Appropriations

The 13 appropriations bills form the "building blocks" of the budget process.
Even though by the end of the twentieth century they constituted less than one-
third of federal expenditures and were scheduled to drop even further as entitlements took up more of the budget, they still were the focus of major budget
battles. Appropriations were controversial because they involved one of the major tradeoffs in the budget between domestic discretionary and defense expenditures, because they contained social programs that were the target for
conservatives who wished to limit government, and because they were of great
interest to legislators who wanted to benefit their constituents or achieve specific agendas.

Appropriations committees and their subcommittees bring different casts of
characters into the budget debate and divide spending into separate provinces. As
limits became more constrained and as committee membership changed to include more members of Congress in marginal seats, appropriations committees
and subcommittees became advocates of spending rather than guardians of the
public purse. For example, in 1996, John Myers (R-Ind.), chair of the House
Energy and Water Appropriations Subcommittee, refused to mark up his bill until
he got more money, and he was able to increase his allocation twice, moving from
a billion dollar cut from the previous year to a $92 million increase.[23] The corre-
sponding Senate subcommittee went ahead and added $887 million more, in-
creasing funding even beyond the president's request.[24] An oddity of this story was
that the chair of the Senate subcommittee was also chair of the Senate Budget
Committee, thus fulfilling simultaneously the roles of rationer and claimant!

Each appropriation bill has its own dynamic, based on the different kinds of
spending included in it. From year to year the lines of conflict became more predictable. The appropriations debates were running battles on funding tradeoffs,

---

[21]"Road Bills Keep Republicans Divided While Clinton Plays Budget Hawk," *Congressional Quarterly Weekly Report*, April 25, 1998, p. 1069.

[22]Alan Ota, "Conferees Trim Bill, Near Agreement, but Clinton Still Threatens Veto," *Congressional Quarterly Weekly Report*, May 16, 1998, p. 1269.

[23]Jonathan Weisman, "Myers Goes for More Funds—and a Little Revenge," *Congressonal Quarterly Weekly Report*, June 22, 1996, p. 175.

[24]*Congressional Quarterly Weekly Report*, July 13, 1996, p. 1958.

ideological agendas, and special interests. For example, the bill for Veterans Administration-Housing and Urban Development and Independent Agencies made tradeoffs in favor of veterans' benefits against housing and space programs. The Energy and Water bill pitted energy research against nuclear weapons research and cleanup of nuclear facilities.

There were inevitably attacks on presidential priorities and programs. Programs such as the Legal Services Corporation, Americorps, Goals 2000, and the National Endowment for the Arts, were regularly deleted, and then funding was restored in later negotiations. There was an unending feud over funding for international organizations. The largest and most controversial bill, for Labor-Health and Human Services-Education, was the annual scene of an ugly fight in which Republicans deliberately targeted social and education programs, provoking immediate confrontation with the White House. In 1998, when the constraints of the caps made it impossible to fund the president's initiatives or even to maintain programs at their original level, the House Subcommittee Chair, John Edward Porter III (R-Ill.), maintained that "We must choose priorities. It's our job to choose which programs work for people and which don't." David Obey (D-Wis.) saw things differently, claiming that the bill took money from "the weakest and most vulnerable" to solve the political problems of the majority party.[25] That year the bill passed neither House.

The escalating conflict was intensified by attempts to add nonfinancial riders to the appropriations bills. Over the years, these became familiar, although new ones also cropped up. They seemed primarily symbolic, as their regular removal in the bargaining process surely indicated their slim chances of passage, but they could be significant hindrances to passage of the bills, and could be used as bargaining chips. The Interior bill was the target for all kinds of riders on the environment, which could be extraordinarily detailed. For example in 1996, the Interior bill hit near showdown on a rider to bar enforcement of environmental protection habitat for the marbled murrelet on 40,000 acres in California.[26] Abortion restrictions in the Foreign Operations bill, education vouchers in the District of Columbia bill, sampling techniques in the census in the Commerce bill, and national testing in the schools, embryo research, and gun control in Labor-Health and Human Services-Education, all became familiar stumbling blocks to passage of appropriations.

But the appropriations bills also offer opportunities too good to pass up. It is impossible to do justice in a short space to the number and variety of special projects inserted in appropriations bills by eager members on both sides of the House. For example, the 1996 House and Senate drafts of the Energy and Water bill contained over a billion dollars on water and flood control projects, and in the House, 380 members requested over 2,500 items. Funding for environmental cleanup also reflected membership on that subcommittee of powerful state interests from Washington and South Carolina.[27] The tug of constituency politics maintained its

[25]Sue Kirchhoff, "GOP Throws Down Gauntlet," *Congressional Quarterly Weekly Report*, June 27, 1998, pp. 1758–59.

[26]Allan Freedman, "Trouble May Be in Store for Interior Bill," *Congressional Quarterly Weekly Report*, June 15, 1996, p. 1664.

[27]*Congressional Quarterly Weekly Report*, July 13, 1996, p. 1958.

attraction, and representatives and senators fought hard for their projects: a sea wall in Chicago, a levee repair project in Washington, a border station in Montana, a federal prison in Kentucky, an ocean research center in Hawaii, a brain institute in Florida. The reaction of Senator Stevens (R-Alaska), chair of the Senate Appropriations Committee, to a proposal to build a research station at the South Pole (instead of Barrow, Alaska) was quite clear on the issue: "How," he asked, "do I explain [this] to my Eskimo people?"[28]

All these controversies slowed down and impeded the appropriations process, and in no year between 1995 and 1999 were the appropriations bills completed on time. Only in 1997 was it possible to gain passage and presidential signature for the 13 appropriations bills; in the other years, huge omnibus appropriations bills covered several of the separate measures.

In 1999, the appropriations process was, according to point of view, a new era in federal budgeting, an opportunity lost, an exercise in willing self-deceit, or the same wearying old game. With the prospect of around one trillion dollars in budget surpluses over the next 10 years, appropriations spending was squeezed—by the budget caps of the 1997 agreement, and by the notion adopted by both parties that the part of the surplus attributable to social security could not be touched. Worse, the remaining razor thin surplus could only be maintained by adhering to the single cap on defense and domestic discretionary spending. If the Republican majority insisted (as they did) on a raise for defense, this meant severe reciprocal cuts in domestic programs, which appropriations chairs insisted were not viable.[29]

The array of budgetary gimmicks that followed from this formula fooled no one, legitimized transparent pretenses, and further eroded the authority of the appropriations process. Rather than deliberately weighing program priorities, the appropriations committees were involved in tricks to make spending above the caps appear below the caps. Emergency spending (which would not count against the caps) came to embrace not only real emergencies—hurricane relief in Central America, the war in Kosovo—but blatant pretexts—veterans' health care, the 2001 census, farm relief.[30] Sometimes these might be quite fictional, such as the maneuvering for "saving" the first year's funding for a project to harvest wild mushrooms in national forests by postponing its start.[31] Or money could be found by not passing some benefit that had been promised but not enacted, so it could be scored at any level at all, such as veterans' benefits for smoking related diseases.

Expenditures could be pushed into the following year, an old game that had also been used the previous year. For example, the last payday for certain defense personnel was delayed, and payments to contractors were slowed up.[32] But

---

[28]*Congressional Quarterly Weekly Report,* October 4, 1997, p. 2408.

[29]*New York Times,* May 24, 1999, p. A30.

[30]Eric Pianin and Juliet Eilperin, "How To Bust a Budget Cap," *Washington Post National Weekly Edition,* August 2, 1999, p. 30.

[31]David Rogers, "Despite Surplus Boasts, Lawmakers Search for Revenues," *Wall Street Journal,* September 2, 1999, p. A26.

[32]*New York Times,* October 11, 1999, p. A10.

some proposals were too blatant to sustain: Criticism forced withdrawal of a scheme to spread payments for the Earned Income Tax Credit over a year instead of providing a lump sum.[33] And a proposal for a 13 month "year" to make the figures come out right was also withdrawn. Finally in desperation to avoid dipping into the "social security surplus," the Republicans proposed across-the-board cuts, initially quite high, but eventually one percent of all programs.[34] After a presidential veto, to save face, the cut was negotiated down to 0.38 percent, an inconsequential amount, but a recognition of inability on the part of Congress to make policy.[35]

By the end of the fiscal year, it was obvious that the caps would be breached and the on-budget surplus would be exceeded. To avoid points of order, earlier appropriations "borrowed" from later ones, so that the last bill in line, Labor-Health and Human Services-Education, which funded most of the social programs and presidential priorities, was facing cuts equivalent to nearly one quarter of its previous year's discretionary spending level.[36] Only two appropriations bills had reached the president.

Over the next month, under continuing resolutions, compromises were reached on all but five appropriations bills. At dispute was about $7 billion in spending and several policy issues.[37] In the end, both sides claimed victory as the five bills were rolled into an omnibus package. Republicans gained a $17 billion increase for defense and raises for health research and education. Among other provisions, the White House gained its priorities for hiring more police officers and teachers, as well as increases for transportation spending, money for the Middle East peace agreement, and long-disputed funding for the United Nations. Predictably, both parties were split in the vote on the omnibus measure, minorities rejecting the compromises made by their leaders. Predictably, also, the appropriations bills apparently set a record for special interest items (estimated at $14.65 billion).[38] Corporate lobbyists did particularly well, as in the chaotic end to the budget process, Republican and Democratic lawmakers quietly gave "their bipartisan blessing to assorted plums for auto companies, defense contractors, utilities, cotton farmers, shipbuilders, chemical companies and even a West Virginia business that sells armor-piercing ammunition."[39] As usual, there were last minute end-runs, as members of Congress tried to exert leverage in an effort to protect or benefit their constituents.

---

[33]Tim Weiner, "Criticism Appears To Doom Republican Budget Tactic," New York Times, October 1, 1999, p. A22.

[34]Tim Weiner and Richard Stevenson, "One Wide-Reaching Slash Could Settle Budget Battle," New York Times, October 11, 1999, p. A10.

[35]"As House Passes Budget, Clinton Savors a Win," Wall Street Journal, November 19, 1999, p. A22.

[36]David Rogers, "GOP Accepts Higher Spending Levels Rather than Risk Budget-Process Delay," Wall Street Journal, September 15, 1999, p. A22.

[37]Tim Weiner, "Congress and the President on the Cusp of Budget Accord," New York Times, November 17, 1999, p. A18.

[38]Lizette Alvarez, "Congress on Record Course for 'Pork' with Alaska in a Class of Its Own," New York Times, November 19, 1999, p. A5

[39]Dan Morgan and Juliet Eilperin, "Looking Out for the Big Guy: Windfalls for Businesses are Quietly Tucked into Appropriations Bills," Washington Post National Weekly Edition, November 1, 1999, p. 30.

The leaders of both parties were self-congratulatory, but in fact, according to CBO, they had not fulfilled their promises, either to maintain spending within the caps or to avoid using the social security surplus. Whereas previously CBO had predicted a $37.5 billion on-budget surplus, it now calculated an over $19 billion deficit, and with all the stratagems, it would be necessary to take at least $17 billion out of social security funds.[40] Even discounting emergency spending, CBO calculated that spending was over $16 billion above the caps.[41]

It might be argued that the appropriations process (which in effect *was* the budget process in 1999) has broken down, in that all the hours of debate have often been passed over or ignored by narrow negotiations at the end of the process, and that haggling and power play have taken the place of reasoned discussion of priorities. How, then, might we characterize a budget process, every one of whose main elements seems to have fared so poorly?

CHARACTERISTICS OF THE BUDGET PROCESS

There is no longer any single word or concept that adequately characterizes the budgetary process of the U.S. government. It is simultaneously powerful, yet impotent. Its institutions and practices are highly structured, but often do not work in the ways intended. It is complex, reflecting different kinds of revenues and expenditures and the large number of interacting participants, yet there is an underlying order segmenting decisions in predictable patterns. Its politics are polarized, but institutional checks and balances moderate radicalism and influence policies toward the center. In short, the budgetary process is a process of opposites.

The Budgetary Process Is Powerful Yet Impotent

The federal budget disposes annually of an incredible amount of resources—over $1.7 trillion dollars, far more than the budget of any other country in the world. It exercises a huge influence on the economy, on regional development, and on the lives of individuals. It manages enormous programs in the realms of social security, health, pensions, and defense, which have lifted millions of people out of poverty and provided livelihood for millions more. The grand politics of the budgetary process determines large blocks of expenditures, as well as making revenue decisions that shift enormous amounts of resources in or out of the public sector. But the budgetary process is also powerful in accomplishing smaller things. The "little" politics of programs have dollar tags that anywhere except the federal budget would be considered huge. Here, budget debates are concerned with substantive objectives and accomplishments. They include local projects, but also national programs whose implementation and benefits are local. No less than grand politics, program politics are of intense interest to advocates, and attract sustained lobbying from outside government.

Yet the federal budget often seems to go its own way, and unpredictably at that. Its determinations have enormous economic consequences, but it often seems a

---

[40]*Wall Street Journal,* December 3, 1999, p. C23.

[41]*New York Times,* December 3, 1999, p. A27.

prisoner of the economy. Changes in key economic indicators often have far greater impact than heavily fought-over program cuts. Projections are uncertain—note how rapidly the forecasts of deepening deficits were reversed to a picture of accumulating surpluses. Both revenues and expenditures seem to take on a life of their own, a result of the close relationship of contemporary budgets and volatile economies.

The Budgetary Process Is Structured Yet Formalistic

To cope with budgetary challenges, a variety of different processes and institutions have emerged by a process of accretion that has layered one reform upon earlier ones. The reforms have generally been concerned with gaining greater control over the budget. A budget is essentially a centralizing mechanism that tries to bring together revenues and expenditures in time and place, and subordinate them to central authority. In contrast, Congress is concerned with representation and decentralization of power. Since 1974, reforms have endeavored to increase centralization, initially to gain cohesive action against deficits, and later to drive through policies agreed by the majority leadership. But a monolithic budget process is unacceptable to Congress, so that institutions do not necessarily work as intended.

So there is a good deal of formalism—a word describing a situation where reality diverges from form, a kind of looking-glass world where things are never the way they seem. The president's budget, conceived as an authoritative workplan, is just an opening bid in competition with a rival, the congressional budget resolution. Budget resolutions, intended as aggregates, often include details and seem irrelevant to the decisions they should govern. Agreements embrace future goals with only the haziest of ideas about how or whether they will be implemented. Timetables slip, and budget cycles run into each other as appropriations are unfinished well into the year to which they apply. Continuing resolutions are regular, not exceptional. Supplemental appropriations are an ad hoc accepted means of doing business and achieving all kinds of purposes. Emergency spending may mean anything at all, and riders that have little or no relationship to the funding issues are attached to any kind of budget measure.

Substance is often no less formalistic than process: Figures are difficult to grasp. There is a constant confusion between nominal and "real" figures. At one point, debate is about a freeze, for example, last year's expenditures are the same as this year's; the next moment, the "freeze" becomes a "freeze below the inflation rate," or a cut. This works quite well in reference to the past, where the rate of inflation is at least known, but in planning for the future, the baseline for cuts or increases is really an imaginary number, based on future assumptions about inflation, expected workload, and program eligibility. The higher the projected baseline and the further it is projected into the future, the more money is required to "keep up" with it, and the larger the cuts needed to meet a target such as balancing the budget. The trouble is that economic projections are shaky, and the longer the projection, the shakier it is. Small errors can cause large swings in budget balance. Yet projections of huge surpluses are now treated as facts, and decisions are based on them. In addition, the caps on spending have spawned all kinds of fictions, including offsets, emergencies, postponements and other gimmickry.

And the distinctions between budget authority and outlays allow for perpetual confusions. Budgets increasingly seem to consist of sliding assumptions, promises, hopes and fears, rather than solid foundations.[42]

The Budgetary Process Is Complex Yet Segmented

The complexity of the budget process derives not only from the maze of processes and institutions, but from the large number of variables affecting decisions, and the multiple interactions among them. Both expenditures and revenues take a number of different forms—discretionary spending, entitlements, interest payments, loans and loan guarantees, tax expenditures—and each has an impact on the unified budget and deficit/surplus. Each is governed by different decision processes, which whatever their substantive utility, help avoid conflicts by compartmentalizing choices so that critical budget elements are separated and do not usually come face to face. The participatory nature of Congress, the loosely integrated executive branch, and the existence of issue networks, have meant a large number of different groups and individuals with power to add, subtract, demand, deny, bargain, impede, and otherwise influence outcomes. In other words, the budget is porous and open to interests.

Yet the different spending and revenue elements of the budget do not behave either randomly or according to a single description. They are subject to different rules, and the ways they are grouped (for example, among and within appropriations) help determine the lines of competition among them. While once incrementalism was an adequate description of budgetary behavior and outcomes, and much of the budget still appears to fit incrementalist theory,[43] it also seems that different parts of the budget behave in different ways.

From an exhaustive analysis of 2,266 accounts covering on-and off-budget outlays from 1962 to 1995, Maureen Berner has concluded that in the long run, incrementalism still applies to the core programs of government, which constitute 70 percent of the budget. Outlays for these programs are stable, grow slowly, and do not compete for gains. A second group, dominated by social services, appears more vulnerable to politics, reforms, budget cuts, and economic fluctuations. Finally, an "unstable" sector includes a variety of somewhat unpredictable spending. These groupings cut across conventional entitlement/discretionary

---

[42]The United States General Accounting Office has suggested criteria for effective budgeting that concern clarification of information about the long-term impact of decisions and tradeoffs at all levels, as well as accountability and transparency. (See Statement of Susan J. Irving, Associate Director Budget Issues, United States General Accounting Office, "Budget Process: Evolution and Challenges," before the House of Representatives Budget Committee, July 11, 1996, p. 8 GAO/T-AIMD-96-129.) A recent proposal for reform, H.R. 853, has suggested including reports on long-term budgetary trends by the Office of Management and Budget and the Congressional Budget Office in the budget.

[43]See Joseph White, "(Almost) Nothing New under the Sun: Why the Work of Budgeting Remains Incremental" in Naomi Caiden and Joseph White (eds.), *Budgeting, Policy, Politics: An Appreciation of Aaron Wildavsky* (New Brunswick, N.J.: Transaction, Inc., 1995, pp. 111–32; Andrew Weiss and Edward Woodhouse, "Reforming Incrementalism: A Constructive Response to Critics," *Policy Sciences*, Vol. 25 1992, pp. 255–73.

spending lines, suggesting a more political than institutional explanation for budget outcomes.[44]

Budgetary Politics Are Polarized but Moderated

Over the last 30 years or so, observers of Congress generally agree that the political environment has become increasingly polarized, and instances of bipartisanship have been exceptional. The lines of cleavage seem to affect almost every issue, although many interests cut across ideological lines and politicians vary in the intensity of their commitment. In each party a more moderate core is flanked by increasingly radical outliers, so that party leaders have to balance support on every issue, as well as gain consent from the opposing side. Budget debates rage over grand politics—tax cuts, defense, entitlements—as well as smaller but nonetheless ideological issues—environment and social programs.

Yet budget protagonists are forced to work within the constitutional system of checks and balances, or more accurately, shared powers. The Constitution gives Congress the power to make appropriations and to borrow and raise taxes, but the president may veto its actions. The combination of legislative and executive autonomy and shared powers is a recipe for deadlock where different parties control the presidency and Congress, particularly where there is heightened partisanship and neither party holds an overwhelming majority or is entirely cohesive.

But the built-in institutional sharing of power over the budget may also be a moderating influence. President and Congress (unless the congressional majority is large enough to override a veto) are forced to negotiate their differences if they wish to avoid breakdown in government. The effect in practice has been to narrow the differences between the two sides. As the Democratic president has moved closer in position to the Republican leadership of Congress, areas of consensus have emerged—a balanced budget, tax cuts, entitlement reform, welfare reform, defense increases, and limited government. The lines of division have turned into matters of degree, while the controversies that have so impeded orderly budgeting actually turn on social and ideological issues for which the budget process is a convenient and potentially powerful forum. The fate of the attack on government programs by the Republicans in 1995 is a case in point. Instead of radical transformation, things are much the way they were, and several major programs targeted for extinction have not only survived, but apparently have even increased their budgets.[45]

The emergence of a surplus, despite the chaotic budget process of 1999, may also have brought a degree of consensus. Both parties agreed to segregate the social security surplus, and even though they did not really avoid a deficit, the amounts involved in the context of previous deficits (which had been offset by social security surpluses) or the budget as a whole, were really negligible. The budget really is

---

[44]Maureen Berner, "Incrementalism, Congressional Power Structures and Budget Deals—What Really Matters to Budget Policy? Insights from a Behavioral Analysis of the U.S. Federal Budget from 1962–1995." Paper prepared for the 1999 Annual Meeting of the Midwest Political Science Association, April 9, 1999, p. 36.

[45]See Michael Grunwald, "Thin Skins for Cutting Pork," *Washington Post National Weekly Edition*, August 9, 1999, p. 12, for a table showing changes in outlays for selected federal programs; Jonathan Rauch, "Lean Budget, Bloated Government," *New York Times*, November 17, 1999, p. A29.

more or less in balance, and if things go well, even the relatively minor deficit might be wiped out, as happened the previous year.[46] But if it took such enormous strain to bridge such a small gap, what will happen when the gap is much larger, either because an economic downturn adversely affects revenues, or simply because the caps demand much larger cuts in future years if there is to be a surplus at all?

Does a budget of opposites "work"? Or is the current situation simply the result of a rather evenly divided politics, which might be amended by an election returning a president and decisive congressional majority from the same party? Or is the budget process in fact failing, and inappropriate if the future turns out to be different from the past?

---

[46]Tim Weiner, "On Paper, Budget Balances Without Customary Raid on Social Security," *New York Times*, October 13, 1999, p. A18.

Glossary[1]

appropriated entitlements Budget authority provided in annual appropriations, although payment must be made to all eligible people who apply. Examples of appropriated entitlements are medicaid, Supplemental Security Income, Aid to Families with Dependent Children, and veterans compensation.

appropriation An act of Congress that permits federal agencies to incur obligations and to make payments out of the Treasury for specified purposes. Appropriations are one form of budget authority.

appropriation act A statute that provides funds for federal programs. An appropriation act generally follows enactment of authorizing legislation unless the authorizing legislation itself provides the budget authority.

authorization (authorizing legislation) Substantive legislation enacted by Congress that sets up or continues legal operation of a federal program or agency either indefinitely or for a specific period of time, or sanctions a particular type of obligation or expenditure within a program. Authorizing legislation is usually a prerequisite for subsequent appropriations or other kinds of budget authority to be contained in appropriation acts. Such legislation may limit the amount of budget authority to be provided subsequently or may authorize the appropriation of "such sums as may be necessary." Budget authority may be provided in the authorization (see "backdoor authority"), which eliminates the need for subsequent appropriations or requires only an appropriation to liquidate contract authority or reduce outstanding debt.

backdoor authority Budget authority provided in legislation outside the appropriations process. The most common forms of backdoor authority are authority to borrow (borrowing authority), contract authority, and entitlements. In some cases (e.g., interest on the public debt), a permanent appropriation is provided that becomes available without current actions by the Congress.

backdoor spending Authority of federal agencies to spend money through the Treasury rather than going through the appropriations process.

borrowing authority Statutory authority (substantive or appropriation) that permits a federal agency to incur obligations and to make payments for specified purposes out of borrowed monies. Section 401 of the Congressional Budget Act of 1974 limits new borrowing authority (except for certain instances) to such extent or in such amounts as are provided in appropriation acts.

---

[1]Most of the definitions of these terms are taken verbatim or adapted from *A Glossary of Terms Used in the Federal Budget Process and Related Accounting, Economic, and Tax Terms*, U.S. General Accounting Office, March 1981, 3rd ed., PAD–81–27. Terms of more recent origin have been defined by Dean Hammer.

budget amendment A formal request submitted to the Congress by the president, after his formal budget transmittal but prior to completion of appropriation action by the Congress, that revises previous requests, such as the amount of budget authority.

budget authority Authority provided by law to enter into obligations that will result in immediate or future outlays involving federal government funds. Budget authority does not include authority to insure or guarantee the repayment of indebtedness incurred by another person or government. The basic forms of budget authority are appropriations, authority to borrow, and contract authority. Budget authority may be classified by the period of availability (one-year, multiyear, no-year), by the timing of congressional action (current or permanent), or by the manner of determining the amount available (definite or indefinite).

capital budget A divided budget with investment in capital assets excluded from calculation of the budget surplus or deficit. A capital budget provides for separating financing of capital or investment expenditures from current or operating expenditures.

concurrent resolution on the budget Under the Congressional Budget Act of 1974, a resolution passed by both houses of Congress, but not requiring the signature of the president, which sets forth, reaffirms, or revises the congressional budget for the U. S. government for a fiscal year. There were two such resolutions required preceding each fiscal year. The first required concurrent resolution, due by May 15, established the congressional budget. The second required concurrent resolution, due by September 15, reaffirmed or revised it. Other concurrent resolutions for a fiscal year could be adopted at any time following the first required concurrent resolution for that fiscal year.

The Balanced Budget Act of 1985 revised this process. Only one annual budget resolution is required, with action by both houses scheduled to be completed by April 15. The resolution now contains figures for the five succeeding fiscal years.

continuing resolution Legislation enacted by the Congress to provide budget authority for specific ongoing activities in cases where the regular fiscal year appropriations for such activities have not been enacted by the beginning of the fiscal year. The continuing resolution usually specifies a maximum rate at which the agency may incur obligations, based on the rate of the prior year, the president's budget request, or an appropriation bill passed by either or both houses of the Congress.

contract authority A form of budget authority under which contracts or other obligations may be entered into in advance of an appropriation or in excess of amounts otherwise available in a revolving fund. Contract authority must be funded by a subsequent appropriation or the use of revolving fund collections to liquidate the obligations. Appropriations to liquidate contract authority are not classified as budget authority since they are not available for obligation. Section 401 of the Congressional Budget Act of 1974 limits new contract authority, with few exceptions, to such extent or in such amounts as are provided in appropriation acts.

current policy budget Projections of the estimated budget authority and outlays for the upcoming fiscal year to operate federal programs at the level implied by enacted appropriations and authorizations of the current fiscal year without policy changes, but adjusted for inflation, changes in the numbers and kinds of beneficiaries, and in some instances to reflect the continuation of certain programs scheduled to terminate.

current services estimates Estimated budget authority and outlays for the upcoming fiscal year based on continuation of existing levels of service, that is, assuming that all programs and activities will be carried on at the same level as in the fiscal year in progress and without policy changes in such programs and activities. These estimates of budget authority and outlays, accompanied by the underlying economic and programmatic assumptions on which they are based (such as the rate of inflation, the rate of real economic growth, the unemployment rate, program caseloads, and pay increases), are transmitted by the president to the Congress when the budget is submitted.

deferral of budget authority Any action or inaction by an officer or employee of the U. S. government that temporarily withholds, delays, or effectively precludes the obligation or expenditure of budget authority, including authority to obligate by contract in advance of appropriations as specifically authorized by law and including the establishment of reserves under the Anti-Deficiency Act as amended by the Impoundment Control Act. The president must provide a special message to Congress reporting a proposed deferral of budget authority. Deferrals may not extend beyond the end of the fiscal year in which the message reporting the deferral is transmitted. Deferrals can be overturned only by Congress passing a law, which the president must sign.

entitlements Legislation that requires the payment of benefits to any person or unit of government that meets the eligibility requirements established by such law. Authorizations for entitlements constitute a binding obligation on the part of the federal government, and eligible recipients have legal recourse if the obligation is not fulfilled.

expenditures See OUTLAYS.

fazio rule House procedure whereby appropriation subcommittees cannot be subject to points of order under Section 602(a) for total spending if their spending proposals are within their allocations for discretionary (not mandatory) budget authority from the Appropriations Committee's 602(b) process.

fiscal policy Federal government policies with respect to taxes, spending, and debt management, intended to promote the nation's macro-economic goals, particularly with respect to employment, gross national product, price level stability, and equilibrium in balance of payments. The budget process is a major vehicle for determining and implementing federal fiscal policy. The other major component of federal economic policy is monetary policy.

fiscal year Any yearly accounting period, without regard to its relationship to a calendar year. The fiscal year for the federal government begins on October 1 and ends on September 30. The fiscal year is designated by the calendar year in which it ends (e.g., Fiscal Year 2000 is the fiscal year ending September 30, 2000).

impoundment Any action or inaction by an officer or employee of the U.S. government that precludes the obligation or expenditure of budget authority provided by Congress. Two kinds of impoundment are rescission and deferral.

loan guarantee A loan guarantee is an agreement by which the government pledges to pay part or all of the loan principal and interest to a lender or holder of a security, in the event of default by a third-party borrower. The subsidy costs of new loan guarantees are now counted in the budget.

multiyear budgeting A budget planning process designed to make sure that the long-range consequences of budget decisions are identified and reflected in the budget totals.

obligational authority The sum of budget authority provided for a given fiscal year, balance of amounts brought forward from prior years that remain available for obligation, and amounts authorized to be credited to a specific fund or account during that year, including transfers between funds or accounts.

off-budget outlays Outlays of off-budget federal entities whose transactions have been excluded from the budget totals under provisions of law, even though these outlays are part of total government spending.

offsets Requirement that an appropriation subcommittee's spending that exceeds the amount allocated to it by the Budget Resolution under Section 602(b) be matched by a reduction in other outlays and/or an increase in revenues equivalent to the amount of spending being added. Offsets may also apply to making up decreases in revenue proposed in tax legislation.

offsetting receipts All collections deposited into receipt accounts that are offset against budget authority and outlays rather than reflected as budget receipts in computing budget totals. Under current budgetary usage, cash collections not deposited into receipt accounts (such as revolving fund receipts and reimbursements) are deducted from outlays at the account level. These transactions are offsetting collections but are not classified as "offsetting receipts."

outlays The amount of checks issued, interest accrued on most public debt, or other payments, net of refunds and reimbursements. Total budget outlays consist of the sum of the outlays from appropriations and funds included in the unified budget, less offsetting receipts. The outlays of off-budget federal entities are excluded from the unified budget under provisions of law, even though these outlays are part of total government spending.

PAYGO A process for keeping expenditures within major elements of the budget by requiring that additions to outlays above amounts set by budget resolutions or in law be made up by new sources of revenue or by reductions elsewhere within (and only within) that category. (See also "offsets".)

permanent appropriations Authority to spend provided in authorizing legislation without the need for subsequent annual appropriations. Examples include medicare, social security, and interest on the public debt.

planning program budgeting system (PPBS) A budgetary process that initially sets out goals (the planning phase), develops and approves programs for reaching these objectives (the programming phase), and prices and allocates inputs required for reaching these objectives (the budgetary phase).

president's budget A proposed budget for a particular fiscal year transmitted to the Congress by the president in accordance with the Budget and Accounting Act of 1921, as amended.

reconciliation process A process used by Congress to reconcile amounts determined by tax, spending, and debt legislation for a given fiscal year with the ceilings enacted in the required concurrent resolution on the budget for that year. Section 310 of the Congressional Budget Act of 1974 as amended provides that the required concurrent resolution on the budget, which sets binding totals for the budget, may direct committees to determine and recommend changes to laws, bills, and resolutions, as required to conform with the binding totals for budget authority, revenues, and the public debt. Such changes are incorporated into either a reconciliation resolution or a reconciliation bill.

reprogramming Utilization of funds in an appropriation account for purposes other than those contemplated at the time of the appropriation. Reprogramming is generally preceded by consultation between federal agencies and the appropriate congressional committees. It involves formal notification and, in some instances, opportunity for disapproval by congressional committees.

rescission A bill or joint resolution that cancels, in whole or in part, budget authority previously granted by Congress. Rescissions proposed by the president must be transmitted in a special message to Congress. Under Section 1012 of the Congressional Budget and Impoundment Control Act of 1974, unless both houses of Congress complete action on a rescission bill within 45 days of continuous session after receipt of the proposal, the budget authority must be made available for obligation.

sequestration Under the Balanced Budget Act of 1985, the withholding of budget authority, according to an established formula, up to the amount required to be cut to meet the deficit target.

supplemental appropriation An act appropriating funds in addition to those in an annual appropriation act. Supplemental appropriations provide additional budget authority beyond original estimates for programs or activities (including new programs authorized after the date of the original appropriation act).

transfer of funds When specifically authorized in law, all or part of the budget authority in one account may be transferred to another account.

trust fund Funds collected and used by the federal government for carrying out specific purposes and programs according to terms of a trust agreement or statute, such as the social security trust fund.

unified budget The current form of the budget of the federal government (beginning with the 1969 budget) in which receipts and outlays from federal funds and trust funds are consolidated. When these fund groups are consolidated to display budget totals, transactions that are outlays of one fund group for payment to the other fund group (i.e., interfund transactions) are deducted to avoid double-counting. Transactions of off-budget federal entities are not included in the unified budget.

zero-base budgeting Zero-base budgeting for analysis of alternative methods of operation at various levels of effort, including the possibility that the activity in question will not be funded at all.

Guide To Acronyms

AFDC	Aid to Families with Dependent Children
BEA	Budget Enforcement Act of 1990 (Title XIII)
BOB	Bureau of the Budget
CBO	Congressional Budget Office
CCC	Commodity Credit Corporation
CEA	Council of Economic Advisers
CFO	chief financial officer
COLAs	cost-of-living adjustments
CR	continuing resolution
CRS	Congressional Research Service
DOD	Department of Defense
DRB	Defense Resources Board
E&E	Emergency and Extraordinary
EOP	Executive Office of the President
EPA	Environmental Protection Agency
FAA	Federal Aviation Administration
FFB	Federal Financing Bank
GAO	Government Accounting Office
GNP	gross national product
GPRA	Government Performance and Results Act
GRH	Gramm–Rudman–Hollings Deficit Reduction Act
GSEs	government-sponsored enterprises
HBC	House Budget Committee

JCS	Joint Chiefs of Staff
JSPD	Joint Services Planning Document
MDA	maximum deficit amount
NASA	National Aeronautics and Space Administration
NEC	National Economic Commission
NPR	National Performance Review
OBRA	Omnibus Budget Reconciliation Act of 1990
OECD	Organization for Economic Co-Operation and Development
OMB	Office of Management and Budget
OSD	Office of the Secretary of Defense
OSHA	Occupational Health and Safety Administration
PDMs	program decision memoranda
POMs	program objective memoranda
PPB	planning, programming, and budgeting
RFC	Reconstruction Finance Corporation
RIF	reduction in force
SBC	Senate Budget Committee
WIC	Women, Infants, and Children
ZBB	zero-base budgeting

Select Bibliography

Aaron, Henry. *Social Security and the Budget: Proceedings of the First Conference of the National Academy of Social Insurance,* New York: University Press of America, 1990.

Aaron, Henry and Barry Bosworth, "Preparing for the Baby Boomers' Retirement." In Robert Reischauer ed. *Setting National Priorities: Budget Choices for the Next Century.* Washington, D.C.: Brookings Institution, 1997, pp. 263–302.

Aaron, Henry and Robert Reischauer. *Countdown to Reform: The Great Social Security Debate.* New York: Century Foundation, 1998.

Adams, Gordon. *The Politics of Defense Contracting: The Iron Triangle.* New Brunswick, N.J.: Transaction, Inc. 1982.

_____. *The Role of Defense Budgets in Civil Military Relations.* Washington, D.C.: Defense Budget Project, 1992.

Antos, Joseph. "Preparing for the Retirement of the Baby Boomers." In Robert Reischauer, Stuart Butler, and Judith Lave. *Medicare: Preparing for the Challenges of the 21ˢᵗ Century.* Washington, D.C.: National Academy of Social Insurance, 1997, pp. 43–45.

Art, Robert J. "Congress and the Defense Budget: Enhancing Policy Oversight." *Political Science Quarterly,* Vol. 100, No. 2 (Summer 1985), pp. 227–48.

Asbell, Bernard. *The Senate Nobody Knows.* Garden City, N.Y.: Doubleday, 1978.

Aspin, Les. "Congress vs. Department of Defense." In Thomas M. Franck, ed. *The Tethered Presidency.* New York: New York University, 1981.

Axelrod, Donald. *Shadow Government.* New York: Wiley, 1992.

Ball, Robert. "The Original Understanding on Social Security: Implications for Later Developments." In Theodore Marmur and Jerry Mashaw, eds. *Social Security: Beyond the Rhetoric of Crisis.* Princeton, N.J.: Princeton University Press, 1988, pp. 17–39.

Banks, William and Jeffrey Straussman. "Defense Contingency Budgeting in the Post-Cold-War World." *Public Administration Review,* Vol. 59 (March/April 1999), pp. 135–45.

Barth, Peter. *The Tragedy of Black Lung: Federal Compensation for Occupational Disease.* Kalamazoo, Mich.: W. E. Upjohn, Institute for Employment Research, 1979.

Berman, Larry. *The Office of Management and Budget and the Presidency.* Princeton, N.J.: Princeton University Press, 1979.

Bernardi, Richard. "The Base Closure and Realignment Commission: A Rational or Political Decision Process?" *Public Budgeting and Finance,* Vol. 16 (Spring 1996), pp. 37–48.

Berner, Maureen. "Incrementalism, Congressional Power Structures and Budget Deals — What Really Matters to Budget Policy? Insights from a Behavioral Analysis of the U.S. Federal Budget from 1962–1995." Paper prepared for the 1999 Annual Meeting of the Midwest Political Science Association, 1999.

Betts, Richard. *Military Readiness: Concepts, Choices, Consequences.* Washington, D.C.: Brookings Institution, 1995.

Bickley, James M. "The Federal Financing Bank: Assessments of Its Effectiveness and Budgetary Status." *Public Budgeting and Finance*, Vol. 5, No. 4 (Winter 1985), pp. 51–63.

Birnbaum, Jeffrey H. and Alan S. Murray. *Showdown at Gucci Gulch: Lawmakers, Lobbyists, and the Unlikely Triumph of Tax Reform*. New York: Random House, 1987.

Bolles, Albert S. *A Financial History of the United States, 1774–89*. New York: Appleton, 1879.

———. *The Financial History of the United States from 1861 to 1885*. New York: Appleton, 1886.

Borcherding, Thomas. "A Hundred Years of Public Spending, 1870–1970." In Thomas Borcherding, ed. *Budgets and Bureaucrats: The Sources of Government Growth*. Durham, N.C.: Duke University Press, 1977.

Borg, Sten G. and Francis G. Castles. "The Influence of the Political Right on Public Income Maintenance Expenditure and Equality." *Political Studies*, Vol. 29 (December 1981), pp. 604–21.

Bovbjerg, Randall R. and John Holahan. *Medicaid in the Reagan Era: Federal Policy and State Choices*. Washington, D.C.: Urban Institute, 1982.

Bramlett, Robert W. "The Federal Accounting Standards Advisory Board." *Public Budgeting and Finance*, Vol. 11 (Winter 1991), pp. 11–19.

Bramlett, Robert and Frank Rexford. "The Federal Accounting Standards Advisory Board: A View of Its Role One Year Later." *Public Budgeting and Finance*, Vol. 12 (Winter 1992), pp. 87–101.

Braybrooke, David and Charles E. Lindblom. *A Strategy of Decision*. New York: Free Press, 1963.

Brummett, John. *Highwire: The Education of Bill Clinton*. New York: Hyperion, 1994.

Bruner, Jerome S., Jacqueline J. Goodnow, and George A. Austin. *A Study of Thinking*. New York: Wiley, 1956.

Bryner, Gary. *Politics and Public Morality*. New York: Norton, 1998.

Buchanan, James M. and Richard E. Wagner. *Democracy in Deficit: The Political Legacy of Keynes*. New York: Academic Press, 1977.

Buck, A. E. "The Development of the Budget Idea in the United States." *Annals of the American Academy of Political and Social Science*, Vol. 63 (May 1924).

———. *Public Budgeting*. New York: Harper, 1929.

Bullock, Charles. "The Finances of the United States from 1775–1789 with Special Reference to the Budget." In Frederick Turner, ed. *Bulletin of the University of Wisconsin, Vol. 1, 1894–1896*. Madison: University of Wisconsin Press, 1897.

Bunch, Beverly. "Current Practices and Issues in Capital Budgeting and Reporting." *Public Budgeting and Finance*, Vol. 16 (Summer 1996) pp. 7–25.

Burkhead, Jesse. *Government Budgeting*. New York: Wiley, 1956.

Caiden, Naomi. "After the Earthquake: The President's Budget for FY 1996." *Public Budgeting and Finance*, Vol. 15 (Summer 1995), pp. 3–17.

———. "The Myth of the Annual Budget." *Public Administration Review*, Vol. 42 (November/December 1982), pp. 516–23.

———. "The Politics of Subtraction." In Allen Schick, ed. *Making Economic Policy in Congress*. Washington, D.C.: American Enterprise Institute, 1984, pp. 100–130.

———. "The New Rules of the Federal Budget Game." *Public Administration Review*, Vol. 44 (March/April 1984), pp. 109–17.

———. "Paradox, Ambiguity and Enigma: The Strange Case of the Executive Budget and the United States Constitution." *Public Administration Review*, Vol. 47 (January/February 1987), pp. 84–92.

Caiden, Naomi and Joseph White, eds. *Budgeting, Policy, Politics: An Appreciation of Aaron Wildavsky*. New Brunswick, N.J: Transaction, Inc., 1995.

Caiden, Naomi and Aaron Wildavsky. *Planning and Budgeting in Poor Countries*. New York: Wiley, 1974. Paperback edition by Transaction, Inc., New Brunswick, N.J., 1980.

Cavanaugh, Francis X. *The Truth about the National Debt: Five Myths and One Reality*. Cambridge Mass.: Harvard Business School Press, 1999.

Clarke, Gary. "Medicaid Fiscal Stresses and the States: A Medical Director's Perspective." In Diane Rowland, Judith Feder, and Alina Salganicoff, eds. *Medicaid Financing Crisis: Balancing Responsibilities, Priorities and Dollars.* AAAS Press, 1994, pp. 155–78.

Cleveland, Frederick A. "Leadership and Criticism." *Proceedings of the Academy of Political Science,* Vol. 8 (1918–1920).

Cleveland, Frederick A. and Arthur E. Buck. *The Budget and Responsible Government.* New York: Macmillan, 1920.

Cogan, John F. *The Budget Puzzle: Understanding Federal Spending.* Stanford, Calif.: Stanford University Press, 1994.

Conlan, Timothy. *From Federalism to Devolution: Twenty-Five Years of Intergovernmental Reform.* Washington D.C.: Brookings Institution, 1998.

Cuny, Thomas J. "Federal Credit Reform." *Public Budgeting and Finance,* Vol. 11 (Summer 1991), pp. 19–32.

———. "The Pending Revolution in Federal Accounting Standards." *Public Budgeting and Finance,* Vol. 15 (Fall 1995), pp. 22–34.

Curro, Michael J. "Federal Financial Management and Budgeting: NPR Recommendations and GAO Views." *Public Budgeting and Finance,* Vol. 15 (Spring 1995) pp. 19–26.

Cutler, David. "Restructuring Medicare for the Future." In Robert Reischauer, ed. *Setting National Priorities: Budget Choices for the Next Century.* Washington, D.C.: Brookings Institution, 1997, pp. 197–234.

Darman, Richard. *Who's in Control? Polar Politics and the Sensible Center.* New York: Simon and Schuster, 1996.

Davis, Edward. "The Evolution of Federal Spending Controls: A Brief Overview." *Public Budgeting and Finance,* Vol. 17 (Fall 1997), pp. 10–24.

Davis, Otto A., M. A. H. Dempster, and Aaron Wildavsky. "On the Process of Budgeting II: An Empirical Study of Congressional Appropriations." In R. F. Byrne, A. Charnes, W. W. Cooper, A. A. Davis, and Dorthy Gilford, eds. *Studies in Budgeting.* Amsterdam: North Holland, 1971, pp. 292–375.

———. "Toward a Predictive Theory of the Federal Budgetary Process." *The British Journal of Political Science,* Vol. 4, Part 4 (October 1974), pp. 419–52.

Dawes, Charles G. *The First Year of the Budget of the United States.* New York: Harper, 1923.

Dempster, M. A. H. and Aaron Wildavsky. "On Change: Or, There Is No Magic Size for an Increment." *Political Studies,* Vol. 27 (September 1979), pp. 371–89.

Derickson, Alan. "The Origins of the Black Lung Insurgency." *Journal of Public Health Policy,* Vol. 4, No. 1 (March 1983).

Derthick, Martha. *Uncontrollable Spending for Social Services Grants.* Washington, D.C.: Brookings Institution, 1975.

———. *Policymaking for Social Security.* Washington, D.C.: Brookings Institution, 1979.

DiLorenzo, Thomas. *Underground Government: The Offbudget Public Sector.* Washington, D.C.: Cato Institute, 1983.

Doyle, Richard. "Congress, the Deficit and Budget Reconciliation." *Public Budgeting and Finance,* Vol. 16 (Winter 1996), pp. 59–81.

Doyle, Richard and Jerry L. McCaffery. "The Budget Enforcement Act in 1992: Necessary but Not Sufficient." *Public Budgeting and Finance,* Vol. 13 (Summer 1993), pp. 20–37.

Eisner, Robert. *How Real Is the Federal Deficit?* New York: Free Press, 1986.

———. "A Balanced Budget Crusade." *The Public Interest* (Winter 1996), pp. 85–92.

———. *The Great Deficit Scares: The Federal Budget, Trade, and Social Security.* New York: Century Foundation Press, 1997.

Ellwood, John W., ed. *Reductions in U.S. Domestic Spending: How They Affect State and Local Governments.* New Brunswick, N.J.: Transaction, Inc., 1982.

———. "The Great Exception: The Congressional Budget Process in an Age of Decentralization." In Lawrence Dodd and Bruce Oppenheimer, eds. *Congress Reconsidered,* 3rd ed. Washington, D.C.: CQ Press, 1985.

Ellwood, John W. and James A. Thurber. "The New Congressional Budget Process: The Hows and Whys of House-Senate Differences." In Lawrence Dodd and Bruce Oppenheimer, eds. *Congress Reconsidered.* New York: Praeger, 1977, pp. 163–92.

Enthoven, Alain C. and Wayne K. Smith. *How Much Is Enough?* New York: Harper & Row, 1971.

Evans, Diana. "Policy and Pork: The Use of Pork Barrel Projects To Build Policy Coalitions in the House of Representatives." *American Journal of Political Science,* Vol 38 (1994), pp. 894–917.

Evans, C. Lawrence and Walter Oleszek. *Congress under Fire: Reform Politics and the Republican Majority.* Boston: Houghton Mifflin, 1997.

Fenno, Richard F., Jr. "The House Appropriations Committee as a Political System: The Problem of Integration." *The American Political Science Review,* Vol. 56 (June 1962), pp. 310–24.

———. *The Power of the Purse: Appropriations Politics in Congress.* Boston: Little, Brown, 1966.

_____. *The Emergence of a Senate Leader: Pete Domenici and the Reagan Budget.* Washington, D.C.: CQ Press, 1991.

Ferejohn, John A. "Logrolling in an Institutional Context: A Case Study of Food Stamps Legislation." Working Papers in Political Science, P–5–85. Palo Alto, Calif.: Hoover Institute, 1985.

Fiorina, Morris. *Congress—Keystone of the Washington Establishment.* New Haven, Conn.: Yale University Press, 1977.

Fisher, Louis. *President and Congress.* New York: Free Press, 1972.

———. *Presidential Spending Power.* Princeton: Princeton University Press, 1975.

———. "The Authorization-Appropriation Process in Congress: Formal Rules and Informal Practices." *Catholic University Law Review,* Vol. 29, No. 5 (1979), pp. 52–105.

———. "In Dubious Battle? Congress and the Budget." *The Brookings Bulletin,* Vol. 17 (Spring 1981), pp. 6–10.

———. "The Budget Act of 1974: A Further Loss of Spending Control." In Thomas Wander et al, eds. *Congressional Budgeting.* Baltimore: Johns Hopkins University Press, 1984, pp. 170–89.

———. *Constitutional Conflicts Between Congress and the President.* Princeton: Princeton University Press, 1985.

_____. "Line-Item Veto of 1996: Heads-Up from the States." *Public Budgeting and Finance,* Vol. 17 (Summer 1997), pp. 3–17.

_____. "Biennial Budgeting in the Federal Government." *Public Budgeting and Finance,* Vol. 17 (Fall 1997), pp. 87–97.

Fisher, Louis and Neal Devins. "How Successfully Can the States' Item Veto Be Transferred to the President?" *Georgetown Law Journal,* Vol. 75, No. 1 (October 1986), pp. 159–97.

Fisher, Louis and Philip Joyce. "Introduction: Reflections on Two Decades of Congressional Budgeting." *Public Budgeting and Finance,* Vol. 17 (Fall 1997), pp. 3–9.

Fitzpatrick, Edward Augustus. *Budget Making in a Democracy.* New York: Macmillan, 1918.

Forsythe, Dall W. *Taxation and Political Change in the Young Nation 1781–1833.* New York: Columbia University Press, 1977.

Fox, Ronald J. *Arming America: How the U.S. Buys Weapons.* Cambridge: Harvard University Press, 1974.

Gansler, Jacques S. "How To Improve the Acquisition of Weapons." In Robert J. Art et al, eds. *Reorganizing America's Defense.* Washington, D.C.: Pergamon Brassey, 1985.

Giddens, Anthony. *The Third Way: The Renewal of Social Democracy.* Oxford: Blackwell Publishers, 1998.

Gilmour, Robert. "Central Legislative Clearance: A Revised Perspective." *Public Administration Review,* Vol. 31 (March/April 1971), pp. 150–58.

Gimpel, James. *Fulfilling the Contract: The First Hundred Days.* Boston: Allyn and Bacon, 1996.

Gordon, Cameron. "The Fables and Foibles of Federal Capital Budgeting." *Public Budgeting and Finance*, Vol. 18 (Fall 1998), pp. 54–72.

Gore, Albert. *Reinventing Government: From Red Tape to Results: Creating a Government That Works Better and Costs Less. Report on the National Performance Review*. New York: Times Books, 1993.

Greenfield, Margaret. *Medicare and Medicaid: The 1965 and 1967 Social Security Amendments*. Westport, Conn.: Greenwood, 1968.

Greenstein Robert and Paul Leonard. *A New Direction: The Clinton Budget and Economic Spending Plan*. Washington, D.C.: Center on Budget and Policy Priorities, 1993.

Greider, William. "The Education of David Stockman." *The Atlantic Monthly*, (December 1981), pp. 27–54.

Guess, George and Kenneth Koford. "Inflation, Recession and the Federal Budget Deficit (or, Blaming Economic Problems on a Statistical Mirage)." *Policy Sciences*, Vol. 17 (1984), pp. 385–402.

Hager, George and Eric Pianin. *Mirage*. New York: Random House, 1997.

Hammond, Thomas H. and Jack H. Knott. *A Zero-Based Look at Zero-Base Budgeting*. New Brunswick, N.J.: Transaction, Inc., 1979.

Harper, Edwin L., Fred A. Kramer, and Andrew M. Rouse. "Implementation and the Use of PPB in Sixteen Federal Agencies." *Public Administration Review*, Vol. 29 (November/December 1969).

Harrington, Michael. "Building Arms Control into the National Security Process." *Arms Control Today*, (February 1975).

Hartman, Robert W. "Multiyear Budget Planning." In Joseph A. Pechman, ed. *Setting National Priorities: The 1979 Budget*. Washington, D.C.: Brookings Institution, 1978.

———. "Congress and Budget-Making," *Political Science Quarterly*, Vol. 97, No. 3 (Fall 1982), pp. 381–402.

———. "Making Budget Decisions." In Joseph A. Pechman, ed. *Setting National Priorities: The 1983 Budget*. Washington, D.C.: Brookings Institution, 1982.

———. "Budget Summit 1990: The Role of Economic and Budget Analysis." Paper prepared for the Association for Public Policy Analysis and Management Conference, October 18–20, 1990.

Heclo, Hugh. "Executive Budget Making." In Gregory B. Mills and John L. Palmer, eds. *Federal Budget Policy in the 1980s*. Washington, D.C.: The Urban Institute, 1984.

Heclo, Hugh and Aaron Wildavsky. *The Private Government of Public Money: Community and Policy inside British Political Administration*, 2nd ed. London: Macmillan, 1981.

Hitch, Charles. *Decision-Making for Defense*. Berkeley, Calif.: University of California Press, 1970.

Holahan, John, Teresa Coughlin, Leighton Ku, David Heslam, and Collin Winterbottom. "Understanding the Recent Growth in Medicaid Spending." In Diane Rowland, Judith Feder, and Alina Salganicoff, eds. *Medicaid Financing Crisis: Balancing Responsibilities, Priorities and Dollars*. AAAS Press, 1994, pp. 23–41.

Howard, Christopher. *The Hidden Welfare State*. Princeton, N.J.: Princeton University Press, 1999.

Hush, Lawrence W. "The Federal, and the State and Local Roles in Government Expenditures." *Public Budgeting and Finance*, Vol. 13 (Summer 1993), pp. 38–55.

Ippolito, Dennis S. *Hidden Spending: The Politics of Federal Credit Programs*. Chapel Hill N.C.: University of North Carolina Press, 1984.

———. *Uncertain Legacies: Federal Budget Policy from Roosevelt through Reagan*. Charlottesville, Va.: University Press of Virginia, 1990.

Johnson, Bruce. "From Analyst to Negotiator: The OMB's New Role." *Journal of Policy Analysis and Management*, Vol. 3, No. 4 (1984).

———. "OMB and the Budget Examiner: Changes in the Reagan Era." *Public Budgeting and Finance*, Vol. 9 (Winter 1988), pp. 3–21.

———. "The OMB Budget Examiner and the Congressional Budget Process." *Public Budgeting and Finance*, Vol. 9 (Spring 1989), pp. 5–14.

Johnson, Loch and Kevin Scheid. "Spending for Spies: Intelligence Budgeting in the Aftermath of the Cold War." *Public Budgeting and Finance*, Vol. 17 (Winter 1997), pp. 7–27.

Johnston, Jocelyn. "The Medicaid Mandates of the 1980s: An Intergovernmental Perspective." *Public Budgeting and Finance*, Vol. 17 (Spring 1997), pp. 3–34.

Jones, L. R. "Policy Development, Planning, and Resource Allocation in the Department of Defense." *Public Budgeting and Finance*, Vol. 11 (Fall 1991), pp. 15–27.

Jones, L. R. and Glen Bixler. *Mission Budgeting To Realign National Defense*. Greenwich, Conn.: JAI Press, 1992.

Jones, L. R. and Jerry L. McCaffery. "Federal Financial Management Reform and the Chief Financial Officers Act." *Public Budgeting and Finance*, Vol. 12 (Winter 1992), pp. 75–86.

———. "Implementation of the Federal Chief Financial Officers Act." *Public Budgeting and Finance*, Vol. 13 (Spring 1993), pp. 68–76.

_____. "Implementing the Chief Financial Officers Act and the Government Performance and Results Act in the Federal Government." *Public Budgeting and Finance* Vol. 17 (Spring 1997), pp. 35–55.

_____. "Financial Management Reform in the Federal Government." In Roy Meyers, ed. *Handbook of Government Budgeting*. San Francisco: Jossey Bass, 1999, pp. 53–81.

Joyce, Philip. "Jesse Burkhead and the Multiple Uses of Federal Budgets: A Contemporary Perspective." *Public Budgeting and Finance*, Vol. 16 (Summer 1996), pp. 59–78.

_____. "The Federal Line-Item Veto Experiment: After the Supreme Court Ruling, What's Next?" *Public Budgeting and Finance*, Vol. 18 (Winter 1998), pp. 3–21.

Joyce, Philip and Robert Reischauer. "The Federal Line-Item Veto: What Is It and What Will It Do?" *Public Administration Review*, Vol. 57 (March/April 1997), pp. 95–104.

Kamlet, Mark S. and David C. Mowery. "The Budgetary Base in Federal Resource Allocation." *American Journal of Political Science*, Vol. 24, No. 4 (November 1980), pp. 806–21.

———. "Budgetary Side Payments and Government Growth: 1953–1968." *American Journal of Political Science*, Vol. 27, No. 4 (November 1983), pp. 636–64.

———. "Contradictions of Congressional Budget Reform: Problem of Congressional Emulation of Executive Branch." Typescript, 1984.

———. "The First Decade of the Congressional Budget Act: Legislative Imitation and Adaptation in Budgeting." *Policy Sciences*, Vol. 18, No. 4 (December 1985), pp. 313–34.

———. "Influences on Executive and Congressional Budgetary Priorities, 1953–1981." *The American Political Science Review*, Vol. 81, No. 1 (March 1987), pp. 155–73.

Kamlet, Mark S., David C. Mowery, and Tsai-Tsu Su. "Whom Do You Trust? An Analysis of Executive and Congressional Economic Forecasts." *Journal of Policy Analysis and Management*, Vol. 6, No. 3 (1987), pp. 365–84.

Kanter, Arnold. *Defense Politics*. Chicago: University of Chicago Press, 1975.

Kaufmann, William W. *A Reasonable Defense*. Washington, D.C.: Brookings Institution, 1986.

Keith, Robert and Edward Davis. "Congress and Continuing Appropriations: New Variations on an Old Theme." *Public Budgeting and Finance*, Vol. 5 (Spring 1985).

Kellman, Steve. "The Grace Commission: How Much Waste in Government?" *The Public Interest*, No. 78 (Winter 1985).

Kettl, Donald. *Deficit Politics: Public Budgeting in Its Institutional Context*. New York: Macmillan, 1992.

Key, V. O., Jr. "The Lack of a Budgetary Theory." *The American Political Science Review*, Vol. 34 (December 1940), pp. 1137–44.

Kim, Sun Kil. "The Politics of a Congressional Budgetary Process Backdoor Spending." *Western Political Quarterly*, Vol. 21 (December 1968), pp. 606–23.

Kimmel, Lewis H. *Federal Budget and Fiscal Policy 1789–1958*. Washington, D.C.: Brookings Institution, 1959.

King, Ronald. "Tax Expenditures and Systematic Public Policy." Paper presented for delivery at the Annual Meeting of the American Political Science Association, Denver, Colo., September 2–5, 1982.

Kingson, Eric and Edward D. Berkowitz. *Social Security and Medicare.* Westport, Conn.: Praegar, 1999.

Kingson, Eric and James Schulz, eds. *Social Security in the Twenty-First Century.* Oxford: Oxford University Press, 1996.

Kliman, Albert J. and Louis Fisher. "Budget Reform Proposals in the NPR Report." *Public Budgeting and Finance,* Vol. 15 (Spring 1995), pp. 27–38.

Kogan, Richard. "The Budget Enforcement Act of 1990: A Technical Explanation." November 1, 1990, unpublished.

Korb, Lawrence. "The Budget Process in the Department of Defense 1947–77: The Strengths and Weaknesses of Three Systems." *Public Administration Review,* Vol. 37 (July/August 1977), pp. 334–36.

———. "The Process and Problems of Linking Policy and Force Structure through the Defense Budget Process." In Robert Harkavy and Edward Kolodziej, eds. *American Security Policy and Policy Making.* Lexington, Mass.: Lexington Books, 1980.

Lawton, Frederick J. "Legislative-Executive Relationships in Budgeting as Viewed by the Executive." *Public Administration Review,* Vol. 13 (Summer 1953), pp. 169–76.

Lekachman, Robert. *The Age of Keynes.* New York: McGraw-Hill, 1966.

LeLoup, Lance. "Discretion in National Budgeting: Controlling the Controllables." *Policy Analysis,* Vol. 4, No. 4 (Fall 1978), 455–75.

LeLoup, Lance, Carolyn Long, and James Giardano. "President Clinton's Fiscal 1998 Budget: Political and Constitutional Paths to Balance." *Public Budgeting and Finance,* Vol. 18 (Spring 1998), pp. 3–32.

LeLoup, Lance, Barbara Luck Graham, and Stacey Barwick. "Deficit Politics and Constitutional Government: The Impact of Gramm–Rudman–Hollings." *Public Budgeting and Finance,* Vol. 7, No. 1 (Spring 1987), pp. 83–104.

LeLoup, Lance and Patrick Taylor. "The Policy Constraints of Deficit Reduction: President Clinton's 1995 Budget." *Public Budgeting and Finance,* Vol. 14 (Summer 1994), pp. 3–25.

Leonard, Brad, Joe Cook, and Jane McNeil. "The Role of Budget and Financial Reform in Making Government Work Better and Cost Less." *Public Budgeting and Finance,* Vol. 15 (Spring 1995), pp. 4–18.

Leonard, Herman B. *Checks Unbalanced: The Quiet Side of Public Spending.* New York: Basic Books, 1986.

Levine, Charles H. and Irene Rubin, eds. *Fiscal Stress and Public Policy.* Beverly Hills: Sage Publications, 1980.

Levy, Frank. *Dollars and Dreams: The Changing American Income Distribution.* New York: Russell Sage Foundation, 1987.

Lewis, Verne B. "Toward a Theory of Budgeting." *Public Administration Review,* Vol. 12 (Winter 1952), pp. 42–54.

Lindblom, Charles E. "Decision-Making in Taxation and Expenditure." In *Public Finances: Needs, Sources and Utilization,* Princeton: Princeton University Press, 1961, pp. 295–336.

———. "The Science of 'Muddling Through.'" *Public Administration Review,* Vol. 19 (Spring 1959), pp. 79–88.

Lindsay, James M. "Congress and Defense Policy: 1961 to 1986." *Armed Forces & Society,* Vol. 13, No. 3 (Spring 1987).

Long, Stephen. "Causes of Soaring Medicaid Spending 1988–1991." In Diane Rowland, Judith Feder, and Alina Salganicoff, eds. *Medicaid Financing Crisis: Balancing Responsibilities, Priorities, and Dollars.* AAAS Press, 1994, pp. 3–21.

Maas, Arthur. "In Accord with the Program of the President?" In Carl Friedrich and Kenneth Galbraith, eds. *Public Policy,* Vol. 4. (Cambridge, Mass.: Graduate School of Public Administration, 1954), pp. 77–93.

MacMahon, Arthur. "Congressional Oversight of Administration." *Political Science Quarterly,* Vol. 53 (June and September 1943), pp. 161–90, 380–414.

————. "Woodrow Wilson: Political Leader and Administrator." In Earl Latham, ed. *The Philosophy and Policies of Woodrow Wilson*. Chicago: University of Chicago Press, 1958, pp. 100–22.

Manley, John F. "The Conservative Coalition in Congress." *American Behavioral Scientist*, Vol. 17, No. 2 (November/December 1973), pp. 223–48.

Mann, Thomas and Norman Ornstein. *Renewing Congress: A Second Report*. Washington, D.C.: American Enterprise Institute and Brookings Institution, 1993.

Marmor, Theodore. "Coping with a Creeping Crisis: Medicare at Twenty." In Theodore Marmor and Jerry Mashaw, eds. *Social Security: Beyond the Rhetoric of Crisis*. Princeton, N.J.: Princeton University Press, 1998, pp. 177–99.

————. *The Politics of Medicare*. Hawthorne, N.Y.: Aldine de Gruyter, 1999.

Marini, John. *The Politics of Budget Control: Congress, the Presidency, and the Growth of the Administrative State*. Washington, D.C.: Crane Russak, 1992.

Martin, Bernard, Joseph Wholey, and Roy Meyers. "The New Equation at OMB: M + B = RMO." *Public Budgeting and Finance*, Vol. 15 (Winter 1995), pp. 86–96.

Marvick, L. Dwaine. *Congressional Appropriation Politics*. Ph.D. Dissertation, Columbia University, 1952.

Marx, Fritz Morstein. "The Bureau of the Budget: Its Evolution and Present Role." *The American Political Science Review*, Vol. 39, No. 4 (August 1945), pp. 653–84.

————. "The Bureau of the Budget: Its Evolution and Present Role, II." *The American Political Science Review*, Vol. 39 (October 1945), pp. 869–98.

Mayhew, David. *Congress: The Electoral Connection*. New Haven: Yale University Press, 1974.

McMurtry, Virginia. "The Impoundment Control Act of 1974: Restraining or Reviving Presidential Power." *Public Budgeting and Finance*, Vol. 17 (Fall 1997), pp. 39–61.

Meyer, Jack A. "Budget Cuts in the Reagan Administration: A Question of Fairness." In D. Lee Bauden, ed. *The Social Contract Revisited*. Washington, D.C.: The Urban Institute, 1984, pp. 33–64.

Meyers, Roy T. "Federal Budgeting and Finance in 1991: The Future Is Now." *Public Budgeting and Finance*, Vol. 12 (Summer 1992), pp. 3–16.

————. *Strategic Budgeting*. Ann Arbor, Mich.: University of Michigan Press, 1994.

————. "Late Appropriations and Government Shutdowns: Frequency, Causes, Consequences and Remedies." *Public Budgeting and Finance*, Vol. 17 (Fall 1997), pp. 25–38.

————. "Strategies for Spending Advocates." In Roy Meyers, ed. *Handbook of Government Budgeting*. San Francisco: Jossey Bass, 1999, pp. 548–67.

Miles, Jerome A. "The Congressional Budget and Impoundment Control Act: A Departmental Budget Officer's View." *The Bureaucrat*, Vol. 5, No. 4 (January 1977).

Mills, Gregory B. and John L. Palmer. *The Deficit Dilemma*. Washington, D.C.: The Urban Institute, 1983.

————, eds. *Federal Budget Policy in the 1980s*. Washington, D.C.: The Urban Institute, 1984.

Minarik, Joseph J. and Rudolph G. Penner. "Fiscal Choices." In Isabel V. Sawhill, ed. *Challenge to Leadership*. Washington, D.C.: The Urban Institute, 1988.

Moore, Marilyn and Janemarie Mulveny. *Entitlements and the Elderly: Protecting Promises, Recognizing Realities*. Washington, D.C.: The Urban Institute, 1996.

Mosher, Frederick C. *Program Budgeting: Theory and Practice, with Particular Reference to the U.S. Department of the Army*. Chicago: Public Administration Service, 1954.

————. *The GAO: The Quest for Accountability in American Government*. Boulder, Colo.: Westview Press, 1979.

————. *A Tale of Two Agencies: A Comparative Analysis of the General Accounting Office and the Office of Management and Budget*. Baton Rouge, La.: Louisiana State University Press, 1984.

Mowery, David S., Mark S. Kamlet, and John P. Crecine. "Presidential Management of Budgetary and Fiscal Policymaking." *Political Science Quarterly*, Vol. 95, No. 1 (Fall 1980), pp. 395–425.

Moynihan, Daniel P. *The Politics of a Guaranteed Income*. New York: Random House, 1973.

Myers, Margaret G. *A Financial History of the United States.* New York: Columbia University Press, 1970.

Myers, Robert J. *Medicare.* Bryn Mawr, Penn.: McCahan Foundation, 1970.

Naylor, E. E. *The Federal Budget System in Operation.* Washington, D.C.: Hayworth Printing, 1941.

Neustadt, Richard. "Presidency and Legislation: The Growth of Central Clearance. *The American Political Science Review,* Vol. 48 (September 1954), pp. 641–71.

——. "Presidency and Legislation: Planning the President's Program." *The American Political Science Review,* Vol. 49 (December 1955), pp. 980–1021.

Niskanen, William A. *Bureaucracy and Representative Government.* Chicago: University of Chicago Press, 1971.

——. "Deficits, Government Spending and Inflation: What Is the Evidence?" *Journal of Monetary Economics,* Vol. 4 (August 1978), pp. 591–602.

Nissenson, Allen and Richard Rettig. "Medicare's End-Stage Renal Disease Program: Current Status and Future Prospects." *Health Affairs,* Vol. 18 (January/February 1999), pp. 167–68.

Oak, Dale P. "An Overview of Adjustments to the Budget Enforcement Act Discretionary Spending Caps." *Public Budgeting and Finance,* Vol. 15 (Fall 1995), pp. 35–55.

O'Lessker, Karl. "The Clinton Budget for FY 1994: Taking Aim at the Deficit." *Public Budgeting and Finance,* Vol. 13 (Summer 1993), pp. 7–37.

Oleszek, Walter. *Congressional Procedures and the Policy Process.* Washington, D.C.: CQ Press, 1996.

Orms, Van Doorn, Ronald Boster, and Robert Fleegler. "The Federal Budget and Economic Management." In Roy Meyers, ed. *Handbook of Government Budgeting.* San Francisco: Jossey Bass, 1999, pp. 197–226.

Ornstein, Norman J. and Shirley Elder. "The B-1 Bomber: Organizing at the Grassroots." In Eston White, ed. *Studies in Defense.* Washington, D.C.: National Defense University Press, 1983.

Palazzolo, Daniel. *The Speaker and the Budget: Leadership in the Post-Reform House of Representatives.* Pittsburgh: University of Pittsburgh Press, 1992.

——. *Done Deal? The Politics of the 1997 Budget Agreement.* New York: Chatham House, 1999.

Pariser, David B. "Implementing Federal Credit Reform: Challenges Facing Public Sector Financial Managers." *Public Budgeting and Finance,* Vol. 12 (Winter 1992), pp. 19–34.

Pascall, Glenn. *The Trillion Dollar Budget.* Seattle: University of Washington Press, 1985.

Patashnik, Eric. "Ideas, Inheritances, and the Dynamics of Budgetary Change." *Governance,* Vol. 12 (April 1999), pp. 147–74.

——. "Budgeting More, Deciding Less." *The Public Interest,* No. 138 (Winter 2000), pp. 65–128.

——. *Putting Trust in the U.S. Budget: Federal Trust Funds and the Politics of Commitment.* Cambridge: Cambridge University Press, 2000.

Penner, Rudolph G. "Forecasting Budget Totals: Why Can't We Get It Right?" In Michael J. Boskin and Aaron Wildavsky, eds. *The Federal Budget: Economics and Politics.* San Francisco: Institute for Contemporary Studies, 1982, pp. 89–110.

Penner, Rudolph and Alan Abramson. *Broken Purse Strings: Congressional Budgeting 1974–1988.* Washington, D.C.: The Urban Institute, 1988.

Perloff, Harvey Stephen. *Modern Budget Policies: A Study of the Budget Process in Present-Day Society.* Ph.D. Dissertation submitted to the Departments of Government and Economics, Harvard University, December 1, 1939.

Persil, Herbert. "From the Field: Federal Agency Budget Officers: Who Needs Them?" *Public Budgeting and Finance,* Vol. 18 (Winter 1998), pp. 114–21.

Peters, Jean. "Reconciliation 1982: What Happened?" *PS.* Vol. 14, No. 4 (Fall 1981), pp. 732–36.

Peterson, Peter. *Facing Up: How To Rescue the Economy from Crushing Debt and Restore the American Dream.* New York: Simon and Schuster, 1993.

Phaup, Marvin. "Accounting for Federal Credit: A Better Way." *Public Budgeting and Finance,* Vol. 5, No. 3 (Autumn 1985), pp. 29–39.

"Credit Reform, Negative Subsidies, and FHA." *Public Budgeting and Finance*, Vol. 16 (Spring 1996), pp. 23–36.

_____. "The President's Commission To Study Capital Budgeting: An Interim Review." *Public Budgeting and Finance*, Vol. 18 (Fall 1998), pp. 1–10.

Popick, Bernard. "The Social Security Disability Program. III. The Black Lung Benefits—An Administrative Case Study." *Journal of Occupational Medicine*, Vol. 13, No. 7 (July 1971).

Posner, Paul, Trina Lewis, and Hannah Laufe. "Budgeting for Federal Capital." *Public Budgeting and Finance*, Vol. 18 (Fall 1998), pp. 11–23.

Potter, Jim. *The American Economy between the World Wars*. New York: Wiley, 1974.

Reese, Catherine. "The Line-Item Veto in Practice in Ten Southern States." *Public Administration Review*, Vol. 57 (November/December 1997), pp. 510–16.

Reischauer, Robert. "Mickey Mouse or Superman? The Congressional Budget Process During the Reagan Administration." Paper presented to the Association for Public Policy Management, Philadelphia, October 20–22, 1983.

_____. "The Congressional Budget Process." In Gregory Mills and John Palmer, eds. *Federal Budget Policy in the 1980s*. Washington, D.C.: The Urban Institute, 1984, pp. 385–413.

_____, ed. *Setting National Priorities: Budget Choices for the Next Century*. Washington, D.C.: Brookings Institution, 1997.

_____. "The Unfulfillable Promise: Cutting Nondefense Discretionary Spending." In Robert Reischauer, ed. *Setting National Priorities: Budget Choices for the Next Century*. Washington, D.C.: Brookings Institution, 1997, pp. 123–54.

Reischauer, Robert, Stuart Butler, and Judith Lave, eds. *Medicare: Preparing for the Challenges of the 21ˢᵗ Century*. Washington, D.C.: National Academy of Social Insurance, 1998.

Rettig, R. A. "The Policy Debate on Patient Care for Victims of End-Stage Renal Disease." *Law and Contemporary Problems*, Vol. 40, No. 4 (Autumn 1976).

Rieselbach, Leroy. *Congressional Reform: The Changing Modern Congress*. Washington, D.C.: CQ Press, 1994.

Rivlin, Alice M. "The Political Economy of Budget Choices: A View from Congress." Paper presented at the American Economic Association meeting, December 29, 1981.

———. "Reform of the Budget Process." *The American Economic Review*, Vol. 74, No. 2 (May 1984), pp. 133–37.

Rovner, Mark. *Defense Dollars and Sense*. Washington, D.C.: Common Cause, 1983.

Rowland, Diane, Judith Feder, and Alina Salganicoff, eds. *Medicaid Financing Crisis: Balancing Responsibilities, Priorities, and Dollars*. AAAS Press, 1993.

Rubin, Irene S. "Budgeting for Our Times: Target Base Budgeting." *Public Budgeting and Finance*, Vol. 11 (Fall 1991), pp. 5–14.

———. *Shrinking the Federal Government: The Effect of Cutbacks on Five Federal Agencies*. New York: Longman, 1985.

Saturno, James and Richard Forgette. "The Balanced Budget Amendment: How Would It Be Enforced?" *Public Budgeting and Finance*, Vol. 18 (Spring 1998), pp. 33–53.

Savage, James. "Deficits and the Economy: The Case of the Clinton Administration and Interest Rates." In Naomi Caiden and Joseph White, eds. *Budgeting, Policy, Politics: An Appreciation of Aaron Wildavsky*. New Brunswick, N.J.: Transaction Inc., 1995, pp. 93–110.

_____, ed. "Symposium: President Clinton's Budget and Fiscal Policy: An Evaluation Two Budgets Later." *Public Budgeting and Finance*, Vol. 14 (Fall 1994), pp. 3–40.

Sawicki, Max. *The End of Welfare: Consequences of Federal Devolution for the Nation*. Armonk, N.Y.: M. E. Sharpe, 1999.

Shanks, J. Merrill and Warren Miller. "Policy Direction and Performance Evaluation: Complementary Explanations of the Reagan Elections." Presented to the Annual Meeting of the American Political Science Association, New Orleans, August 29–September 1, 1985.

Schick, Allen. "The Road to PPB: The Stages of Budget Reform." In *Public Administration Review,* December 1966, pp. 243–58.

———. "The Budget Bureau That Was: Thoughts on the Rise, Decline, and Future of a Presidential Agency." *Law and Contemporary Problems,* Vol. 35 (Summer 1970), pp. 519–39.

———. "Budgetary Adaptations to Resource Scarcity." In Charles H. Levine and Irene Rubin, eds. *Fiscal Stress and Public Policy.* Beverly Hills: Sage Publications, 1980.

———. *Congress and Money.* Washington, D.C.: The Urban Institute, 1980.

———. *Reconciliation and the Congressional Budget Process.* Washington, D.C.: American Enterprise Institute, 1981.

———, ed. *Perspectives on Budgeting.* American Society for Public Administration, 1980.

———. "Controlling the Budget by Statute: An Imperfect but Workable Process." In Alvin Rabushka and William Craig Stubblebine, eds. *Constraining Federal Taxing and Spending.* Stanford, Calif.: Hoover Institution, 1982.

———. *Making Economic Policy in Congress.* Washington, D.C.: American Enterprise Institute, 1983.

———. "Controlling the 'Uncontrollables': Budgeting for Health Care in an Age of Mega-Deficits." Paper prepared for American Enterprise Institute Pew Fellows Conference, November 1985.

———. "The Evolution of Congressional Budgeting." In Allen Schick, ed. *Crisis in the Budget Process.* Washington, D.C.: American Enterprise Institute, 1986.

———. *The Capacity to Budget.* Washington, D.C.: The Urban Institute, 1990.

———. "From the Old Politics of Budgeting to the New." In Naomi Caiden and Joseph White, eds. *Budgeting, Policy, Politics: An Appreciation of Aaron Wildavsky.* New Brunswick, N.J.: Transaction, Inc., 1995, pp. 133–42.

The Federal Budget: Politics, Policy, Process. Washington, D.C.: Brookings Institution, 1995.

Schier, Steven E. "Thinking about the Macroeconomy: The House and Senate Budget Committees in the 1980s." Paper presented for 1985 Annual Meeting of American Political Science Association, New Orleans, August 29–September 1, 1985.

Shultz, William J. and M. R. Caine. *Financial Development of the United States.* New York: Prentice-Hall, 1937.

Seligman, Edwin R. A. *The Income Tax.* New York: Macmillan, 1921.

Simon, Herbert A. "The Criterion of Efficiency." In *Administrative Behavior,* 2nd ed. New York, Macmillan, 1957, pp. 172–97.

———. *Models of Man.* New York: Wiley, 1957.

Simon, Herbert A., Donald Smithburg, and Victor Thompson. "The Struggle for Existence." In *Public Administration.* New York: Knopf, 1950, pp. 381–422.

Sinclair, Barbara. *Unorthodox Lawmaking.* Washington, D.C.: CQ Press, 1997.

Smith, David. *Paying for Medicare: The Politics of Reform.* Hawthorne, N.Y.: Aldine de Gruyter, 1992.

Smithies, Arthur. *The Budgetary Process in the United States.* New York: McGraw-Hill, 1955.

Stein, Herbert. *The Fiscal Revolution in America.* Chicago: University of Chicago Press, 1969.

Stein, Robert and Kenneth Bickers. *Perpetuating the Pork Barrel: Policy Subsystems and American Democracy.* New York: Cambridge University Press, 1995.

Stewart, Charles Haines, III. *The Politics of Structural Reform: Reforming Budgetary Structure in the House, 1865–1921.* Dissertation submitted to Stanford University, August 1985.

Stockman, David. "The Social Pork Barrel." *The Public Interest,* No. 39 (Spring 1975), pp. 3–30.

———. *The Triumph of Politics.* New York: Harper & Row, 1986.

Stone, Deborah. *The Disabled State.* Philadelphia: Temple University Press, 1984.

Strahan, Randall. *New Ways and Means: Reform and Change in a Congressional Committee.* Chapel Hill, N.C.: University of North Carolina Press, 1990.

Tarschys, Daniel L. "The Growth of Public Expenditures: Nine Modes of Explanation." *Scandinavian Political Studies.* Vol. 10 (1975), pp. 9–31.

————. "Curbing Public Expenditures: Current Trends." *Journal of Public Policy*, Vol. 5 (1985), pp. 23–67.

Thompson, Fred and L. R. Jones. *Reinventing the Pentagon: How the New Public Management Can Bring Institutional Renewal.* San Francisco: Jossey Bass, 1994.

Thompson, James D. and Arthur Tuden. "Strategies, Structures, and Processes of Organizational Decision." In J. D. Thompson et al, eds. *Comparative Studies in Administration.* Pittsburgh: University of Pittsburgh Press, 1959.

Thurber, James. "The Impact of Budget Reform on Presidential and Congressional Governance." In James Thurber, ed. *Divided Democracy: Cooperation and Conflict between the President and Congress.* Washington, D.C.: CQ Press, 1991, pp. 145–70.

————. "If the Game Is Too Hard, Change the Rules: Congressional Budget Reform in the 1990s." In James Thurber and Roger Davidson, eds. *Remaking Congress: Change and Stability in the 1990s.* Washington, D.C.: CQ Press, 1995, pp. 130–44.

————. "Congressional Budget Reform: Impact on the Appropriations Committees." *Public Budgeting and Finance*, Vol. 17 (Fall 1997), pp. 62–73.

————. "Centralization, Devolution, and Turf Protection in the Congressional Budget Process." In Lawrence Dodd and Bruce Oppenheimer, eds. *Congress Reconsidered.* Washington, D.C.: CQ Press, 1997, pp. 325–46.

Thurber, James and Samantha Durst. "Delay, Deadlock and Deficits: Evaluating Congressional Budget Reform." In Thomas Lynch, ed. *Federal Budget and Financial Management Reform.* Westport, Conn.: Greenwood Press, 1991, pp. 78–118.

Thurmaier, Kurt. "Decisive Decision Making in the Executive Budget Process: Analyzing the Political and Economic Propensities of Central Budget Bureau Analysts." *Public Administration Review,* Vol. 55 (September/October 1995), pp. 448–61.

Tobin, James. "The Future of Social Security: One Economist's Assessment." Working Paper #4, Project on the Federal Social Role, National Conference on Social Welfare, Washington, D.C., 1985.

Tomkin, Shelley Lynne. *Inside OMB: Politics and Process in the President's Budget Office.* Armonk, N.Y.: M.E. Sharpe, 1998.

True, James. "Is the National Budget Controllable?" *Public Budgeting and Finance*, Vol. 15 (Summer 1995), pp. 18–32.

————. "Attention, Inertia, and Equity in the Social Security Program." *Journal of Public Administration Research and Theory*, Vol. 9 (September 1999), pp. 571–96.

Tyszkiewicz, Mary and Stephen Daggett. *A Defense Budget Primer.* Washington, D.C.: Congressional Research Service, 1998.

Verba, Sidney and Gary R. Orren. *Equality in America: The View from the Top.* Cambridge: Harvard University Press, 1985.

Waldo, Dwight. *The Administrative State.* New York: Ronald Press, 1948.

Walker, Robert. "William A. Jump: The Staff Officer as a Personality." *Public Administration Review,* Vol. 14 (Autumn 1954), pp. 233–46.

Walker, Wallace Earl. *Changing Organizational Culture: Strategy, Structure, and Professionalism in the U.S. General Accounting Office.* Knoxville, University of Tennessee Press, 1986.

Weaver, R. Kent. "Controlling Entitlements." In John E. Chubb and Paul E. Peterson, eds. *The New Direction in American Politics.* Washington, D.C.: Brookings Institution, 1985.

Webber, Carolyn and Aaron Wildavsky. *A History of Taxation and Expenditure in the Western World.* New York: Simon and Schuster, 1986.

Weicher, John C. *Entitlement Issues in the Domestic Budget.* Washington, D.C.: American Enterprise Institute, 1985.

Weiss, Andrew and Edward Woodhouse. "Reforming Incrementalism: A Constructive Response to Critics." *Policy Sciences*, Vol. 25, (1992), pp. 255–73.

White, Joseph. "What Budgeting Cannot Do: Lessons of Reagan's and Other Years." In Irene Rubin, ed. *New Directions in Budget Theory.* Albany, N.Y.: SUNY Press, 1988, pp. 165–202.

———. "Better News Than They Think." *San Diego Union,* October 7, 1990.

———. "(Almost) Nothing New Under the Sun: Why the Work of Budgeting Remains Incremental." In Naomi Caiden and Joseph White, eds. *Budgeting, Policy, Politics: An Appreciation of Aaron Wildavsky.* New Brunswick, N.J.: Transaction, Inc., 1995, pp. 111–32.

———. "Budgeting and Health Policymaking." In Thomas Mann and Norman Ornstein, eds. *Intensive Care: How Congress Shapes Health Policy.* Washington, D.C.: American Enterprise Institute and Brookings Institution, 1995.

———. "Entitlement Budgeting vs. Bureau Budgeting." *Public Administration Review,* Vol. 58 (November/December 1998), pp. 510–21.

———. "'Saving' Medicare—From What?" Paper delivered at the Annual Meeting of the American Political Science Association, Boston, September 1998.

———. "Budgeting for Entitlements." In Roy Meyers, ed., *Handbook of Government Budgeting.* San Francisco: Jossey Bass, 1999, pp. 678–98.

White, Joseph and Aaron Wildavsky. *The Deficit and the Public Interest.* Berkeley: University of California Press, 1990.

———. "How to Fix the Deficit—Really." *The Public Interest,* No. 94 (Winter 1989), pp. 3–24.

White, Leonard D. *The Jeffersonians: A Study in Administrative History, 1801–1829.* New York: Macmillan, 1951.

———. *The Jacksonians: A Study in Administrative History, 1829–1861.* New York: Macmillan, 1954.

———. *The Federalists: A Study in Administrative History.* New York: Macmillan, 1961.

Wildavsky, Aaron. *Dixon–Yates: A Study in Power Politics.* New Haven, Conn.: Yale University Press, 1962.

———. *The Politics of the Budgetary Process.* Boston: Little, Brown, 1964; revised 4th ed., 1984.

———. "The Political Economy of Efficiency: Cost-Benefit Analysis, Systems Analysis, and Program Budgeting." *Public Administration Review,* Vol. 26, No. 4 (December 1966), pp. 292–310.

———. "Rescuing Policy Analysis from PPBS." *Public Administration Review,* Vol. 29, No. 2 (March/April 1969), pp. 189–202.

———. *The Budgeting and Evaluation of Federal Recreation Programs, or Money Doesn't Grow on Trees.* With Jeanne Nienaber. New York: Basic Books, 1973.

———. *Budgeting: A Comparative Theory of Budgetary Processes.* Boston: Little, Brown, 1975; revised 2nd ed., Transaction, Inc., 1986.

———. "Doing Better and Feeling Worse: The Political Pathology of Health Policy." *Daedalus,* (Winter 1976), pp. 105–23.

———. "Ask Not What Budgeting Does to Society but What Society Does to Budgeting." Introduction to the second edition of *National Journal Reprints.* Washington, D.C., 1977.

———. "A Budget for All Seasons? Why the Traditional Budget Lasts." *Public Administration Review,* Vol. 38 (November/December 1978), pp. 501–09. Also in B. Geist, ed. *State Audit: Developments in Public Accountability.* London: Macmillan, 1981, pp. 253–68.

———. *Speaking Truth to Power.* Boston: Little, Brown, 1979.

———. *How To Limit Government Spending.* Los Angeles and Berkeley: University of California Press, 1980.

———. "Budgets as Compromises among Social Orders." In Michael J. Boskin and Aaron Wildavsky, eds. *The Federal Budget: Economics and Politics.* San Francisco, Institute for Contemporary Studies Press, 1982, pp. 21–38.

———. "Modelling the U.S. Federal Spending Process: Overview and Implications." With Michael Dempster. In R. C. O. Matthews and G. B. Stafford, eds. *The Grants Economy and Collective Consumption.* London: Macmillan, 1983, pp. 267–309.

——. "The Transformation of Budgetary Norms." *Australian Journal of Public Administration,* Vol. XLII, No. 4 (December 1983), pp. 421–32.

——. "The Unanticipated Consequences of the 1984 Presidential Election." *Tax Notes,* Vol. 24, No. 2 (July 9, 1984), pp. 193–200.

——. "Budgets as Social Orders." *Research in Urban Policy,* Vol. 1 (1985), pp. 183–97.

——. "A Cultural Theory of Expenditure Growth and (Un)Balanced Budgets." *Journal of Public Economics,* Vol. 28 (1985), pp. 349–57.

——. "Item Veto without a Global Spending Limit: Locking the Treasury after the Dollars Have Fled." *Notre Dame Journal of Law, Ethics and Public Policy,* Vol. 1, No. 2 (1985), pp. 165–76.

——. "The Logic of Public Sector Growth." In Jan-Erik Lane, ed. *State and Market.* London: Sage Publications, Ltd., 1985, pp. 231–70.

Willoughby, William Franklin. *The National Budget System with Suggestions for Its Improvement.* Baltimore: Johns Hopkins University Press, 1927.

Wilmerding, Lucius W., Jr. *The Spending Power: A History of the Efforts of Congress To Control Expenditures.* New Haven, Conn.: Yale University Press, 1943.

Wilson, Woodrow. *Congressional Government: A Study in American Politics.* Boston: Houghton Mifflin, 1895.

Witte, John F. "Tax Philosophy and Income Equality." In Robert A. Solo and Charles Anderson, eds. *Value Judgment and Income Distribution.* New York: Praeger, 1981, pp. 340–78.

——. *The Politics and Development of the Federal Income Tax.* Madison, Wis.: University of Wisconsin Press, 1985.

Wolf, John F. "The Item Veto in the American Constitutional System." *Georgetown Law Journal,* Vol. 25 (1936).

Wye, Christopher. "The Office of Management and Budget: A Continuing Search for Useful Information." In Christopher Wye and Richard Samichsen, eds., *Evaluation in the Federal Government: Changes, Trends and Opportunities.* San Francisco: Jossey Bass, pp. 65–72.

Young, James Sterling. *The Washington Community, 1802–1828.* New York: Columbia University Press, 1966.

Zigler, Edward and Jeanette Valentine, eds., *Project Head Start: A Legacy of the War on Poverty.* New York: Free Press, 1979.

Zigler, Edward and S. Muenchow. *Head Start: The Inside Story of America's Most Successful Educational Experiment.* New York: Basic Books, 1992.

Credits

Excerpt, p. xii: From Naomi Caiden, "Foreword," *Budgeting, Policy, Politics* (New Brunswick, N.J.: Transaction Publishers, 1995). Reprinted by permission of Transaction Publishers, Copyright © by Transaction Publishers; all rights reserved.

Excerpt, p. 44: From Allen Schick, "From the Old Politics of Budgeting to the New," *Budgeting, Policy, Politics* (New Brunswick, N.J.: Transaction Publishers, 1995), p. 134. Reprinted by permission of Transaction Publishers, Copyright © by Transaction Publishers; all rights reserved.

Chapter 2, pp. 25-41 This chapter incorporates much of the material from Chapter 7, "Balanced Regimes, Balanced Budgets: Why America Was So Different," in *A History of Taxation and Expenditure in the Western World* by Carolyn Webber and Aaron Wildavsky (New York: Simon & Schuster, 1986). Copyright ©1986 by Carolyn Webber and Aaron Wildavsky. By permission.

Excerpts, pp. 109, 111: From Bruce Johnson, "The Increasing Role of the Office of Management and Budget in the Congressional Budget Process." Paper prepared for the 5th Annual Conference of the Association for Public Policy Analysis and Management, Philadelphia, October 21–22, 1983, pp. 6, 7–8. This paper later appeared in revised form under the title "From Analyst to Negotiator: The OMB's New Role," in *Journal of Policy Analysis and Management,* copyright © 1984 by the Association for Public Policy Analysis and Management. Vol. 3, no. 4 (1984), pp. 501–515. Reprinted by permission.

List, p. 123: From *National Journal,* January 11, 1986. Reprinted by permission.

Table 6.2, p. 130: Copyright, February 3, 1986. *U.S. News & World Report.* Reprinted by permission.

Excerpt, p. 145-146: From Allen Schick, *The Federal Budget: Politics, Policy, Process* (Washington, DC: Brookings Institution, 1995), p. 3. Copyright © by Brookings Institution. Reprinted by permission.

Table 7.2, p. 162: From "Fiscal 1996 Budget Resolution: New Discretionary Spending Caps in the Congressional Budget Resolution," *Congressional Quarterly Weekly Report,* July 15, 1995, p. 2044. Reprinted by permission.

Chart, p. 159: From "The Budget Process," *Congressional Quarterly Weekly Report*, May 15, 1995, p.1305. Reprinted by permission.

Index